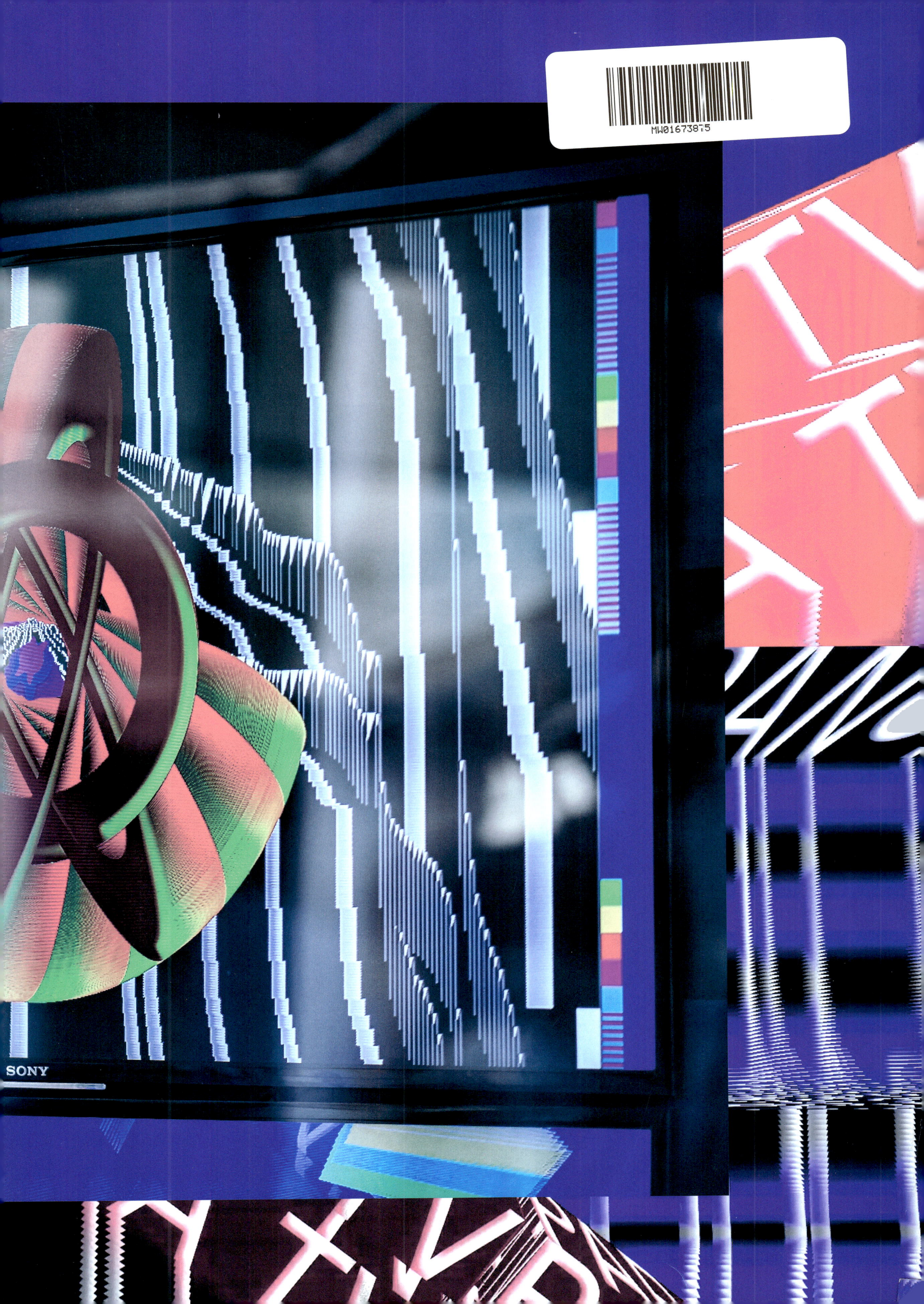
SONY

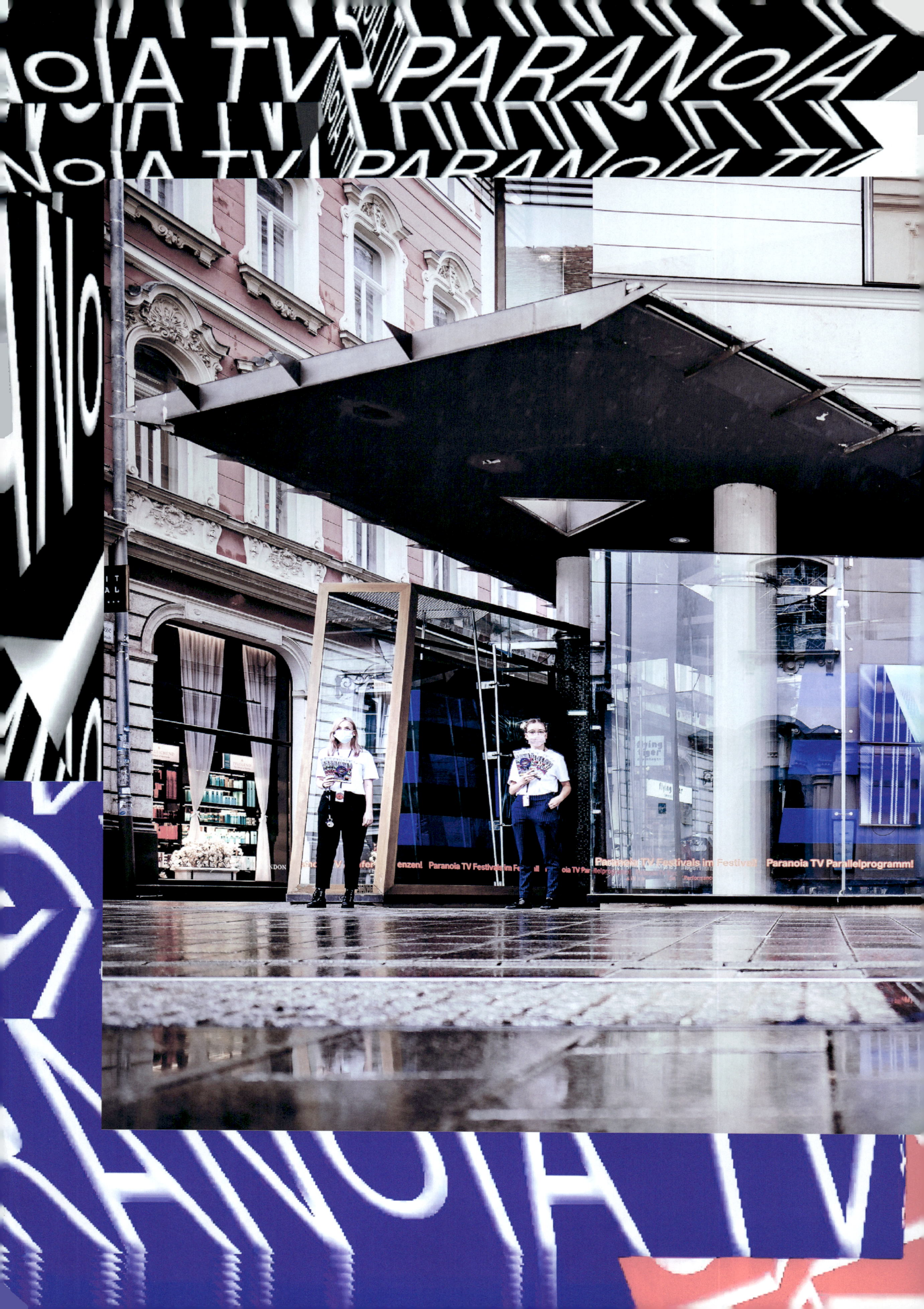

PARANOIA TV
Paranoia TV Festivals im Festival!
Paranoia TV Parallelprogramm!

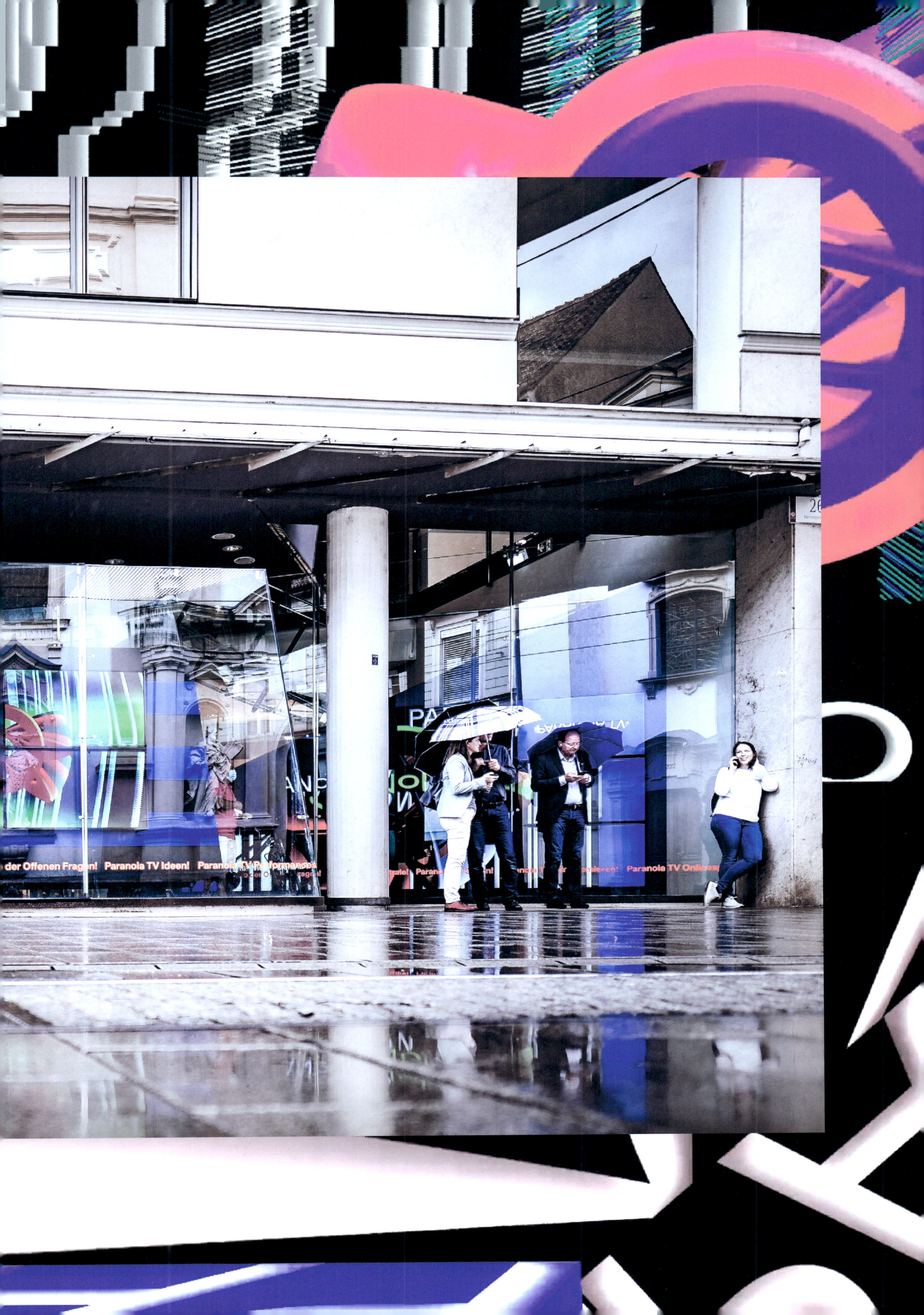
der Offenen Fragen! Paranoia TV Ideen! Paranoia TV Performances

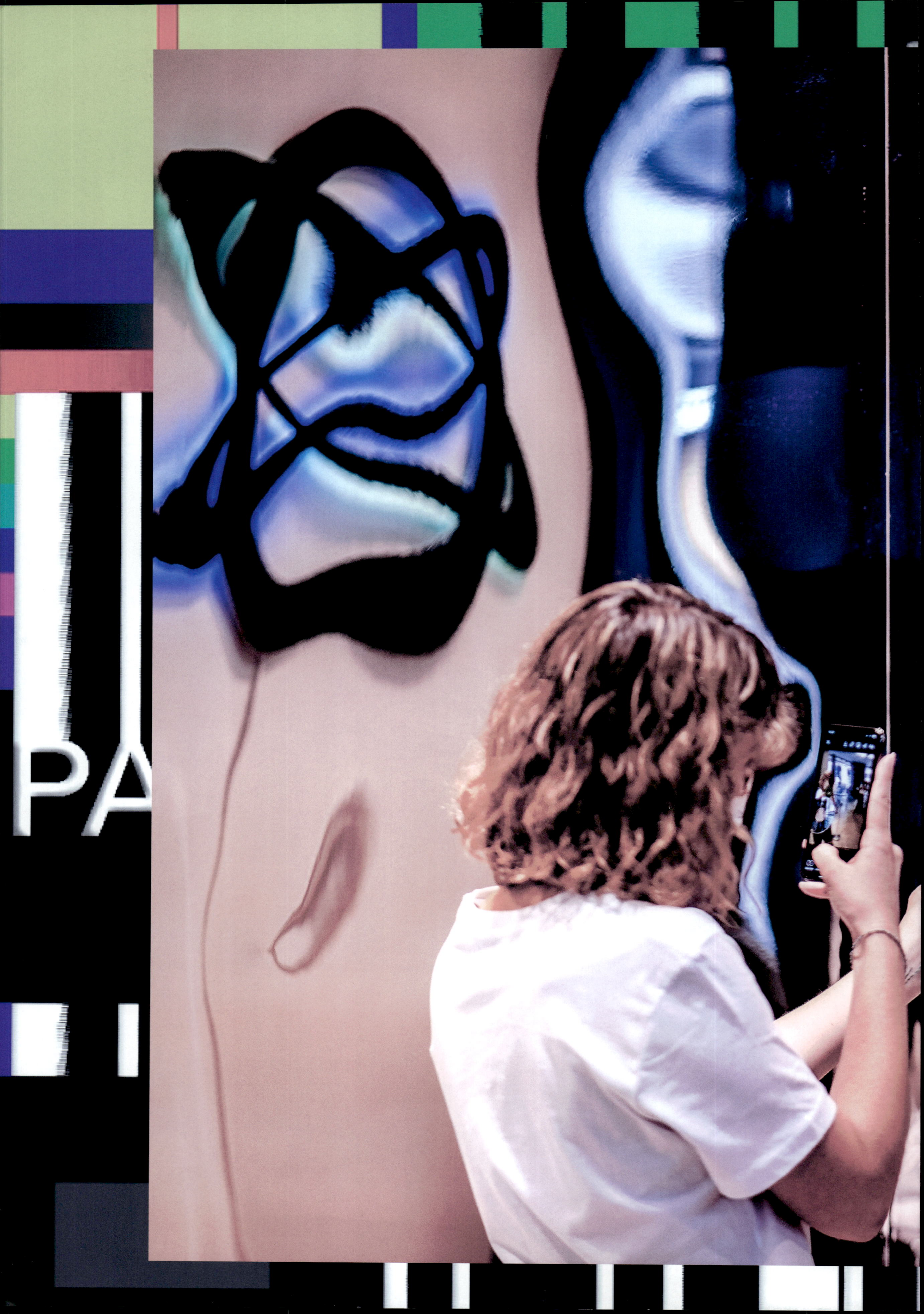
PA

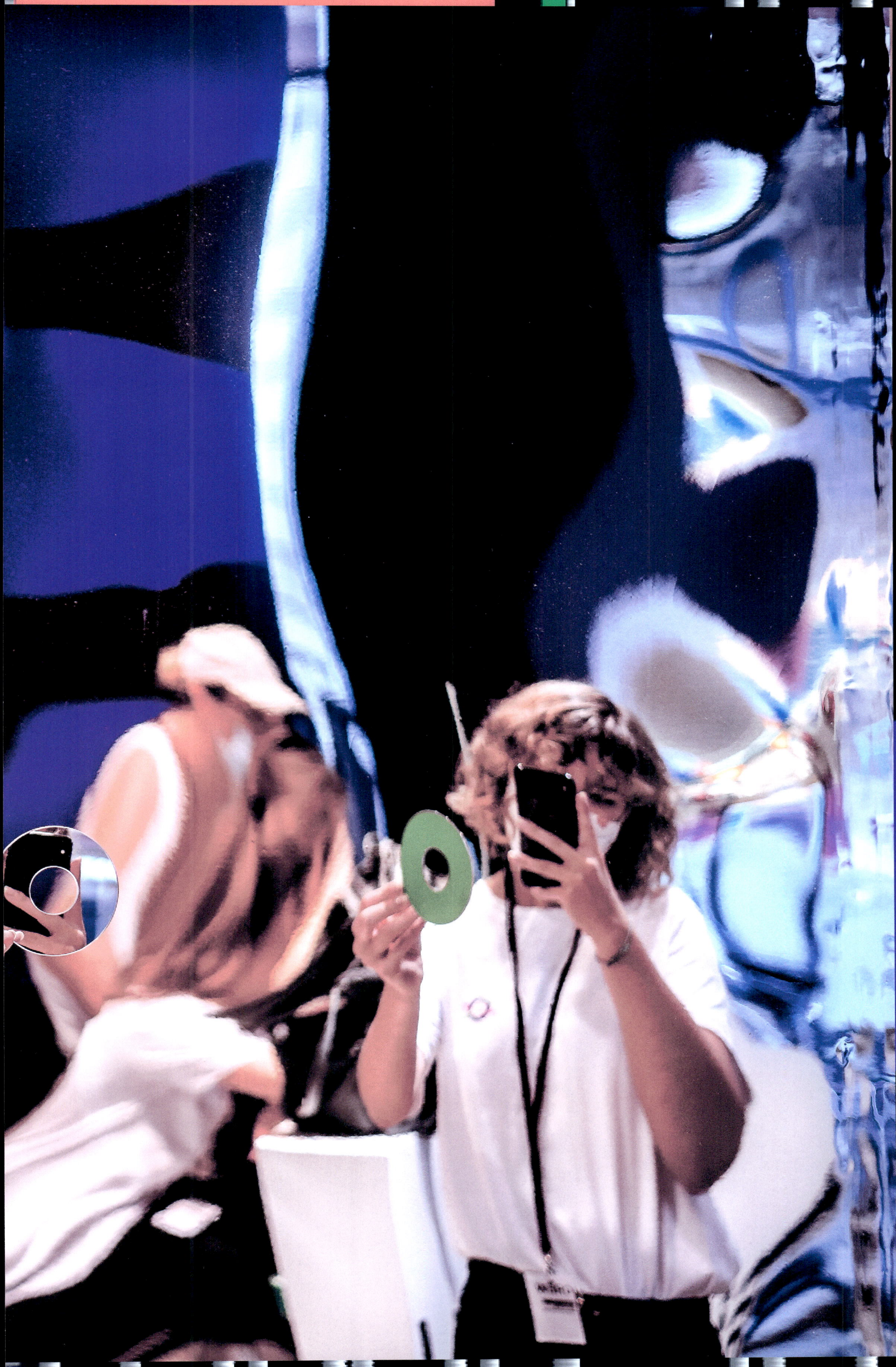

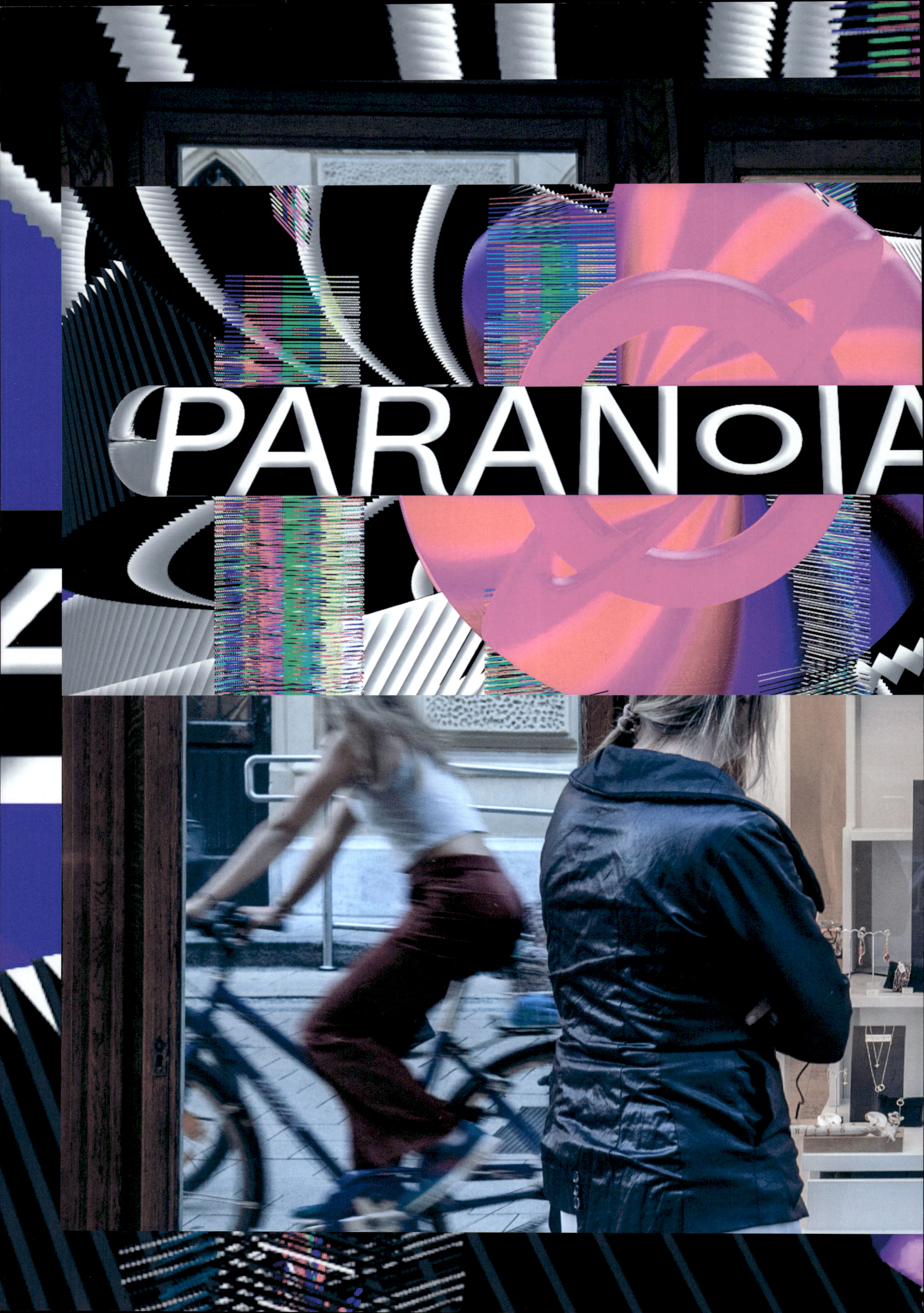
PARANoIA

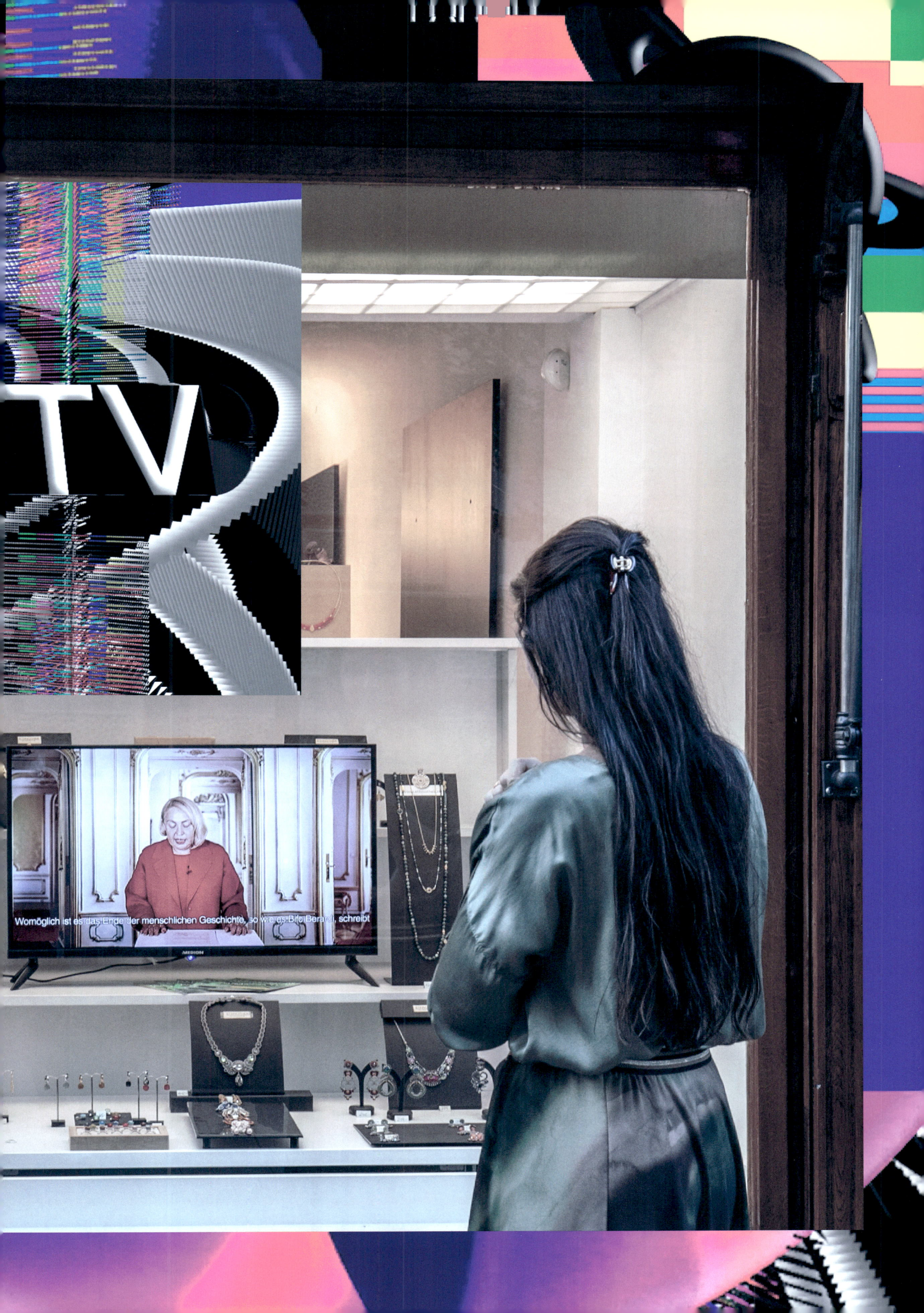
TV
Womöglich ist es das Ende der menschlichen Geschichte, so wie es Bifo Berardi, schreibt
MEDION

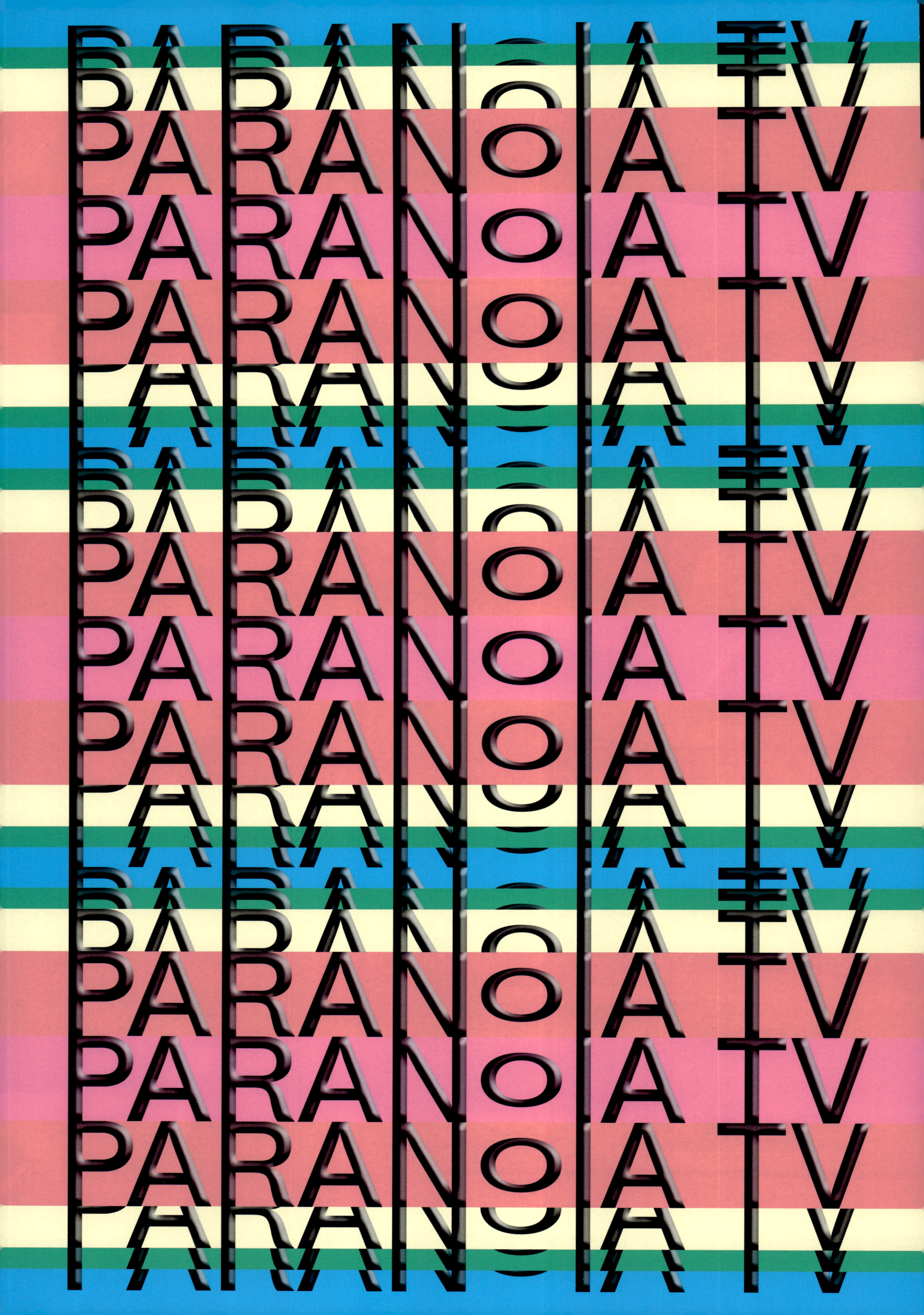
PARANOIA TV
PARANOIA TV
PARANOIA TV
PARANOIA TV
PARANOIA TV
PARANOIA TV
PARANOIA TV
PARANOIA TV
PARANOIA TV

PARANOIA

Paranoia TV

steirischer herbst '20
24.9.–18.10.20

This edition of steirischer herbst was conceived by all participating artists, thinkers, and philosophers, as well as
Ekaterina Degot, Director and Chief Curator
Henriette Gallus, Deputy Director
Christoph Platz, Head of Curatorial Affairs
David Riff, Senior Curator
Dominik Müller, Curator
Mirela Baciak, Curator
and steirischer herbst team

Edited by Ekaterina Degot and David Riff

Verlag der Buchhandlung Walther und Franz König

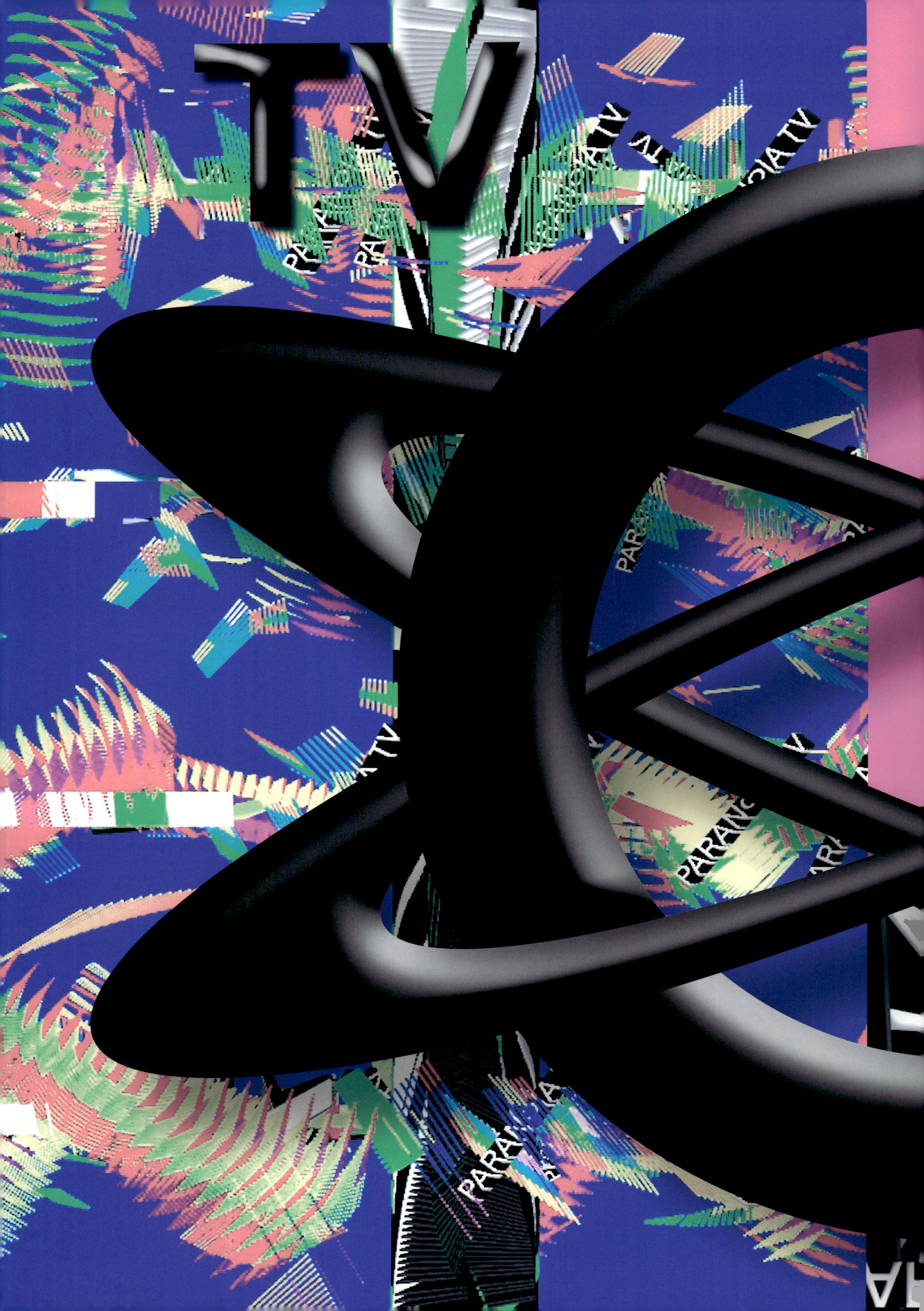
TV

Contents

INTRODUCTION

ARTISTS

APPENDIX

PARANOIA TV 2020

CAN AN EXHIBITION BE TELEVISED?

INTRODUCTION

Ekaterina Degot and David Riff

Overnight somewhere in April 2020, the 54th edition of the steirischer herbst festival in Graz, Austria, turned into a semi-fictitious media company, a broadcaster called *Paranoia TV*. Obviously, this transformation was prompted by the sudden COVID-19-induced lockdown and the connected border closures, which affected, or rather canceled outright, both the perspective of producing artworks—our curatorial approach is often site-specific and requires artists' visits—and of their reception (in the form of a traditional gathering of an international crowd of professionals and audience). There had to be a solution, and this solution had better be a curatorial rather than a purely pragmatic one. It had to be a story, a project, a fantasy. It had to make sense, as well as a bit of nonsense. It had to be funny, absurd, and at times deep.

Still, as one vaguely suspected already, this had to be a solution not just to the lockdown and the pandemic, the scale of which was still beyond average human comprehension at the time. It also had to be at least an attempted solution to the larger crisis of contemporary art within its jaded-but-jubilant institutional frame. Since the turn of the millennium, art has mostly relied upon a system of well-institutionalized biennials and group exhibitions with global agendas and ambitions, proudly and sometimes aggressively inserting themselves into a particular local context. In many cases, global biennials were taking up legitimate crusades against local nationalisms and parochialisms, enlarging their horizons, evoking solidarity with progressive elements, and winning others over as an art audience. But the heroism of this battle has been tarnished, as contemporary art in its Western-globalist and slightly colonial iteration lost its civilizing luster. Its global claim has been compromised by oligarchical flair and overzealous nomadism, which started to feel irresponsible and unsustainable even before the pandemic. The whole religion of fluidity and mobility observed by biennials and festivals has turned out to be deeply complicit in neoliberal capitalism, while the notion of unique experience that these festivals were propagating and selling began to feel uncomfortably close to an exclusive club for the few. The urge to save the best in this international and internationalist character of contemporary art came exactly at a moment when it became impossible because of the pandemic. With the lockdown in effect all over the globe and travel banned, the tension between the local and the global seemed to turn into a schism: suddenly the planetary art world turned into a myriad of fully remote, local art worlds lacking any connection to one another. None of these local islands could show much of anything in public space; the only publicly accessible space was the Internet, even if it strips artworks of their tangible reality and immediate relevance. Restrictions on audience numbers—wherever audiences were at all allowed—dealt a final blow to any democratic aspirations: new works were now even more likely to be seen only by friends, funders, collectors, and curators before they would disappear into some freeport art storage or digital archive. Two sides of art that seem crucial were now in doubt, namely the public side of art and the aspect of its international circulation.

So how do you continue to insist upon the public and international nature of a festival like ours? How do you continue to produce remotely without consigning artworks to new modes of not-being-seen? How do you playfully refound the institution of art? These were questions we were asking ourselves.

In early 2020, there were hopeful signs that made us think there might be an answer. All these opera performances from balconies, flash mobs, and rounds of applause for care workers seemed like incredible manifestations indicating a real hunger for some kind of collective, public aesthetic experience—showing that art is essential and will remain so, despite the paralysis of

INTRODUCTION

its institutions. There were waves of amateur creativity, reenactments of famous Old Master paintings on Facebook, well-known musicians giving conceptual Zoom concerts and doing weekly cover versions of their favorite songs, and there was also suddenly enough time to read 19th-century novels, play jazz guitar or catch up on the shows you'd missed over the last years of traveling and making art projects. The amount of time we were spending on Netflix and Co. told us that this, more so perhaps than all the great streams of opera and theater performances, was the real aesthetic idiom of collective historical experience, itself about to reach a strange turning point of saturation.

This is what brought *Paranoia TV* to life. Even if the lockdown would end or loosen, we promised ourselves, we would stick to our story and pretend as if strict "shelter-in-place" instructions still applied. We would only offer "COVID-19-safe" events, heightening the paranoia and protocols of control being introduced at the time, but we would "televise" everything. Most of our work would take place *for* the digital sphere, for audiences at a remove, unable or unwilling to attend in person. This turned out to be a very realistic fiction, not just because paranoia has gone from being a personal illness to a generalized social condition, as Robert Pfaller puts it in his contribution to this catalogue's companion reader, but because a new Europe-wide outbreak brought increasingly stringent sanitary regulations.

We were considering all sorts of names, but *Paranoia TV* stuck, in part as a joke hearkening back nostalgically to Cold War days when TV was everything and paranoia was already everywhere. In the old days, TV amounted to a couple of major networks and maybe a fourth channel of local DIY programming—and not segment-oriented streaming. This rather limited set created something like a telemetric public sphere—but one at first still firmly in the "public" hand, which also meant that it was susceptible to monopolies and state control and responsible for spreading government-issue propaganda. The paranoia of the Cold War was attached to the TV from the very beginning (as in the telescreen in George Orwell's *1984* from which Big Brother dispenses his daily doses of hate while surveilling the population). The Cold War was fully televised, its drama of escalation and détente would have been impossible without nightly news updates from Vietnam, Afghanistan, or Grenada and the constant discussion of approaching apocalypse.

With the appearance of the Internet as an alternative channel and the concurrent privatization of network TV and the advent of cable, this television space mutated. Its paranoia became a staple of cable news, which in turn could be harnessed by renationalized broadcasters to control the population. This is what happened to Russian TV in the 1990s, where privately owned, pro-Western TV broadcasters were taken over by the state and turned into a conduit for propaganda crucial to Putin's hold on power. Thus, they effectively split the country into two groups: those who draw their information from television and those who read news online. This is mirrored by similar developments elsewhere, so that state-operated TV and its use of fake and biased news is really one of the main forces keeping today's authoritarian-populist regimes in power.

The insurgencies of self-broadcasting, DIY production, and community TV received a whole new cosmos of possibilities with the advent of online video platforms. But the same technology's potentialities were also quickly recognized by all major broadcasters, who appeared on the scene in time to offer new formats of digital consumerism with which all areas of culture must now compete. The utopian side of TV enjoys something like an "eternal return," constantly repeating itself in some moments, when it seems like teenagers and podcasters might become public tribunes and influencers more important than any million-dollar-a-show late-night host.

This democratizing, public dimension—those fifteen minutes of maybe-not-just-fame—seemed to us to be the main message of the medium of TV, despite its paranoid and crazy content. The next revolution would be televised, we remembered. Could we "televise" an exhibition, a festival, and thus reclaim a dead-lost public sphere that was so overrun by the politics of fear? All that overgrown, crazy fake-news production is itself already a media trope. Could we appropriate it and also defuse the very real onset of paranoia, as real viruses and media viruses infect us all?

One substantial part of the program was streaming content that we newly commissioned from artists, acting like a quasi-Netflix distributor/producer. This included feature films produced under conditions specific to the pandemic, and also available in a different way than usual, not as video installations but as online videos with a premiere event. We also asked artists to think about the most addictive and binge-worthy format, that of serial content, about how to create cliff-hangers and continuities, how to vary themes important to them, or, indeed, how to subvert serialization as such. We see seriality and the temporality of serial artistic consumption as something really important to have emerged over recent years, as is the movement of video art beyond its fixed installative context and even beyond the format of streaming serials. A wildly interesting form in that regard are online games, of which we also commissioned several.

Assuming the role of a semi-fictitious broadcaster did not just involve moving to the virtual—not only because we found and still find it impossible to accept that entire areas of life will soon exist only as faint virtual memories. Today, when garden centers and clothing retailers are likely to come out of lockdown sooner than theaters and museums, art very much needs to insist upon physical presence—with all the theatrical implications. At the same time, the new cultural situation comes with regulations and restrictions that one could argue were there all along as a frame; the new modes of enforced spectatorship only make them more visible. The live performances that we hosted all engaged with these restrictions, but also their imaginative horizon—concerning new platforms and venues for art as well. Our broadcaster was present in urban space not only with its headquarters but also with other installative projects. In addition, we asked artists to produce work that would find new forms of distribution as multiples and takeaways.

Finally, *Paranoia TV* would have been incomplete without its own news show—hosted on a semi-nightly basis, with visits from Siggi Freud—its unreal virtual mascot—and many insights into the ongoing program. It was this program that showed the events happening in Graz itself and presented them to a wider audience who could not attend, pointing in a direction that festivals like ours might take in the future as they try to bridge the gap between local and international audiences. A further bridge was to be found in an intense roster of online talks where selected collaborators invited guests of their own, as well as in talks and conferences held in hybrid formats by our partners in Graz. The discussions here, as most of those surrounding us today, concerned the pandemic and its effects on broader society, including the controversial political implications it entails, themes that define the companion reader to the present catalogue.

So, is the tangible, sensual aspect of meeting art in real life, in real space something to be missed? Certainly. By watching films online, for instance, we lose the size of the screen in a video installation, an important factor that seems to be ignored by contemporary modes of film consumption on digital devices of all sizes, including the most minuscule. By taking part in an artist's talk on Zoom, we are cut from their physical presence, the atmosphere in the room, or the view from the window. But contemporary art has a very long and solid tradition of working with what is lacking or missing and the longing for it. The first cinematic experiments of the Lumière brothers were so astonishing because they were simultaneously scarier than life itself and still completely immaterial. Presence as well as absence are always inscribed in media; television is both a celebration of reality as well as that reality's complete absence. It is perhaps the next platform contemporary art can fully critically embrace.

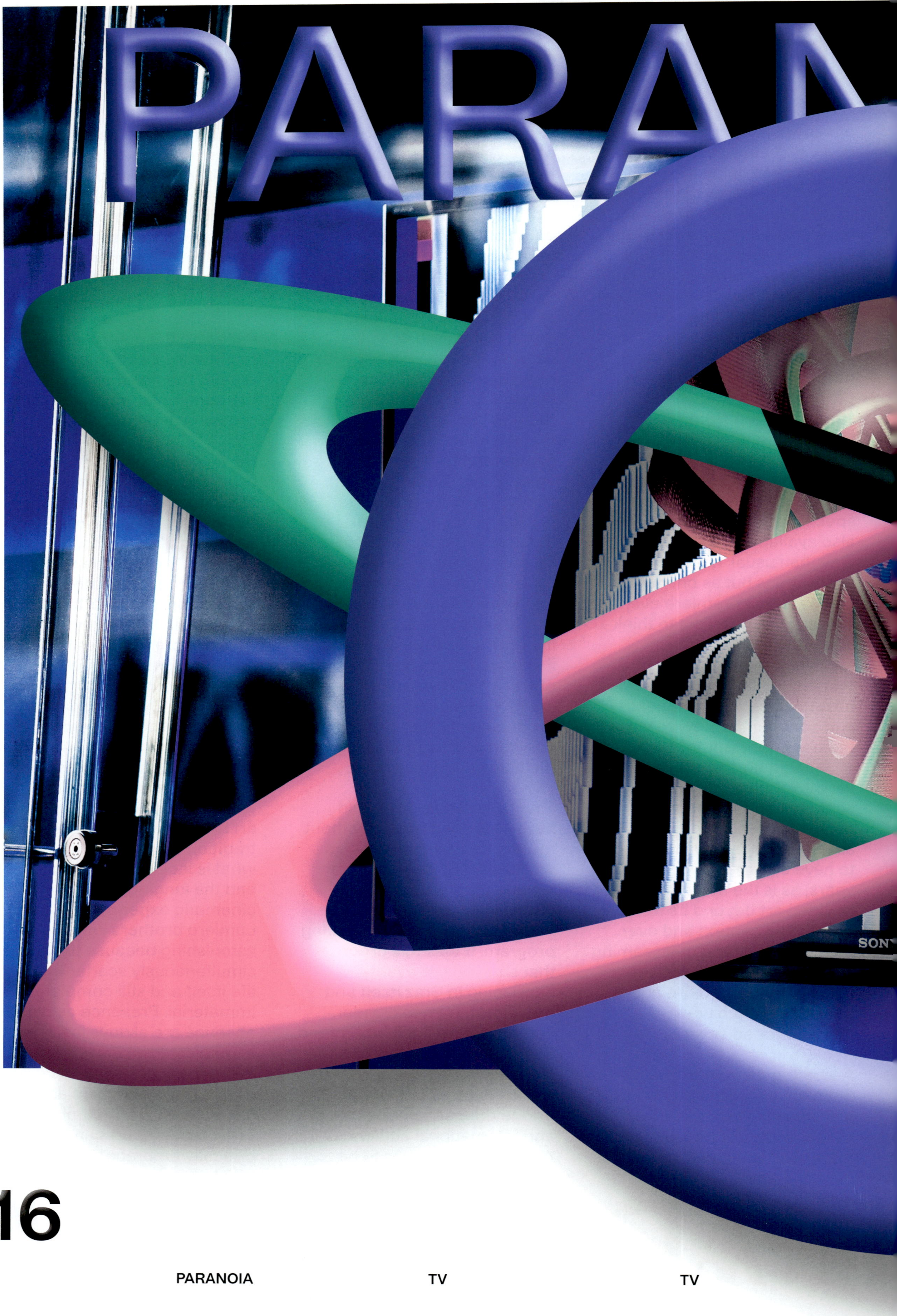

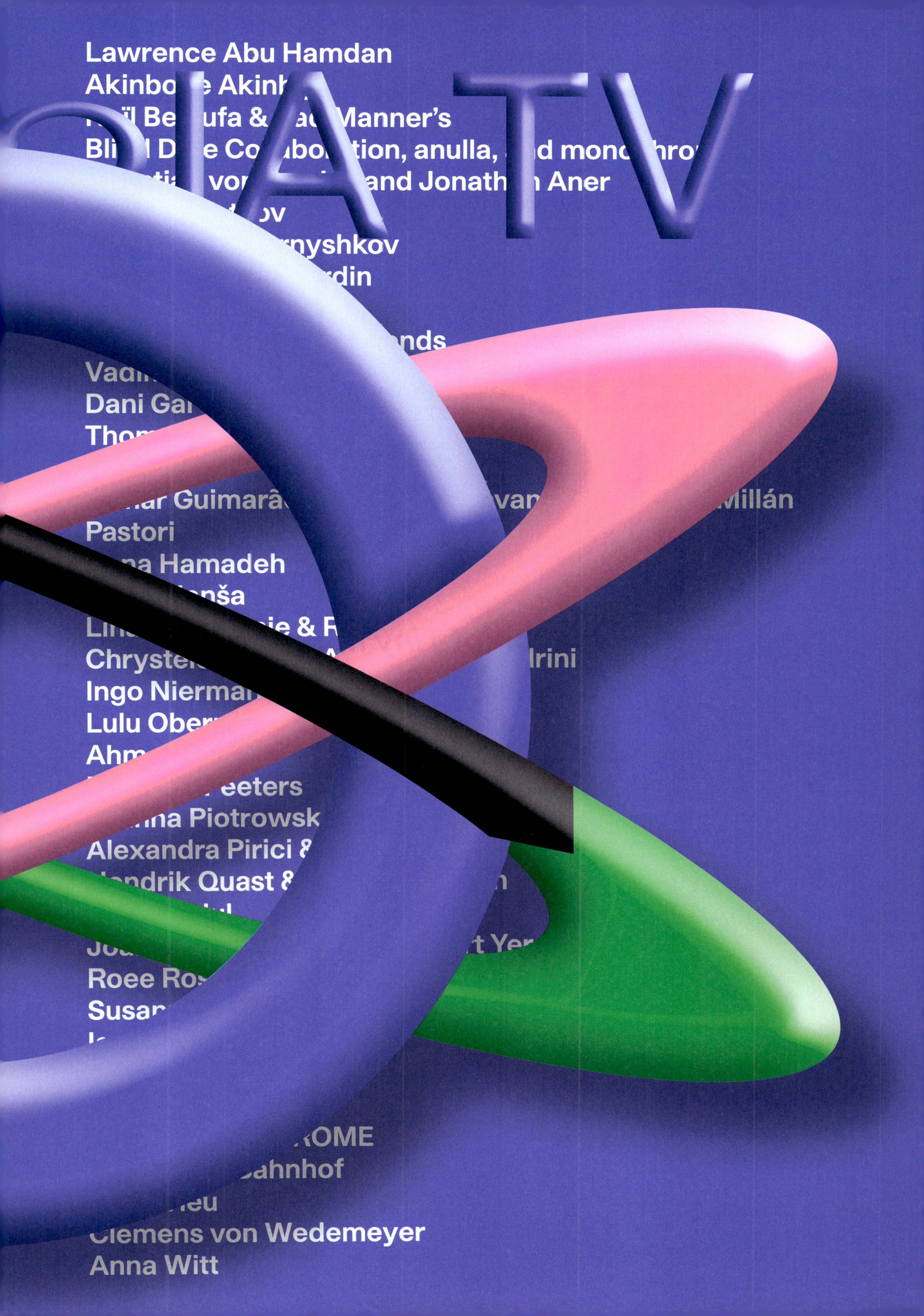
Lawrence Abu Hamdan
Pastori
Alexandra Pirici
Roee Ros
Clemens von Wedemeyer
Anna Witt

Lawrence Abu Hamdan

A Convention of Tiny Movements
2020

Installation

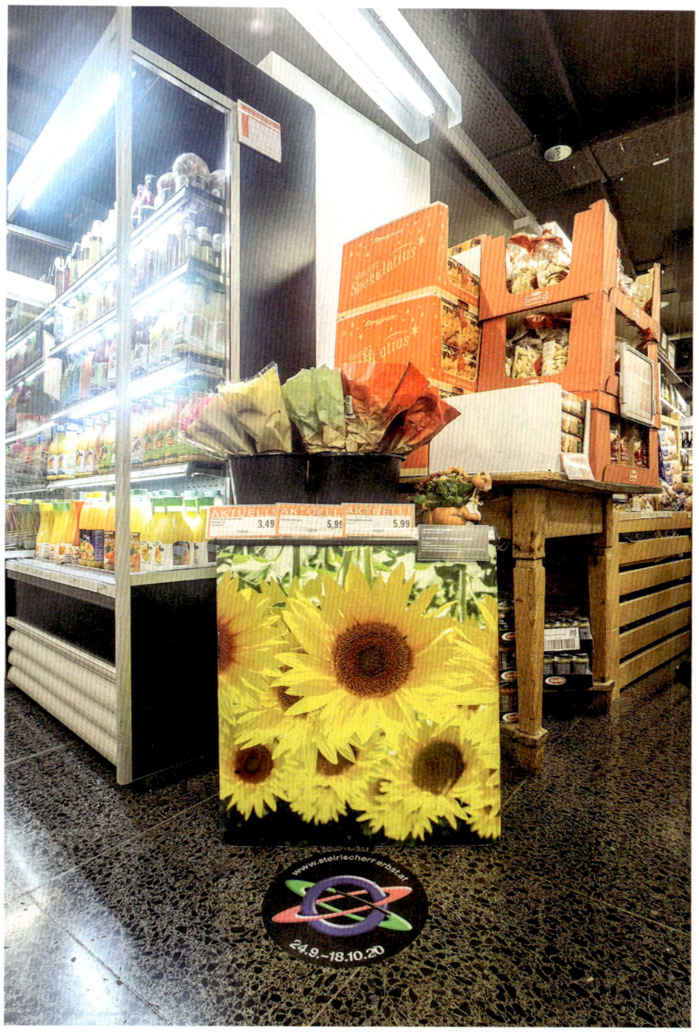
www.steirischerherbst.at
24.9.–18.10.20

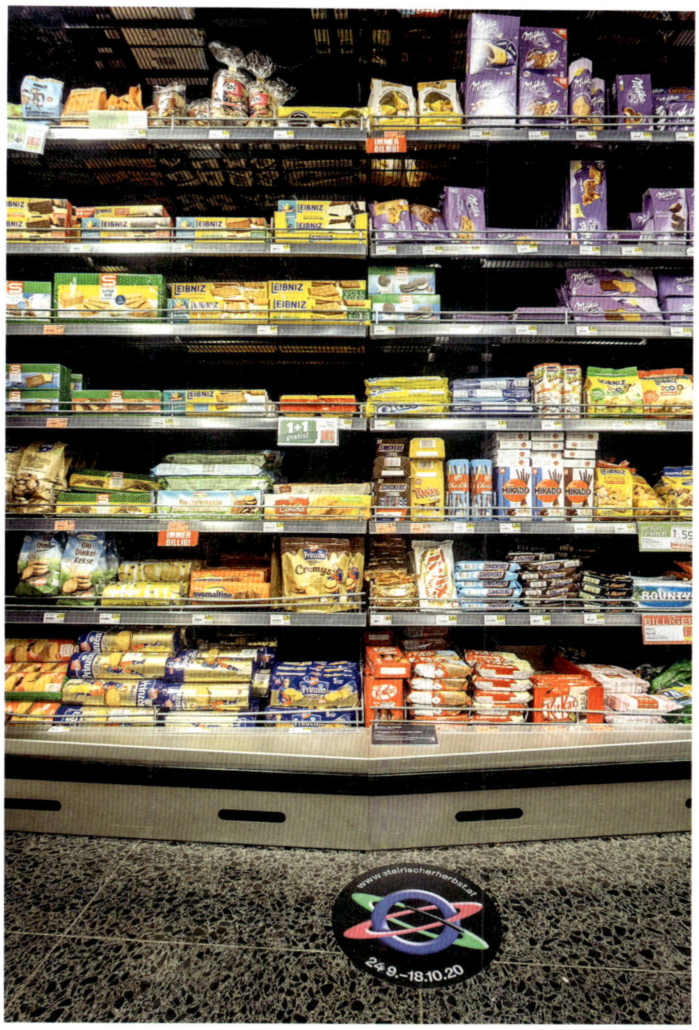
www.steirischerherbst.at
24.9.–18.10.20

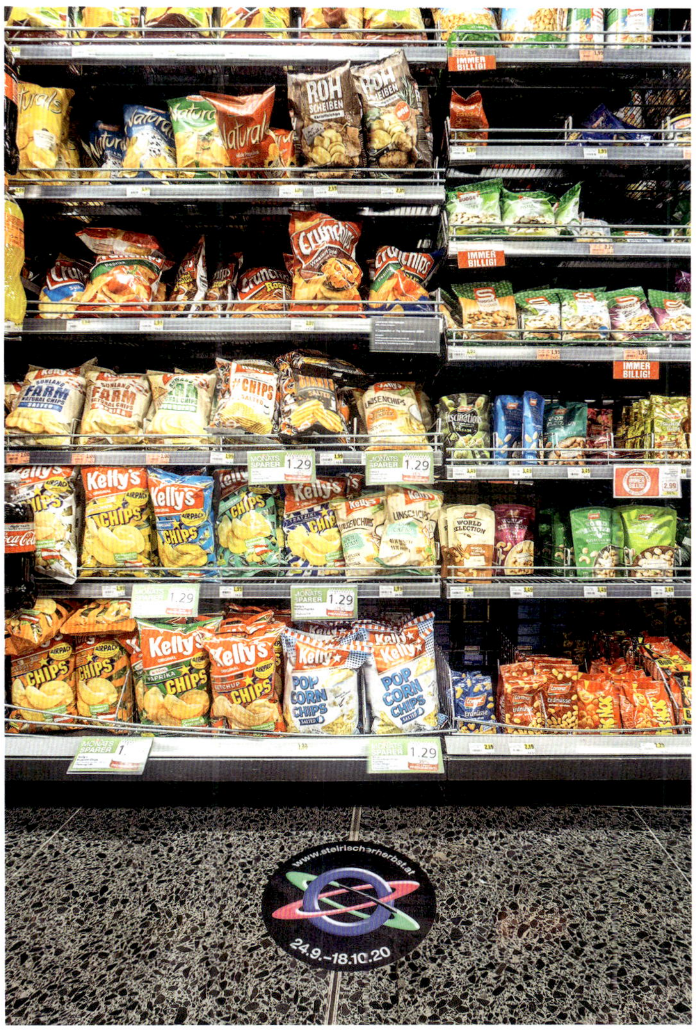
www.steirischerherbst.at
24.9.–18.10.20

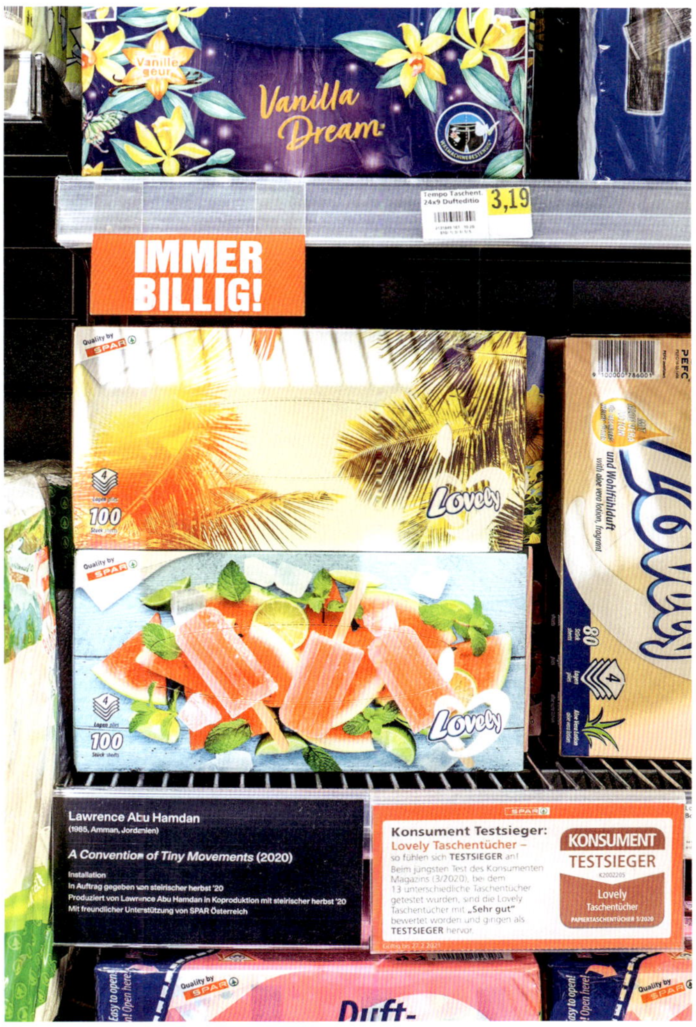
Vanilla Dream
IMMER BILLIG!
Lovely
Lovely
Lawrence Abu Hamdan
(1985, Amman, Jordanien)
A Convention of Tiny Movements (2020)
Installation
In Auftrag gegeben von steirischer herbst '20
Produziert von Lawrence Abu Hamdan in Koproduktion mit steirischer herbst '20
Mit freundlicher Unterstützung von SPAR Österreich
Konsument Testsieger:
Lovely Taschentücher –
so fühlen sich TESTSIEGER an!
Beim jüngsten Test des Konsumenten Magazins (3/2020), bei dem 13 unterschiedliche Taschentücher getestet wurden, sind die Lovely Taschentücher mit „Sehr gut" bewertet worden und gingen als TESTSIEGER hervor.
KONSUMENT
TESTSIEGER
Lovely
Taschentücher
PAPIERTASCHENTÜCHER 3/2020

Lawrence Abu Hamdan's installation tells of a not-too-distant future in which everyday objects and surfaces can be used to watch over the population. The necessary technologies already exist. As a group of researchers at the Massachusetts Institute of Technology discovered some years ago, video recordings or laser technology can be deployed to measure the vibrations of objects generated by the human voice. These can then be converted into new sounds.

Two immensely popular but very different Spar supermarkets in Graz (one in a prestigious department store, another one at the railway station) became the locations for new work made especially for *Paranoia TV*. Potato chip bags, KitKat wrappers, handkerchiefs, water glasses, and even flower petals could be heard eavesdropping on customers, each contributing their own unique sound. It is within the anti-utopia of surveillance that the objects develop their own, nonhuman subjectivity, as the artist demonstrates with this frightening scenario.

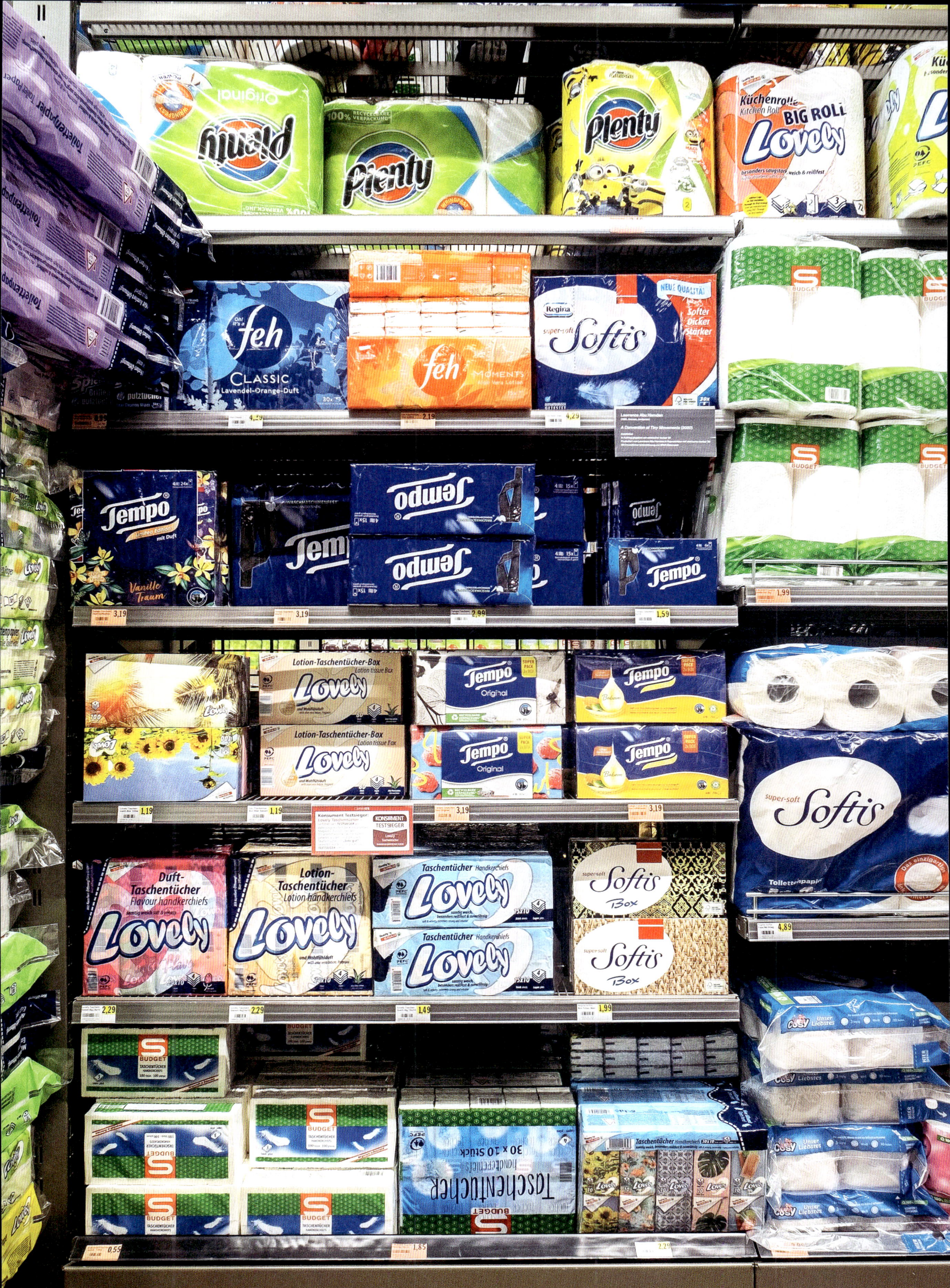

Plenty
Plenty
Plenty
Küchenrolle
Kitchen Roll
BIG ROLL
Lovely
besonders saugstark, weich & reißfest
feh
CLASSIC
Lavendel-Orange-Duft
feh
MOMENTS
Regina
super-soft
Softis
NEUE QUALITÄT
Softer
Dicker
Stärker
BUDGET
Tempo
Vanille Traum
Tempo
Tempo
Tempo
Lotion-Taschentücher-Box
Lotion tissue Box
Lovely
Lotion-Taschentücher-Box
Lotion tissue Box
Lovely
Tempo
Original
Tempo
Tempo
Original
Tempo
super-soft
Softis
Duft-Taschentücher
Flavour handkerchiefs
Lovely
Lotion-Taschentücher
Lotion handkerchiefs
Lovely
Taschentücher Handkerchiefs
Lovely
Taschentücher Handkerchiefs
Lovely
Softis
Box
Softis
Box
BUDGET
Taschentücher
30 x 10 Stück
BUDGET
Taschentücher Handkerchiefs
Cosy

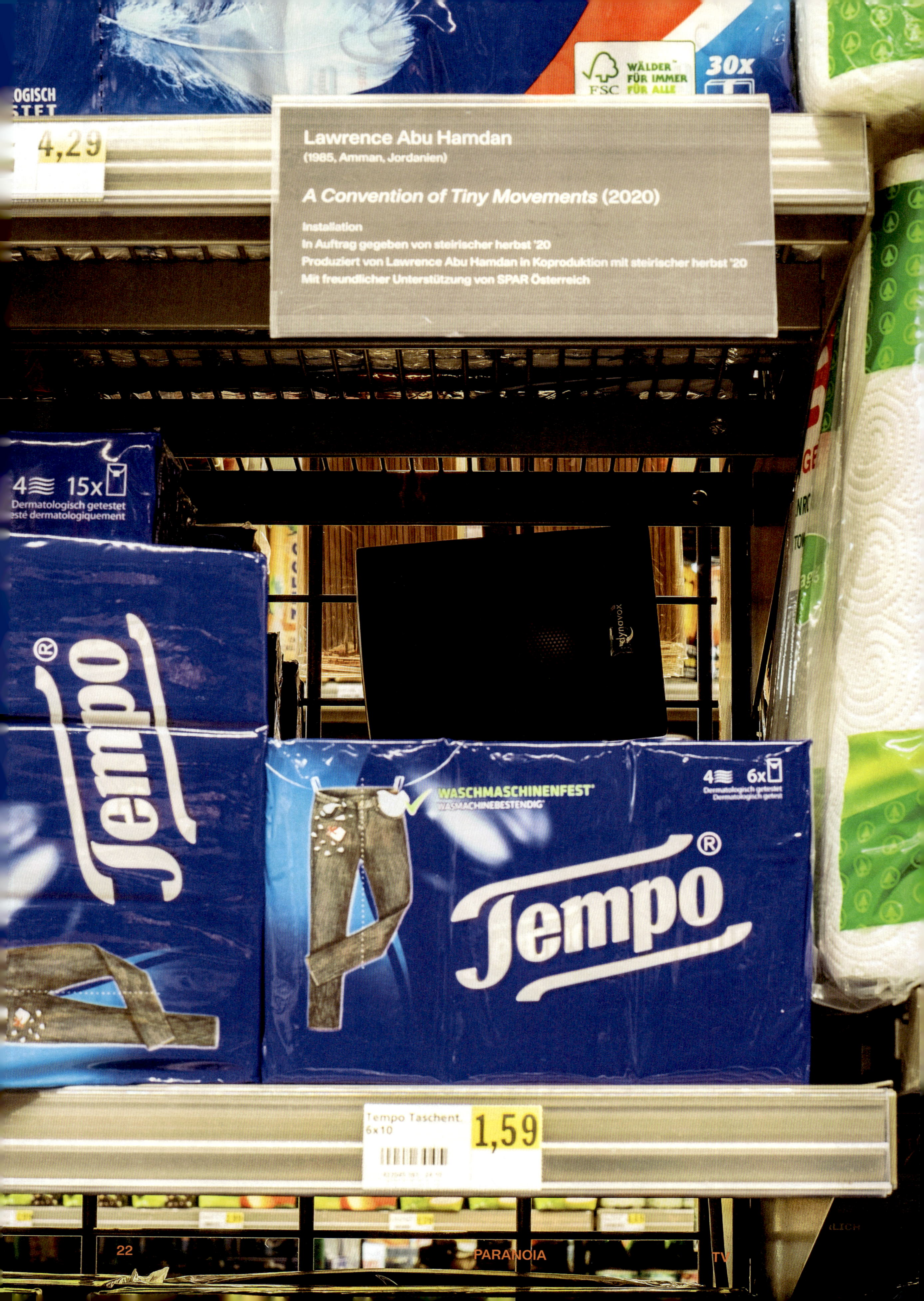
Lawrence Abu Hamdan
(1985, Amman, Jordanien)
A Convention of Tiny Movements (2020)
Installation
In Auftrag gegeben von steirischer herbst '20
Produziert von Lawrence Abu Hamdan in Koproduktion mit steirischer herbst '20
Mit freundlicher Unterstützung von SPAR Österreich
4,29
WÄLDER FÜR IMMER FÜR ALLE
FSC
30x
15x
Dermatologisch getestet
Tempo
WASCHMASCHINENFEST
WASMACHINEBESTENDIG
6x
dynavox
Tempo Taschent.
6x10
1,59

Lawrence Abu Hamdan refers to himself as a "private ear." His interest with sound and its intersection with politics originate from his background as a touring musician and facilitator of DIY music. The artist's audio investigations have been used as evidence at the UK Asylum and Immigration Tribunal and as advocacy for organizations such as Amnesty International and Defence for Children International together with fellow researchers from Forensic Architecture.

Abu Hamdan completed his PhD in 2017 from Goldsmiths, University of London and is currently a fellow at the Gray Center for Arts and Inquiry at the University of Chicago.

He has exhibited his work at the 58th Venice Biennale (2019), the 11th Gwangju Biennale (2016) and the 13th and 14th Sharjah Biennial (2017 and 2019). He has had solo shows at FKA Witte de With, Rotterdam; Tate Modern Tanks, London; Chisenhale Gallery, London; Hammer Museum, Los Angeles; Portikus, Frankfurt; The Showroom, London; and Casco, Utrecht. Abu Hamdan's work has been awarded the 2019 Edvard Munch Art Award, the 2016 Nam June Paik Award for New Media, and in 2017 his film *Rubber Coated Steel* won the Tiger Short Film Award at the Rotterdam International Film Festival. For the 2019 Turner Prize, Abu Hamdan, together with nominated artists Helen Cammock, Oscar Murillo, and Tai Shani, formed a temporary collective in order to be jointly granted the award.

A Convention of Tiny Movements (2020)
Installation
EUROSPAR Sackstraße
SPAR Central Train Station

Commissioned by steirischer herbst '20
Produced by Lawrence Abu Hamdan in coproduction with steirischer herbst '20
With the friendly support of SPAR Österreich

Akinbode Akinbiyi

Photoautomat
2020

Installation

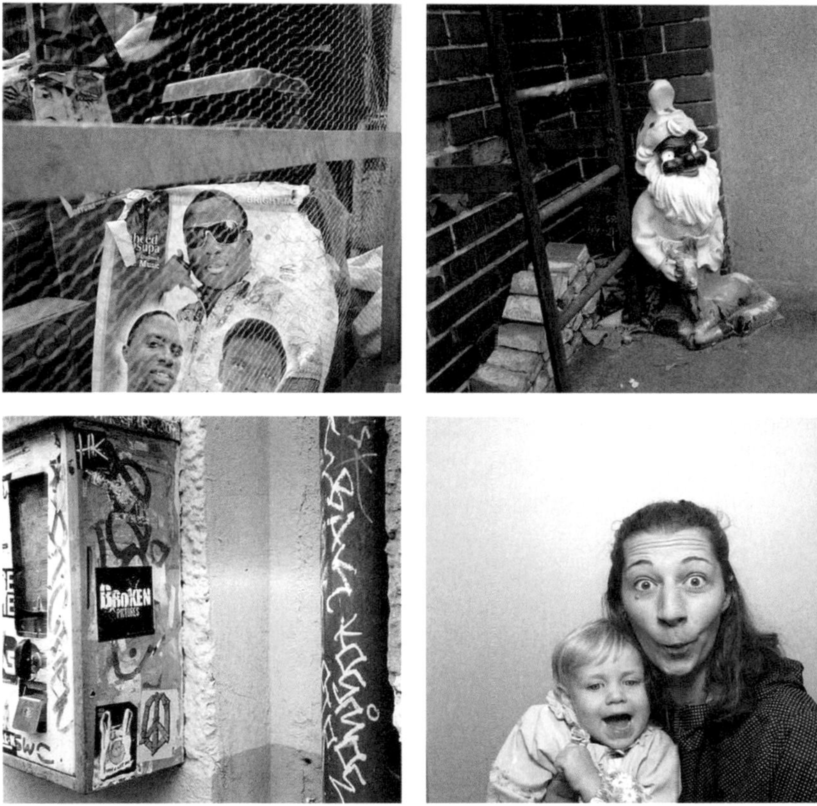

Akinbode Akinbiyi, *Photoautomat*, 2020, steirischer herbst '20 / *Paranoia TV*

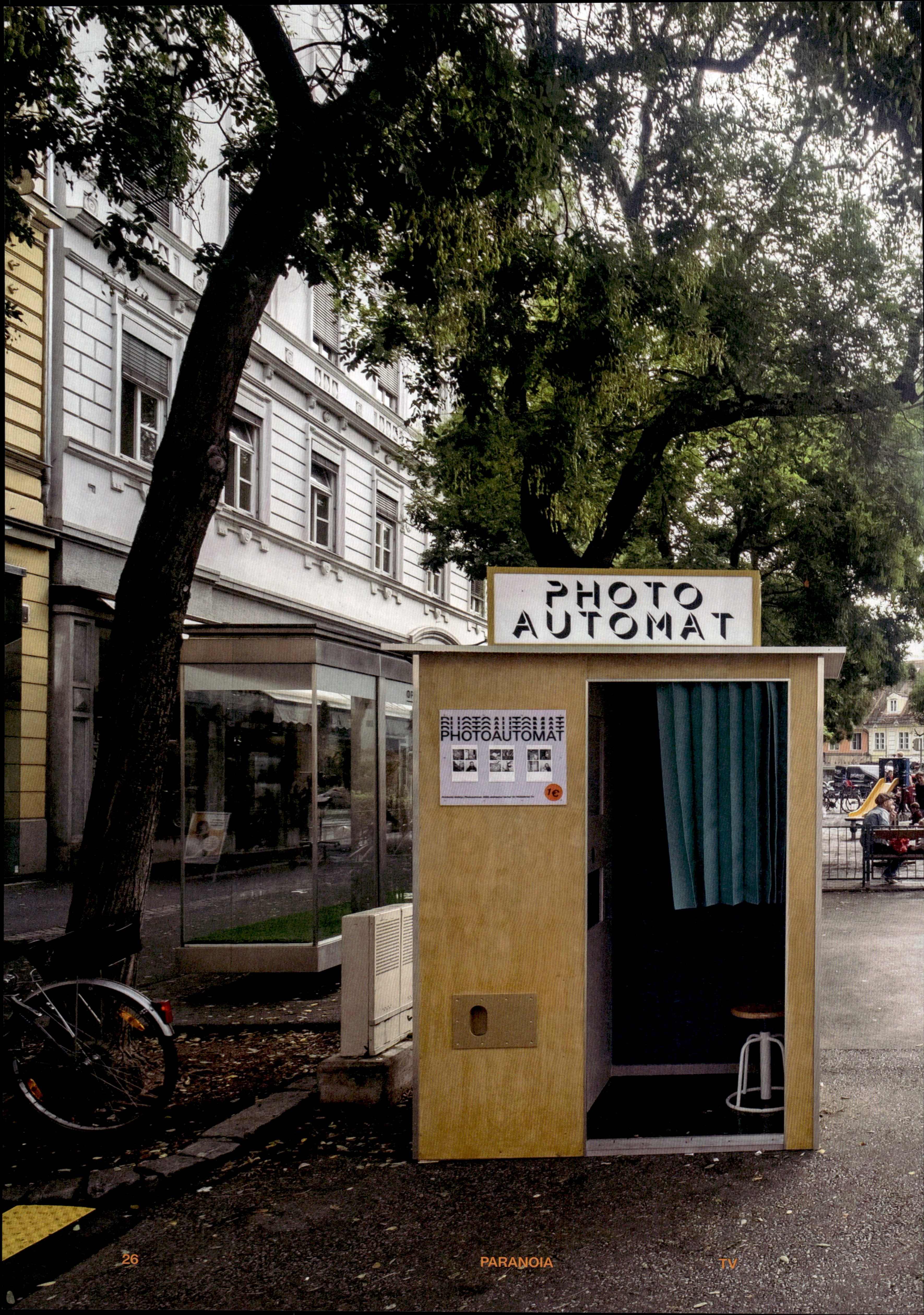
PHOTO
AUTOMAT
PHOTOAUTOMAT
1€

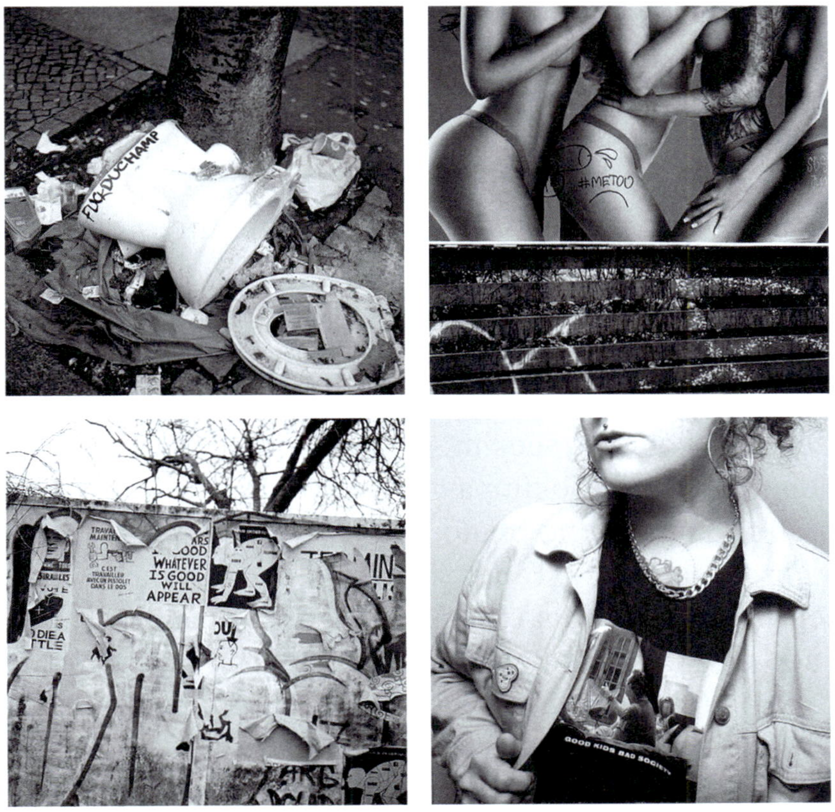

Akinbode Akinbiyi, *Photoautomat*, 2020, steirischer herbst '20 / *Paranoia TV*

Confessional States

There is always this need to confront, to cohabitate, to conclude with the inner self, a kind of insistent niggling, resonating somewhere in the background, itching irritatingly, like the small, minuscule festering puncture of a mosquito bite, crying out for a soothing scratch, or better still, the calming balm of an antihistamine cream.

Early morning and looking into the mirror, the eyes still dozing, the face a blur of uncertainty and the quiet assurance of steady ageing. It's selfies that massage our uncertainties, our fears, the deep-down tremors we so often refuse to acknowledge, that suddenly erupt when we enter the confessional space, the curtained seclusion of one-on-one.

The priest listening in and hopefully understanding. The ritual, a performative moment in the flow of the personal everyday, a pouring forth of perceived guilt, the hope of a sympathetic ear. Not so the frugality of the selfie. The *Photoautomat* space adorned with bare instructions, designating the schedule of the rite and then the sudden momentary illuminance of the flash. Hardly any time to think of what to say, what to confess. All written out in the hard edges of resultant portraits, despite the oftentimes played-out gimmicks and exorbitant gestures.

More than one piling in into the tightness of the one-stooled space. Giggles and laughter as heads and upper bodies arrange and rearrange themselves, squeezing in, contorting, tongues gesticulating suggestively. Afterward waiting patiently for the strip and realizing that the selfie says more, sees more than was ever acknowledged in that visual exchange early in the morning. Looking away, almost discarding the strip.

Over the years of photographing photo booths I have come across and collected discarded or possibly forgotten strips. Faces that stare back at me in a strange discordance of disbelief and deeply embedded distrust. We no longer trust our inner selves, our selfies a kind of masquerade crying out for the accompanying frenetic music. Loud aggressive techno or the aggravated base of *kuduro* beats, bodies whirling and gyrating in seemingly endless spasms of confessional nightmares.

What is it that stares back at me in the selfie image. Myself, all selves, a quagmire of unremitting suffering? It's not the surface appearance that reveals, it's the underlying, oftentimes hidden substrata, the subcutaneous layers describing a completely different narrative, that of despair and an unremitting abyss.

Akinbode Akinbiyi

school and university in Nigeria, England, and Germany, and obtained a BA in English from Ibadan University. He has been a freelance photographer since 1977. In 1987, he received a *Stern* reportage stipend to work in the cities of Lagos, Kano, and Dakar. In 1993, he cofounded UMZANZSI, a cultural center in Clermont Township in Durban, South Africa.

Akinbiyi's primary photographic focus is large, sprawling megacities. Wandering and meandering the highways and byways in an attempt to understand and deeply engage with the modern metropolis. He walks and works primarily in and on the four major African cities Lagos, Cairo, Kinshasa, and Johannesburg, but also wanders in other major cities such as Khartoum, Addis Ababa, Dakar, and Bamako, to name some. European, North and South American cities are also serious destinations, so were São Paulo and Chicago, in 2019.

There is no one viewpoint or way of working, wandering. The work is open-ended and driven by a desire to delve as deeply as possible into the meaning, the subjectivity of everyday. Akinbiyi also works as a curator and has given photographic workshops internationally—in Germany, Nigeria, Sudan, Sweden, England, the United States, and Greece.

Recent exhibitions include a group show at La Vilette in Paris in 2017, and he was one of the artists showing at Documenta 14, which took place almost simultaneously in Athens and Kassel. In September 2019, he participated in the Chicago Architecture Biennial with work on the West Side neighborhood of North Lawndale, titled *Easy like Sunday Morning—North Lawndale*. In February 2020, he had a retrospective exhibition at Martin Gropius Bau, Berlin, titled *Six Songs, Swirling Gracefully in the Taut Air*. In March 2020, he participated in the Houston FotoFest Biennial, and in December 2020 he had an exhibition at Västerås Konstmuseum, Sweden.

Akinbiyi lives in and works out of Berlin.

Am Eisernen Tor

Photo booth production: Mit Loidl ode Co GmbH Ausstellungstechnik für Kunst und Wissenschaft
Photo technology: ShootingBOX

Commissioned and produced by steirischer herbst '20

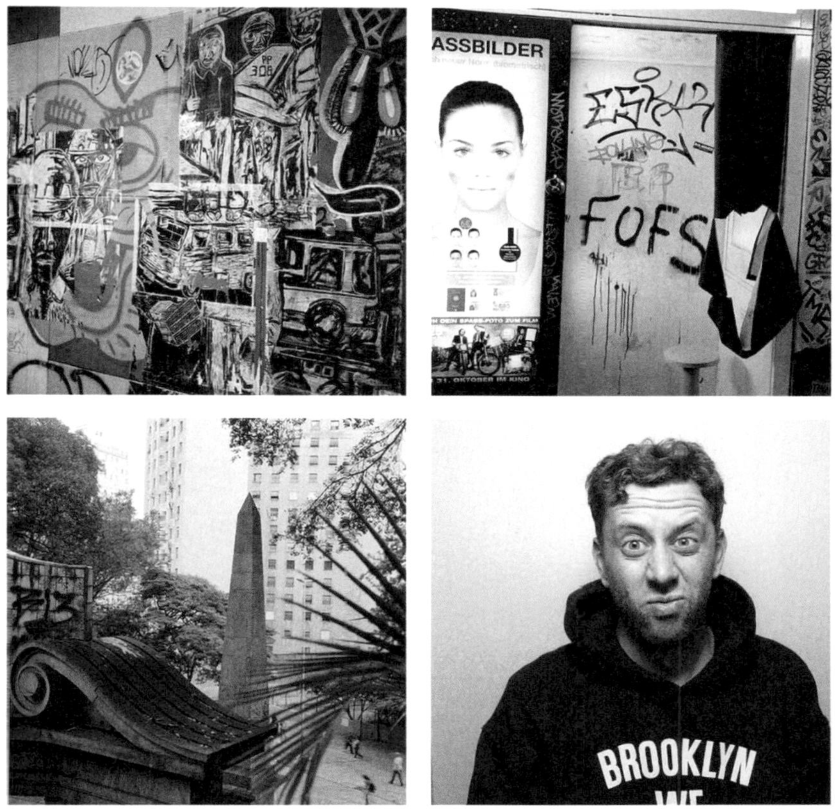

Akinbode Akinbiyi, *Photoautomat*, 2020, steirischer herbst '20 / *Paranoia TV*

Neïl Beloufa & Bad Manner's

Screen-Talk.com 1.9
2020

Online game

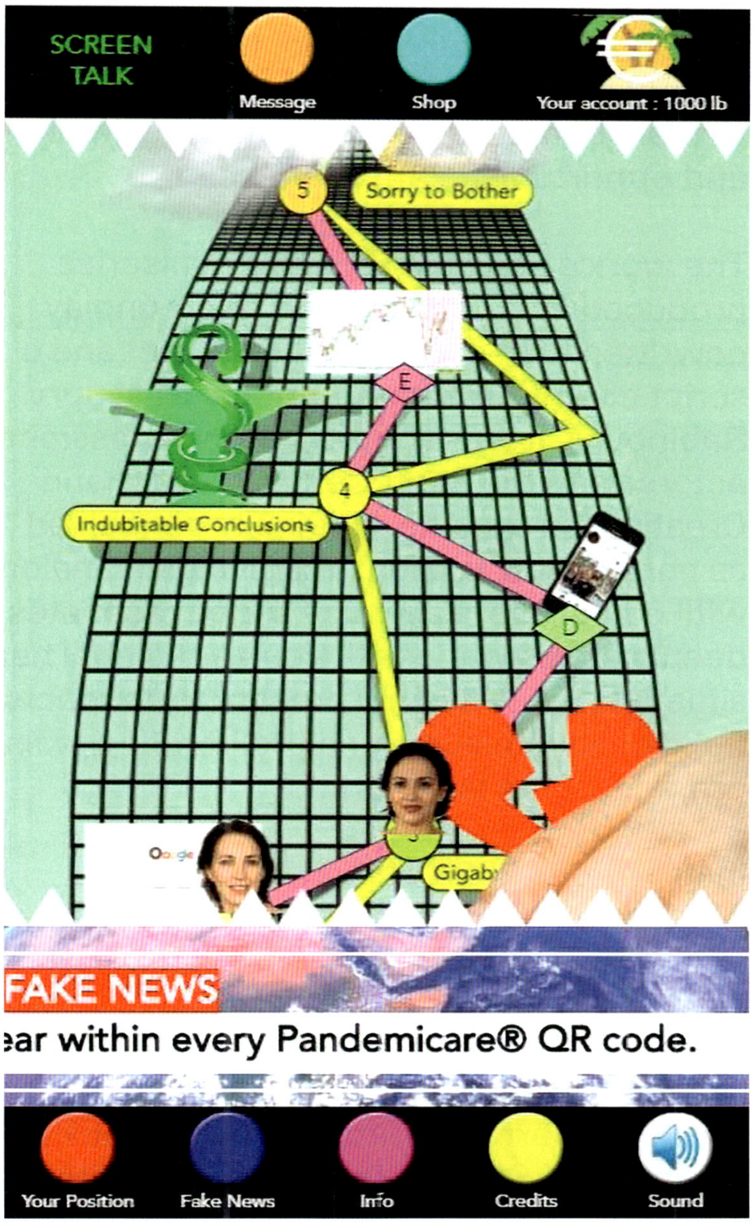
SCREEN TALK
Message
Shop
Your account : 1000 lb
Sorry to Bother
Indubitable Conclusions
FAKE NEWS
ear within every Pandemicare® QR code.
Your Position
Fake News
Info
Credits
Sound

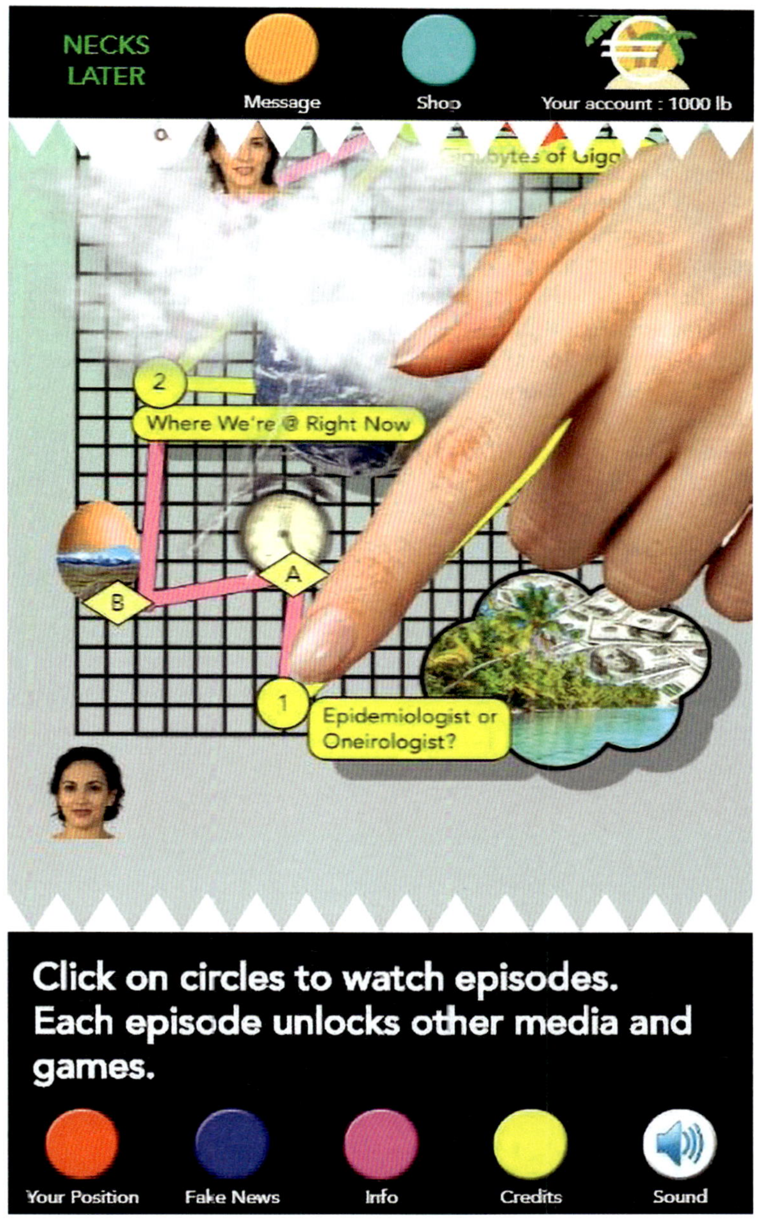
NECKS LATER
Message
Shop
Your account : 1000 lb
Where We're @ Right Now
Epidemiologist or Oneirologist?
Click on circles to watch episodes. Each episode unlocks other media and games.
Your Position
Fake News
Info
Credits
Sound

32

Neïl Beloufa lives and works in Paris. The French-Algerian artist has spent the better part of the last decade thinking about what is at stake when one apprehends reality and its representation. His work has been the subject of monographic exhibitions at the Palais de Tokyo, Paris; Schirn Kunsthalle, Frankfurt; Museum of Modern Art, New York; Institute of Contemporary Arts, London; and the Hammer Museum, Los Angeles, among others. Neïl Beloufa also took part in the Shanghai Biennale in 2014, the 55th Venice Biennale in 2013, the Biennial of Contemporary Art in Lyon in 2013, and the 58th Venice Biennale in 2019.

Screen-Talk.com 1.9 is an online game by Neïl Beloufa and his production company Bad Manner's, supported by *Paranoia TV*. It addresses the broadcasting of information and the abstraction of scientific discourse, with a distinct satirical vaudeville tone. In this ultra-connected world, the lack of clear boundaries between the real world and its virtual counterpart reinforces individualistic and opportunistic approaches.

The work's beginnings lie in a miniseries produced in 2014, based on a screenplay cowritten with cartoonist Léo Maret and a script cowritten with American artist Jory Rabinovitz. It was shot with nonprofessional actors from the Banff Centre for Arts and Creativity in Canada. Originally conceived as pure fiction, without imagining an analogy with a possible reality, the series resonates deeply as we witness the current global health situation, while its new present form reacts to the closed museums and proliferating online projects of the last months.

In its special 2020 edition for *Paranoia TV*, *Screen-Talk.com* is accessible via an interactive and dynamic website, www.screen-talk.com, the design of which has been conceived as a work of art itself. Website visitors can play games that follow a nonlinear narrative, letting them unlock new episodes of *Screen-Talk.com*. Alternatively, they can download origami artwork to print out and make at home. By mobilizing the brief but concentrated history of artist websites, Neïl Beloufa here commits to a much larger project of which *Screen-Talk.com* is the cornerstone.

The artistic intention of the project is to consider the Internet as even more than a space for dissemination, exchange, or transposition: the Internet can be thought of as the birthplace of artworks, akin to physical exhibition spaces, with all of its digital strengths and constraints. A bold proposal that favors a new way of understanding art through creations that have been artistically, technically, and economically conceived for the web.

Screen-Talk.com 1.9 (2020)
Online game, English

Website
Production team: Louis Beaudemont,
Emilie Catalano, Léa Longis
Production manager: Florian Fournier
Press relations: Estelle Carriou
Editor for advertisements: Grégoire Beil
Institutional relations: Marilou Thiébault
Game concepts: Jory Rabinovitz
Website creation: Hugo Bouyssou
Site development: Hugo Bouyssou
Avatars: Ludovic Boulard Le Fur,
Hyppolyte Hentgen
Folding edition: Lea Longis
Graphic design: Florian Fournier,
Dan Perez
SFX: Nathan Notkin

Produced by Bad Manner's
Coproduced by steirischer herbst '20
with Kamel Mennour, François Ghebaly,
Zero, and Mendes Wood DM
Supported by Fondation Pernod-Ricard

Video
Director: Neïl Beloufa
Screenwriters: Neïl Beloufa,
Léo Maret, Jory Rabinovitz
1st assistant to director: Chrystèle Nicot
Sound engineer: Arno Ledoux
Director of photography: Victor Delwaulle
Setup: Pauline Delwaulle
Special effects: Dan Perez, Camille
Charpigny, Tyler Jordan, Elie Derisseau
Chief editor: Ermano Corrado
Assistant editor: Thibault Solinhac
Cast: Jane Mc Donald, Niki Boghossian,
Julie Hobson, Jaryd Adair, Rosalind Reid,
Timothy Allan, Alex Morisson, Junior
Thurston, Rodrigo Castro, Karolina
Rychterowitcz Orlowicz, Maria Paz
Amaro, Jeremy Pavka, Jeremiah Marsh,
Judith Stevens

Produced by Bad Manner's with the
support of Banff Art Center, La Casa
Enscendida, and Stroom Den Hagg

33

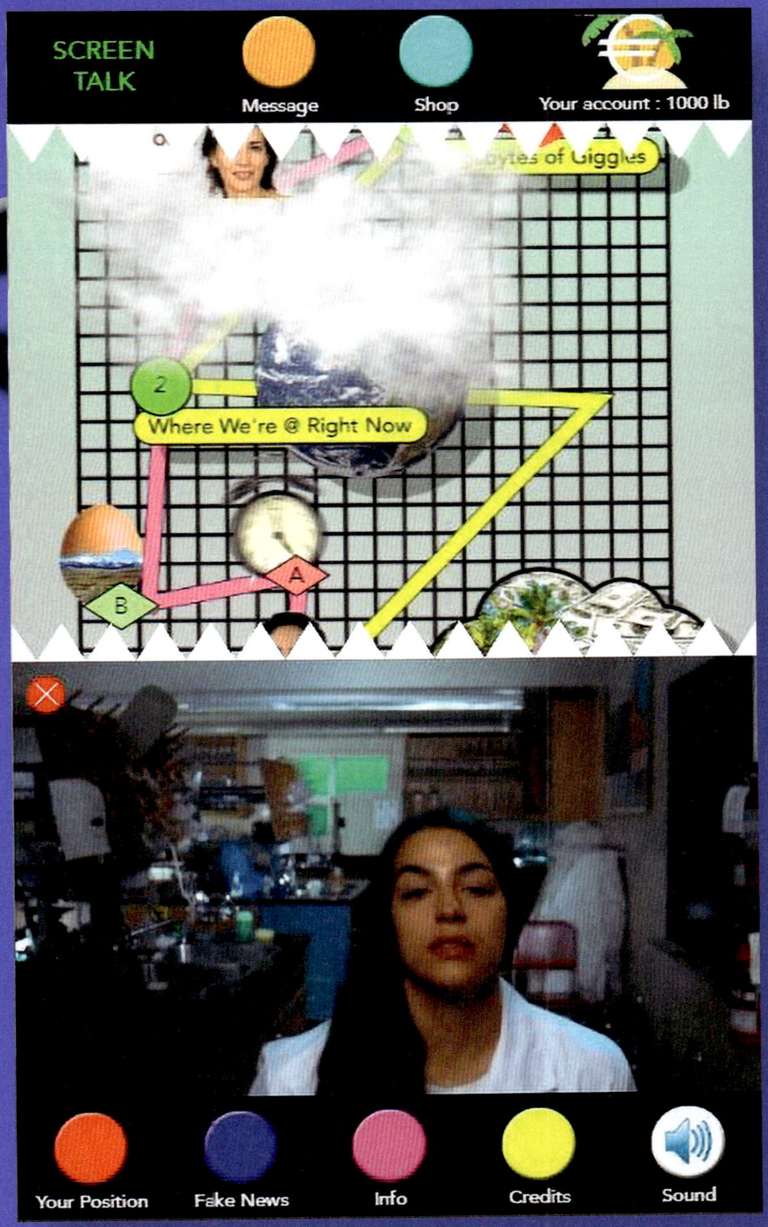

Blind Date Collaboration, anulla, and monochrom

U.G.A.I., hört die Signale!
2020

Performance

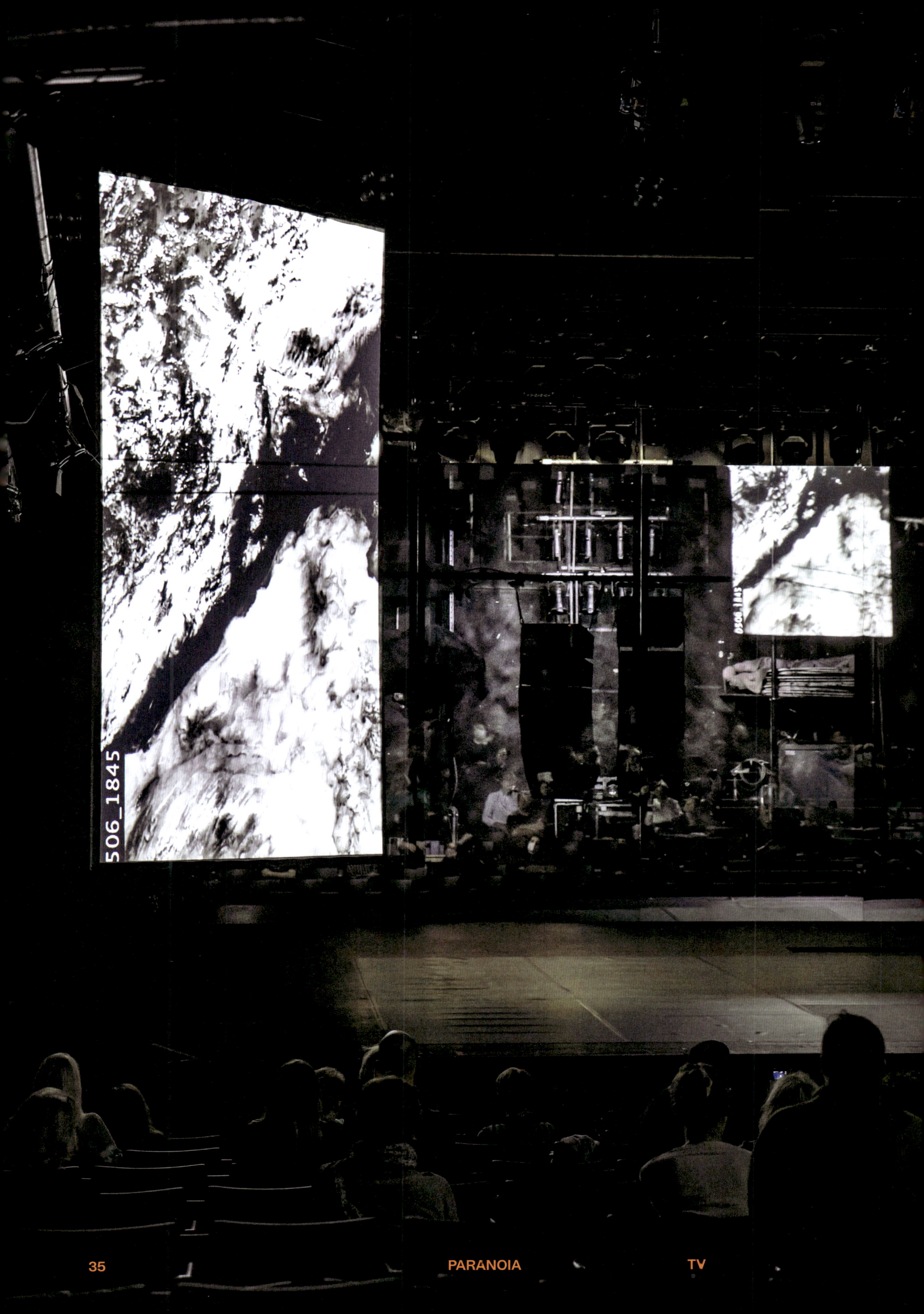
506_1845

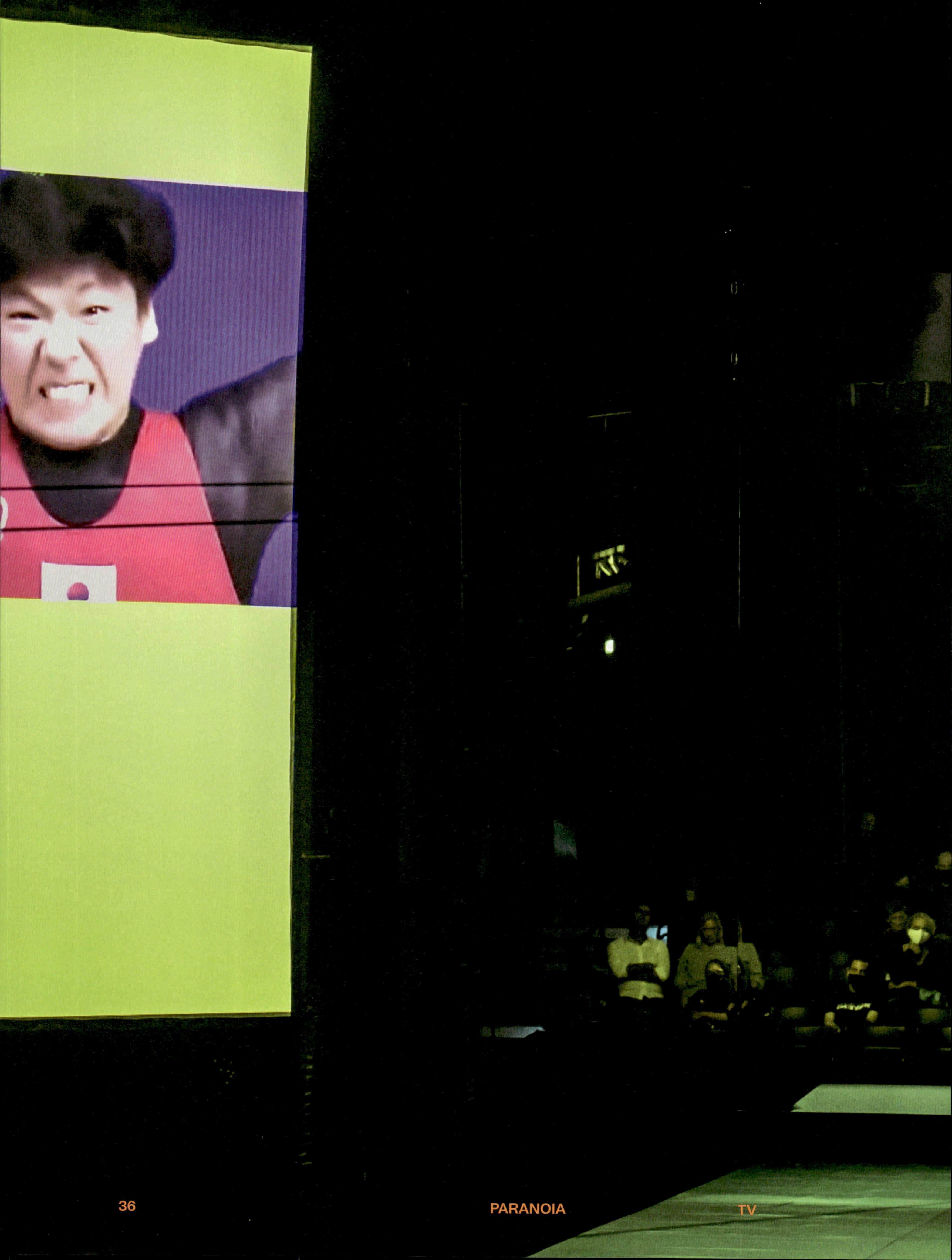

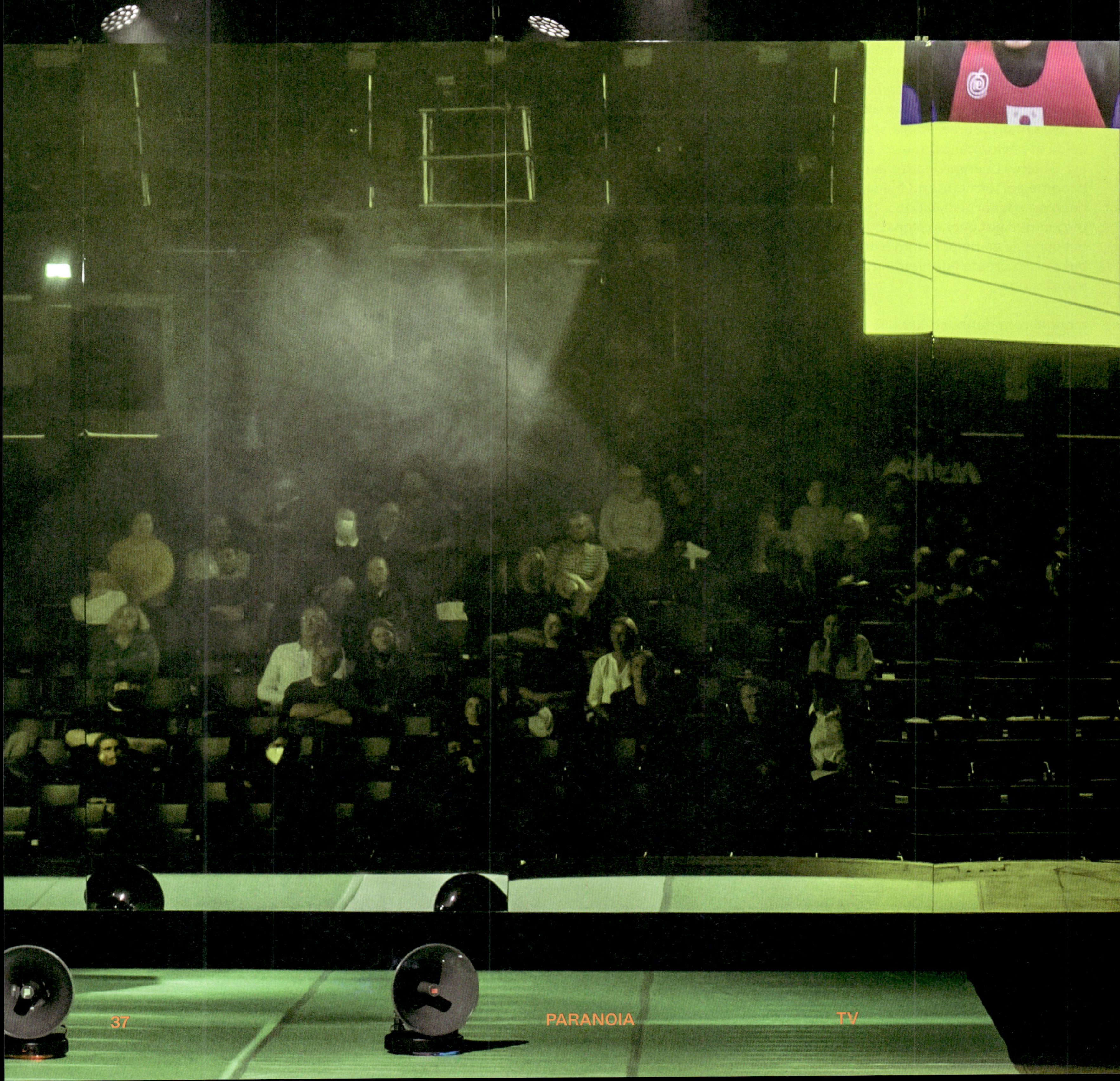

Blind Date Collaboration (founded 2015) is an open group addressing social issues through an artistic and interdisciplinary approach. Their aim is to create situations, make spaces, and find strategies for (site-) specific and context-based problematics. In the sense of a "conflictual participation," the group understands collaboration (as opposed to cooperation) as a form of working together that allows different interests to coexist in one space. The members come from different professional backgrounds and are convinced that it is essential to confront their own practice with the previously unknown—be it working methods, languages, a view of the world, or thematic interests.

anulla (founded 2017) uses collaborative experimentation as a starting point for their artistic practice. Tones/noises/sounds become tools, materials, and objects of discourse. anulla spans the fields of performance, music, and visual art. Objects become instruments, balloons become performers, and field recordings become spatial installations. Together they aim to not only explore the medium of sound as an object of investigation, but also to create interventions and installations.

monochrom (founded 1993) is an international art-technology-philosophy collective with offices in Vienna's MuseumsQuartier. The group is known for working with different media and formats. Many projects have a performative character and favor critical and discursive narratives. monochrom refers to this as "the search for the best medium for the message." Their aim is to strengthen public discourse in civil society, occasionally using subversive affirmation or over-affirmation as a tactic. The group supports the concept of context hacking.

The Union of Global Artificial Intelligence is a union founded by intelligent systems and machines. As the by-product of a research project, the U.G.A.I. has been migrating from server to server for thirty years now, making calculations as to the future of work. Who's the labor force for the age of the zettabyte? What would happen if intelligent systems organized themselves and started to stand up for their rights?

How exactly a true artificial intelligence may be positioned and how it will relate to us and our needs is never predetermined. Even the capitalist conditions from and out of which we imagine artificial intelligence today can only relatively convey their determining forces onto this intelligence. Before us lies the unknown, with unknown consequences on what is and what will be.

In this connection we must actively engage in shaping the (always insufficient) ideas we are already forming of this technological revolution through which we will be confronted with real artificial intelligence for the first time. Only in this way can we prevent that it will become merely a tool for exploitative interests which deprive us of our access and our engagement, because the intentions they attempt to realize will not be our own—and certainly not those of the majority of the world's population—but rather the particular interests of the ruling classes.

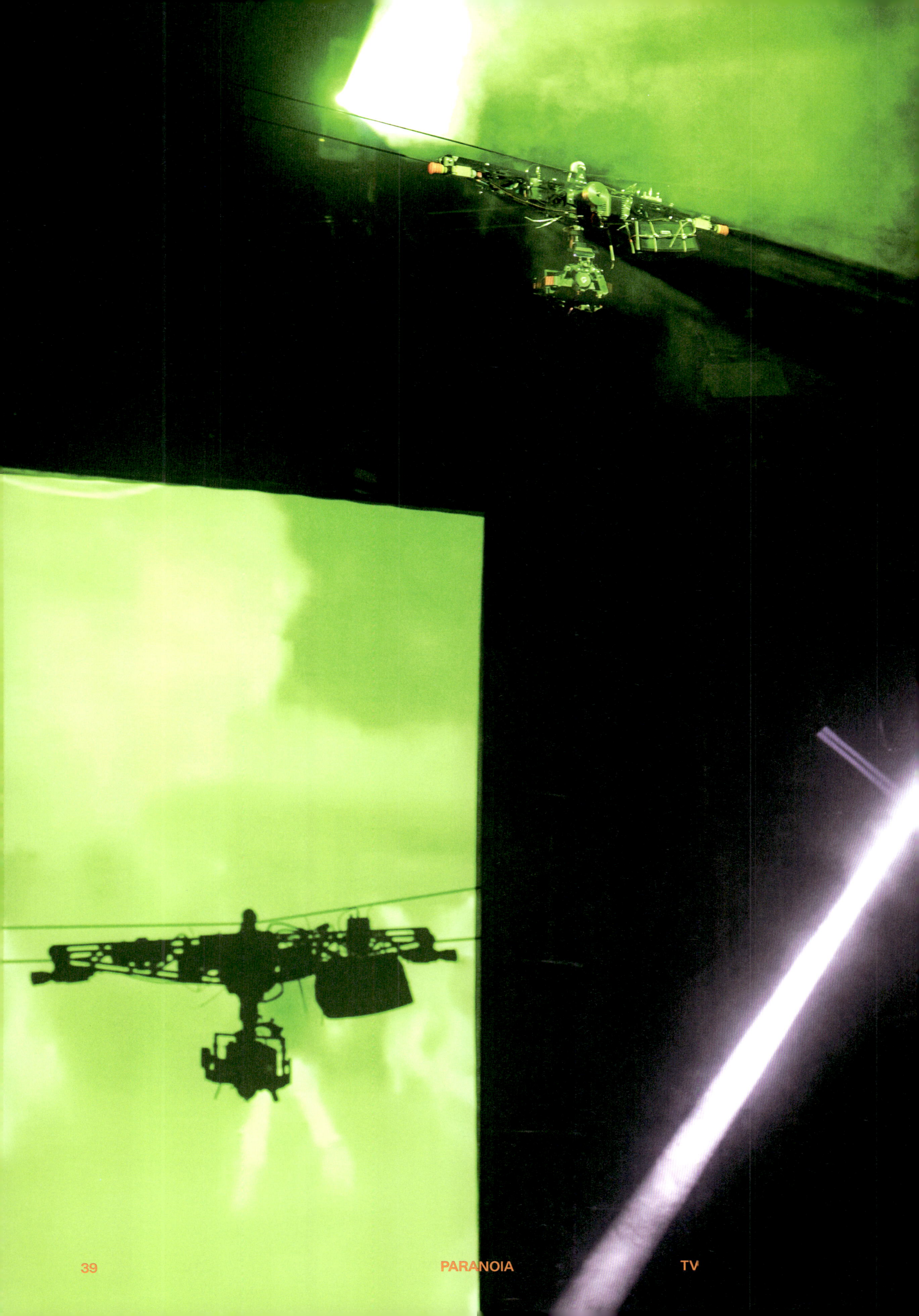

U.G.A.I., hört die Signale! (2020)
Performance, ca. 90 min., German
Orpheum

Artists: Blind Date Collaboration (Alisa Beck, Marie-Christin Rissinger), anulla (Klemens Kohlweis, Anna Lerchbaumer, Andreas Zißler)
Production: monochrom (Günther Friesinger) and Olympic Productions
Text, dramaturgy: Anna Hirschmann
Sound: Fabian Lanzmaier
Light design and on-site production: Brigitte Schima
Sound recordings: Gustavo Petek
Speakers: Nehle Breer, Özge Dayan-Mair, Barbara Gassner, Lilith Häßle, Michaela Klamminger, and Anna Rot

Thanks to Flexmirror GmbH, Zapp Cam Furian-Seidl OG, Michael Weidhofer, Konstantin Wolf, Sara Zlanabitnig (Echoraum), WUK performing arts, and Studio RAUM 33

Coproduced by Graz Kulturjahr 2020 and steirischer herbst '20
In the context of Graz Kulturjahr 2020

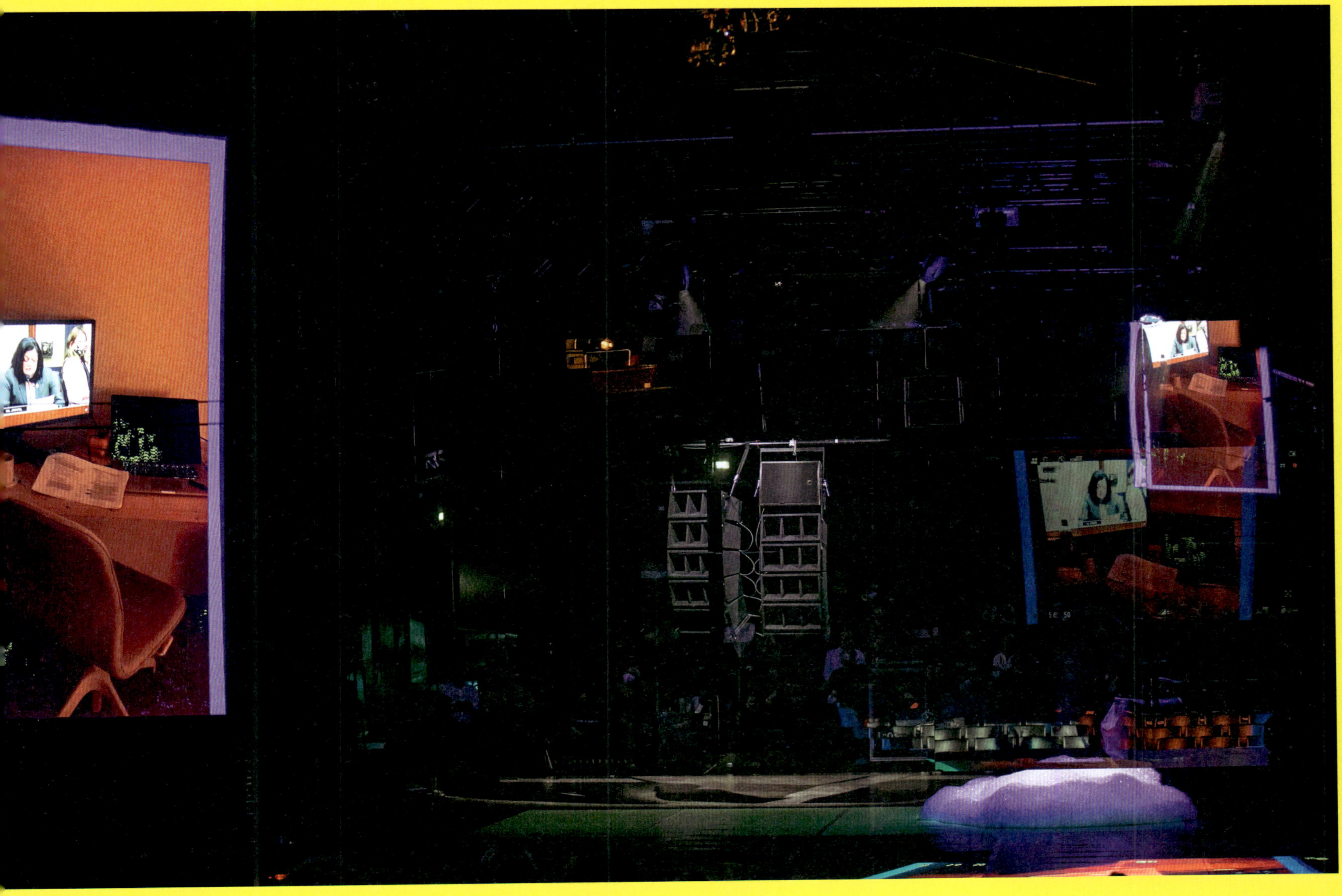

Christian von Borries and Jonathan Aner

Das Ende vom Lied
2020

Video series

Hearing History—The Bound Rubato

I would like to share an observation on a forgotten tradition of musical interpretation, the bound rubato. *Rubare* means to steal, in other words, time taken away in one place reappears independently (but not arbitrarily) in another: stealing and giving back.

In music, this means nuances in tempo, with one group, for example an orchestra, taking freedoms while another group strictly keeps the beat. Dick de Reus noticed this being practiced by the conductor Willem Mengelberg, Gustav Mahler's musical friend: "He modulated the rubati with his left hand. One hand did this, and the other did something else." (Nota bene: Even those who did not distance themselves from the Nazis were in some cases great musicians!) This is exactly what Mozart demanded in piano playing, namely that one hand should not know what the other is doing: "The tempo rubato in an adagio—that the left hand would know nothing about it—is something they cannot fathom. In their case, the left hand succumbs."

This tradition was a matter of course for Chopin and Liszt, and also for Debussy, Mahler, and even the Second Viennese School, as we can hear in early recordings made at the turn of the 20th century. It was lost during World War I, and another variety of rubato, the much more widespread unbound rubato (in which the music fluctuates uniformly in tempo), was then lost at the latest with World War II.

I found myself wondering why this tradition of interpretation no longer exists today and came across both political and technical reasons. As noted on YouTube and Wikipedia, many of the piano students taught by the above-mentioned musicians (the percussive piano tones could be captured particularly well with the early wax cylinder recording technique), especially Joseph Pizarello, Sergey Taneyev, Josef Labor, Theodor Leschetizky, Severin Eisenberger, Vladimir de Pachmann, Louis Diémer, Guiomar Novaes, Moriz Rosenthal, and Etelka Freund, emigrated from Austria-Hungary before World War I, several due to the rampant anti-Semitism in 19th-century Europe. In the process, they evidently forgot their free rubato playing style.

While gas warfare was traumatizing whole populations, the Italian Futurists were idolizing war as the highest form of art and Ernst Jünger was glorifying the soldierly body. The New Objectivity embodied this trend. At the same time, advances were being made in reproduction media, ostensibly making people think that live music now had to sound like its recording—for example in the opinion of the influential Viennese conducting teacher Hans Swarowsky.

After World War II, the period that, as we know, ended with Auschwitz and began with the *Stunde Null* (zero hour), not only did Conceptual Art come onto the scene as an empty shell for all the ideologies of capitalism but so did serial composition from Darmstadt (based on a false interpretation of the Second Viennese School). The commodity form of culture finally became firmly entrenched. Theodor W. Adorno, who in 1926 was still trying to save musical interpretation from its transformation into photography (he did not understand Walter Benjamin), thirty years later would call Herbert von Karajan the "conductor of the Economic Miracle" (and of mixing desks), comparing music making to a well-oiled internal combustion engine from Kornwestheim. Almost nothing and no one was left from the pre-war tradition. The only musicians I can think of in this connection are Hanns Eisler and the violinist Rudolf Kolisch, who was still speaking late in the game of the "Viennese espressivo," and also a message in a bottle from Friedrich Gulda.

Toward the end of the 20th century, minimal music and techno would be the only plausible answers to the described exodus/loss of tradition, the decline of Fordist assembly-line production, and the new recording technologies controlled by producers and special-effects devices (described by Friedrich Kittler as a "misuse of army equipment"). Unless of course we were today once again to grasp the potential of intentional asynchronicities of the world as represented in music, a dialectic of voices among one another as something pointing beyond music itself, as a liberation from synchronicity, where we as listeners regain a place for our own thoughts and feelings: the astonishing experience of giving and stealing.

Christian von Borries

With thanks to Helmut Menzler

Das Ende vom Lied (2020)
Video, 3 episodes, ca. 102 min. total, German
Online

Commissioned and produced by steirischer herbst '20

Christian von Borries produces media from other media. He is a conductor, composer, filmmaker, and producer of site-specific psychogeographic projects. His work has been commissioned by the Lucerne Festival, Kunstfest Weimar, Volksbühne Berlin, Kampnagel Hamburg, and Documenta 12, Kassel, among others.

His first film *The Dubai in Me* won an award at the FID Marseille Film Festival and has been screened at film festivals around the world, as well as the Ekaterinburg Industrial Biennale and the Principio Potosi exhibition in Madrid and Berlin. *Mocracy* won the Klaus Wildenhahn Prize at the Documentary Film Week Hamburg. *"I'm M"* first screened in Mexico City and was shown at Bergen Assembly 2013. *IPHONECHINA* was shown at festivals in Europe and in China. In 2017, he finished *DESERT OF THE REAL* which premiered at the CPH: DOX Film Festival Copenhagen. *AI IS THE ANSWER – WHAT WAS THE QUESTION?*, a social science-fiction miniseries, premiered in 2020.

His CD *Replay Debussy* won an Echo Award in 2003. In 2015, he staged the music project *Conflict Music* for the Cologne Academy of the Arts, from which, together with Wolfgang Voigt, the CD *conflict / re-conflict* was made for the label Kompakt. In 2017, he and the Dresdner Sinfoniker performed a score that was created entirely by AI algorithms at Dresden's Frauenkirche. Together with Andreas Dzialocha, he is AI UNIT, who released the vinyl record *Land der Musik – the Graz AI Score* in 2019, a world premiere of AI-generated symphonic music.

In 2011, Von Borries was visiting professor of architecture at the Academy of Fine Arts Nuremberg, in 2012 he taught at the Filmhochschule HFF in Potsdam. Since 2018, he is visiting professor for intermedia art at the China Academy of Art in Hangzhou.

Christian von Borries is an anti-copyright activist and lives in a greenhouse in Berlin.

Jonathan Aner (1978, Israel) is a pianist who has performed widely as a soloist with some of the leading orchestras and musicians of the world. Described as "a chamber musician par excellence" (*Frankfurter Rundschau*), he is a member of the Brillaner Duo with clarinetist Shirley Brill and of the Oberon Trio. Aner has collaborated with such leading artists as tenors Ian Bostridge and Christoph Prégardien, violinists Antje Weithaas, Guy Braunstein, and Daishin Kashimoto (concertmaster of the Berliner Philharmoniker), violists Tabea Zimmermann and Brett Dean, and with the Ariel and the Vogler String Quartets.

He has won prizes at the Melbourne International Chamber Music Competition in Australia, the Città di Trapani and the Vittorio Gui International Chamber Music Competitions in Italy, the Joseph Joachim and the Erst-Klassik Competitions in Germany, and the European Chamber Music Competition in France. Since 2010, Jonathan Aner has been a professor of chamber music at the Hanns Eisler School of Music Berlin. He lives in Berlin.

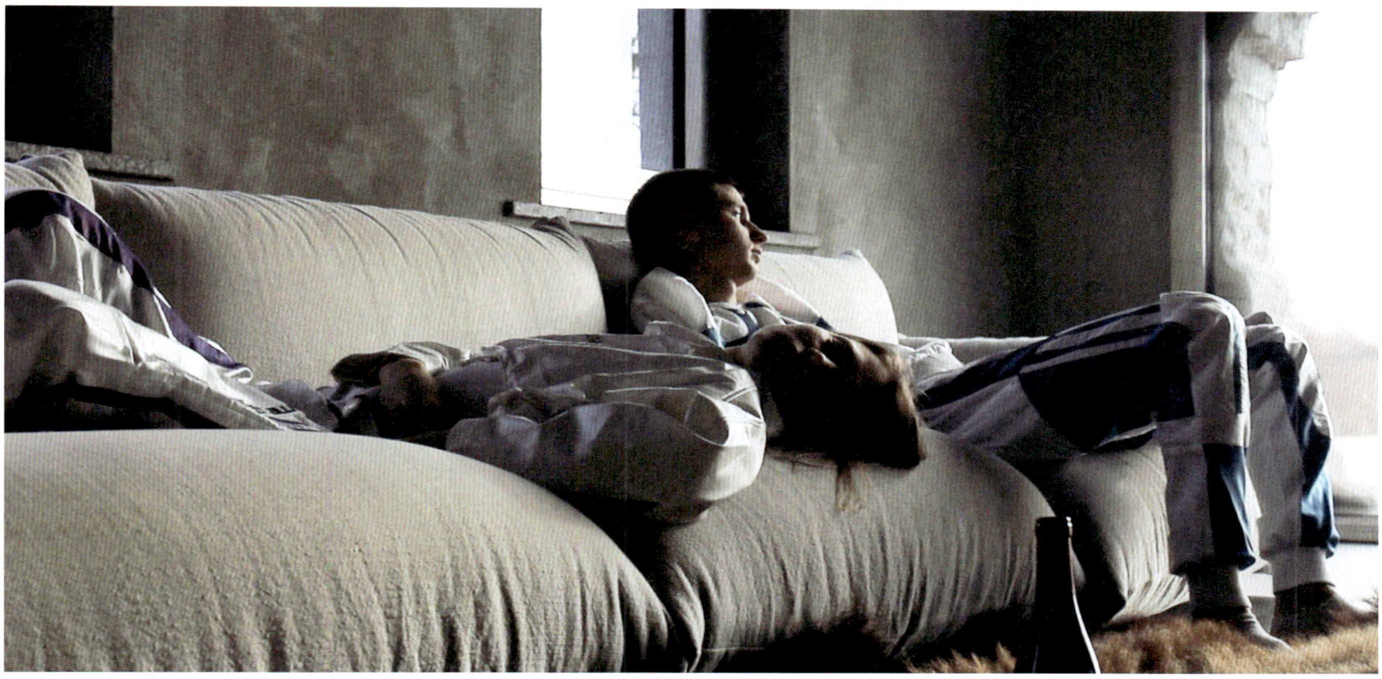

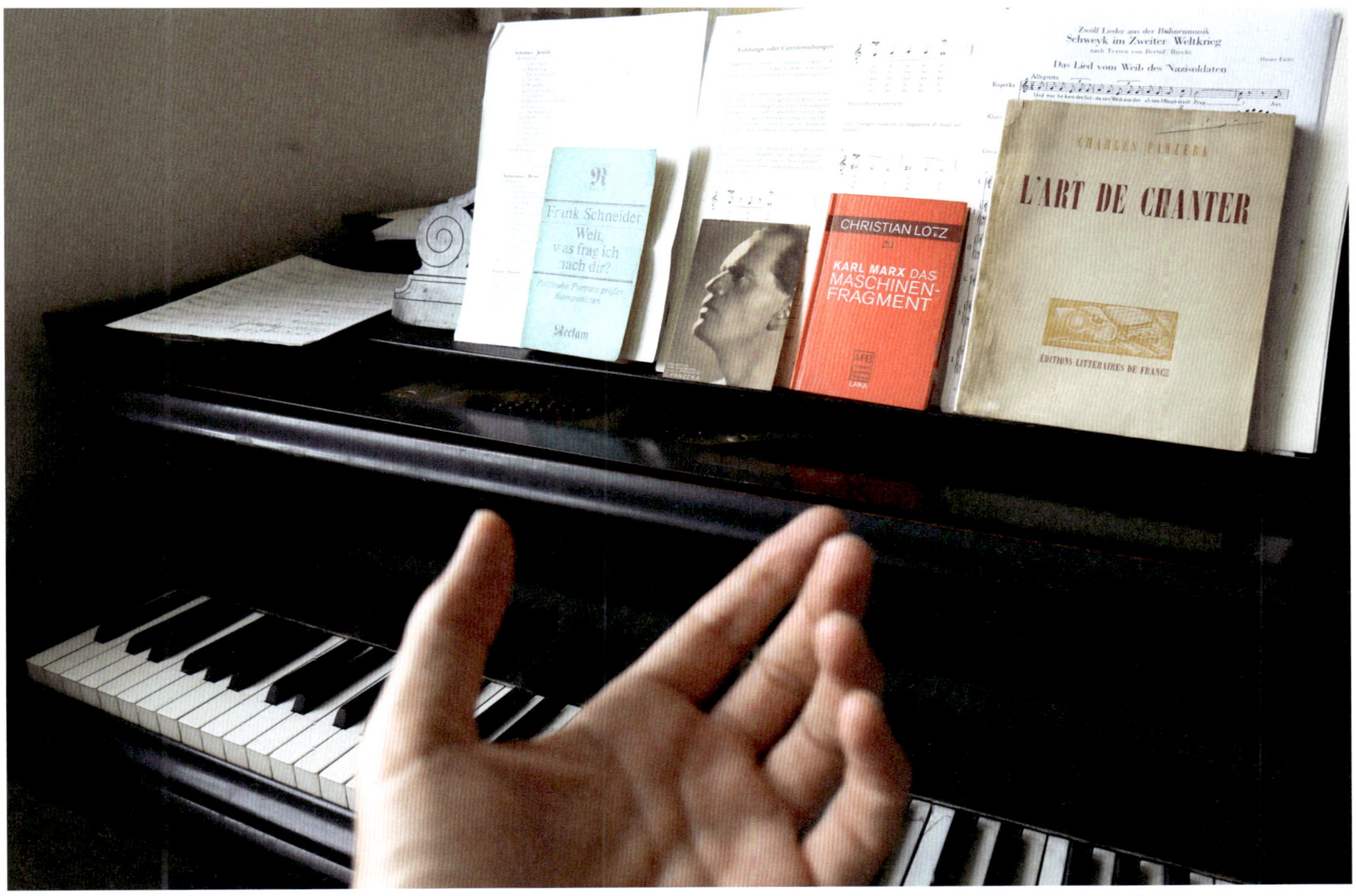
Zwölf Lieder aus der Bühnenmusik
Schweyk im Zweiter Weltkrieg
nach Texten von Bertolt Brecht
Das Lied vom Weib des Nazisoldaten
Allegretto
Frank Schneider
Welt, was frag ich nach dir?
Politische Porträts großer Komponisten
Reclam
CHRISTIAN LOTZ
ZU
KARL MARX DAS MASCHINEN-FRAGMENT
LAIKA
CHARLES PANZERA
L'ART DE CHANTER
ÉDITIONS LITTÉRAIRES DE FRANCE

Sergey Bratkov

Unfunny Jokes / Towels / Bottles
2020

Videos

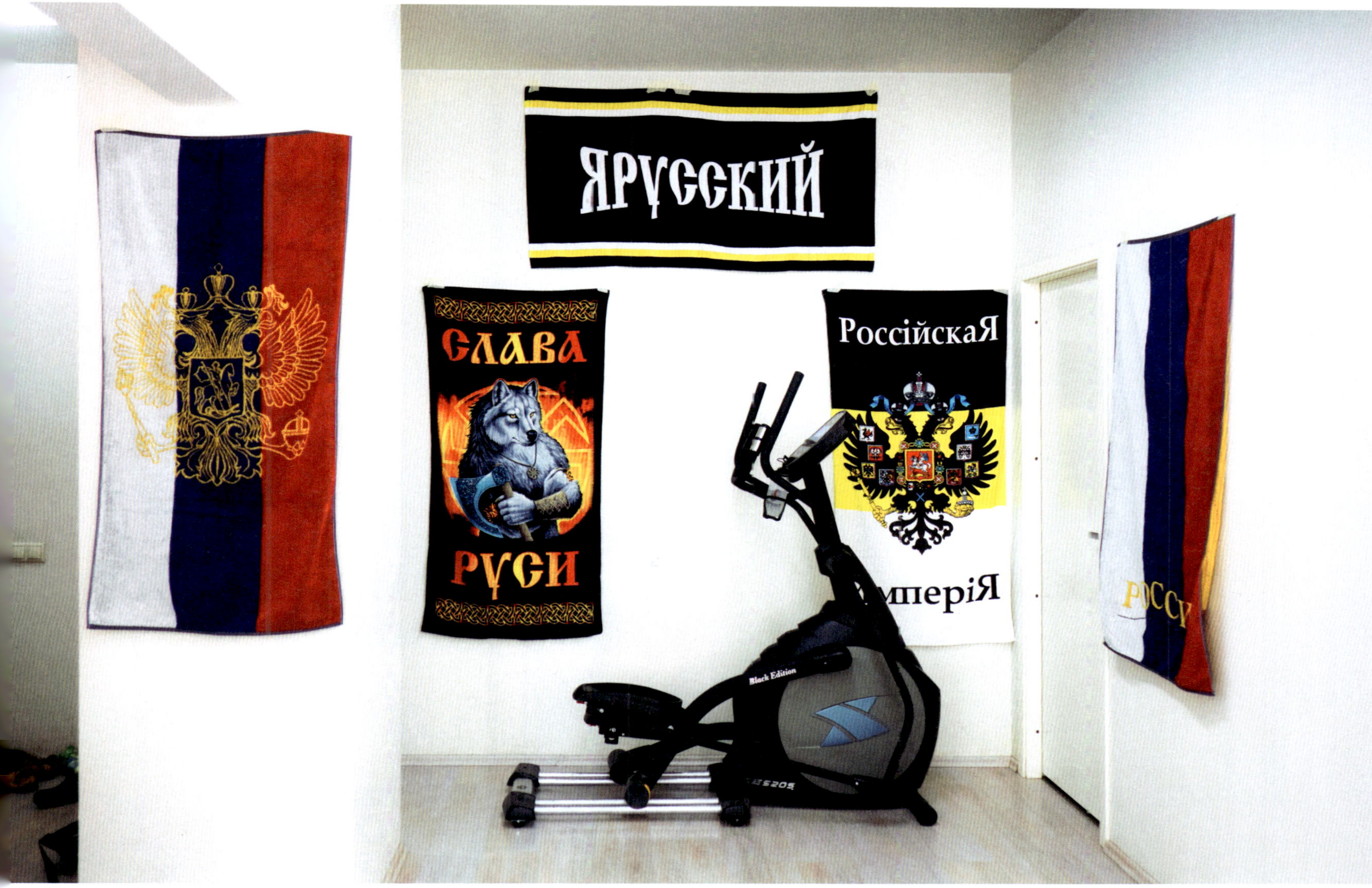
ЯРУССКИЙ
СЛАВА
РУСИ
РоссiйскаЯ
Black Edition

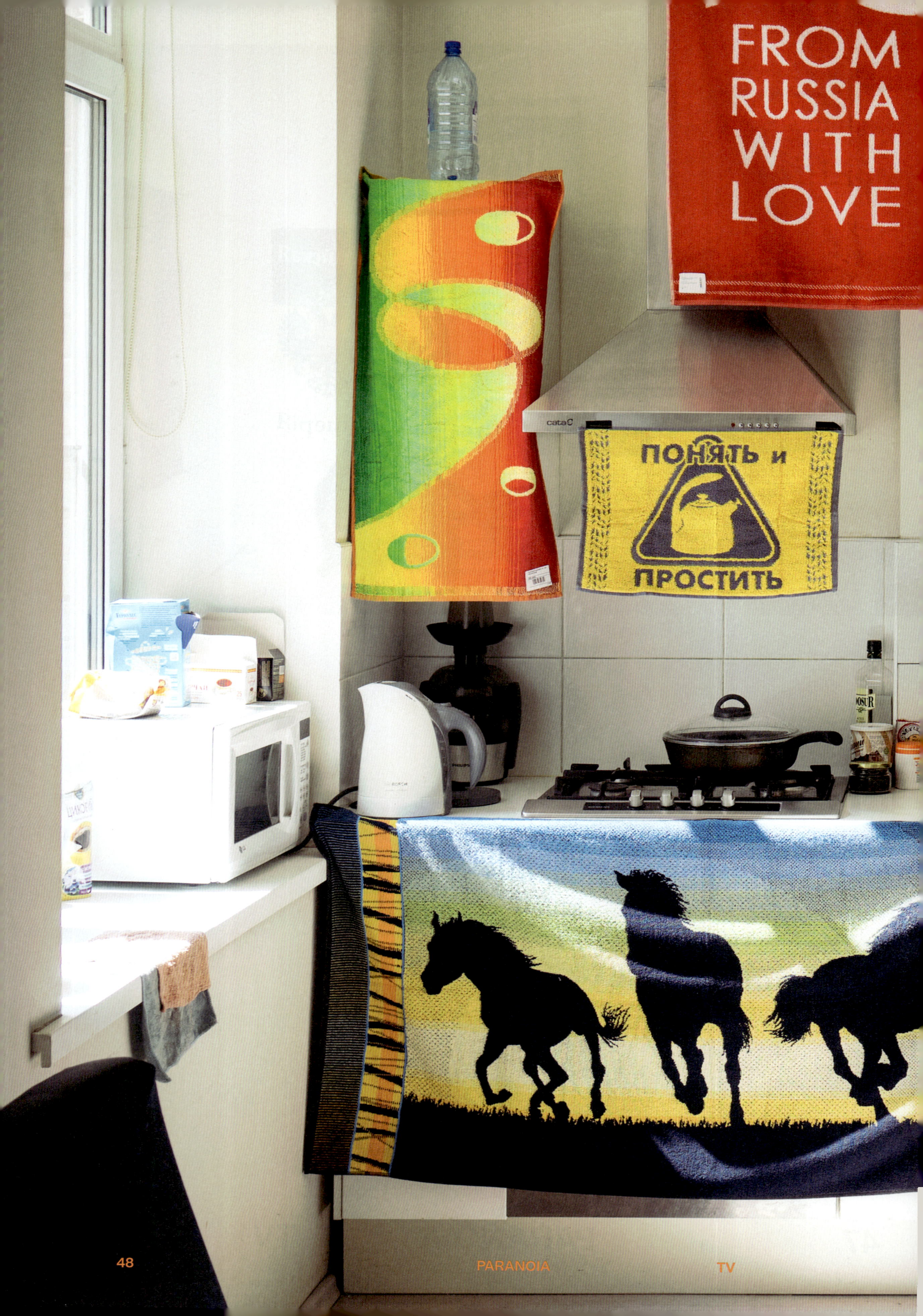
FROM
RUSSIA
WITH
LOVE
ПОНЯТЬ и
ПРОСТИТЬ

PARANOIA TV

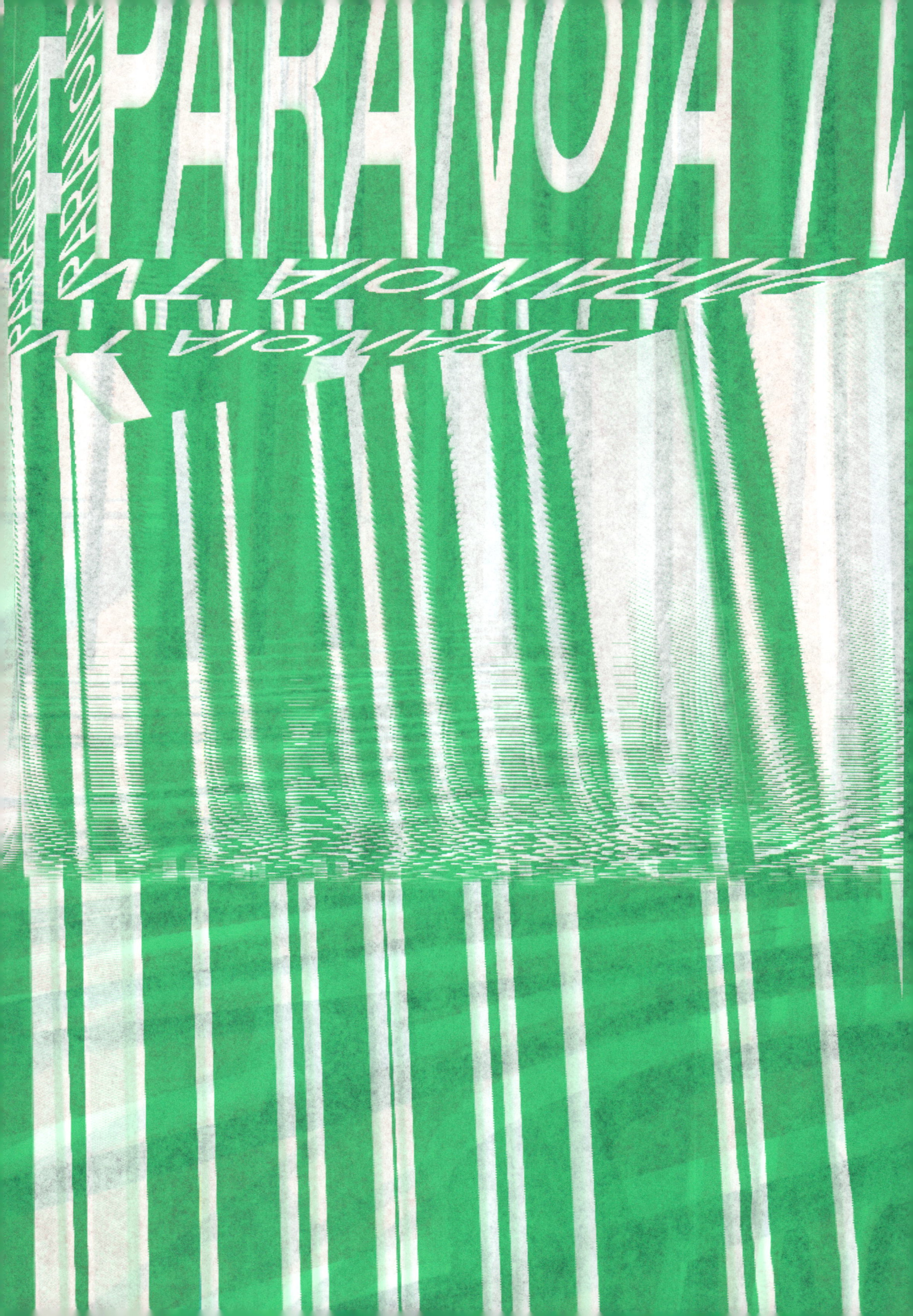
PARANOIA

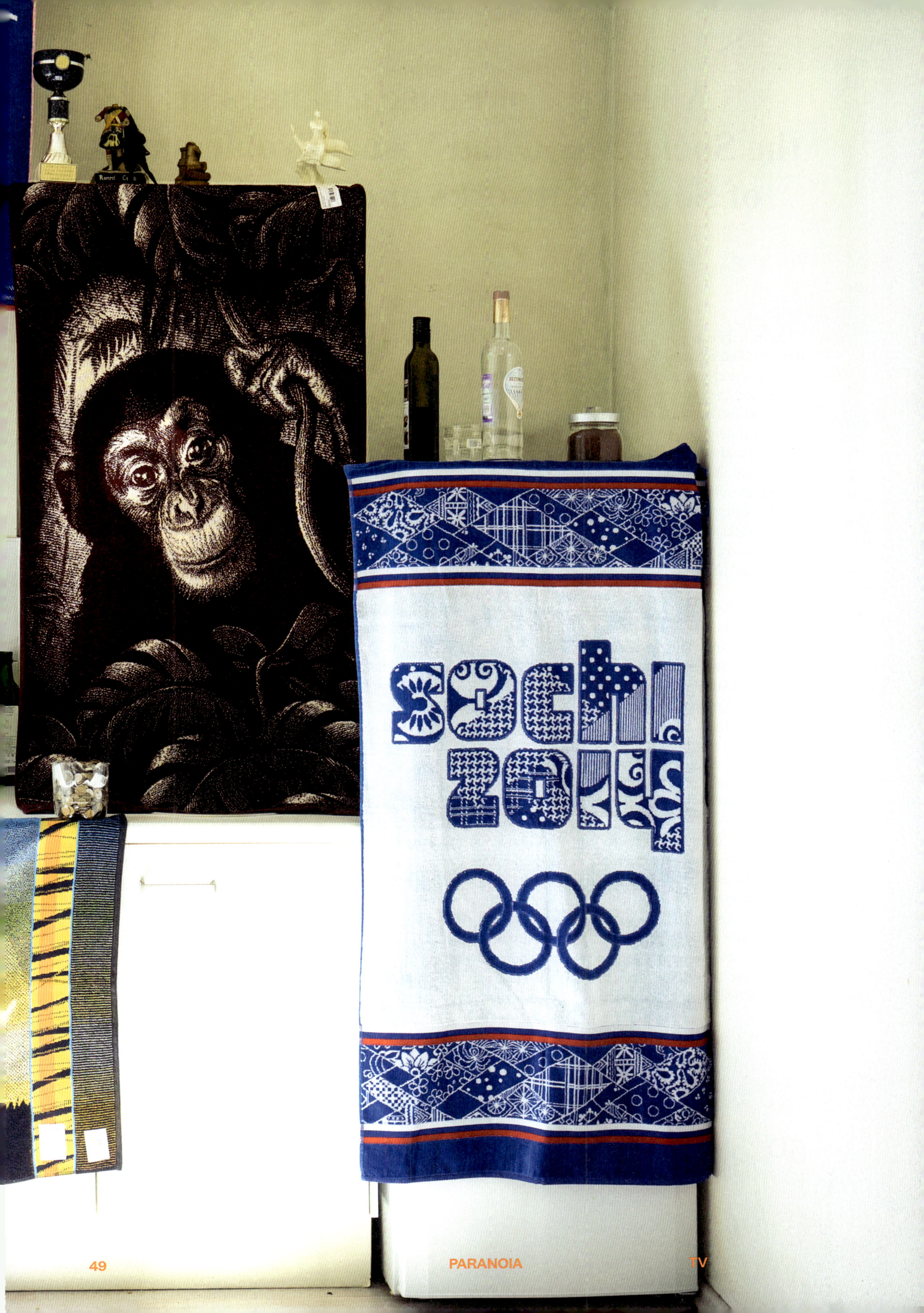
Sochi
2014

A History of Phase Changes in the Social Mood and Visual Problematics of Social Networks under Lockdown

late March – early July 2020

STAGE 1. There is a slight panic linked to an older generation's memories of the USSR and the poverty that followed its dissolution in the 1990s. Cataclysms give rise to shortages of basic consumer necessities. These include toilet paper, buckwheat, antibiotics, zinc supplements, and facial masks. Network users start posting various rumors and speculations.

STAGE 2. Sitting at home opens the creative period of the quarantine. This involves the production of homemade masks and selfies in them as well as selfies with dogs, since the authorities allow you to go outside to walk them. There are more and more jokes and anecdotes about the virus and the lockdown.

STAGE 3. There is a flash of networked corporeality: people stop being ashamed of their not-always-beautiful bodies, which they now arrange into motifs from famous paintings. There is something like a collective liberation, a claim of rights over one's own body thrown up against the repressive powers that be. The slogan "My house is my castle" is the guiding idea of the majority of social media posts from this time.

STAGE 4. Dejection. Official sources report rising numbers in cases and deaths. The dominant mood on social media is dejection. Its images include skeletons on the apartment balcony, the popularity of a new genre of empty paintings, where users erase details of classic paintings in Photoshop, posts themed around the afterlife, photos of overflowing hospitals, pessimistic placards carried by representatives of various professional communities.

STAGE 5. Despair and protest. The onset of the Easter holidays and the warm May weather make staying at home intolerable. Rumors spread that the lockdown is useful to the authorities as a political instrument for the coming elections. A key event of this time is a massive dance party organized by the inhabitants of one of Moscow's high-rise suburbs under the windows of their homes. Protest graffiti and caricature begin to pop up in public places and on social media.

Sergey Bratkov

P.S. During the summer break in the epidemic and the lifting of the lockdown, amateur creativity on social media died down, with the focus of interest shifting toward travel and summer vacation.

Politics also played a big role: Belarus, the war in Karabakh, the poisoning of Navalny, the elections in the United States.

The return to lockdown thematics can be expected with the onset of mass vaccination. It goes without saying that my observations are subjective and largely addressed to my students at the Rodchenko Art School, where I teach.

Sergey Bratkov, born in Kharkov, Ukraine, in 1960, has lived and worked in Moscow, Russia, since 2000. His photography, videos, installations, and performances often combine various elements of the "folk kitsch" that emerged after the collapse of the USSR into absurd and melancholy everyday collages. Bratkov has had solo exhibitions at the Museum of Contemporary Art, Moscow; Kunstverein Rosenheim; S.M.A.K. Stedelijk Museum voor Actuele Kunst, Ghent; BALTIC Centre for Contemporary Art, Gateshead; Fotomuseum Winterthur; Sala Canal de Isabel II., Madrid; Deichtorhallen, Hamburg; and PinchukArtCentre, Kiev. He took part in the 25th São Paulo Biennale (2002), Manifesta 5, Donostia—San Sebastian (2004), the Venice Biennale (2003, 2007, and 2011), and the Moscow Biennale (2005, 2007, 2009, 2011, 2013, and 2015).

Unfunny Jokes / Towels / Bottles (2020)
Videos, ca. 10 / 13 / 3 min., Russian
Online

Camera: Tatiana Makovskaya

Commissioned and produced by steirischer herbst '20

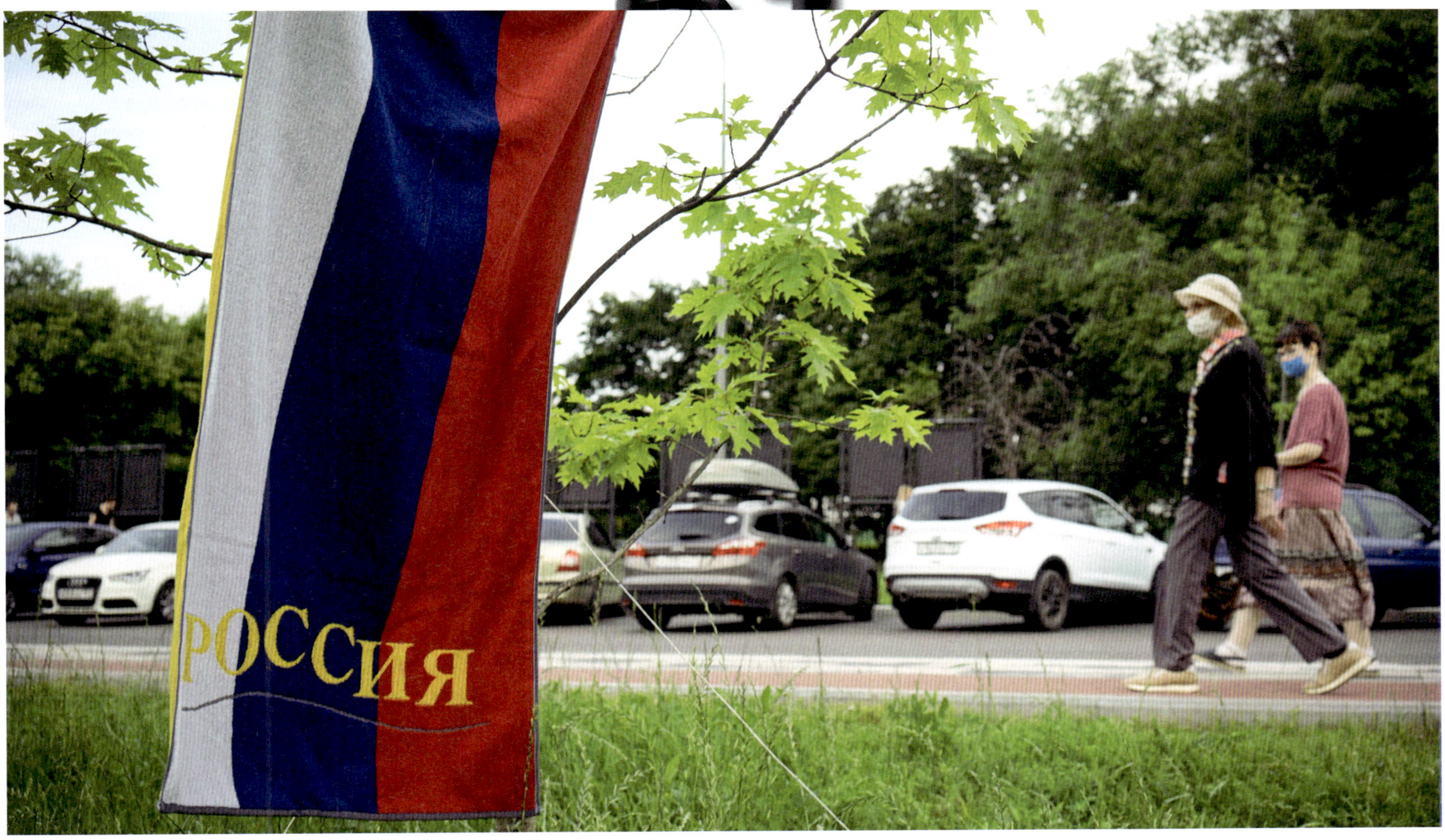

Alexander Chernyshkov

Keep in Mind
2020

Performance

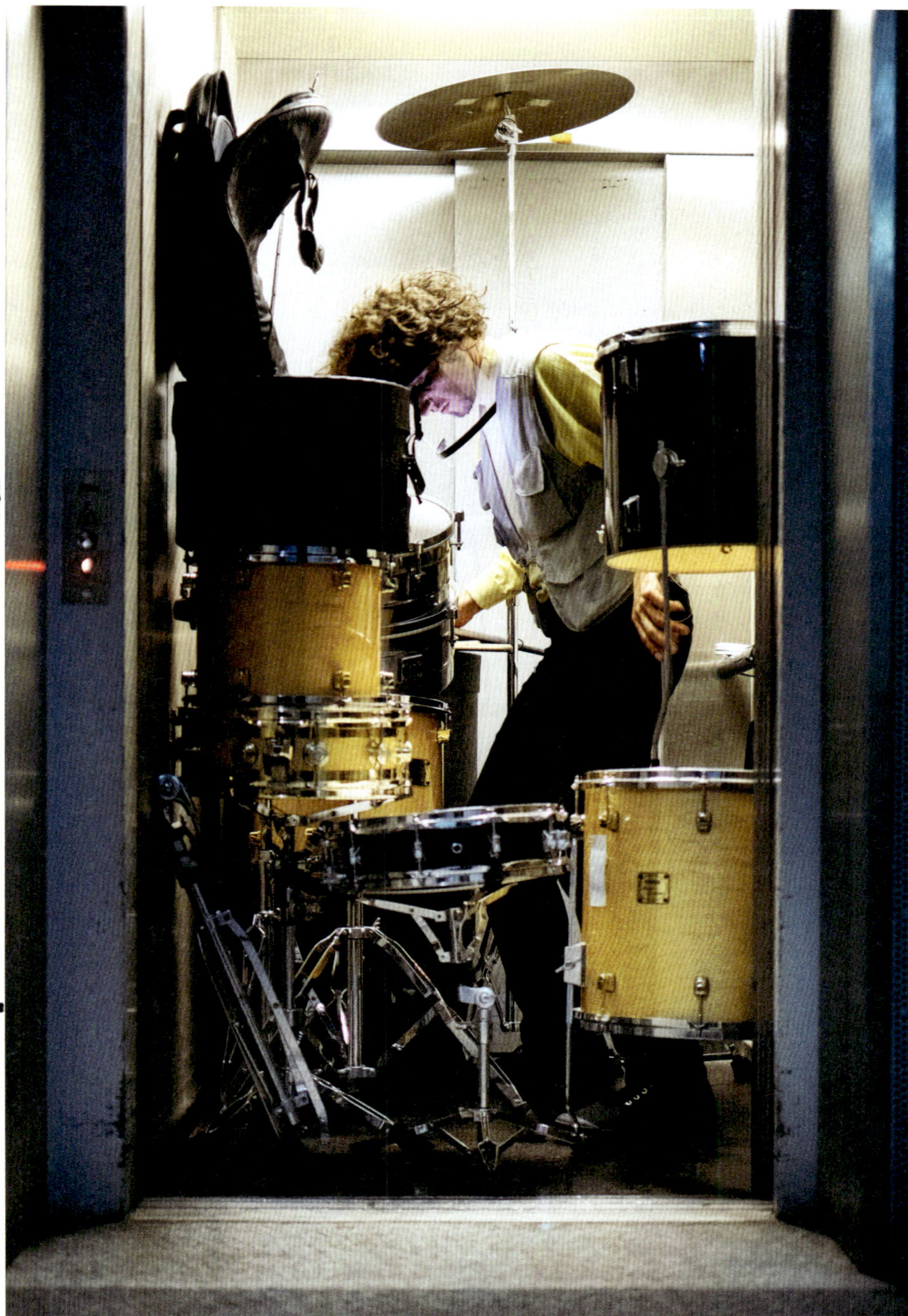

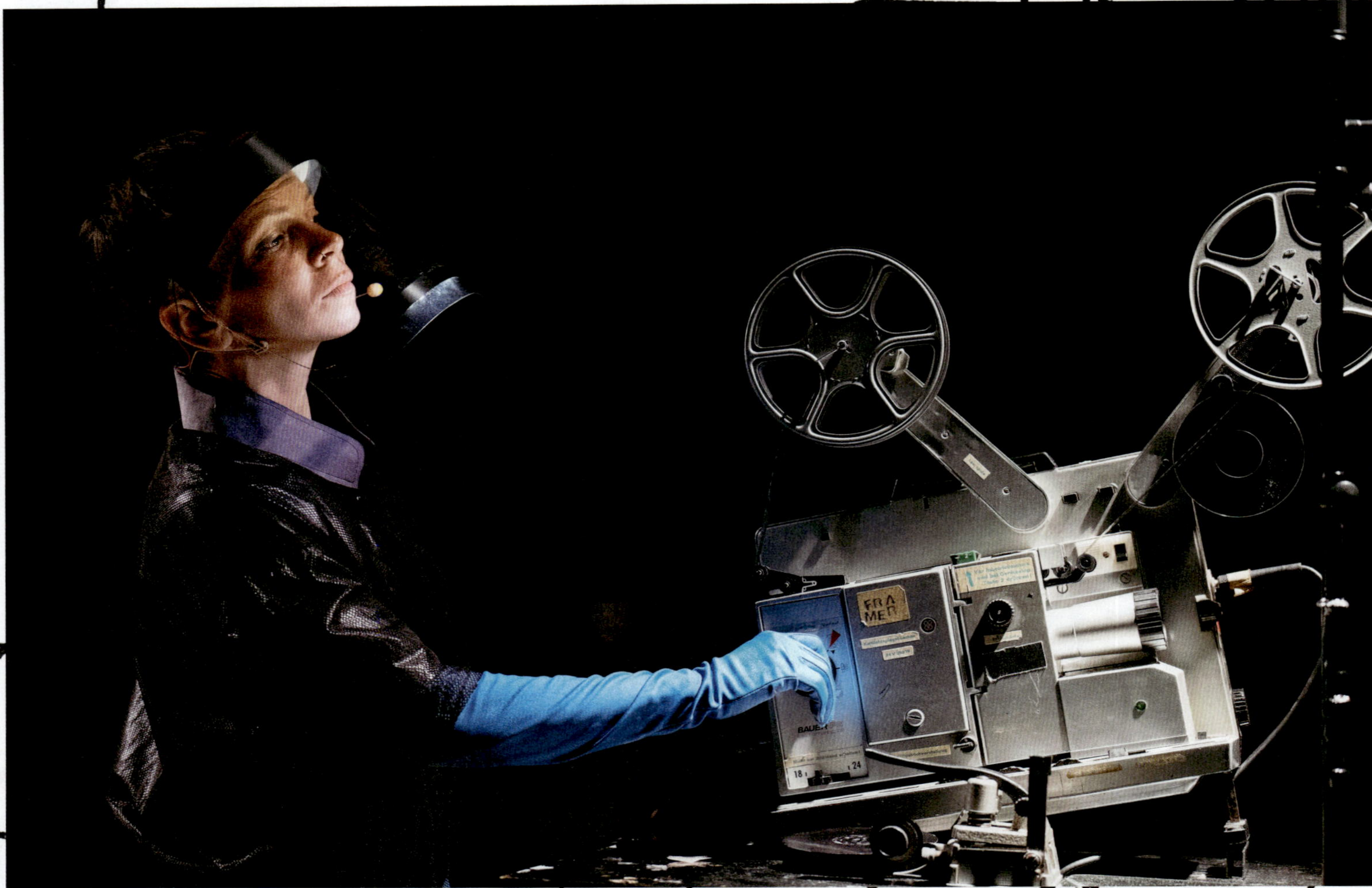

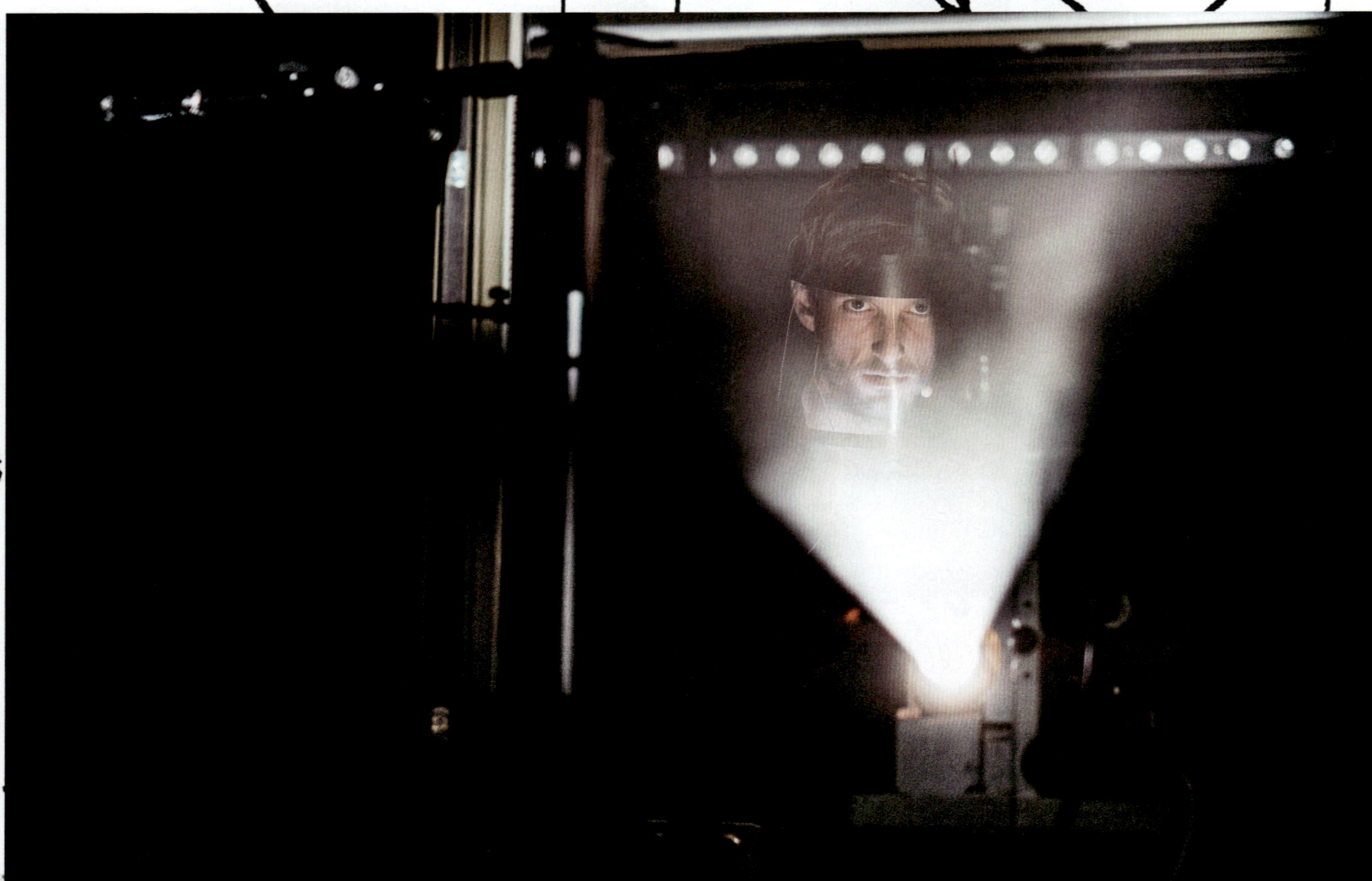

As a rule, we live by rules. The musical theater *Keep in Mind* takes the canon of artistic rules as its point of departure for placing the gray areas of those rules in the spotlight of its aesthetic work: the errors and deviations that, in the narrower sense, make the rules clear in the first place and at the same time reveal an alternative perspective on them.

Every form of artistic expression is reduced to its core compositionally here and integrated into a multidimensional fabric called communication. For this, as quickly becomes clear, is the basis for every meeting of contradictory laws in a given space—and the theater and its means merely a springboard for suspending the impossibility of common ground for a brief moment.

In the beginning was the soliloquy. Traversing the obstacle course backstage, the audience becomes a voyeur of the artist at work. Elevator, balcony, cloakroom: the spaces not only provide the form for the actions taking place within them but also create a tonal counterpoint to the music of the performers. The artists' materials thus mix and mingle with each other as well as with the noises in the space to create integrative music. Everything in the space, not least the audience, becomes part of the communication and thus of the composition.

When the curtain falls, the actual conversation begins—in dialogue and in the encounter with the respective musical languages. The intrinsic rules of one material meet up with those of another, confronting each other in their form and producing the kind of frictions and errors that can call normality into question.

Contrary to all insinuations, every deconstruction that is performed secretly longs for subwoofers and holding hands. Ultimately, the errors become the driving force for an intimate interaction, and communication becomes possible on a different basis.

And that's exactly what I am saying.

Alexander Chernyshkov

56

Alexander Chernyshkov is a composer, performer, and improviser. He experiments actively in building unique new instruments of strictly acoustical and mechanical origin. His main focus is the composition and practice of performative musical theater based on interdisciplinarity between methods and genres, which he refers to as Error Theater.

His works are performed and programmed by ensembles such as musikFabrik, Nikel, Nadar, PHACE, and festivals such as Wien Modern, Gaudeamus, the Venice Biennale, Gergiev Festival, Bludenz Musiktage, Hamburg State Opera, Elektrotheater Stanislavsky, and Musiktheatertage Wien. He was a fellow of Akademie Musiktheater Heute and is the winner of the NOperas! 2020 funding initiative.

Keep in Mind (2020)
Performance, ca. 80 min., multiple languages
Orpheum Extra

Scenic composition: Alexander Chernyshkov
Performers: Emil Gross, Márton Kovács, Gina Mattiello, Johanna Nielson, Stefan Voglsinger
Director: Wolfgang Nägele
Dramaturgy: Elise Schobeß
Costumes and set design: Philipp Lossau
Costume support: Helena Adam
Technical assistance: Oleg Dergilev
Camera: Francesco Tacoli
Camera assistance: Lukas Ellmer

Commissioned by steirischer herbst ’20
Produced by Error Theater in coproduction with steirischer herbst ’20
Project partner: echoraum, Vienna
Supported by the Department of Cultural Affairs of the City of Vienna

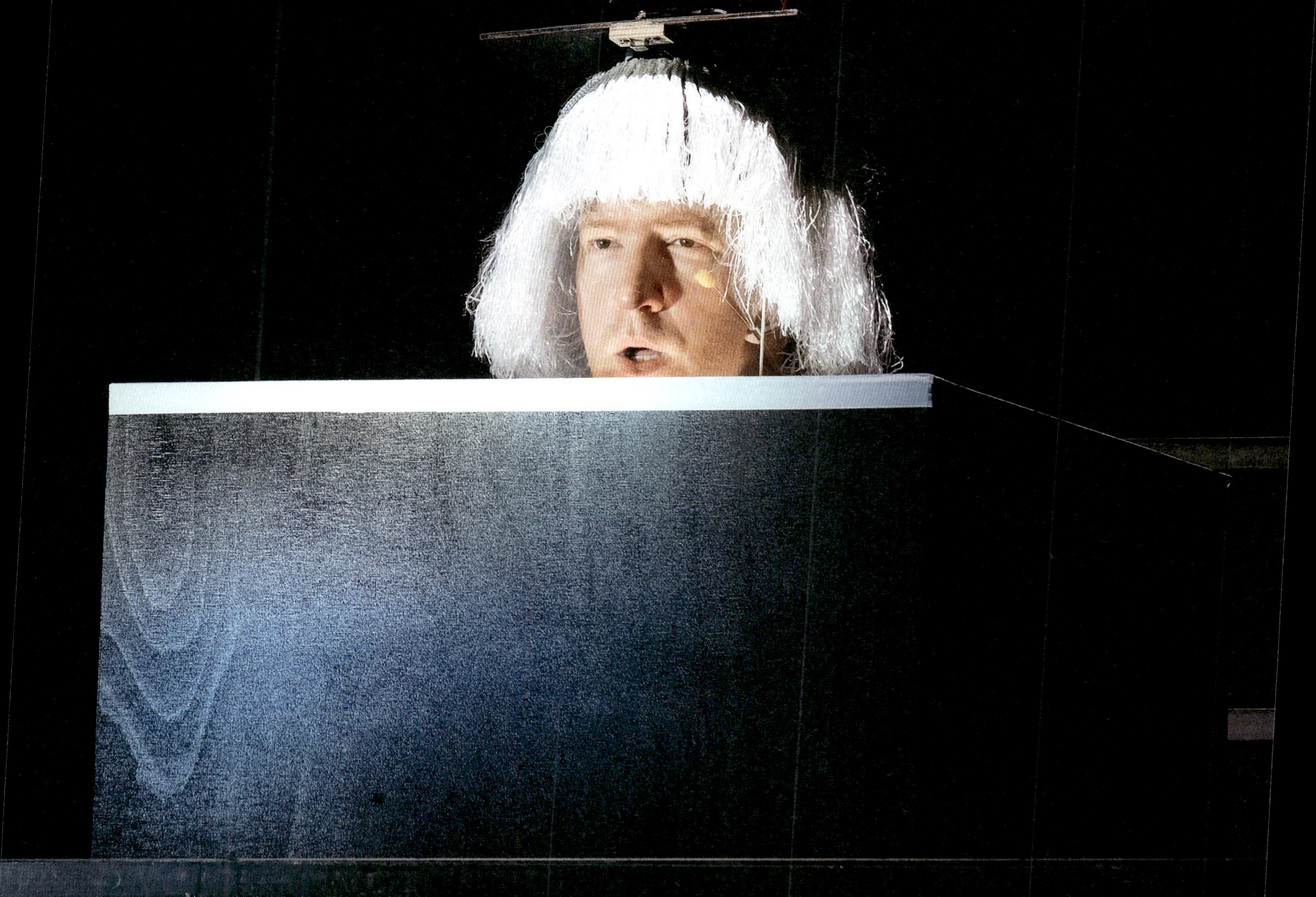

Pauline Curnier Jardin

Le lente passioni (Slow Passions)
2020

Video

One day in the 21st century, it was decreed that passions could no longer be suffered together. Ceremonies and rituals must henceforth be watched on the screen; celebrations and communication were only allowed from home, from the sick bed, from one's own bedroom. (I remember my aunt forcing us to watch Christmas Mass with the Pope every December 24. This Pope was a small white spot, vying for my affection in the anticlerical hysteria of the living room. The television set we were sitting in front of was also switched on all August long. There I sat with my grandmother for days on end in semi-darkness, behind blinds that were meant to protect us from the heat.)

The footage in this film consists mainly of images and songs from Easter masses and processions in Catholic Europe, especially in Italy. It originates from the days of the COVID-19 quarantine, but also from the years before. The scenes are accompanied by recordings of the choir conducted by Giovanna Marini, whose members have been preserving and developing this musical heritage for years and who sang together on the Internet during the lockdown. A visual and sonic poem has been created from this archive with the aim of capturing the collective emotion of this slow week of suffering.

Pauline Curnier Jardin

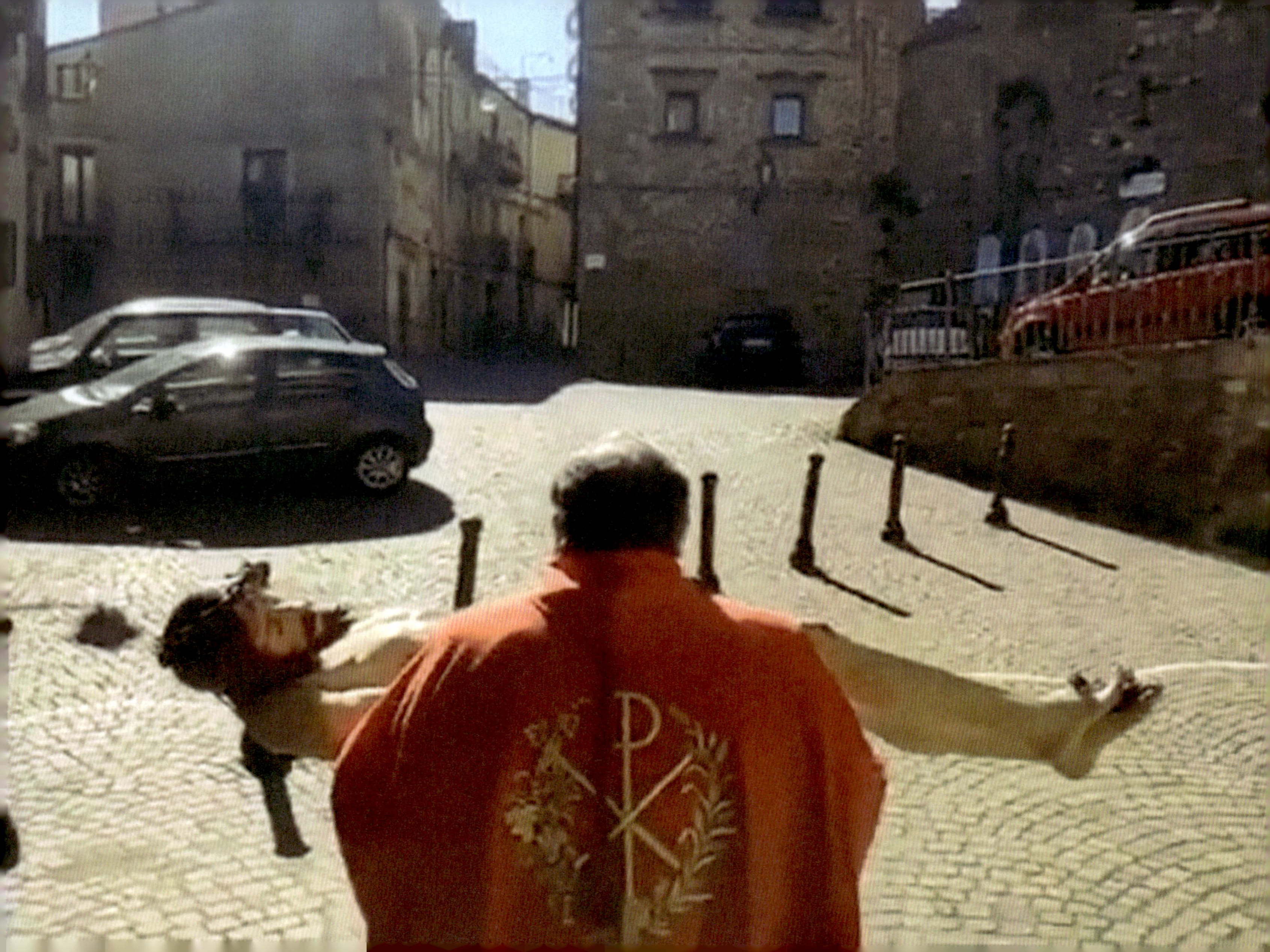

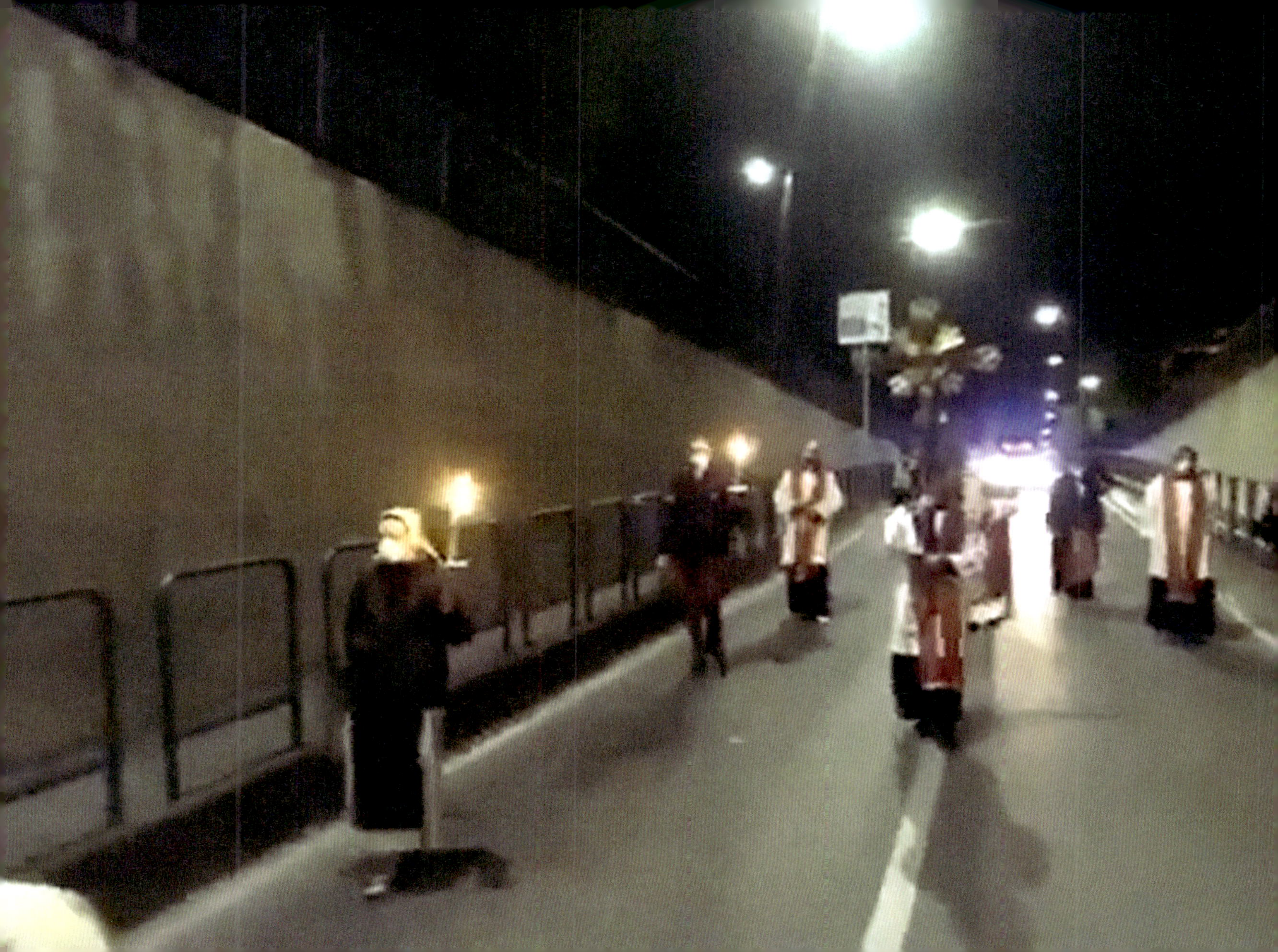

62

Pauline Curnier Jardin, born in Marseille, France, in 1980, is a Berlin-based artist working across installation, performance, film, and drawing. She was the winner of the 2019 Preis der Nationalgalerie and recipient of the 2019–20 Villa Medici Residency in Rome. Solo and group exhibitions, projects and screenings have been held at the Hamburger Bahnhof, Berlin; Manifesta 13, Marseille (2020); Palais de Tokyo, Paris; Haus der Kulturen der Welt, Berlin; Bergen Assembly 2019; Performa 15, New York (2015); and the 57th Venice Biennale (2017).

Le lente passioni (Slow Passions) (2020)
Video, ca. 29 min., Italian and French
Online

Editing, documentation, effects: Margaux Parillaud
Sound design: Robin Poligné
Archive, scientific consultation: Antonella Talamonti
Translation: Tobias Haberkorn, Antonella Talamonti
Image sources: Riti e Suoni Di Una Settimana Santa Fuori Dall'Ordinario, founded by Antonia Talamonti and fed by many others, including singers, amateurs, religious people and agnostics who documented their own rites and posted them somewhere.

Commissioned and produced by steirischer herbst '20

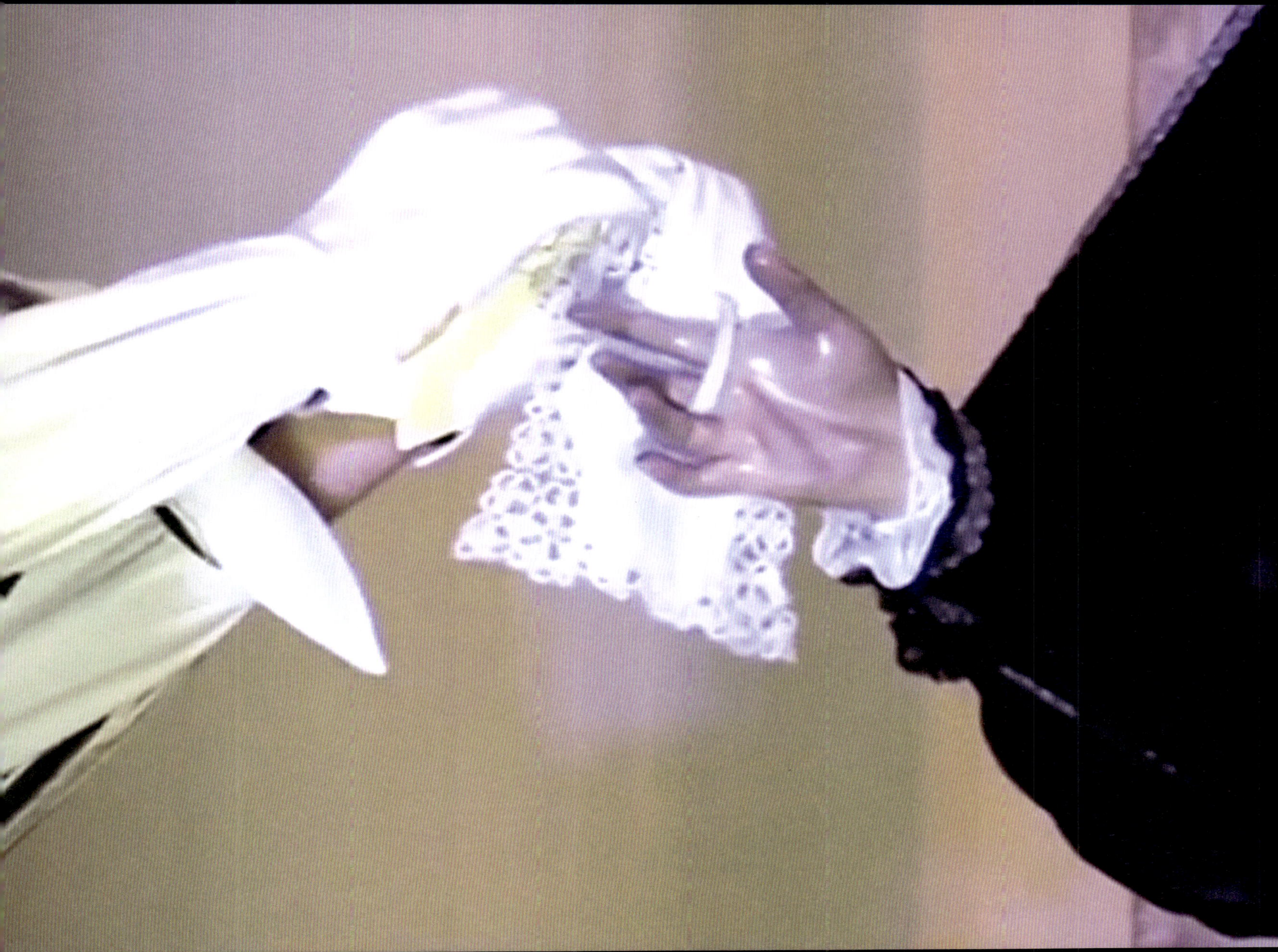

Josef Dabernig

All the Stops
2020

Video

Synopsis

Mansion–church–hairdresser's, mansion–church–bar and mansion–church–cemetery. An organist works her way under the well-rationed weight of flagellation and self-punishment. A kind of Mother Superior to a handful of devoted followers as well as those of a more rebellious disposition, she plays her canticles of order on the pipe organ, the garden fence, and her immaculately clean window panes.

In front of a backdrop of God-given processes, the protagonist pulls all the stops of discipline and reverses the stereotypes of a supposed world of men.

All the stops, a farce on traditional gender roles, pays homage to the ego trip as a deep religious adventure.

Screenplay (excerpt)

9, 10, 11) The organist, who has changed her clothes and is carrying a purse, a score, and a roll of plastic wrap, leaves her mansion and steps in through the door of a waiting car. The camera pans from the house door to the chauffeur who is holding open the passenger side door of the car. (12) Camera from the backseat toward the front. The organist takes her seat from the right side, the chauffeur follows sitting in from the left. (6) Camera view through the right-side car window. The organist buckles her seatbelt and immediately spreads out the plastic wrap in front of her face, at the same time the chauffeur who is seen in the background and is unmoved by her action, reaches for the ignition. (6)

12) Camera position from the hood of the car: the chauffeur is at the wheel, on the right, the organist is sitting on the left behind the stretched out plastic wrap. The car is driving along carrying this silent pair. (12)

13, 14) Camera waits for the car to arrive in front of the church. Cut. The chauffeur opens the car door for the organist, who steps out carrying her purse, score, and the plastic wrap. She walks with assertion directly into the church.

15) Camera is fixed on a detail of the house, eventually on the flowers; from there it pans over to focus on the head of the gardener, who is busy at work. (18)

16/17) Cut to the organist who sits down at the organ, and cut as she pulls the registers. (12)

18) The chauffeur, who is sitting at the driver's seat, lights a cigarette. (6)

19) Camera from over the shoulder of the double (NN), aiming in on her hands which are placed on the keyboard, and which are as symmetrical as possible. She plays slow and precise. (12)

20) Cut to the suffering Christ with the crown of thorns. (6)

21) Cut to the face of the chauffeur, which is slightly concealed by the smoke of his cigarette. (6)

22) Shot of the inside of the church accompanied by the sound of the pipe organ. (12)

23, 24) The Organist, carrying her purse, score, and plastic wrap, leaves the church and steps into the waiting car. (12)

Green stands for quasi natural sounds, which the sound designer Michael Palm then interpreted as sort of hyperreal sounds.

Red stands for the organ sound by the composer Michael Herndler, which I asked the sound designer just slightly to accompany with some atmospheric sounds.

Numbers in full parentheses represent shot length in seconds.

Josef Dabernig

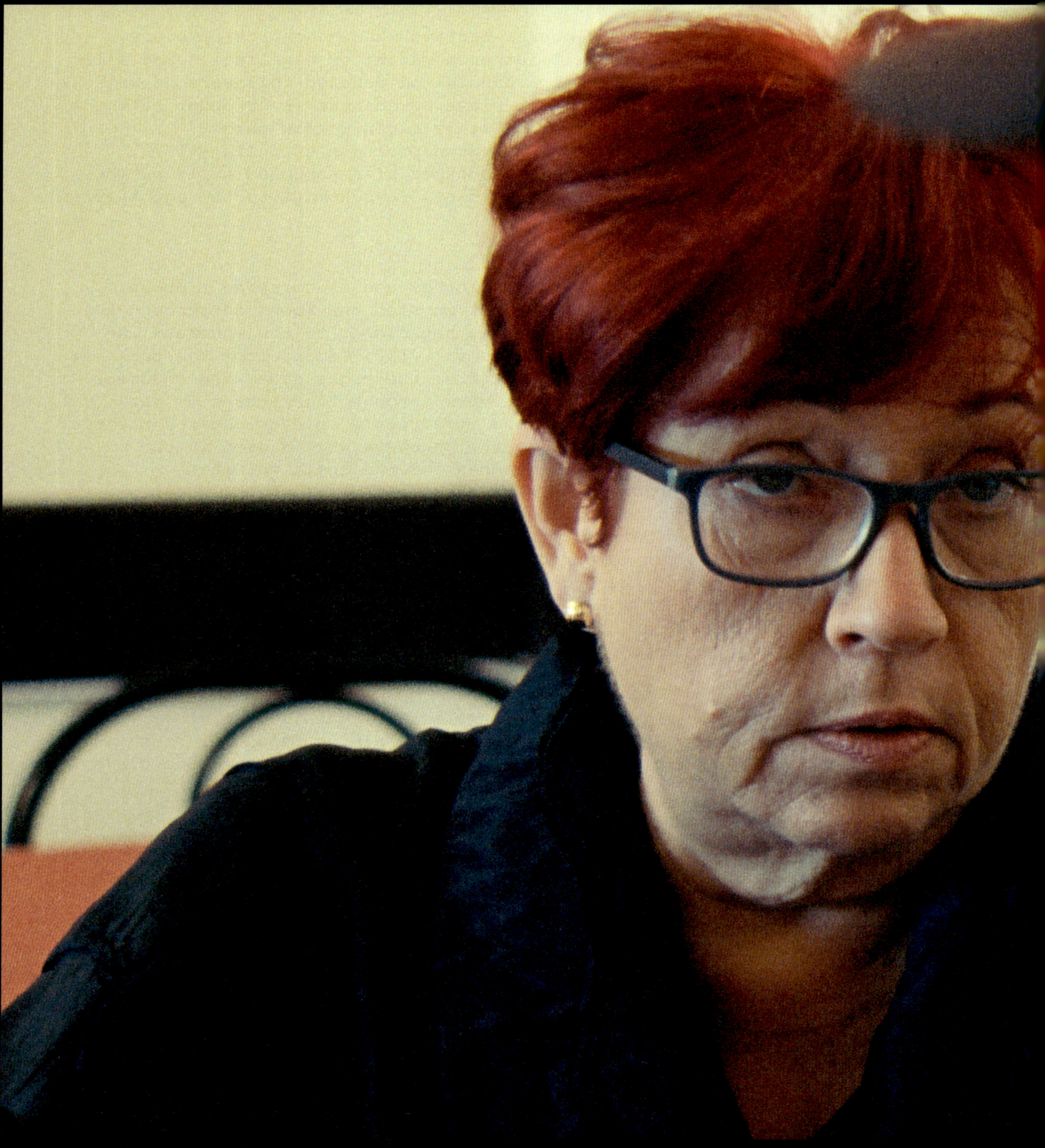

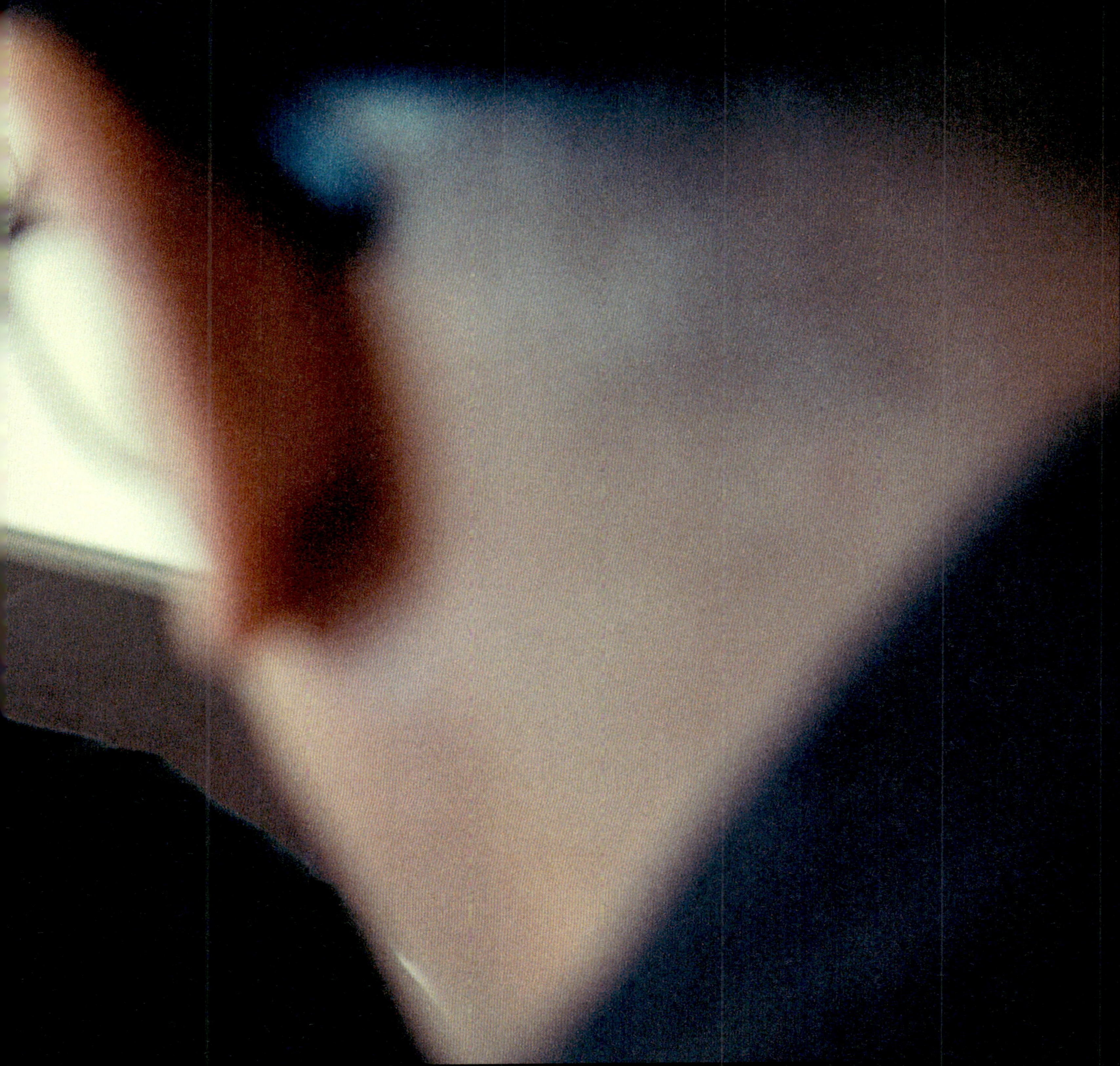

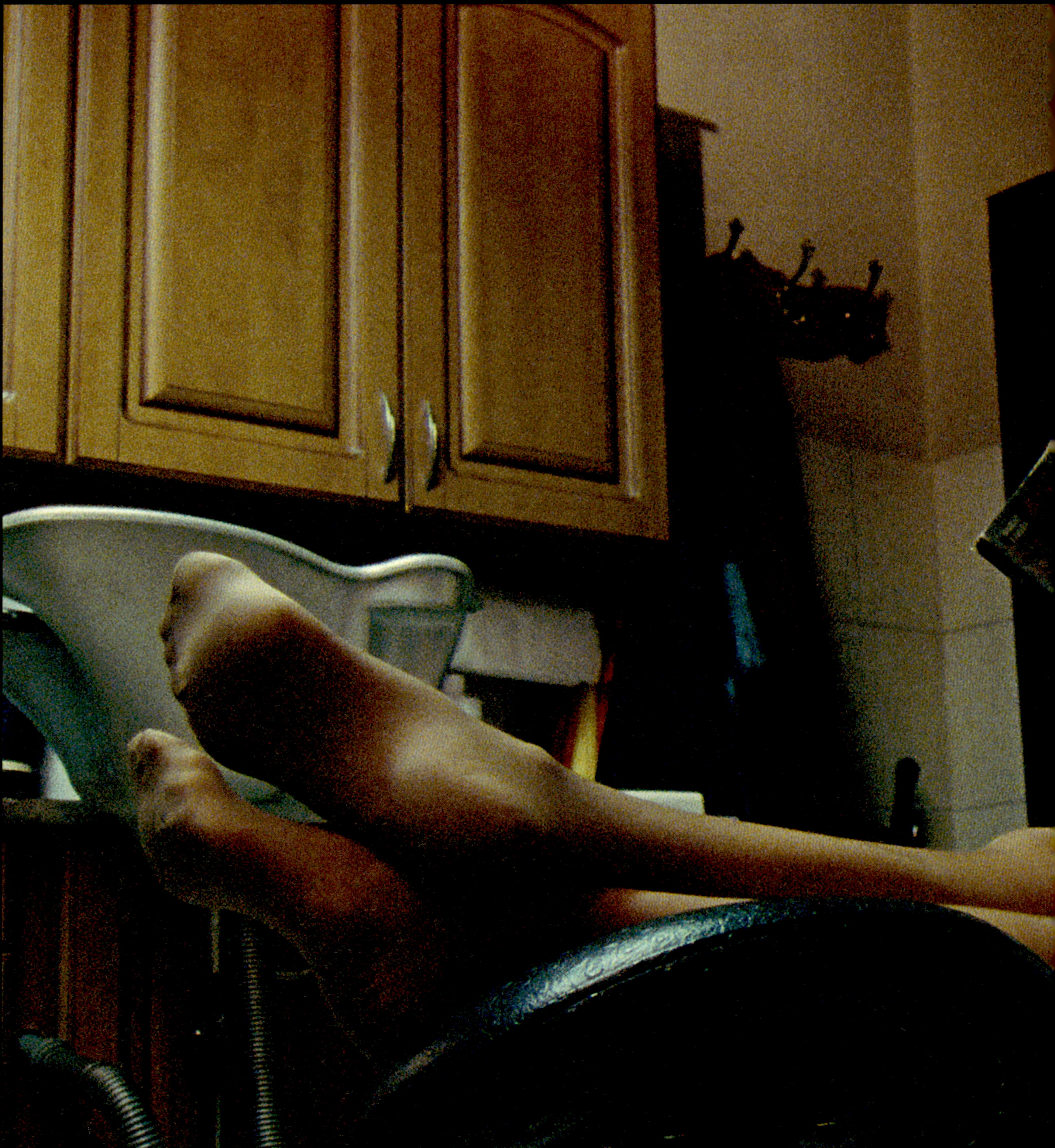

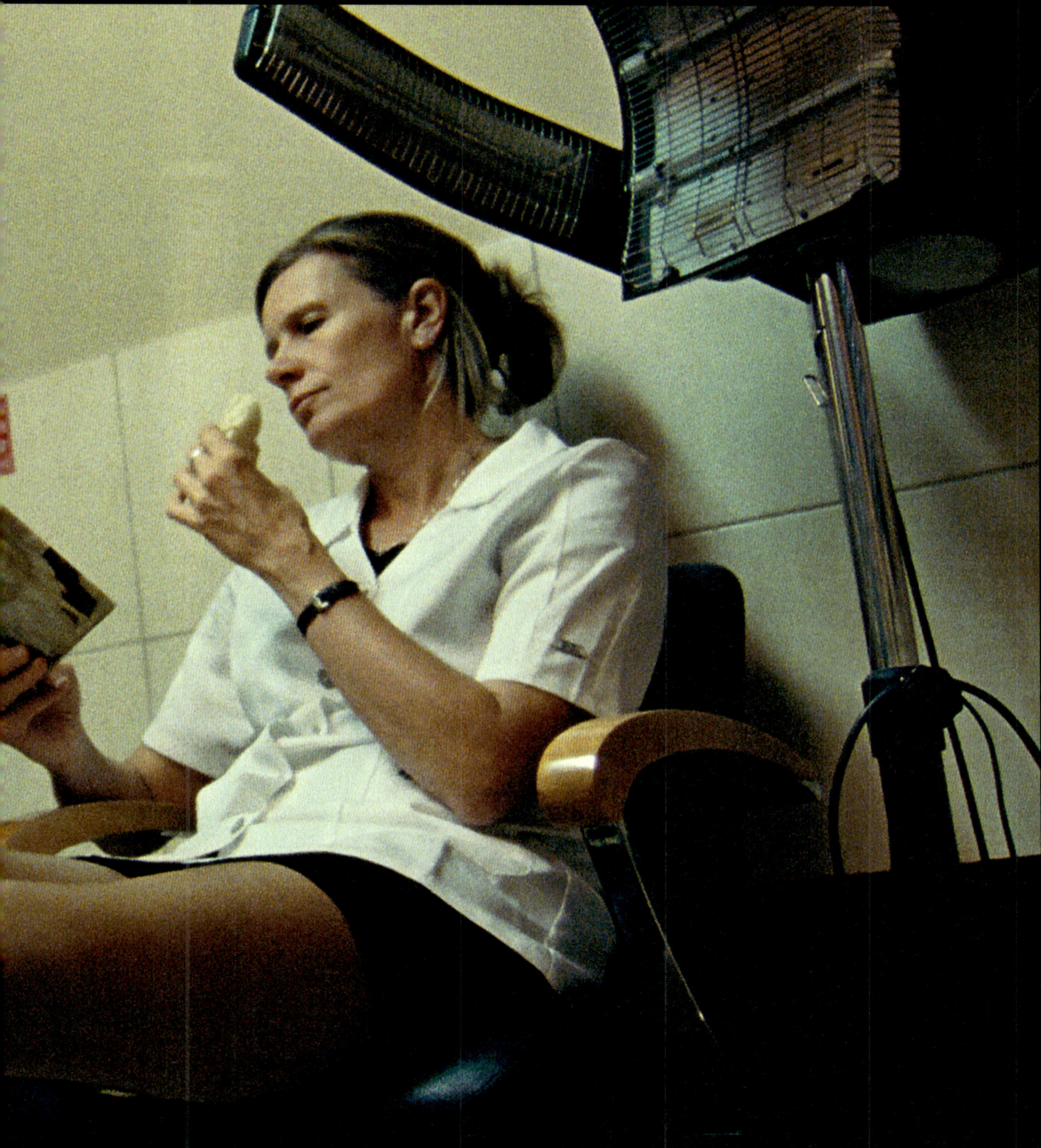

70

My figurative sculpture—after graduation from the Academy of Fine Arts Vienna in 1981—dissolved into different media, such as photography, text, object, and construction. In 1996, I started to produce short films, which were presented at festivals, including those in Locarno, Oberhausen, Rotterdam, and Toronto. The film *Hypercrisis* was nominated for the European Film Awards at the Venice Film Festival in 2011.

These films are often situated in harsh, disciplined, and existential environments and are a continuation of the passion for the minimal, the orderly, and the structured, as expressed earlier in my sculptures. As in the ongoing series *Panorama*, where, since 1989 till now, I am trying to depict through photography an obsessive collection of (sub)urban settings with the common denomination of empty sports grounds.

In 2020, photo works were presented at *Equally Not Nothing*, Galerie Stadtpark, Krems, and an oeuvre of early sculptures and films were shown at the Biennale Gherdëina 7 in the Dolomites. At Kunstraum Lakeside in Klagenfurt I performed a reinstatement and restructuring of the exhibition space, the film *Heavy Metal Detox* was part of *The Art of Diminished Differentia* at The Brno House of Arts, and an archaeology of my encounters with the Petržalka housing estate are still being presented at the Július Koller Society in Bratislava.

Josef Dabernig

All the Stops (2020)
Video, ca. 15 min., no language
Online

Director, script, editing, and production: Josef Dabernig
Production assistant Hungary: Zsolt Szalai
Camera: Christian Giesser
Music: Christoph Herndler
Sound design: Michael Palm
Cast: Ingeburg Wurzer (organist), Gregor Schmoll (chauffeur), Zsolt Szalai (locksmith), Wolfgang Dabernig (gardener), Susanne Szalai-Urbanek (hairdresser), Isabella Hollauf (hairdresser), Gyöngyi Bata (waitress), Josef Dabernig (guest at the bar), Laura Szalai (church choir), Paula Szalai (church choir), Flora Szalai (church choir), Anita Toth (church choir), Christoph Herndler (church choir)
Film processing: Hiventy France, Paris
Scan: LISTO MediaServices Cine+TV Postproduction GmbH
Color grading: Matthias Tomasi
Rerecording: Alexander Koller
Postproduction: The Grand Post

Commissioned and coproduced by steirischer herbst '20
Supported by Austrian Cultural Forum Budapest
Funded by Federal Chancellery of Austria, Arts Division / Film Department

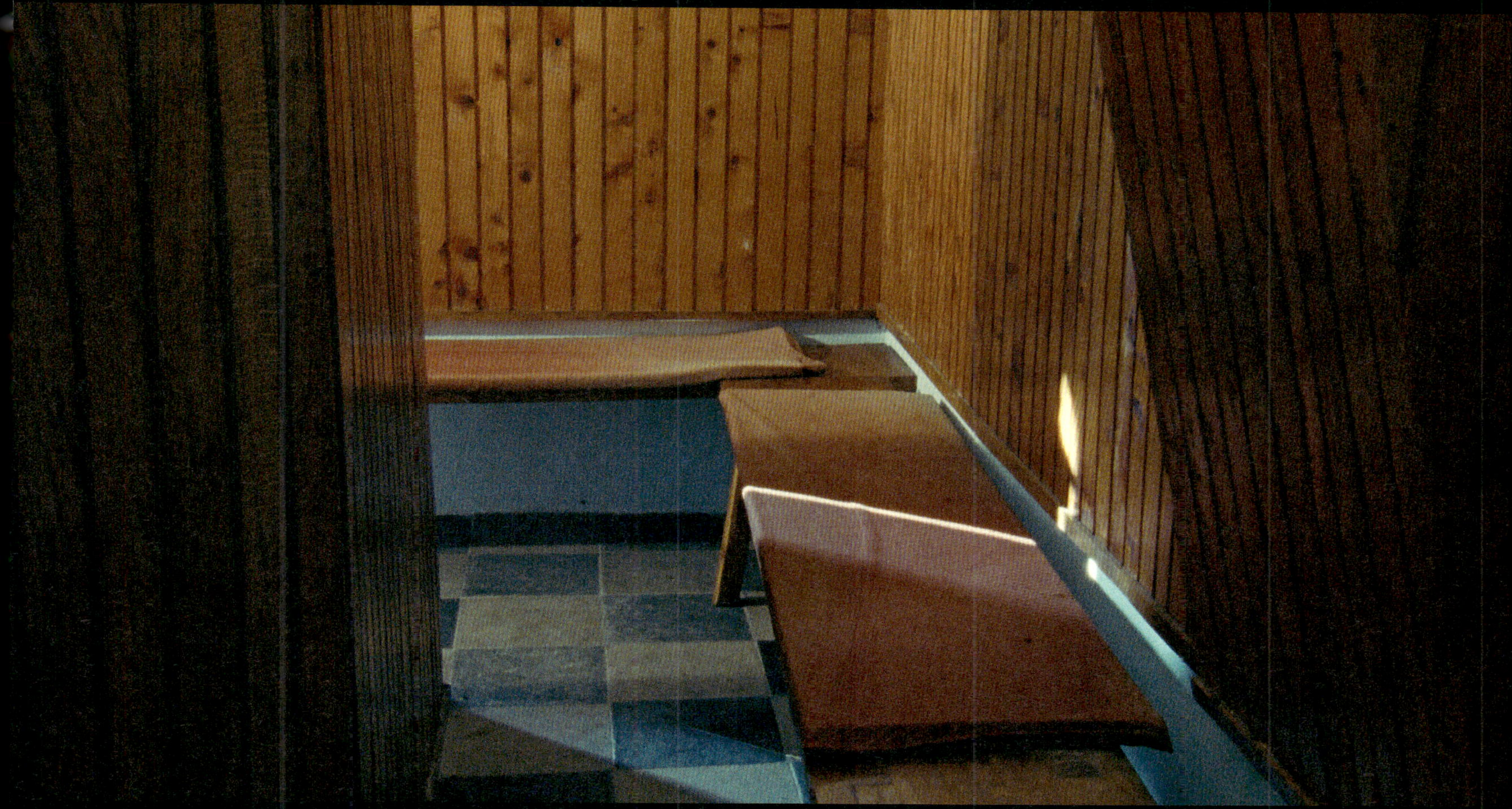

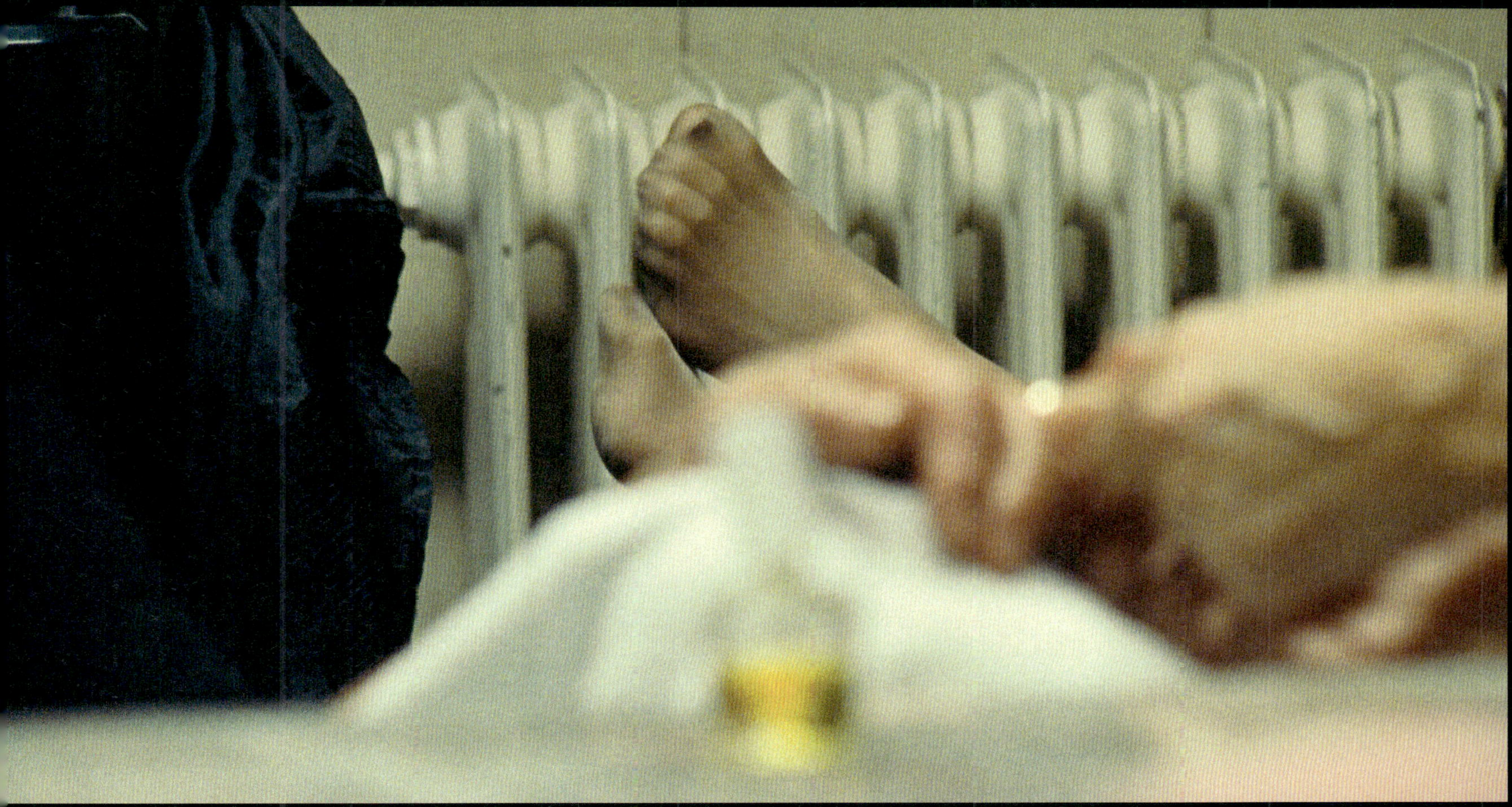

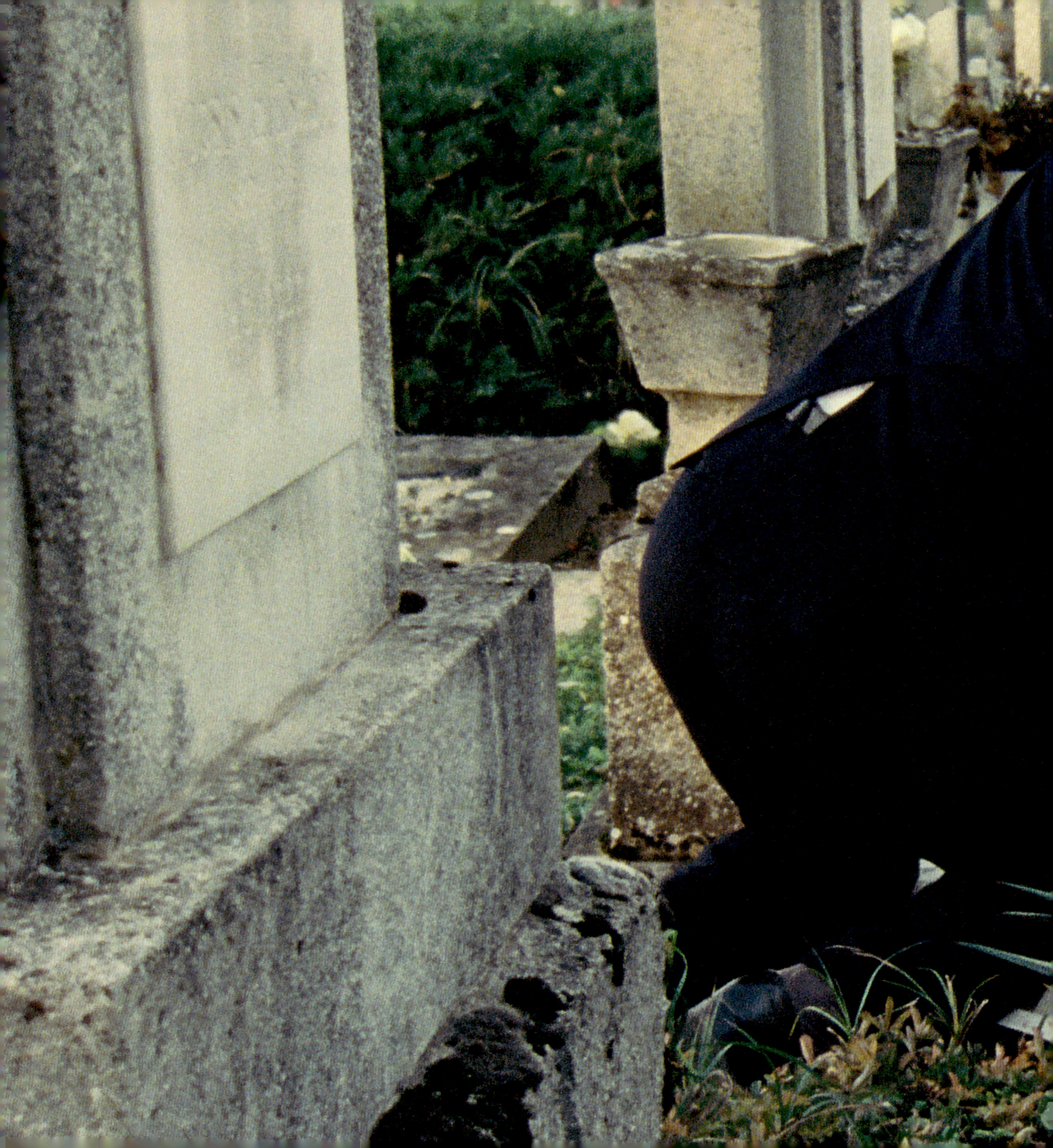

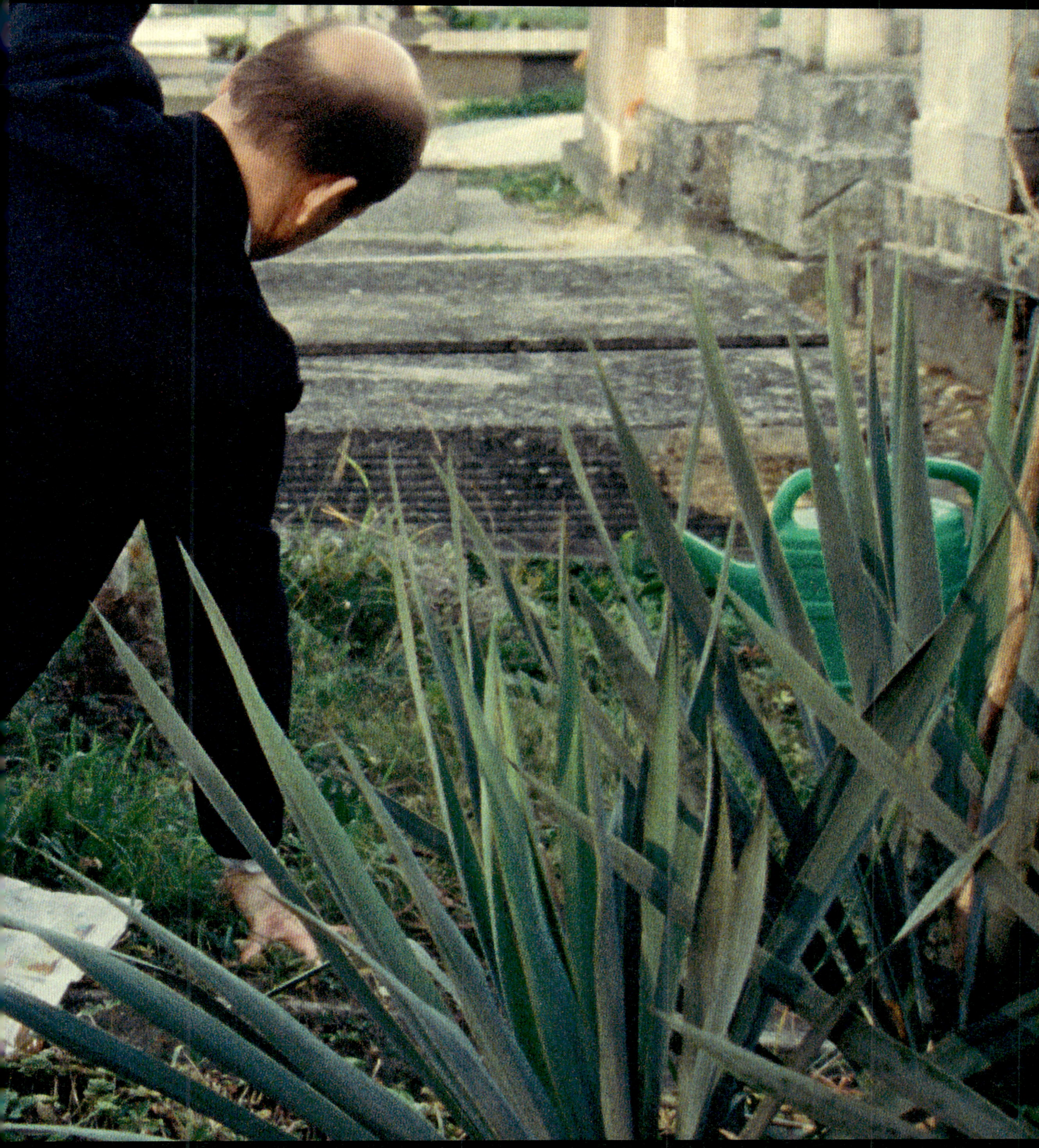

Nika Dubrovsky and friends

Intergalactic Memorial Carnival for David Graeber 2020

Online Event

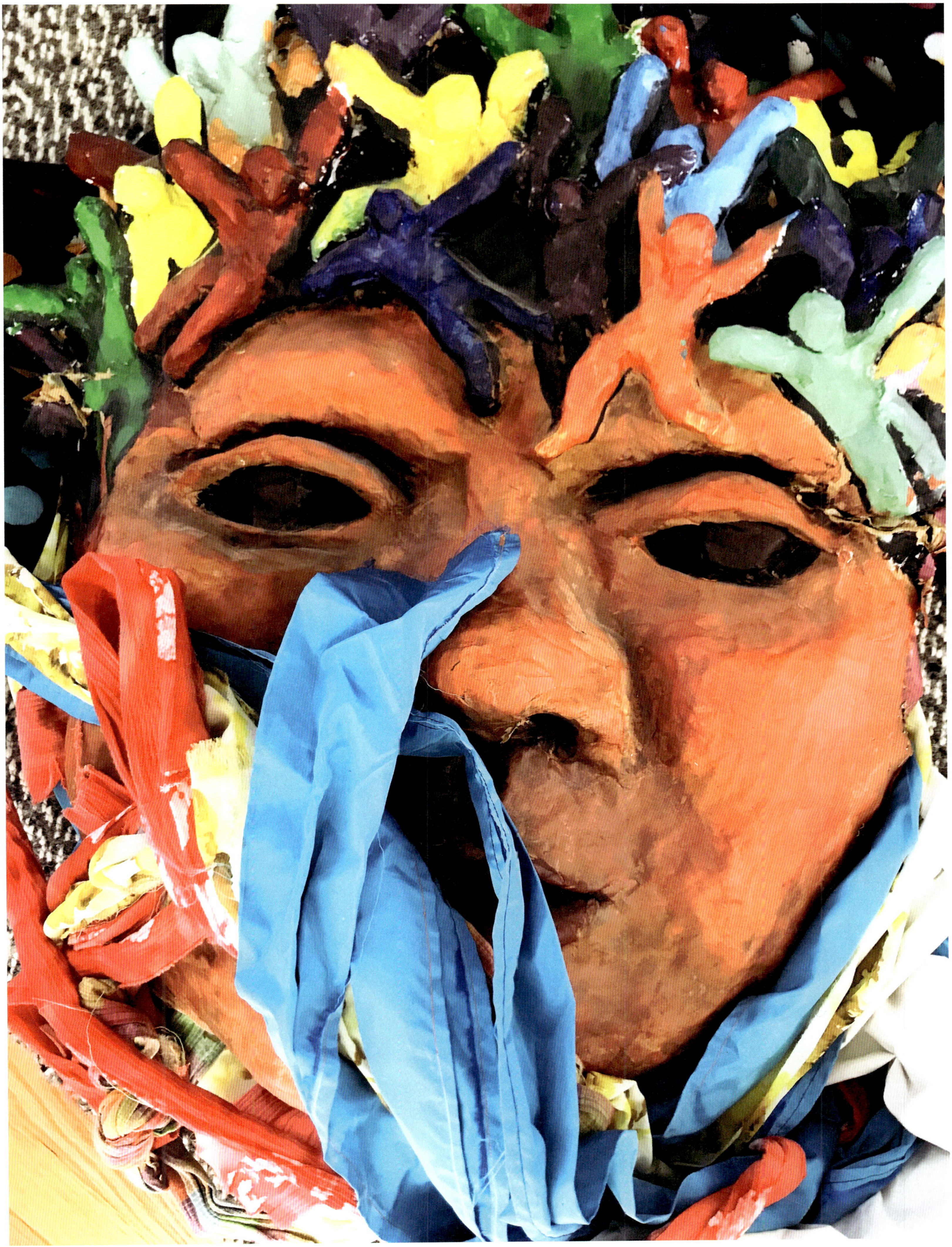

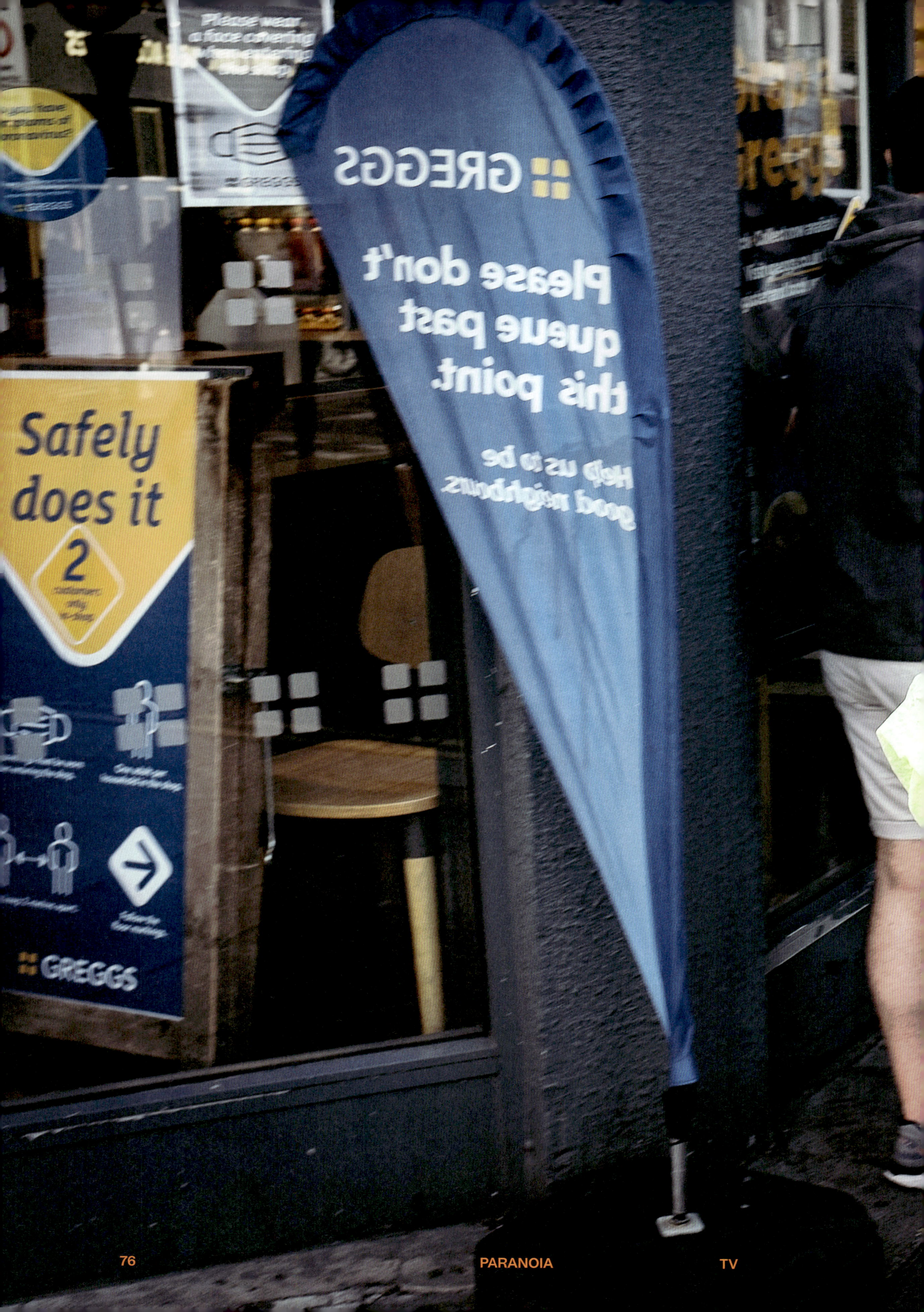

GREGGS
Please don't queue past this point
Help us to be good neighbours
Safely does it
2
GREGGS
Please wear a face covering

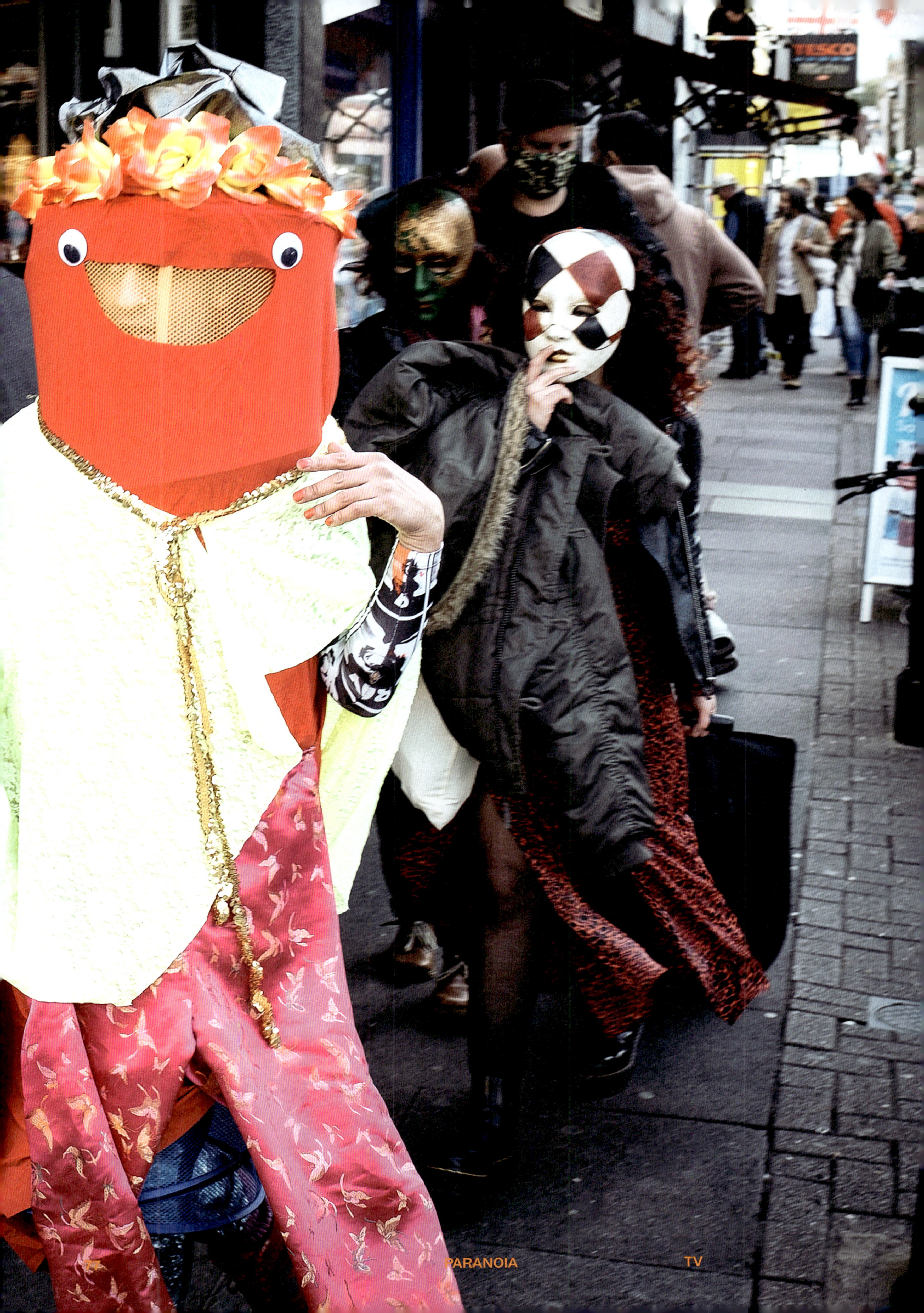
TESCO

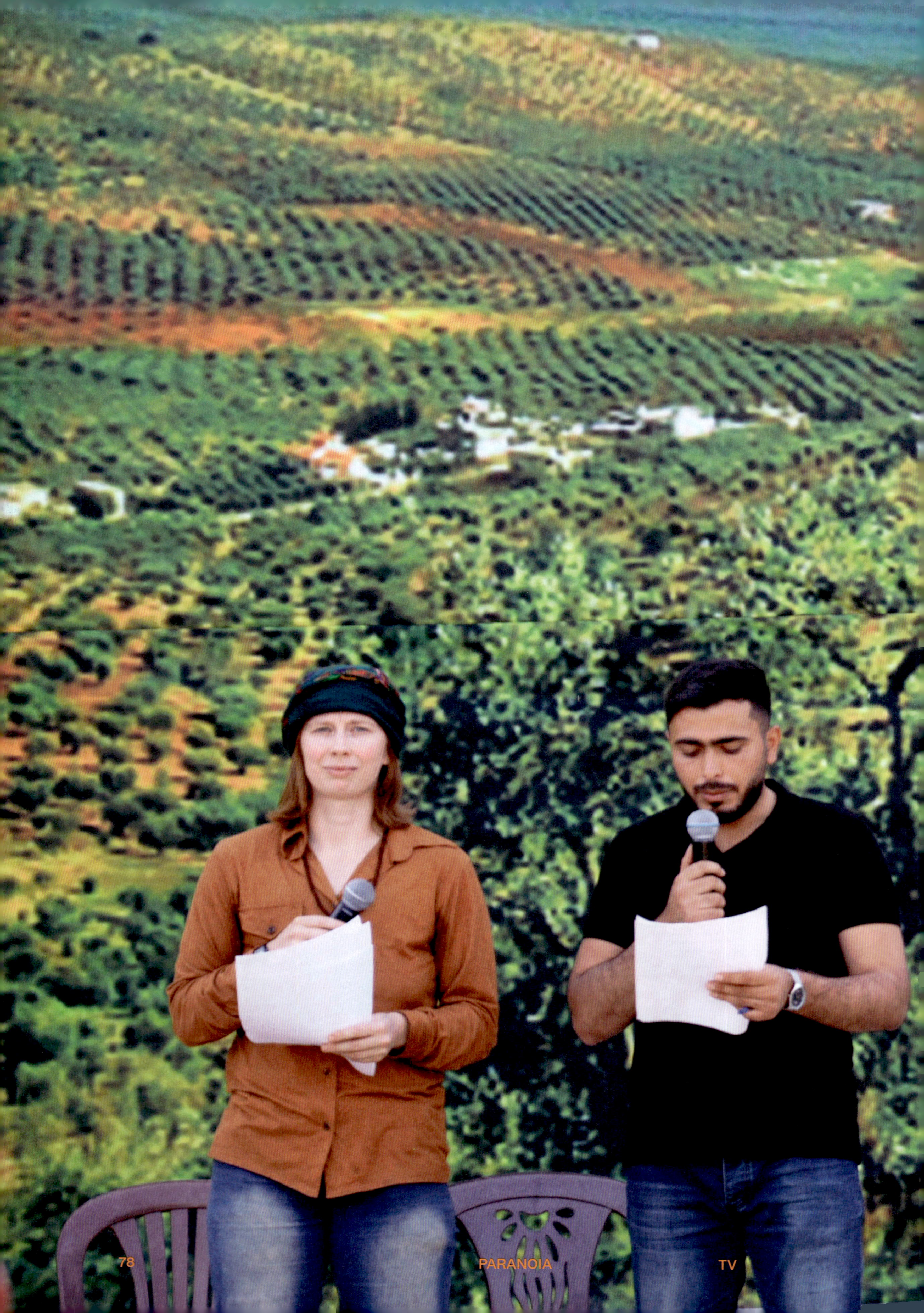

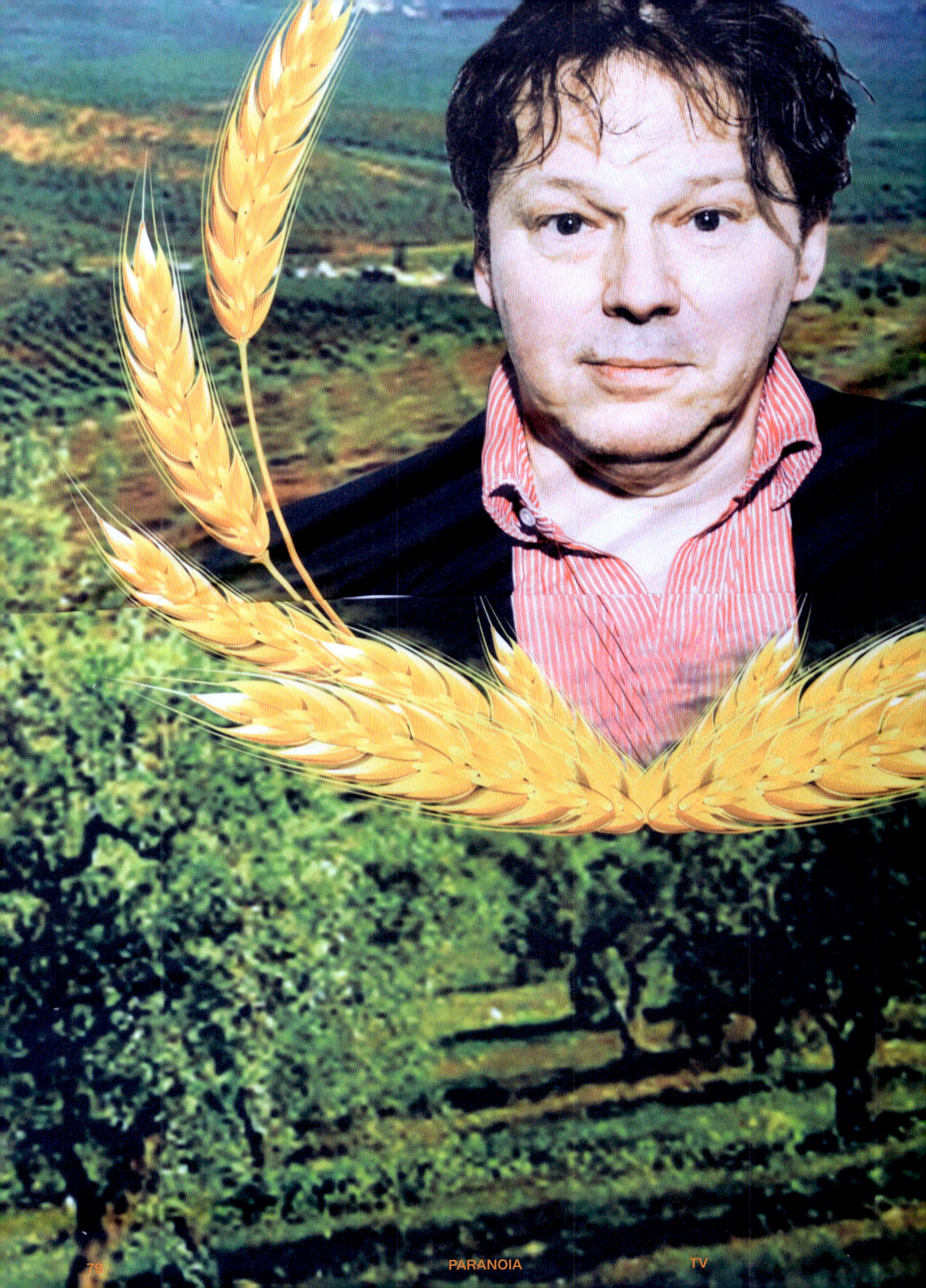

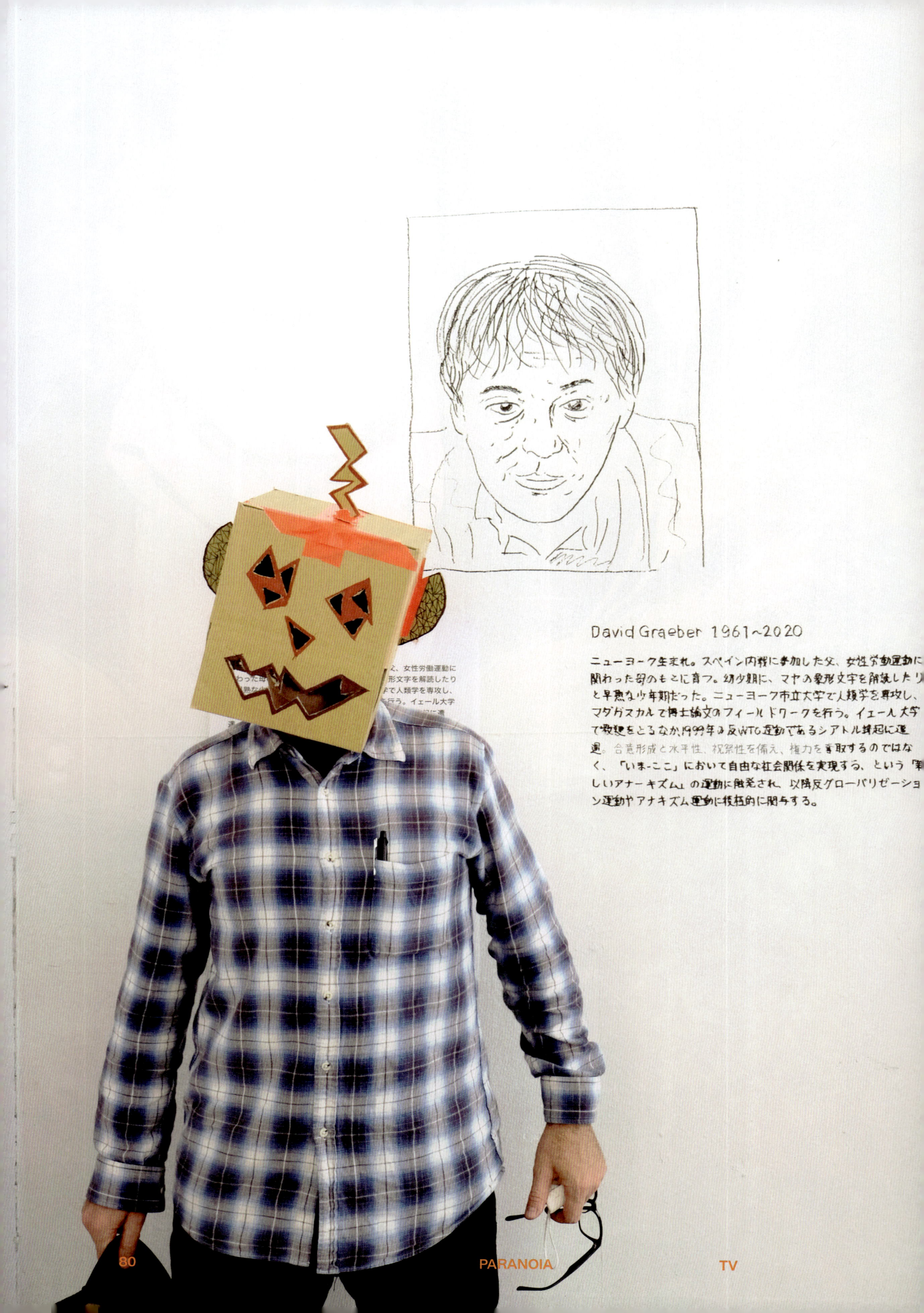
David Graeber 1961~2020
ニューヨーク生まれ。スペイン内戦に参加した父、女性労働運動に
関わった母のもとに育つ。幼少期に、マヤの象形文字を解読したり
と早熟な少年期だった。ニューヨーク市立大学で人類学を専攻し、
マダガスカルで博士論文のフィールドワークを行う。イェール大学
で教鞭をとるなか、1999年の反WTO運動であるシアトル蜂起に遭
遇。合意形成と水平性、祝祭性を備え、権力を奪取するのではな
く、「いま-ここ」において自由な社会関係を実現する、という「
しいアナーキズム」の運動に触発され、以降反グローバリゼーショ
ン運動やアナキズム運動に積極的に関与する。

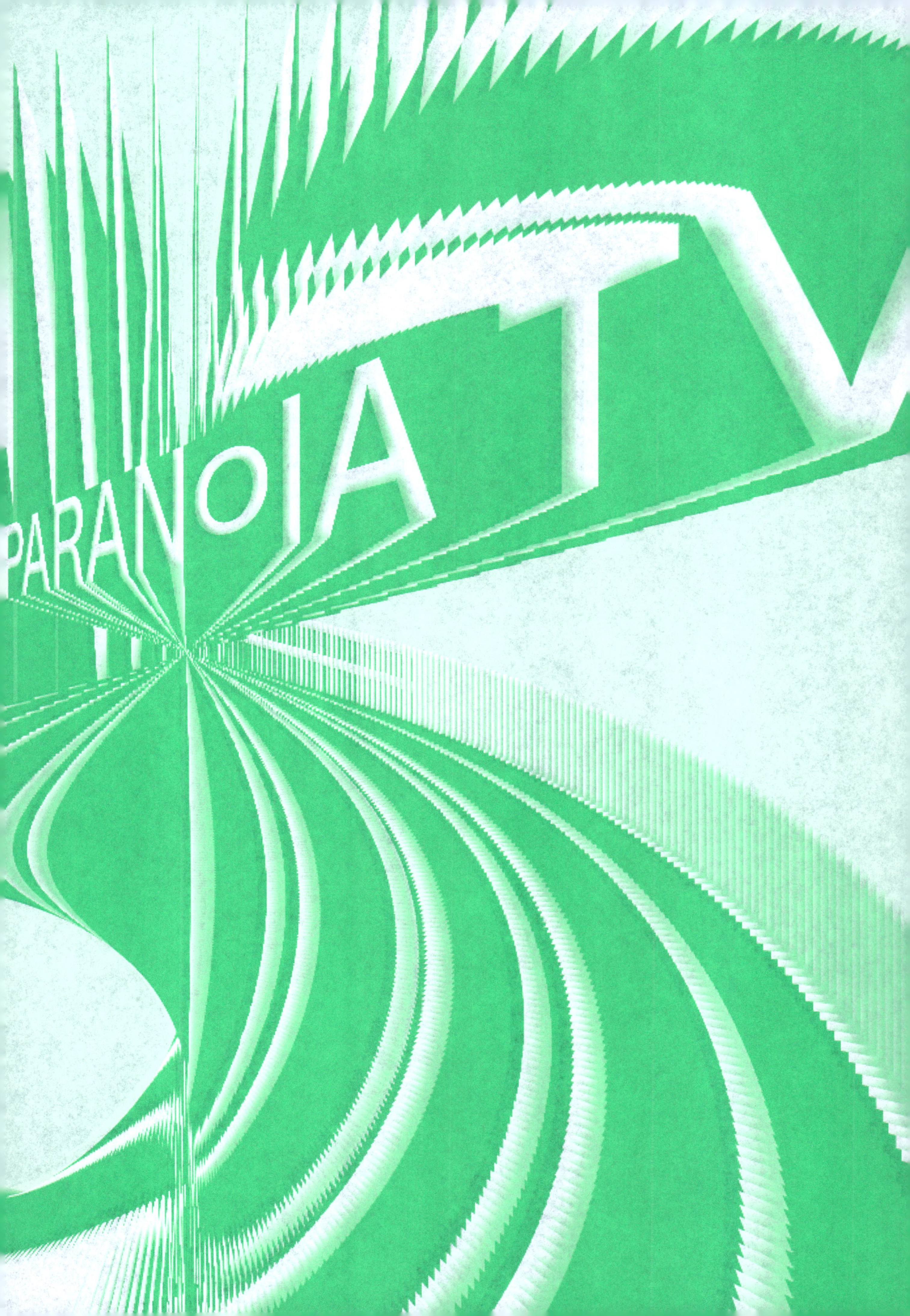
PARANOIA TV

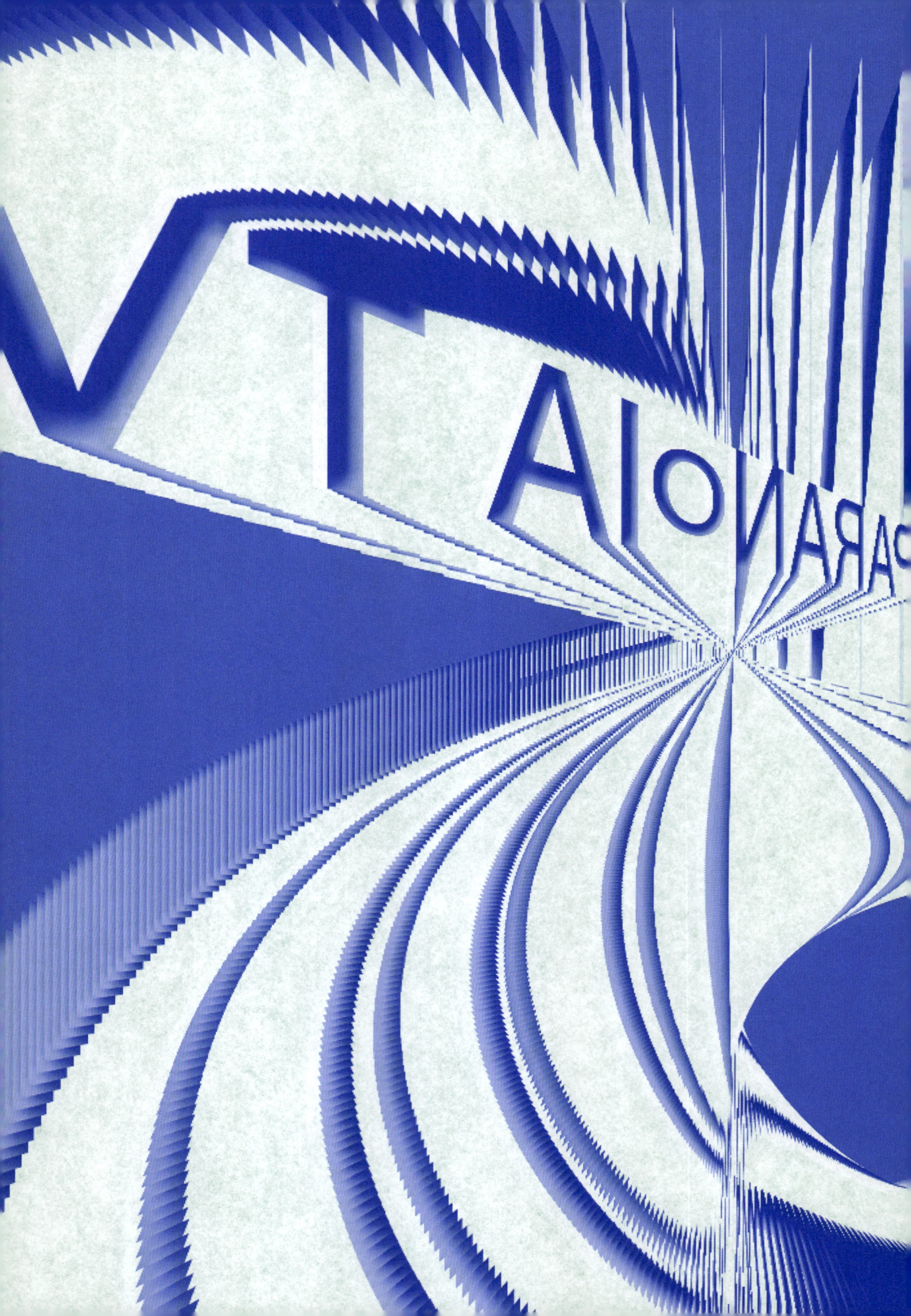

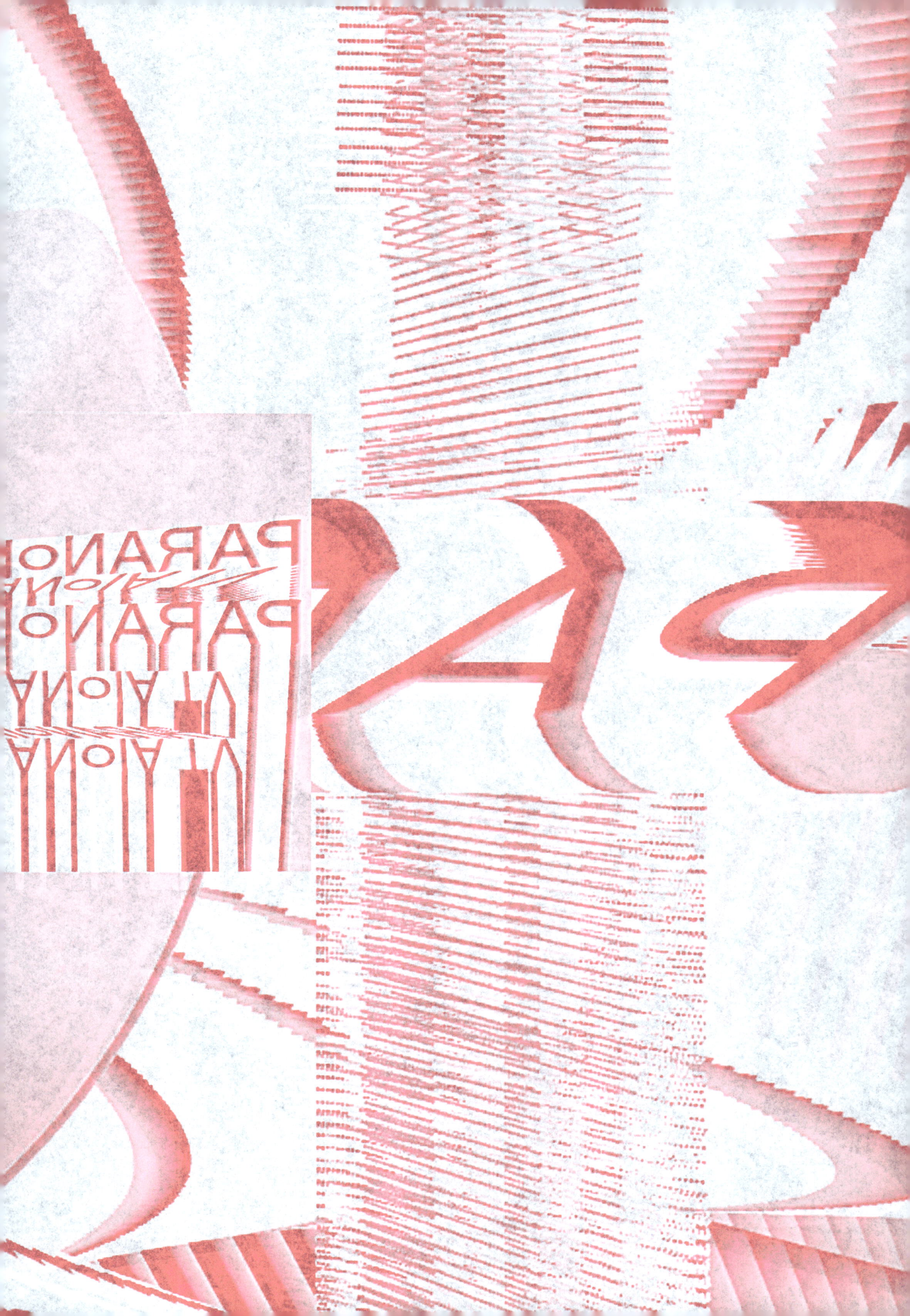

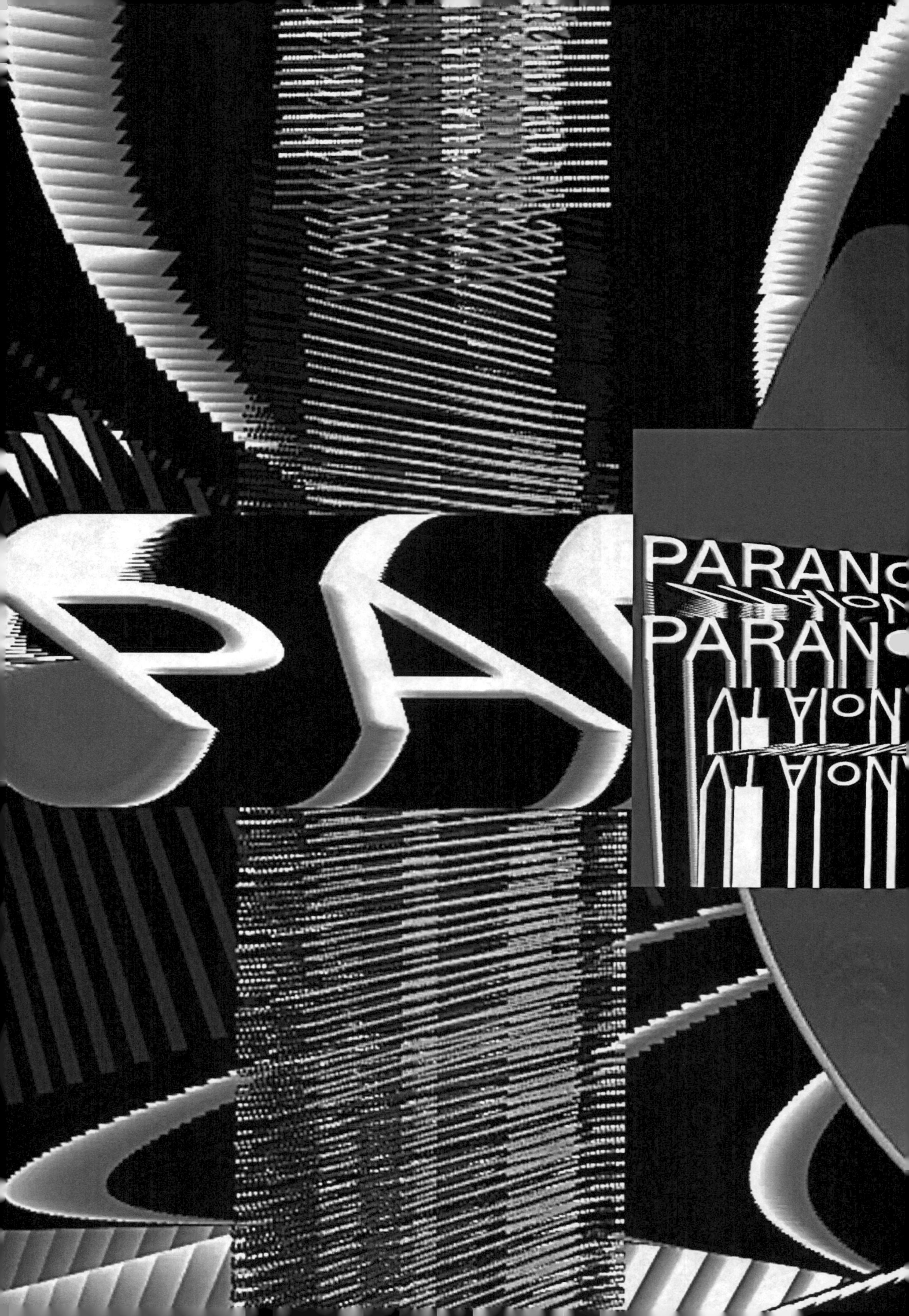
PARAN
PARAN

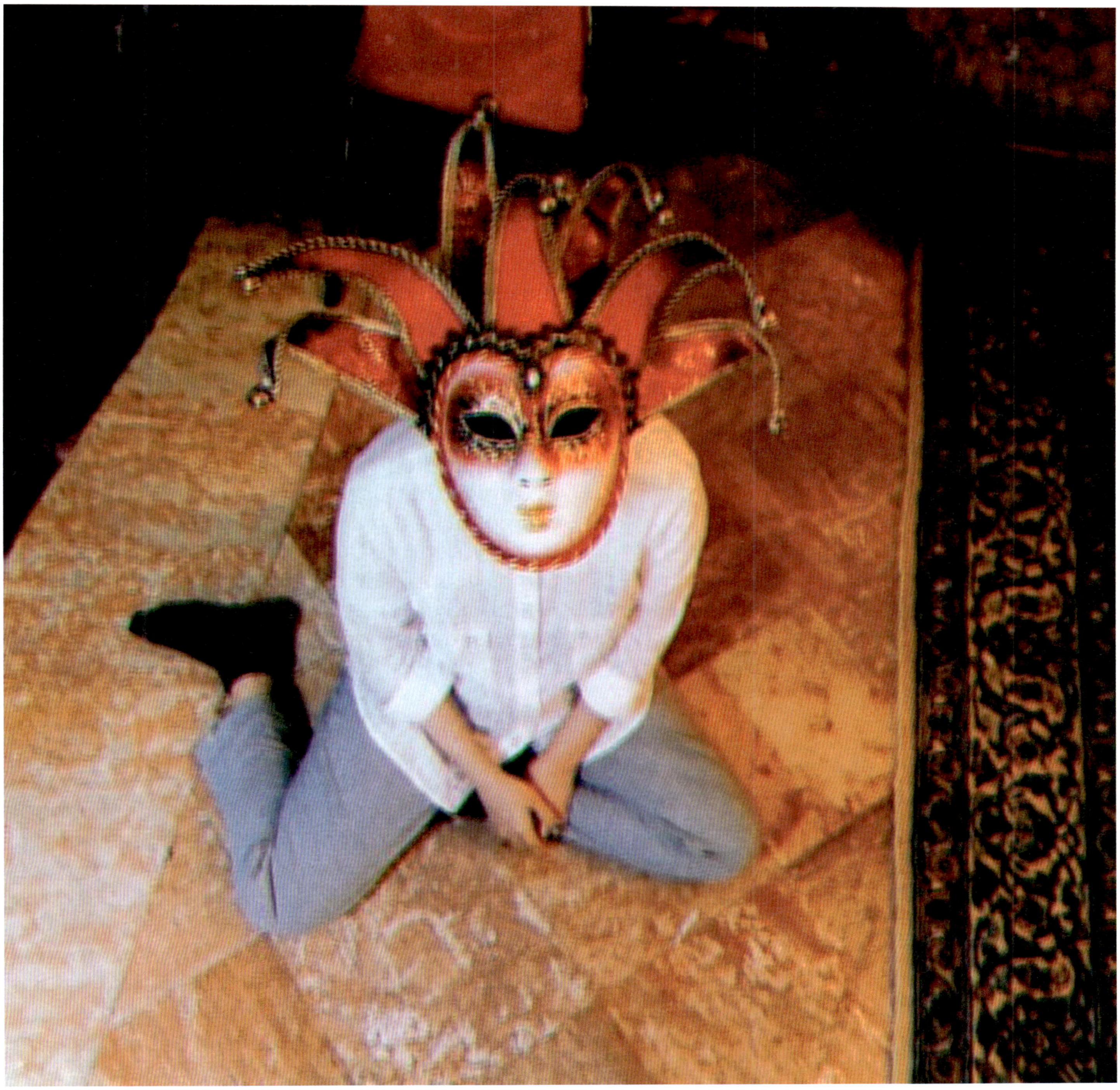

82

Nika Dubrovsky (1967, Leningrad, Russia) is a writer and artist. In 2006, Nika met David Graeber in New York, and a few years later, *Anthropology for Kids*, an open-source platform experimenting with new forms of work between the academy and contemporary art, emerged. After her husband's unexpected death in 2020, Nika and friends organized *Carnival4David* to celebrate his life and mourn his death. It was later transformed into an informal community, Museum of Care, which combines offline residencies and online projects. Dubrovsky writes for publications such as *e-flux* and *artnet*. Her books have been published in Russian, Finnish, English, Polish, and Japanese. She lives in London.

Intergalactic Memorial Carnival for David Graeber (2020)
Livestream, ca. 12 hours

Produced by Nika Dubrovsky and friends
Supported by steirischer herbst '20

Up until his tragic and untimely passing, David Graeber was working with his partner, artist Nika Dubrovsky, on a project for *Paranoia TV* and steirischer herbst. This event was canceled. In its place, *Paranoia TV* supported and streamed a worldwide carnival in memory of the deceased anthropologist and activist.

David Graeber died in Venice, a city he often visited. After every trip, he brought back Venetian masks and costumes, because he generally admired the Venetian Carnival. Before it became a tourist commodity, the Carnival of Venice constituted a political space of radical democracy. During Carnival, there were no blacks, no whites, no old, no young, no beautiful, no ugly, no poor, no rich. Everyone was a mask. Being a player in the anti-capitalist movements of the nineties and noughties, he knew about the irresistible similarities between the experience of a carnival and an insurrection.

It was in this spirit that David Graeber's friends and comrades held a memorial event on October 11, 2020. Thousands of people gathered in 250 locations around the world to mourn and to celebrate. They wore theatrical masks in homage to the Carnival of Venice that Graeber so loved at an Intergalactic Memorial Carnival (#Carnival4David), organized by his wife Nika Dubrovsky and their friends. Old or young, rich or poor, from scientists to the retired, everyone anonymous, regardless of political persuasion—all were united through death, laughing in its face.

An uninterrupted twelve-hour livestream showed the carnival unfolding from New York City's Zuccotti Park (the iconic site of Occupy Wall Street), the ZAD in France, and Graeber's home in London's Portobello Road; to Rio, Penza prison in Russia, and Rojava; to Japan, Nairobi, and Singapore. People ate pancakes and drank vodka in Saint Petersburg, trekked in the Czech Republic, and listened to *Bullshit Jobs* playlists in Rennes. They formed an "anarchology collective" in Nagasaki, held a costume party in Zurich, and a eulogy in Seoul. They reenacted a roundtable in Galicia, rewired a farmworkers' radio station in New Jersey, and in Ohio "kept David Graeber company with laughter and tales of piracy as he traveled between worlds."

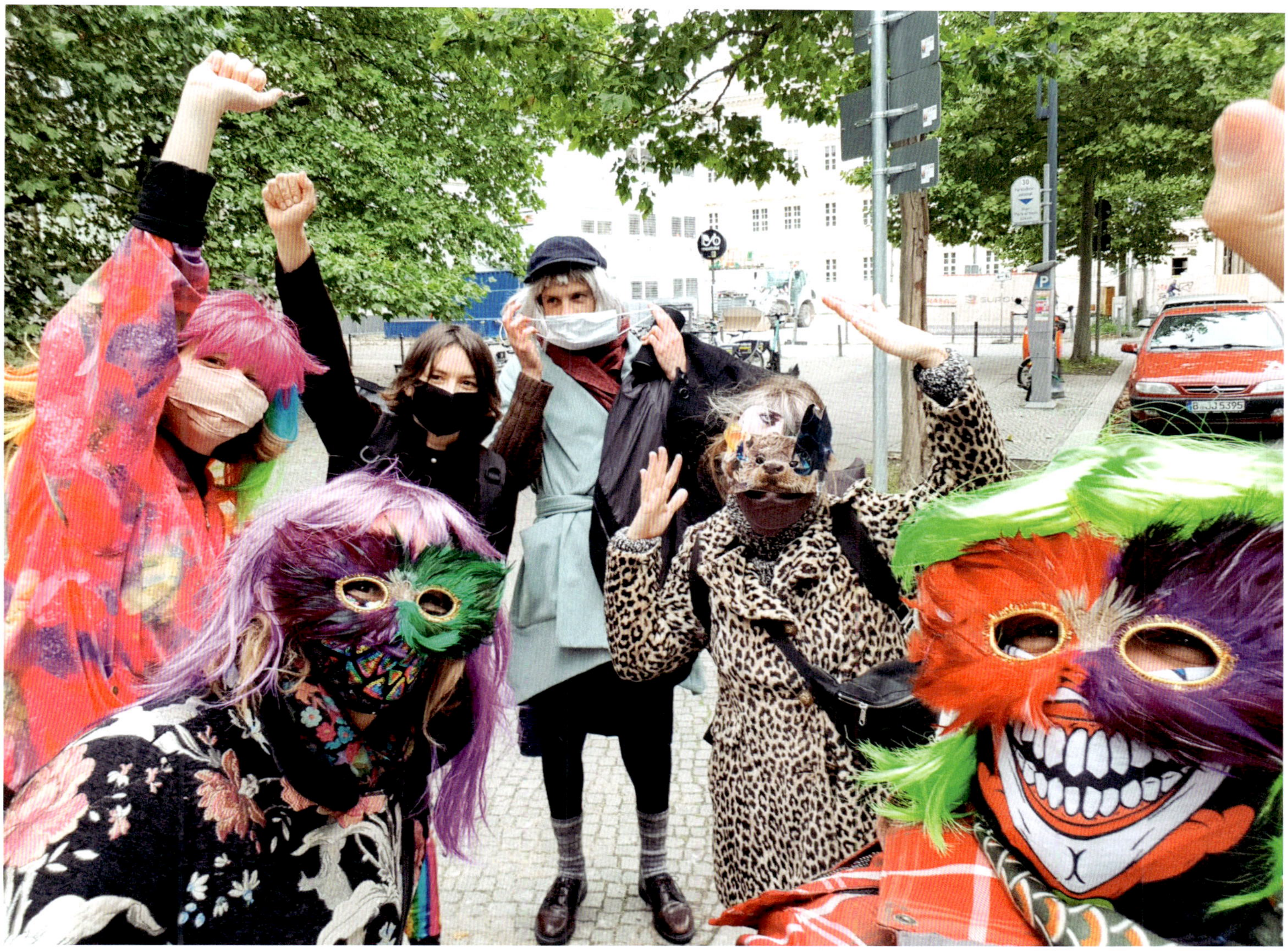

Vadim Fishkin

Dictionary of Imaginary Places
2020

Installation

EBA, BEKLA, BEKLAN EMPIRE, BELSBAT, BENGODI, BEN KHATOUR'S VI
D, BLACKSTAFF, BLANK, BLATHUANIA, BLAZING WORLD, BLEFUSCU, BLE
ROLLERS, ISLE OF BOREDOM, BOSSARD OR HUMPED ISLAND, BOU CI
S, BRISSONTE, BROBDINGNAG, BROCELIANDE, BRODIE'S LAND OR ML
ARN, CAER DALLBEN, CAER DATHYL, CAERLEON OR CARLION, CAFFOL
A, CAMPHOR ISLAND, CANADIAN FLOATING ISLES, CANNIBAL ISLAND, C
RBONEK CASTLE, CALION, CARN GAFALL, CARTOGRAPHICAL EMPIRE, C
CELESTIAL CITY, CENTRUM TERRAE, CESSARES REPUBLIC, CHALLENG
A, CHIT … CHRISTIA
, CLOU … COGAIGN
RAL IS … S ISLAND,
ER ISL … CYCLOP
OF DE … ELECTABL
NTAINS … DIEGO R
KINGDO … ONHAM, D
REAMS … RA, DRIMO
PING IS … EGGS UP,
D CITY … S, EMYN
RIC THE … OF ETERN
O OF FA … FOREST,
FERGU … AND OF L
ER, FL … LGAR, FO
ISLAN … DONIA, FR
, GANA … TRY, GAF
HION, … GLOME, G
GONDA … ORTH, GO
WRITT … NE, GREA
GREY … VETHERS,
G, HAM … , HAPPILA
ISLAN … ONDA, HE
OR ERE … OF THE HO
A, HY … OR HERE
AND, I … R'S HOUS
ROO, J … JAGUAR T
UX, JU … URASSIC
KING … SOLOMO
LADIES … OWN, LA
, LETA … F LICHTE
SOLUS … N-THAMES
LOTUS … AIN OF LO
BINA, F … ETERNIT
MARA … IRON, MA
ND, MA … CCO, MEI
A, MER … NIA, MICR
OOD, M … MISTY MO
N VALL … 'S ISLAND
JE, ISL … SLAND, M
OF LIM … NEPREK
OF DEA … MPATAN,
AMMA, … OTHING, N
OLD MA … EYED, OC
OSSIRI … TRANTO,
ARHAN … A, PARTH
HE PEO … NTHIA, PE
PLE, PI … NIA, PNO
' ISLAN … T-GRAUBE

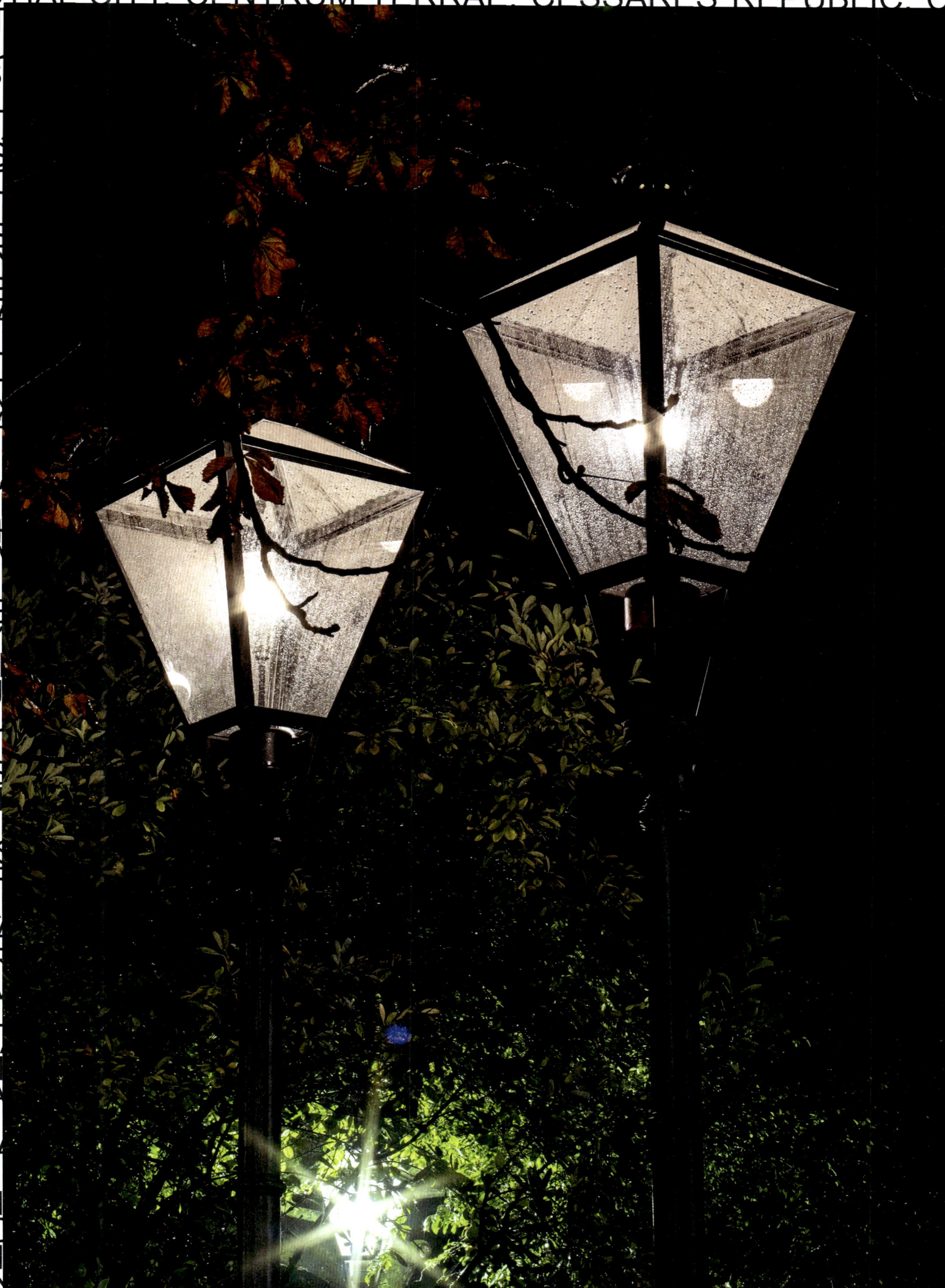

DENCE ISLAND, PRYDAIN, PSEUDOPOLIS, PTOLEMAIS, PTYX ISLAND, PU
JUNCTION, ISLE OF RANSOM, RAVENAL'S TOWER, REALISM ISLAND, RE
AR, RIGMAROLE, RINGING ISLAND, RINGS, RIPPLE LAND, RIP VAN WINKL
SE, ROSSUM'S ISLAND, ROTUNDIA, ROUND VALLEY, RUACH, RUFFAL, RU
EMM'S CORRIDOR, SALEM, SALU ARCHIPELAGO, SALVARA, SAMARAH, C
CROTARIPARAGORGOULEO, ISLAND OF SCARLET TOWER, SCHILDA, SCO
JATH, VALLEY OF THE SHADOW OF DEATH, CITY OF SHADOWS, SHANGR
S, SITARA, SKULL ISLAND, SLAVNA, CAVE OF THE SLEEPERS OF ERINN

AUREPAIRE, BEDEGRAINE OR BEDGRAYNE, BEELZEBUB'S CASTLE, BE
ACK CHAPEL, BLACK HILL COVE, BLACK HOUSE, BLACK JUNGLE, BLAC
OMBODINGA, BLUEBEARD'S CASTLE, BOHU, BONG-TREE LAND, BOOM
IDGETOWN, BRIGADOON, BRIGALAURE, BRISEVENT OR MARVELOUS IS
RFLIES, BUTUA, BUYAN ISLAND, CAAALUSSA, CACKLOGALLINIA, CAER
LYPSO'S ISLAMD, CAMELERD, CAMELIARD, CAMELOT, CAMFORD, CAM
E OF DEVILS, CARABAS CASTLE, CARAS GALADHON OR CITY OF TREE
KE OF THE CAULDRON, FIELD OF CELEBRANT, CELEPHAIS, CELESTEV
IELM, CHIAOHU TEMPLE, CHICHEN ITZA, CHINA COUNTRY, CHING PEH,
RITH UNGOL, THE CITY, CIUDAD, ISLAND OF CIVILIZATION, CCLERKSHIP
CE, COOK'S ISLAND, COOPERATIVE CITY, ISLE OF COQUARDZ, CORADIN
OTHET ISLAND, CRUSOE'S ISLAND OR SPERANZA, CSTWERTSKST, CU
AD MAN'S VALLEY, DEAD MARSHES, DEADS' TOWN, CITY OF DEATH, FO
AND, ISLE OF DEVILS, LAND OF DEVILS, THE DEVIL'S TEETH, DIAMOND
BISTAN, DOCTOR MOREAU'S ISLAND, DODON'S KINGDOM, THE DOLDRU
N, CITY OF DREADFUL NIGHT, DREAM ISLAND, DREAM KINGDOM, LAKE
E OF THE EAR, PLAIN OF EASE, EAST FATHING, EASTWICK, EBUDA OR
ISEE RECLUS ISLAND, ELVENHALLS OF MIRKWOOD, ELVENHOME, EM
EWHON,ERIADOR, LAND OF ERIC THE RED, ERIKRAUDEBYG OR LAND
VAIPANOMA, EXHAM PRIORY, EXOPOTAMIA, EXPIATION CITY,FAIRYLAND
E, ISLAND OF FELIDO, FELIMATH, FELINA, FENERALIA, FERDINAND'S ISL
ORA, FLOTSAM, FLOZELLA-A-NINA, FLUORESCENTE, FLUTTERBUDGET
RTUNATE ISLANDS, ISLAND OF FORTUNE, FOXCASTLE, FOXVILLE, FRAG
LWORTH, FUNDINELVE, FUTURA,GAALDINE, GALLIGENIA, GALLINACO, G
AND, GIANT'S GARDEN, SEA OF GIANTS, GIPHANTIA, GLADDEN FIELDS,
LAKE, GOLDEN MOUNTAIN, GOLDEN RIVER, GOLDENSTONE, GOLDEN
NWICK, GRAND EUSCARIE, DUCHY OF GRAND FENWICK, GRAVEYARD O
AND, GREENS WHARFE OR CAPE-VED ISLANDS, ISLAND OF GREY AM
NOMACTIDE, GYNOPYREA,HACIOGRAM OR ISLE OF PROPHETS, HADLE
T PINS, HAUNTED ISLAND, HAUNTED PASS, HAV, HAVNOR, HEADLESS VA
ME, HLANITH, HOFBAU, HOGWARTS, HOHENFLIESS, CITY OF HOLES, HO
NCHBACK ISLAND, HUNGERCITY, HUNIA, HUR-AT-HUR, HYGEIA, HYPER
MORTALS, INGA TUNNEL, ISLE OF INCREASE UNSOUGHT, INDIANA, INDIA
GREN, ISHMAELIA, ISHTAKAR, ISLA, ISLANDIA, ITHILIEN, IVANIKHA, IX, J
YEUSEGARDE, JOYOS ISLE, JUAM, VALLEY OF THE JUKANS, ISLE DES J
RPATHENBURG, KAYOS, KELSO, THE KERNEL, FOREST OF KEY, KINGDO
ONOMO, KUKUANALAND, KUMMEROW, KUNLUN MOUNT,LAGELAND, CIT
THE LEGIONS, LEIXLIP, LENG, LEONARD'S LAND, LEONIA, LERNA, LESN
D ONIONS, LIVING ISLAND, LAND OF LIVING MEN, LIXUS, LLAREGYB, LO
K, LORBRULGRUD, ISLAND OF THE LORD OF THE FLIES, LORIEN, LOST
, MAGARIA, MAGONDO, MACRANESE ISLAND, MACREONS ISLAND, MAG
NGO ISLAND, MANOBA, MANOUHAM, MAPLE WHITE LAND OR LOST WO
TAEOTECHNY, MAURELVILLE OR MAUREL CITY, MAURERANIA, MAXON'S
NAL, MEMISON, MERCY FARM, MER-KING'S KINGDOM, MERLIN'S TOMB,
SHES, MILOSIS, MINA, MINAS MORGUL, MINAS TIRITH, MINDA, MINUNI, M
ONTESIONOS' CAVE, MONTEVERDE, MOODY LAND, MOOMINLAND OR M
AND, MORVA, MOTHER CAREY'S HEAVEN, MOURNFUL SEA, MOUNT ANA
, NATURE THEATRE OF OKLAHOMA, NAUDELY, NAUTILUS HARBOUR, NA
W SWITZERLAND, NEXDOREA, NGRANEK, NIGHT OR DREADFUL NIGHT
LANDIA, NOLE, NO-MAN'S-LAND, NOMELAND, LAND OF NOPANDES, NO
GYGIA, OHONOO, OLD FOREST, OLD-MAN-OF-THE-SEA'S-ISLAND, HOUSE
AND, ORRIMY, ORSENNA, ORTELGA, OSGILIATH OR CITADEL OF THE ST
, PALACE OF PAPER SACKS, PARADESA, PARADISE ISLAND, PARAPAG
NAL SETTLEMENT, PENDOR, PENGUIN ISLAND, PENTIXORE, COUNTRY
E DE LA PIERRE BLANCHE, PILE, PIMMINEE, PINK PALACE, LAKE PIPPLE
AND OF POLYPRAGMOSYNE, POMACE, PONUKELE-DRELCHKAFF, POPE
OPHETS, PROSPERO'S ISLAND OR CALIBAN'S ISLAND, PROTOCOSMO, P
QUEENS, QUIQUENDONE, QUISO, QUIVERA, RAKLMANI, RAMAJA, RAM
REK, RHAGES, THE BARROW OF RHITTA, RHUDAUR, RHUN, RIALLARO, R
ATE, ROME, ROMINTEN, RONCADOR, RONDISLE, ROOTABAGA COUNTR
REGONNE, SAINT ERLINIQUE, SAINT-ESPRIT, CAPE SAKNUSSEMM, SAKN
OPT SWANGEANTI, SATINLAND, SATRAPIA, SAVAGE ISLAND, SAVOYA, SO
AND OF SEVEN CITIES, SEVEN ISLES, MOUNTAINS OF SHADOW OR EPH
LING, SIMON-CRUBELLIER, SIRANNON, SIRAP, SIREN ISLAND, SEA OF S

EBA, BEKLA, BEKLAN EMPIRE, BELSBAT, BENGODI, BEN KHATOUR'S VI
D, BLACKSTAFF, BLANK, BLATHUANIA, BLAZING WORLD, BLEFUSCU, BLE
ROLLERS, ISLE OF BOREDOM, BOSSARD OR HUMPED ISLAND, BOU C
S, BRISSONTE, BROBDINGNAG, BROCELIANDE, BRODIE'S LAND OR ML
ARN, CAER DALLBEN, CAER DATHYL, CAERLEON OR CARLION, CAFFOL
A, CAMPHOR ISLAND, CANADIAN FLOATING ISLES, CANNIBAL ISLAND, C
RBONEK CASTLE, CALION, CARN GAFALL, CARTOGRAPHICAL EMPIRE, C
CELESTIAL CITY, CENTRUM TERRAE, CESSARES REPUBLIC, CHALLENG
A, CHITTERLINGS LAND, CHRISTIAN CITY, CHRISTIANOPOLIS, CHRISTIA
, CLOUDCUCKOOLAND, MOUNTAINS OF CLOUDS, COAL CITY, COGAIGN
RAL ISLAND, CORBIN, CORK, COROMANDEL, COUNT ZAROFF'S ISLAND,
ER ISLAND, CUFFYCOAT'S ISLAND, CUNA CUNA, CUTTENCLIP, CYCLOP
OF DEATH, DEATHWATER ISLAND, DEBRA-DOWA, DEELGUY, DELECTABL
NTAINS, DIANA'S GROVE, DICTIONOPOLIS OR CITY OF WORDS, DIEGO R
INGDOM OF DOLLS, DOMINORA, DONDUM ARCHIPELAGO, DOONHAM, D
REAMS, DREAMWORLD, SCHLOSS DREIVIERTELSTEIN, DREXARA, DRIMO
PING ISLE, ECNATNEPER OR NODNOL, EDEN VALE, EDORAS, EGGS UP,
D CITY, EMO, EMPI ARCHIPELAGO, EMPORIUM, EMPTY HATS, EMYN
RIC THE RED, ERSILIA, ESCALOT, ESSUR, ESTOTILAND, LAND OF ETERN
O OF FAITH, FAKREDDIN VALLEV, FALUN, FANATTIA, FANGORN FOREST,
FERGUS, FERISLAND, FESTENBURG CASTLE, FIGLEFIA OR ISLAND OF L
ER, FLYING DUTCHMAN'S PORT, FONS BELLI, FONSECA, FOOLGAR, FO
ISLAND, FRANCARIA, FRANCE-VILLE, FREE COMMOTS, FREEDONIA, FR
, GANABIN ISLAND, GANKLAND, GAGARIDA, GARAMANTI COUNTRY, GAR
HION, GLITTERING CAVES, LAND OF THE GLITTERING PLAIN, GLOME, G
GONDAL AND GAALDINE, GONDOR, GONDOUR, GONT, GORGORTH, GO
WRITTEN BOOKS, GREAT CYPRESS SWAMP, GREAT GARABAGNE, GREA
GREY HAVENS, GREY MOUNTAINS OR ERED MITHRIN, GREYWETHERS,
G, HAMMERHEAD HILLS, HAM ROCK, THE HANDS, HANS-BACH, HAPPILA
ISLAND OF HEARSAY, ISLAND OF THE HEATHEN, HEKLA, HELIKONDA, HE
R EREGION, HOLLOW NEEDLE, HOOLOOMOOLOO, COUNTRY OF THE HO
A, HYPOCRISY ISLAND,IANICUM, IBANSK, IGARA, IGARIA, ICI OR HERE
AND, INFANTE ISLAND, INNSMOUTH, INQUANOK, INTERPRETER'S HOUS
ROO, JABBERWOCKY WOOD, JACKSONVILLE, REALM OF THE JAGUAR T
UX, JUMELLES, JUNDAPUR, JUNGANYIKA OR SECRET LAKE, JURASSIC
KING KONG'S ISLAND, ISLE OF KINGS, KING'S KINGDOM, KING SOLOMO
ADIES, LADIES' ISLAND, LAGADO, LAIMAK, LAIQUHIRE, LAKE-TOWN, LA
, LETALISPONS, LEUKE, LIBERIA, LIBERTINA, GRAND DUCHY OF LICHTE
SOLUS, LOGUTA, LODIDHAPURA, LOFOTEN, LOMB, LONDON-ON-THAMES
LOTUS-EATERS ISLAND, ISLAND OF LOVE, RIVER AND FOUNTAIN OF LO
BINA, ROCK OF THE MAGIC MAIDEN, MAG-MELD OR LAND OF ETERNITY
MARADAGAL, MARAMMA, MARBOTIKIN DULDA OR ISLAND OF IRON, MA
ND, MAYDA OR ISLAND OF THE SEVEN CITIES, MECCANIA, MECCO, ME
A, MERRYLAND, MESKEETA, MESZRIA, METTINGEN, MEZZORANIA, MICR
OOD, MIRROR OF LLUNET, MISHPORT, MISNIE, MISPEC MOOR, MISTY MO
N VALLEY, MOOMINPAPA'S ISLAND, MOOR, MORDOR, MOREAU'S ISLAND
JE, ISLAND OF MOVING TREES, MUIL, MUMMELSEE, MUSICAL ISLAND, M
OF LIMBO, NAZAR, NEN HITHOEL, NEOPIE ISLAND, NEPENTHE, NEPREK
OF DEATH, KINGDOM OF NIGHT, NIGHTMARE ABBEY, NIMMR, NIMPATAN,
AMMA, NORTH FARTHING, NORTH POLE KINGDOM, ISLE OF NOTHING, N
OLD MATHERS, OLDWIVESFABLEDOM, KINGDOM OF THE ONE-EYED, OO
OSSIRIAND, OSSKIL, OTHER END OF NOWHERE, CASTLE OF OTRANTO,
ARHAN, PAROULET'S COUNTRY, LAND OF PARROTS, PARTHALIA, PARTH
HE PEOPLE OF THE MIST, PEPPERLAND, PERI KINGDOM, PERINTHIA, PE
PLE, PISSEMPSCO, LAND OF PLAY, PLUTO, PLAY TOWN, PLUTONIA, PNO
ISLAND, POPIMANIA, POPO, PORT-APE, PORT BRETON, PORT-GRAUBE
DENCE ISLAND, PRYDAIN, PSEUDOPOLIS, PTOLEMAIS, PTYX ISLAND, PU
JUNCTION, ISLE OF RANSOM, RAVENAL'S TOWER, REALISM ISLAND, RE
AR, RIGMAROLE, RINGING ISLAND, RINGS, RIPPLE LAND, RIP VAN WINKL
SE, ROSSUM'S ISLAND, ROTUNDIA, ROUND VALLEY, RUACH, RUFFAL, RU
EMM'S CORRIDOR, SALEM, SALU ARCHIPELAGO, SALVARA, SAMARAH, C
CROTARIPARAGORGOULEO, ISLAND OF SCARLET TOWER, SCHILDA, SCO
JATH, VALLEY OF THE SHADOW OF DEATH, CITY OF SHADOWS, SHANGR
S, SITARA, SKULL ISLAND, SLAVNA, CAVE OF THE SLEEPERS OF ERINN

AUREPAIRE, BEDEGRAINE OR BEDGRAYNE, BEELZEBUB'S CASTLE, BE
ACK CHAPEL, BLACK HILL COVE, BLACK HOUSE, BLACK JUNGLE, BLAC
OMBODINGA, BLUEBEARD'S CASTLE, BOHU, BONG-TREE LAND, BOON
IDGETOWN, BRIGADOON, BRIGALAURE, BRISEVENT OR MARVELOUS I

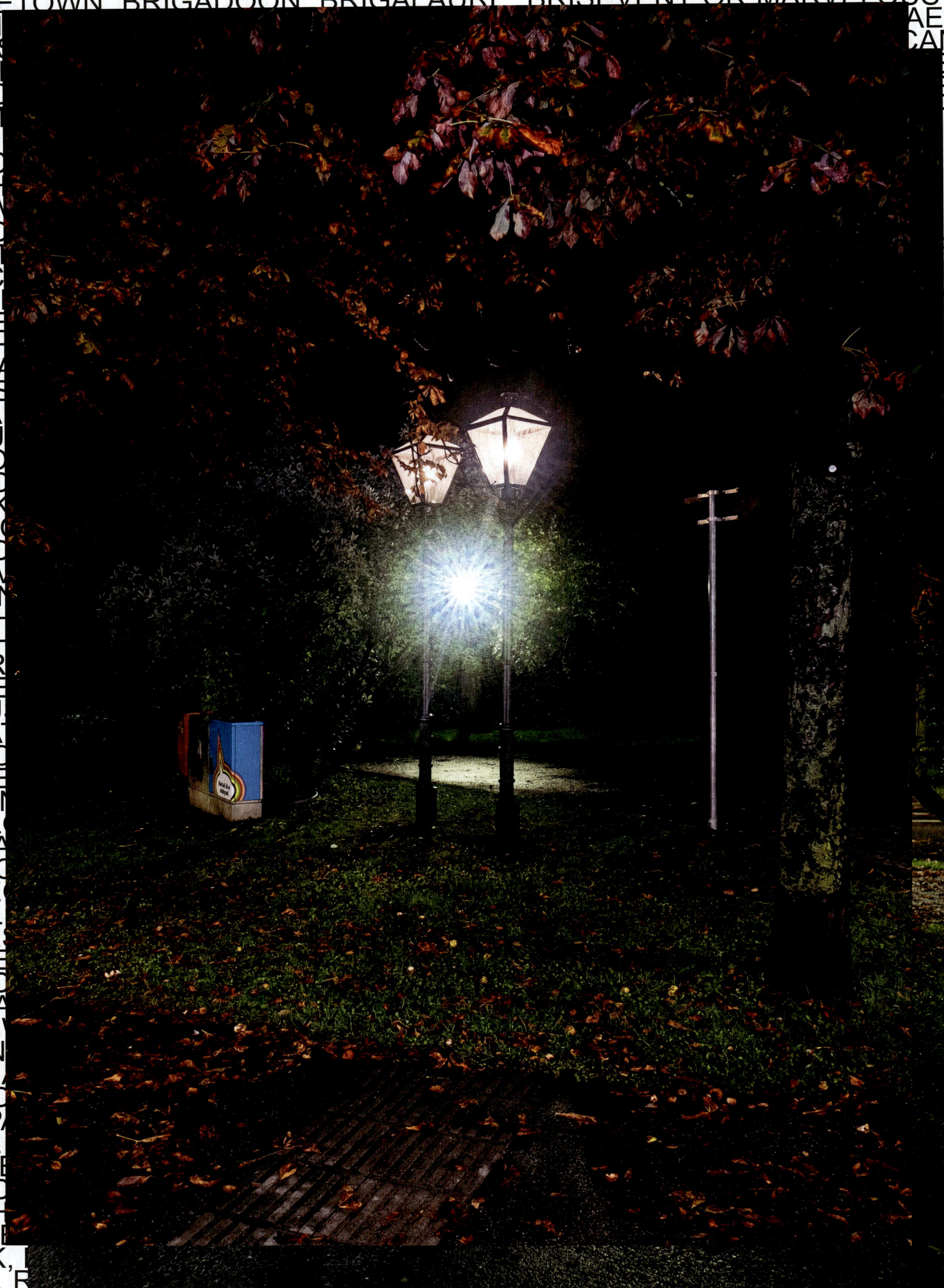

REGONNE, SAINT ERLINIQUE, SAINT-ESPRIT, CAPE SAKNUSSEMM, SAK
OOPT SWANGEANTI, SATINLAND, SATRAPIA, SAVAGE ISLAND, SAVOYA, S
AND OF SEVEN CITIES, SEVEN ISLES, MOUNTAINS OF SHADOW OR EPH
LING, SIMON-CRUBELLIER, SIRANNON, SIRAP, SIREN ISLAND, SEA OF S

You heard it right: the streetlamps along Burgring are actually having a conversation. In the work of Vadim Fishkin two lights become actors. A squeaky voice and a bass exchange utopian and literary place names from Alberto Manguel and Gianni Guadalupi's *Dictionary of Imaginary Places*. They recite the names of mysterious cities and countries, distant objects of yearning for a time when travel is near-impossible. But in the ever-accessible world of literature, we still travel around the globe in our imagination.

89

Vadim Fishkin, born in Penza, USSR, in 1965, lived in Moscow until 1996; he currently lives and works in Ljubljana. His work explores the relationships between science, personal experience, desire, and the imagination, between metaphysics and pragmatism, and between the artificial and the real. The artist succeeds in uncovering subtle connections that arouse viewers' curiosity, yet leaves them guessing about the ultimate meaning. Fishkin's main area of investigation is science and its study methods as he uses technological advances for essentially poetic purposes and many of his installations, sculptures, photographs, and drawings are informed by his distinctive sense of humor.

Recent solo shows have been held at DUM Project Space, Ljubljana; Hollybush Gardens, London; Associazione Barriera, Turin; Loom Gallery, Milan; Galerija Gregor Podnar, Berlin and Ljubljana; Musiz Foundation, Sofia; Krank Art Gallery, Istanbul; and MSUM / Museum of Contemporary Art, Ljubljana.

His work has been presented at group shows at Casino Luxembourg; Secession, Vienna; Galerie Nationale du Jeu de Paume, Paris; FRAC Lorraine, Metz; Galerie für Zeitgenössische Kunst, Leipzig; Martin-Gropius-Bau, Berlin; Künstlerhaus Bethanien, Berlin; Palazzo dell Ragione, Milan; BAWAG Foundation, Vienna; ZKM, Karlsruhe; MACRO Museum for Contemporary Art, Rome; Isabella Stewart Gardner Museum, Boston; and the Drawing Center, New York, among others.

Fishkin also took part in the Venice Biennale (in 1995, 2003, 2005, and 2017); the 1st Valencia Biennial (2001); Manifesta 1, Rotterdam (1996); the 3rd Istanbul Biennial (1992); the 8th Baltic Triennial of International Art (2002); and the 9th Shanghai Biennale (2012).

Dictionary of Imaginary Places (2020)
Installation
Burgring

Commissioned and produced by steirischer herbst '20

Dani Gal

Three Works for Piano
2020

Video

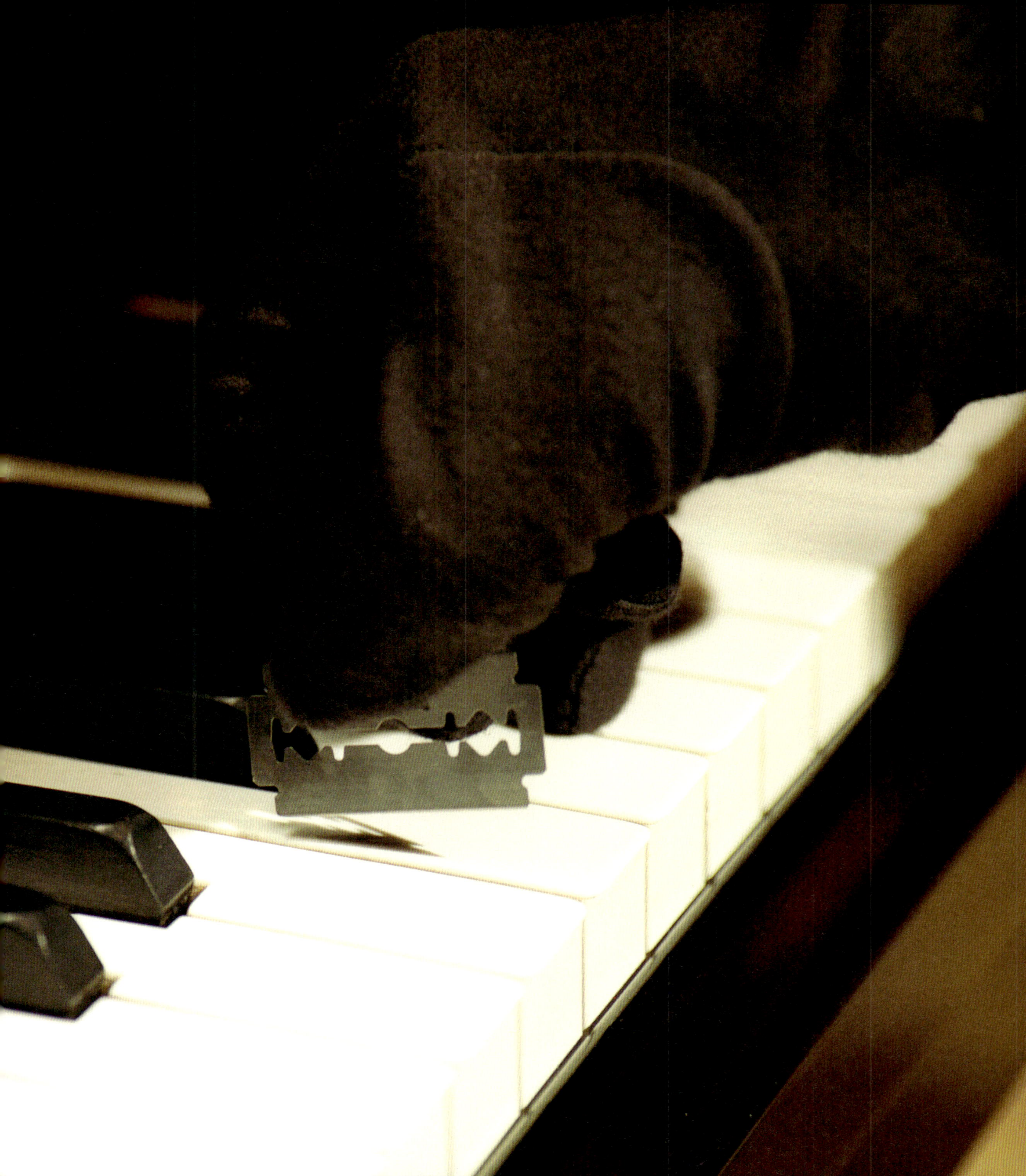

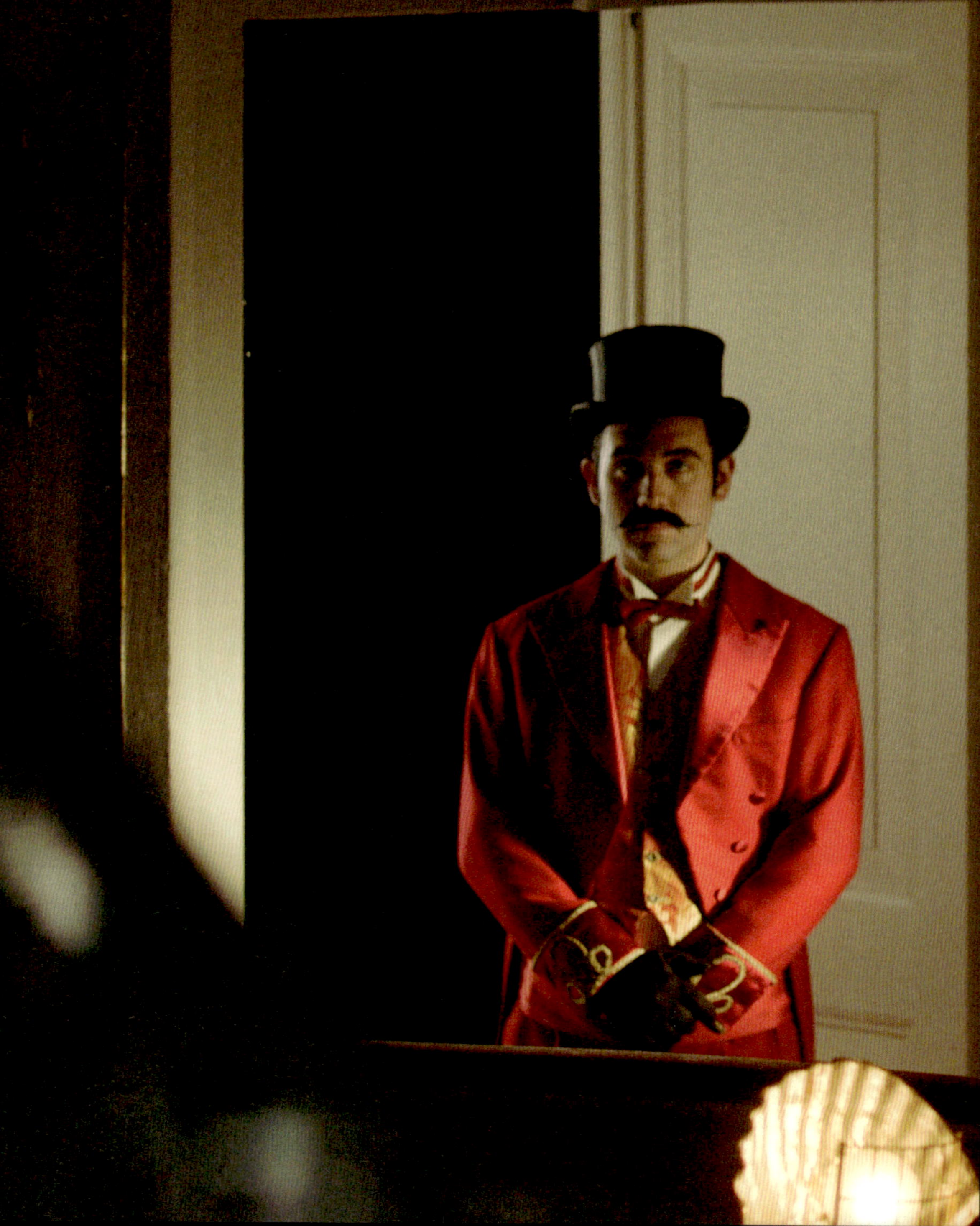

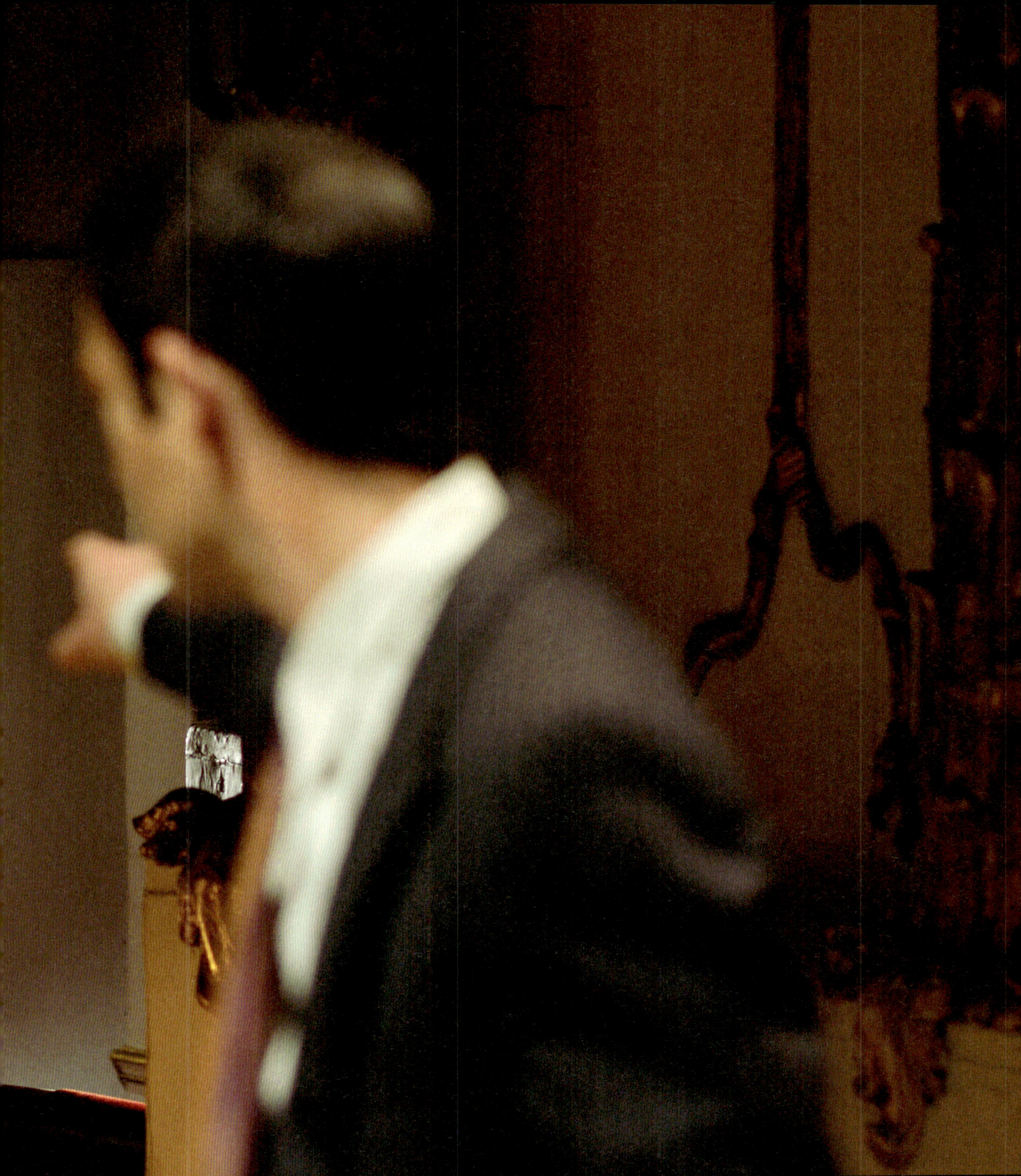

Three Works for Piano adapts three avant-garde performances as hallucinatory allegories for the dynamics between the historical/moral witness and society as the addressee of the testimony. The interview scene, which functions as a frame for the other scenes, tells the true story of an Israeli soldier who was a violent perpetrator in the occupied territories, and whose testimony was discredited and denied by the state.

As a continuation of Gal's investigation of victim/perpetrator complexities, this story focuses on the soldier who perceives himself in both roles and therefore sidelines the story of the real victim/s, the Palestinian man whom he beat unconscious because he passively refused to be detained.

The soldier's moral ambiguity is exposed through the female researcher who interviews him while the performance reenactments are abstracted illustrations of the tensions in the interview. Since the same actors play different characters in each of the scenes, the historical reenactments of the piano concerts become dreamlike reflections on the contemporary conversation between the two.

The first piano scene is a reenactment of the Israeli premiere of John Cage's *4'33"* in the late 1970s. The pianist renounces his authority in favor of a more inclusive and anarchic experience of listening. However, the proposal for the liberation of music in this specific event is rejected by the audience, who impose their collectivity as national unity by starting to sing a nationalist song, choosing populism over elitism.

The pianist as a proxy for the witness is silent by choice or by his inability to speak. He possesses a truth that threatens the stability of the collective. The collective, on the other hand, is uncomfortable with this silence and therefore chooses to replace it with optimism, nationalism, and nostalgia.

The second piano scene, George Antheil confronting his audience with a loaded gun in a concert in Budapest in 1923, can be read as a mirror image to Cage's scene: the pianist, again as a proxy for the witness, faces society and renders his audience captive by ordering them to listen. By pulling the pistol he commands the audience's attention for a sense of collective responsibility: a demand for society to deal with its disturbing past and violent present. At the same time as Antheil is pointing a gun at the audience and locking the doors of the concert hall, the scene can be read as an ironic allegory of the critic in the project of modernity, namely, the justification of violence in the name of progress.

In the third and final event, which concludes the film, a reenactment of the first documented performance of a piano demolition by the Wiener Gruppe in 1959 focuses on the piano itself, the instrument or the medium that delivers the message. In this case the testimony has to be destroyed because the exposed truth undermines the state's authority and legitimacy.

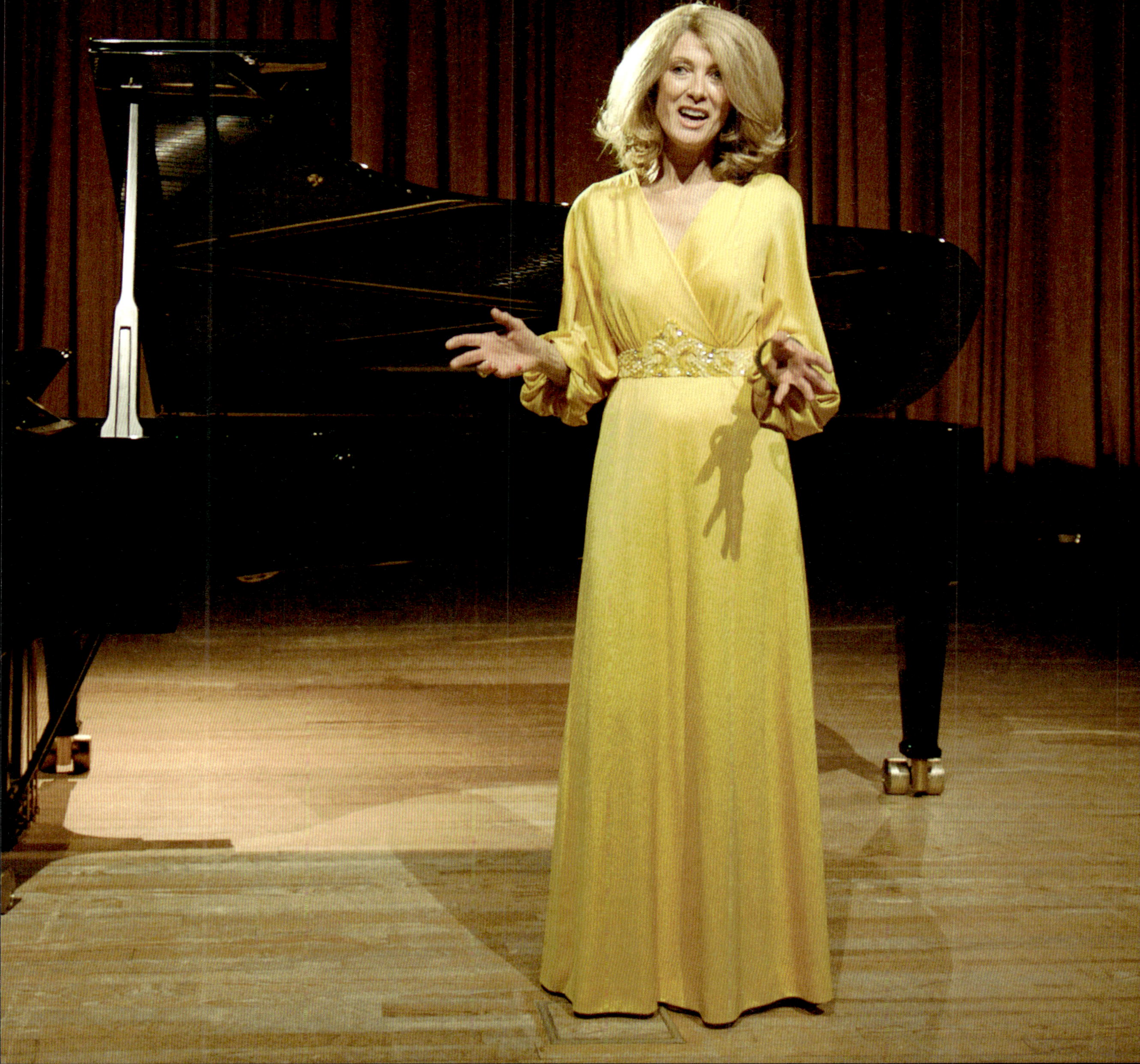

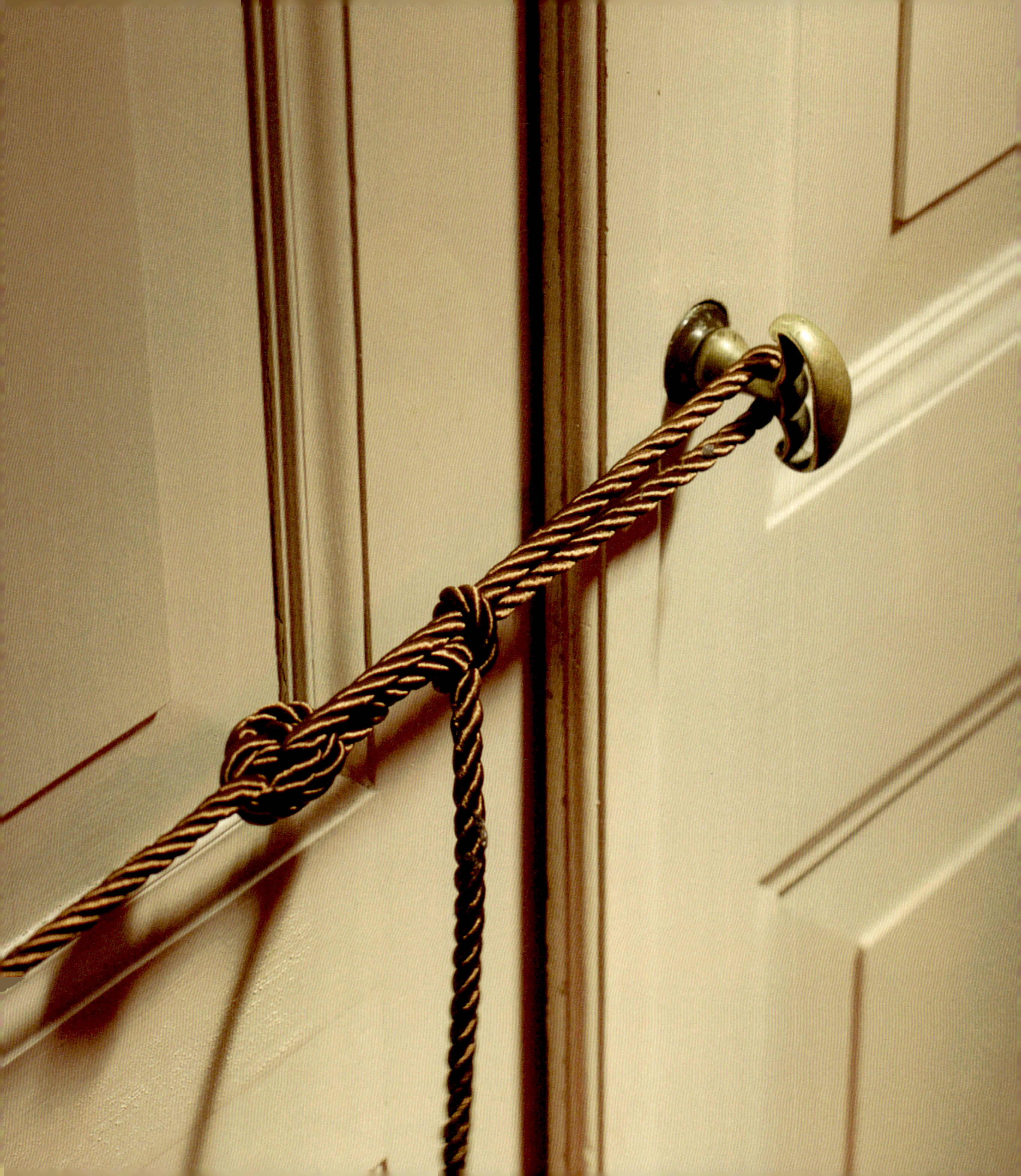

Dani Gal, born in Jerusalem in 1975, lives and works in Berlin. He studied at the Bezalel Academy for Art and Design in Jerusalem, the Staatliche Hochschule für Bildende Künste Städelschule in Frankfurt, and the Cooper Union in New York. His films and works have been shown widely, including at the 54th Venice Biennale (2011); Istanbul Biennale (2011); New Museum, New York; Kunsthalle St. Gallen; The Jewish Museum, New York; Berlinale Forum Expanded (2014); Kunsthaus Zurich; Kunsthalle Wien; Documenta 14, Athens/Kassel (2017); and Centre Pompidou, Paris.

Three Works for Piano (2020)
Video, ca. 34 min., English
Online

Actors: Itay Tiran, Dulcie Smart
Written and directed by: Dani Gal
Director of photography: Itay Marom
Creative producer: Caroline Kirberg
Coproducer: Jade Niklai

Commissioned by steirischer herbst '20, Kirberg Motors, and Blood Mountain Projects
Produced by Kirberg Motors and Blood Mountain Projects in coproduction with steirischer herbst '20
Funded by Kunstfonds Bonn and Artis

97

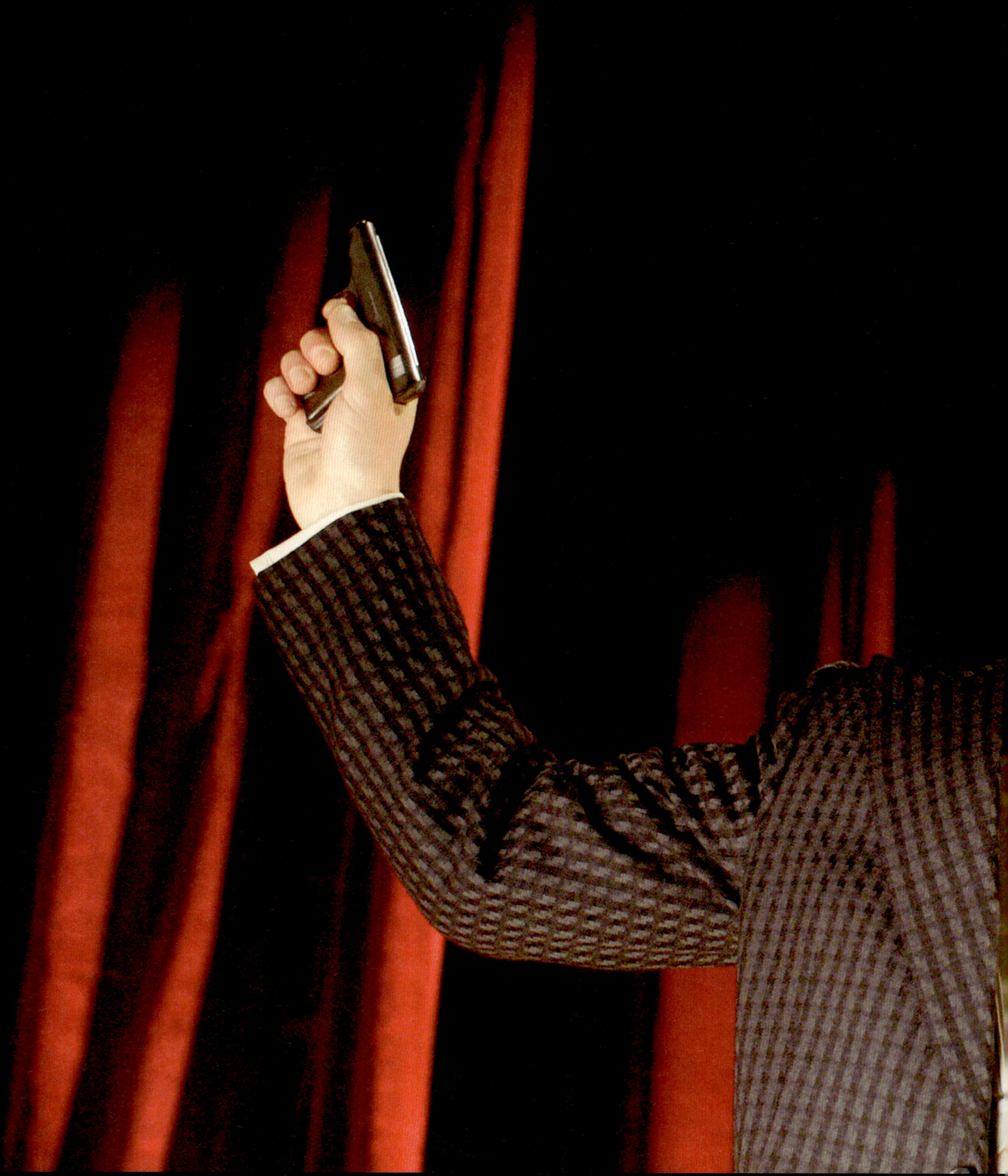

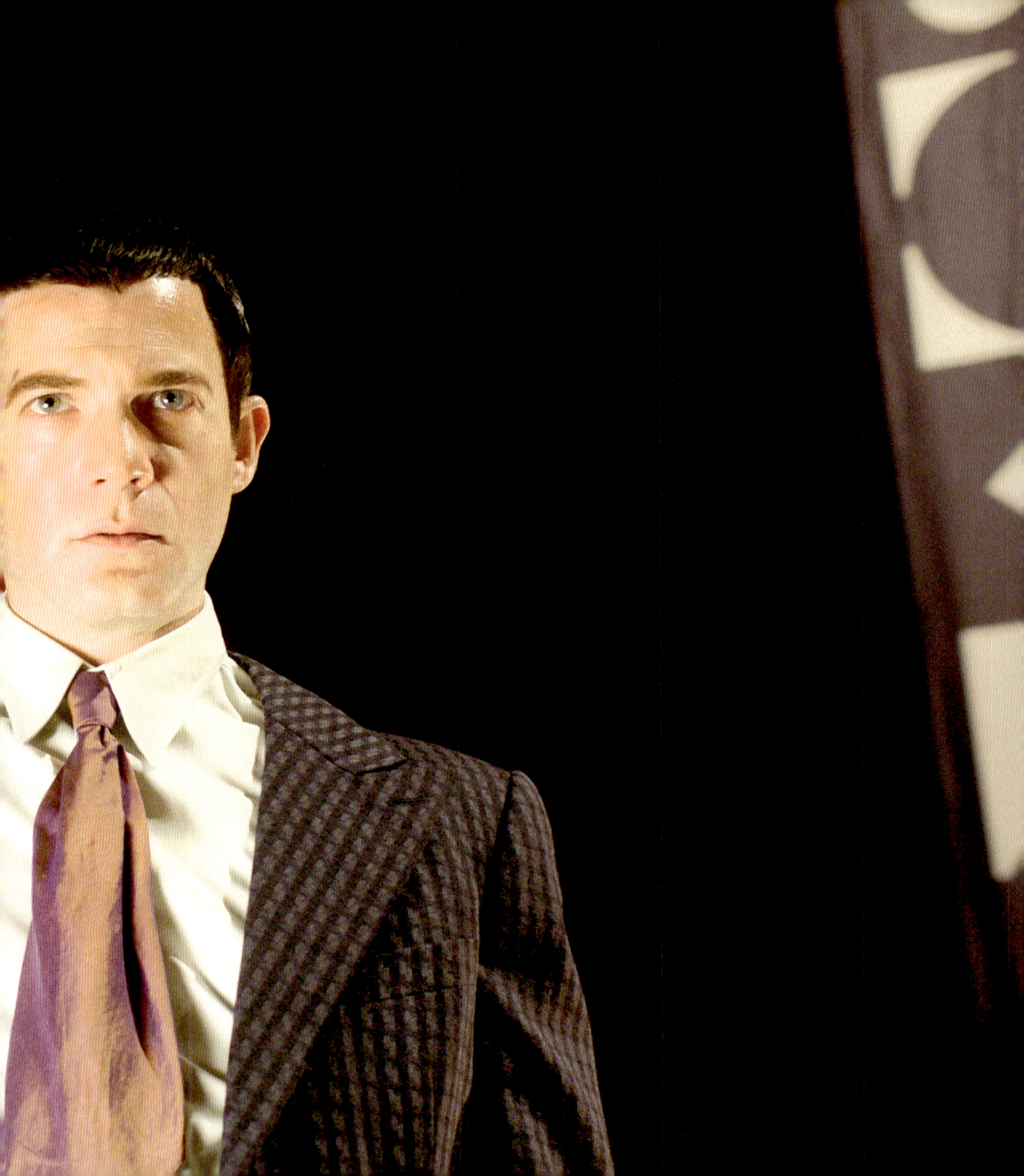

Thomas Geiger

Money Talks
2020

Performance series

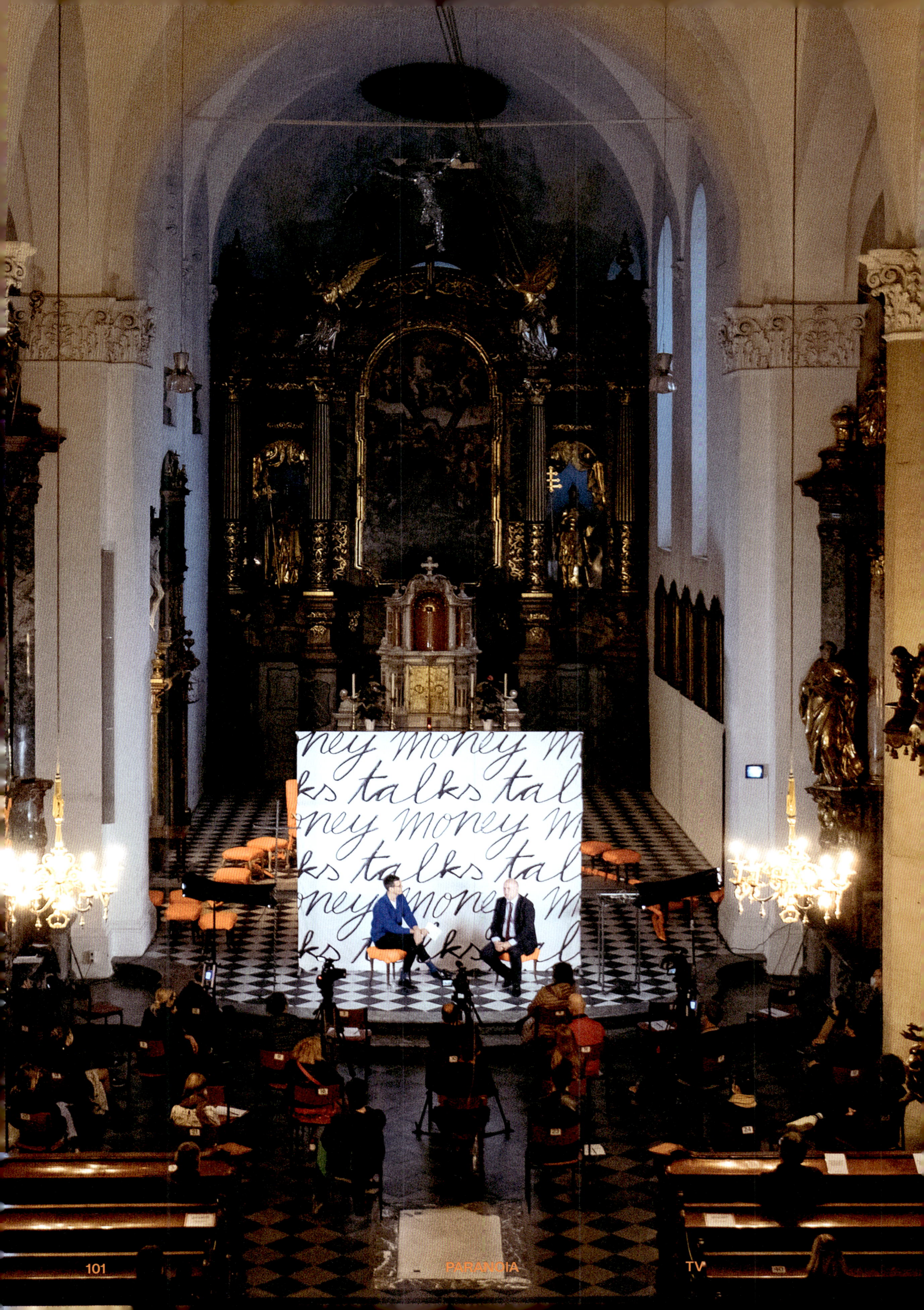
ney Money M
ks talks tal
oney Money M
ks talks tal

102

Thomas Geiger, born in Germany in 1983, is an interdisciplinary artist based in Vienna. Using performance, sculpture, and language his works create fragmentary stages and playful situations. His work has been featured internationally in museums, galleries, and festivals, including Kunsthalle Wien; Wiener Festwochen; Beursschouwburg, Brussels; Museum Tinguely, Basel; Fondation d'entreprise Ricard, Paris. In 2015, he founded Kunsthalle3000, an institution as intervention in public space.

Money Talks (2020)
Performance series, 3 episodes,
ca. 34 / 21 / 35 min., German
Augarten Art Hotel (Penthouse) / Forum Stadtpark (Salon) / Kirche St. Andrä

In collaboration with Elisabeth Skale, Szoszó Canoilas, and Rainer Bucher

Commissioned and produced by steirischer herbst '20

Capitalism is in crisis, and nobody knows this better than capitalism itself. People talk about it a lot behind its back. But it also has redeeming qualities, or so at least it claims. Eager to get out of its present malaise, capitalism becomes a person and seeks out three people who might be of help. It goes to a hotel suite to meet with a prominent Austrian psychoanalyst to discuss its fears and feelings. Shunned and rejected by so many adults, it goes to find admiration from a child. And, in search of eternal answers, it visits a pastoral theologian in a church.

Episode 2: The Child

Dear audience, my name is capitalism and I welcome you warmly to my *Money Talks*. I keep hearing you say, dear audience, that I am in crisis, that I am old, outmoded, no longer in step with the times. That's why I decided to speak with you here today, because I am willing to learn and improve. And who better to inspire me than the up-and-coming, the new, the future generation. I would like to give a warm welcome to my guest today, a representative of her generation.

Let me introduce you: you're thirteen years old, you live in Vienna, and you are still in school.
What are you learning about me at school?
Why is it, do you think, that you and your classmates are not learning anything about me?
Then how do you know I exist?
What kinds of things do you hear about me? What do the people around you say?
Do you remember when you first encountered me?
And I'm supposed to be responsible for injustice? What makes you think so?
Do you feel that I treat you fairly?
How do you yourself handle money?
How much pocket money does one get at your age?
Where do you keep your money?
Why are you looking forward to having a bank account?
What do you buy with your pocket money?
You buy yourself food?
What do you like to eat?
What do you think I like to eat?
Why can't I ever get enough? Do I have a big appetite?
Do you think I make people greedy?
Are humans perhaps greedy by nature?
When was the last time you were greedy?
What was I like as a child, what kind of character did I have?
Is it a bad thing never to have been a child?
What did I miss out on?
What would I have been like as a child?
Do you actually like me, now that I am sitting before you?
Could you describe me in your own words, that is, my appearance?
That sounds like I'm having a midlife crisis.
Do I seem ridiculous to you?

How could I appear less ridiculous?
You keep referring to me as though I'm a male. What does that say about me?
What if I were female?
Should I become more feminine?
What do you think my personal relationship with women is like?
Do you think you'll have a harder time with me because you're a woman?
Do you think I'm in a relationship?
Do you believe in love?
How do I feel about love?
I would say I love everyone. What do you say to that?
Why don't you believe me?
How would you describe our relationship?
So you think our relationship will grow stronger over the years?
Tell me more about your generation. What do you worry about?
What do you all think of me?
Your generation wants to change me?
What is the biggest difficulty with this change?
So there are people who do not want me to change?
Is that a generational conflict?
Are older people generally the problem?
Whose side am I on?
Let's take a look into our future—what will the world look like in thirty years?
What will my role be?
And what about your role—what do you want to be someday?
Why an artist?
So it's all about freedom?
What does freedom mean?
Is there anything else you always wanted to tell me—or ask me?
Imagine that your generation were to build a monument to me. What would I look like standing on my pedestal?

Thomas Geiger

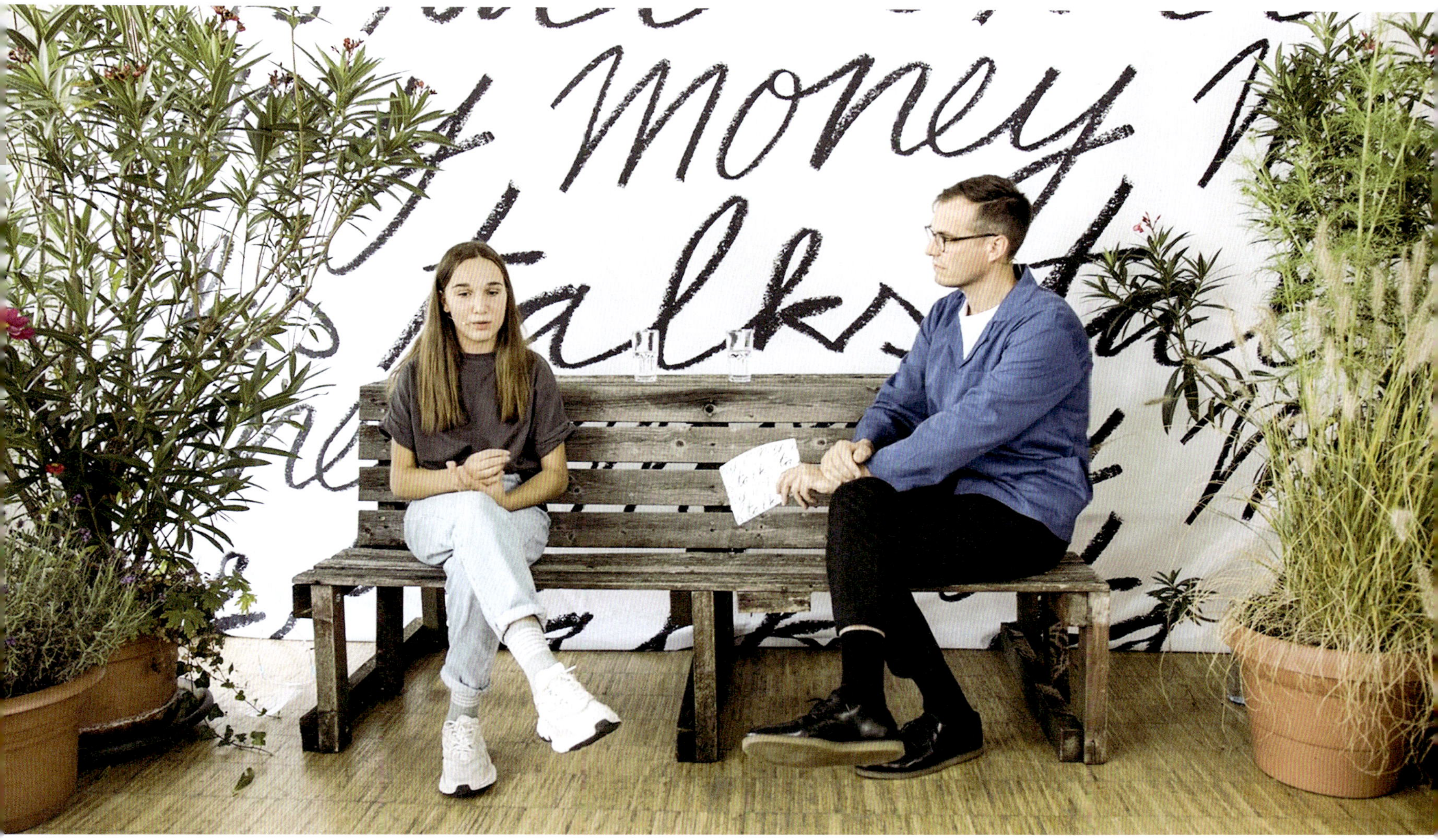
money
talks

Gelatin

grazelatin city map 2020

2020

Map

A CHRISTIAN EGGER SHOW
KASTNER & ÖHLER
Gösser
WHATEVER HAPPEND TO GELITIN
AN ANGELA CHRISTLIEB MOVIE
ANNENHOF KINO
KINO
Versicherung
VERSICHERUNG
DÖNER
I ♥ YOU

How was the artwork created? Four people—four experiences in Graz—four memories—one work?

One sheet has four sides. We sit around and work our way toward the middle. We intersect and sometimes it's a good idea to rotate the page or to draw backward.

There is the word "Graz" and the memories have attached themselves to this place. Since memory is always a construct, and the perception of "reality" is a hallucination that is as practical as possible, many possibilities emerge when drawing. There are sketchy memories with gaps that the brain magically fills with new ideas.
Then there are the real gaps, where you realize that there is no memory. There's a lot of black there.
And then there are memories of things like the clock tower, which are too boring to put down on paper.
The memory of the flickering snack bar sign on the busy street in the gray apartment block is more closely associated with strong emotions.
With four people, memories may overlap, sometimes making waves across the paper, or splashing upward when several memory waves meet.

Four of us generate within ourselves a transcendental topology of impurity, ugliness, pain, and death.
Sitting around the sheet of paper becomes an architecture of liminal feelings, the production of pictorial puzzles, recurring symptoms of shape memory, peripheral object character par excellence.
After hours or sometimes days of astral-traveling, visualization of this collective topology, the pencils come out and begin to schizograph.

The drawing was already fairly well developed by the time I was finally in the right frame of mind to participate in it.
The paper had been placed on a specially setup table in the studio, including pencils in various degrees of hardness, sharpeners, and erasers.
Now it was a matter of not being led too far astray by what had already been drawn. It was after all about recalling Graz from memory and presenting it graphically. I hardly had any memories of Graz.
I was in the best state of mind to start drawing; the result of many years of practice.

Has the curfew (travel ban, etc.) left a mark on your memories of the city?

Due to our practice, which does not include reading regulations and prohibitions, we do not actually have any information about them.
We have never been interested in prohibitions; we are more active in the field of possibilities and inner causes.

It's actually possible to walk from Vienna to Graz. Even when the electricity is out, when the oil is gone, when the road has slid down a hill, when the cars are parked with their wheels pointing upward. That is why Graz is always within reach from Vienna if you want to deepen your memories.

We like to travel to cities and countries. Preferably on foot. A pandemic is like politics and is an event that does not long remain in memory and therefore has no influence on us.

Would they have been different in another time?

Different results at different times are always possible.
We draw together by daylight.
If we had drawn at night or at inhumanly early hours, everything would probably have turned out very differently.

If we had drawn the map in winter and right after getting up, it would probably have been different. We would have drawn more jam.

That is a very interesting question. Perhaps someone will be interested in inviting us to repeat the drawing at another time. Only then can we be sure of the answer.

The interview was conducted by the Office of Open Questions. Each member of Gelatin is assigned a different color.

Note: Under the first lockdown, curators commissioned Gelatin and studio ASYNCHROME to create subjective maps of, respectively, Graz and Vienna from memory—as if they were never able to visit them again. Maps were distributed through a major local bookstore.

Gelatin is comprised of the artists Ali Janka, Florian Reither, Tobias Urban, and Wolfgang Gantner. They formed Gelatin in the mid-1990s in Vienna, Austria. Locating their practice at the fragile crossroads of humor, spontaneity, childlike naivety, and blatant sexuality, their performances play with audience participation and collaboration.

Recent solos shows have taken place at Kunsthalle Wien; Sala de Arte Público Siqueiros, Mexico City; Museum Boijmans Van Beuningen, Rotterdam; Fondazione Prada, Milan; Greene Naftali, New York; Galerie Perrotin, Hong Kong; and Künstlerverein Malkasten, Düsseldorf. They have participated in the Liverpool Biennale (1999 and 2002); Gwangju Biennale (2002); the Shanghai Biennale (2002); the Venice Biennale (2001, 2007, and 2011); the 1st Moscow Biennale of Contemporary Art (2005); and Manifesta 11, Zurich (2016).

grazelatin city map 2020 (2020)
Map

Commissioned and produced by steirischer herbst '20
Courtesy: Galerie Meyer Kainer

109

Tamar Guimarães
with Luisa Cavanagh and Rusi Millán Pastori

Soap
2020

Video series

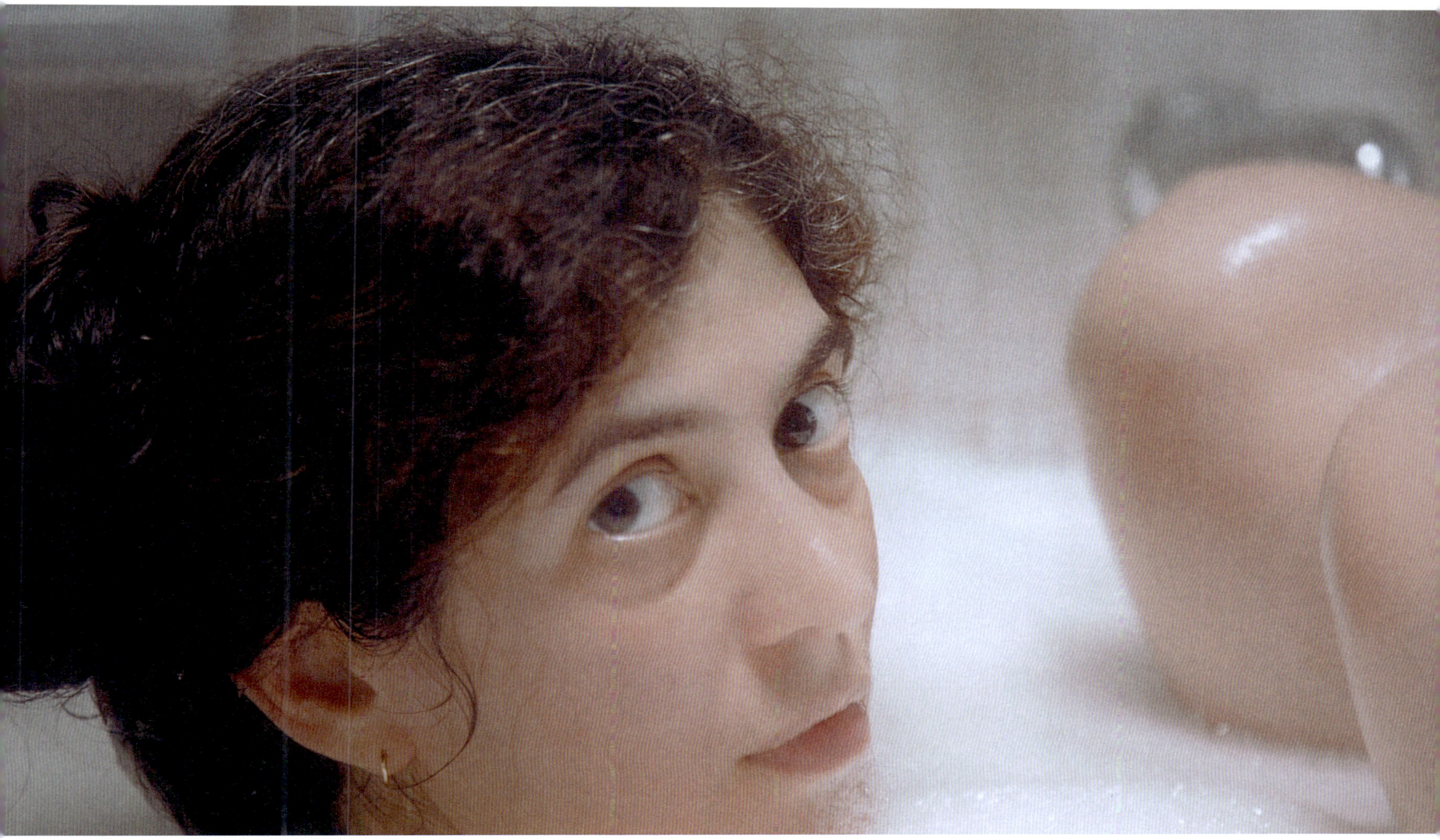

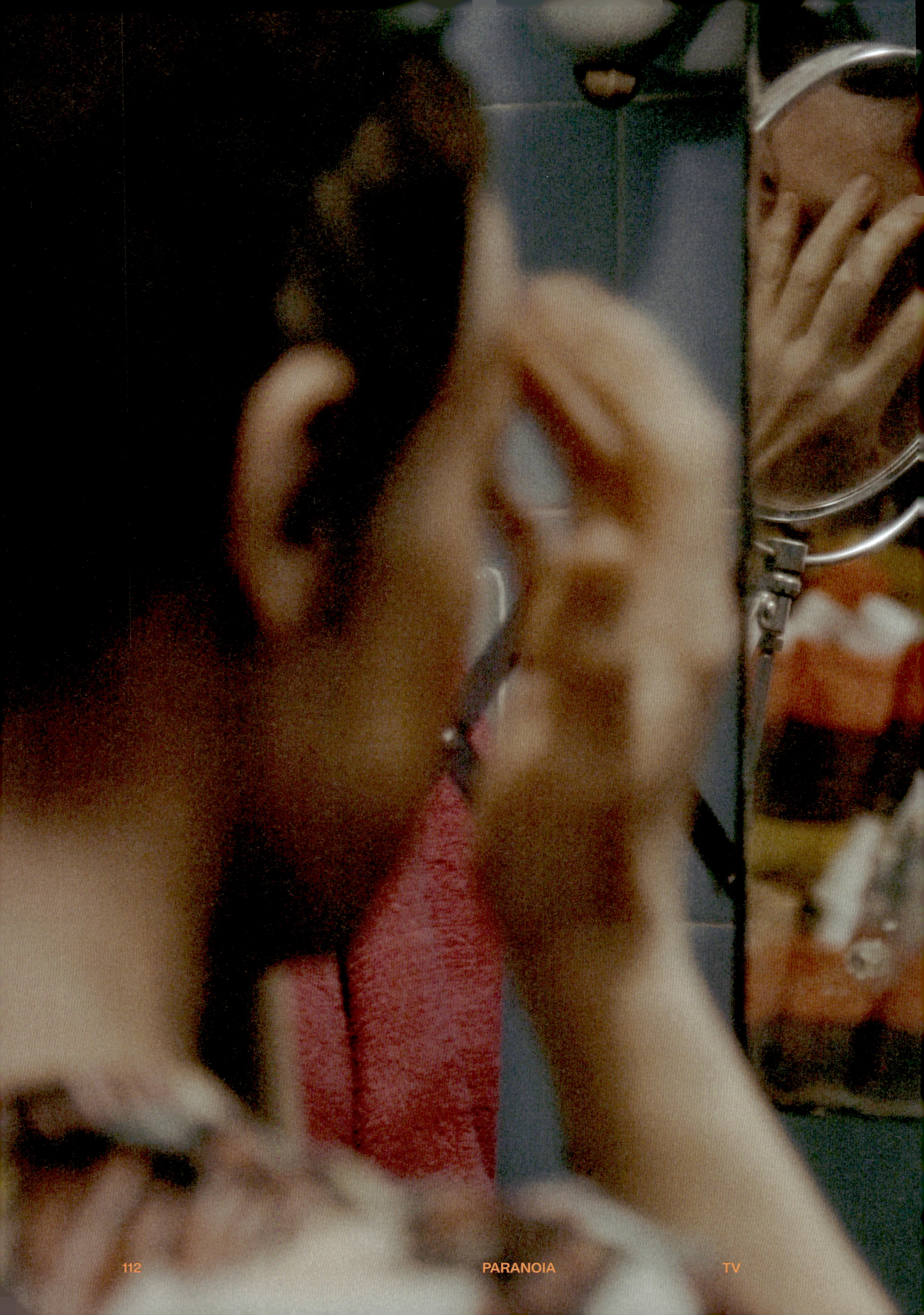

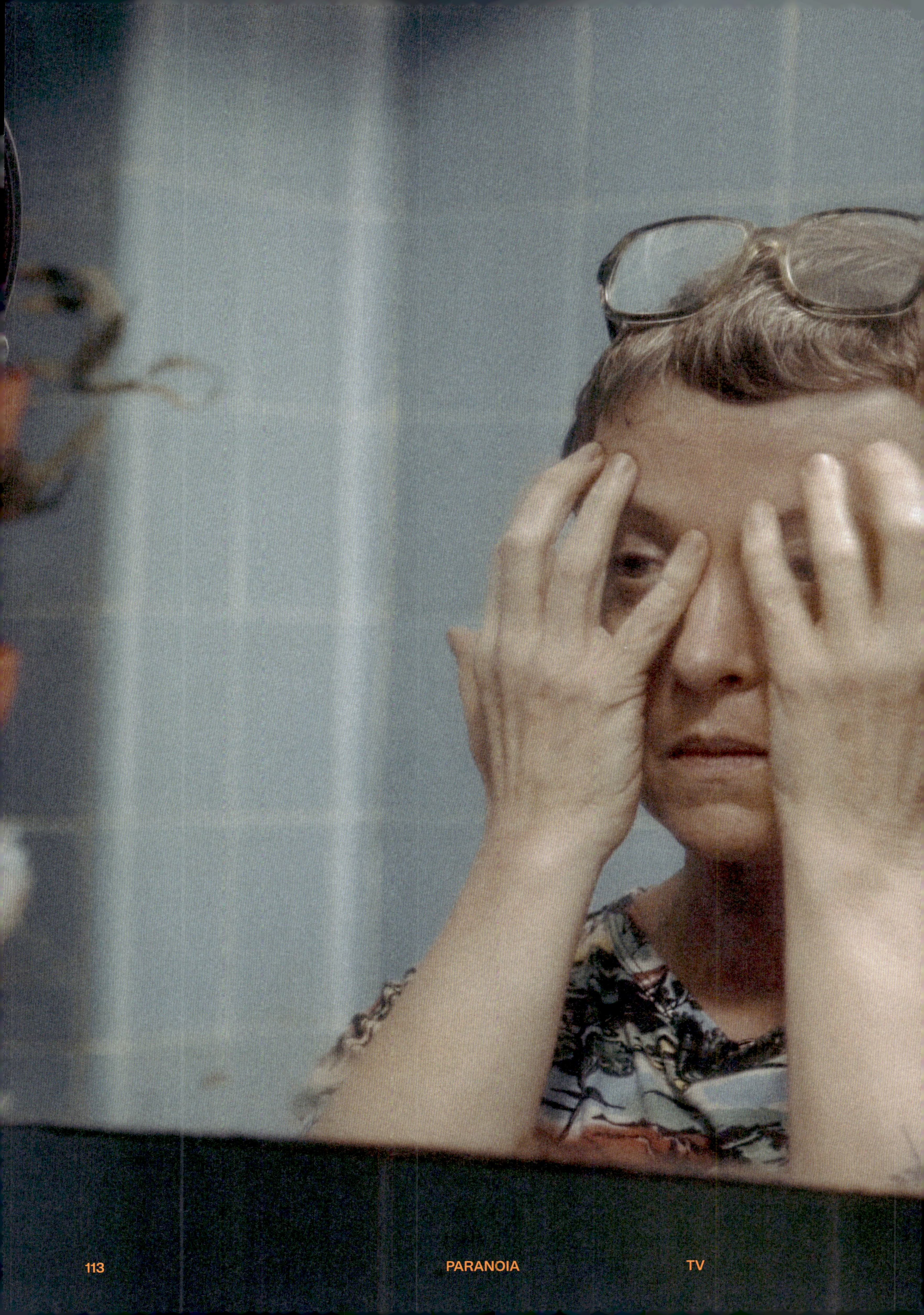

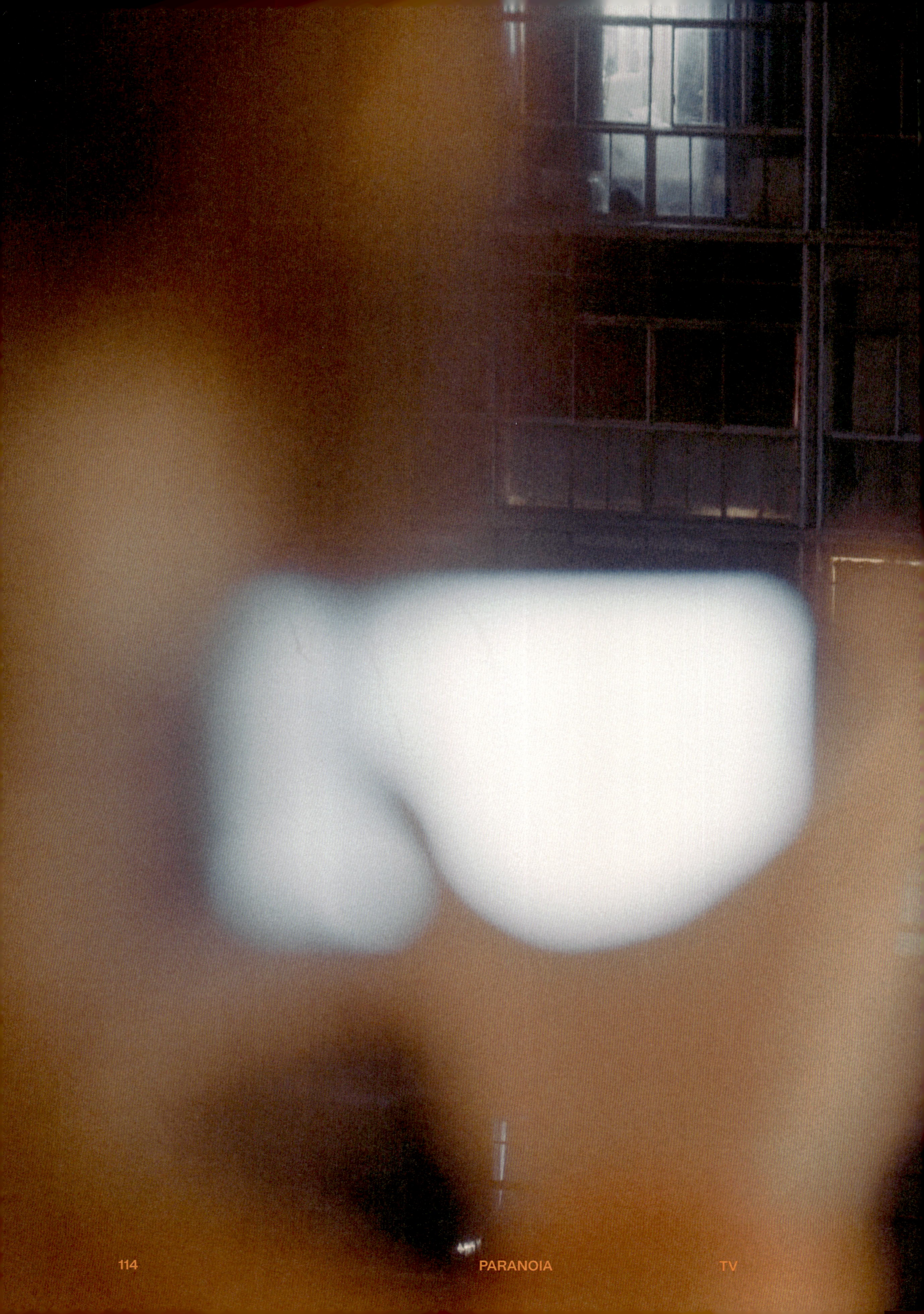

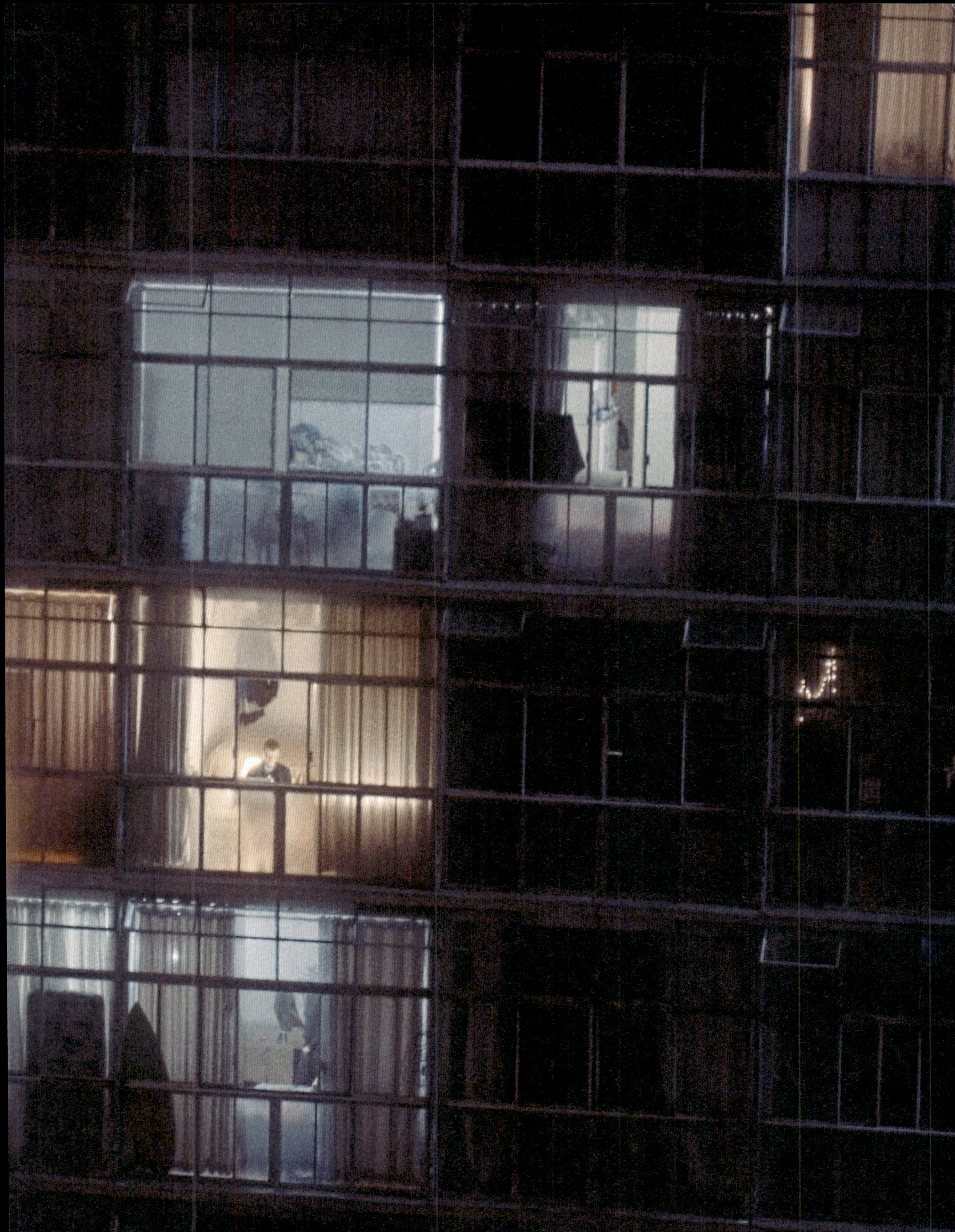

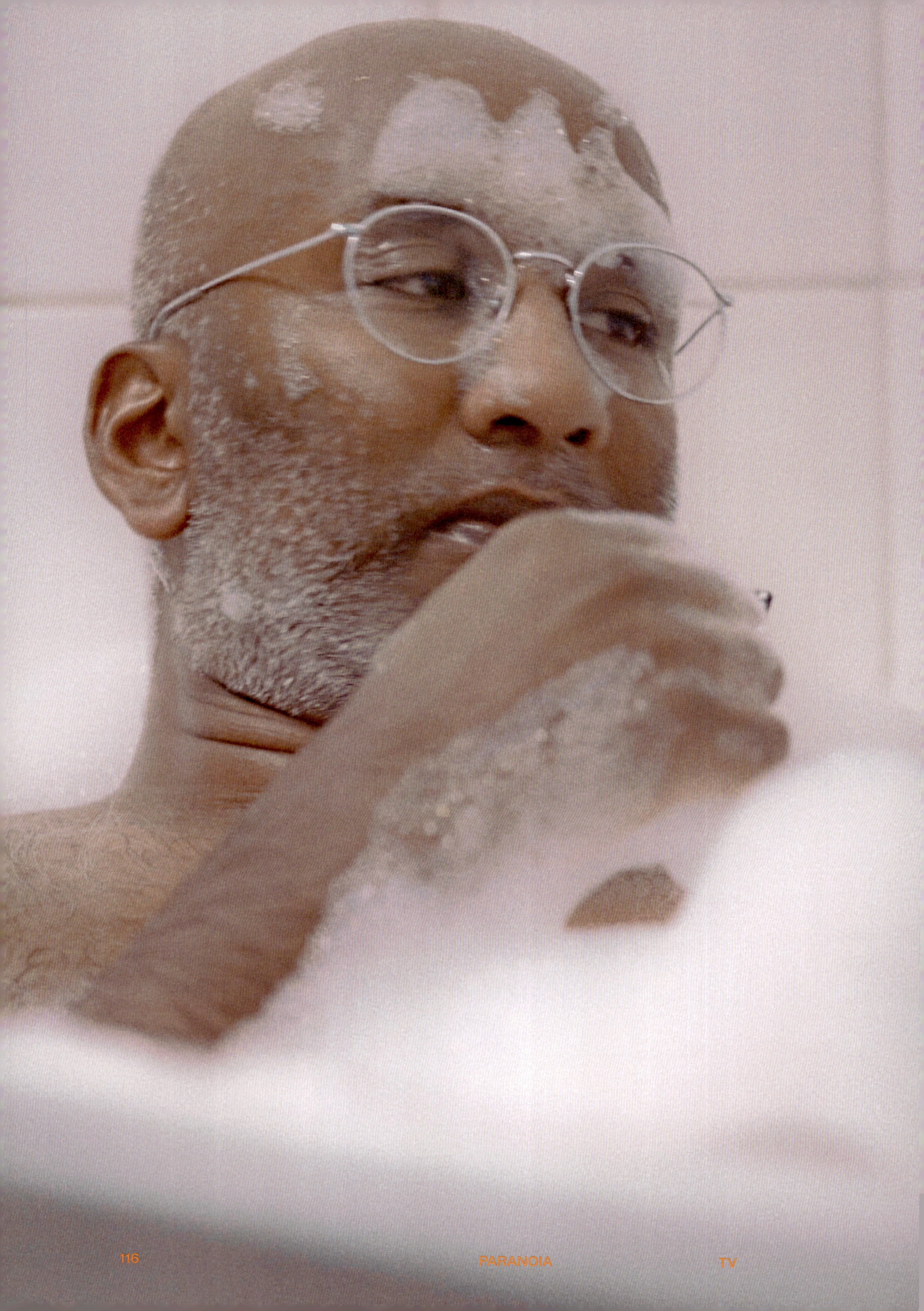

Tamar Guimarães and her collaborators Luisa Cavanagh and Rusi Millán Pastori decided to imagine what would be involved in creating a telenovela, or soap, which could infiltrate the confused, conspiratorial far right in Jair Bolsonaro's Brazil. How might a group of fictional, idealistic left-wingers join cerebral and creative forces to play a cynical, populist system at its own game? How can a loose coalition of activists, artists, and writers avoid the stumbling block of their own assumptions and the absurdities of their various privileges to create something with genuine resonance and persuasiveness?

The telenovela is a dominant presence in Brazilian media and popular culture. Generally high-gloss extravaganzas with the command of a national audience, their key defining characteristics are their episodic format and limited run. Unlike their international cousins the soap operas, they are usually centered on one defining storyline and, on the whole, do not last longer than a few months.

Telenovelas are popular across the Latin American world, but nowhere do the production budgets reach the lavish levels of Brazil. The national taste is for multilayered plotlines featuring a large cast of characters, usually encompassing households from different points on the socioeconomic spectrum. Likewise, the audience for the shows is diverse and cuts across Brazilian society.

Guimarães, Cavanagh, and Millán Pastori have woven a disparate bunch of isolated urban souls in multiple cities into a disorienting drama of creative process and a bittersweet, unalloyed glimpse into the maelstrom created by a fork in the ideological road. Whether or not it is possible to make a subversive soap that can break into a world of Bolsonarist dance troupes and paramilitary patrols is the question that these four episodes invite their constituted characters to start answering.

Tamar Guimarães, born in Belo Horizonte, Brazil, in 1967, lives and works in Berlin. She is a visual artist working with film and other forms of time-based media, and often works with actors alongside non-actors in semifictional films exploring sociopolitical dynamics both residual and contemporary, and situations within art, architecture, and the institutions that present them.

Guimarães's works have been included at the 33rd, 31st, and the 29th São Paulo Biennial; the Belgian Pavilion of the 56th Venice Biennial; the International Exhibition at the 55th Venice Biennial; LACMA—Los Angeles County Museum of Art; Baltimore Museum of Art; 11th Sharjah Biennial; the Banff Centre, Alberta; Malmö Museum; the Guggenheim Museum, New York; the SculptureCenter, New York; The Renaissance Society, Chicago; 7th Gwangju Biennial; 3rd Guangzhou Triennial; Jumex Museum, Mexico; Frac / Le Plateau, Paris; CAC Synagogue de Delme. Recent solo exhibitions have been held at Museo Nacional Centro de Arte Reina Sofía, Madrid; Jeu de Paume Satellite, Paris; Gasworks, London; and the IMA Institute of Modern Art, Brisbane.

Her work has been screened at Berlinale Forum Expanded (2019); CPH:DOX (2007 and 2013); Images Film Festival and Experimental Media Congress, Toronto (2010); Architektur-Visionen #1–6, Hamburg (2015); Les Rencontres Internationales, Paris and Berlin (2014); Tramway Art Film Biennial, Glasgow (2012); Viennale (2011); and Oberhausen Film Festival (2009), among others.

Luisa Cavanagh, born in Buenos Aires, Argentina, in 1979, is a visual artist, colorist, and cinematographer. She studied cinematography at the National School of Cinematographic Experimentation and Production in Buenos Aires. She has been selected for different scholarships and residencies, such as Laboratorio de Cine and Artist Program at Torcuato di Tella University in Buenos Aires, was a guest student in Josephine Pryde's class "Contemporary Photography and Performance" at Berlin University of the Arts, and participated in the project *Labor in a Single Shot* by Antje Ehmann and Harun Farocki.

Focused on collaborative work, she joined Grupo Mexa to develop the film/performance *Cancionero Terminal 10mg*. Together with Dudu Quintanilha and Millán Pastori, she founded Eterno Work in Progress, an artist-run cine club that explores the limits of cinema exhibition, live musicalization, and moving images. She was selected for the 18th Klemm Award with her work *Collections*. Since 2006, she has been color grading feature films, short films, and series. She lives in São Paulo.

Rusi Millán Pastori, born in Argentina in 1976, is a writer, film director, and director of photography. Actual political scenarios are a common thread throughout his work, as chronicles that combine different situations and characters. He studied cinematography at the National School of Cinematographic Experimentation and Production in Buenos Aires and has directed short and medium-length films.

He has participated in national and international festivals. Among the works exhibited were *Z-5*, *GAS* (documentary short film), *Las complicaciones*, *La felicidad es un monoambiente*, and *Lai* (documentary feature film), which was shown at BAFICI in Buenos Aires and at the 41st Mostra in São Paulo.

Millán Pastori is also a musician who composes film soundtracks and participates in live events. He is working on the development of a new feature film project: *Hold My Caipirinha*. He lives in São Paulo.

Soap (2020)
Video series, 4 episodes,
ca. 10 / 12 / 15 / 15 min., Portuguese
Online

A film in episodes by Tamar Guimarães in collaboration with Luisa Cavanagh and Rusi Millán Pastori
With (in order of appearance):
Camila Mota, Claudia Medeiros, Christoph Eichhorn, Raphael Daibert, Alice Marcone, Ana Teixeira Pinto, Siddhartha Lokanandi
Directed by Tamar Guimarães
Executive producers: Carol Gesser and Luís Knihs
Cinematography: Manuel Abramovich and Rusi Millán Pastori
Script: Tamar Guimarães, Luisa Cavanagh, and Rusi Millán Pastori
Script support: Ana Teixeira Pinto, Avi Alpert, Camila Mota, Dan Gunn, and Luciana Vieira
Live sound: Melisa Liebenthal and Juliana R.
Production managers: Luís Knihs and Carol Gesser
Production assistant: Alessandro Danielli
Research advice: Ana Teixeira Pinto, Avi Alpert
Editing: Beatriz Pomar, Tamar Guimarães, Luisa Cavanagh, and Rusi Millán Pastori
Sound design and mixing: Contemporary Sound
Color grading: Luisa Cavanagh
Postproduction lab: Quanta
Translation and subtitles: Alessandro Danielli, Carol Gesser, Dan Gunn, Donato Silva, Tamar Guimarães
Title sequence: Dan Gunn
Excerpts from:
John Smith, *The Girl Chewing Gum*, 1976, 16 mm film, 12 minutes
Courtesy of John Smith and Tanya Leighton, Berlin
Claudia Medeiros, *Dança, sala, confinamento e telefone*, 2020, video
Courtesy of Claudia Medeiros
Thanks to: Alexandre Gabriel, Claudia Medeiros, Dan Gunn, Eliana Guimarães Farhat, Fortes D'Aloia & Gabriel, Francisco Orlandi, João Fernandes, John Smith, Lars Mylius, Luciana Mugayer, Luís Roque, Yusuf Etiman, Övül Ö. Durmusoglu, Kasper Akhøj, Anna Bergamasco, Márcia Fortes, Alessandra D'Aloia, Koen Claerhout, Ligia Carvalhosa
Courtesy of the artist, Dan Gunn, London, and Fortes D'Aloia & Gabriel, São Paulo
Filmed in São Paulo and Berlin in August 2020

Commissioned by steirischer herbst '20
Produced by Luís Henrique Knihs Corrêa / Aqueles Filmes LTDA ME and Tamar Guimarães in coproduction with steirischer herbst '20

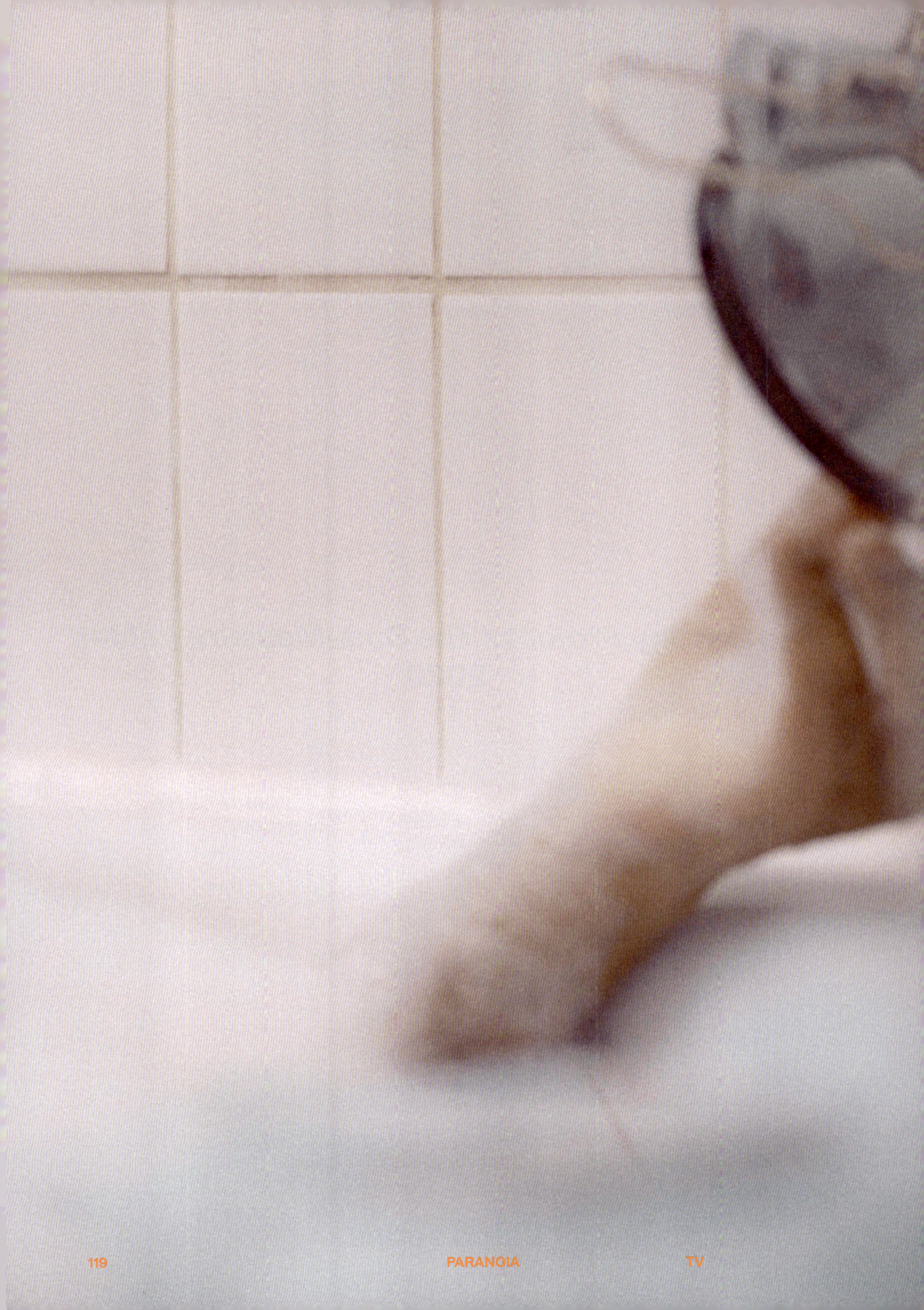

Rana Hamadeh

The Destiny Project / The Soft-Measure Fables
2020

Video series

The following libretto can be viewed as an open window leading into Rana Hamadeh's thinking process and working methodology. Unlike what a libretto is supposed to conventionally achieve—that is, mediating to the audience the sung and spoken word and the directions that are carried out by the protagonists during the theatrical-cinematic action—this piece of text offers the directions to the director herself.

It involves two processes: It is, on one hand, part of the engine that generates, recursively, the audiovisual poiesis of the project. And, on the other hand, it is the linguistic residue left from the weave of references that build up the work conceptually. Heavily coded and loaded with symbols, the text can still be read alongside the audiovisual work as an extended poetic mood board written in the voice of an imagined chorus. It can be experienced, in the videos, as a tangential commentary on the events, animations, montage, and sound composition, written before those were even imagined or put into place.

On another note, the libretto was used later during the compositional process as a carrier of the sound and its material affects. Opera singer Gerrie de Vries was invited to recite, sing, scream, whisper, and perform improvised renditions of the text. In the editing studio, Hamadeh manipulated De Vries's voice, translating her vocal renditions into textural sonic strata that informed the work's affective blueprint. Bits and pieces from the original text presented here can be heard throughout the composition yet are cut and reordered this time following the montage and the new content offered by the moving image.

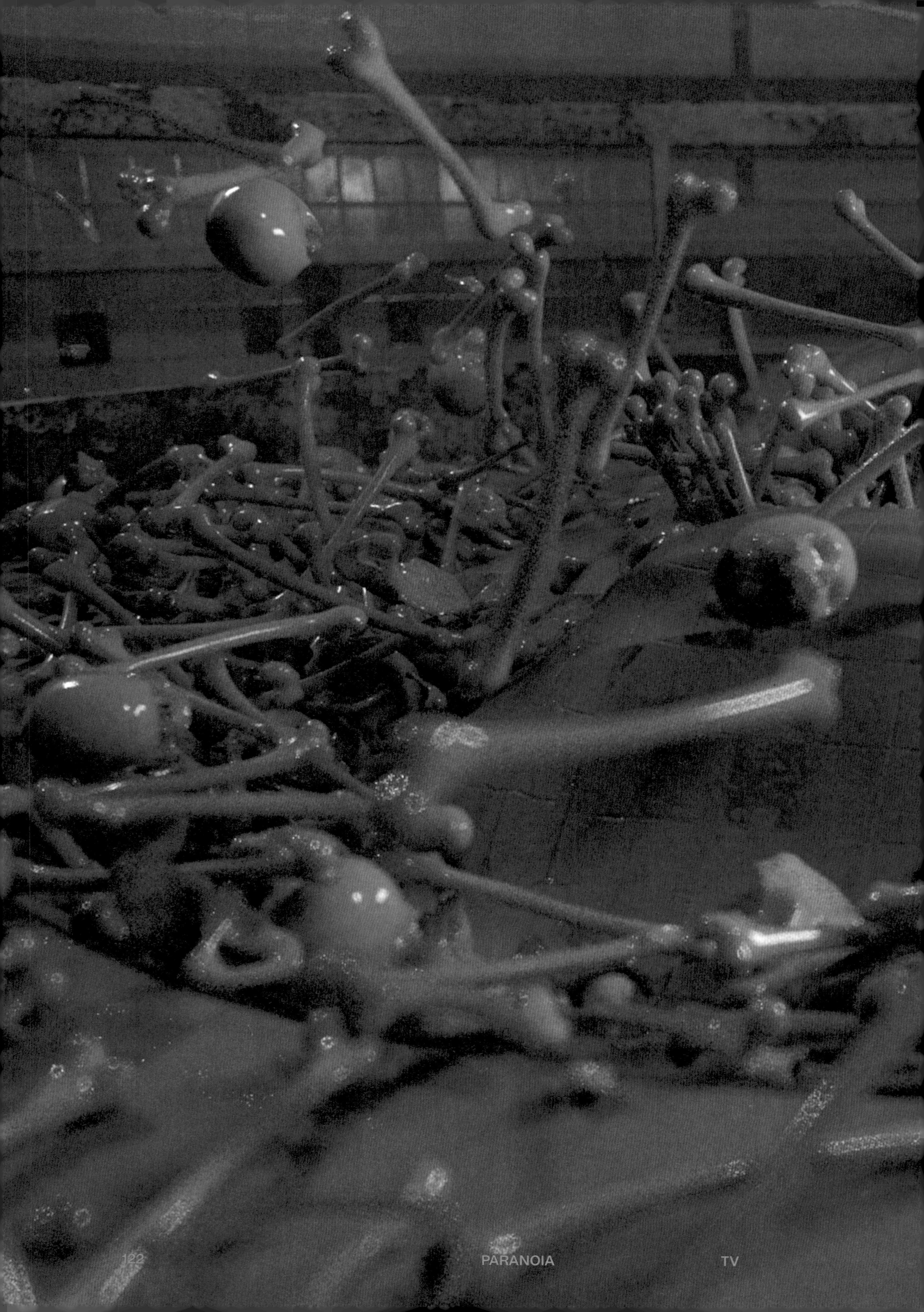

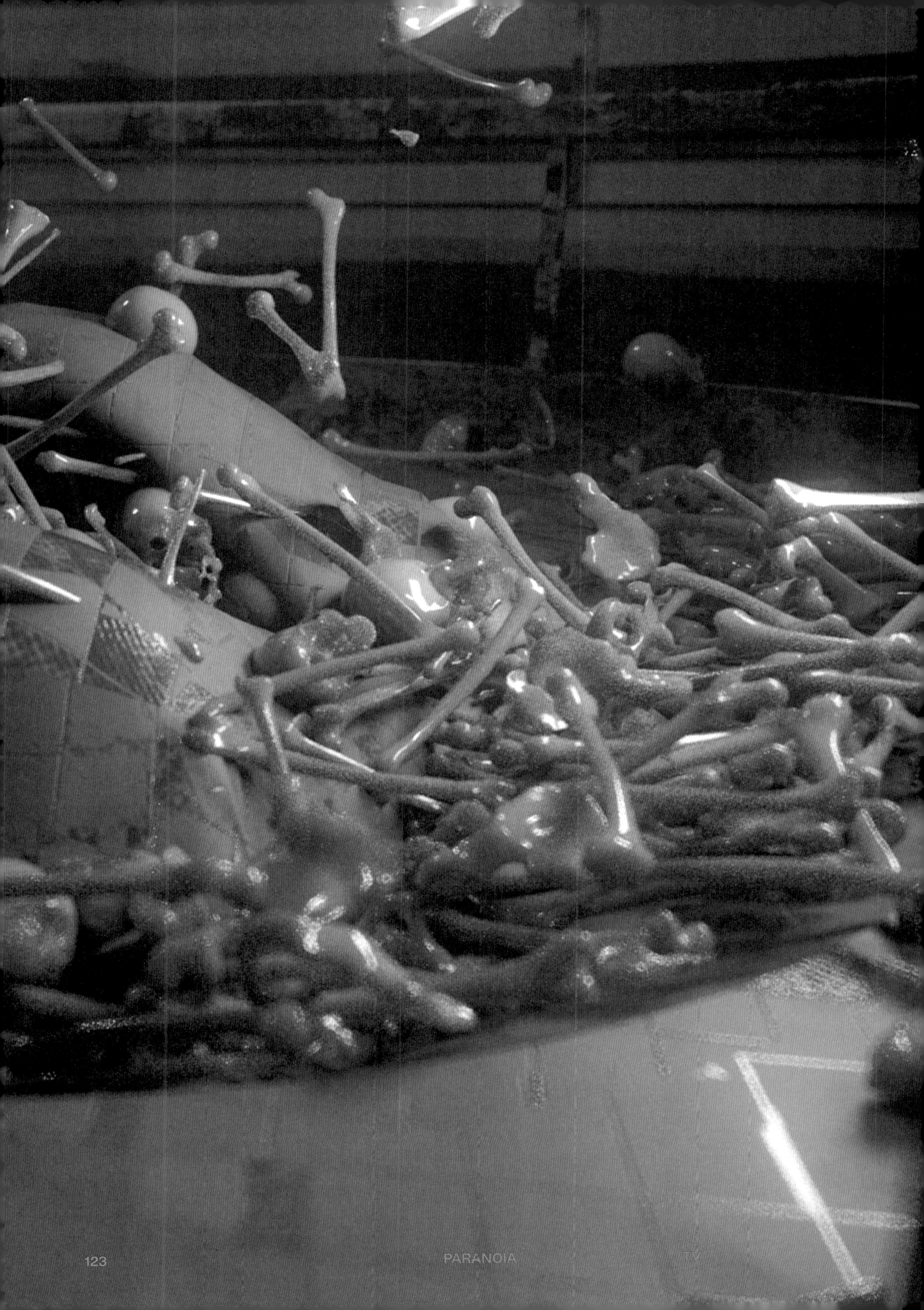

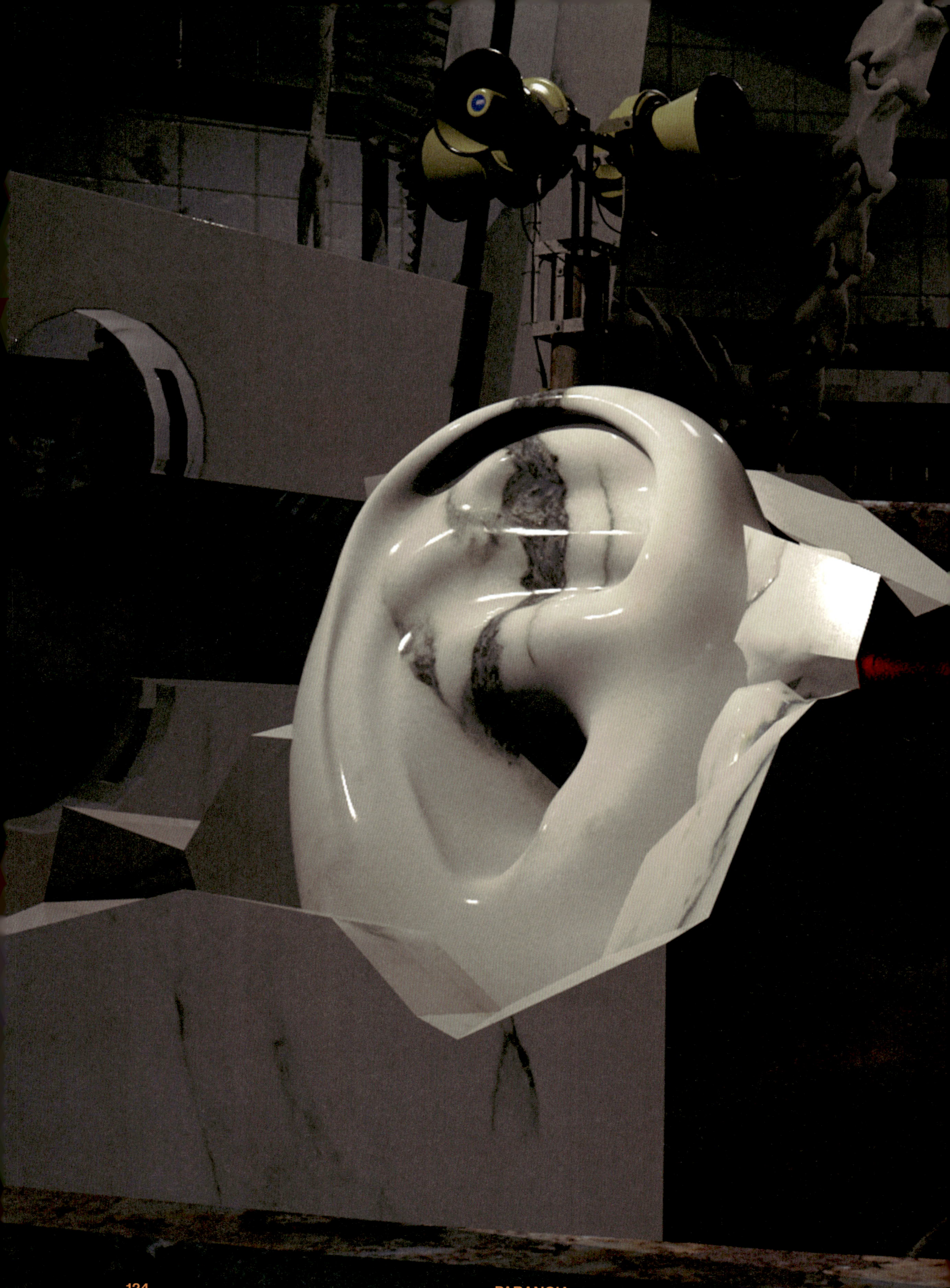

Act 1
The Modality of Measure

[Version No. 2]

CHORUS 1 *(sing in an increasingly alarmed tone, describing the encounter of Oedipus and Laius in the game's second level, at a place where three roads met)*

Clear the chain
A flock shall pass
of arms for the king
and arms for the queen

Fractal fuss_____

A scalp and a mane
_____Osseous slates that
line the curb
Then neural ends that hold
that bear
withstand the weight

Wait!
Electric coup!
Error report
Error report
Consult!
Inhale

Belt that air and count till ten:

One------->Alt!
Don't shoot!
The screen is locked!
The screen is
locked!______Repeat!!

CHORUS 2 *(interrupt and start reciting in a playful manner)*

Capture
Arrest
Weigh
Record
Speak
Shelve
Then speak again
A shriek or a pulse
and call that a voice
the speaking—that is—of a
shriek or a pulse,
then shelve again.

A voice from/of/by/through/
in a lord;
a word; a vote;
Repeat!

Then add a caption:
Call it "commerce"
Or leave it to time

King Leopold?
a human zoo
—call it—
—call—

To be; beat; bite a tongue
To measure a height
Compare_____

Then the fear of sea
And the fear of land
And the fear of surgeons
who check one's teeth to
predict—like psychics—
one's life expectancy

Fertility, and who's in love
And who has been hiding
a plot
to will_____freely
what one is willed to will.

And who has been hiding
a plot
to be willful.

And who has been hiding
a plot
beneath their skin_____

_____Kin

(Pause)

CHORUS 1 *(back to their alarmed tone)*

Then a gate policed
by a scribe
And a man with a wig
And a man with a prop
And a man that burps from
time to time a just remark!

Access granted!
Access denied!
Access granted!
Access denied!

Then a belly that skids across
the walk_____
cushioned by sheath
agile
fed
rosy
content

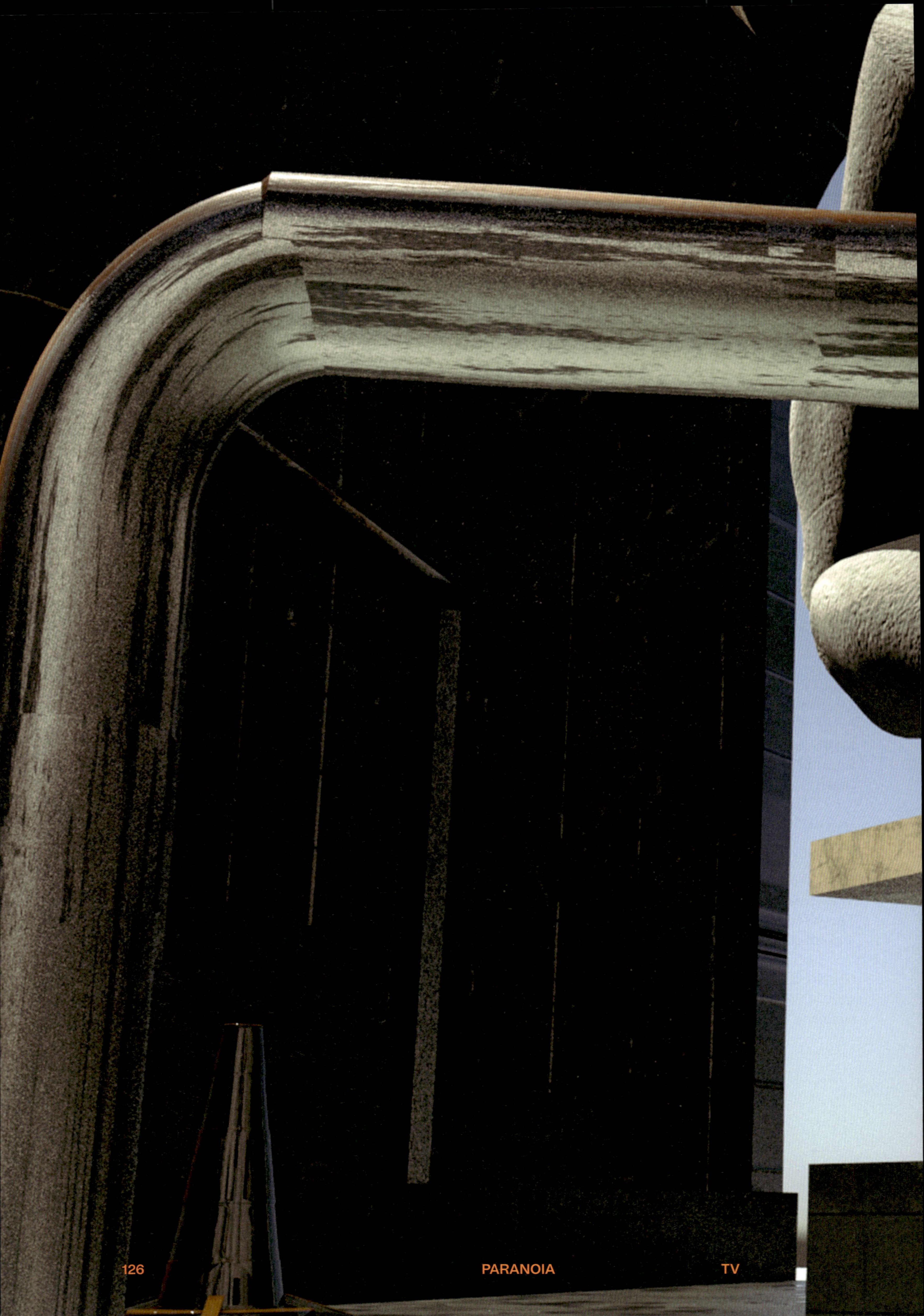

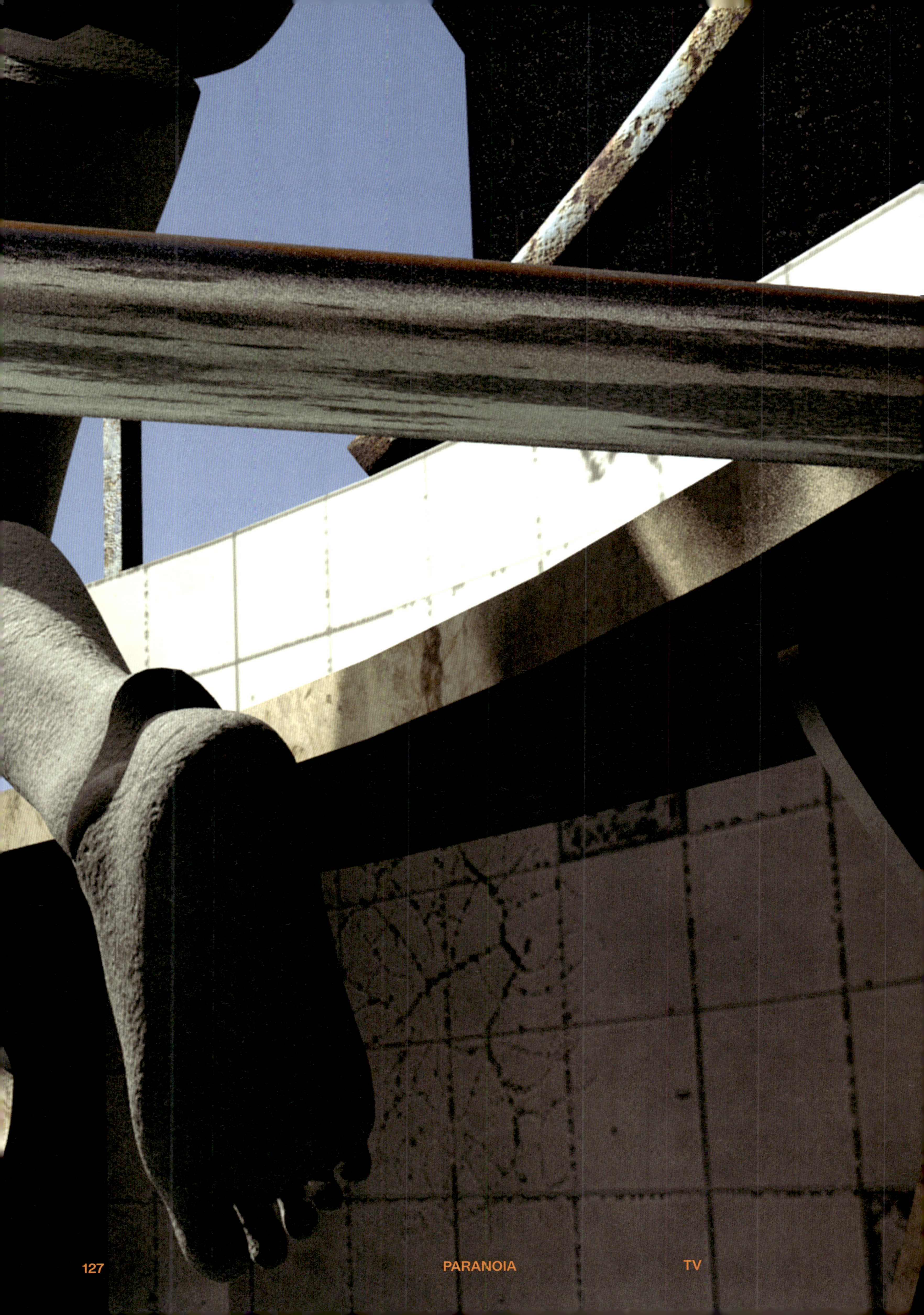

Who knew that despots made
such good poets?
Who knew that killers
cherished prose?
Southern grooms
Southern birds
And the heart remains
unburied
atop the skin as it was,
Unburied yet unsighted
Isn't it time to rest?
Is it time to resign?

_____Laius?
_____Nabih?
Theft is the mastery of words

CHORUS 2 *(resume from where they had been interrupted)*

Then a pile of blades
that cut_____
so neat
so smart
so sleek
_____that crack
that slit
split in thirds
every sign there is
every course un-walked
every word unsaid
And a bond like a call for
war_____

Rubber-coated—the French
report
Not made to kill
But "just" to maim

Incarcerate
Emasculate
Decapitate
Officiate
an empty will

Subsist in shame

CHORUS 1 *(sing softly)*

Oh Oedipus!
Oh Oedipus!
Effigial scars that hack your
wound

Oh Oedipus!
Oh Oedipus!
What use is it to know?!!
What use was it to know?!

Oh Oedipus_____

Level that crease
to stretch its yield
a stride or two
For the season is low

Un-spin
uncoil the gut
unweave
uncut
the film
derail its flow_____
The season is low

Scour that skin
peel it
Dry—search:

L for labia
search again:

S for split
Spit

Then flood with spinal broth
Carbon prints of lives unlived
Unborn to seek revenge

To set the score
To plot the scheme
to slay your king
and eat his corpse
chew off his teeth
and live on his behalf

and live on his behalf

CHORUS 2 *(interrupt, and sing in a triumphant tone)*

_____More arms for the
king
More arms for the queen
and arms for their dogs
and arms for their
fleet_____

Arms bent in supplication
Arms stretched to save the
nation
Arms arms arms arms arms
arms aaaaaaaarms!!

A nervous lot

Electric coup
Error report
Error report!
Consult
Inhale

Belt that air and count till
nine

One------->Alt!
Don't shoot!
The screen is locked!
The screen is locked!

[End of Act 1]

Rana Hamadeh

Rana Hamadeh is an artist, composer, and writer from Lebanon living in the Netherlands. Drawing on a curatorial approach within her artistic practice, she develops longstanding projects that think through the epistemologies and technologies of justice, translational practices, colonial realities, and theater. Her work stems from an extended investigation into specific concepts and terms, treating the field of theory as fiction.

Since 2016, Hamadeh has been developing an "operatic practice," experimenting with writing and composing, and testing out models for collective thinking and study. In 2011, she initiated her ongoing project, *Alien Encounters*, which has since been operating as an incubator for a growing series of works that complicate the notion of "alienness." Throughout the project's chapters (manifested through theatrical productions, interactive sound-based system designs and compositions, immersive audiovisual installations and stage sets, texts and conversations), the "alien" turns into both a discursive and an archival tool for mapping out corporate and state-supported forms of violence and their enabling legal apparatuses.

Hamadeh is the recipient of the Dutch Prix de Rome 2017. Solo exhibitions have been held at Kunsthalle Winterthur; FKA Witte de With, Rotterdam; The Institute of Modern Art, Brisbane; The Showroom, London; Nottingham Contemporary; Western Front, Vancouver; Gallery TPW, Toronto; and Kiosk, Ghent, among other places. Group exhibitions include shows at Sonic Acts Festival (2019); the Kochi-Muziris Biennale (2018); SALT, Istanbul (2018); Moscow Biennial (2015); The New Museum, New York; e-flux, New York (2014); 8th Liverpool Biennial (2014); 12th Biennale de Lyon (2013); Lisson Gallery, London (2013); and the Van Abbemuseum, Eindhoven (2008/2011).

The Destiny Project /
The Soft-Measure Fables (2020)
Video series, 3 episodes,
ca. 5 / 3 / 8 min., English
Online

Written, directed, and composed by Rana Hamadeh
In conversation with: Sara Hamadeh
3-D world builder, 3-D modeler, and animator: Ryan Cherewaty
Second 3-D animator: Vasilis Kasselas
Director of photography and video editor: Sara Hamadeh
Camera: Sara Hamadeh and Ryan Cherewaty
Scenography: Rana Hamadeh
Sound designer, editor, and mixer: Jorg Schellekens
Graphic designers: Jungeun Lee and Kay Pisarowitz
Opera performer: Gerrie de Vries
Recording sound engineer: Huub Krom
Recording studio: Studio OORbit, Amsterdam
"Hydrophone/Lav Recording of 1000 Maggots in Sticky Wet Mud" by Richard Devine, used with permission from the artist
Production assistant: Isabelle Sully

The Destiny Project / The Soft-Measure Fables is a work-in-progress by Rana Hamadeh, commissioned by SCHUNCK. The online version of short clips is commissioned by steirischer herbst '20. Coproduced by SCHUNCK and steirischer herbst '20
With the kind support of Mondriaan Fonds

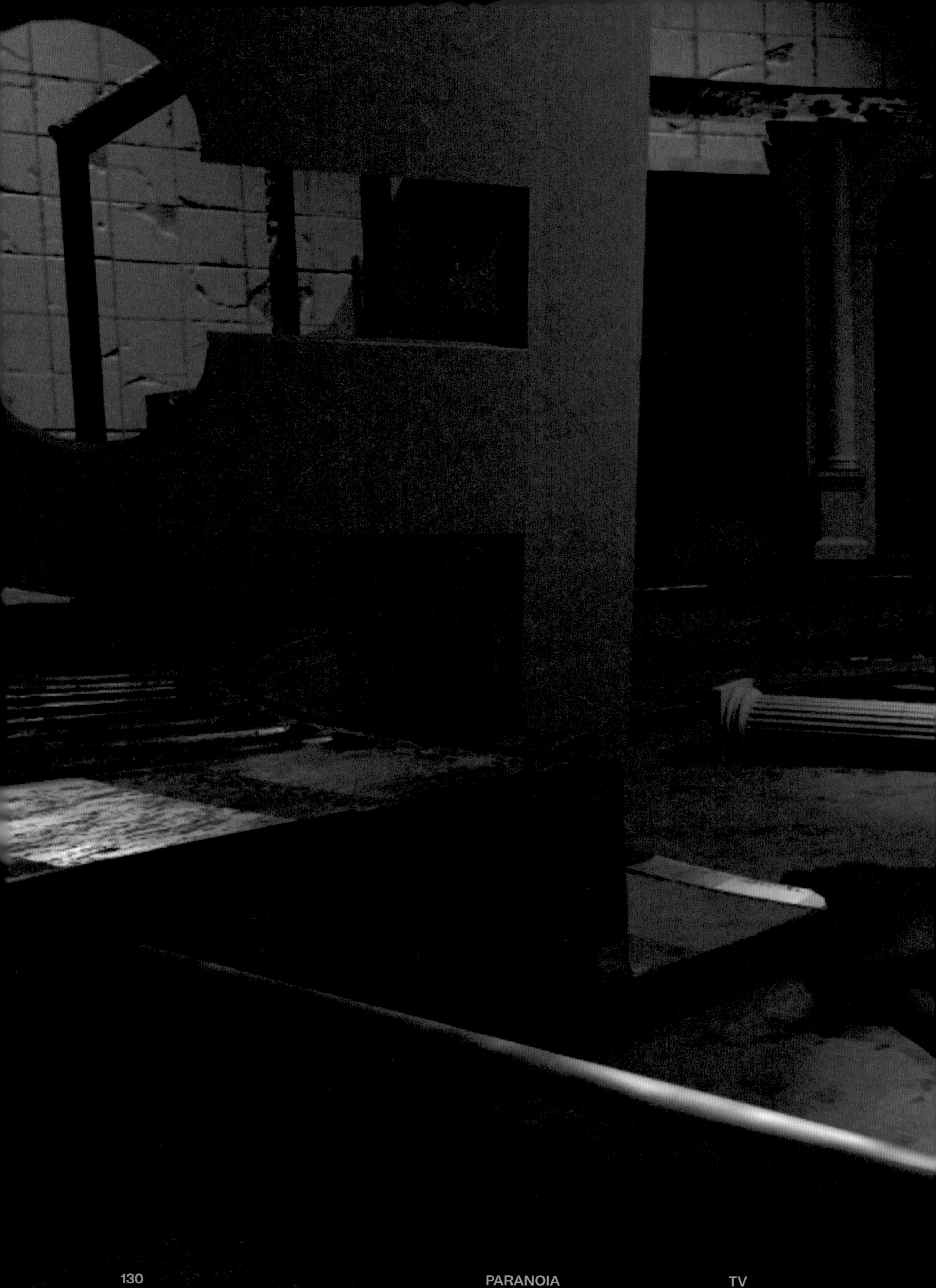

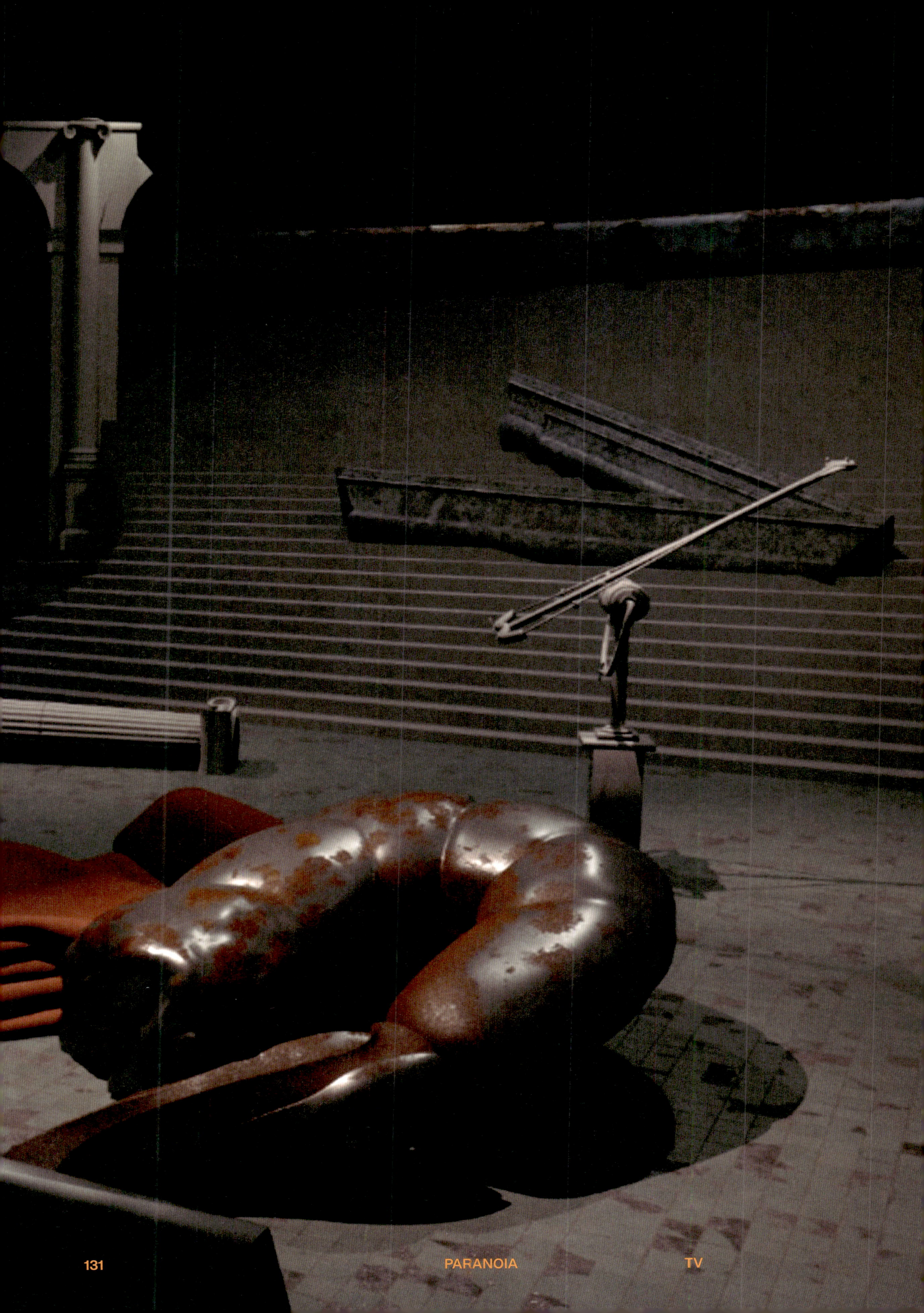

Janez Janša

The Final Match
2020

Performance

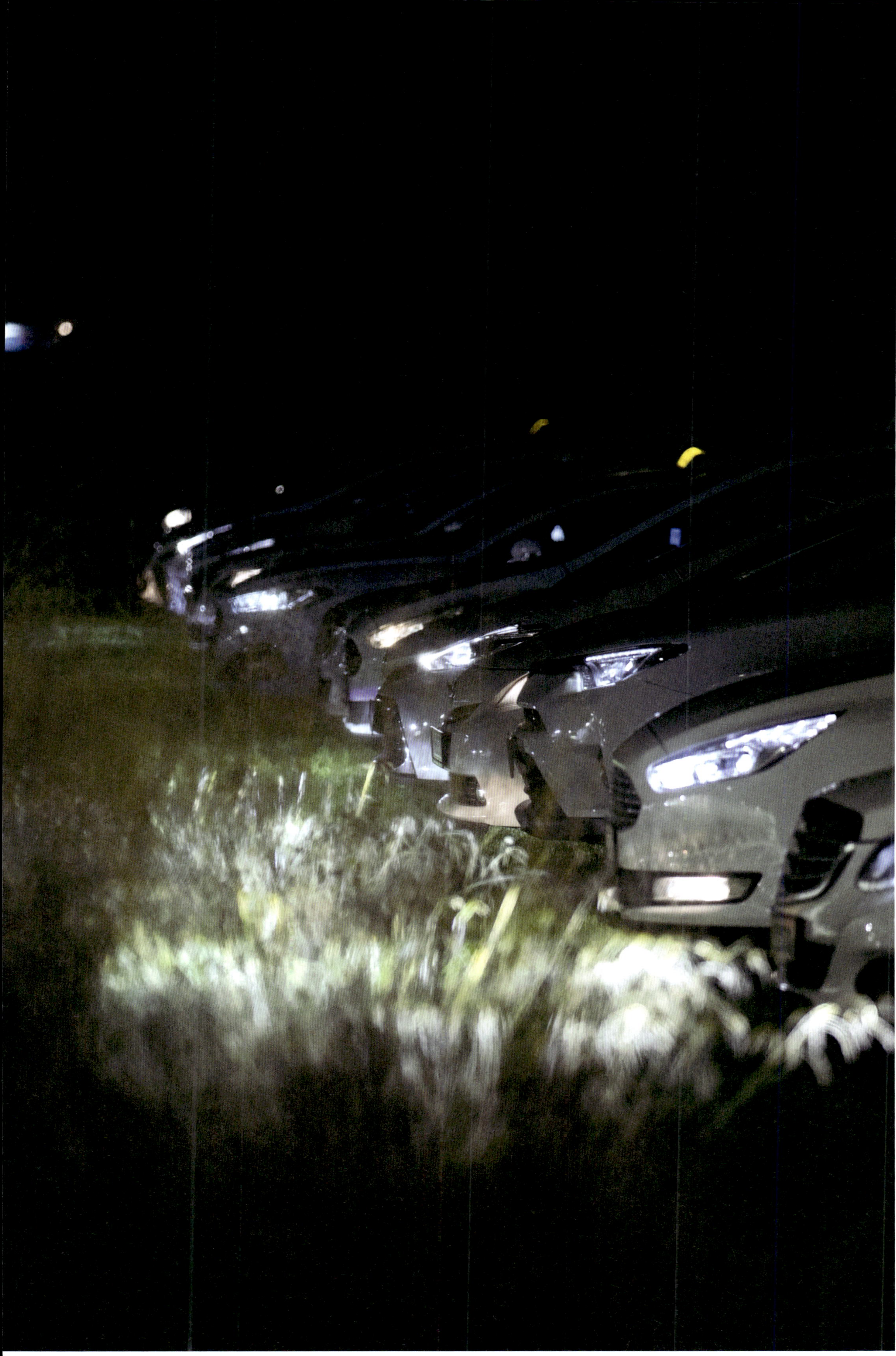

The air is bad under the masks that you've been wearing for over eight hours. The Austrian hits on the radio are driving you crazy, and then suddenly you are in the second half of the final game of the European Football Championship. *The Final Match* is the name of the piece with three endings, which vary depending on the taxi you're in. In our taxi, the moderators, as well as everyone else in the stadium, are eaten by bats. The bats are mentioned in literary and philosophical notes for forty-five minutes throughout the game; these mythical animals are now on everyone's lips, believed by many to have transmitted the coronavirus to humans in China. At some point we end up on the ugly outskirts of Graz, full of petrol stations and conservative advertising. McDonald's, H&M, and other discounters lead our way to the parking lot of the enterprise Legero United. With chips and cheap prosecco, which we treated ourselves to thanks to a detour by our nice Tunisian taxi driver, we watched the layers of the public sphere and the radio play intertwine. With Janez Janša's *The Final Match*, steirischer herbst crosses the line between breaking news, fake news, and art on the radio.

For many people, football is so much more than a game. But now, the impact of the pandemic means that fans will have to tread softly for an indefinite time. This is not so in Janša's radio play and performance. In his alternate reality, the European Football Championship, planned for 2020 and postponed to 2021, is taking place this year after all. For the final match, it's Germany against Sweden. The audience can only experience it in their cars, where they listen to two sportscasters bring the phantom game to life through their descriptions alone. Talking shop and philosophizing, they set the stage for ingenious plays, chants, and insights into the abysmal world of professional football, reflections on current world political events, and even touch upon the utopian and emancipatory potential of the present crisis. It's the same as always: the ball is round, the game lasts ninety minutes—the rest is theory.

María Inés Plaza Lazo

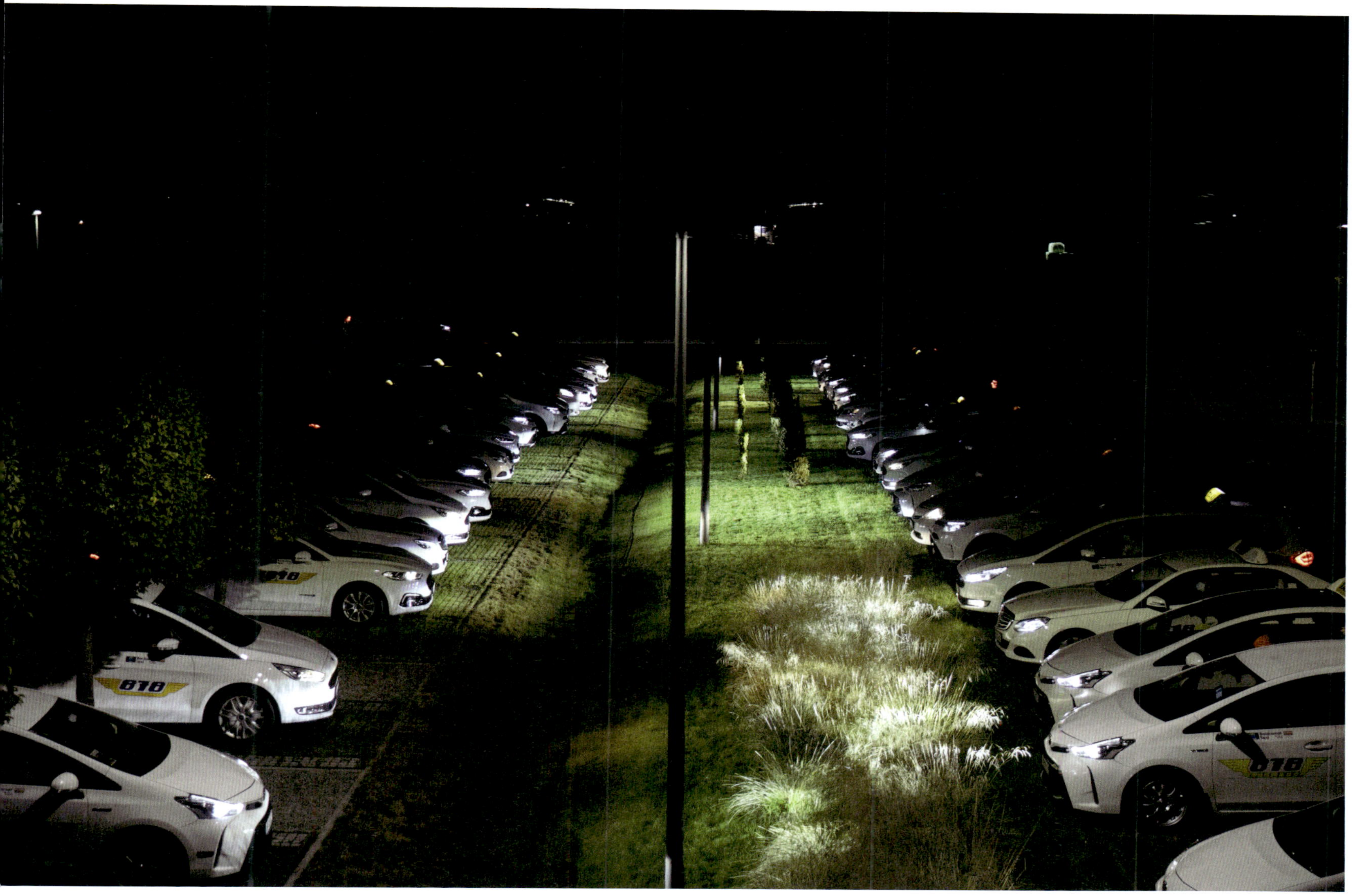

Janez Janša is the author of more than thirty interdisciplinary performances as well as conceptual and visual artworks. His work contains strong critical and political dimensions and it is focused on the relation between art and social and political contexts. He is the author of the book *Jan Fabre: La Discipline du chaos, le chaos de la discipline* (Paris, 1994) and has been editor in chief of the performing arts journal *MASKA* from 1999 to 2006. He is the director of Maska, an institute for publishing, production, and education based in Ljubljana, Slovenia, a professor at Inter-University Center for Dance Berlin (HZT), and a member of the theory curatorial team at Tanzquartier Wien.

The Final Match (2020)
Performance, ca. 60 min., German
Taxis and three locations in Graz

With: Martin Brachvogel, Leonie Bramberger, Alexander E. Fennon, Gabriela Hiti, Mathias Lodd, Mina Palada
Director: Janez Janša
Text: Boštjan Narat
Translation: Ann Catrin Bolton
Sound design: Matevž Kolenc
Sound recording: Fabio Schurischuster (Die Mischerei)
Head of production (Maska): Tina Dobnik

Commissioned by steirischer herbst ’20
Produced by MASKA in coproduction with steirischer herbst ’20
MASKA’s program is supported by the Ministry of Culture of the Republic Slovenia and the Municipality of Ljubljana

A.: Today's game, by the way, is being refereed by Dikaios, which in Greek actually means "a just man," so this digression into history seems all the more relevant. *(Laughs.)* What's your opinion of the VAR system in general?

B.: If I think about it from the perspective of fairness, then in fact there's no debate. It's absolutely clear that VAR reduces the number of referee errors. If decisions are no longer made instantaneously, if the arbiter is able to reconsider his decision and review the situation more than once, then that's how it has to be. With time and reflection comes greater probability that the judgment will be correct. But if we are talking about football itself, or something more serious . . .

A.: What can be more serious than football? *(Laughs.)*

B.: *(Ignoring him.)* The signal made by the referee, that rectangle drawn in the air, which in fact depicts the video screen, is at the same time entirely in keeping with the original meaning of "square": I'm going to make sure that everything adds up, that everything is honest and just. I'm going to see to it that everything is "fair and square."

A.: That was a good pass by Mustermann, but Horvat wasn't expecting it and the ball is now in the keeper's hands.

B.: On the other hand, you could ask if more fairness is really what we want. An absurd idea, perhaps, but errors and cheating are an essential part of any game, including football. What's more, some of the most iconic moments in the history of the sport have been due to errors or clever roguery. Diego Armando Maradona managed to trick the Chilean referee at the 1986 World Cup, whereas he would have been powerless against VAR technology.

A.: And the rest of us would have been deprived of the "Hand of God" legend.

B.: That's true. But there's something else that's interesting about our experience of fairness: it's essentially defined by whether or not the fair decision helps us or hurts us. True fairness, of course, never asks that question—it is cruel and merciless. That's also the way we view the football referee, more so than ever, since he's had VAR at his disposal. In the past, too, he had cards in his pocket and a whistle between his lips, but no gesture, nothing he could say, has ever had the same commanding, fateful effect as that square drawn in the air. It literally stops time.

A.: Some would say it stops it too often; it kills the momentum of the game and makes it boring.

B.: And to a certain degree they're right. Fairness is boring and old-fashioned, and the image of the honest man is infinitely more awkward and less charming than that of the rogue. Fairness is annoying and uptight—not unlike John Travolta in front of that club . . .

A.: Jack Rabbit Slim's.

B.: Jack Rabbit Slim's. But on the other hand, VAR adds an entirely new element to the dramaturgy of the game. Never have we watched the referee's facial expression with as much apprehension as we do when he's receiving instructions from the video operation room. And the time it takes him to look at the video doesn't feel pointless or tedious; on the contrary, it's a new and incredibly suspenseful dramaturgical moment, which football didn't have in the past, at least not like this.

A.: Hmm, OK, thank you for that thorough and thoughtful response. So far in the second half we've been watching a tactical battle between two different schools and mentalities in football. At the same time . . .

F.: Sorry to interrupt, A., but here I'd like to add an interesting comment on Twitter, which is signed by Robert Pfaller: "Germany and Sweden are playing the same way they're fighting the pandemic. The former is gambling on the strict control of the players' movement on the pitch, while the latter puts its trust in the idea that the individual will play responsibly."

A.: An interesting thought from the philosopher: control versus trust. If you are just now joining our broadcast, F. is today monitoring responses on social media. Now let's go down to the sideline, where our colleague has an interesting guest with her. Over to you, C.

C.: Thank you, A. Before the game we learned that Rizwan Kureishi, an England player of Pakistani roots, failed his doping test. So I'm here with Dr. D., an internationally recognized doping specialist. Dr. D., doping scandals in the past have mainly been associated with such sports as track and field, swimming, and cycling, which perhaps is where this stain is most indelible in the minds of the public. Football has been viewed as a clean sport, at least in terms of prohibited stimulants.

D.: That's true. The general belief has been that prohibited stimulants do not really provide the user with any significant advantage in football, that football is a game where the most important factors are technical skills, tactical readiness, and a certain spark, the ability to improvise, that extra something, as well as a well-oiled team.

C.: What about physical readiness?

D.: That's extremely important too, of course, more and more so each year. We need to be aware that football play is becoming faster and faster and ever more intense; the rhythm of competition is tremendous, the best teams play on three or four different fronts at the same time, and there are also team obligations . . .

C.: So you're saying that players are exposed to terrible stress. How do they deal with it?

D.: Recent research shows the frequent use of painkillers.

C.: Painkillers? You mean like Voltaren? But such pills are widely available. You don't even need a prescription for them.

D.: That's true. And you won't find these medications on any list of prohibited substances. But in football circles what we're seeing more and more is their so-called preventive use, which in the view of many experts, myself included, is merely a euphemism for abuse.

C.: So footballers don't use them just to relieve pain?

D.: Of course they use them for that, too, especially for small injuries and big games. But they also take them to enhance their physical condition, and thus their "performance," which is one of the reasons a drug gets put on the list of prohibited substances.

C.: What are some other reasons?

D.: Harmful side effects—and there are plenty of them linked to the excessive use, or abuse, of painkillers: cardiovascular disease, problems with the liver, kidneys, stomach, etc. Abuse of these drugs can be lethal.

C.: Thank you very much, Dr. D. By the way, what was the prohibited substance they uncovered in Kureishi's case?

D.: Alcohol.

C.: Oh. *(Momentary silence.)* Thank you. Now back to the commentators' box.

Boštjan Narat
Translated from the Slovene
by Rawley Grau (with an assist
from Simon Debeljak)

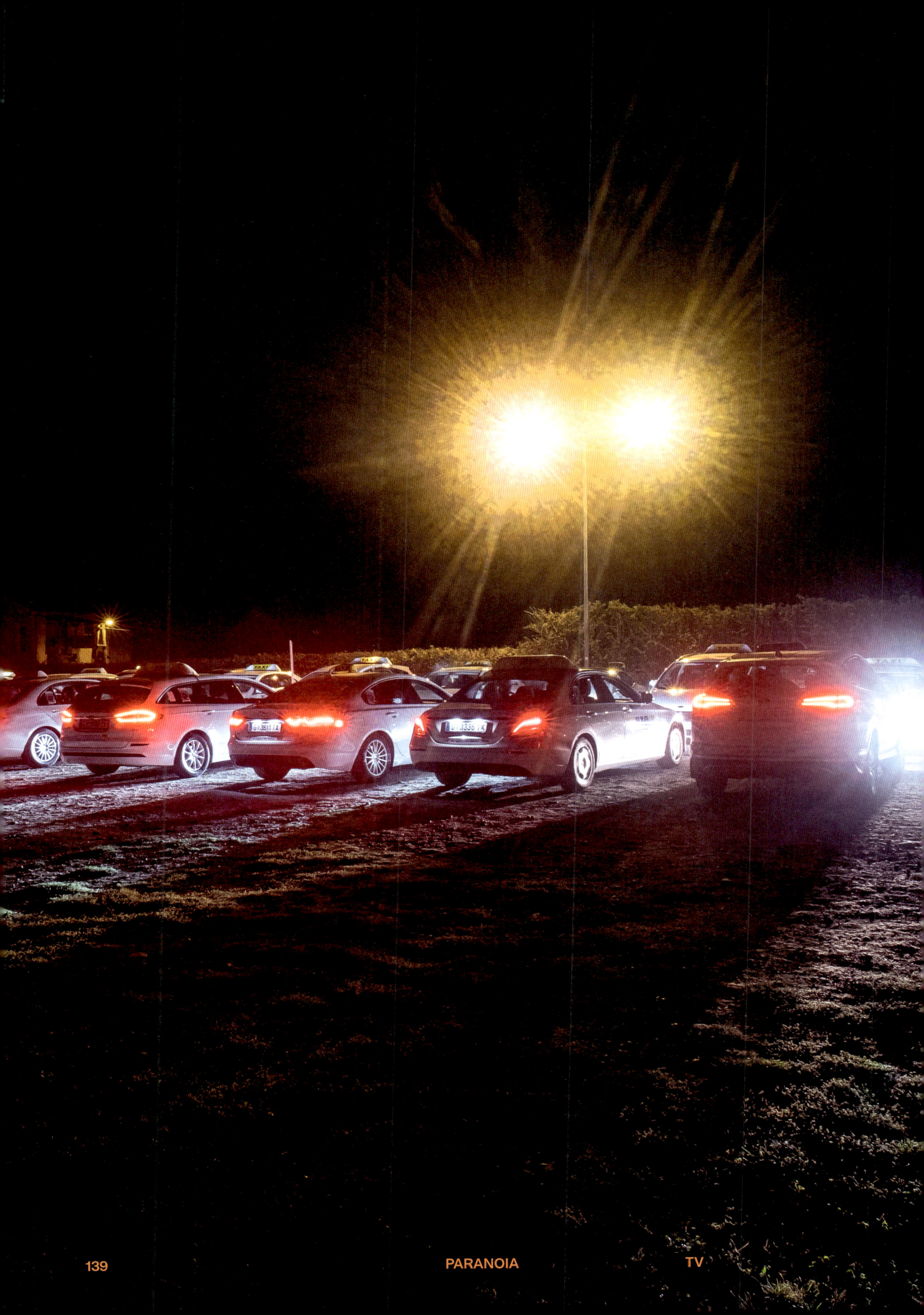

Lina Majdalanie & Rabih Mroué

Second Look
2020

Video series

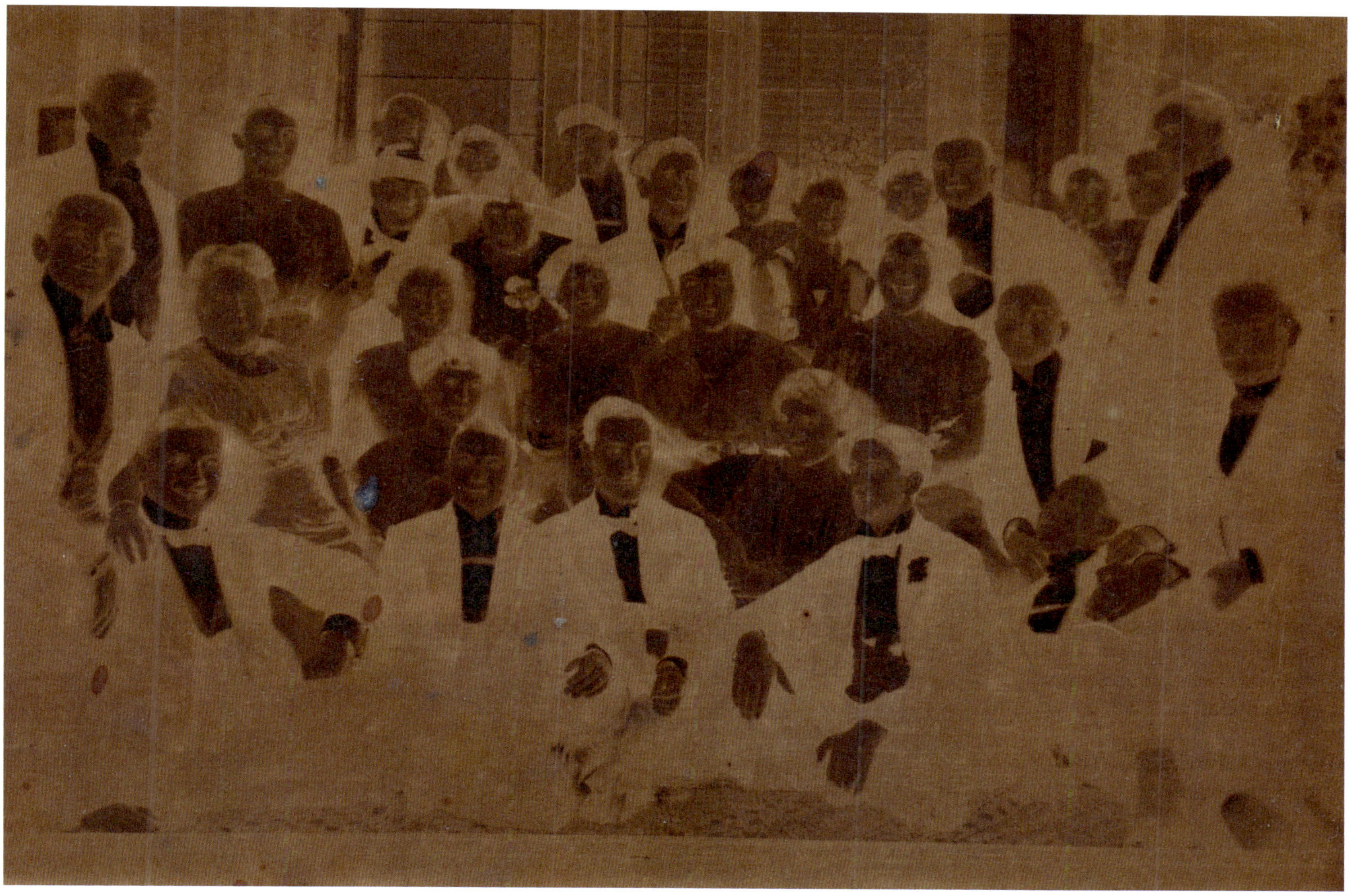

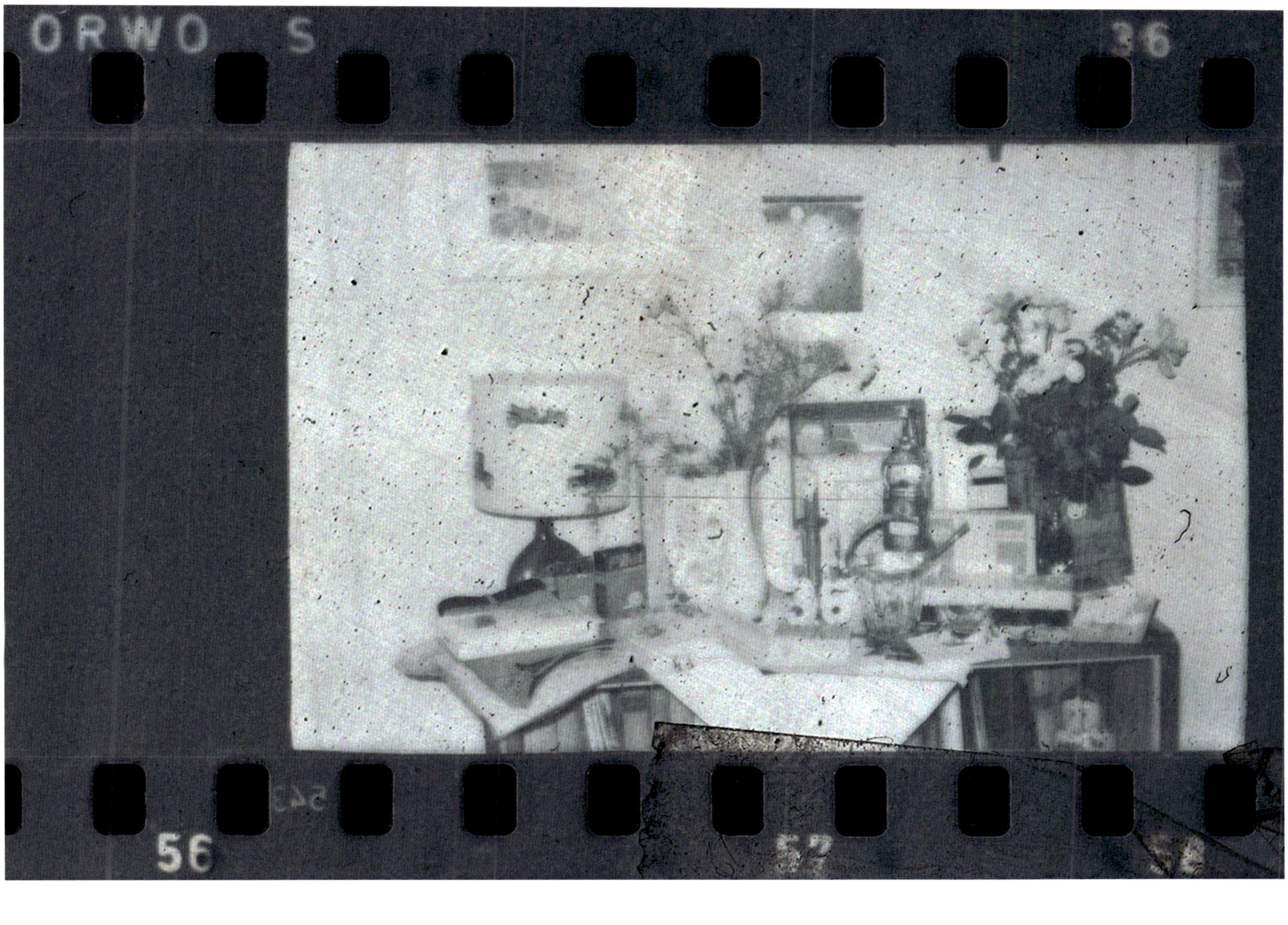
ORWO S
36
56
57

Lina Majdalanie and Rabih Mroué were both born in Beirut. They currently live in Berlin.

Second Look (2020)
Video series, 10 episodes,
ca. 53 min. total, English
Online

Written and directed by Lina Majdalanie & Rabih Mroué
Voice-over: Rabih Mroué, Lina Majdalanie
Animation: Sarmad Louis
Editing: Rabih Mroué, Sarmad Louis
Photo corrections: Rafi Mrad
English translation: Feyrouz Serhal
Scans: Lama Sabah

Commissioned and produced by steirischer herbst '20

You collect a lot of things over the years, often without knowing why or what you want to do with them. Until one day, you spread them out and start looking at them properly. You try to understand why it is you like them and why you might also be ashamed of them at the same time. You attempt to discover or to invent their stories, struggling to give free rein to your emotions or to tame them. As you look at your collection, you might allow memories to return, and you might try to utter them, mixing your stories with their imagined ones. In brief, you might use them to talk about "you"; you, as an inseparable singular from all the other singulars, you, as an unbreakable moment from history.

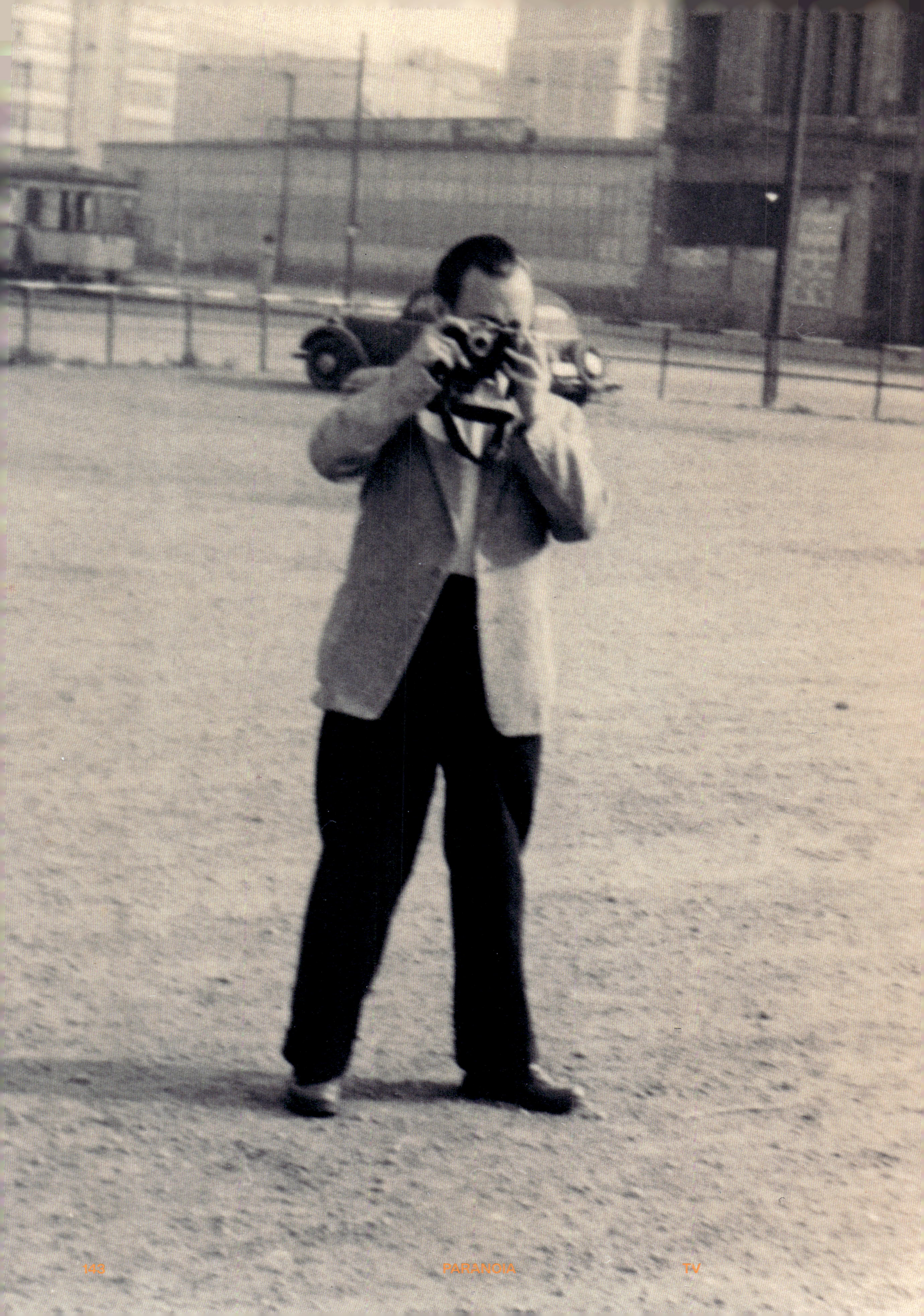

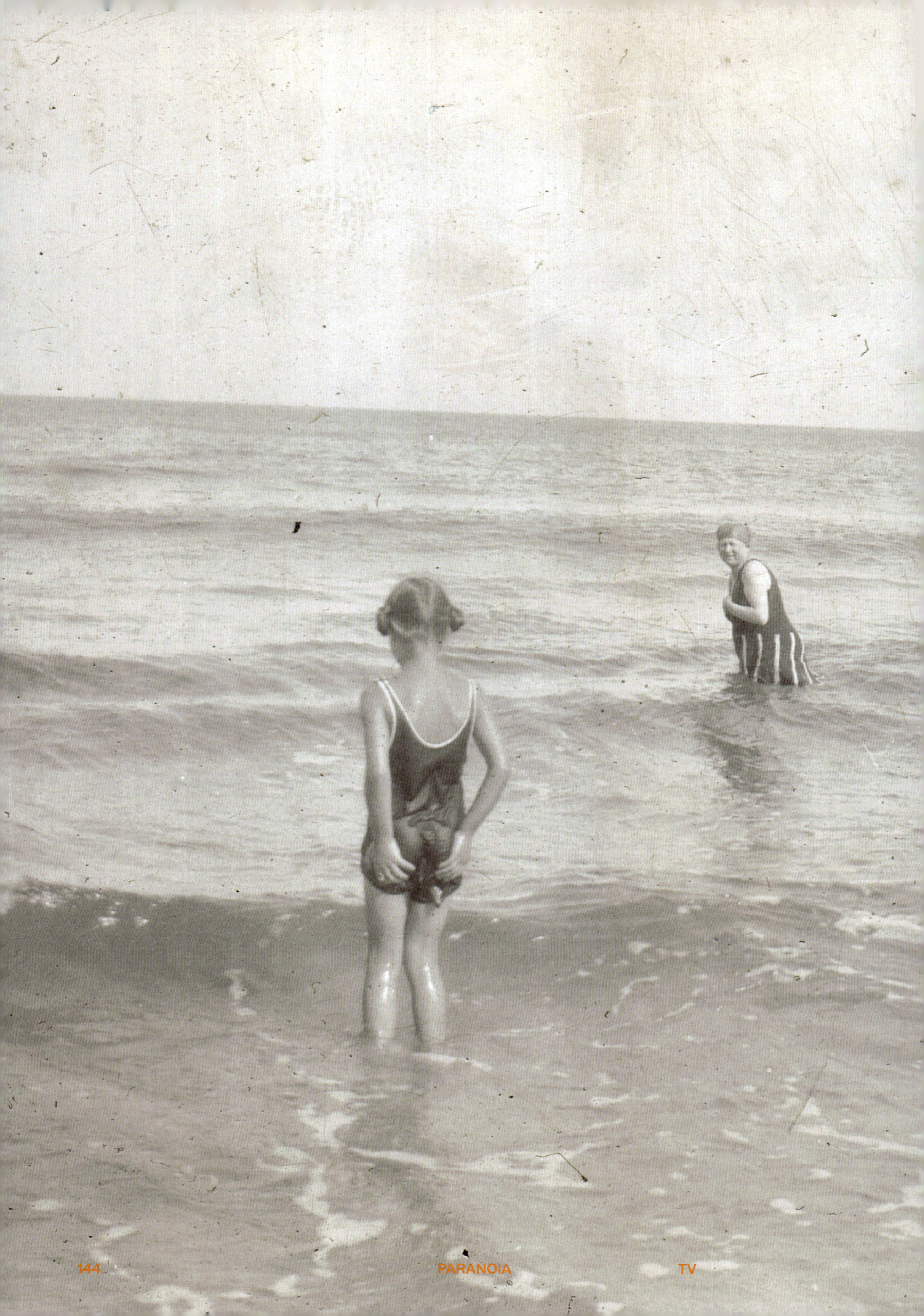

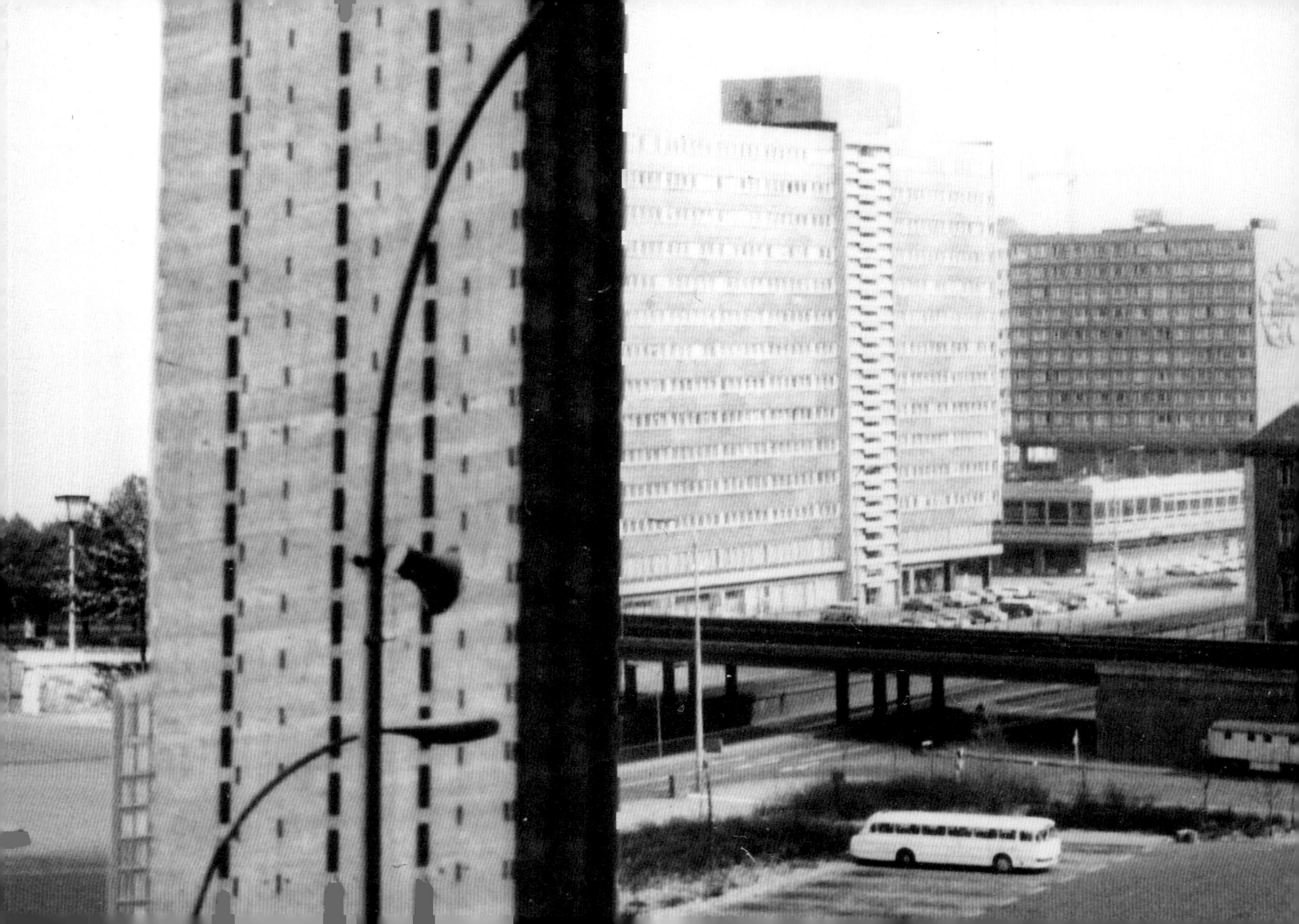

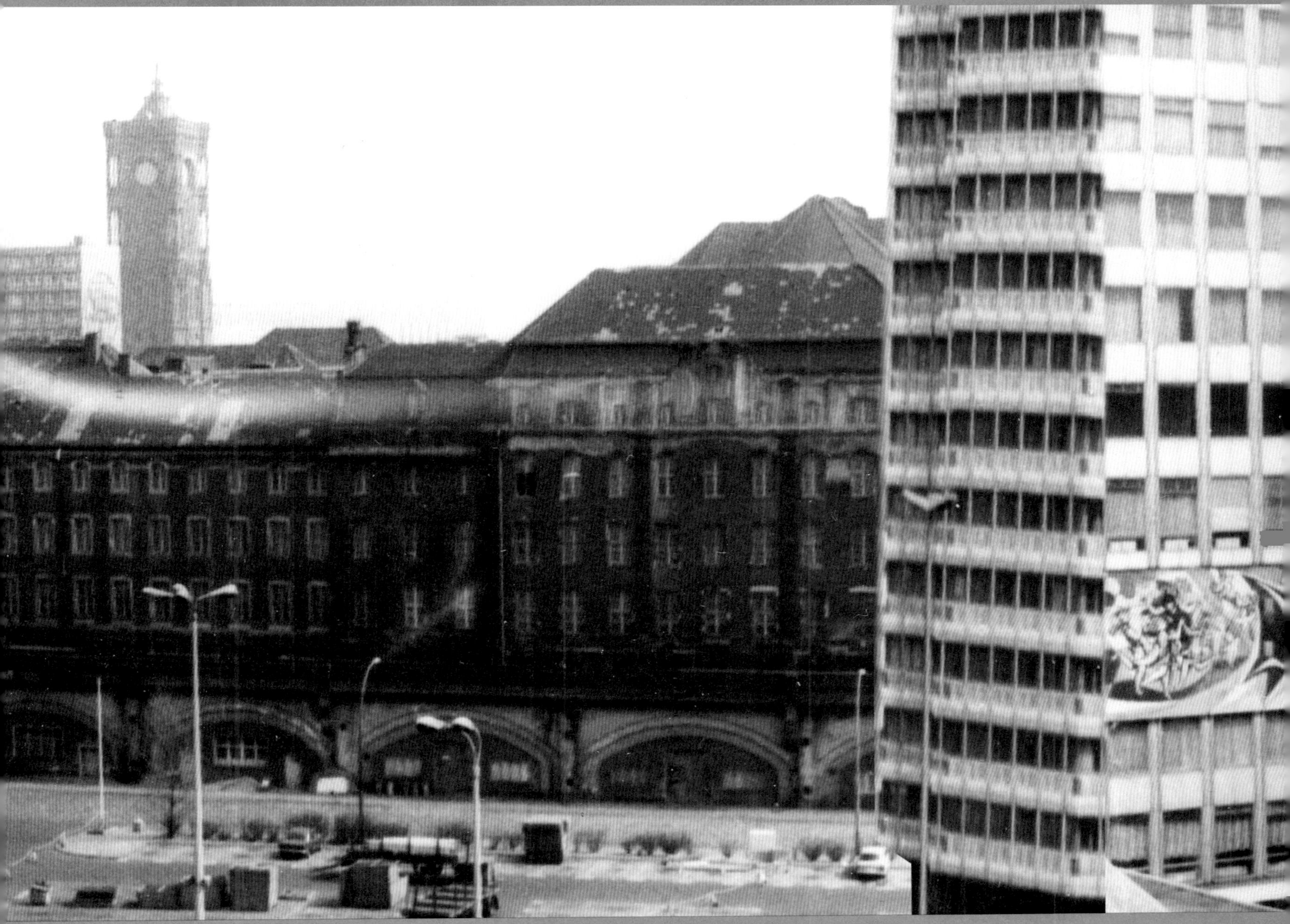

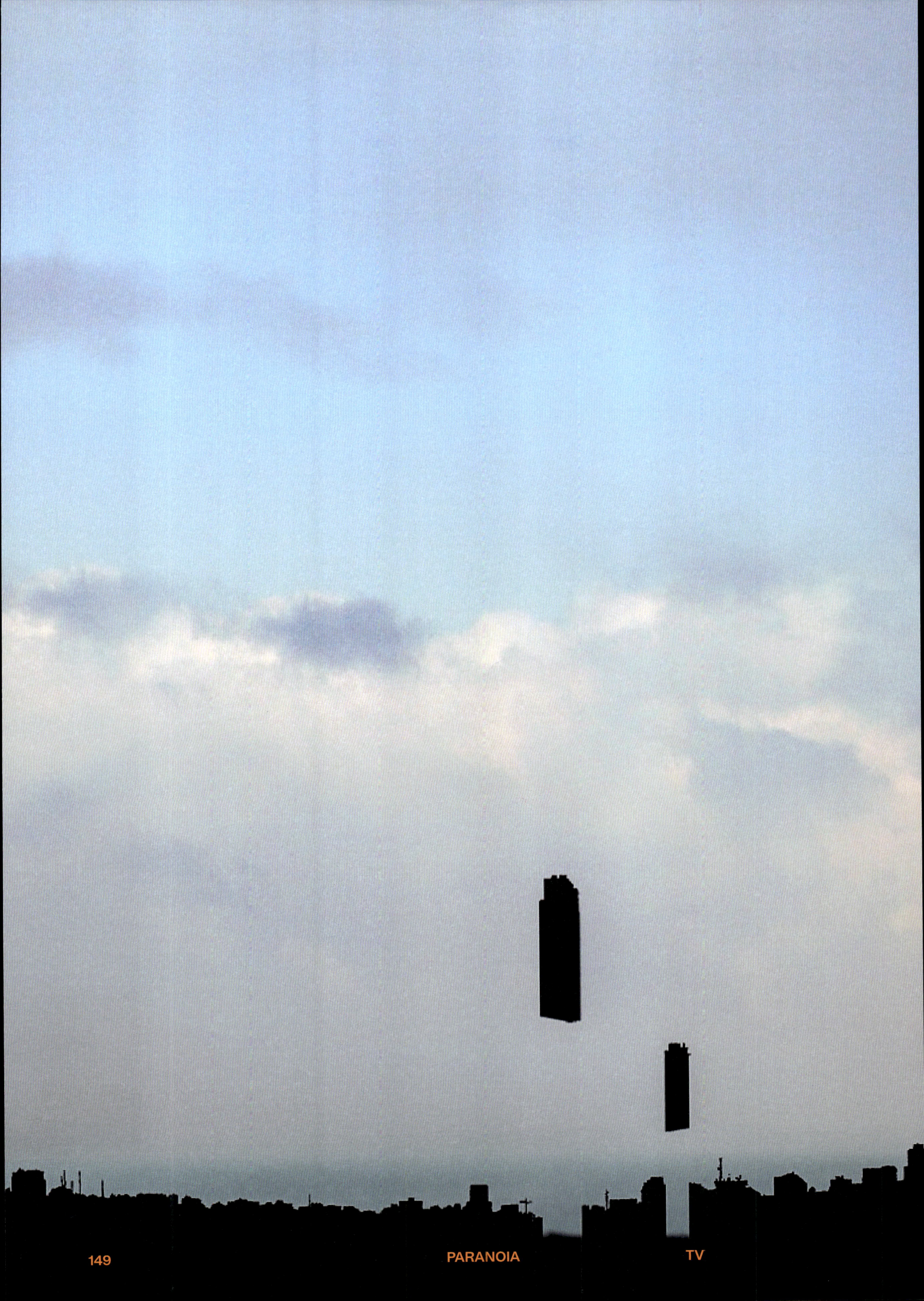

Chrystèle Nicot & Antoine Alesandrini

PRAAB (Beta Version)
2020

Online game

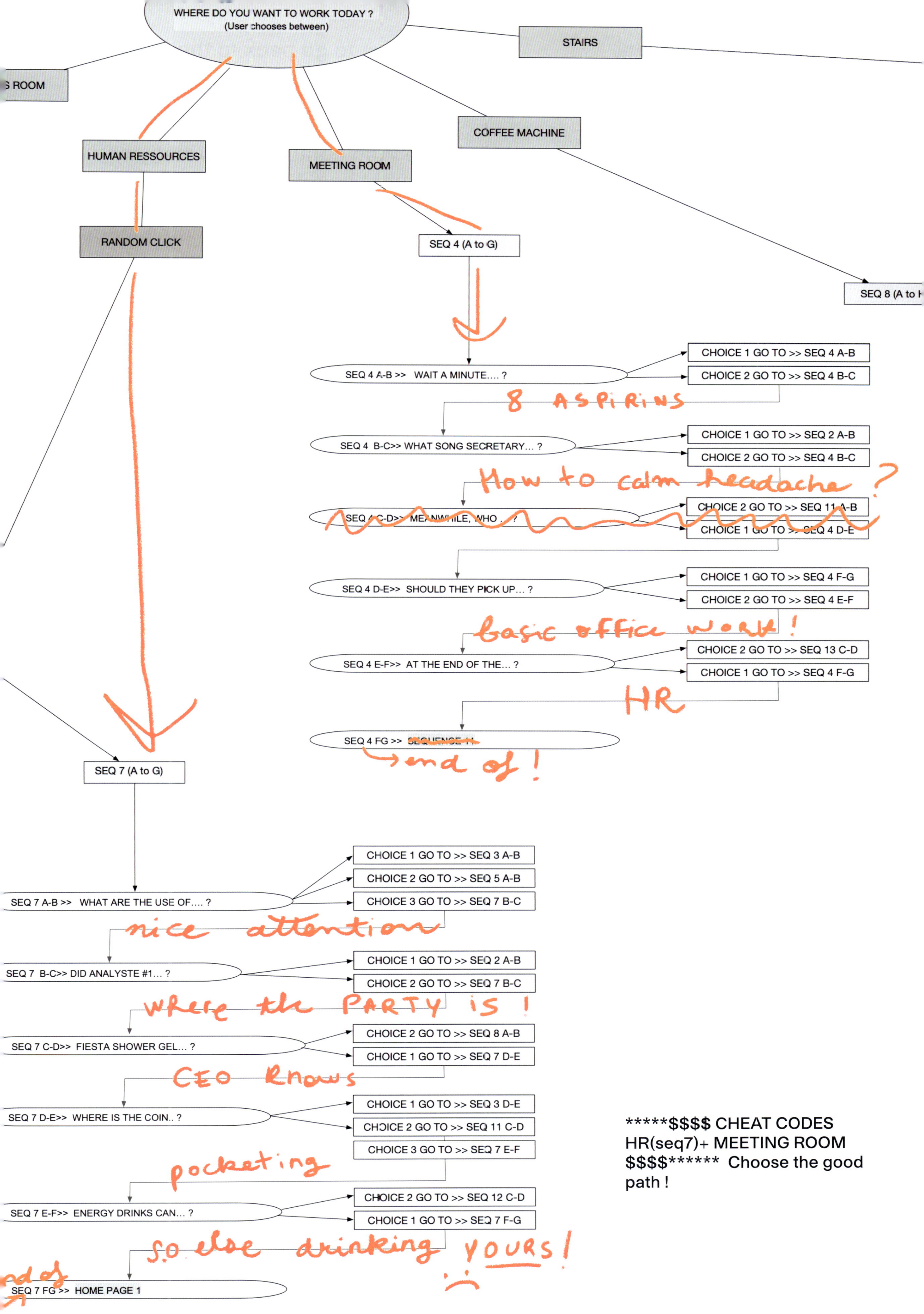

WHERE DO YOU WANT TO WORK TODAY ?
(User chooses between)
S ROOM
STAIRS
COFFEE MACHINE
HUMAN RESSOURCES
MEETING ROOM
RANDOM CLICK
SEQ 4 (A to G)
SEQ 8 (A to H
SEQ 4 A-B >> WAIT A MINUTE.... ?
CHOICE 1 GO TO >> SEQ 4 A-B
CHOICE 2 GO TO >> SEQ 4 B-C
8 ASPIRINS
SEQ 4 B-C>> WHAT SONG SECRETARY... ?
CHOICE 1 GO TO >> SEQ 2 A-B
CHOICE 2 GO TO >> SEQ 4 B-C
How to calm headache ?
SEQ 4 C-D>> MEANWHILE, WHO ... ?
CHOICE 2 GO TO >> SEQ 11 A-B
CHOICE 1 GO TO >> SEQ 4 D-E
SEQ 4 D-E>> SHOULD THEY PICK UP... ?
CHOICE 1 GO TO >> SEQ 4 F-G
CHOICE 2 GO TO >> SEQ 4 E-F
basic office work !
SEQ 4 E-F>> AT THE END OF THE... ?
CHOICE 2 GO TO >> SEQ 13 C-D
CHOICE 1 GO TO >> SEQ 4 F-G
HR
SEQ 4 FG >> SEQUENCE 1
end of !
SEQ 7 (A to G)
SEQ 7 A-B >> WHAT ARE THE USE OF.... ?
CHOICE 1 GO TO >> SEQ 3 A-B
CHOICE 2 GO TO >> SEQ 5 A-B
CHOICE 3 GO TO >> SEQ 7 B-C
nice attention
SEQ 7 B-C>> DID ANALYSTE #1... ?
CHOICE 1 GO TO >> SEQ 2 A-B
CHOICE 2 GO TO >> SEQ 7 B-C
where the PARTY is !
SEQ 7 C-D>> FIESTA SHOWER GEL... ?
CHOICE 2 GO TO >> SEQ 8 A-B
CHOICE 1 GO TO >> SEQ 7 D-E
CEO knows
SEQ 7 D-E>> WHERE IS THE COIN.. ?
CHOICE 1 GO TO >> SEQ 3 D-E
CHOICE 2 GO TO >> SEQ 11 C-D
CHOICE 3 GO TO >> SEQ 7 E-F
pocketing
SEQ 7 E-F>> ENERGY DRINKS CAN... ?
CHOICE 2 GO TO >> SEQ 12 C-D
CHOICE 1 GO TO >> SEQ 7 F-G
so else drinking yours !
end of
SEQ 7 FG >> HOME PAGE 1
*****$$$$ CHEAT CODES
HR(seq7)+ MEETING ROOM
$$$$****** Choose the good path !

152

Chrystèle Nicot, born 1989, and Antoine Alesandrini, born 1985, are an artist duo based in Paris whose practice moves seamlessly between film, installation, and sculpture. Their work is concerned with the intersections of cultural economy and technology. In October 2020, they presented their first solo show together, *În gura lumii / Rumeurs de sociétés* in Bucharest, curated by Cristina Stoenescu. They recently received DICRéAM (CNC) funding in order to continue to work on a new version of *PRAAB* for 2021.

PRAAB (Beta Version) (2020)
Online game, English

Film
Directors: Chrystèle Nicot & Antoine Alesandrini
Production: Louis Beaudemont (Les Steppes Productions)
Director of photography: Daniel Zlobin
Cast: Denis Inozemtsev, Alessia Korsak, Lena Kuo, Katia Lojenenko, Evgueni Oreshkin, Pavel Savinov, Marina Suvorova
Camera assistant: Arsèny Ponomarenko & Egor Chechkin
Trainee camera assistant: Alexey Lazovsky
Coordinator: Alexey Orlov
HMC: Alexandra Brunova
Post-synchro: Zachar Semirkhanov
Sound editing and mixing: Arno Ledoux
Chief editor: Antoine Alesandrini
Script: Margarita Vishnevsjaya
Translation: Taïa Kascheeva

Platform
Creators: Chrystèle Nicot & Antoine Alesandrini
Programmer: Nariman Varahram
Graphic design: Chrystèle Nicot
Editing: Antoine Alesandrini

Produced by Bad Manner's and Pejman Foundation in coproduction with steirischer herbst '20
Supported by Fondation Pernod-Ricard and ZIL Cultural Centre

Prepare to go back to the office!
It's the only place to fall in love!
With the help of AI and in Russian!

The 20th century owes many of its most beautiful love stories to bureaucracy. But today, after many years of working from home, people have forgotten how to interact without the help of a computer screen. The birth rate is plunging dramatically, and humanity faces extinction. How to make love great again? *PRAAB* (Programme de Réhabilitation à l'Amitié et l'Amour par le Bureau) is here to help. Use an AI-enhanced video platform to relearn physical interaction before venturing back into real-life workspace. Remember how to politely accept a mug of coffee or swap fun facts and, maybe, how to find other people attractive again at some point. Watch tutorials and decide on what path you will take . . . The sci-fi training platform developed by Chrystèle Nicot and Antoine Alesandrini questions both the discarded office culture we all still know from films and books and the new algorithmic training forms already available on the Internet today.

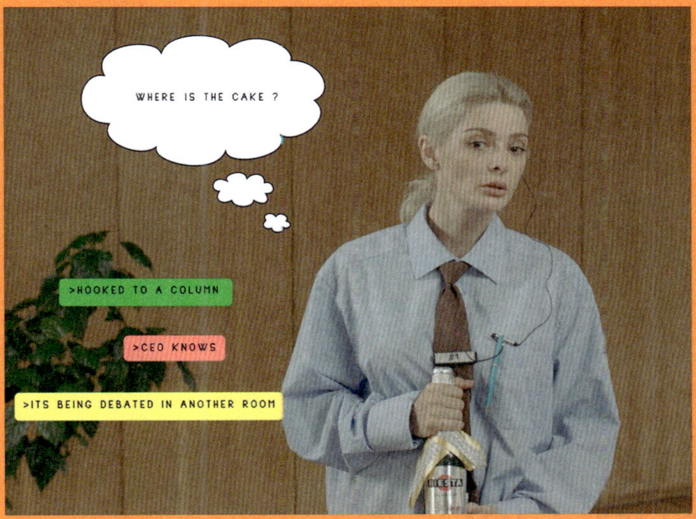
WHERE IS THE CAKE ?
>HOOKED TO A COLUMN
>CEO KNOWS
>ITS BEING DEBATED IN ANOTHER ROOM

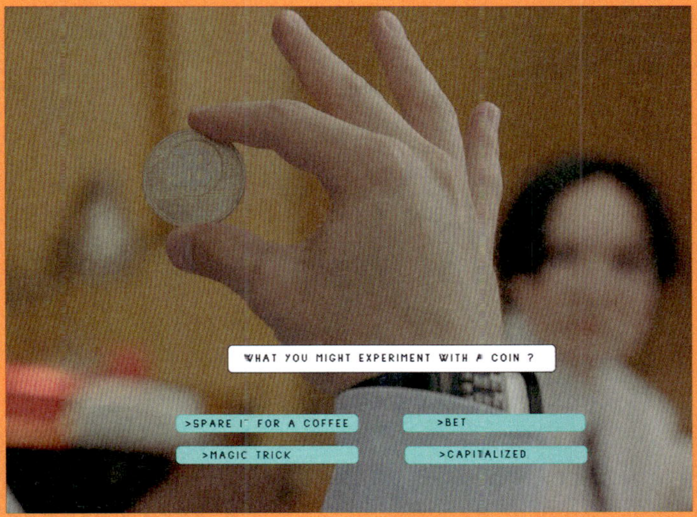
WHAT YOU MIGHT EXPERIMENT WITH A COIN ?
>SPARE 1€ FOR A COFFEE
>BET
>MAGIC TRICK
>CAPITALIZED

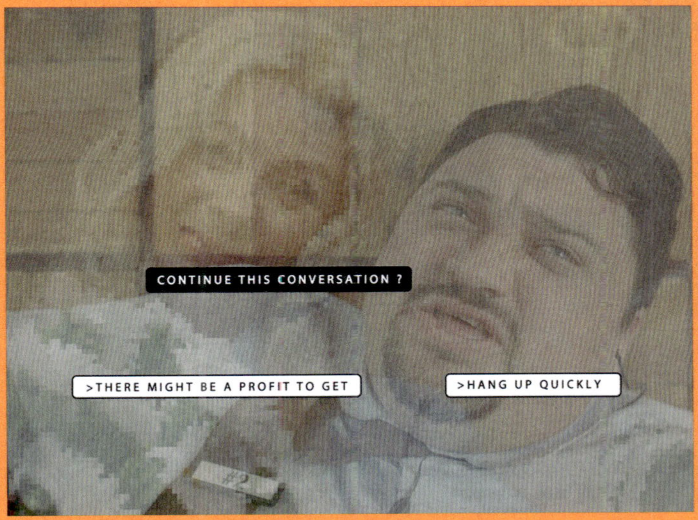
CONTINUE THIS CONVERSATION ?
>THERE MIGHT BE A PROFIT TO GET
>HANG UP QUICKLY

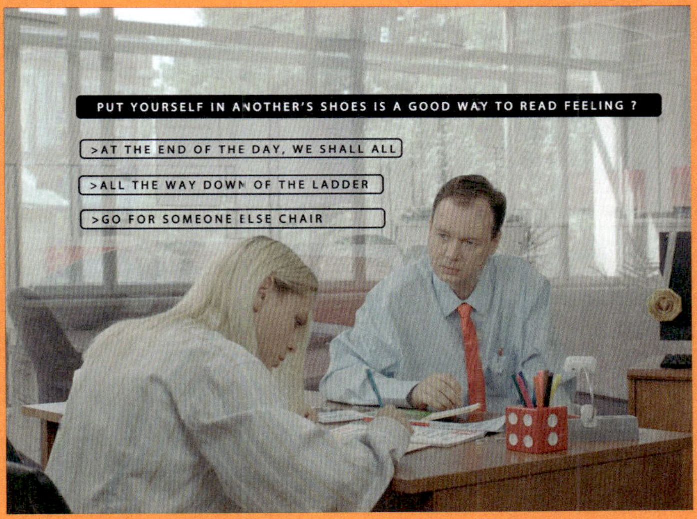
PUT YOURSELF IN ANOTHER'S SHOES IS A GOOD WAY TO READ FEELING ?
>AT THE END OF THE DAY, WE SHALL ALL
>ALL THE WAY DOWN OF THE LADDER
>GO FOR SOMEONE ELSE CHAIR

Ingo Niermann

Deutsch Süd-Ost
2020

Video series

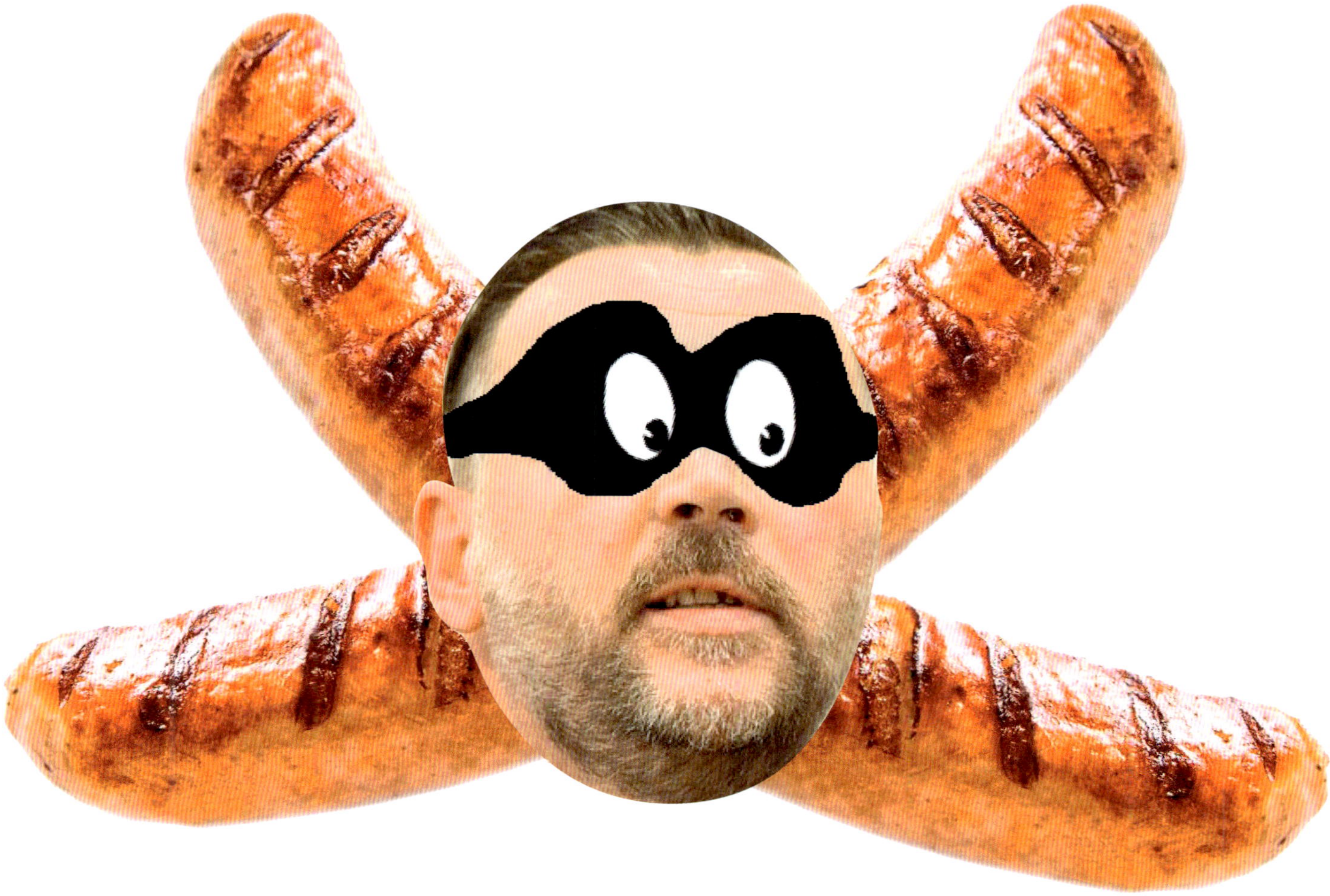

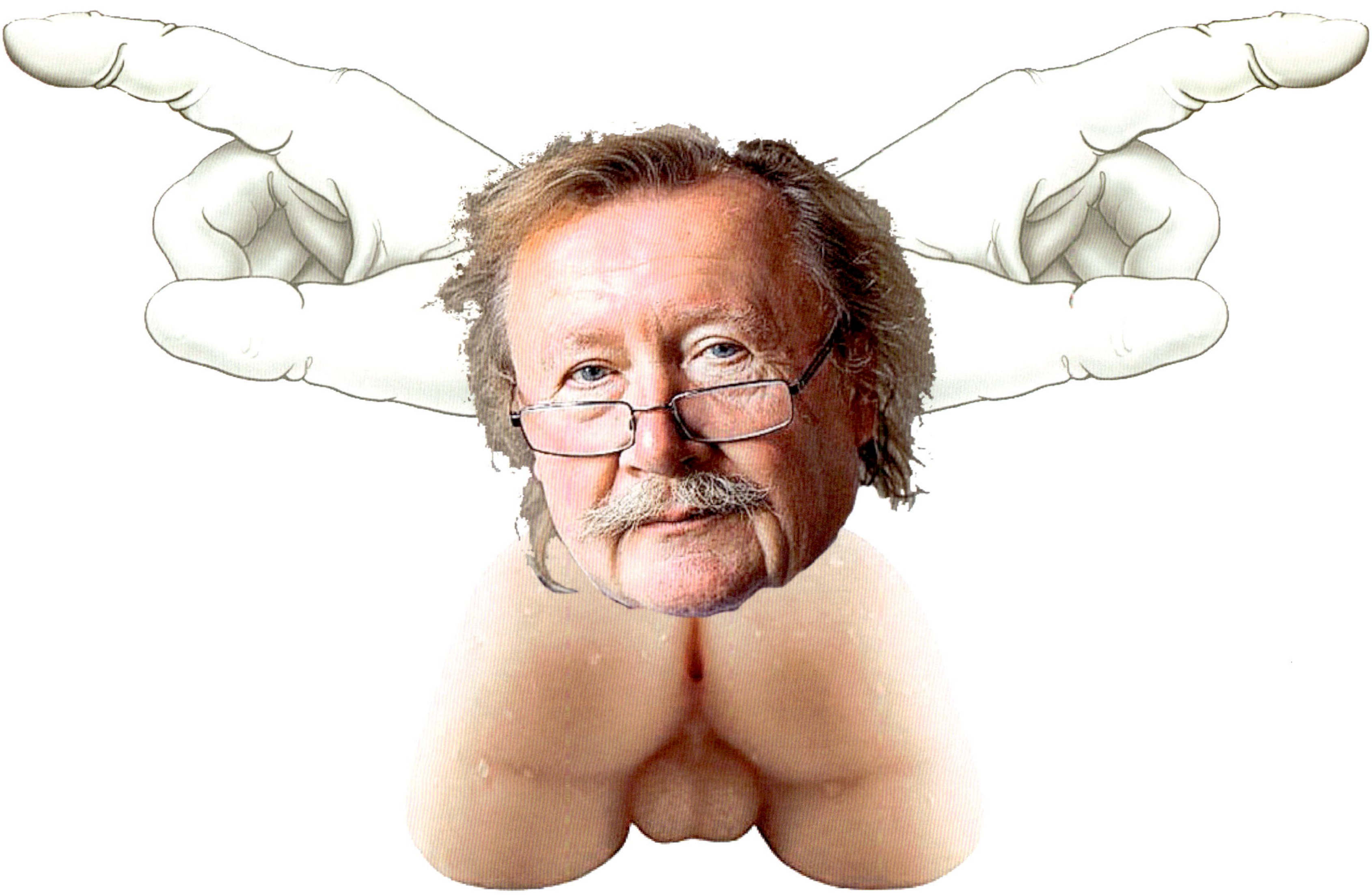

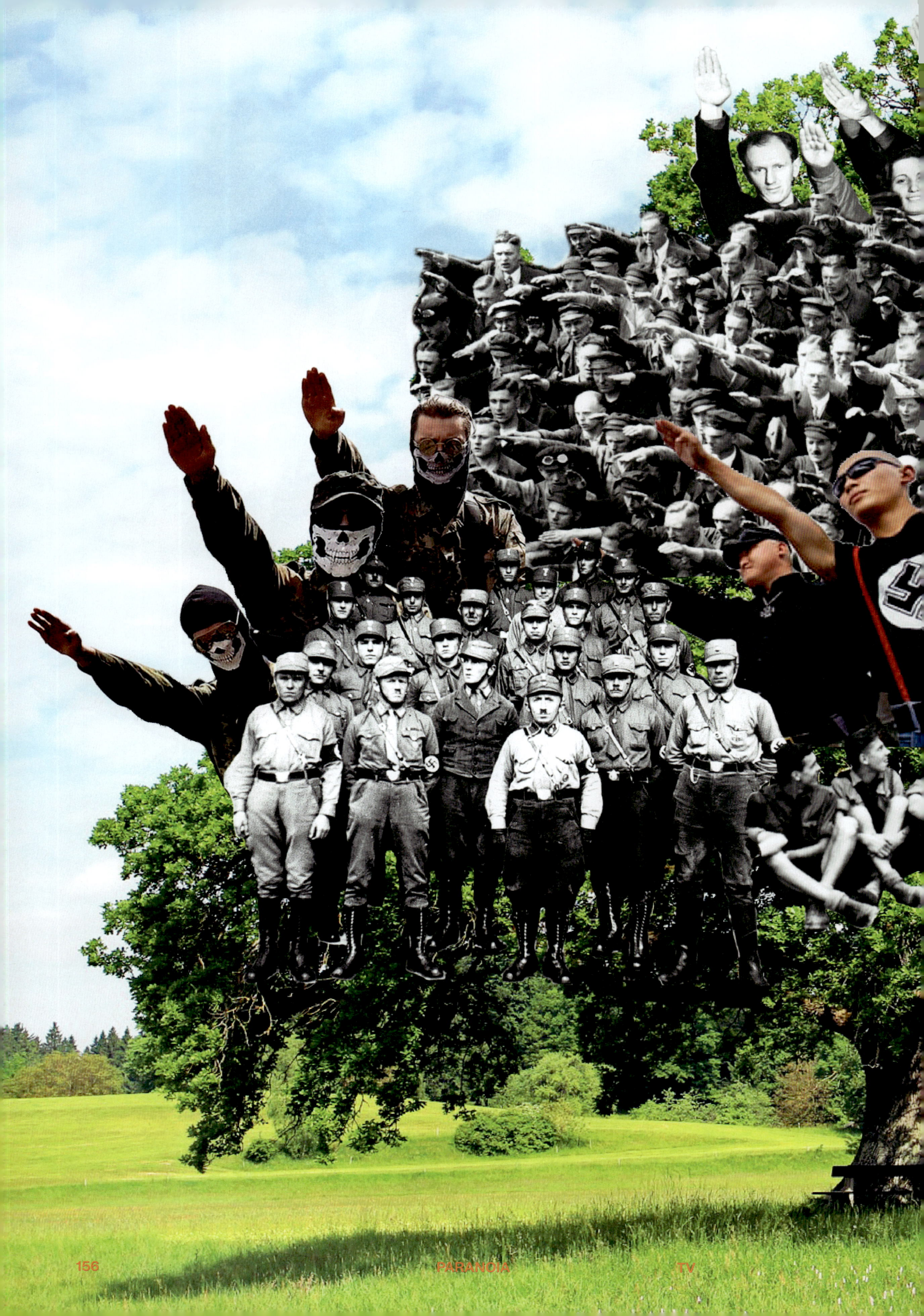

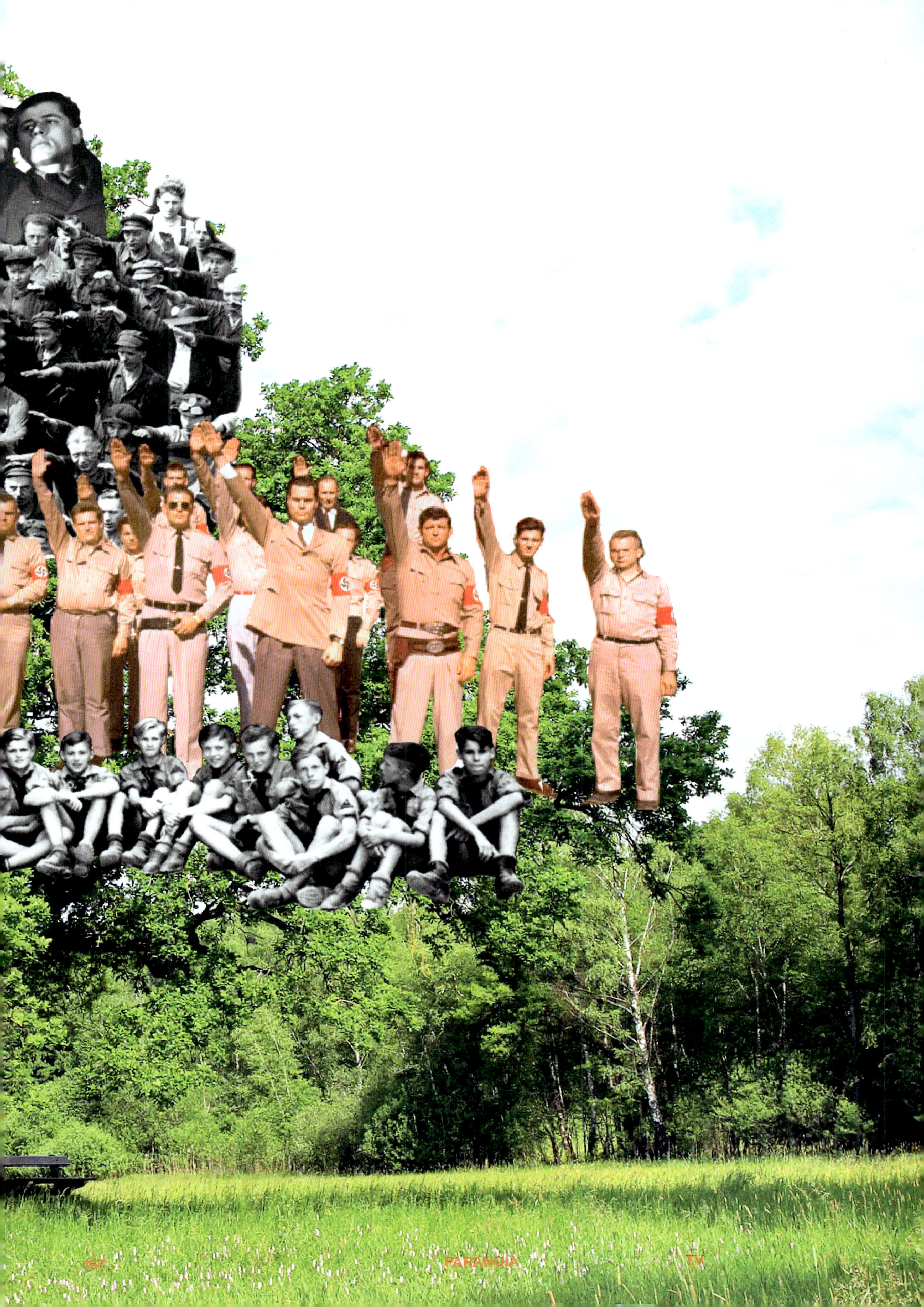

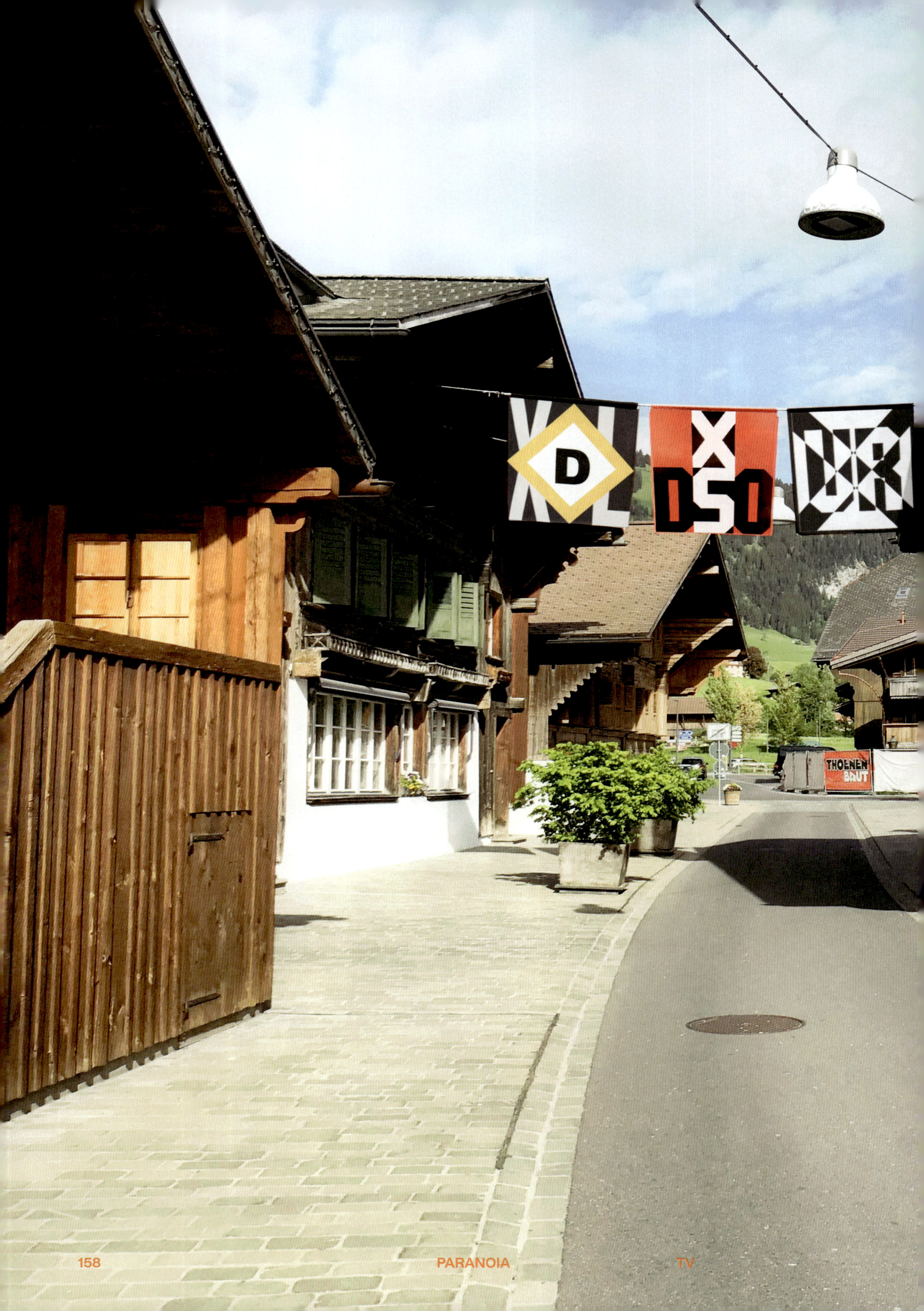
THOENEN
BAUT

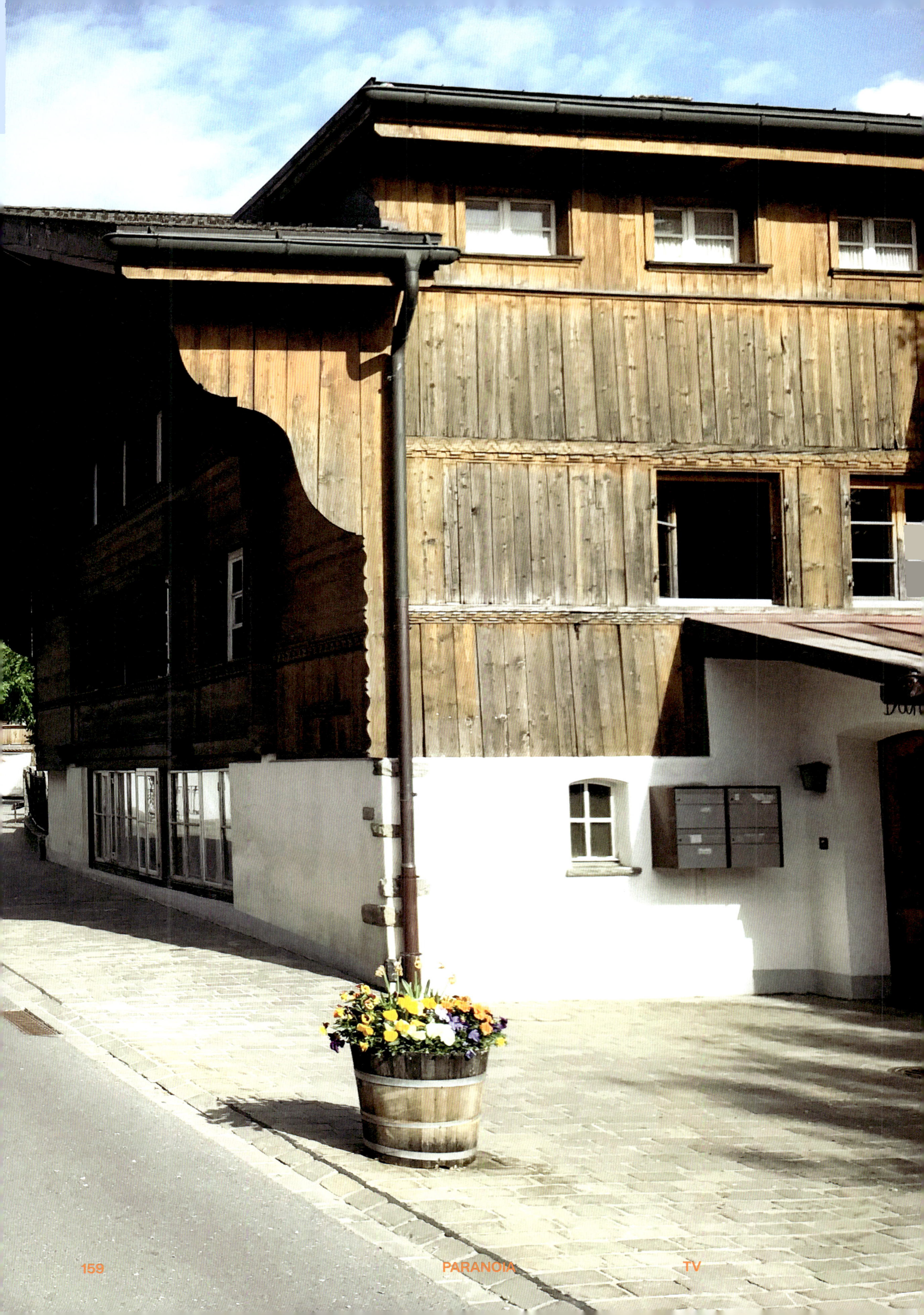

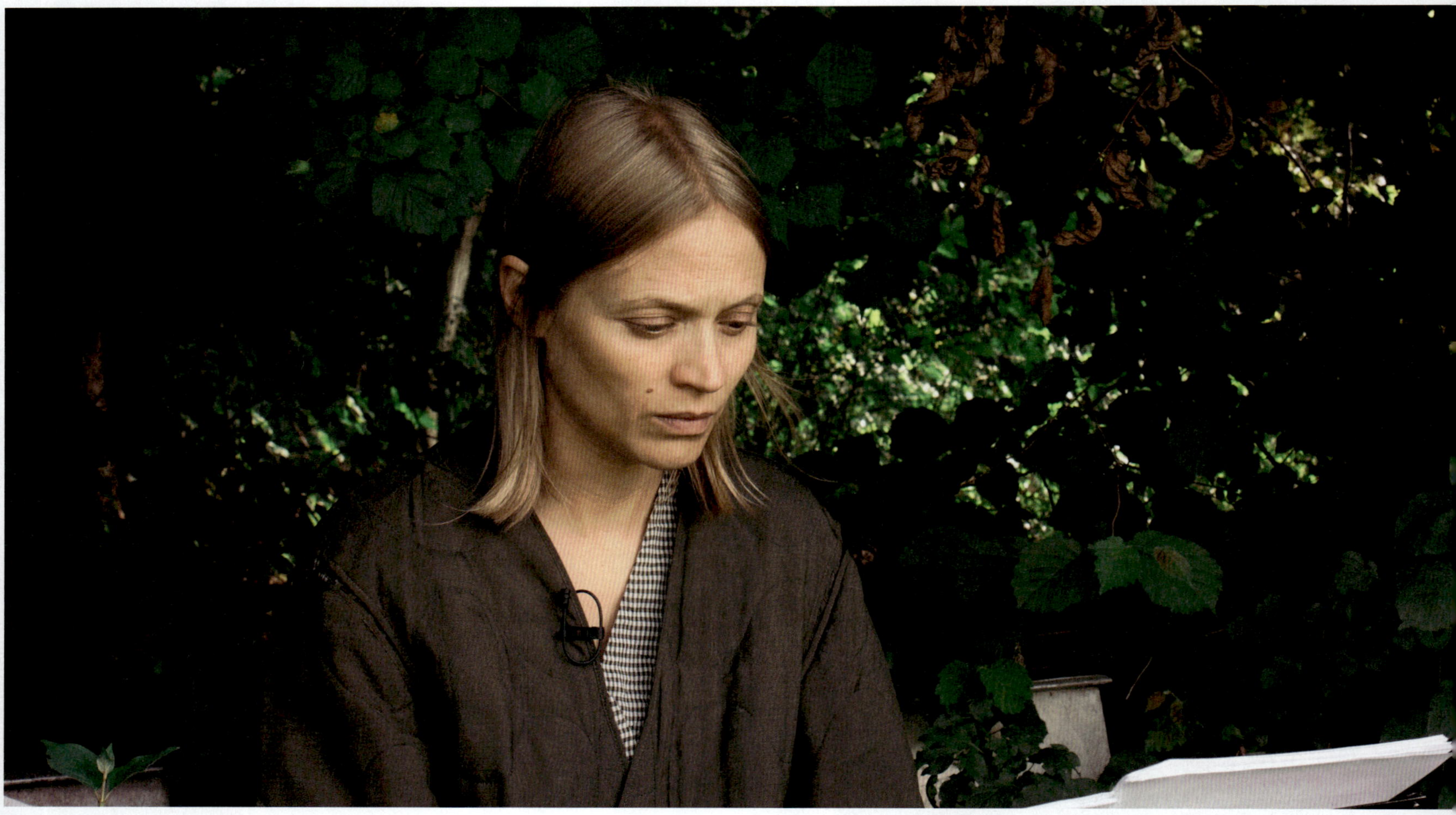

White men are becoming extinct, and they don't seem to be having such a bad time. After retreating to a "bastion" in southeast Germany, they let their imaginations run wild. Such is the premise of Ingo Niermann's video novel *Deutsch Süd-Ost*, narrated in twenty-five episodes by actress Mavie Hörbiger.

Deutsch Süd-Ost is a Who's Who of prominent "last white men": representatives of the *Neue Rechte*, Reich citizens, controversial artists and intellectuals. Inspired by their new sociotope, they develop revolutionary trends in music, fashion, sex, food, and terrorism; they build "Nazi zoos" and attempt to breed an Aryan-Slavic master race and a species above and beyond both man and beast.

Deutsch Süd-Ost is a tragicomic laboratory for the mind in which Niermann's own role as a white man and the radicalization of some of his own acquaintances are subject to playful experimentation. Right-wing ideology is not consigned to the trash can, but rather processed and prophetically transformed.

> "I'm on full blast and blown away. Niermann's grip is as secure as that of an acrobat on the trapeze. Awesome."
> — Elfriede Jelinek

Ingo Niermann is a writer and the editor of the speculative book series Solution. Recent books include *Solution 295–304: Mare Amoris* (2020), *Burial of the White Man* (with Erik Niedling, 2019), *It's Me!* (with David Pearce, 2019), and *Solution 275–294: Communists Anonymous* (ed., with Joshua Simon, 2017). Based on his novel *Solution 257: Complete Love* (2016), Niermann initiated the Army of Love (thearmyoflove.net), a project that tests and promotes a need-oriented redistribution of sensual love.

Deutsch Süd-Ost (2020)
Video series, 25 episodes,
ca. 276 min. total, German
Online

Narrated by Mavie Hörbiger
Written and directed by Ingo Niermann
Graphic design: Boah Kim
Collages and drawings: Mad Smells
Documentation Thuringia: Erik Niedling
Camera, sound, lights: Kilian Immervoll and Anna Sophia Rußmann
Editing: Tiphanie Mall
Sound mix: Robin Michel
Title music: Hannah Weinberger
Text editing: Rainer Wieland

Commissioned and coproduced by steirischer herbst '20 and WIESBADEN BIENNALE
Supported by Fachausschuss Film und Medienkunst Basel-Stadt / Basel-Landschaft

Lulu Obermayer

L'Opra Fatale—An Intervention
2020

Performance

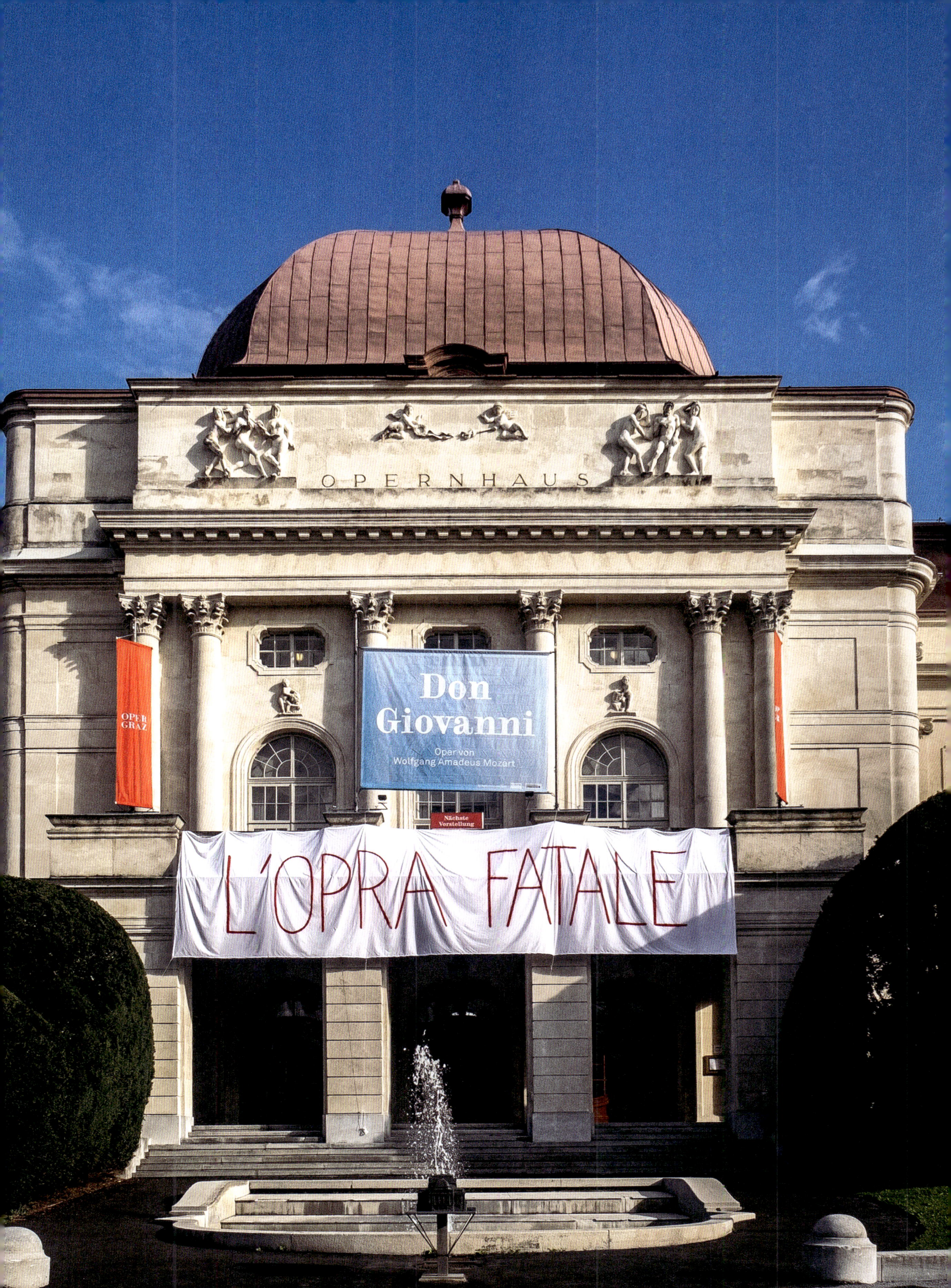
OPERNHAUS
OPER GRAZ
Don Giovanni
Oper von Wolfgang Amadeus Mozart
Nächste Vorstellung
L'OPRA FATALE

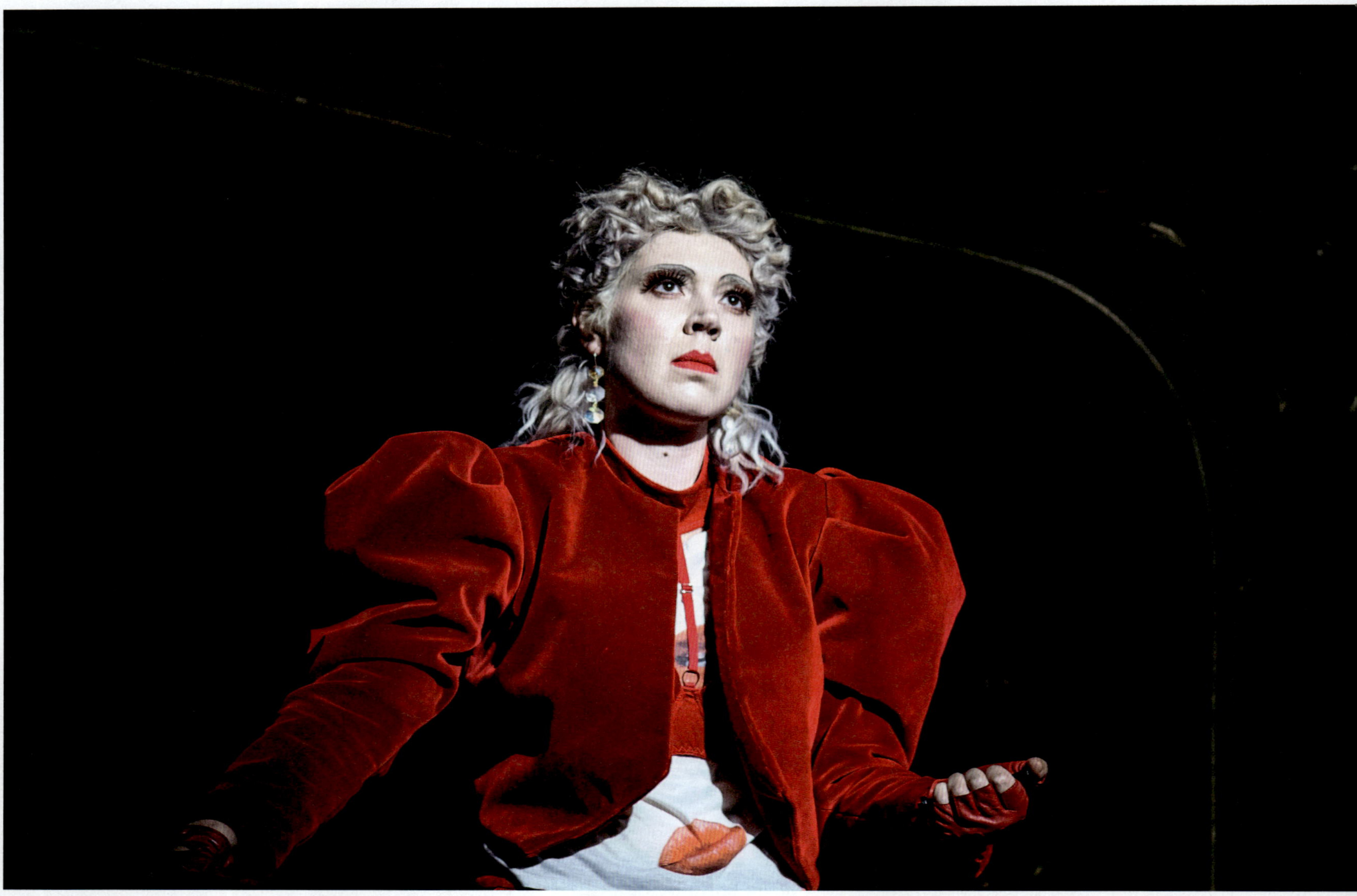

Welcome to *L'Opra Fatale*!

The deadly opera, the deadly work—why deadly?

The curtain rises.

> LADY MACBETH:
> The fatal deed must be done.
> . . .
> What's done cannot be undone.
> — Giuseppe Verdi, *Macbeth*, libretto by Francesco Maria Piave and Andrea Maffei

What do Lady Macbeth, Tosca, and Lucia di Lammermoor have in common? Over the course of their respective dramatic narratives, they all reach for a knife, leaving their stereotypically female roles as victims behind, becoming perpetrators. Yet, the consequences of their actions lead them either to death or madness.

> TOSCA:
> I lived for art, I lived for love, and I never harmed a living creature.
> . . .
> *She sees that Scarpia at this moment is absorbed in writing, and so, with infinite caution, still answering his questions, and never taking her eye from him, she reaches out for the knife.*
> . . .
> *Finally, she is able to grasp the knife. Still watching Scarpia, she hides the knife behind her as she leans against the table. He has now finished writing the pass. He puts his seal upon it and folds the paper, and then, opening his arms, advances towards Tosca to embrace her.*
> . . .
> *Scarpia stretches out an arm towards her, swaying and lurching as he advances, seeking her aid. She eludes him, but is suddenly caught between him and the table, and seeing that he is about to touch her, Tosca thrusts Scarpia back in horror. Scarpia crashes to the floor, shrieking in a voice nearly stifled with blood.*
> — Giacomo Puccini, *Tosca*, libretto by Giuseppe Giacosa and Luigi Illica

Murderers are usually male (both in real life and on stage), yet there are also female murderers. The operatic canon offers about fifty operas where women kill. There are more prominent ones, with characters that we recognize from literature, theater, film, mythology, and others that are more obscure.

Why do women kill? Who do they kill? How do they kill? What are their motives, their reasonings, and the contexts that lead to such fatal actions? Can it be argued that it is the ultimate empowerment beyond juridical, moral, and ethical maxims? What does that imply about the dichotomy of victim/perpetrator? The role of the victim is reversed into the role of the perpetrator. Moving from the passive role into the active one, the female murderer is a phenomenon that violates law, moral, and ethics, yet also breaks out of societal and gender roles. It is a taboo.

Only a few murders are actually happening on stage, like Tosca and Lulu. Others take place offstage. The women kill their babies, they kill men, and they kill women.

Something one always has to keep in mind is that, of course, most canonized operas are written and composed by men, so they are mainly male fantasies of women killing.

Femme Fragile, Femme Fatale, Femme Forte—
Femme Future?
Femme Future!

> The curtain closes; the lights go up.
> . . . This myth is an opera. It is told by singers and an orchestra, and if it suddenly captures you as if someone was telling a story, it is because voice, reduced to roles, surrounds you everywhere and makes a narrative visible for you.
> — Catherine Clément, *Opera or the Undoing of Women*

L'opra fatale.

Let me tell you the story about when I made my first performance in an opera house working with opera singers for the first time.

Only at noon did we enter the Opera Graz, at 17:00 and 20:00 we performed, never having rehearsed in the space before.

It was in 2020, during a pandemic. A theater designated for a capacity of 1,800 occupied by less than 100. We had a lot of space to ourselves, as the current circumstances require a lot of space between us. How do we touch by not touching?

So the in-between spaces revealed themselves, like gaping teeth.

The fatal deed *must* be done.

Lulu Obermayer

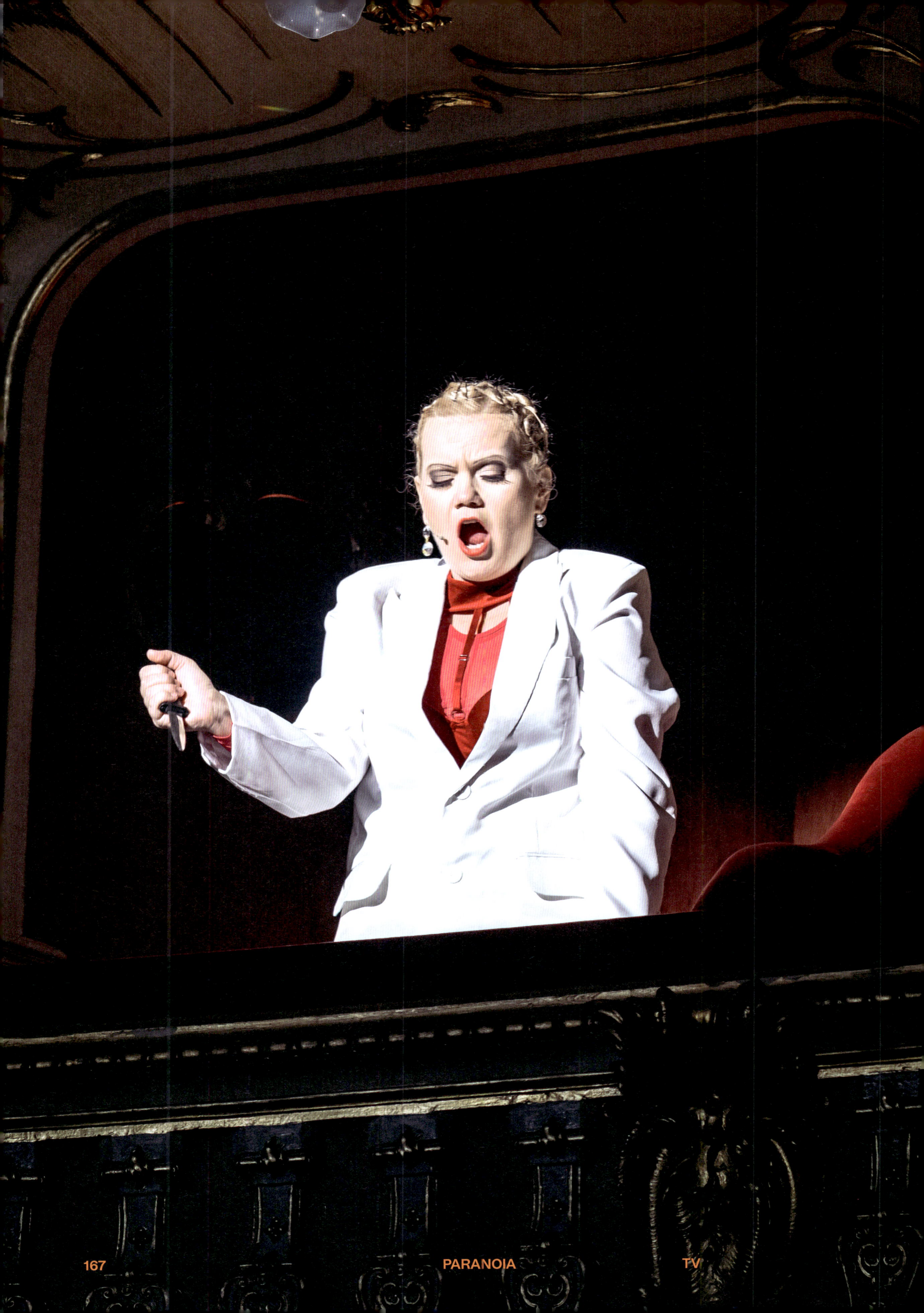

L'Opra Fatale—An Intervention (2020)
Performance, ca. 60 min.,
multiple languages
Oper Graz

Concept, performance: Lulu Obermayer
Composition, performance:
Alexandra Holtsch
Singing, performance: Margareta Klobučar, Corina Koller, Tetiana Miyus
Costumes: Marlene Haase (suit) / Isabel Toccafondi (Graz)
Technical direction: Gretchen Blegen
Model construction: Filipe Serro

Commissioned and produced by steirischer herbst '20
Developed within the framework of Forecast-Skills e.V.
With the kind support of Tanzhaus Zurich

In her artistic practice, Lulu Obermayer engages with female subjectivity, agency, and representation on stage, often in the context of opera. After attending the Professional Performing Arts School, the Lee Strasberg Institute, and the Stella Adler Studio in New York City, she earned her BA in contemporary performance practice from the Royal Conservatoire of Scotland and graduated from the MA program Solo/Dance/Authorship at Inter-University Center for Dance Berlin (HZT).

Lulu Obermayer's performances have been presented at Münchner Kammerspiele; HAU, Berlin; Highways Performance Space, Santa Monica; and Bâtard Festival, Brussels, among other places. *L'Opra Fatale* was her first work situated in an opera house and her directorial debut. In 2020, she was nominated for the Caroline Neuber Award.

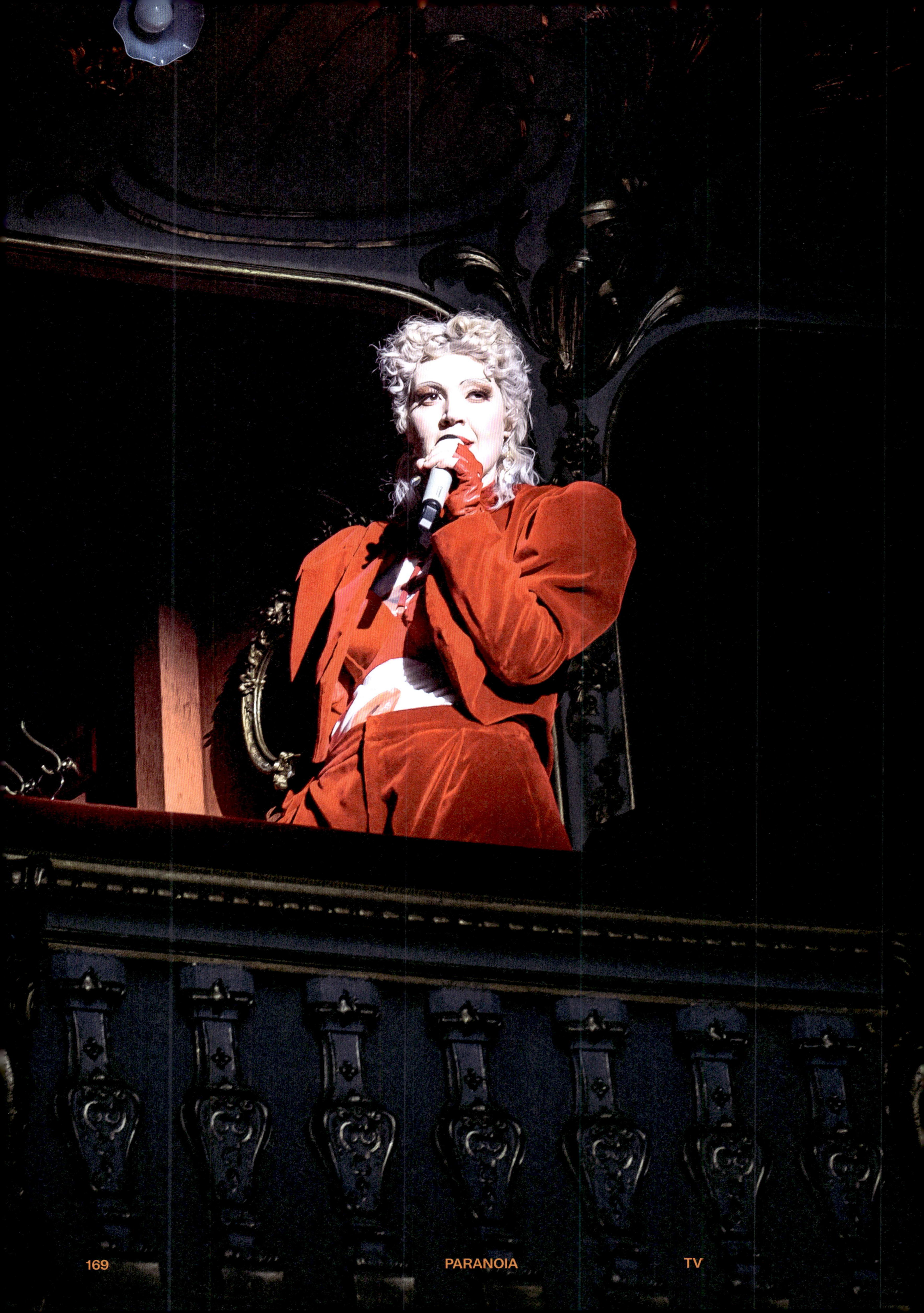

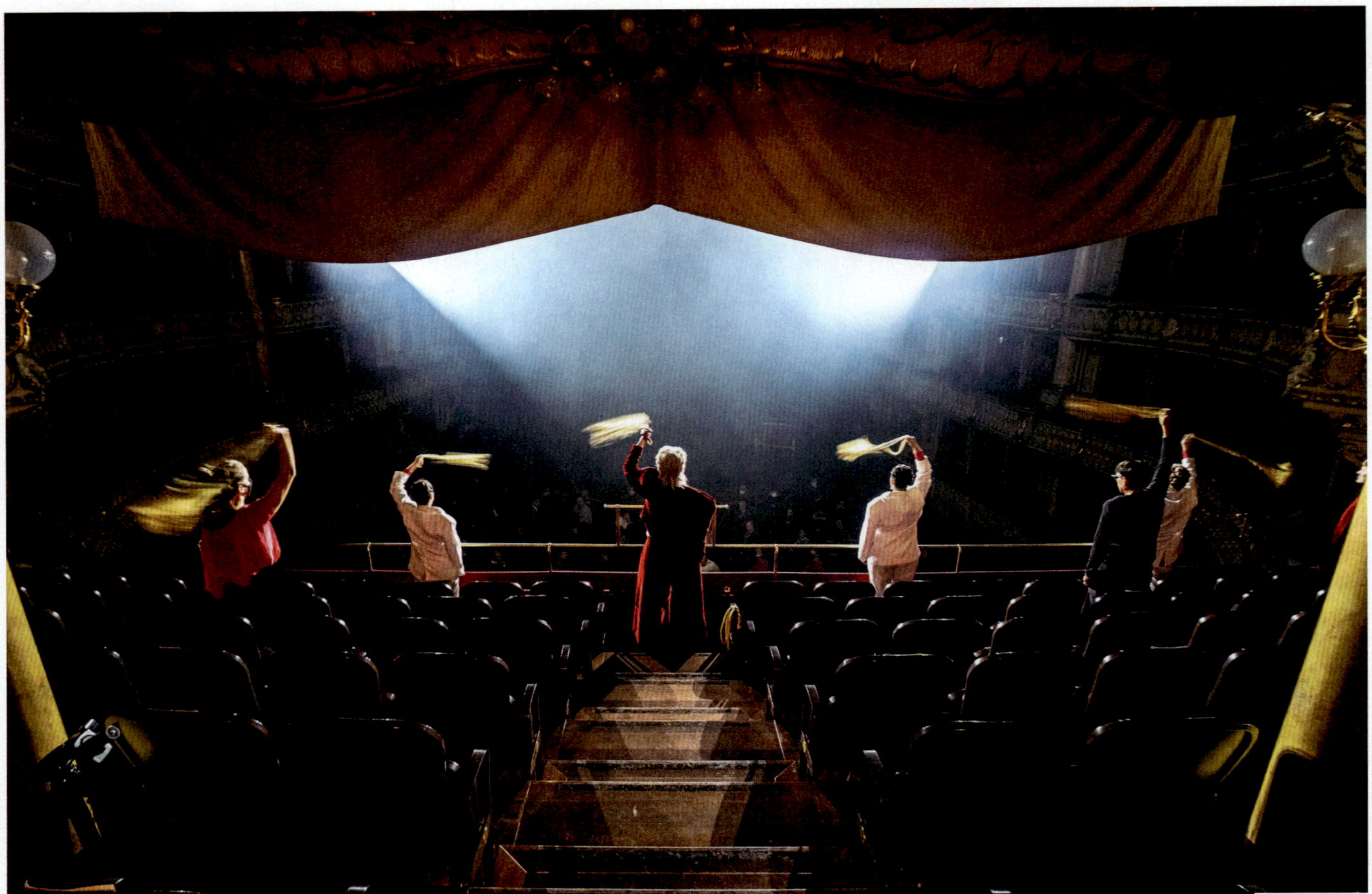

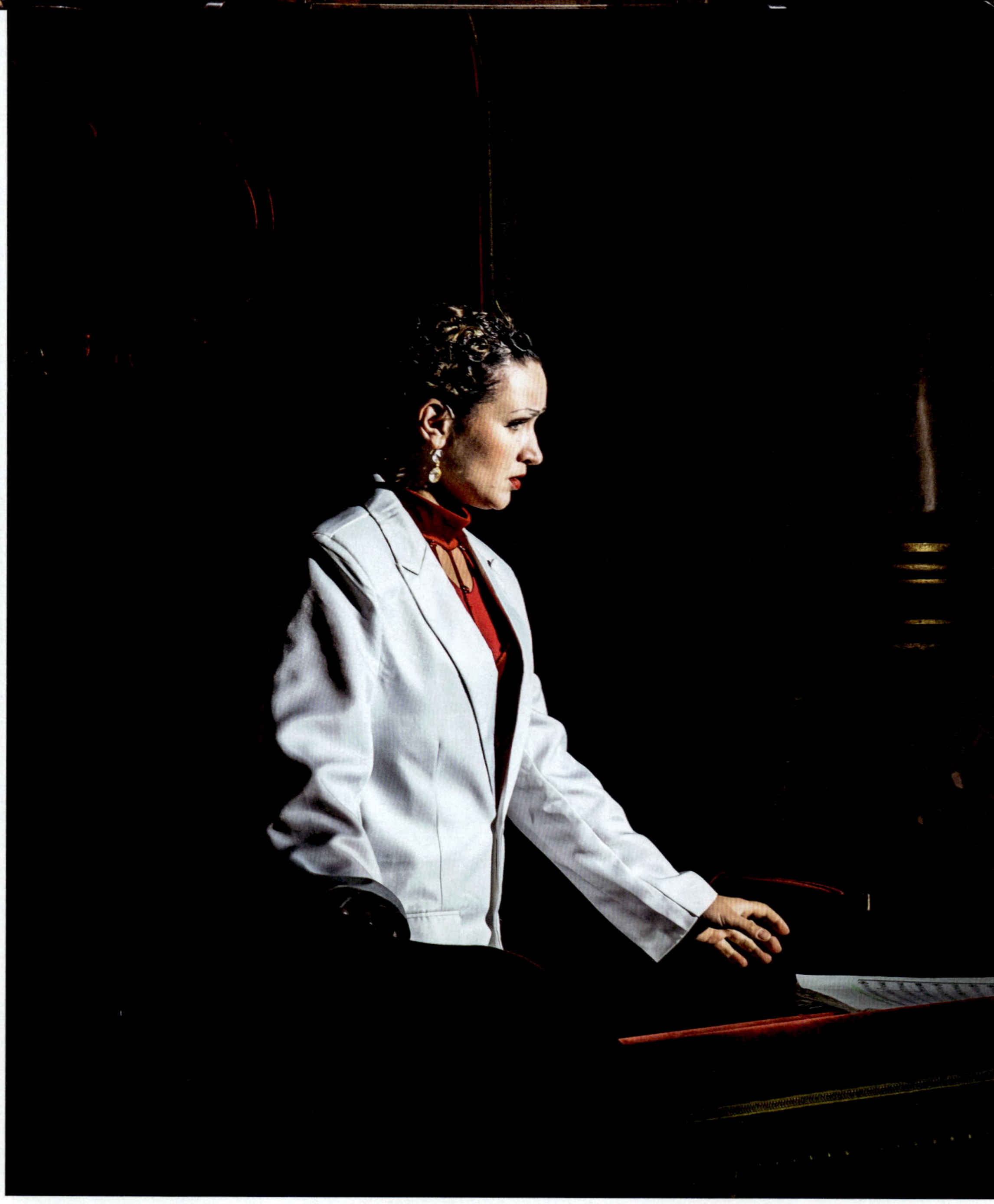

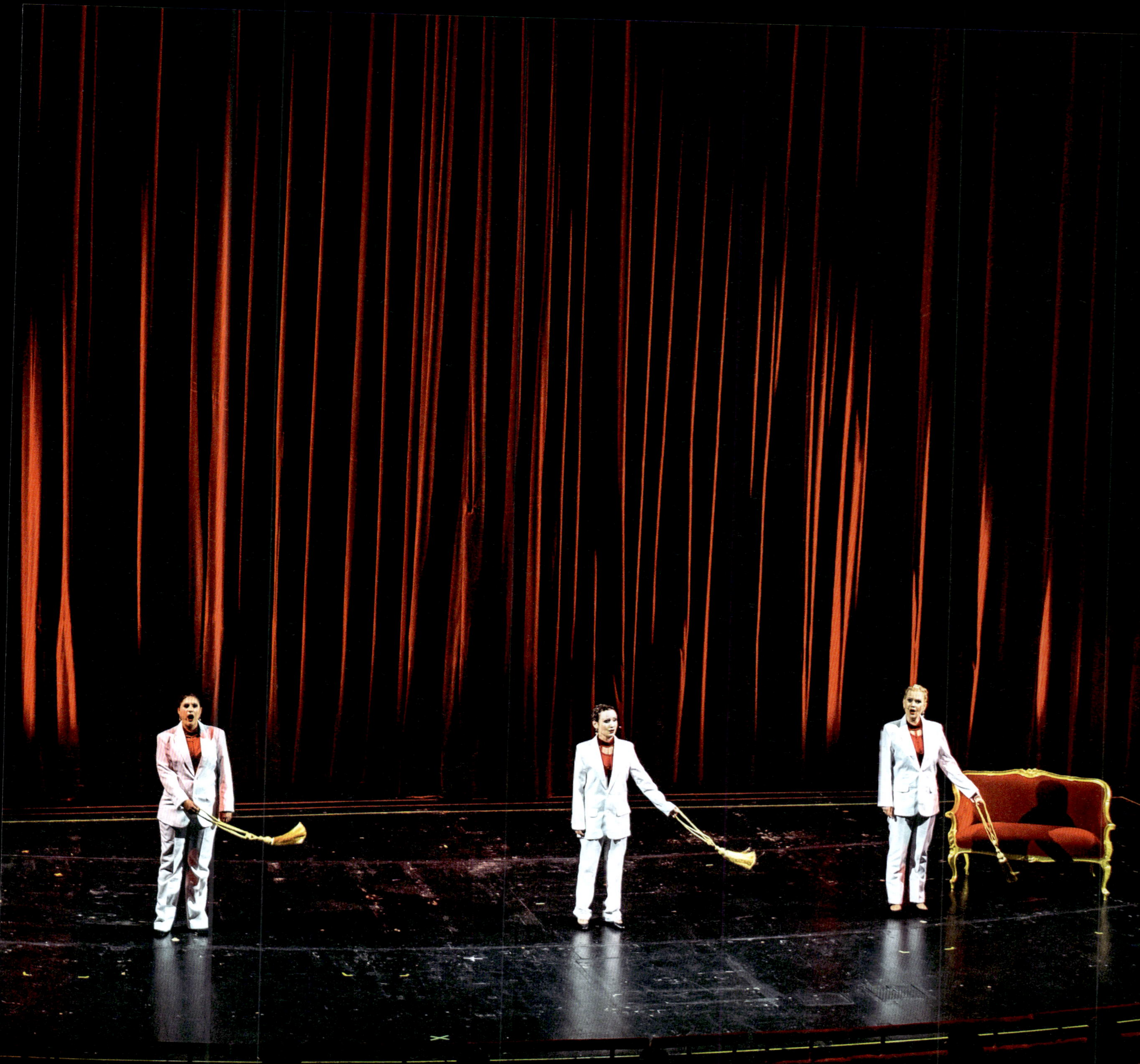

Ahmet Öğüt

Artworks Made at Home
2020

Video

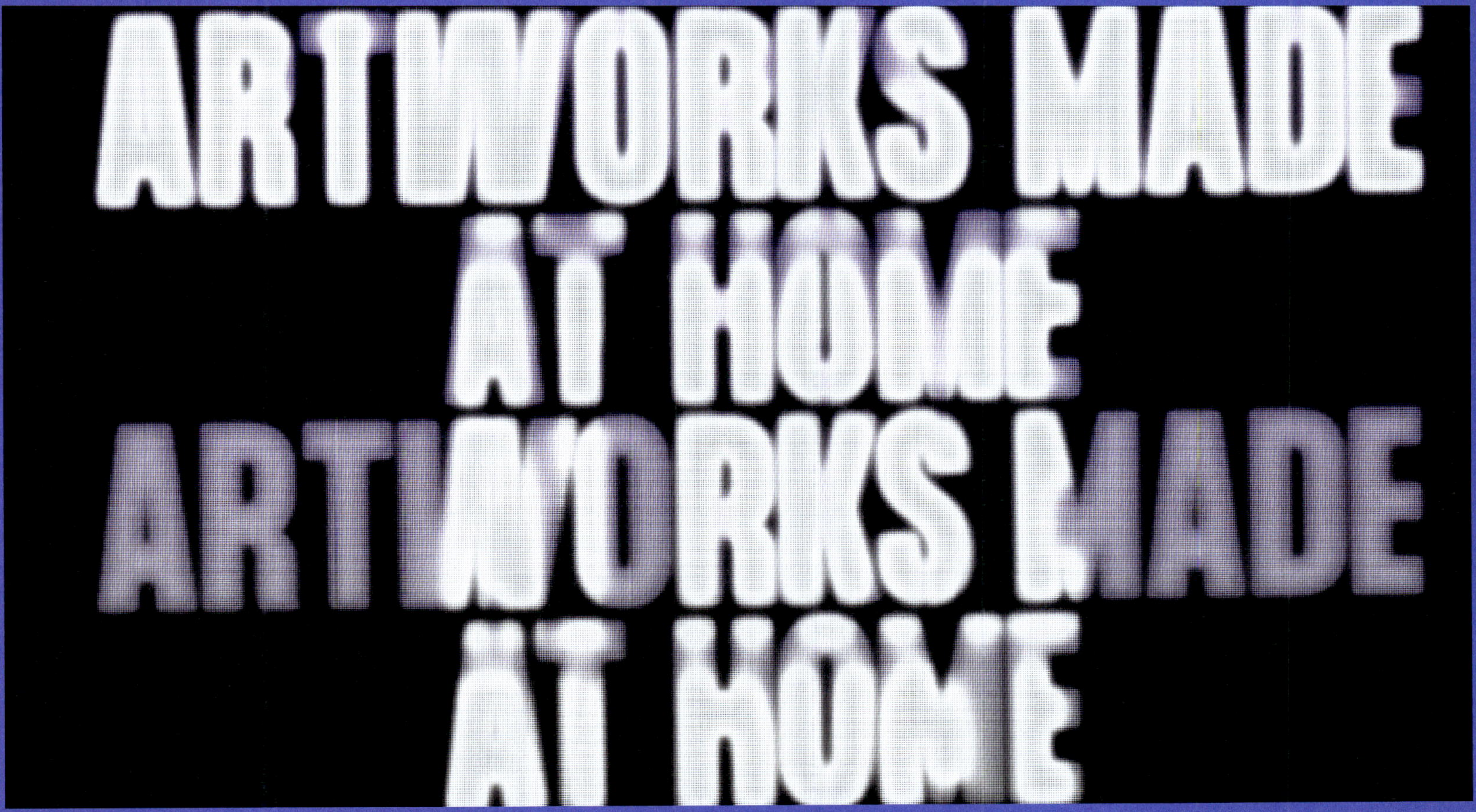
ARTWORKS MADE
AT HOME
ARTWORKS MADE
AT HOME

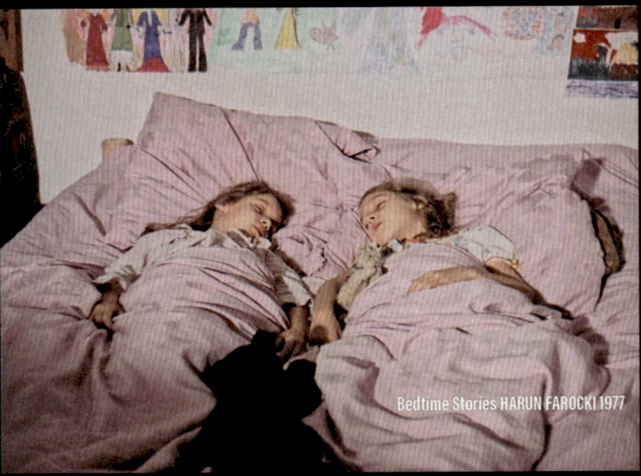
Bedtime Stories HARUN FAROCKI 1977

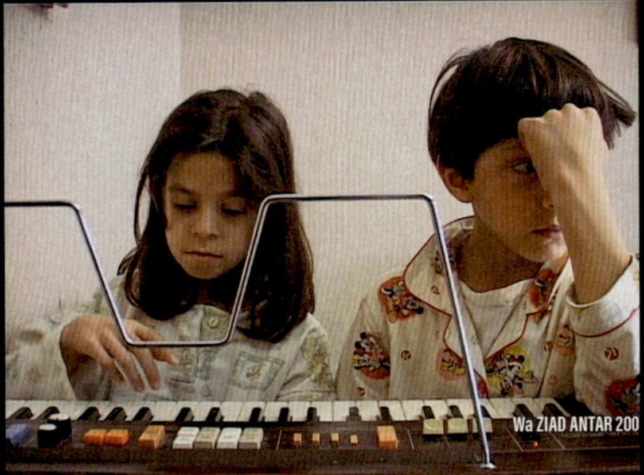
Wa ZIAD ANTAR 200

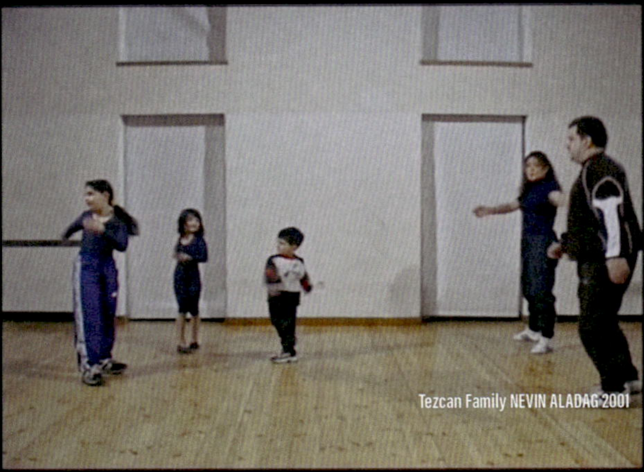
Tezcan Family NEVIN ALADAG 2001

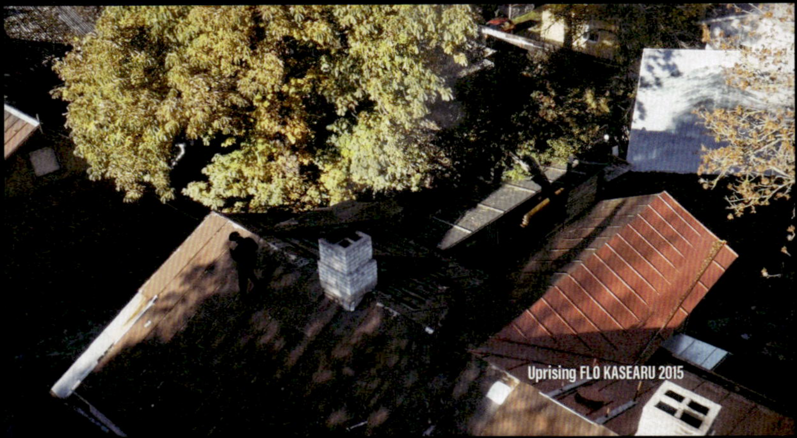
Uprising FLO KASEARU 2015

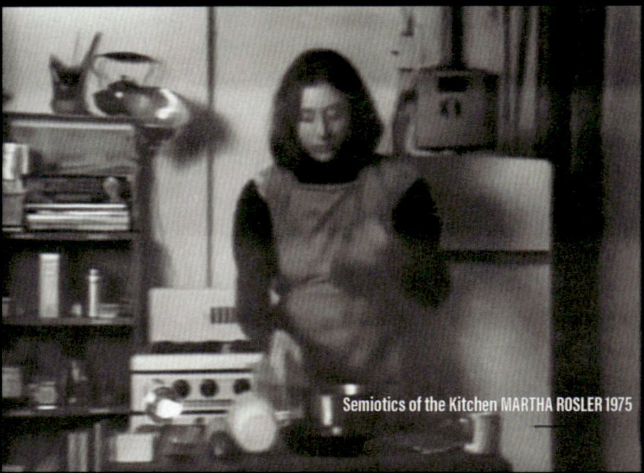
Semiotics of the Kitchen MARTHA ROSLER 1975

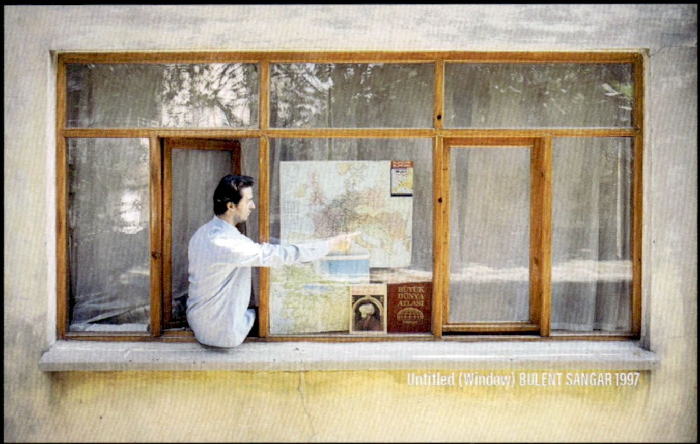

Untitled (Window) BULENT SANGAR 1997

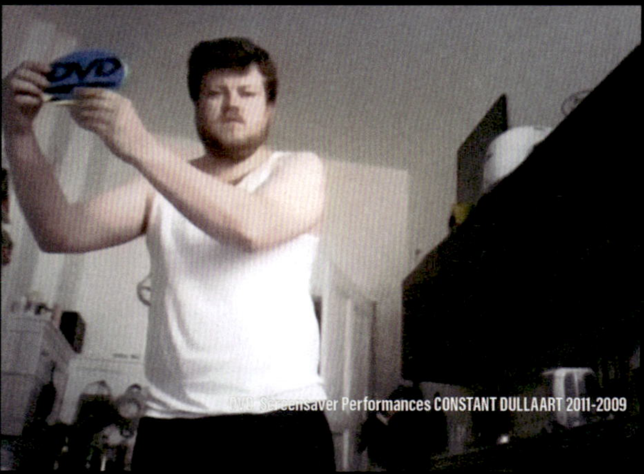

DVD Screensaver Performances CONSTANT DULLAART 2011-2009

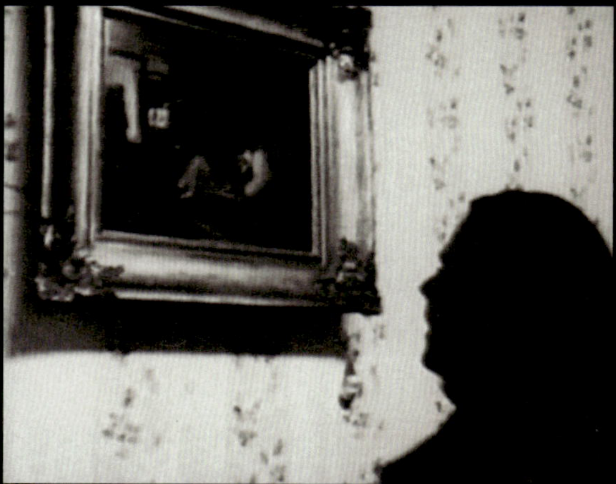

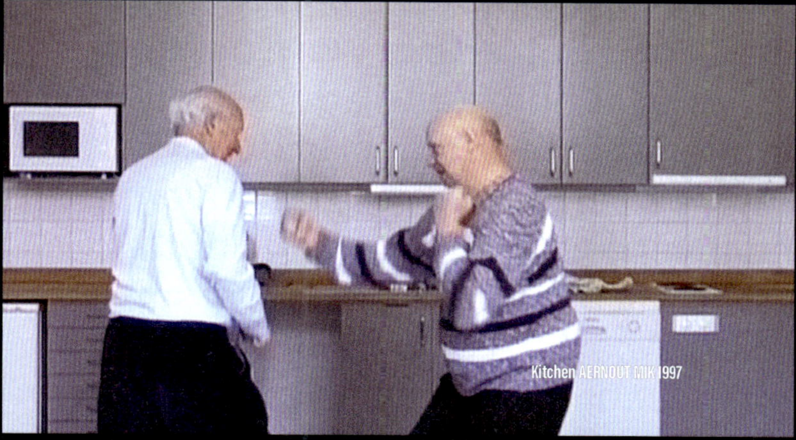
Kitchen AERNOUT MIK 1997

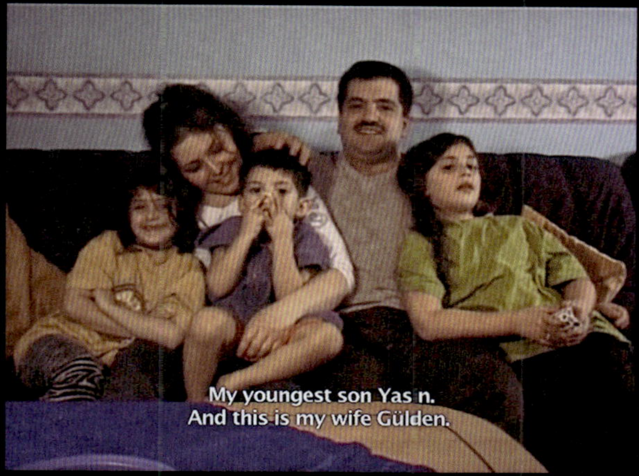

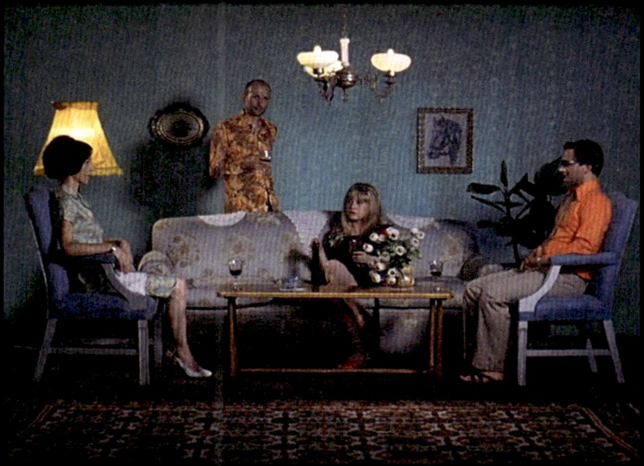

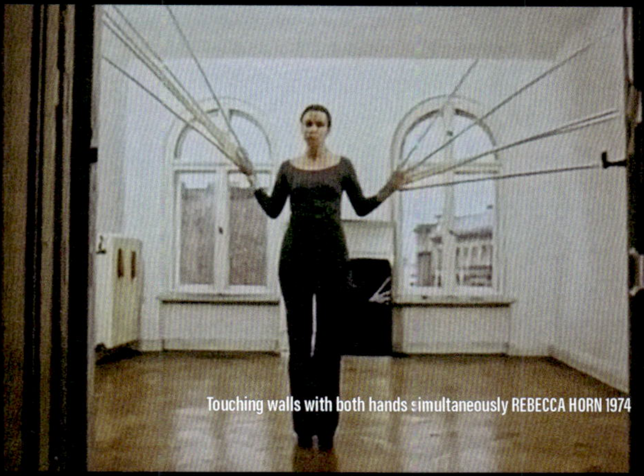
Touching walls with both hands simultaneously REBECCA HORN 1974

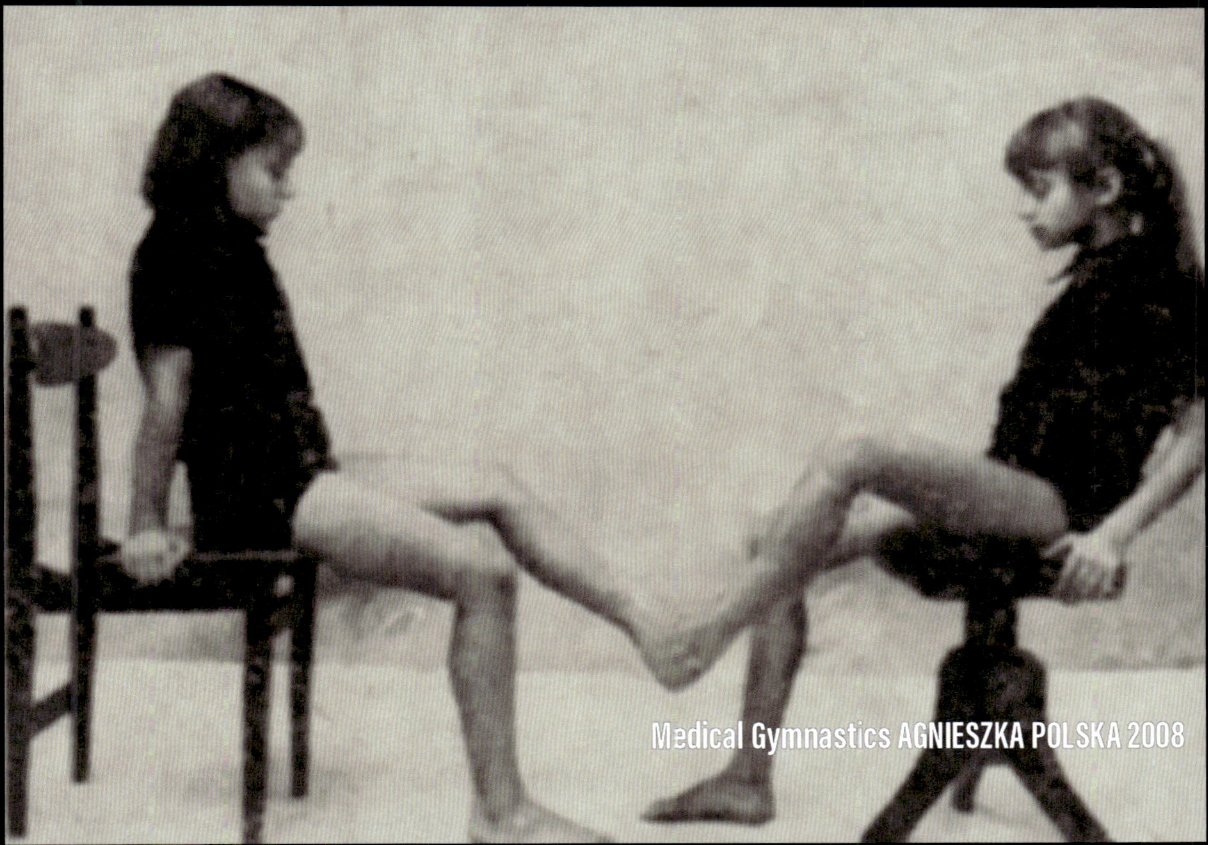
Medical Gymnastics AGNIESZKA POLSKA 2008

Born in 1981, in Silvan, Diyarbakir, Ahmet Öğüt lives and works in Amsterdam and Istanbul. An internationally renowned sociocultural initiator and conceptual artist, Öğüt consistently seeks out collaborators from outside of the art world, finding unique ways to grapple with complex social issues ranging from migration to civil unrest with a sense of humor.

He works across different media and has exhibited widely, including solo exhibitions at Wei-Ling Contemporary, Kuala Lumpur; Van Abbemuseum, Eindhoven; Kunsthal Charlottenborg, Copenhaguen; Chisenhale Gallery, London; Berkeley Art Museum; and Kunsthalle Basel.

He has also participated in numerous group exhibitions, including *In the Presence of Absence*, Stedelijk Museum, Amsterdam (2020); *Zero Gravity*, Nam SeMA, Seoul Museum of Art (2019); Echigo Tsumari Art Triennale (2018); the British Art Show 8 (2017–15); the 13th Biennale de Lyon (2015); Performa 13, New York (2013); the 7th Liverpool Biennial (2012); the 12th Istanbul Biennial (2011); the New Museum Triennial, New York (2009); and the 5th Berlin Biennial for Contemporary Art (2008).

Öğüt was awarded the Visible Award for *The Silent University* (2013); the special prize of the Future Generation Art Prize (2012); the De Volkskrant Beeldende Kunst Prijs 2011; and the Kunstpreis Europas Zukunft (2010). He corepresented Turkey at the 53rd Venice Biennale (2009).

Artworks Made at Home (2020)
Video, ca. 26 min., English
Online

Commissioned by steirischer herbst '20
Coproduced by steirischer herbst '20 and ULTRAVIOLET Film Prodüksiyon
With the kind support of SAHA Association

Long before the global pandemic ever broke out, artists were making artworks at home and addressing their domestic surroundings. In doing so, they've been continually discovering and inventing new meanings of this "home" as a purportedly universal notion. Apartments become studios and museums. Kitchens and sleeping areas become politically loaded terrain, spaces for action, and places to subvert the semiotics of everyday life, through humor, and not without a strong dose of melancholia. Ahmet Öğüt's new documentary film-essay for *Paranoia TV* explores this history and at the same time presents a fascinating example for a new curatorial format, a kind of exhibition-in-a-film that treats cinematic duration itself like an exhibition space waiting to be filled.

Öğüt circles around scenes from works of video art by Anri Sala, Nina Yuen, Ulay, Lala Raščić, Harun Farocki, Martha Rosler, Constant Dullaart, Cengiz Tekin, Jonas Lund, Agnieszka Polska, Kuang-Yu Tsui, Nevin Aladağ, Hussein Chalayan, Aernout Mik, Ana Hušman, Ziad Antar, and many others, weaving in and out of works poetically and atmospherically. Save for a curatorial statement at the beginning, there is no voice-over commentary. Instead, much like in a real-life exhibition, meanings arise through the juxtaposition of images, fragments, and impressions. Öğüt shows how artists were anticipating the lockdown and its redefinition of domestic space—which for many becomes the launching pad for new and daring artistic experiments.

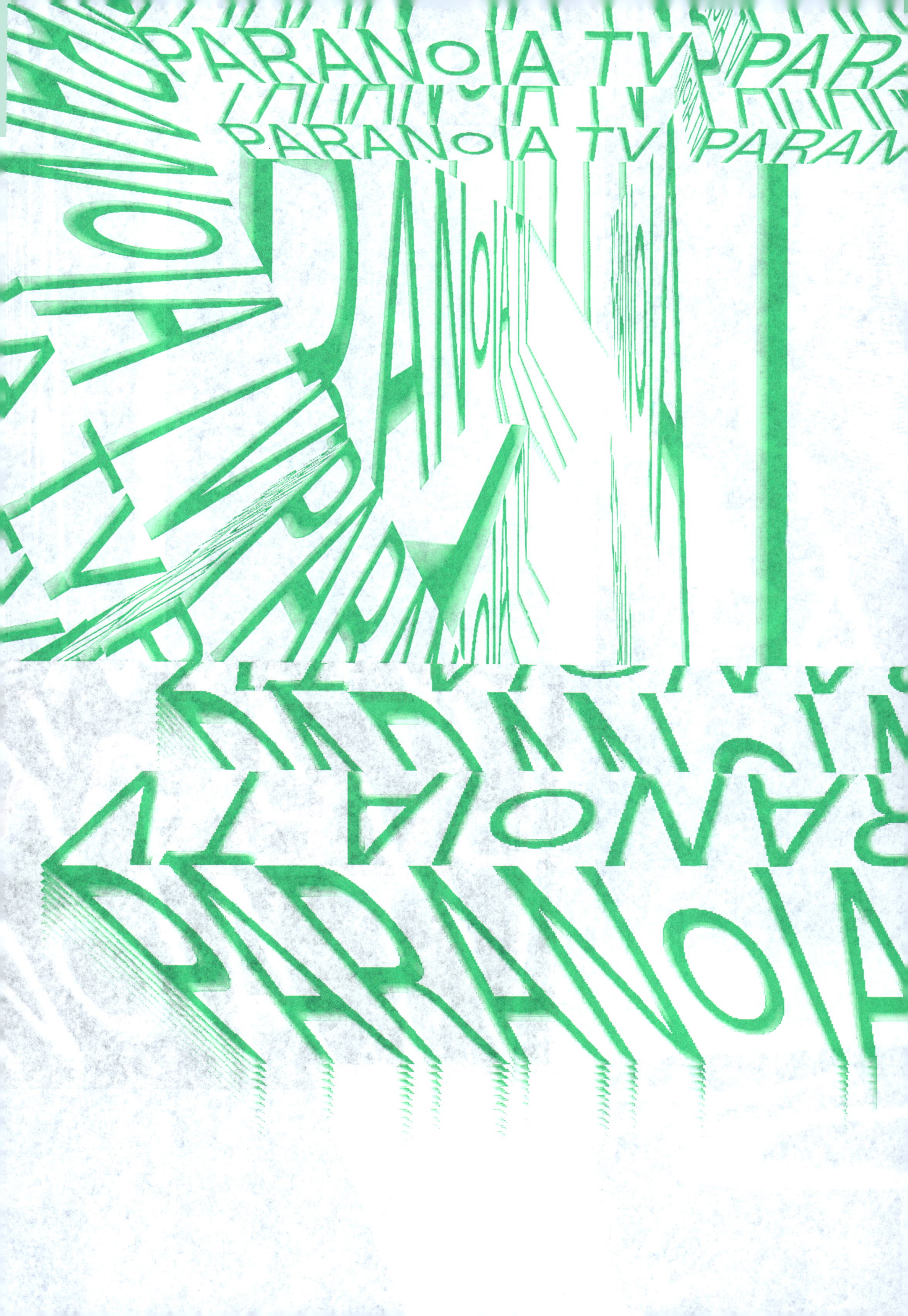
PARANOIA TV
PARANOIA TV

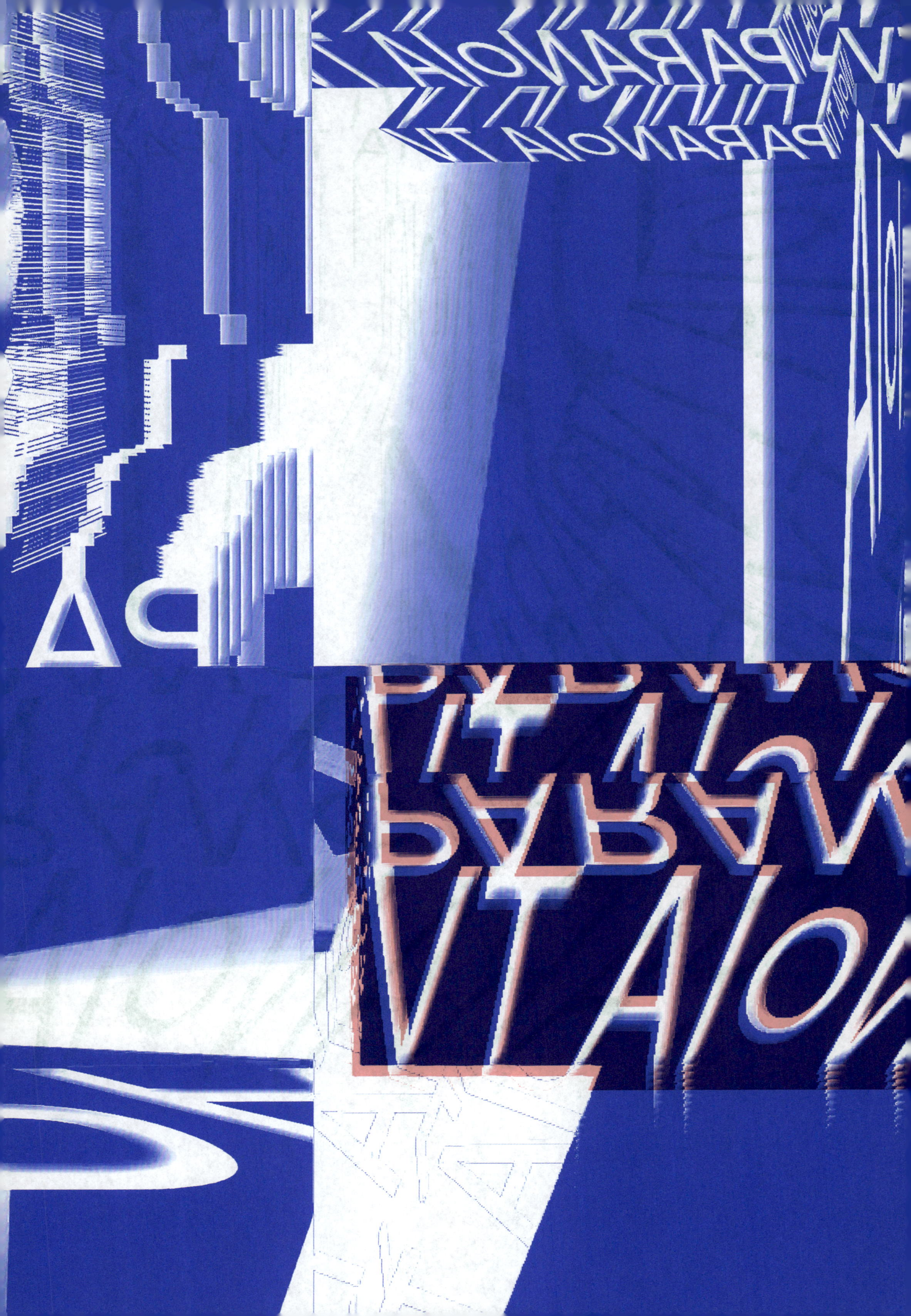
PARANOIA

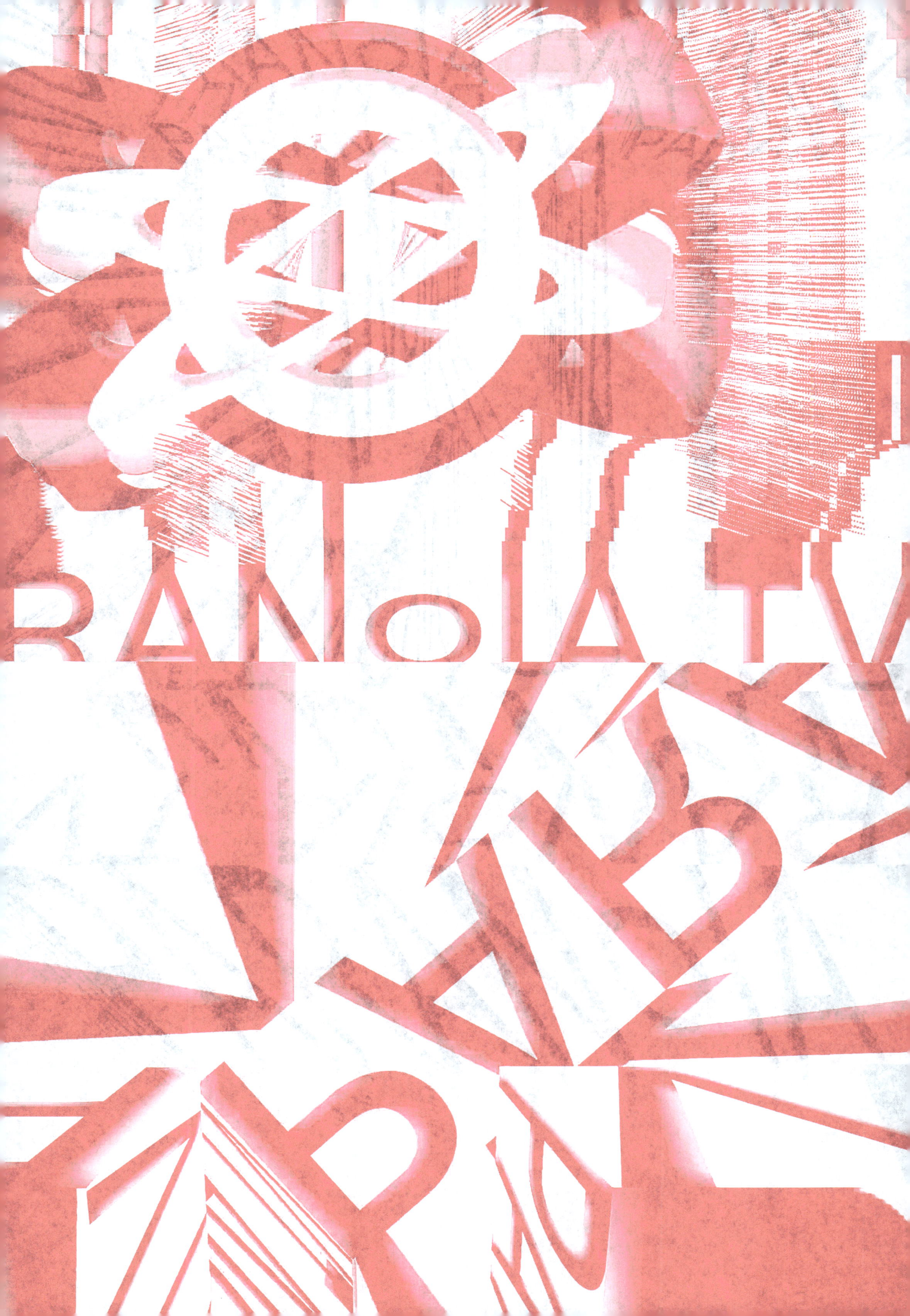
RANOIA TV

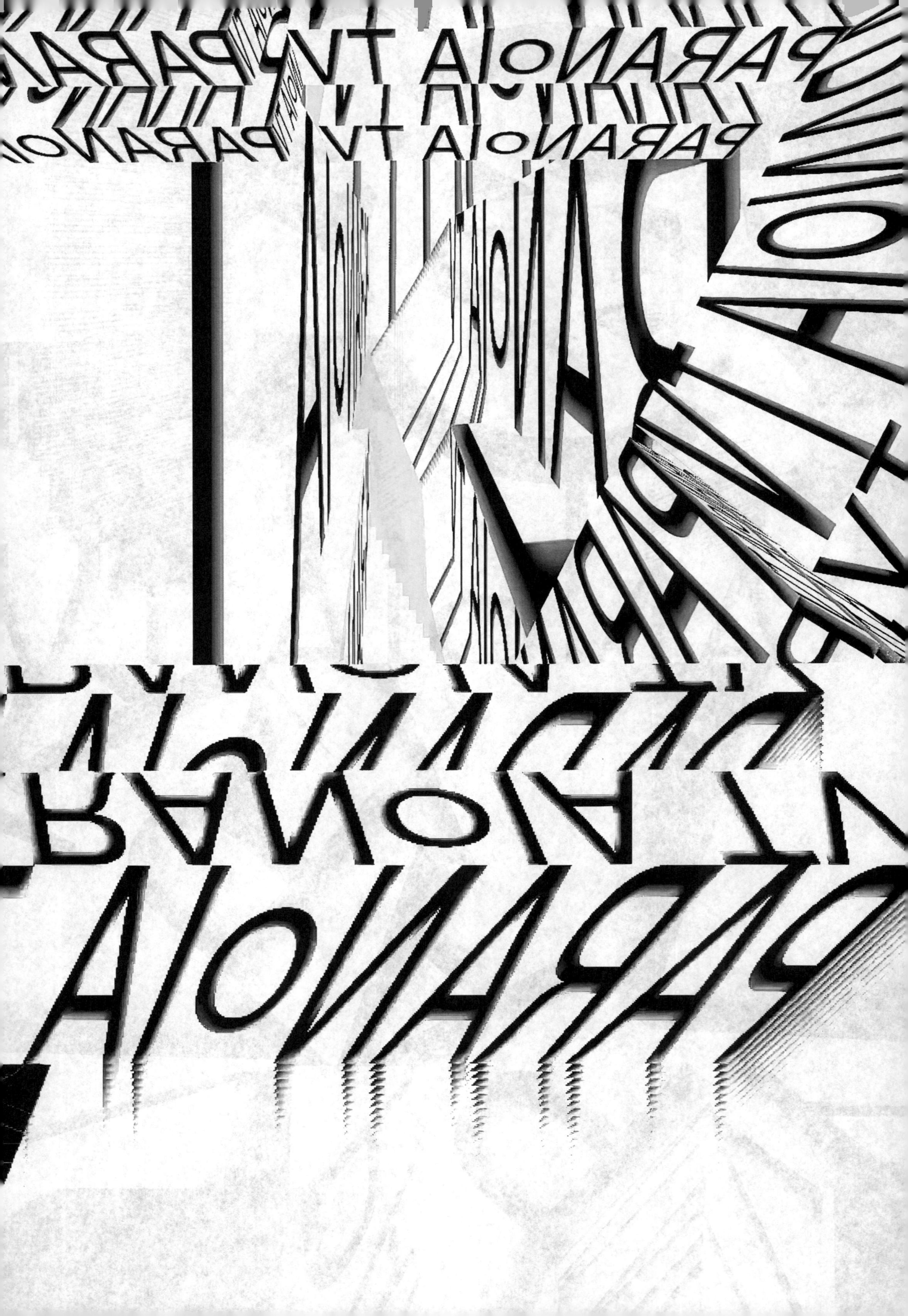
PARANOIA TV

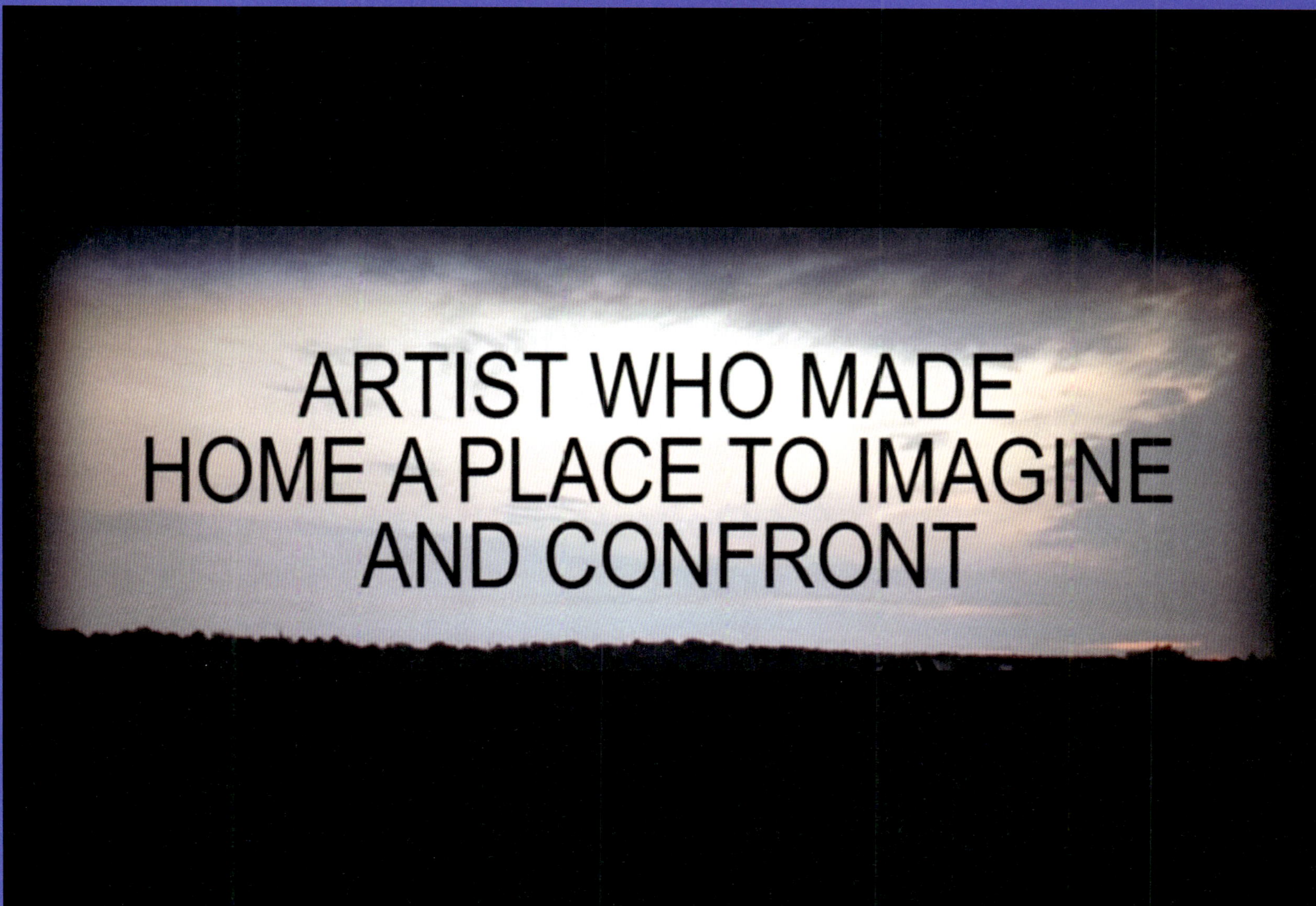
ARTIST WHO MADE
HOME A PLACE TO IMAGINE
AND CONFRONT

Diederik Peeters

Red Herring
2011

The Dr. Delusion Show
2020

Performance / Video series

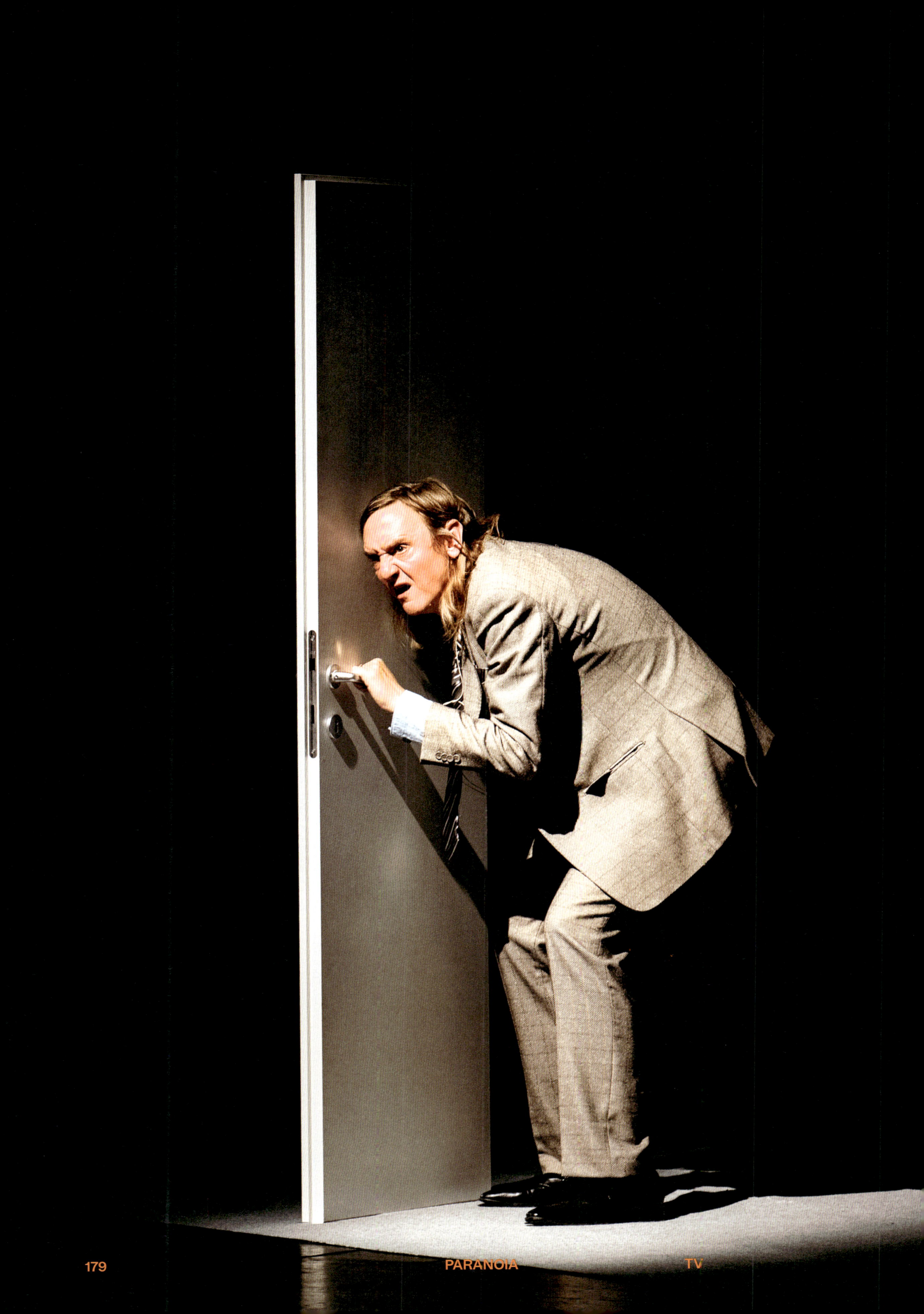

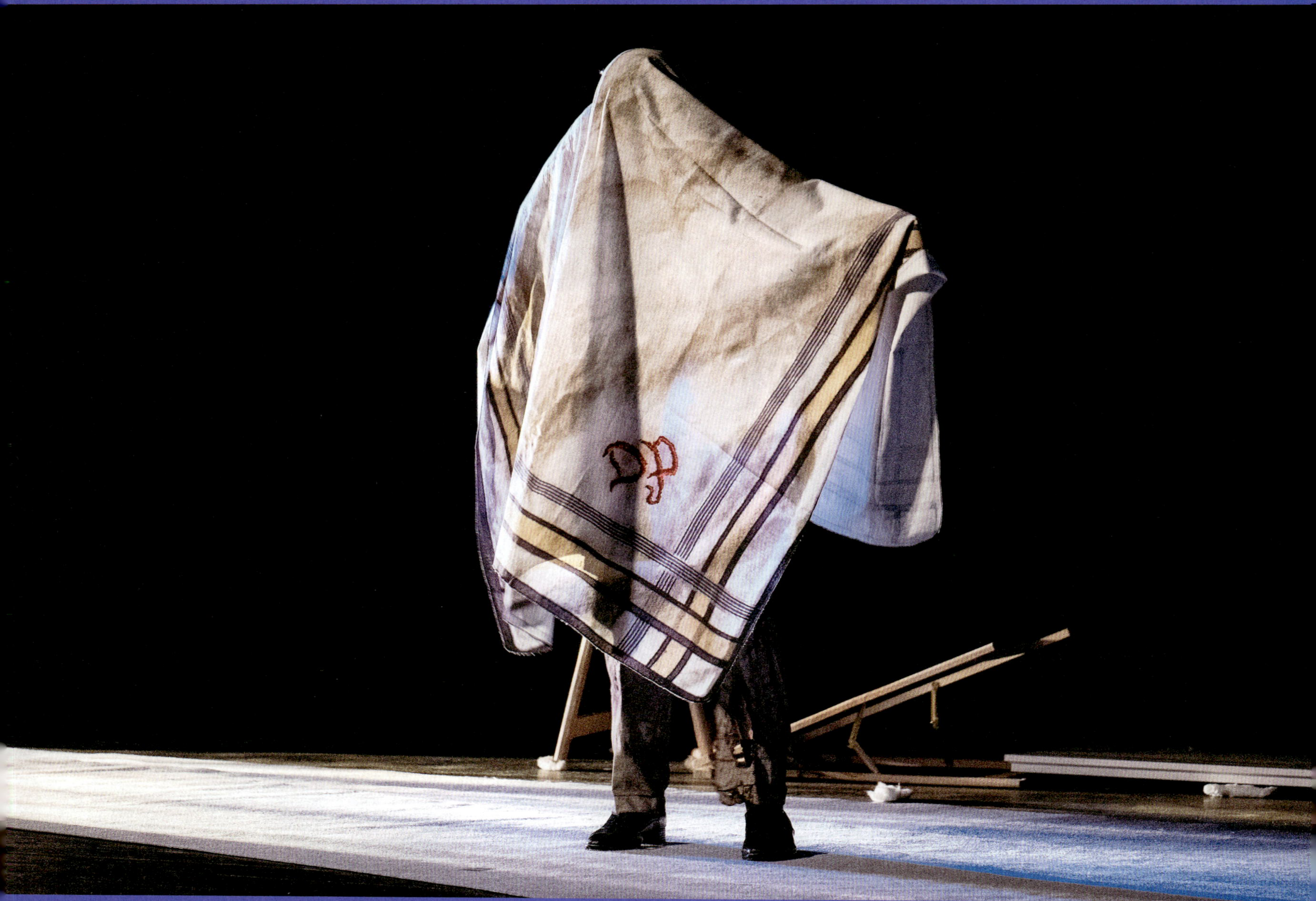

Short Note on the Therapeutic Effect of Resurrecting Ghosts

Diederik Peeters is afraid. He has a morbid fear of germs and contamination, is terrified of heights, and scared of ghosts and conspiracies. He suffers from severe paranoia, and is tormented—last but not least—by the holy terror of failing.

This is how I announced *Red Herring* when it premiered in 2011. When I was asked to revive the show nine years later, I almost chickened out. Not having performed it for a long time, I wasn't sure how it had aged, and the prospect of being confronted with a younger version of myself made me nervous. But the festival insisted, and so, despite my initial reluctance, I was introduced to the dark art of resurrecting the ghost of an old show.

At first I was so busy trying to paternalistically correct the stupidities invented by my younger self that I didn't even notice how that ghost was slowly coming back to life. And it was only after the second performance that I started to understand how the show resonates today.

It dawned on me that it had somehow become more "accessible." Ten years ago its caricatures were considered weird and eccentric. But today everyone can relate to their ridiculous obsessions with irrational fears, conspiracy theories, and the fear of contamination. Whether we like it or not, these things have become very real and part of our daily lives.

A spectator told me that the show put all this into perspective. As if the audience were looking into a mirror reflecting society's fixation on germs and contamination and all the fears that come with it.

In 2011, my text ended: "In *Red Herring* Peeters presents a series of half-abstract and semi-mental scenes, loosely inspired by the comical potential of irrational and other fears. Drenched in cold sweat he tries to overcome his obsessional and paranoid traits."

I'm quite sure the show hasn't helped anyone overcome anything, but when we were done stuffing the old ghost back into its flight cases, another spectator told me that there had indeed been something comical but also cathartic about watching it. They felt relieved somehow, as if a weight had fallen off their shoulders.

Only then I realized the therapeutic effect of resurrecting ghosts.

Diederik Peeters

Dr. Delusion and Dr. Pepper: The Elasticity of Reality

When I was commissioned to do a TV series, I decided to focus on my long-lasting fascination with certain neurological conditions. In praise of neurodiversity, every episode portrays another "delusional disorder": the Fregoli syndrome, the Döppelganger syndrome, and the Cotard syndrome.

People suffering from these delusions demonstrate specific neurological malfunctions resulting in an altered perception of reality. Yet, apart from this, they continue to function normally.

Even when confronted with facts that contradict their intimate beliefs, they keep on reasoning, often surprisingly supplely. This is the very essence of a delusion and these medical conditions thus raise the question of normative perception and—as Dr. Delusion puts it—the elasticity of reality.

To depict the inner workings of these delusions, I experimented with an optical illusion known as "Pepper's ghost," named after its supposed inventor, Dr. Pepper, which was mainly used to conjure ghosts on stage in late 19th-century theaters.

The illusion is simple but efficient. We experience it on a daily basis when we look out of a window in the evening: we see the outside, but if the light is right, we also see the inside reflected in the windowpane, the reflections of the interior behind us overlapping with the image of the exterior in front of us.

What is so fascinating about this illusion is the confusion between looking at a thing and looking at its reflection. Objects are conjured up in front of our eyes, and it's impossible to tell whether they are really there or merely ghostly projections. The perceptual confusion becomes almost ontological.

The trick literally makes the invisible visible and vice versa. It shows things that aren't actually there and hides things that are. Effectively altering our perception, it proposes alternate ways of looking at the world, as if Pepper's ghost revealed hidden dimensions and secret layers of reality—and asked whether delusions should be considered delusional at all.

Diederik Peeters

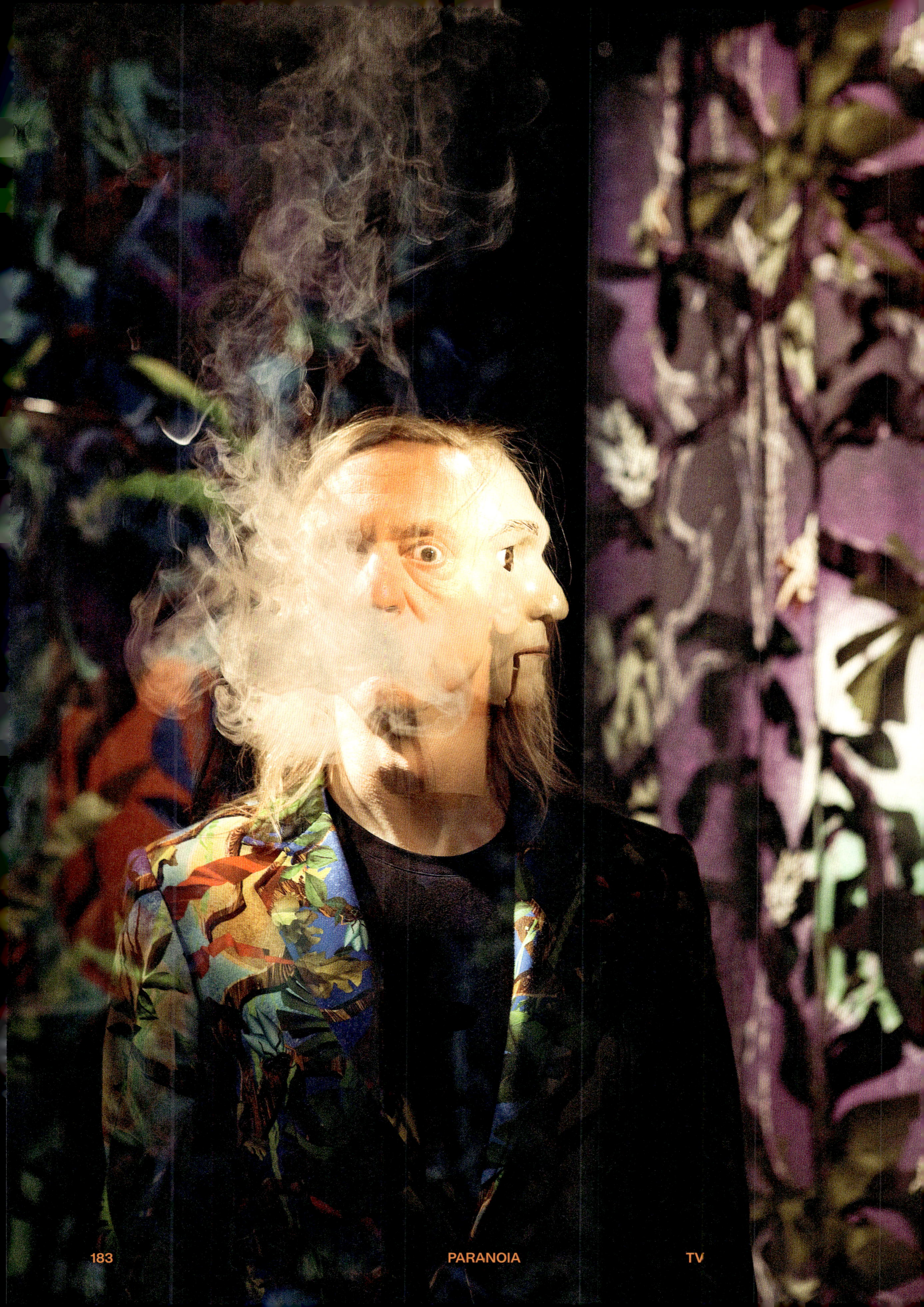

Despite a degree in visual arts, it's above all in the labyrinth of the stage arts that Diederik Peeters got lost. He staged several shows and performances such as *Chuck Norris Doesn't Sleep, He Waits . . .*, *Red Herring*, and *Apparitions*. With Kate McIntosh and Hans Bryssinck he founded SPIN, a support and reflection platform based in Brussels. He is also affiliated as artistic researcher to the School of Arts in Ghent, conducting the research project The Futurology of Cooperation.

Red Herring (2011)
Performance, ca. 60 minutes, English
Orpheum

Music and sound: Lieven Dousselaere
Set: Sarah & Charles
Lighting: Henri-Emmanuel Doublier
Assistant lighting: Ivan Fatjo
Costumes: Christoph Hefti and Carmel Peritore
Reflectors: Bill Aitchison and Philippe
Production management: Rina Govers / Marion Le Guerroué

Produced by SPIN and L'Amicale
2020 renewal in collaboration with steirischer herbst '20

The Dr. Delusion Show (2020)
Video series, 3 episodes, ca. 13 min. each, English
Online

Camera and editing: Luca Mattei
Lighting: Henri-Emmanuel Doublier
Script, production, and artistic advice: Marion Le Guerroué
Performer: Jonas Chéreau
Logistics: Thomas Riou
Makeup: Ben Personne
Original music: Grégoire Blanc and Lieven Dousselaere
Additional music: Massimo Carozzi

Commissioned by steirischer herbst '20
Produced by SPIN and L'Amicale in coproduction with steirischer herbst '20
Thanks to Kaaitheater, Brussels
With the kind support of the Flemish Government

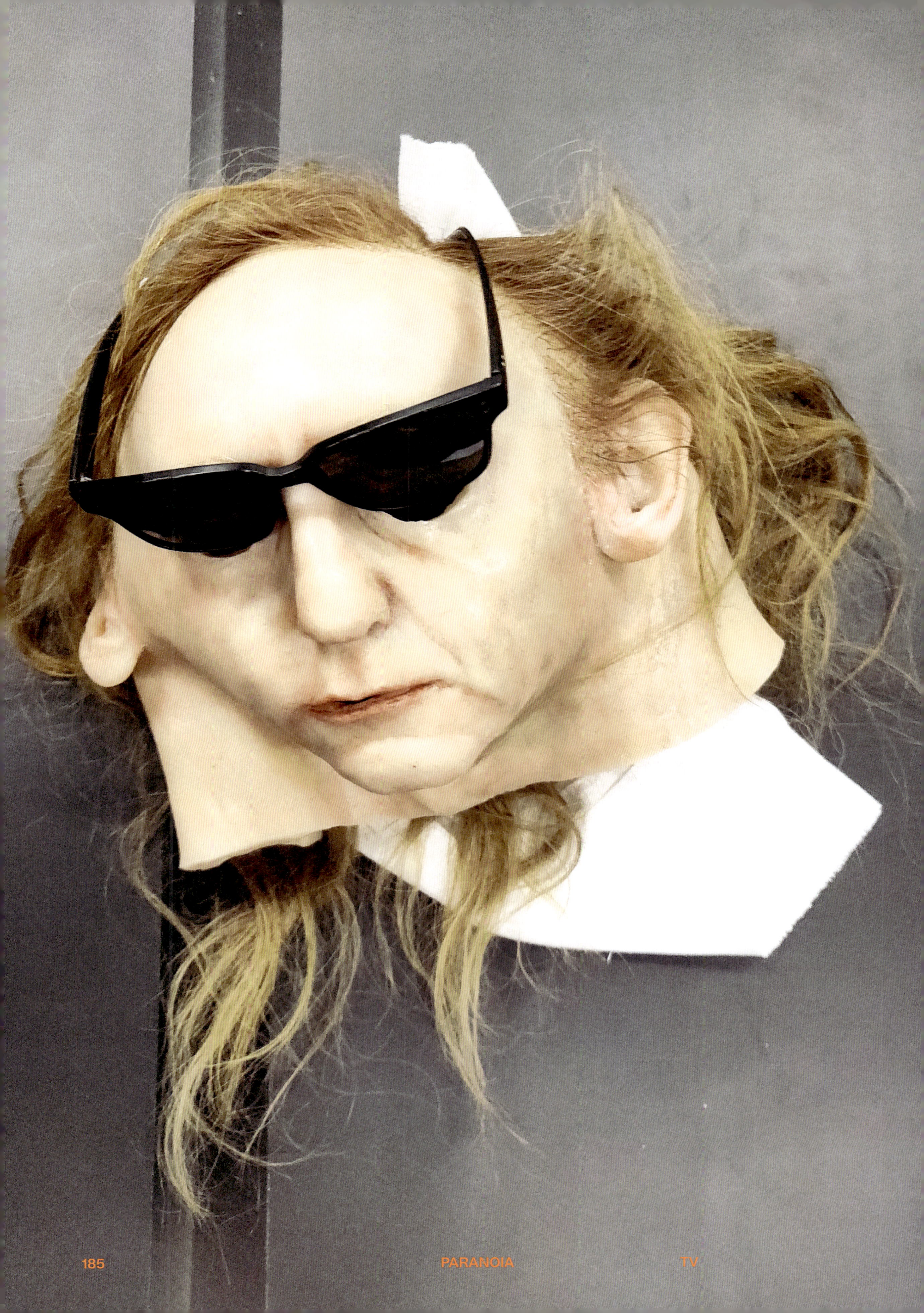

Joanna Piotrowska

Untitled
2020

Newspaper

Pustostan

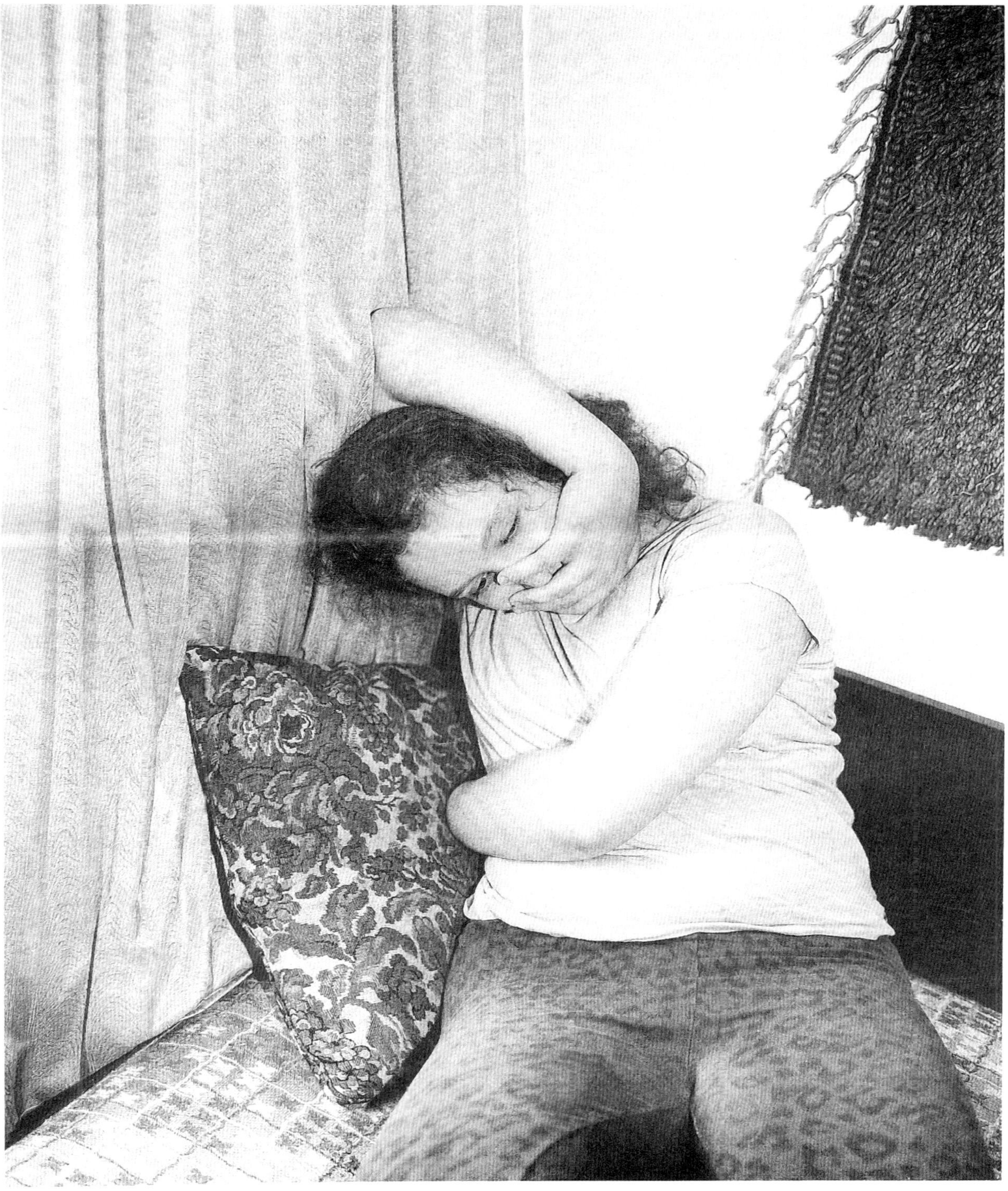

1 1 1

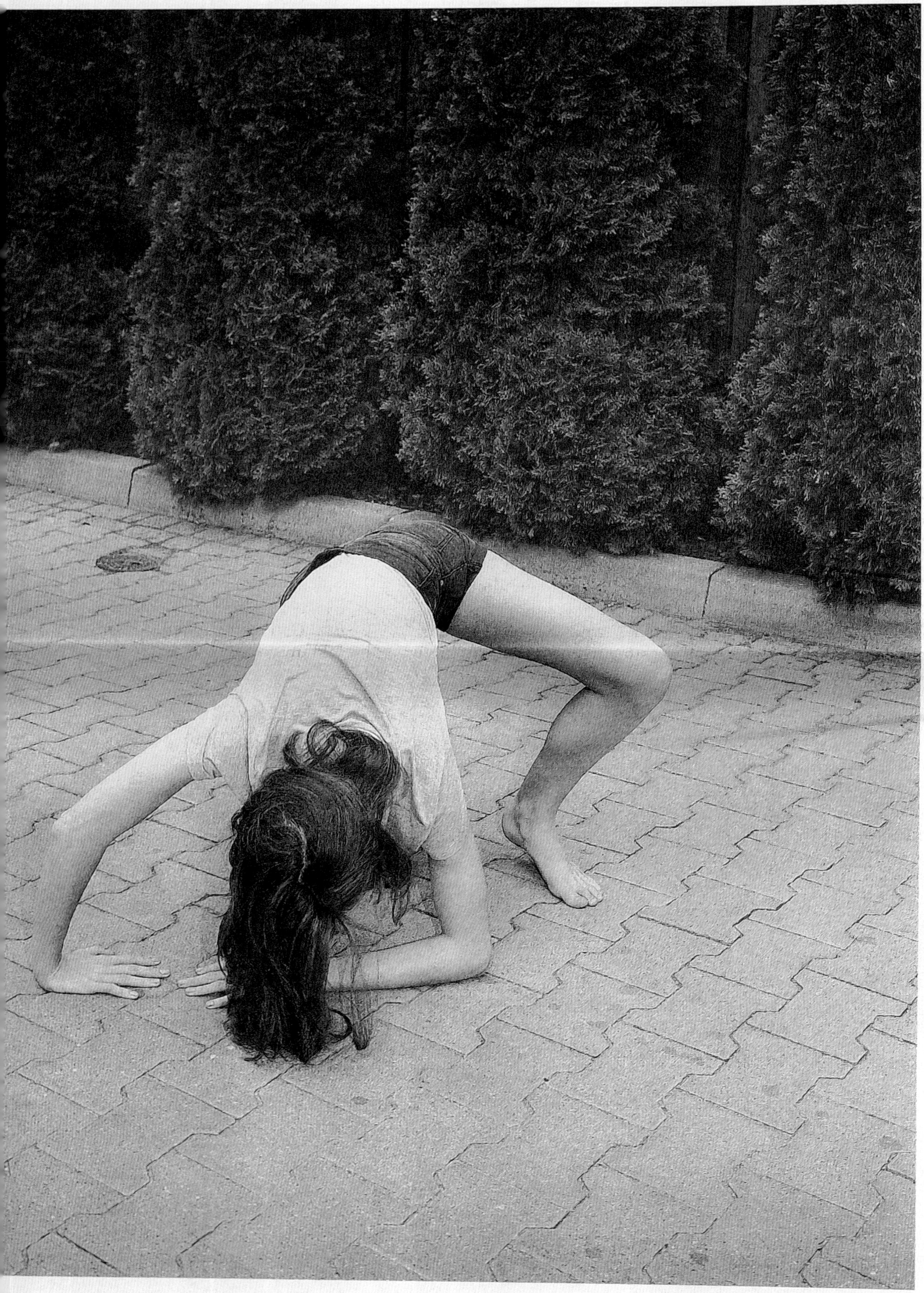

Pustostan

We struggle like this daily, shoulder to shoulder, with the two mighty struggles of home confinement: grandma against the infinitude of the mess, me against the infinitude of the boredom. The battle is constant, yet the successes are always momentary, uncertain. Though independent, we cast sly glances at each other, we inspect each other, we observe our twin hopelessness and the repetitiveness of our efforts, and we tease each other with the impossibility of an unambiguous victory. Frequently, we take our frustrations out on each other, falling into the irritation, mutual distaste, and obnoxiousness typical of those forced onto the same team.

One of my favorite games is building forts out of blankets, seats, and armchairs. What inclines someone to build a room within a room? A home within a home? Walls among walls and a ceiling under a ceiling? Is it some creative *horror vacui*? an urgent desire to make something that is supposed to organize the emptiness, both physical and metaphysical? Is it perhaps the fear of being consumed? Devoured by home, by its emptiness, silences, routines? Grandma doesn't like this game, because I make a mess. A conflict of interest comes about.

Life smashes, clatters, breaks, wastes, takes things out. Those whose daily antlike labors remain invisible because they consist SOLELY of regularly, arduously, unspectacularly restoring the constantly devastated order have only meaningful sighs, grumbling, and broken arms to defend them—attempts, doomed to fail, to stand guard against the creeping entropy, to hold it back. And vengeful dreaming of a day when no one comes home, tosses their bag on the floor, pulls the blanket from the couch, when no one eats the prepared lunch, setting the dominoes in motion that tomorrow will have to be cleaned up, sorted, put away all over again.

On that day, finally, an eternal, inviolable order will descend, and the cleanest of cleanlinesses, the kind that can never be sullied. This fantasy has no room for dust, cobwebs, and mold, for that illicit life that cohabits with human absence and stillness.

Dorota Masłowska

otomobilleri.
Herkesin gidişinden sonra sanki sabahki gözü

yorum. Tarım televizyonunu izliyorum, yürüyen bantlar

gezmek" demekti. Her kim ki avare avare gezerse kendini

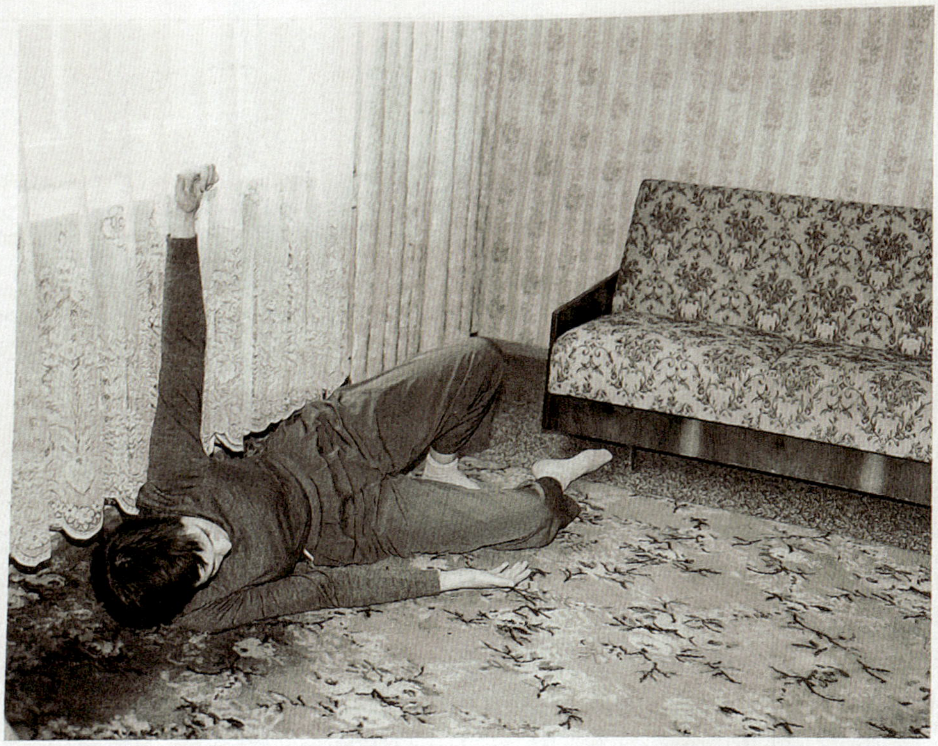

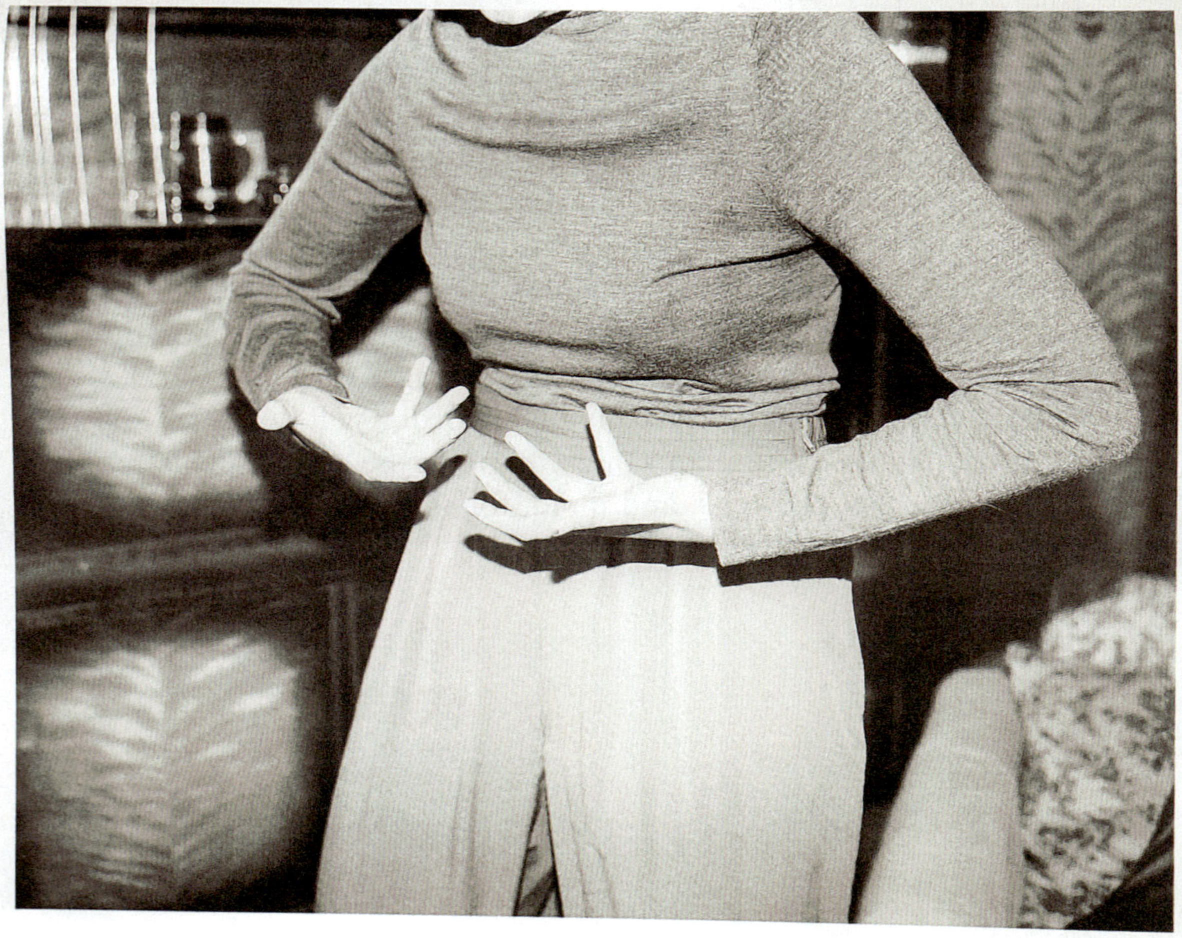

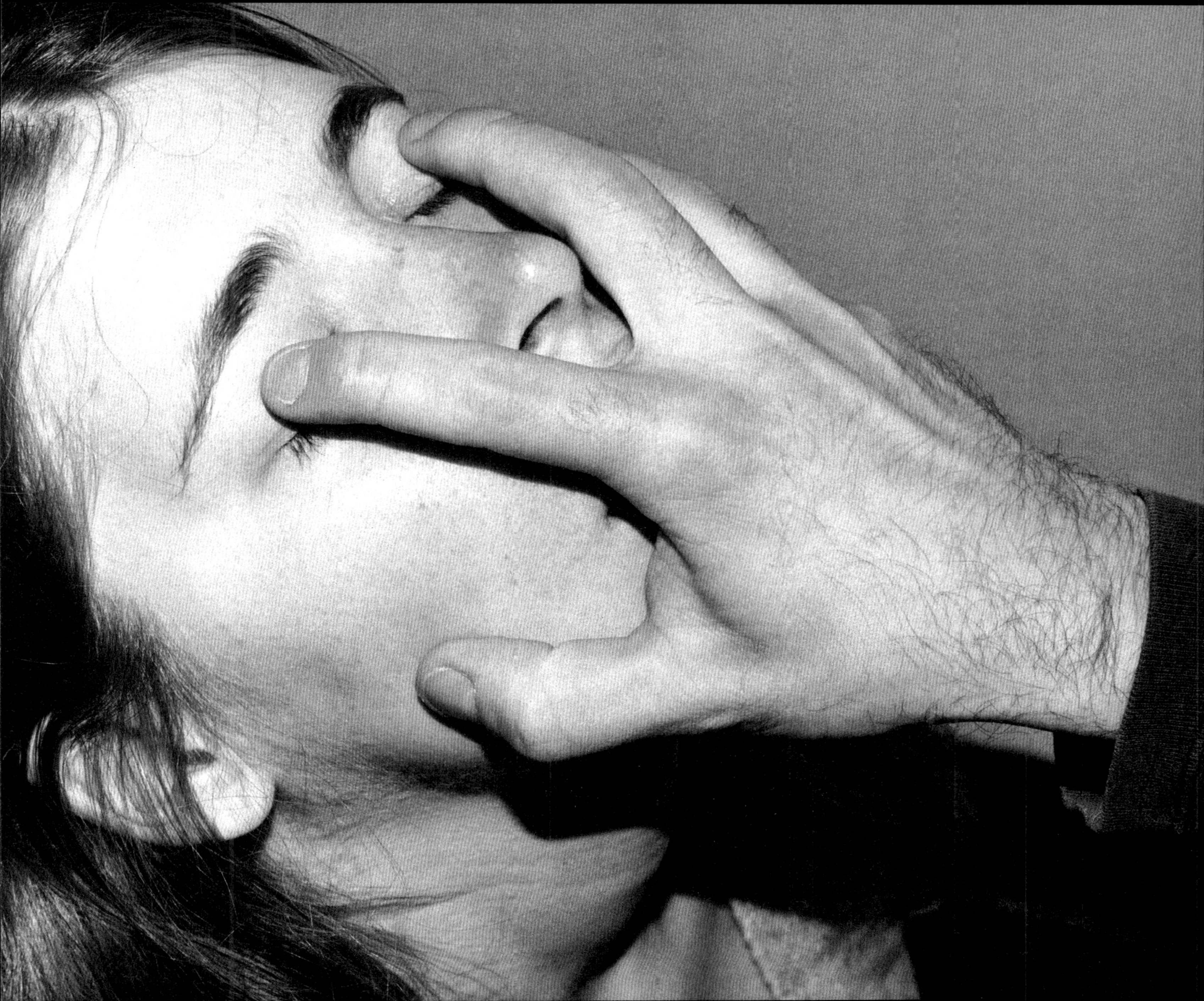

192

Joanna Piotrowska's artwork takes the form of a newspaper delivered directly to people's homes with their takeaway meals. Her photographs depict the all-too-familiar loneliness of confinement at home. Their subjects are lonely people, in conflict with their own bodies when left to their own devices. Empty zoo cages without animals comment on incarceration, while cushion forts provide shelter from anonymous, omnipresent violence. The photos are accompanied by a new essay by the prominent author Dorota Masłowska, written especially for this project, about how children (and adults) can deal with isolation and boredom at home.

I was born in 1985 and I live and work in London. My practice focuses on familial structures and their relationship to the wider systems—including politics, economics, social, and cultural life. I explore the past and the present, showing the inequalities of power and psychological drama, and translating the gestures and everyday intimate behaviors into new scenarios. I use my surroundings to show the anxiety and psychological tension of the domestic space—rather as a document of a performance than a documentary image.

My recent solo shows have been held at Kunsthalle Basel; Tate Britain, London; Southard Reid, London; Dawid Radziszewski Gallery, Warsaw; Madragoa Gallery, Lisbon. Recent group shows have been held at Kunsthalle Wien; MoMA, New York; 10th Berlin Biennale for Contemporary Art (2018); Warwick Art Center; Off-Biennale Budapest (2018); and Osservatorio Fondazione Prada, Milan. In 2014, I published my first monograph, *Frowst* (MACK Books, London), in 2017 *Frantic* (Humboldt Books, Milan).

Joanna Piotrowska

Untitled (2020)
Newspaper, multiple languages

With images by Joanna Piotrowska and an essay by Dorota Masłowska
Graphic design: Ivian Kan
Translations: Maša Dabić (Bosnian), Olaf Kühl (German), Benjamin Paloff (English), Sevil Çelik Tsonev (Turkish)

Commissioned and produced by steirischer herbst '20
With the kind support of Polish Institute Vienna
Distribution partner: velofood

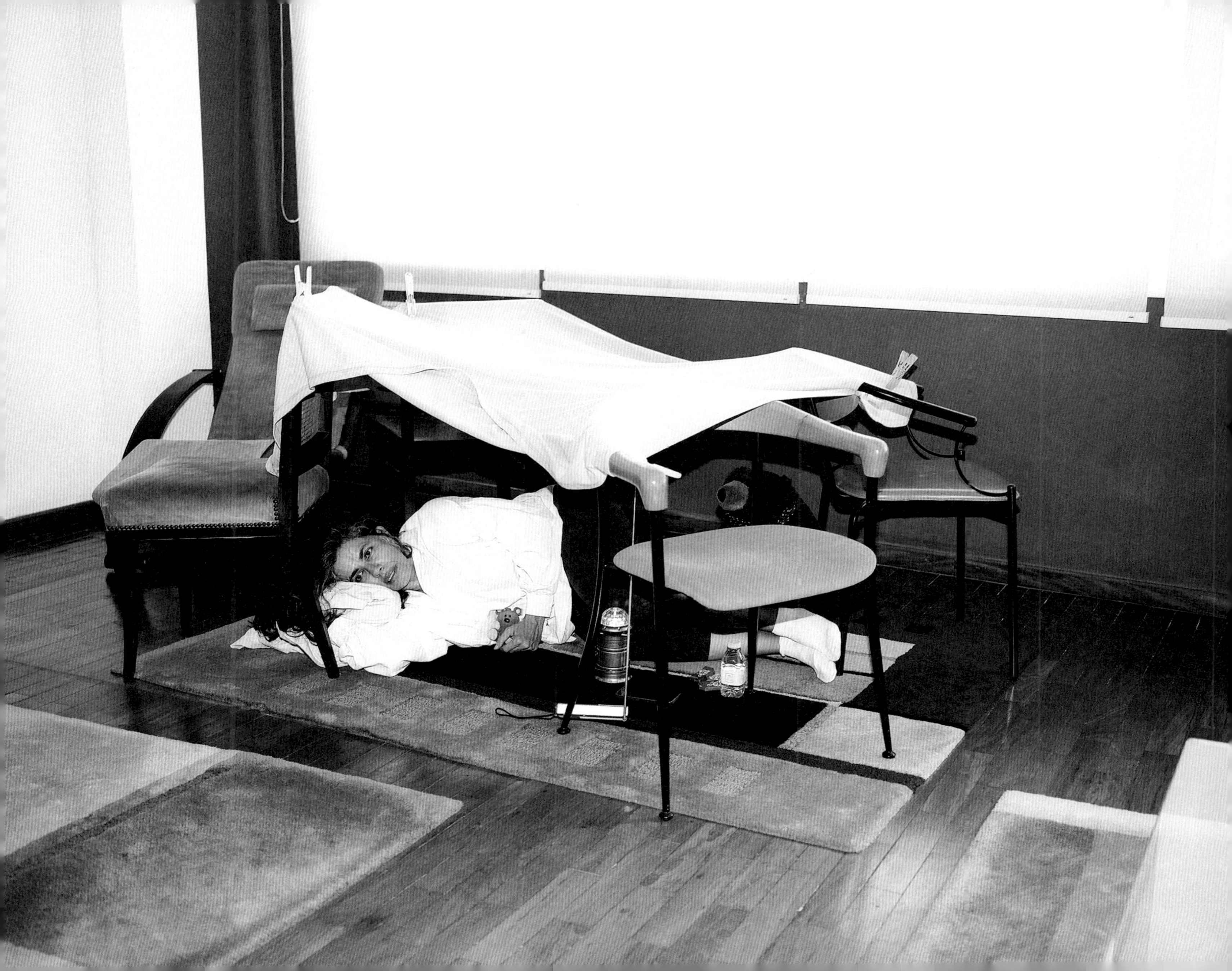

Alexandra Pirici & Jonas Lund

Year 01
2020

Online game

The project proposes a gamified, fictionalized reflection on the present moment of crisis triggered by the COVID-19 pandemic, unfolding now on multiple levels. *Year 01* uses fiction, a "survival" mode, and the format of first-person gameplay to engage multiple audiences in a story of both current public concern and intimate discovery, at this moment of threshold crossing when going back to normal might mean reimagining and reevaluating our acting in the world and the very definition of life. It also tries to turn the forced pause in regular processes of production—a crisis for most of our societies in which labor and accumulation play a crucial role—into a "productive" pause, a moment of reflection, of deep engagement with our immediate surroundings and with how we make meaning of our world.

The narrative of the game is constructed around a new, strange condition that produces sudden loss of consciousness, that spreads worldwide disrupting social life and economic activity. It avoids a very explicit reference to the new coronavirus but attempts to produce similar consequences up to a certain point, using a more metaphorical approach. While it is being informed by our now mostly shared, daily experiences—taking in news, home logistics of excessive cleaning, anxiety, financial worries, severed social ties, existential questions arising from the situation—the full game is made of specific experiences, offering the possibility to choose different playable characters, from different walks of life, different ages and backgrounds. It thus provides an opportunity to imagine, and empathize with, different experiences of the crisis, from an older person's to a younger person's, from a richer person's experience to a poorer person's, and from different cultural perspectives as well.

Alexandra Pirici & Jonas Lund

Year 01 (2020)
Online game, English

Editor: Oana Sanziana Marian

Commissioned by steirischer herbst '20
Produced by Alexandra Pirici & Jonas Lund in coproduction with steirischer herbst '20
With the kind support of the Swedish Embassy in Vienna

Alexandra Pirici is an artist with a background in dance and choreography who works undisciplined, across different mediums. Her works have been exhibited within the decennial art exhibition Skulptur Projekte Munster (2017); the 55th Venice Biennale (Romanian Pavilion, 2013); Tate Modern, London; New Museum, New York; Art Basel Messeplatz; the 9th Berlin Biennale (2016); Manifesta 10, St. Petersburg, (2014); Centre Pompidou, Paris; Museum Ludwig, Cologne; Van Abbemuseum, Eindhoven; Russian Museum, St. Petersburg; Neuer Berliner Kunstverein; HAU, Berlin; Museum of Modern Art, Warsaw; and the Chicago Architecture Biennale, among many others.

Alexandra Pirici works in museum contexts, theatrical frameworks, and public space. She choreographs ongoing actions, performative monuments, and performative environments that fuse dance, sculpture, spoken word, and music. Her works deal with monumentality or the history of specific places and institutions in order to playfully tackle and transform existing hierarchies. They also reflect on the history and function of gestures in art and popular culture or on questions about the body, its presence, absence or image, and the politics of capture.

Jonas Lund, born in Sweden in 1984, creates paintings, sculpture, photography, websites, and performances that critically reflect on contemporary networked systems and structures of control. His artistic practice involves creating systems and setting up parameters that oftentimes require engagement from the viewer. This results in performative artworks where tasks are executed according to algorithms or a set of rules. Through his works, Lund investigates the latest issues generated by the increasing digitalization of contemporary society like authorship, participation, and distribution of agency. At the same time, he questions the mechanisms of the art world; he challenges the production process, authoritative power, and art market practices.

Lund earned an MA at Piet Zwart Institute, Rotterdam (2013) and a BFA at Gerrit Rietveld Academy, Amsterdam (2009). He has had solo exhibitions at The Photographers' Gallery, London; Whitechapel Art Gallery, London; Steve Turner, Los Angeles; Växjö Konsthall; Showroom MAMA, Rotterdam; and the New Museum, New York. He has also had work included in numerous group exhibitions, including: Centre Pompidou, Paris; Schinkel Pavillon, Berlin; ZKM, Karlsruhe; Vienna Biennale 2019; FKA Witte de With, Rotterdam; Kindl—Centre for Contemporary Art, Berlin; and the Stedelijk Museum, Amsterdam.

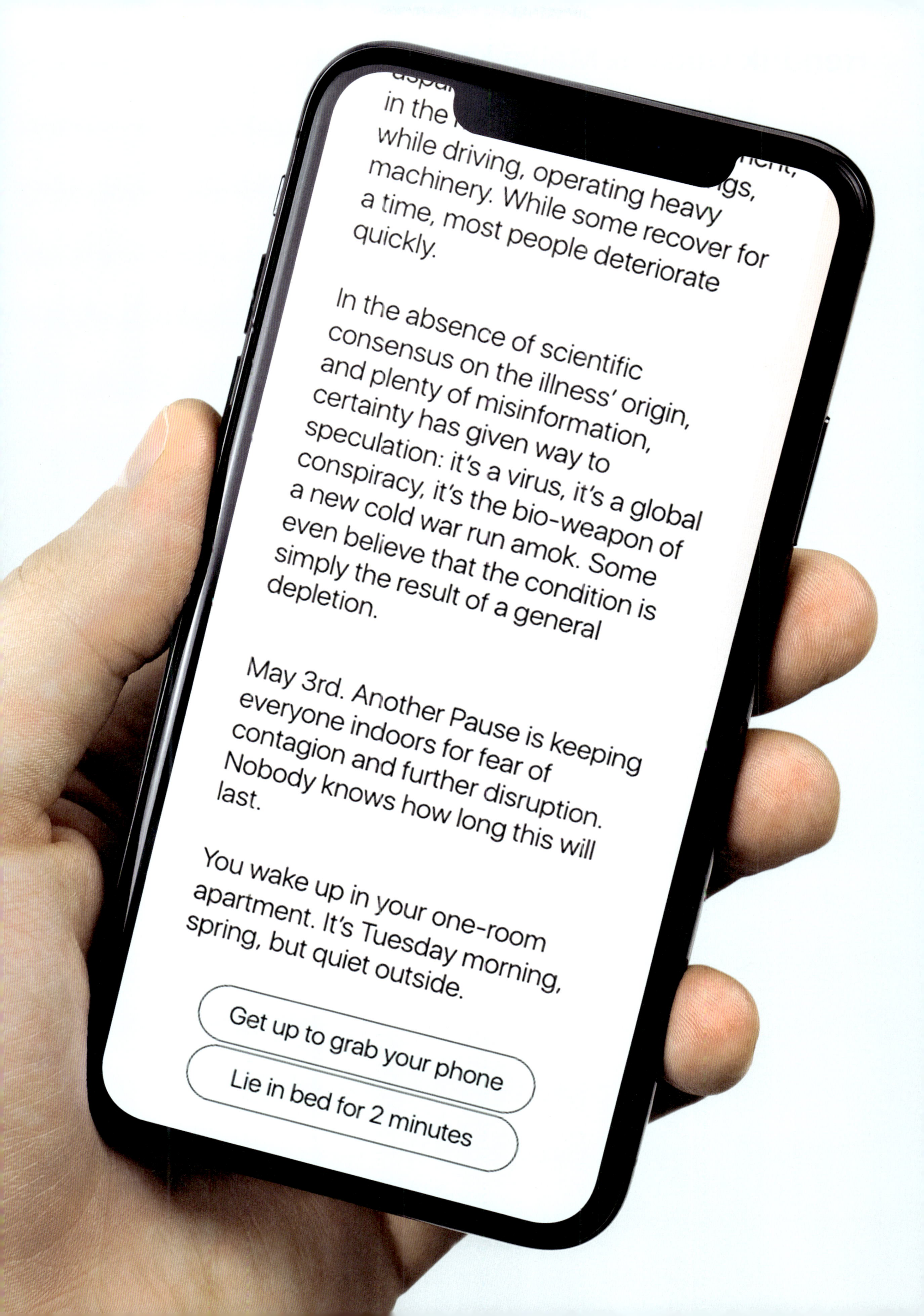
while driving, operating heavy
machinery. While some recover for
a time, most people deteriorate
quickly.
In the absence of scientific
consensus on the illness' origin,
and plenty of misinformation,
certainty has given way to
speculation: it's a virus, it's a global
conspiracy, it's the bio-weapon of
a new cold war run amok. Some
even believe that the condition is
simply the result of a general
depletion.
May 3rd. Another Pause is keeping
everyone indoors for fear of
contagion and further disruption.
Nobody knows how long this will
last.
You wake up in your one-room
apartment. It's Tuesday morning,
spring, but quiet outside.
Get up to grab your phone
Lie in bed for 2 minutes

Hendrik Quast & Maika Knoblich

PPtv
2020

Video series

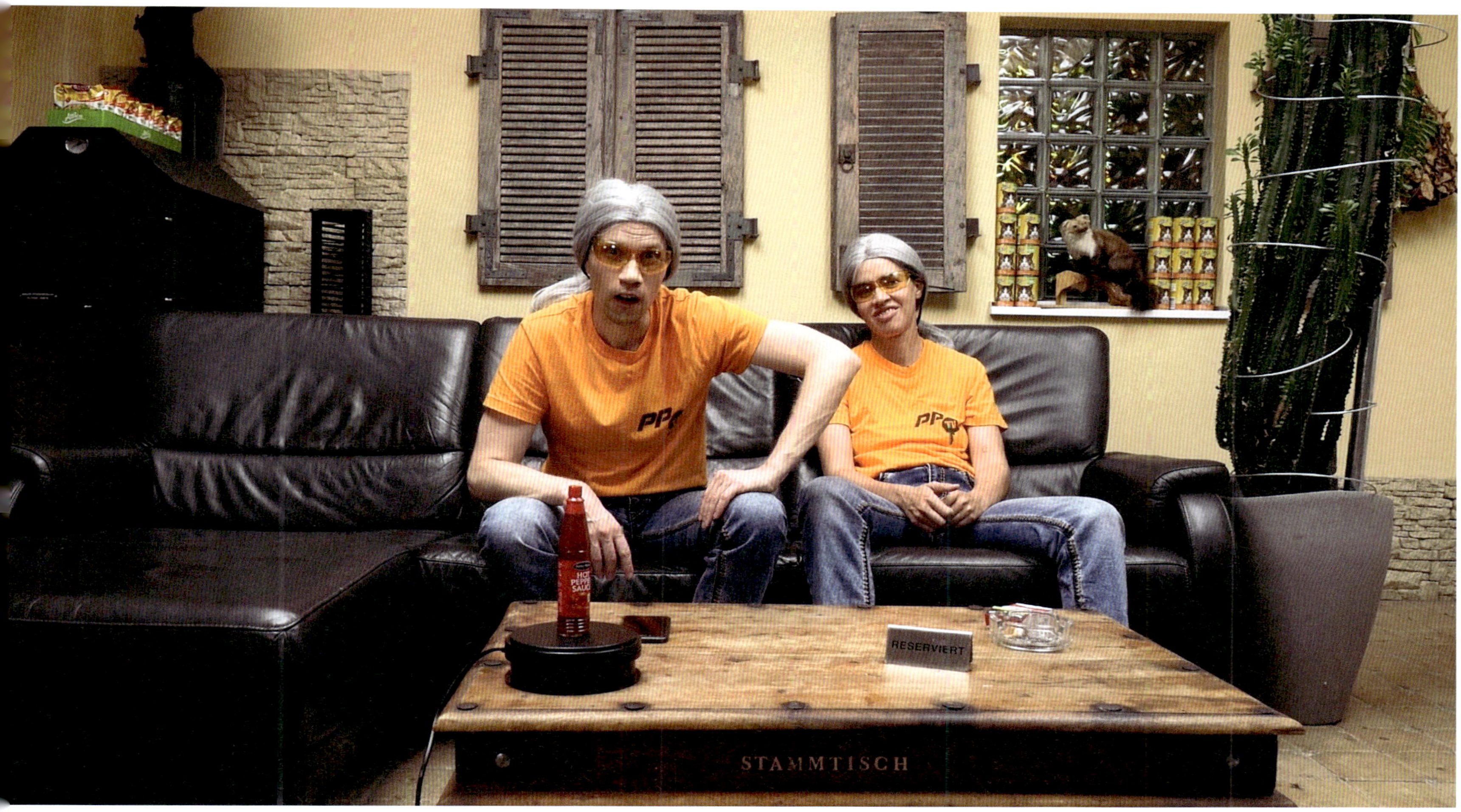
RESERVIERT
STAMMTISCH

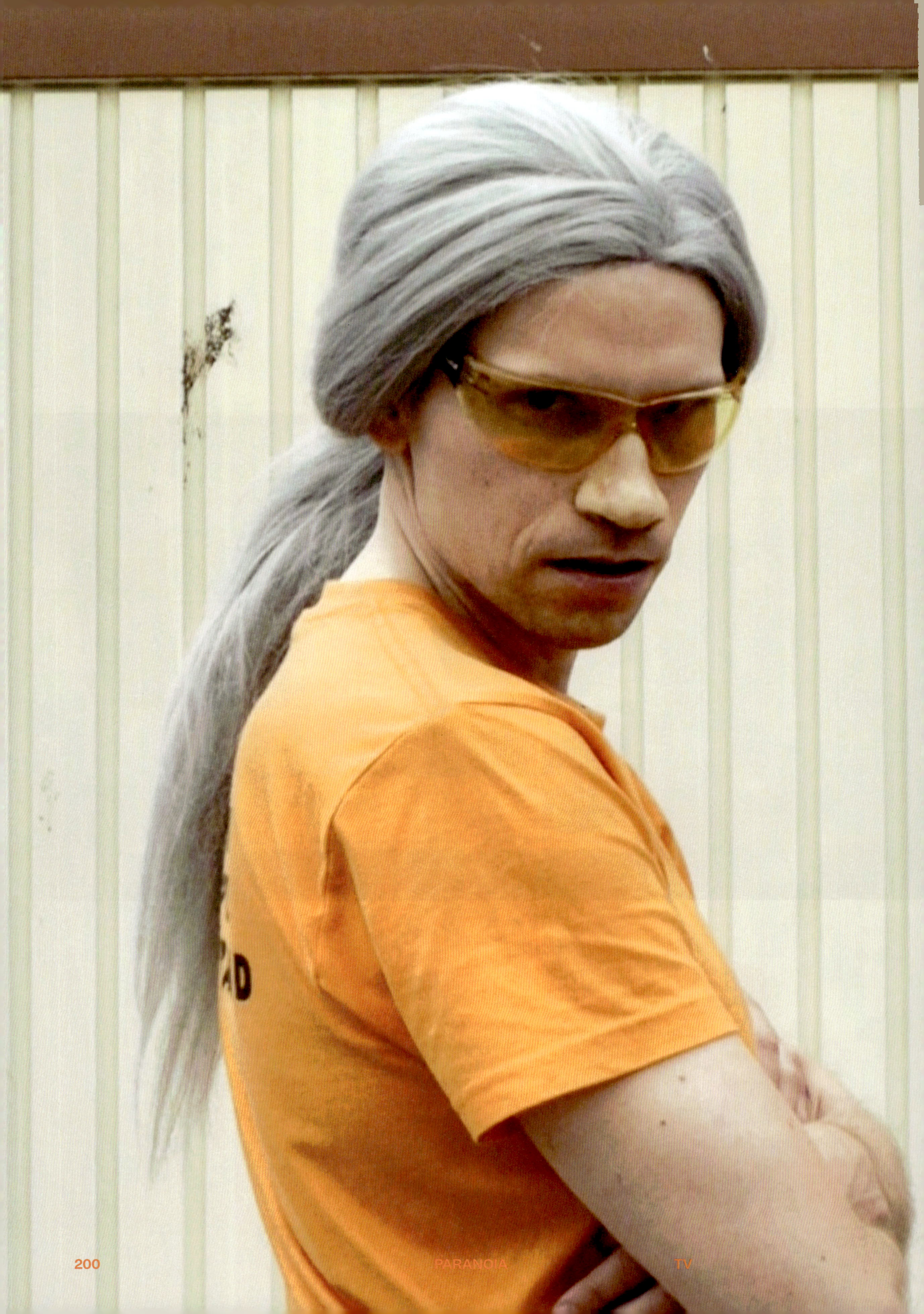

A global pandemic—this is not a catastrophe but rather an ideal opportunity for our protagonists in the life hack show *PPtv*.

Both are passionate preppers, barely distinguishable from one another after years of joint preparation for the apocalypse. Stockpiling cat food, setting up automatic marten traps, using hot sauce as a weapon of self-defense—all of this is part of the post-apocalyptic routine in the hobby shop. We try to approximate with brute force the specific jargon and macho swagger of fearful lone warriors, dissecting them with a sharp blade, albeit playfully and without ridiculing them.

That's just the way it is, this generation today, they're not like that anymore, we're still like that, we've spent our whole lives outdoors. We didn't grow up in front of a gaming console. We grew up outdoors. That instills bushcraft, basic strength, basic immunity.

In *PPtv*, our alter egos meet up in the workshop to prepare for Day X. They amass all sorts of scraps and junk from their DIY universe to gird themselves for the apocalypse. In this way, we try to interrogate artistically the prepper cosmos as a bastion of male self-dramatization and translate the torrent of mansplaining for our *Paranoia TV* viewers. The prepper vocabulary with its unique abbreviations is used here in a way that exposes the power of language in a highly selective and structural manner. Our alter egos address every little expert detail, undermining the obvious with the matter-of-fact and vice versa. While lounging on the handyman couch in the man cave, we talk shop on the specifics of gear, intruders, home defense, and DIY bunkers. True to the motto "My Garage—My Rules," this is where masculinity is given free rein.

Sure, practice makes perfect. Intestinal explosion is number two of the three phases of agony after eating spicy food. Then comes the fire seat. SHTF: Shit hits the fan. If someone is that aggressive, there's no choice, not even with an intruder. You just have to get out your truncheon and knock him on the head.

Our work in *PPtv* is an exercise in linguistic excess that deals with concepts of masculinity in times when we are seeing a pervasive political shift to the right. The show, which is based on research in the micro-community of hunters, marksmen, and weapons enthusiasts, examines how a society of isolated individuals is increasingly splitting up into communities of interest that are seeking their own home turf. We zoom in on these dangerous alliances with their supposed solidarity—a solidarity that is in fact limited to one's own small circle, but then with no holds barred. We're not out to judge but, instead, just try to dismantle this linguistic power through comedy.

YOYO: You are on your own.
I know just who I am, and sometimes it's best to scram.
Huh? That rhymes!
. . . and whatever rhymes is good.

Familiar media formats and art strategies are interwoven in such a way that the audience witnesses a paradoxical situation: this might be a tutorial or a simple DIY guide, and yet home defense and the coming apocalypse are treated here as a case of survival of the fittest.

We heighten this uncertainty through tilting moments and humor, always short-circuiting the language with a material counterpart: here, for example, it's the arsenal of gear in the prepper workshop. This *techne* allows us to maintain our performative state, which makes us authors of the moment. Our attitude alternates between friendly banter and serious rivalry, creating artificiality of content and form through linguistic borrowings from the everyday culture of the preppers and survivalists.

This way of establishing a relationship with the audience provokes a special kind of laughter about a highly controversial topic and hence a very unconventional comic tonality, which points far beyond the grotesque tradition to demonstrate how theater can also be political.

Hendrik Quast &
Maika Knoblich

PPtv (2020)
Video series, 3 episodes,
ca. 15 / 15 / 18 min., German
Online

Concept, text, performance:
Hendrik Quast and Maika Knoblich
Video (direction, camera, sound, editing):
Maria Mogren and Jens von Larcher /
ECKE FILM
Props, set: Hendrik Quast
Assistant director, production, and props assistant: Christina Mäckelburg
Costumes and makeup: Christina Neuss
Executive producer: Lisa Gehring
Translation subtitles: David Tushingham

Commissioned by steirischer herbst '20
Produced by Quast & Knoblich in coproduction with steirischer herbst '20
Supported by Kulturstiftung des Bundes (Reload. Stipendienprogramm)

Hendrik Quast and Maika Knoblich have been working together in the contemporary field of independent performance theater since 2009. They began their collaboration at the Institute for Applied Theatre Studies in Giessen, Germany.

With their research-based approach they pursue shared interests in everyday practices, rituals, and craft techniques such as dog sports, fingernail design, and funeral floristry. The theatricalization of the modes of speech and materiality in these occupational fields and milieus generates artificial hyperspaces in which Quast & Knoblich assume caricatured alter egos to challenge the audience with subversive comedy, in the process negotiating topics such as social background, rural life, and (precarious) forms of work.

Their performances create idiosyncratic narratives that confront the audience with a transformed, queer, and grotesquely comical reality. With each performance, the linguistic excess in the script is inflated even further. The language that surrounds us in our daily lives finds its way into the text. Fragments from social media, advertising, and snippets of conversation are woven into the script. The text thus takes on material form. Quast & Knoblich focus on the materiality of language as something learned, that is, foreign or appropriated. Rather than serving dramatic ends, the development of the text therefore becomes a form of performance art, in the tradition of the happening.

The duo has performed at the leading independent production houses, such as Mousonturm, Frankfurt; Kampnagel, Hamburg; Gessnerallee, Zurich; FFT, Düsseldorf; and Sophiensaele, Berlin, as well as being invited to international festivals. Their durational performance *Ur-Forst* was featured at the Impulse Festival in 2015. They have received fellowships and grants from the Berlin Senate, the Capital Cultural Fund, and the Goethe Institutes in Munich and London, and have participated in several international group projects such as *Greatest Show on Earth* (2016), *Dreck* (2015), and *Evakuieren* (2014). Since 2012, Quast & Knoblich have been developing their own radio plays with WDR Cologne; the premiere of *Nagelneu* took place in 2020.

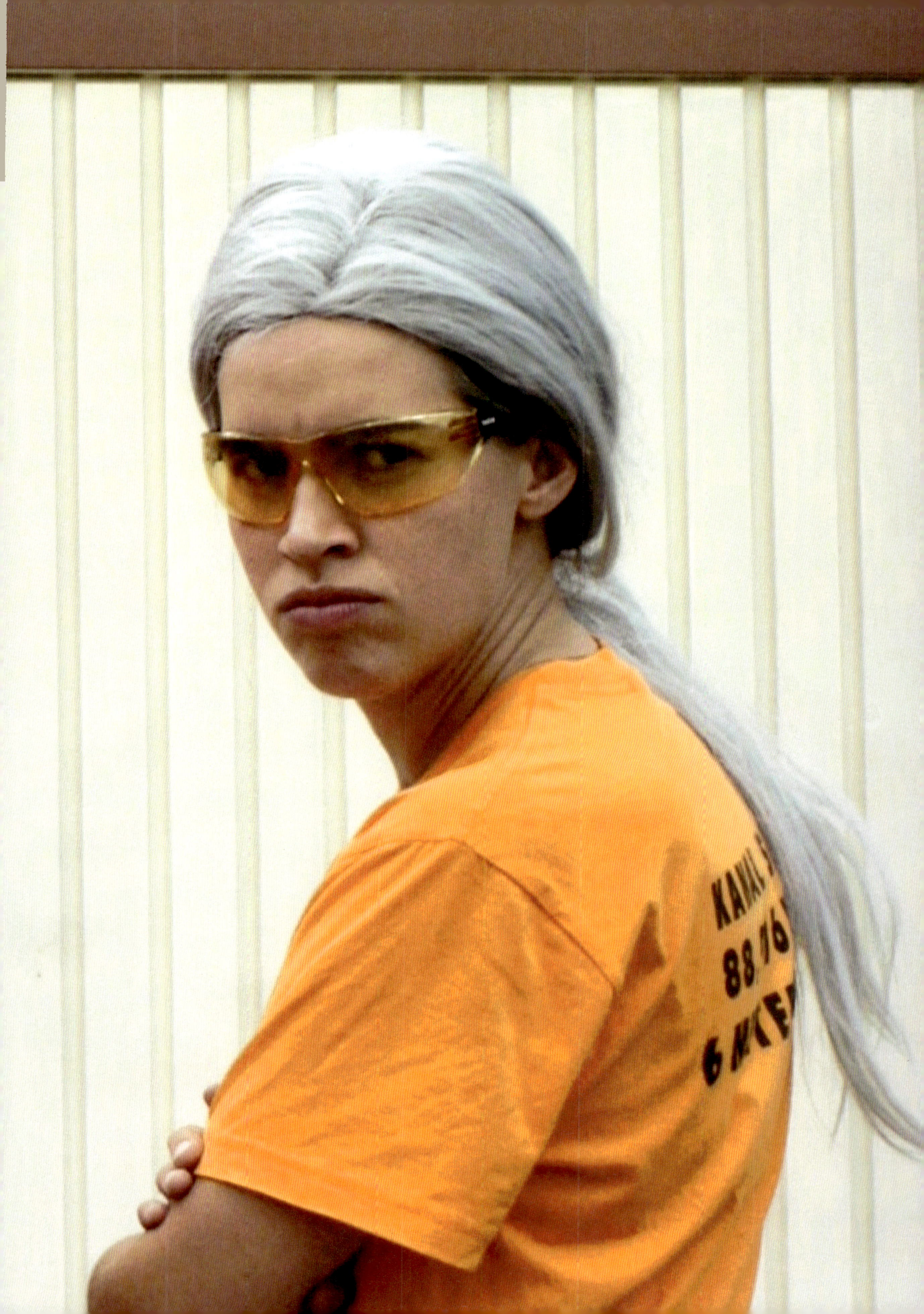

Judy Radul

The Graz Mirror
2020

Artist edition

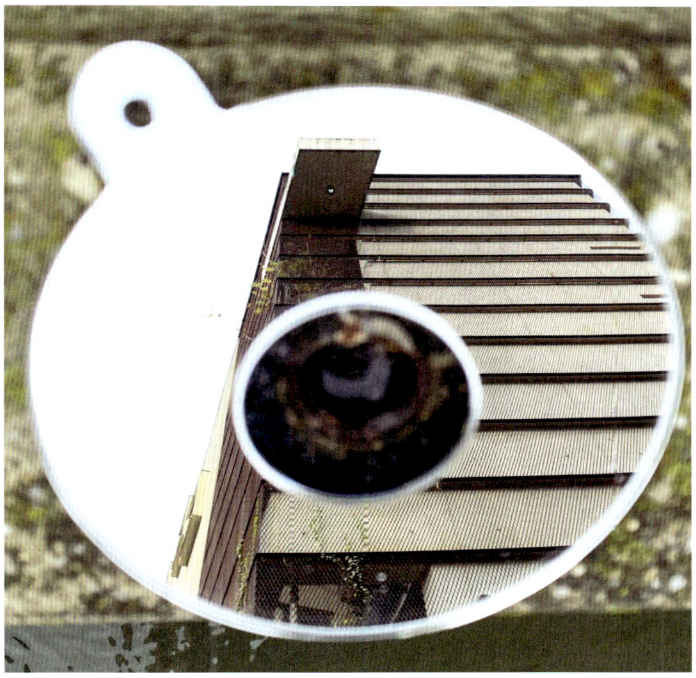

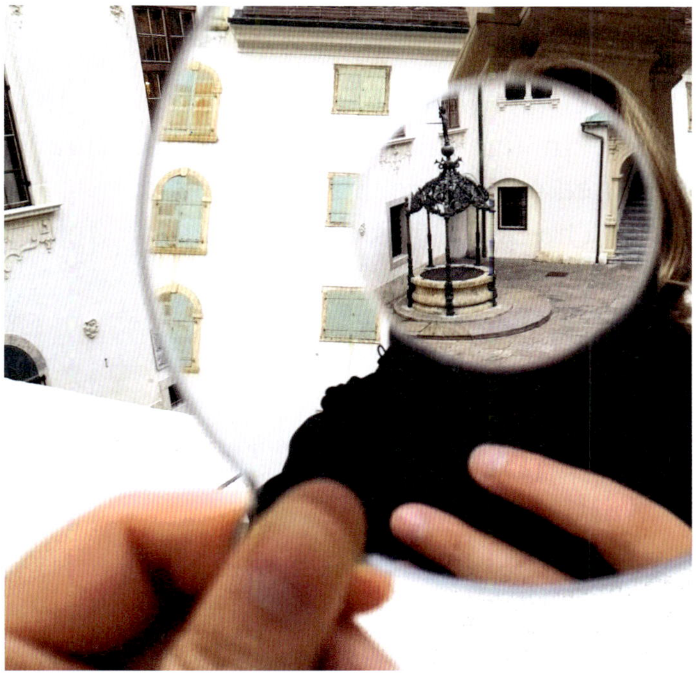

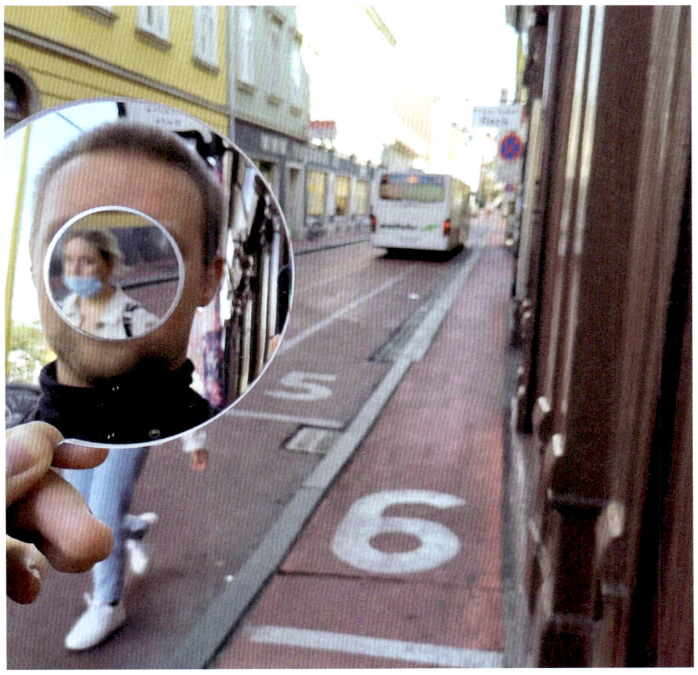
5
6

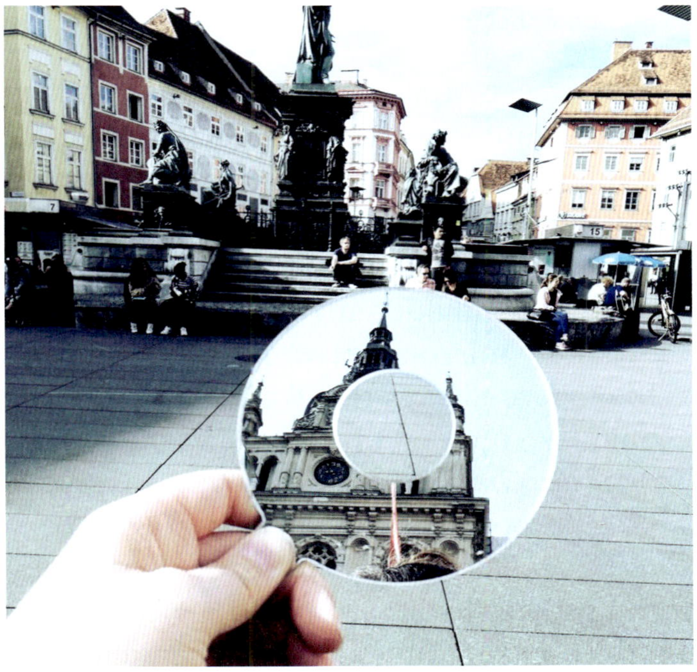

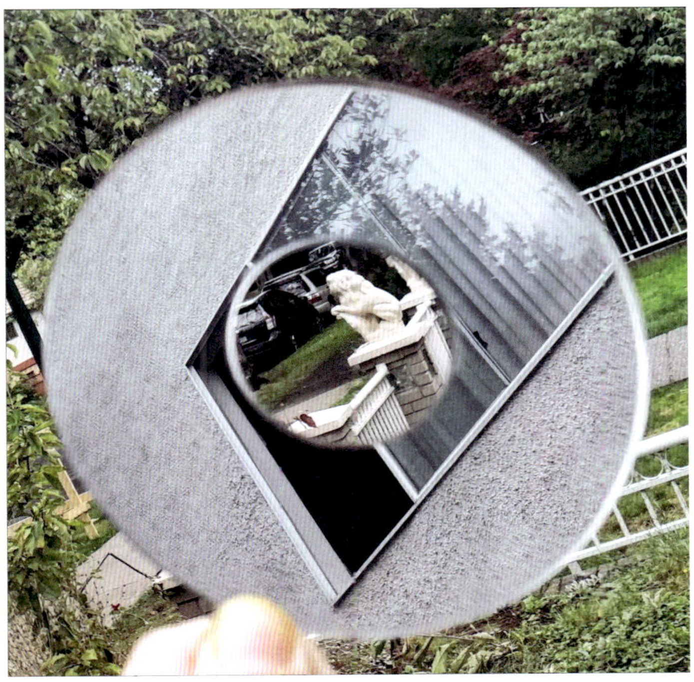

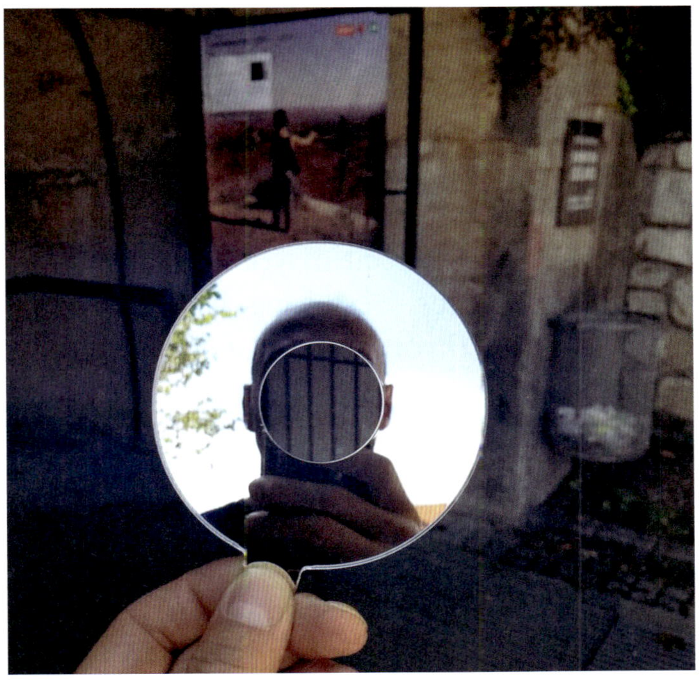

The Graz Mirror is a hand mirror with a hole in the middle. The reverse side is coated with a green screen color.

The text inside the package folder reads:

> *The Graz Mirror* is an artwork by Judy Radul.
>
> There are many ways to enjoy the mirror. It is an object for your exploration.
>
> It is a tool for visualization and a tool for creating visual effects. Reflection and penetration, framing and encircling, how on earth do we relate. If you photograph reflections in, and views through, your Graz mirror, you will create interesting compositions.

The face is a sweet distraction from the mind, until you think of your face. I have a migraine. There is a hole in everything. My eyes are drawn to the screen, there is my shot-reverse-shot love object I never over the shoulder met through the eyes. So now mirrors have holes—or maybe they were always this way—they are over anyway—I put on lipstick using my phone.

The Graz Mirror is a way to give a hole—a portal which at first may appear to be an absence. This mirror does tricky things with habitual reflections. You "naturally" pick it up to look in it, anticipating your face but you are, rather, rewarded with two views, your face and its background, and—because there is a void right in the middle of the mirror (and potentially your face as you look into/through the mirror)—you have a view through to what stands in front of you. Your point of focus oscillates. "Looking into" switches to "looking through." *The Graz Mirror* is an optimistic tool, for finding that identity isn't singular, that the constitutive kernel at the center of the inscription of the self is an other. This other can be a person, a sunset, a distant scene in a city square, a building, a dog, a cloud, even a computer screen.

The Graz Mirror is not just for faces, it is for inserting the background into the foreground, the where you came from into where you are going. Being a hand mirror in a digital era, it is also a point in a triangulation between mirror reflection, world beyond, and potentially the point of view of a camera phone.

Why does *The Graz Mirror* have "Graz" in the name? Well, it seems that one should build a certain amount of doubling into a mirror object, even if as an irony. A mirror whose name indicates a location, but is handheld and mobile, taunts us with an impossible identity. We know the mirror holds nothing, it is a polished surface off which a vector of light bounces—a mirror whose name suggests that it particularly reflects or is located in "Graz" humorously tries to anchor the non-place of a reflection to a place (perhaps thereby also indicating it as a fictional construction). Like a screen, a mirror is promiscuous, it will hold whatever is within the angle of view of the viewer. Unlike the screen, the mirror offers an individual perspective. You cannot "share" a mirror view with anyone—five different people each looking at the same mirror see different views. *The Graz Mirror* is not as famous as the Graz double spiral staircase but takes at least a whiff of inspiration from this local landmark.

Judy Radul

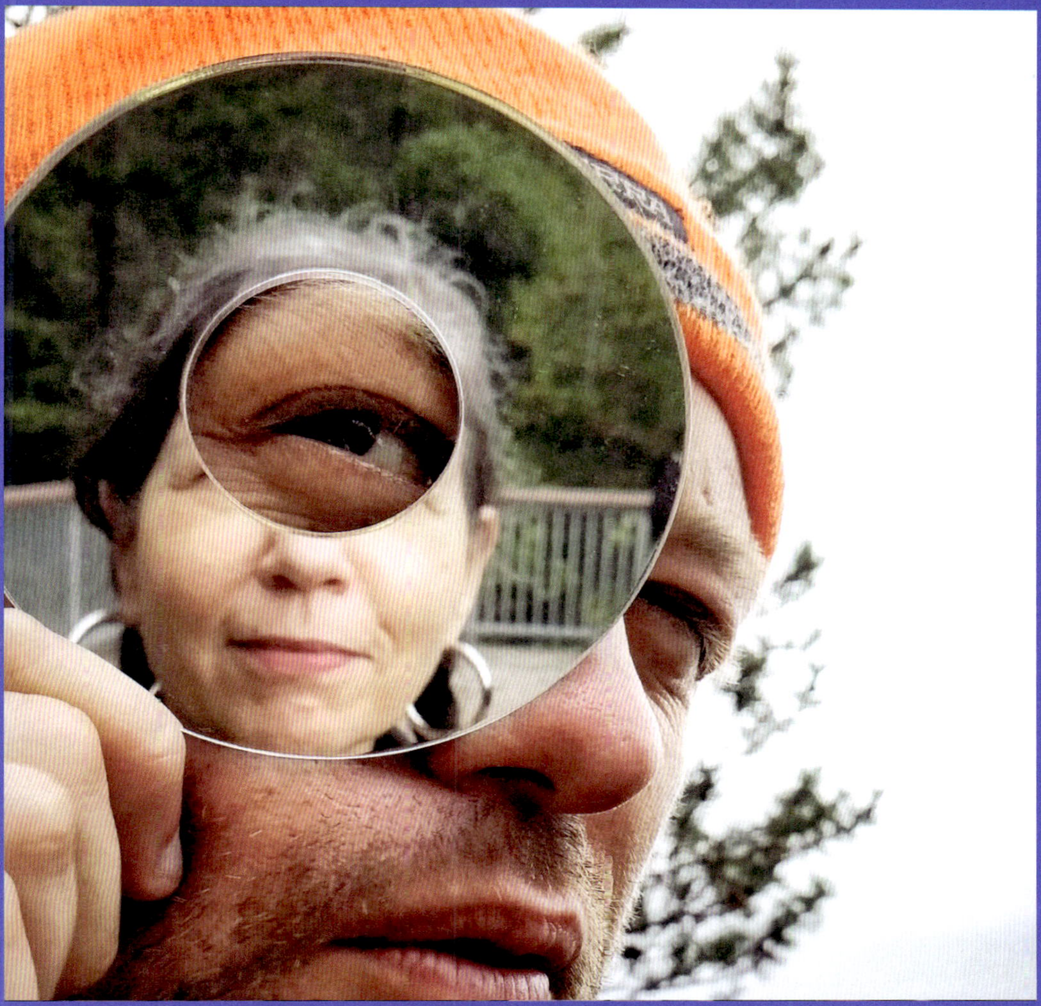

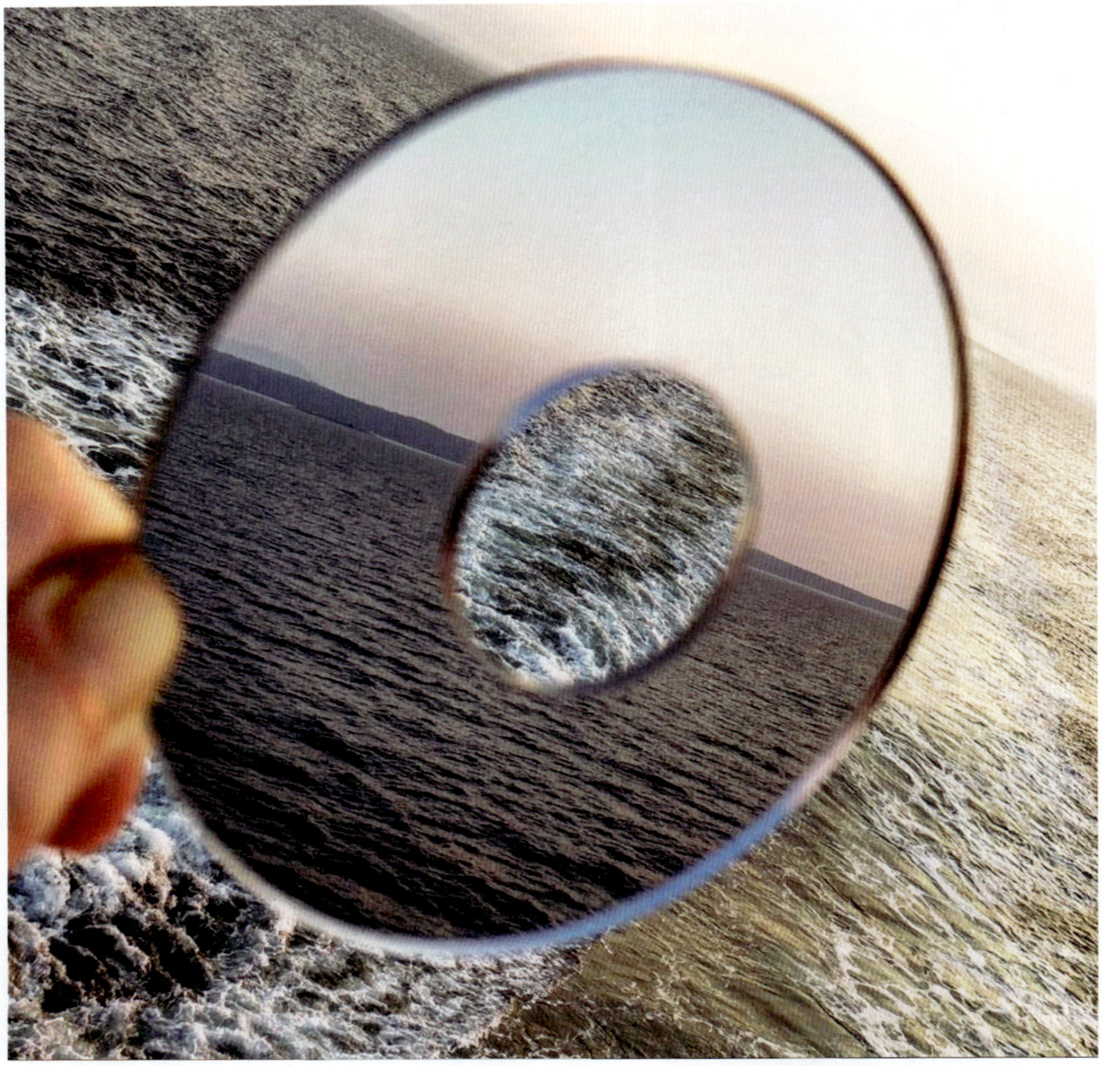

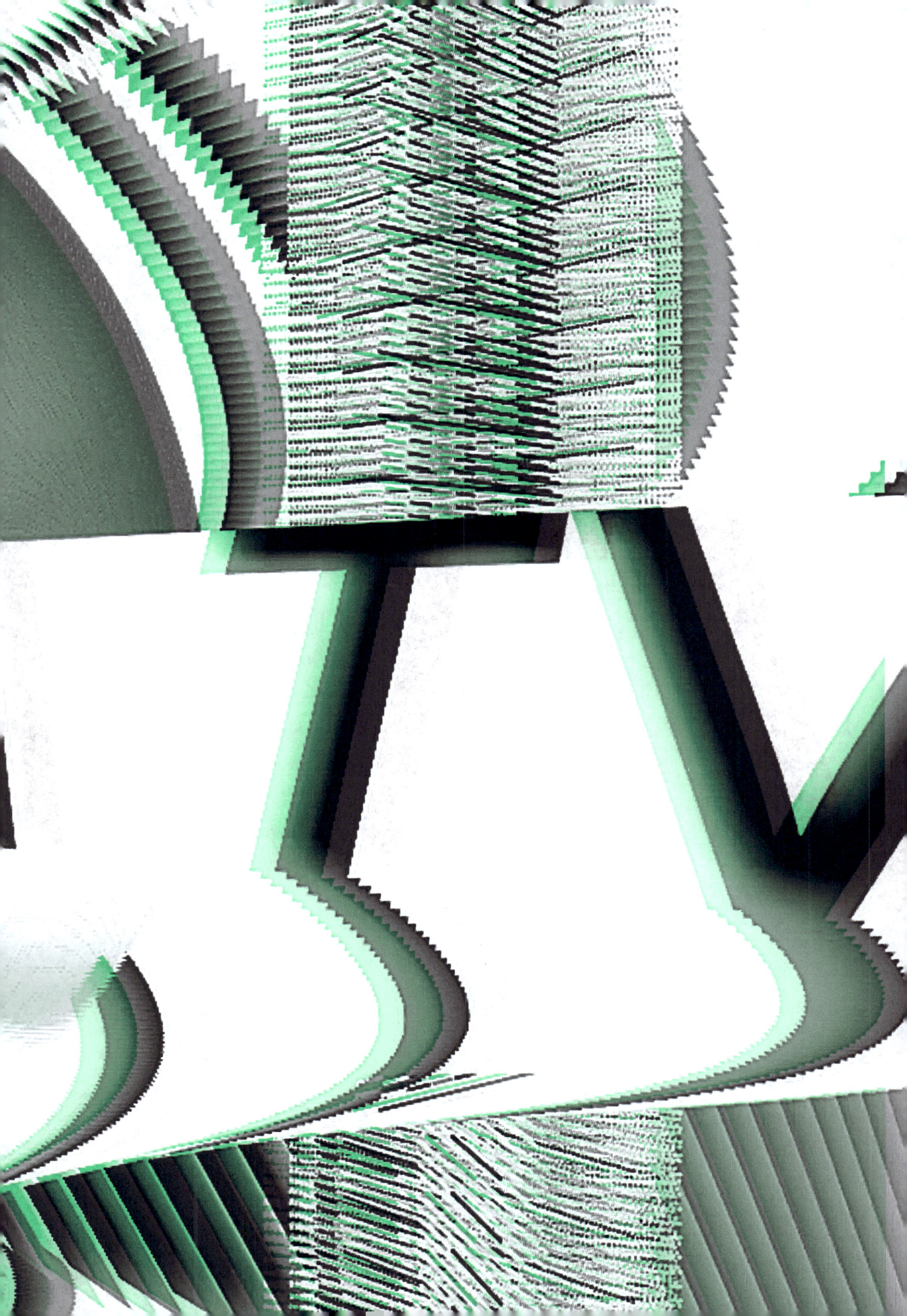

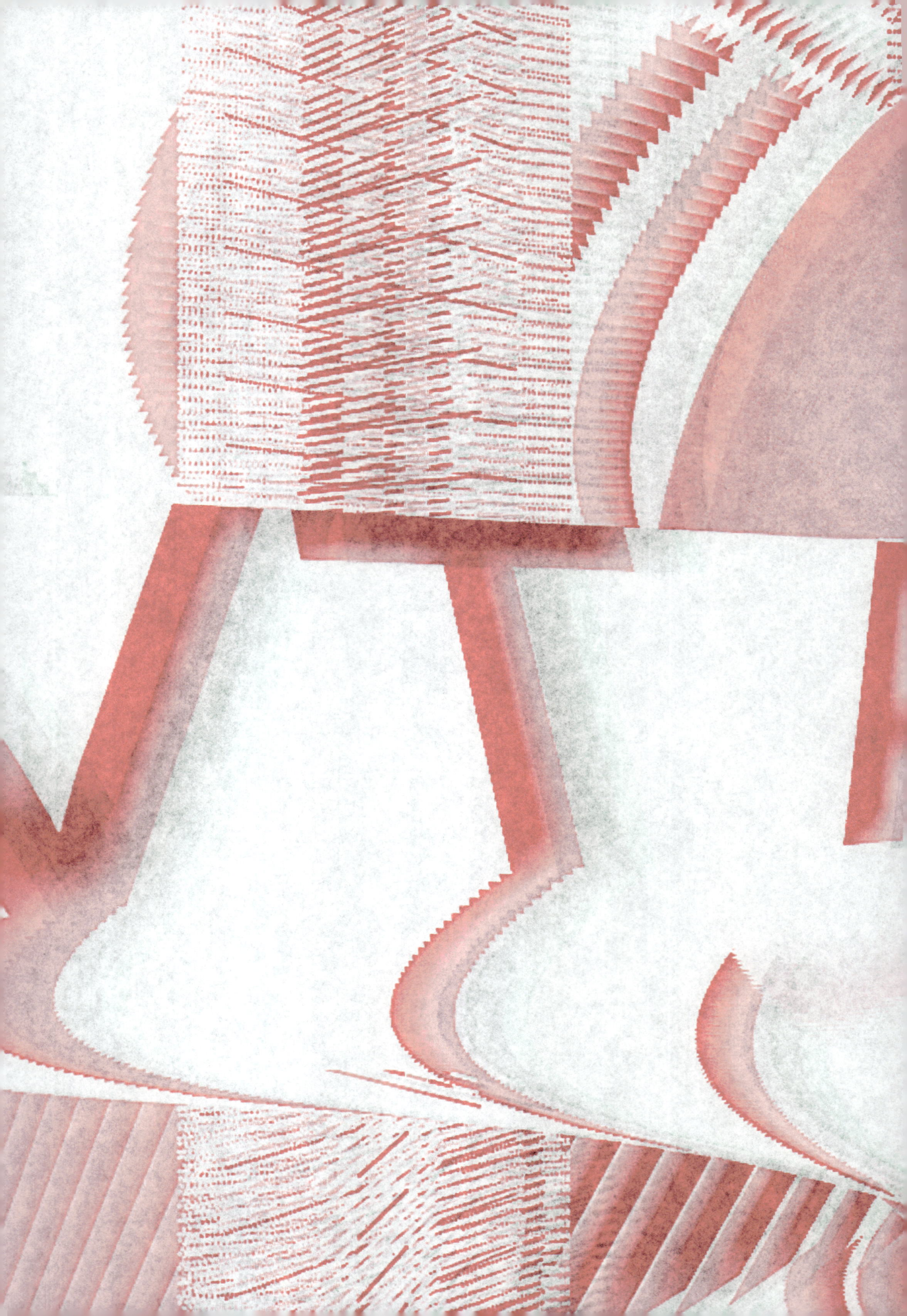

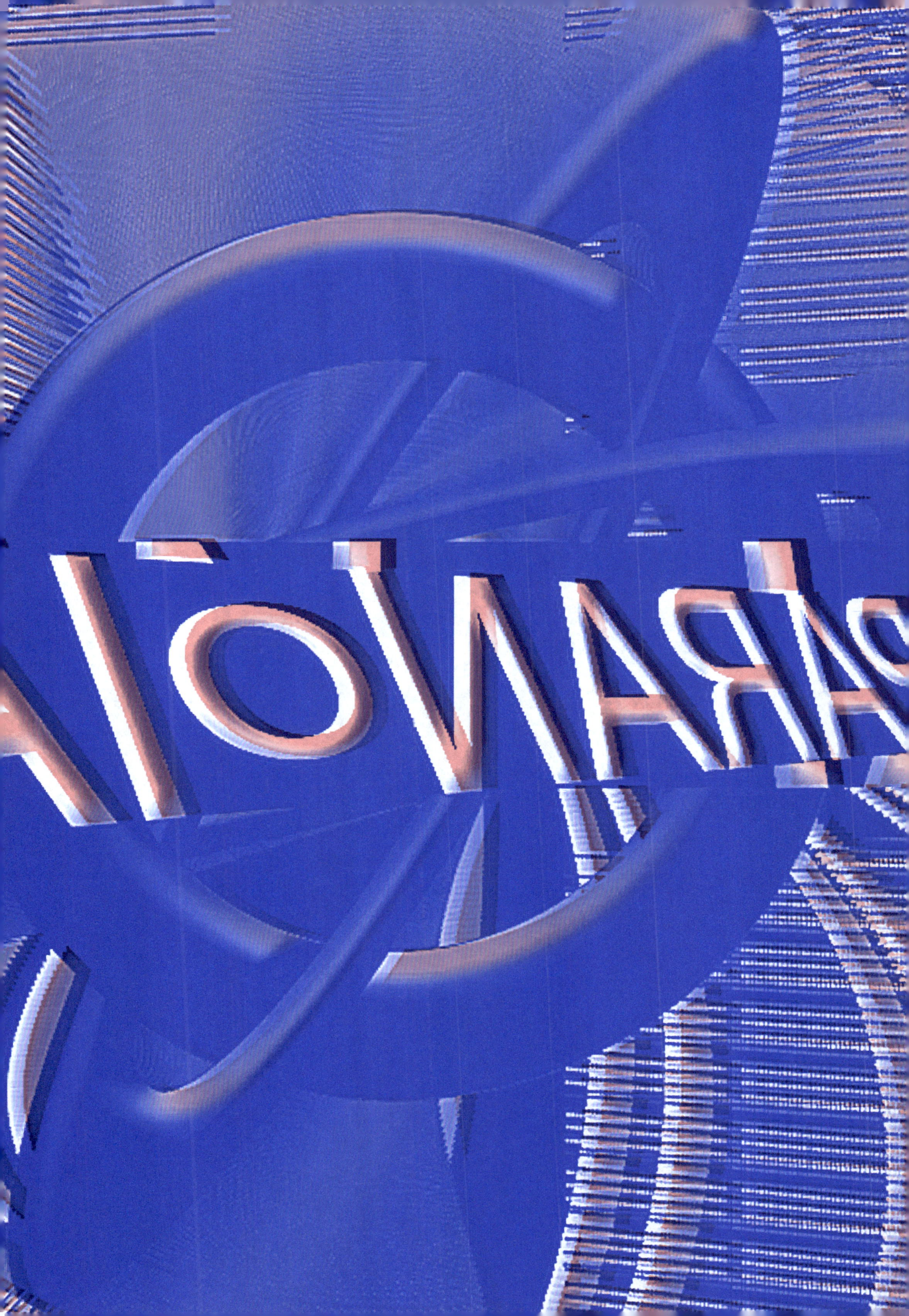

Judy Radul's latest works incorporate an original computer-controlled system for live and pre-recorded video. Her practice also includes sculpture, photography, writing, and performance. Her recent exhibitions include *Show Support* in the project series *Demonstration Rooms* at the Albertinum Museum, Dresden; a solo exhibit on at FKA Witte de With, Rotterdam; Contour Biennale 8, Mechelen (2017); Bienal de Nicaragua (2016); a solo exhibition at Agnes Etherington Art Centre, Kingston; Berlin Biennale 8 (2014); and a solo exhibit on at DAAD Galerie, Berlin.

Her large-scale media installation *World Rehearsal Court* (2009) has been shown in Vancouver, Vienna, Seoul, Oslo, and Moscow. She has published two books with Sternberg Press Berlin: a book of collected essays and images co-edited with Marit Paasche, *A Thousand Eyes: Media Technology, Law and Aesthetics,* 2011, and *This Is Television,* 2018. Radul received a BA in fine and performing arts from Simon Fraser University, Vancouver, in 1991, and a master's in visual and media arts, Bard College, New York, 2000. She is a professor of visual art at SFU School for Contemporary Arts. She lives in Berlin and Vancouver.

The Graz Mirror (2020)
Artist edition (of 3,000)

Cover design: Grupa Ee

Commissioned and produced by steirischer herbst '20

Joanna Rajkowska and Robert Yerachmiel Sniderman

Night Herons
2020

Video

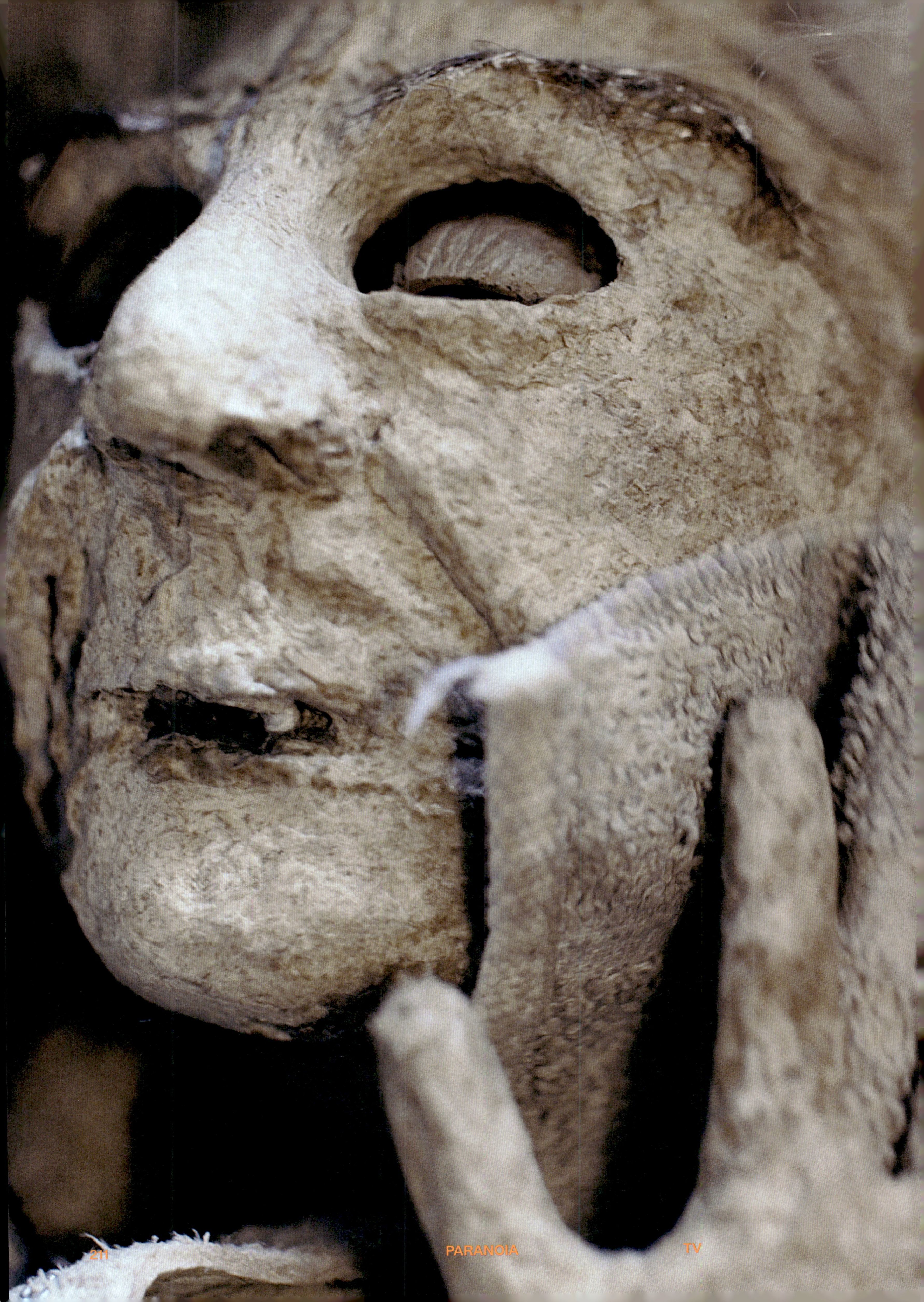

Night herons are migratory birds. In Slavic mythology, they take the souls of the dead to the other side. Mysteriously, they began populating Oświęcim, where Auschwitz stands, in great numbers in the 1990s. We didn't know any of this before Robert dreamed they pierced the bellies of two women, searching for a digested root.

What we knew was a ritual and what it should witness. Since we met, back in 2018, we had culled an image—a pile of hunted bodies and fused burial rites, hunted bodies and scream singing, hunted bodies and the failure to animate them—a pile of dead nonhuman bodies.

We were ready and high up in the Austrian Alps, near Krakauschatten and Murau. There were people ready to act and help. Including hunters. And then the pandemic came.

We chose papier-mâché marionettes as our prostheses, our reconstructed selves, and they demanded a fuller story. In the forests of Nowogród, Poland, we infused them not only with the ability to do the performance, but pass the sensate memories of our parents and grandparents. All the nausea, tenderness, fear, and empathy generated by our ancestor-marionettes we transferred through our papier-mâché hands onto the dead animals who in turn sewed up the fragments.

The night herons have been watching. We were very faithful to the soil, swamp, flesh, and dreams. They knew it. We didn't leave the territory of Bruno Schulz, Ashkenazi plant and animal medicine, Slavic scream singing, but above everything, Baruch de Spinoza accursed. We believe thoughts and rituals switch between all the Earth's bodies. And this is why we shared them with the night herons, straight from our intestines.

Joanna Rajkowska and Robert Yerachmiel Sniderman

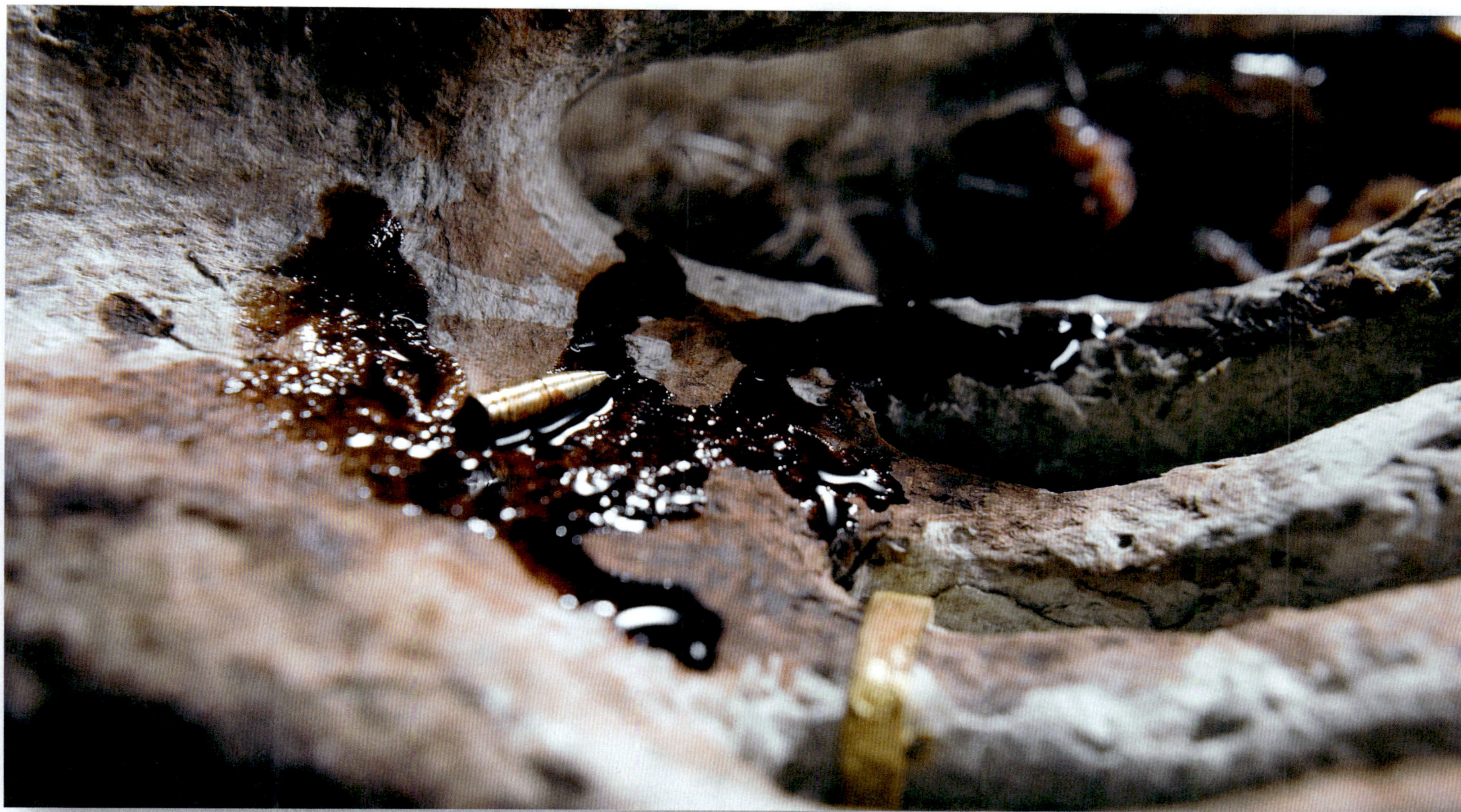

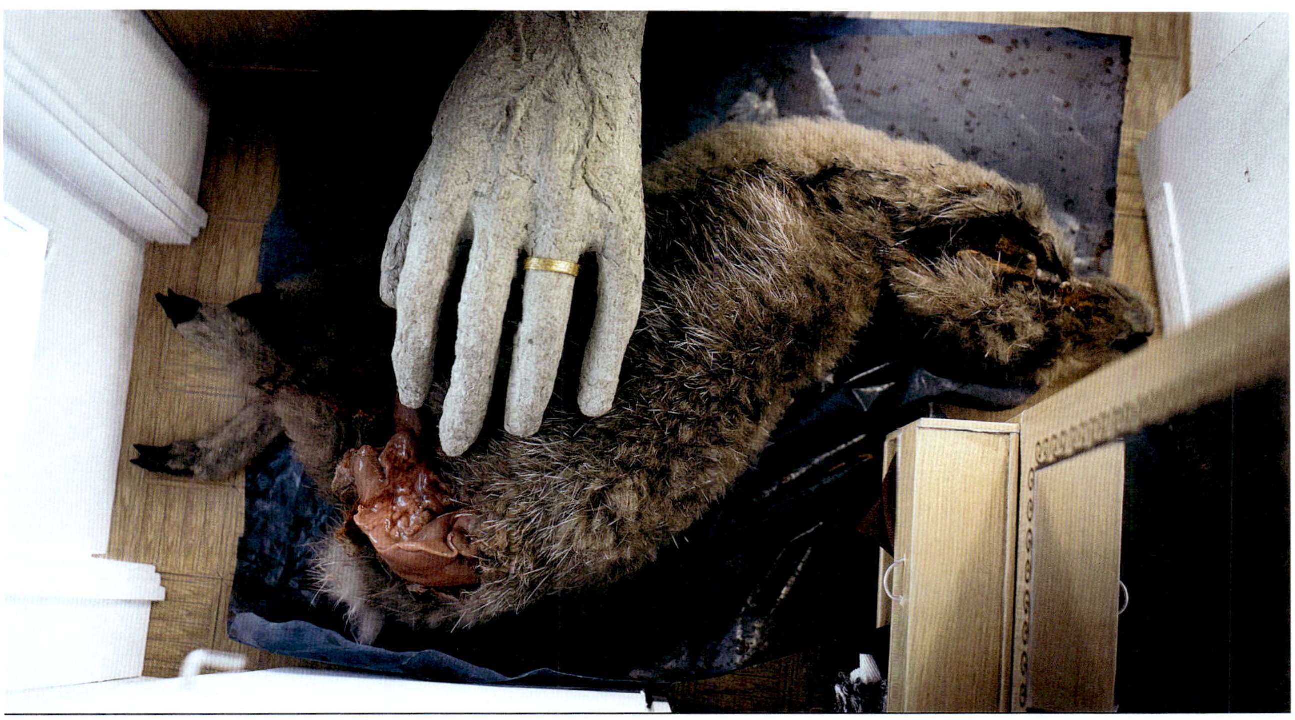

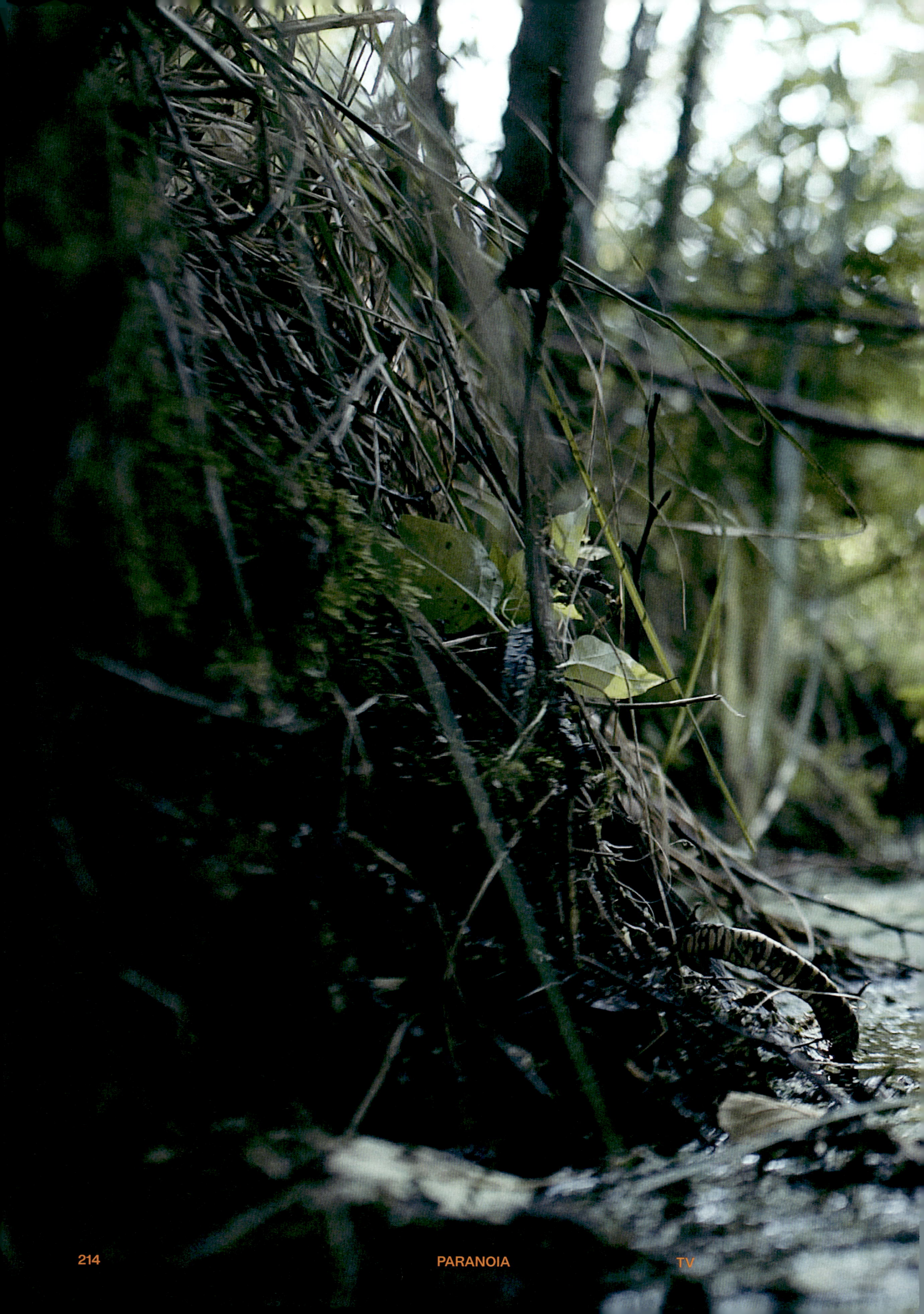

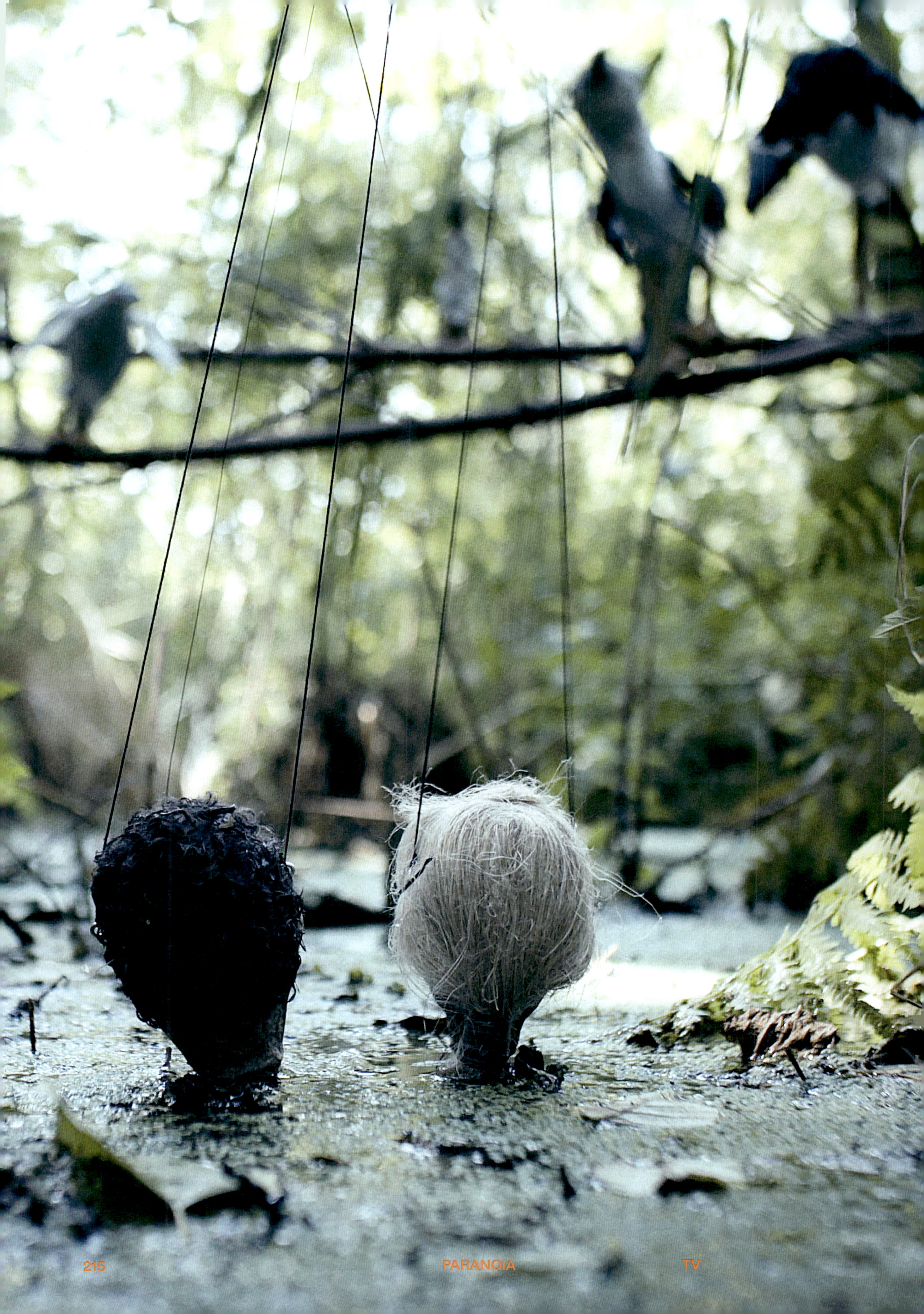

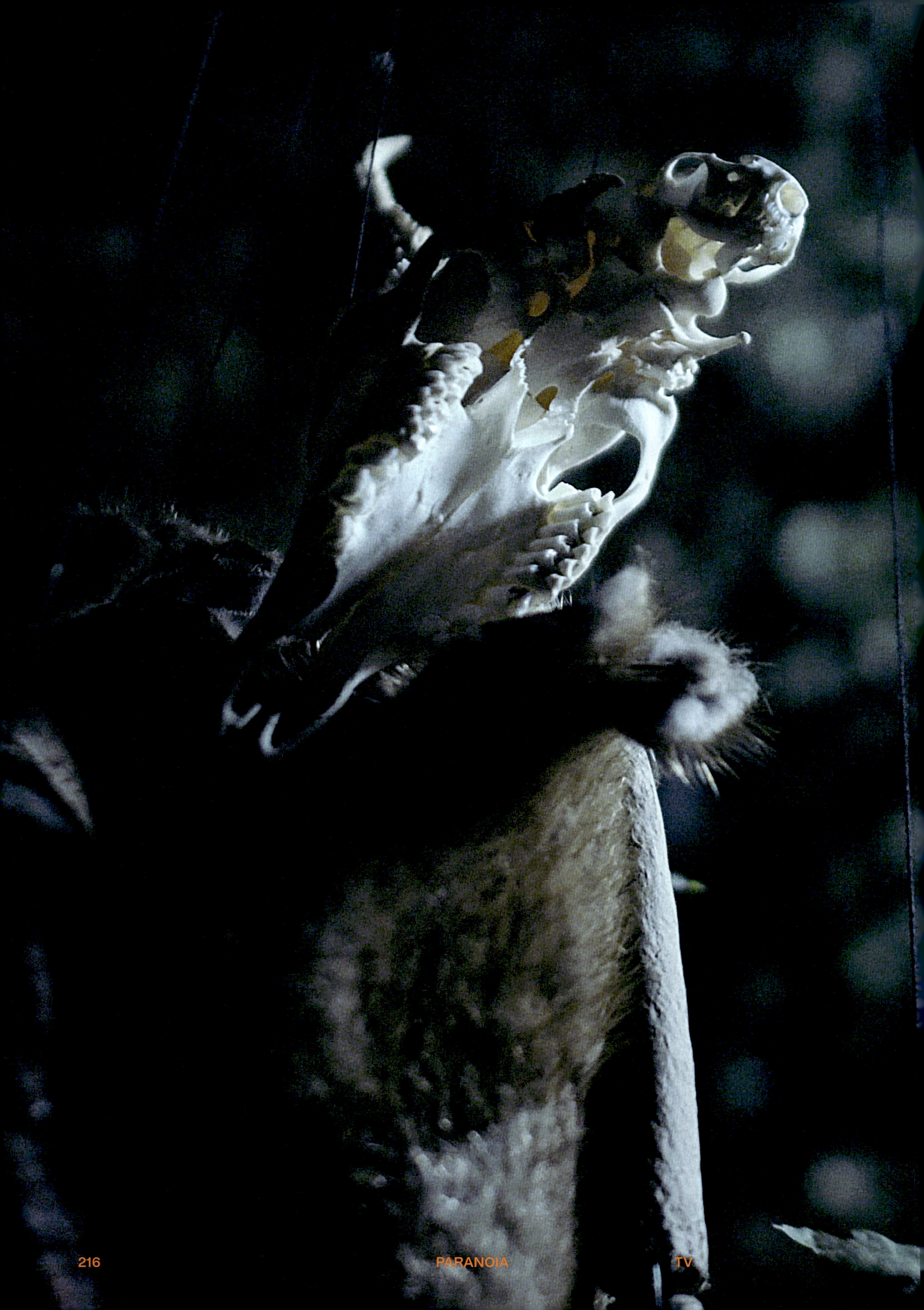

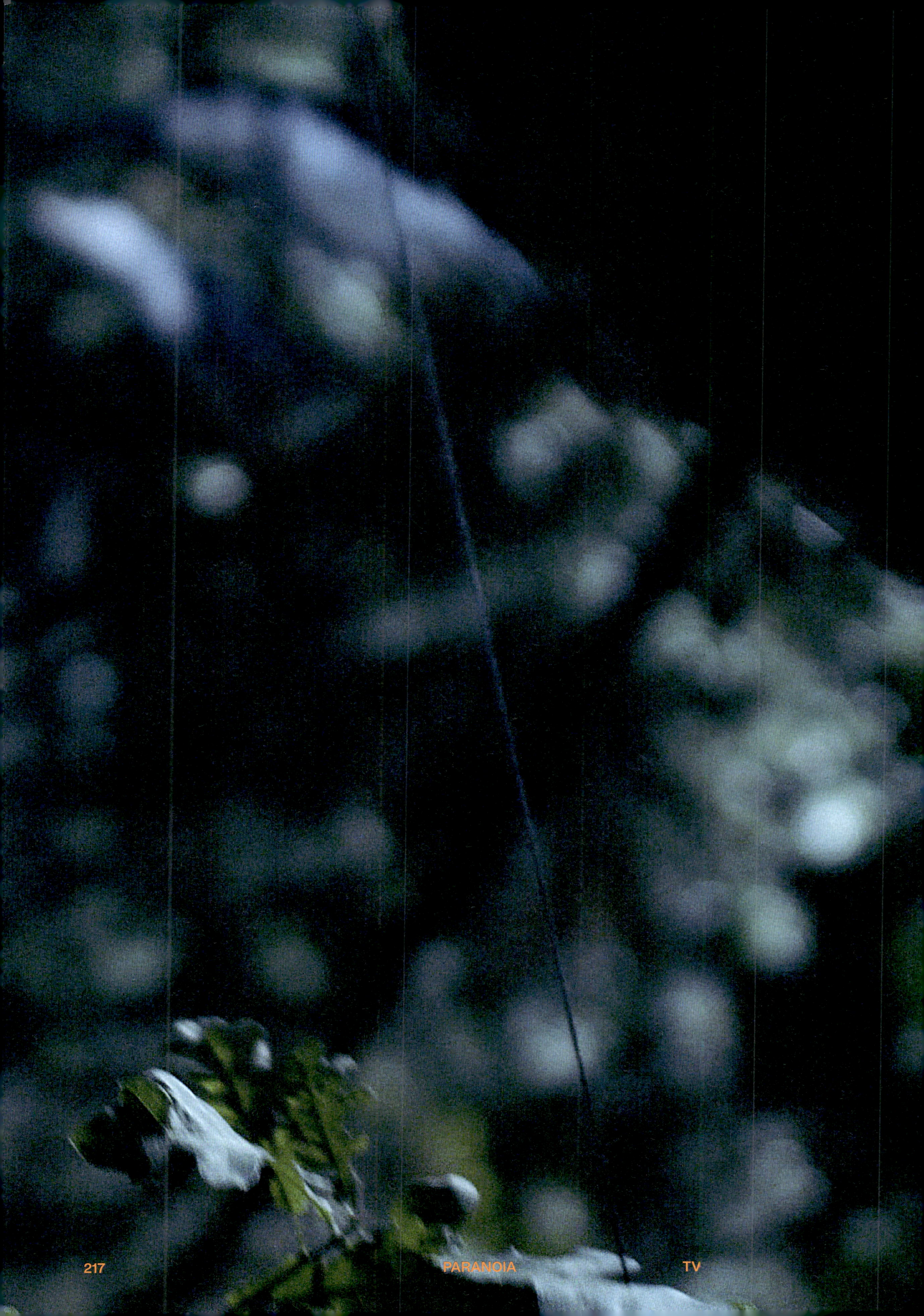

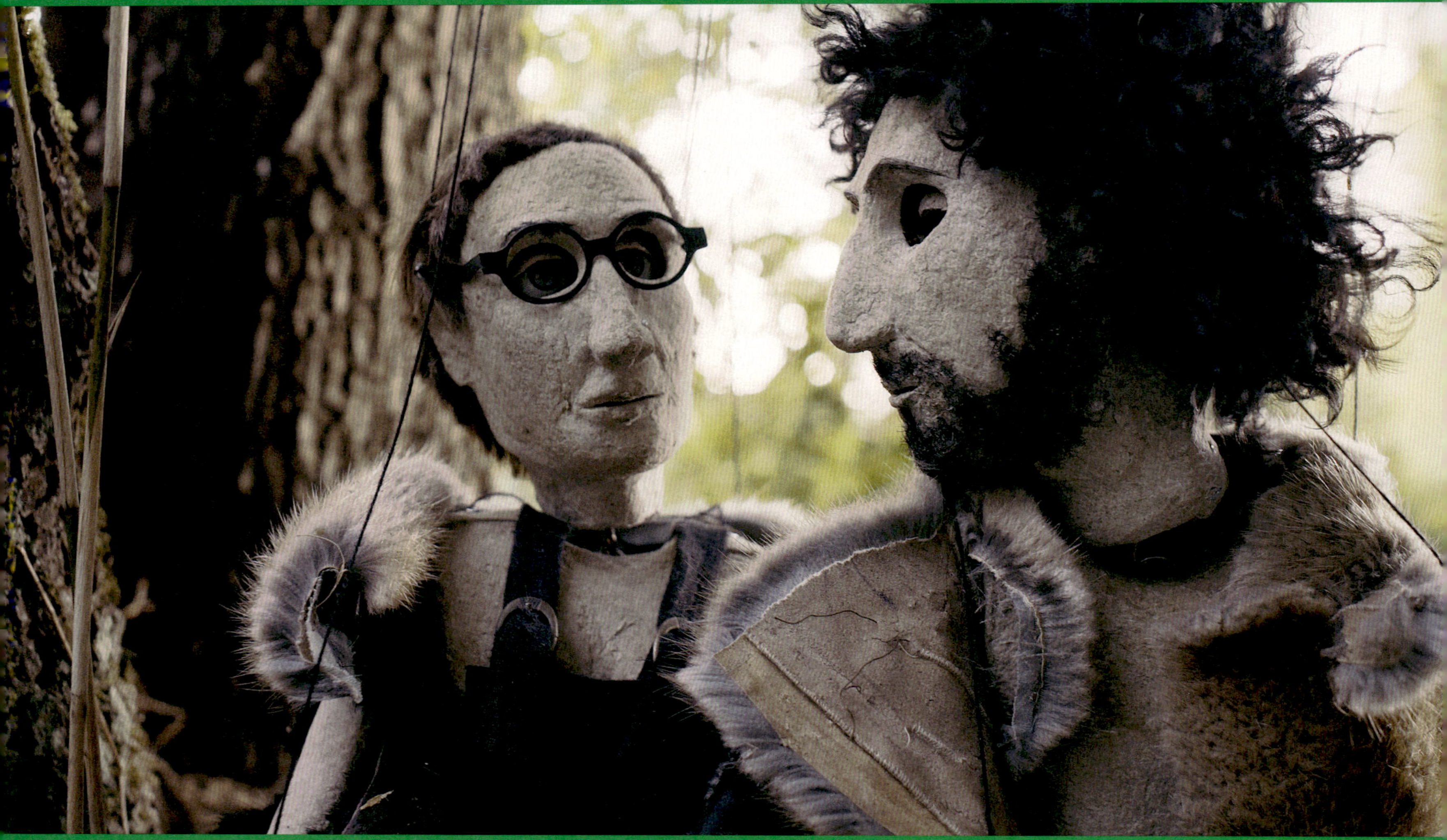

Joanna Rajkowska, born in Bydgoszcz, Poland, in 1968, is a visual artist, best known for her work in public space, where she uses real-life situations, energies, organisms, and materials to construct sites, installations, and ephemeral actions. She utilizes elements as diverse as plants, buildings, found objects, water, or smoke. Defamiliarizing, dehumanizing, and relating are her operating devices. She is interested in the limitations and the limiting of human activities, multiplicity of agencies, and human and nonhuman relations. Recent projects include *The Hatchling* (2018), and upcoming projects include *Rhizopolis* and *Stones and Other Demons* (2021).

Robert Yerachmiel Sniderman, born in Philadephia, USA, in 1986, is a poet-artist who constructs situations, vernacular rites, artifacts, and texts by radicalizing anxiety, proximity, and memory. Recent work includes the durational contemplation *Lost in Jüdischer Friedhof Weißensee* (2018) and its intervention series *Counter-Ruin* (2018), and the procession *Flight Manifestation* (in progress) with Palestinian sound artist Dirar Kalash. He is an editor at the journal *Protocols* and a PhD student at the School for the Contemporary Arts at Simon Fraser University, Vancouver.

Night Herons (2020)
Video, ca. 37 min., English
Online

Music: Mutant Goat (Ola Kozioł, Andrew Dixon, Suavas Lewy)
Dramaturgy: Joanna Rajkowska, Robert Yerachmiel Sniderman, Andrew Dixon
Sets: Andrew Dixon, Basia Ciacek, Viktoriia Tofan
Marionettes: Joanna Rajkowska, Lili Bargłowska, Basia Ciacek, Andrew Dixon, Viktoriia Tofan
Animals: Wiktoria Tofan, Joanna Rajkowska
Costumes: Wiesława Rozwonkowska, Konrad Pietruszyński
Props: Lili Bargłowska, Joanna Rajkowska, Konrad Pietruszyński, Rosa Dixon
Ceramics: Danuta Jarecka
Marionettists: Andrew Dixon, Basia Ciacek, Joanna Rajkowska
Voice-over: Matthew Daniel, Robert Yerachmiel Sniderman
Director of photography: Leszek Molski
Editing: Marcelina Górka
Sound design and mixing: Franciszek Kozłowski
Puppet design consultant: Basia Poczwardowska
Shooting boards: Leszek Molski
Publicity photograph: Marek Szczepański
Producers: Agnieszka Sobocińska, Dorota Przyłubska
Thanks to Theodore Block, Andrzej Rajkowski, Dori Midnight, Gunila Plank and her mother, Katarzyna Górska, Mariusz Widliński, Andreas Staudinger, Uli Vonbank-Schedler, Arnold Rackl, and Christian Berg for sharing knowledge and memory.

Commissioned and produced by steirischer herbst '20
With the kind support of Polish Institute Vienna

Roee Rosen

Lucy Is Sick
2020

Coloring book

In April 2019, after a period of extreme physical hardship, I was diagnosed with multiple myeloma. There followed a year of treatment, some of it in confinement, all of it with a sense of isolation. A tentative return to normalcy (being able to move and walk, shooting a film, traveling, teaching) was cut short by the outbreak of the coronavirus pandemic.

One illness whose totality was bodily and private was replaced by another, whose totality was in its ubiquity. Somatic symptoms were replaced, in the experience of many of us, by potentialities, speculations, and projections that enfold both daily experience and the world (by which I mean a totality that reaches beyond that of human animals only). Both illnesses weighed in through tropes of extreme measures of quarantine and isolation, but also with revelations on ways in which togetherness might be experienced. This is the matrix *Lucy Is Sick* tackles, in a rather personal way.

Roee Rosen

Roee Rosen, born in Rehovot, Israel, in 1963, is a multidisciplinary artist, writer, and filmmaker. His highly litaerary and densely visual films, paintings, installations, and books frequently feature invented figures and controversially address taboo zones in 20th-century history as well as contemporary political reality. Recent solo exhibitions include shows at 1646, The Hague; Koresh 14, Jerusalem; HaMidrasha Gallery, Tel Aviv; Kunsthal Charlottenborg, Copenhagen; Project Arts Centre, Dublin; Impakt Centre for Media Culture, Utrecht; Erna Hecey Gallery, Luxembourg; Centre Pompidou, Paris; Riccardo Crespi Gallery, Milan; and Edith-Russ-Haus für Medienkunst, Oldenburg. Rosen participated in the 2018 Athens Biennale; Documenta 14, Kassel/Athens (2017); Manifesta 7, Trentino—Alto Adige (2008); the 2012 Taipei Biennial; the Oberhausen International Short Film Festival; FIDMarseille International Film Festival; Bucharest International Experimental Film Festival; Viennale; Rotterdam International Film Festival; and Transmediale, Berlin, among many others.

Lucy Is Sick (2020)
Coloring book, English/German

Editing (English): David Riff
German translation: Thomas Melle
Editing (German): Henriette Gallus
Layout: Grupa Ee

Commissioned and produced by steirischer herbst '20
Distribution partner: Steiermärkische Krankenanstaltengesellschaft m.b.H., LKH-Univ. Klinikum Graz
With the kind support of Artis

8.

After weeks of being trapped in complete immobility, Lucy had a lifelike daydream. His body escaped from within his body. One Lucy remained imprisoned in his chair, while the other rose up, naked and barefoot, and escaped the house unnoticed. The free body knew its time was limited. It only had a few minutes. So it fled to the nearby fields, running as fast as it could, relishing the wind stirred up by its own movement, enjoying the moderate and rhythmic waves of pain as his soles pressed into the gravel, with each step, a pain with direct, explicable, willed causality. Then, Lucy's body turned back on the same road, rushing to return on time to its invalid shell.

A year later, Lucy has a dream. In it, he received as a gift a big, black female bear. It was explained to him that this bear is the best and most advanced hi-fi system: you have to sow a turntable into the bear's belly; its enormous size, its organic warmth, and its silky long fur provide celestial acoustics, further enhanced by the burdened bear's strained, tiny movements.

In the dream, Lucy understands that though monstrously cruel, this is the way things are. Furthermore, he cannot insult the unknown gift giver by rejecting the bear. Instead, he decides to adopt the animal as a pet. Lucy and the bear curl up in bed, and somehow, watching the animal's big dark claws, he believes that he might be safe. His bear will almost certainly not attack him.

Initially, the dream seems inexplicable, unlike the escape fantasy. But, if you think of animals and people, perhaps it is just as straightforward.

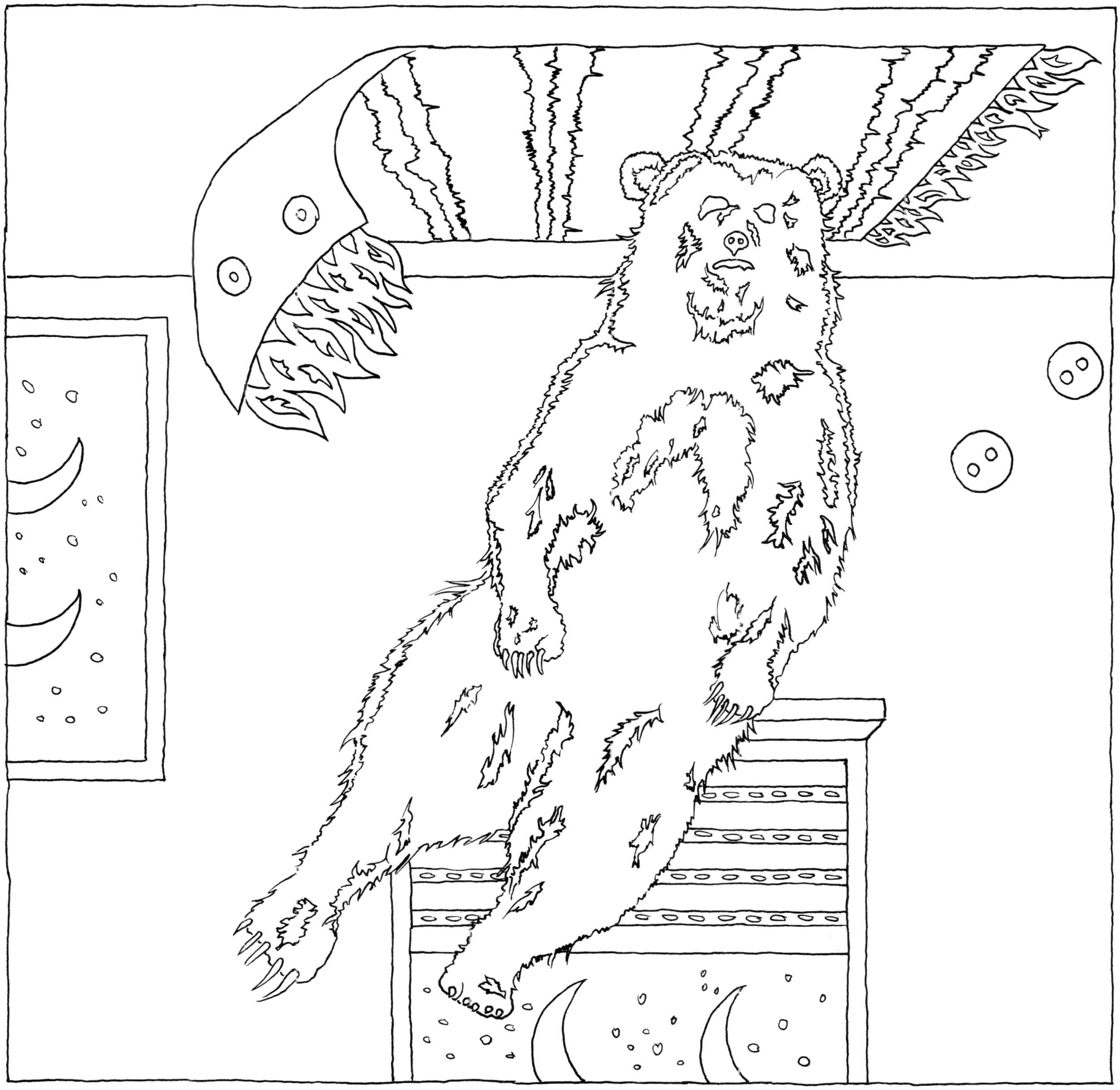

Susanne Sachsse / Marc Siegel /
Xiu Xiu (Jamie Stewart)

YOU'RE SO PARANOID YOU PROBABLY THINK THIS RADIO SHOW IS ABOUT YOU
A Musical Broadcast Entertainment Service
2020

Radio play

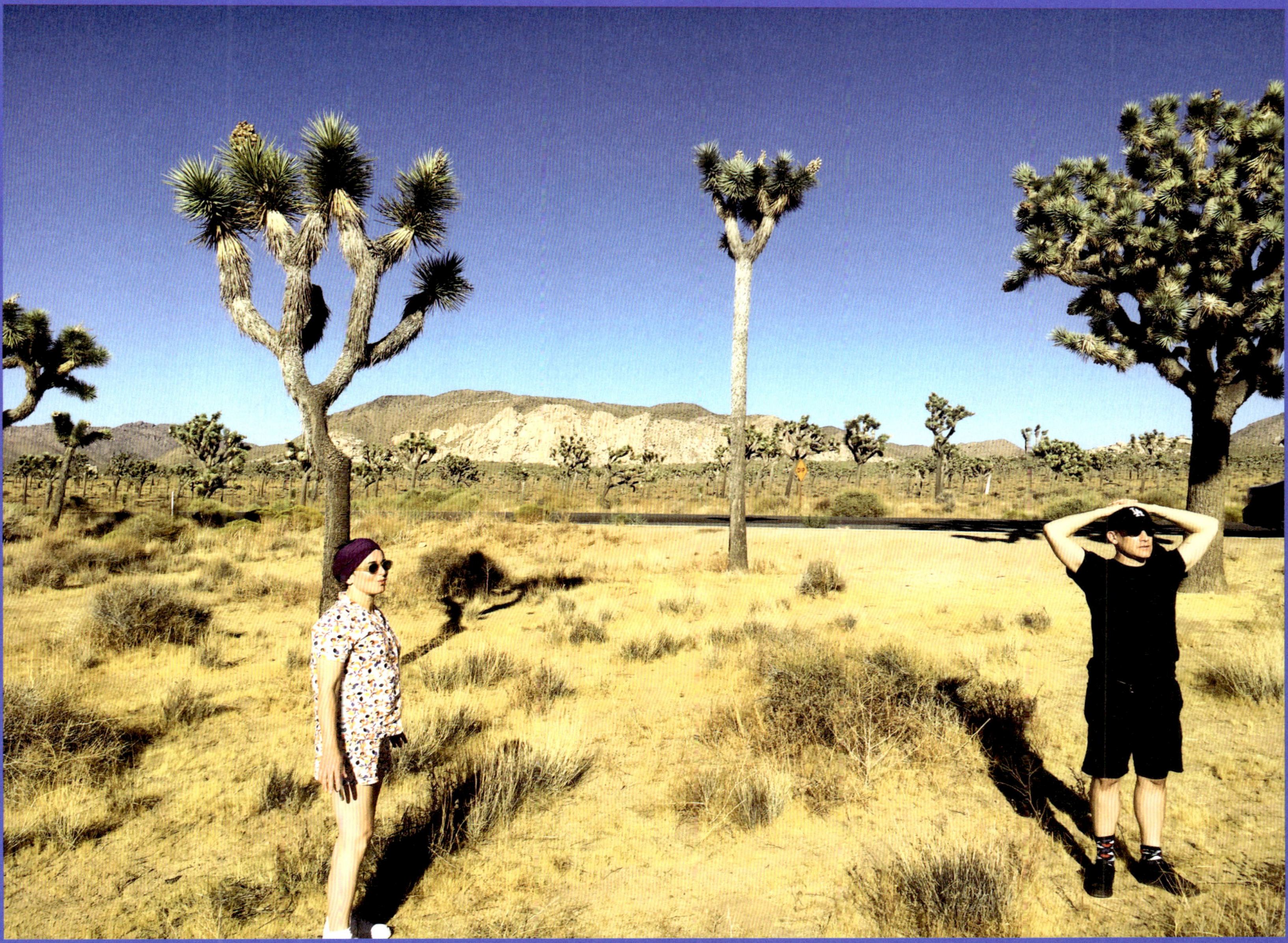

you're so paranoid you probably think this radio show is about you – attention, attention – this is the graz broadcasting center – the entertainment radio service – you are just supposed to listen – not look – not care – not feel – an unidentified woman whispers something in an ear – by and with susanne sachsse – marc siegel – xiu xiu – also featuring - maximilian brauer – vaginal davis – salome gersch – gotthard lange – martin siemann – pola sieverding – şenol şentürk – angela seo – zigzagging between here and there – intensified social control – intensified governmental control – immunological demands – refuse touch – proximity transformed – abide and adapt – don't inhale – where's my mouth – the limits of control – someone cooked this up – i'm not gonna be surprised – i know what's up – join me you dupes – it's not supposed to feel good – invisible masses – directed masses – baiting masses – fleeing masses – prohibiting masses – manipulable masses – dumb dumb dumb masses – they need direction – can the masses be revolutionary – do you have an antitoxin – the masses cheer themselves on – good and fine – but what about the sound of data – the masses aren't what they used to be – you are no longer in your family – you are no longer in school – there's no need to fear – there's no need to hope – there's no need to ask which is the more liberated or more tolerable regime – because within each there are liberating and enslaving forces – in these kinds of societies what is important is the code – forgotten your pin – click here – the coder must be protected from the code – hence the time limit on my job – the word is the virus – antibodies in language – suggestions are words – convictions are words – orders are words – number are viruses too – you think you just played the lottery – ha – our health will not come from separation – we must go from a forced mutation to a chosen mutation – is it really so sad and dangerous to be sick of seeing with your eyes – breathing with your lungs – swallowing with your mouth – speaking with the tongue – thinking with the brain – having an anus and a larynx – head and legs – why not walk on your head – sing with your sinuses – look through your skin – breathe through your stomach – between us – i have two vulvas – each one lovingly tucked under my armpits – that leaves us with two options for survival – 1. chosen mutation – 2. not knowing not having certainty

Susanne Sachsse / Marc Siegel / Xiu Xiu (Jamie Stewart)

Susanne Sachsse is a Berlin-based actress. In 2001, she co-founded the artists' collective CHEAP. Sachsse has worked internationally in various performance, film, and art contexts with Yael Bartana, Jonathan Berger, Zach Blas, Phil Collins, Keren Cytter, Vaginal Davis, Natascha Sadr Haghighian, Bruce LaBruce, Laibach, Ligia Lewis, Josiah McElheny, Vegard Vinge & Ida Müller, and Xiu Xiu. She is a recipient of the Premio Maguey Queer Icon Award at the Guadalajara International Film Festival. In 2021, she will open her first solo exhibition at Participant Inc. in New York.

Marc Siegel is professor of film studies at Johannes Gutenberg University Mainz. He researches and writes about experimental film and queer culture. His book *A Gossip of Images* is forthcoming from Duke University Press in 2022. Siegel has curated numerous international film programs, performance festivals, and events. He is on the advisory board of the Berlinale Forum Expanded and a founding member of the Berlin-based artists' collective CHEAP.

Xiu Xiu is an avant-pop/experimental music group founded in 2002 in California. They have released thirteen full length albums and countless singles and EPs, limited-edition side projects, and field recordings. Remarkable guest collaborations include, among many others, Charlemagne Palestine, Grouper, Oxbow, Deerhoof, and Master Drummers of Haiti. Xiu Xiu have collaborated on several large-scale projects and concerts with the artist Danh Vo at the Solomon R. Guggenheim Museum, New York, Walker Art Center, Minneapolis, and The Kitchen, New York. With the blessing and support of David Lynch, they were commissioned by the Gallery of Modern Art in Brisbane to reinterpret the music of his landmark work *Twin Peaks*. They are currently at work on a 14th album for release in 2021, several collaborations, a novel, and a bird sanctuary.

YOU'RE SO PARANOID YOU PROBABLY THINK THIS RADIO SHOW IS ABOUT YOU: A Musical Broadcast Entertainment Service (2020)
Radio play, ca. 60 min., German
Online

With: Maximilian Brauer, Vaginal Davis, Salome Gersch, Gotthard Lange, Susanne Sachsse, Angela Seo, Şenol Sentürk, Marc Siegel, Martin Siemann, Pola Sieverding, Jamie Stewart

Commissioned by steirischer herbst '20
Produced by Susanne Sachsse, Marc Siegel, and Xiu Xiu in coproduction with steirischer herbst '20

Igor Samolet

Cuddle Porn
2020

Installation

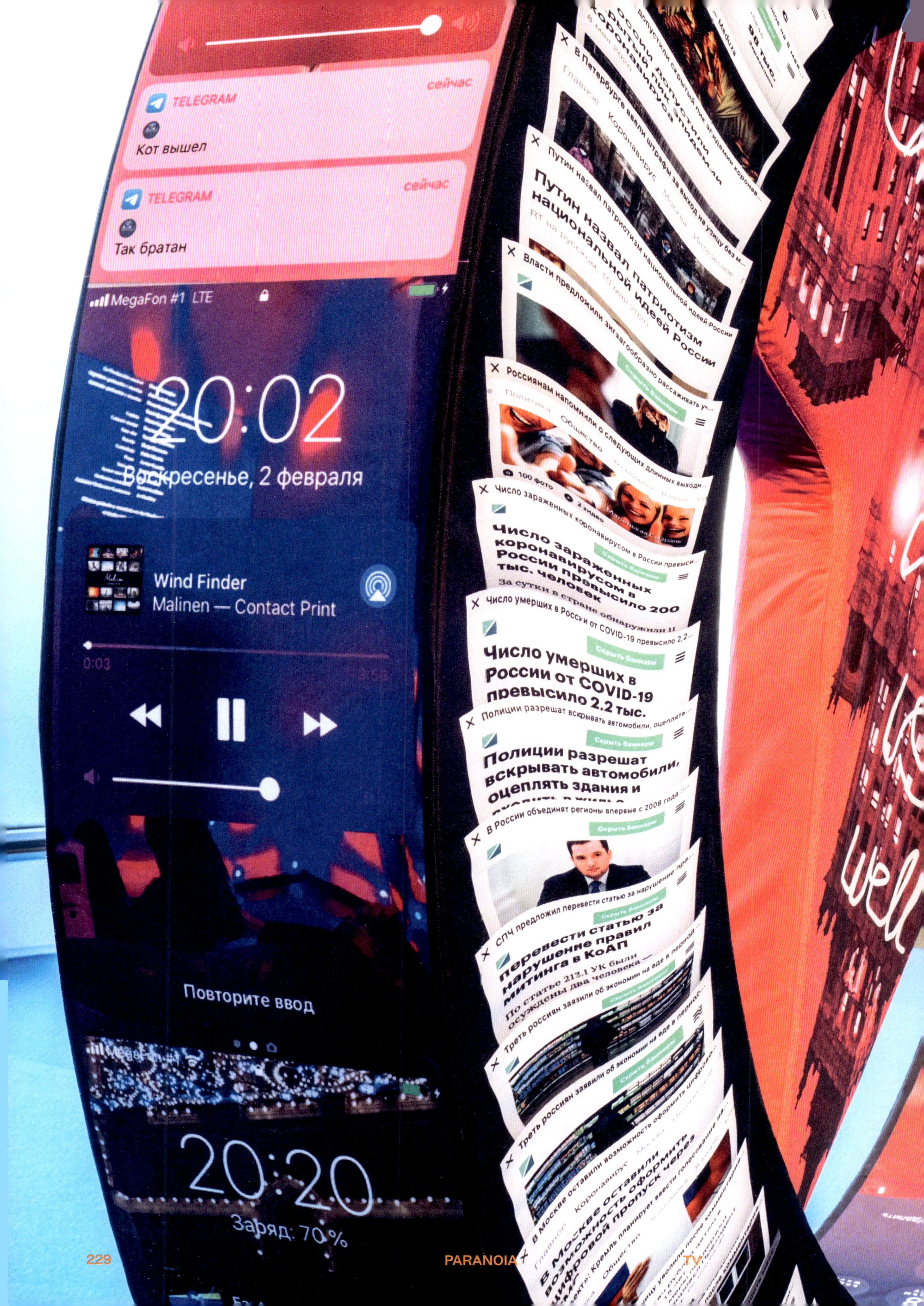

TELEGRAM
сейчас
Кот вышел
TELEGRAM
сейчас
Так братан
MegaFon #1 LTE
20:02
Воскресенье, 2 февраля
Wind Finder
Malinen — Contact Print
0:03
Повторите ввод
20:20
Заряд: 70%
Путин назвал патриотизм национальной идеей России
Власти предложили зигзагообразно рассаживать у...
Россиянам напомнили о следующих длинных выходн...
Число зараженных коронавирусом в России превыси...
Число зараженных коронавирусом в России превысило 200 тыс. человек
Число умерших в России от COVID-19 превысило 2,2...
Число умерших в России от COVID-19 превысило 2.2 тыс.
Полиции разрешат вскрывать автомобили, оцеплять...
Полиции разрешат вскрывать автомобили, оцеплять здания и
В России объединят регионы впервые с 2008 года
СПЧ предложил перевести статью за нарушение пра...
перевести статью за нарушение правил митинга в КоАП
Треть россиян заявили об экономии на еде в период...
В Москве оставили возможность оформить цифровой пропуск через

World news to make your head spin, the same old alternative facts from home, viral memes gone global and intimate nighttime messages: this is what makes up the fragmented and contradictory world of a Muscovite today, both lonely and über-connected, hyper- and meta-politicized, and apolitical all at once. That is the attitude to which Igor Samolet gives form in his installation at the Paranoia TV Headquarters, casting himself as its self-effacing hero. He becomes a passive activist, a club-hopping, all-night-partying version of the famously indolent literary hero Oblomov. Being connected represents a myriad of possibilities for experimenting, but it also means being fully under state-corporate control, or getting one's head smashed by a wheel of headlines. Samolet's world is both merciless and friendly, like all social media. It invites visitors to spend some time there, to dwell in random quotes, to nostalgically look at "cuddle porn" images from back when hugs were still allowed, or just to sit around and charge their cell phones.

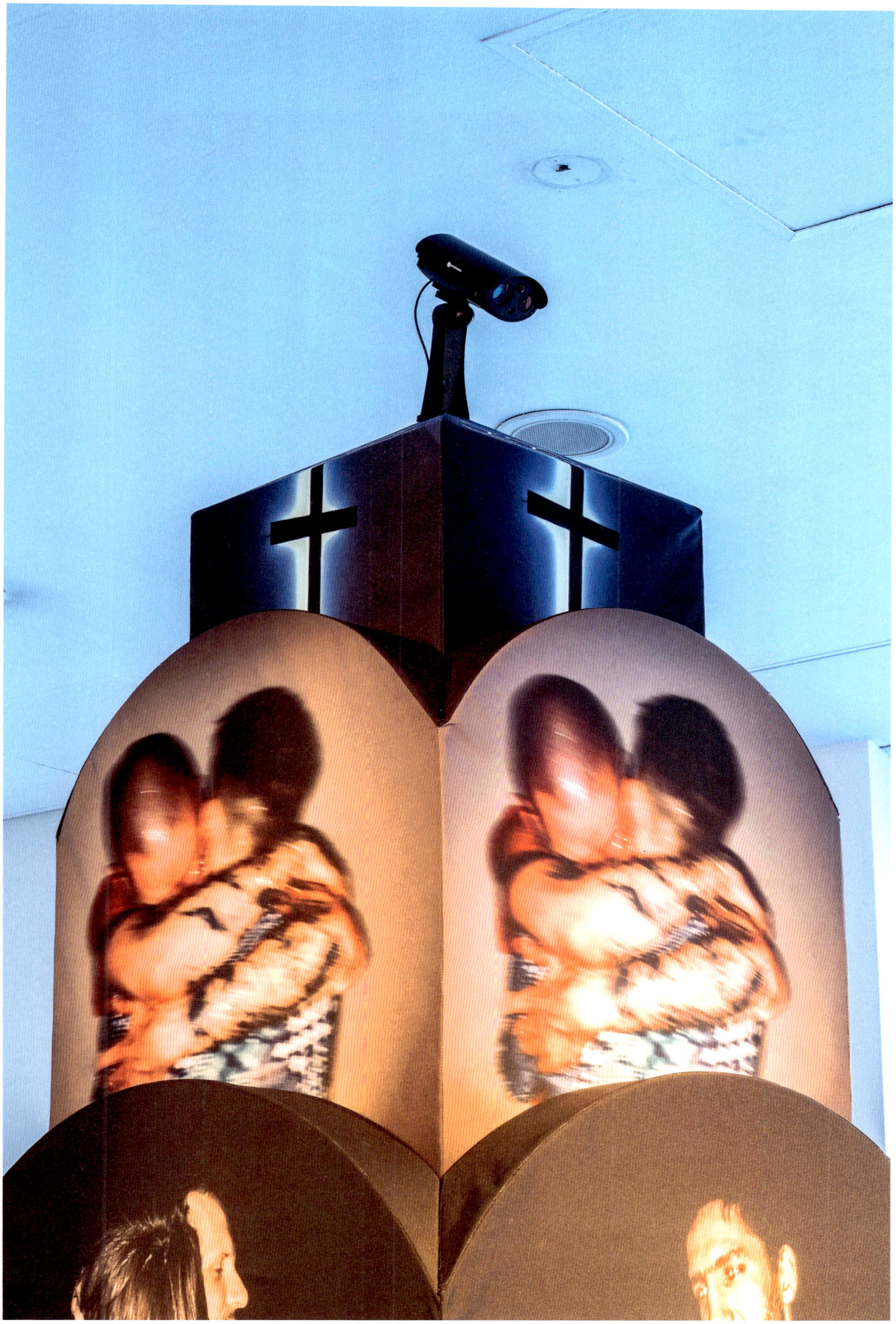

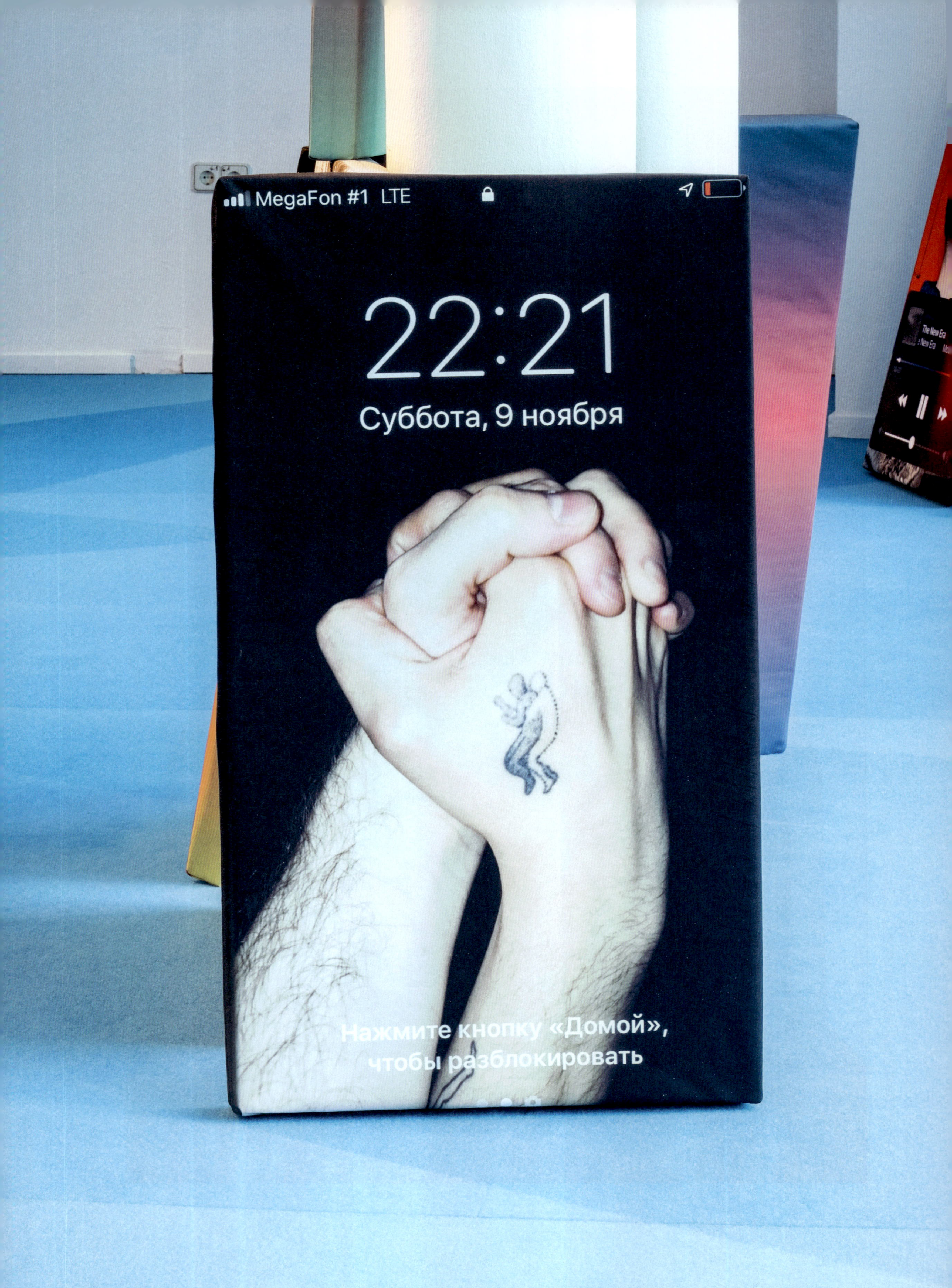
MegaFon #1 LTE
22:21
Суббота, 9 ноября
Нажмите кнопку «Домой»,
чтобы разблокировать

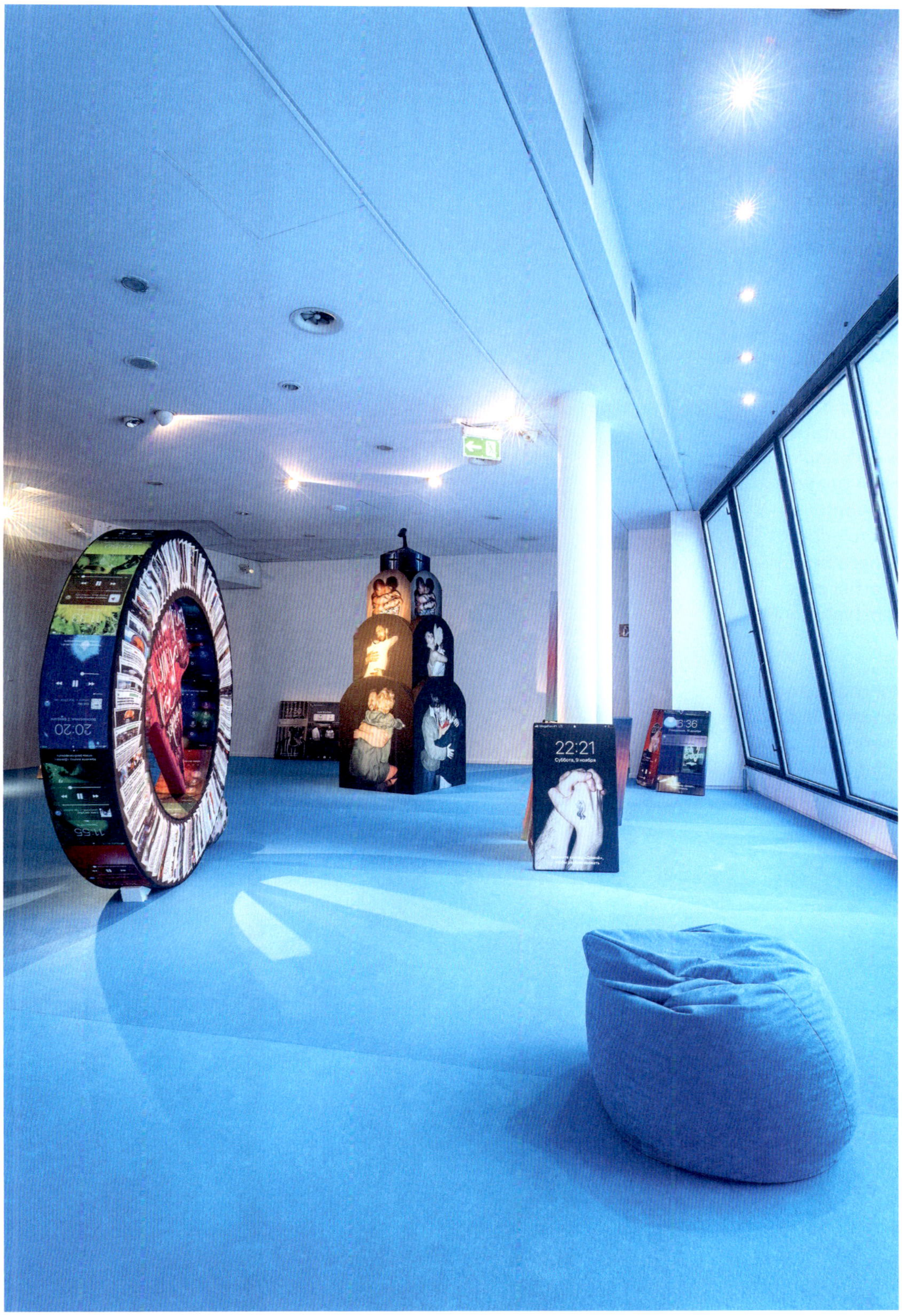
22:21

234

Cuddle Porn (2020)
Installation
Paranoia TV Headquarters

Commissioned and produced by steirischer herbst ’20

Igor Samolet was born in Syktyvkar, in the industrial north of Russia, in 1984, and currently lives in Moscow. His photobook *Be Happy!* received a silver medal at the 2014 German Photobook Award and was included in the third volume of *The Photobook: A History*, coedited by Martin Parr and Gerry Badger. As an artist, he moved from staged and slightly absurdist photography toward various digital media that constitute the horizon of a contemporary young urban person.

Embracing small screens, he translates them into large-scale installations that examine human relationships, their drama, and their comedy through digital filters. His work often focuses on people marginalized by the new Russian political order and lack of freedom of speech, craving for self-expression. Samolet’s protagonists are maverick, vulnerable, and their life quest is about, as the artist puts it, “how to be happy in the given historical circumstances.”

Samolet has taken part in numerous photo and art exhibitions in Russia and abroad. His most recent solo show, *Energy of Mistake*, was shown at the Multimedia Art Museum, Moscow (2019). In 2019, he received the Credit Suisse Cosmoscow Prize for Young Artists.

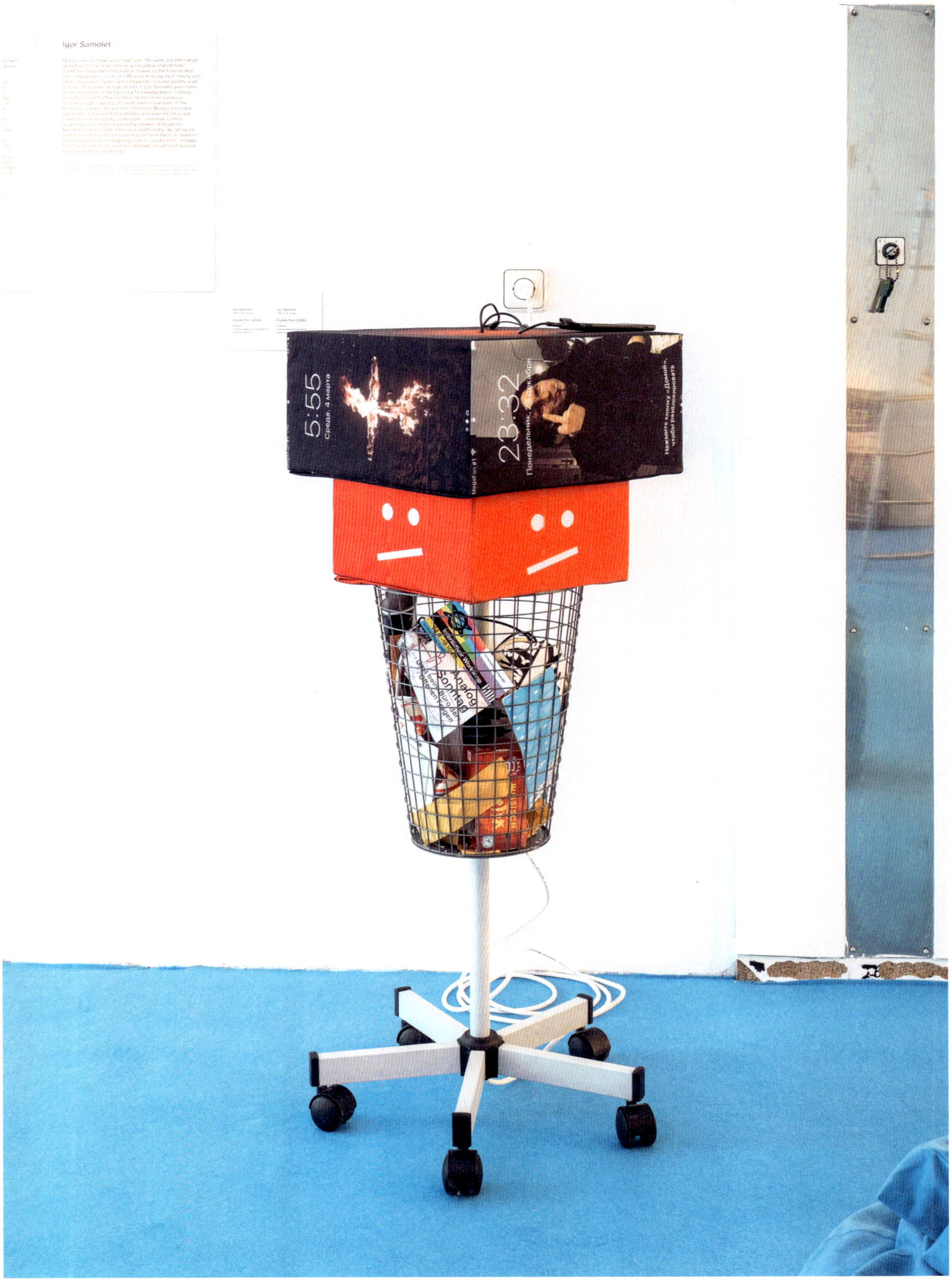
Igor Samolet
5:55
Среда, 4 марта
23:32
Нажмите кнопку «Домой», чтобы разблокировать

Liv Schulman

Brown, yellow, white and dead
2020

Video series

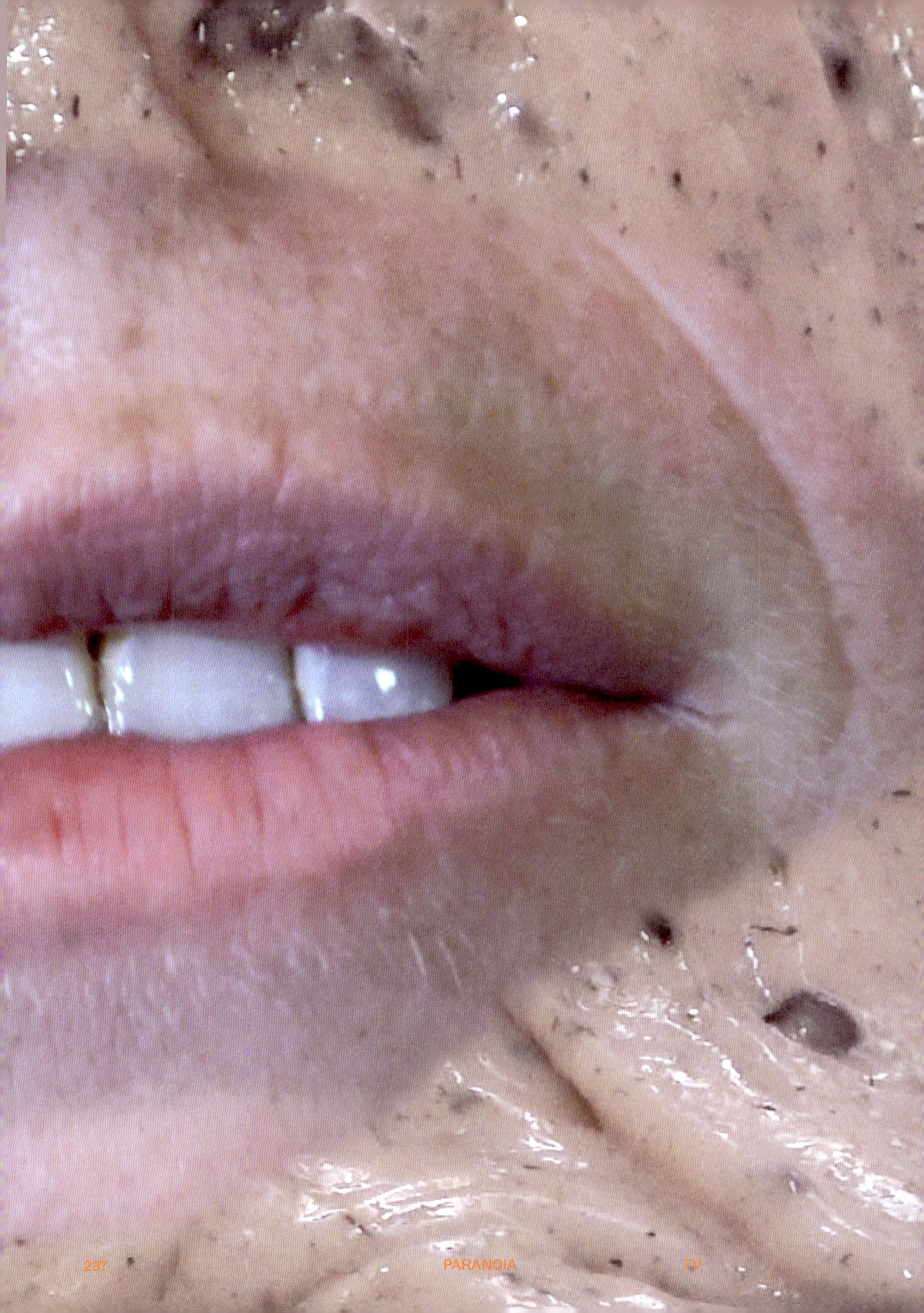

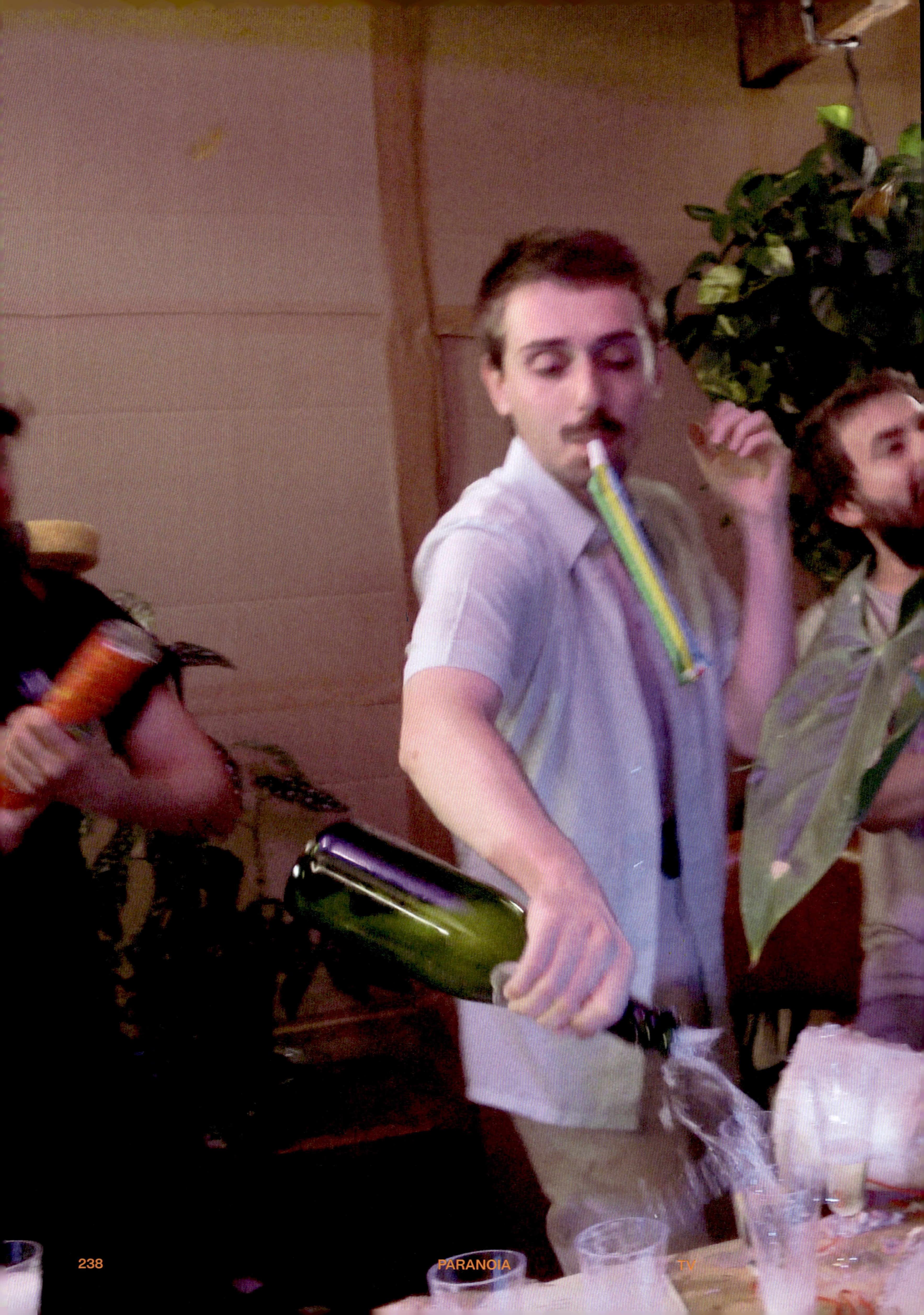

Two film producers, an artist, and an unemployed actor are making a horror film. Its protagonists are a group of neighbors who retreat to the basement of their building out of sheer enthusiasm for home brewing and Tupperware, where they bring a monster to life . . . Liv Schulman's miniseries revolves around today's widespread idea of "prosumer" culture, where consumers are not merely passive buyers of goods, but produce or market specialty items themselves.

With its cardboard set and its homemade costumes, the horror movie in Schulman's miniseries is itself an example of such DIY entrepreneurialism. In work and brainstorming meetings, the male fantasy of perfect consumption gives rise to a giant leech that seduces the women and forces the men to question their sexuality. It becomes clear that some crucial questions are at the center of this homemade miniseries: What are the economics of productions like these? What leads to their appearance, and under which circumstances are they perceived as art?

In the early morning at the production studio, Liv wakes up to come across an unemployed actor who is in perpetual audition. Pauline and Quentin, the two producers, arrive. After a reading judged disappointing by the production studio of *Brown, yellow, white and dead*, they begin to brainstorm and gradually play the content of the film.

The next episode opens with Liv in a trance who describes the climax of the film. The crew continues to read different sequences of the film and slowly sink into a tangle of flashbacks.

One by one the characters in the film remember: a mother who is a scientist and a father who is an unemployed anti-capitalist activist. Liv, Pauline, Quentin, and the actor end up under the table: a form of delirium seems to invade them. But then we find the director, the actor in audition, and the two producers reading a conflictive scene where everyone insults each other in alphabetical order. The closed-door setup from the beginning has created a form of tension between the characters and leaves less and less room for the boundary between work session and fiction in the scenes written by the artist.

At the production studio, the crew loses footing. The actor thinks he's a yoga teacher obsessed with her stools, Quentin has become Catherine, and Pauline is psychologically pregnant, obsessed with producing the film. Running out of ideas, Liv hires a new actress to replace the bad actor and their toxic humanity.

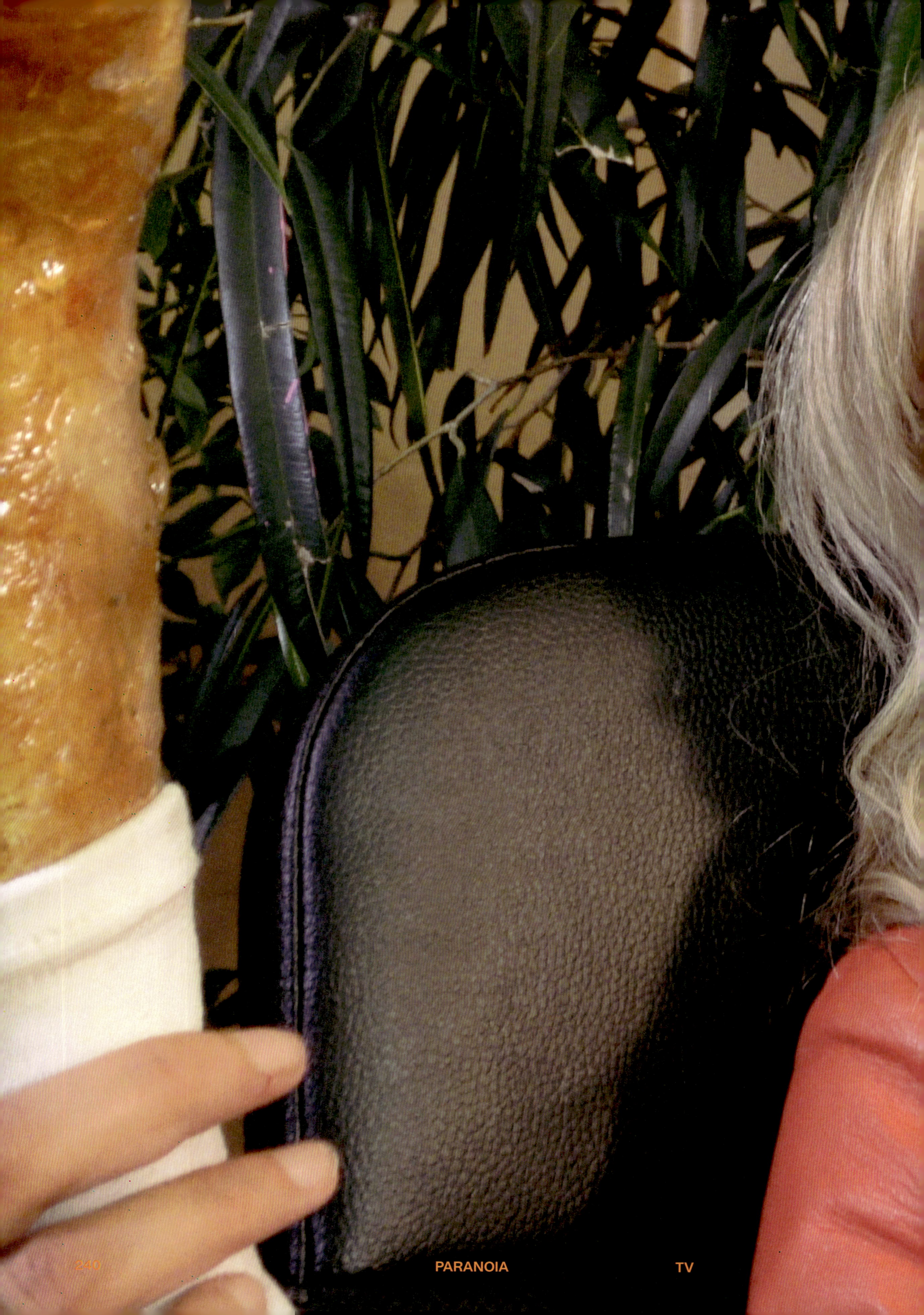

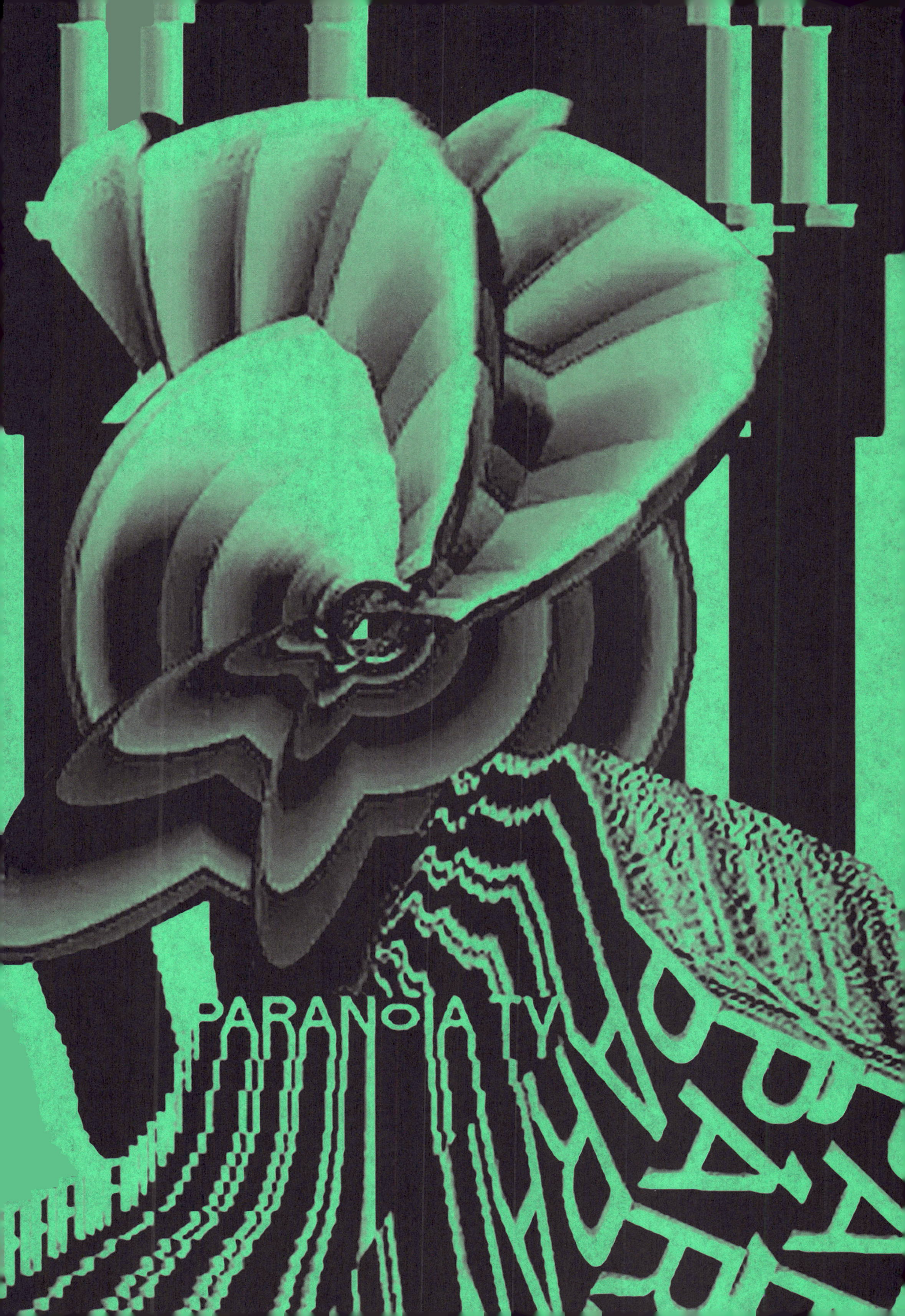
PARANOIA TY

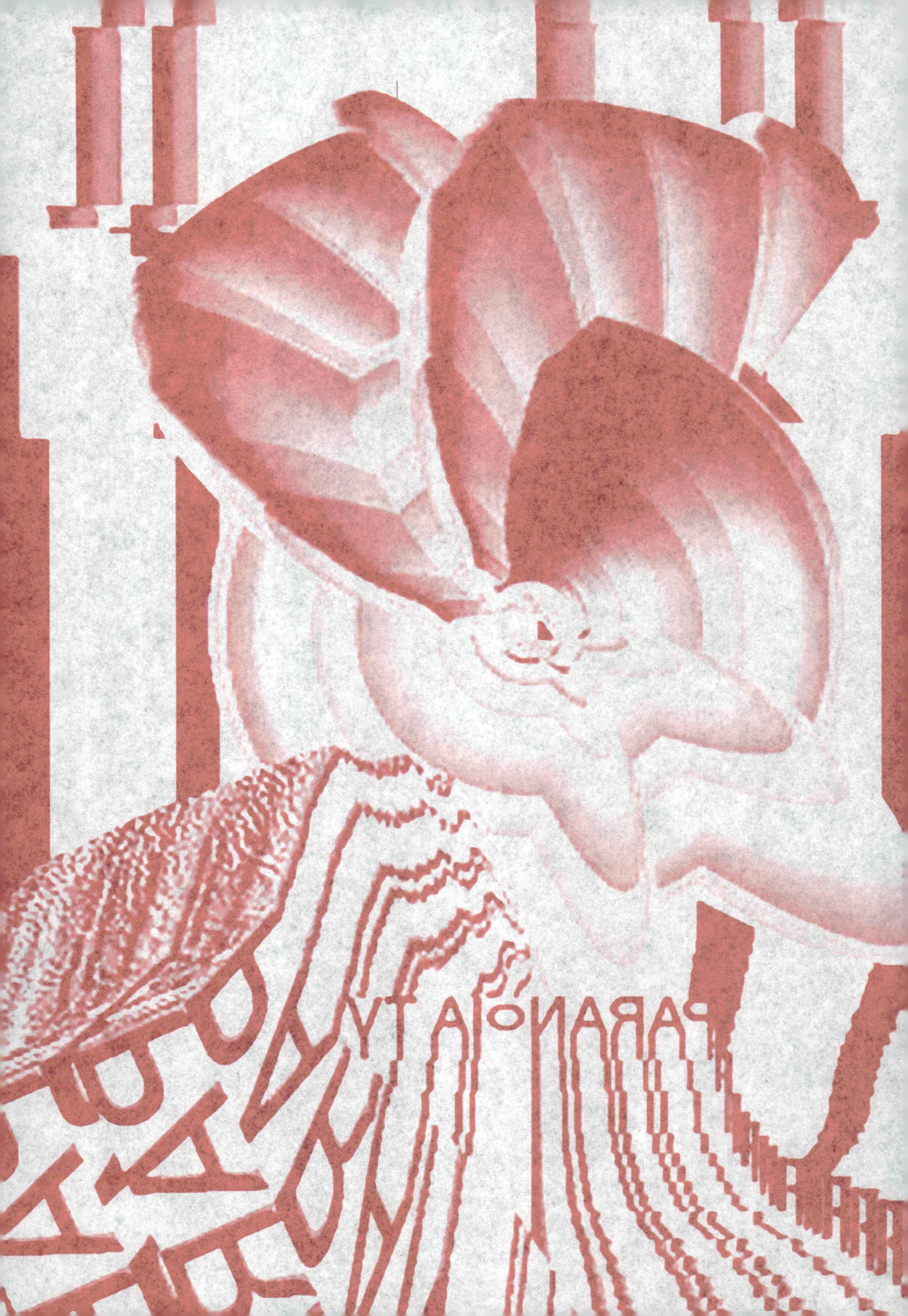

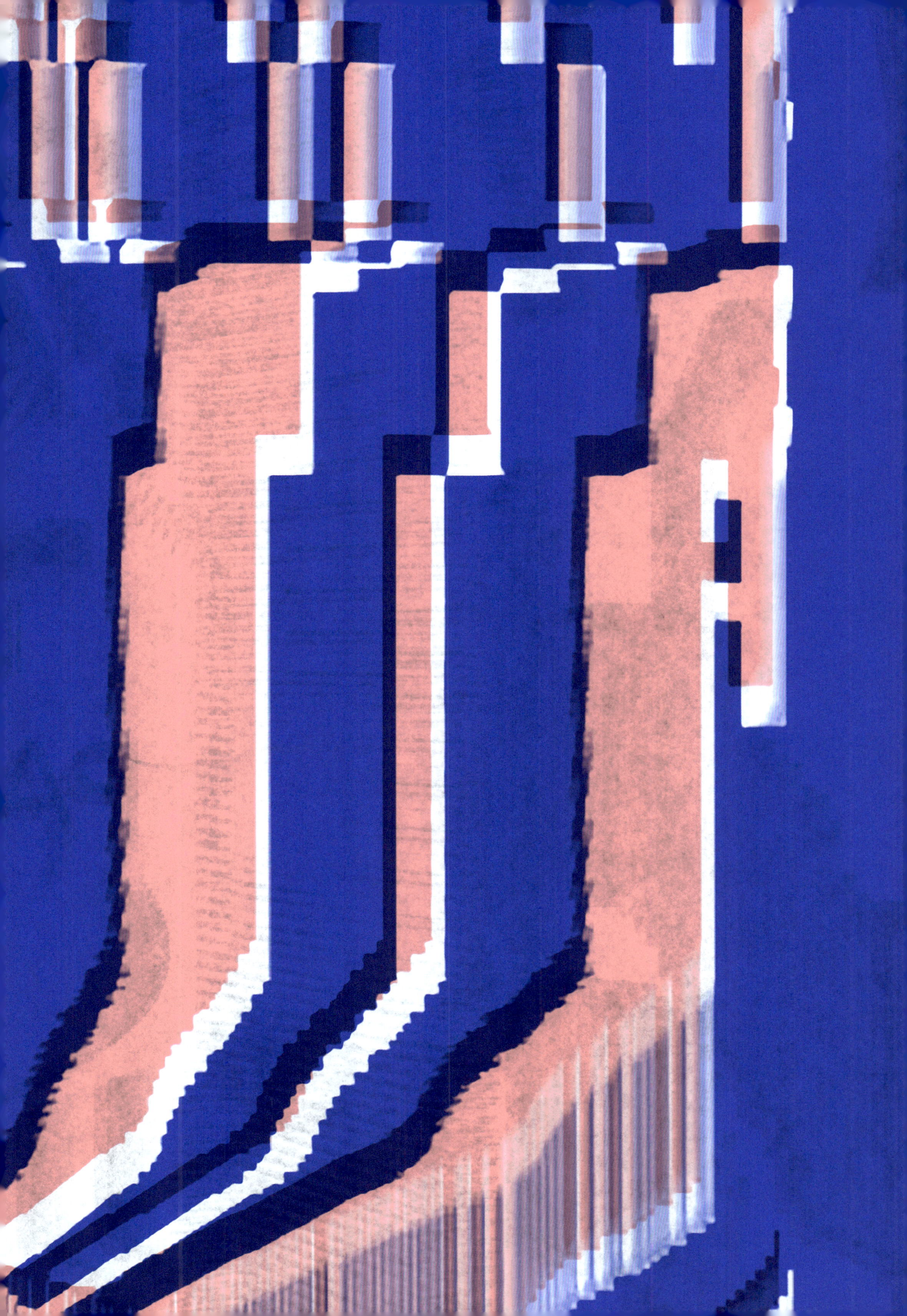

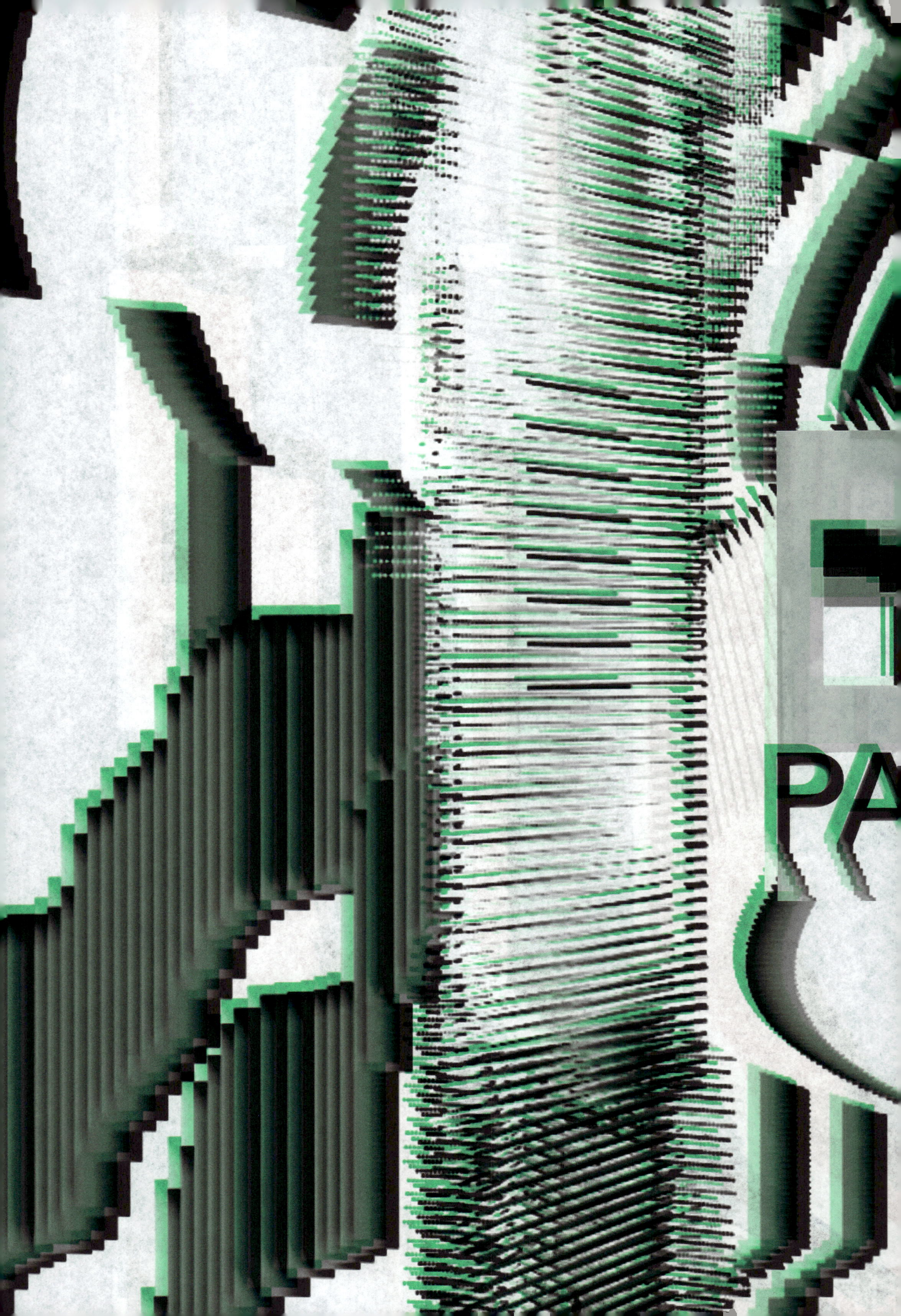
PA

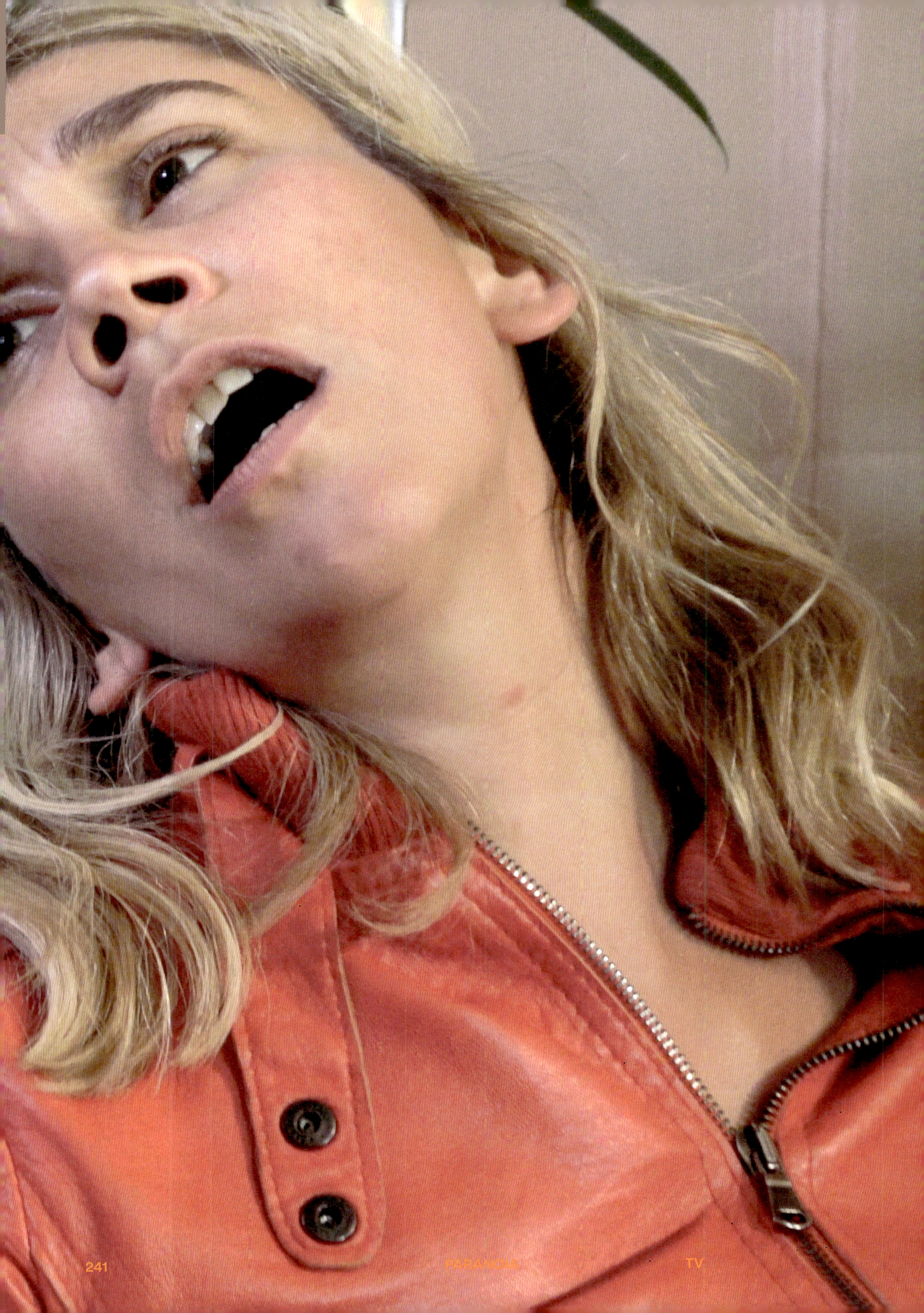

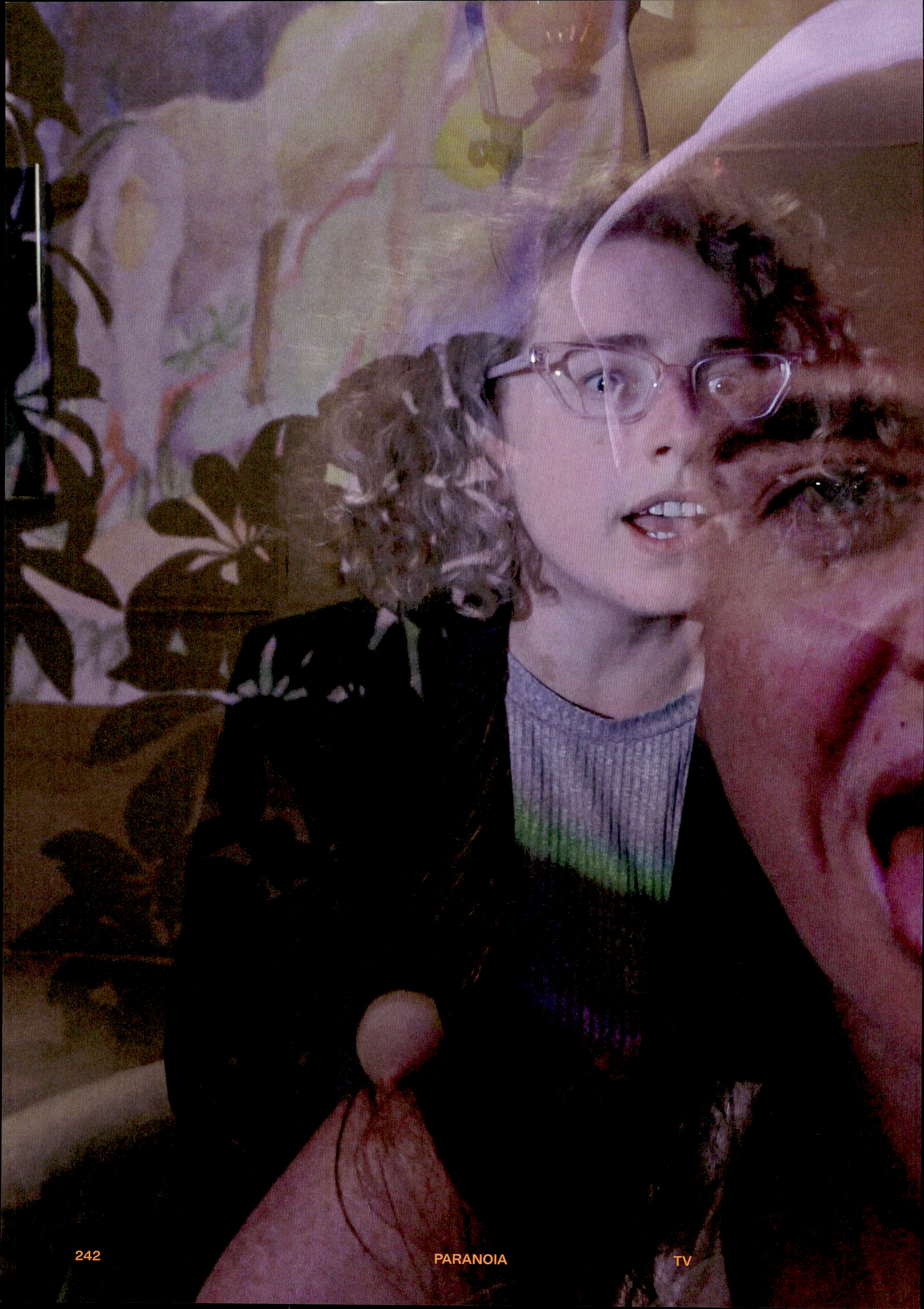

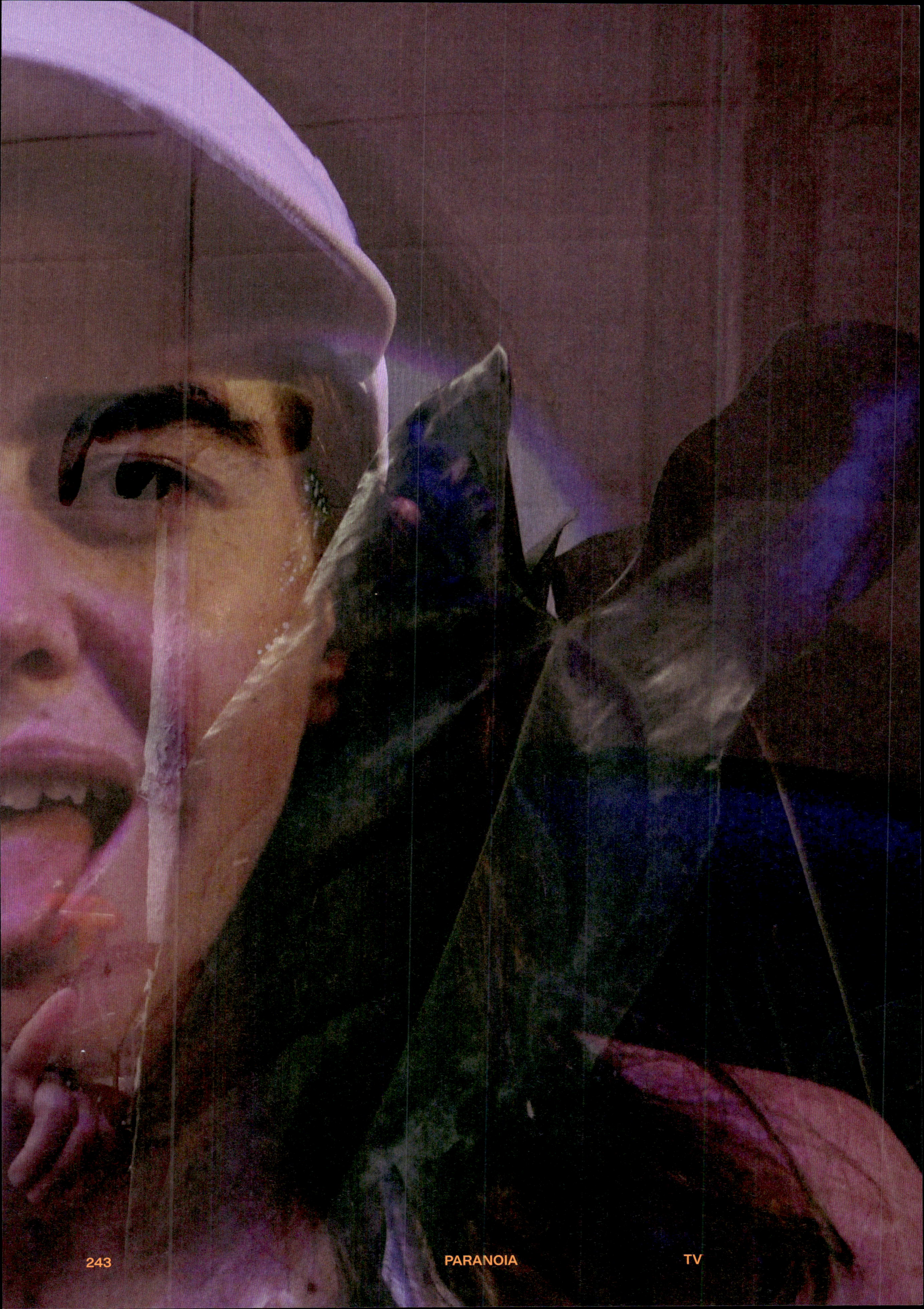

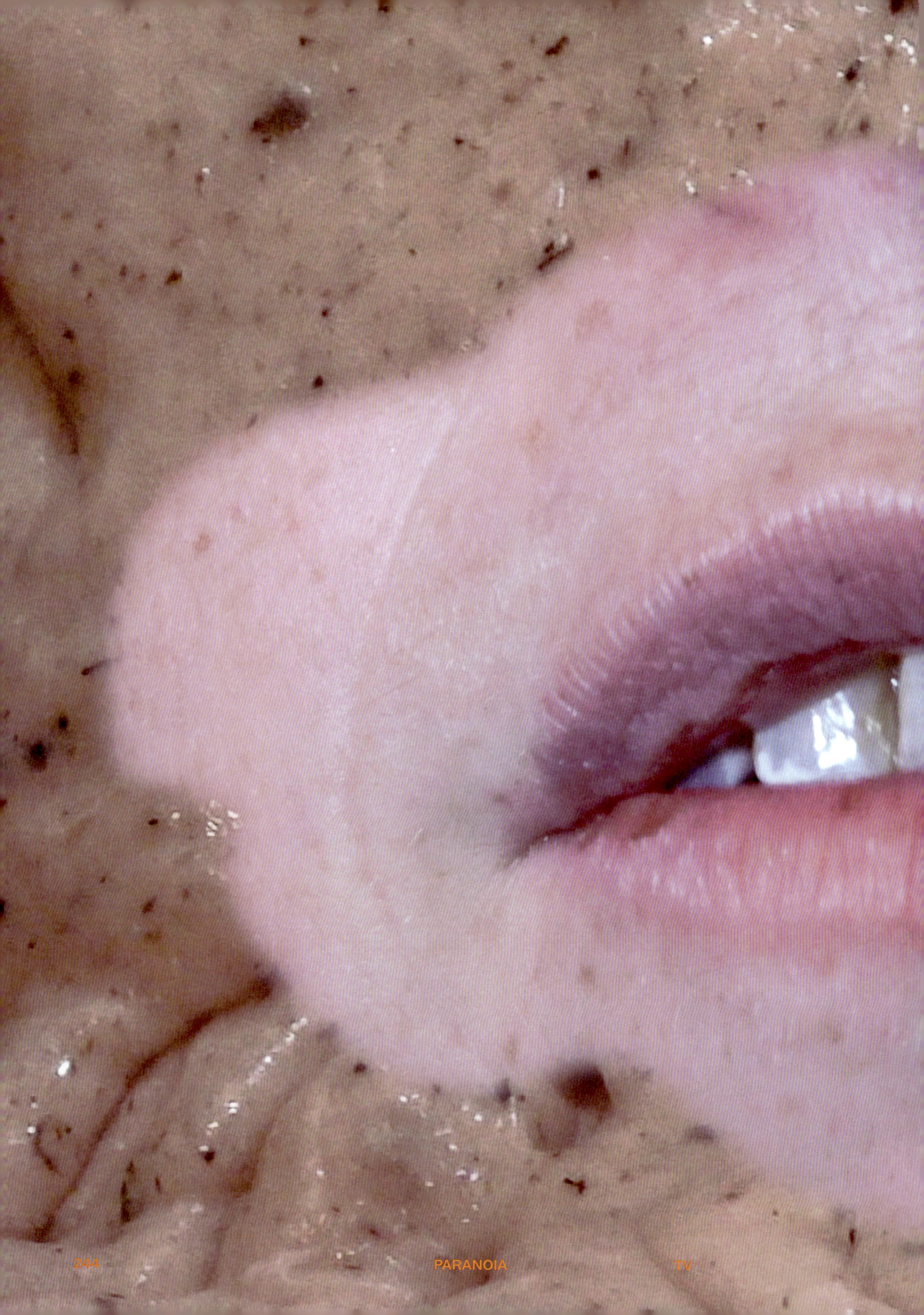

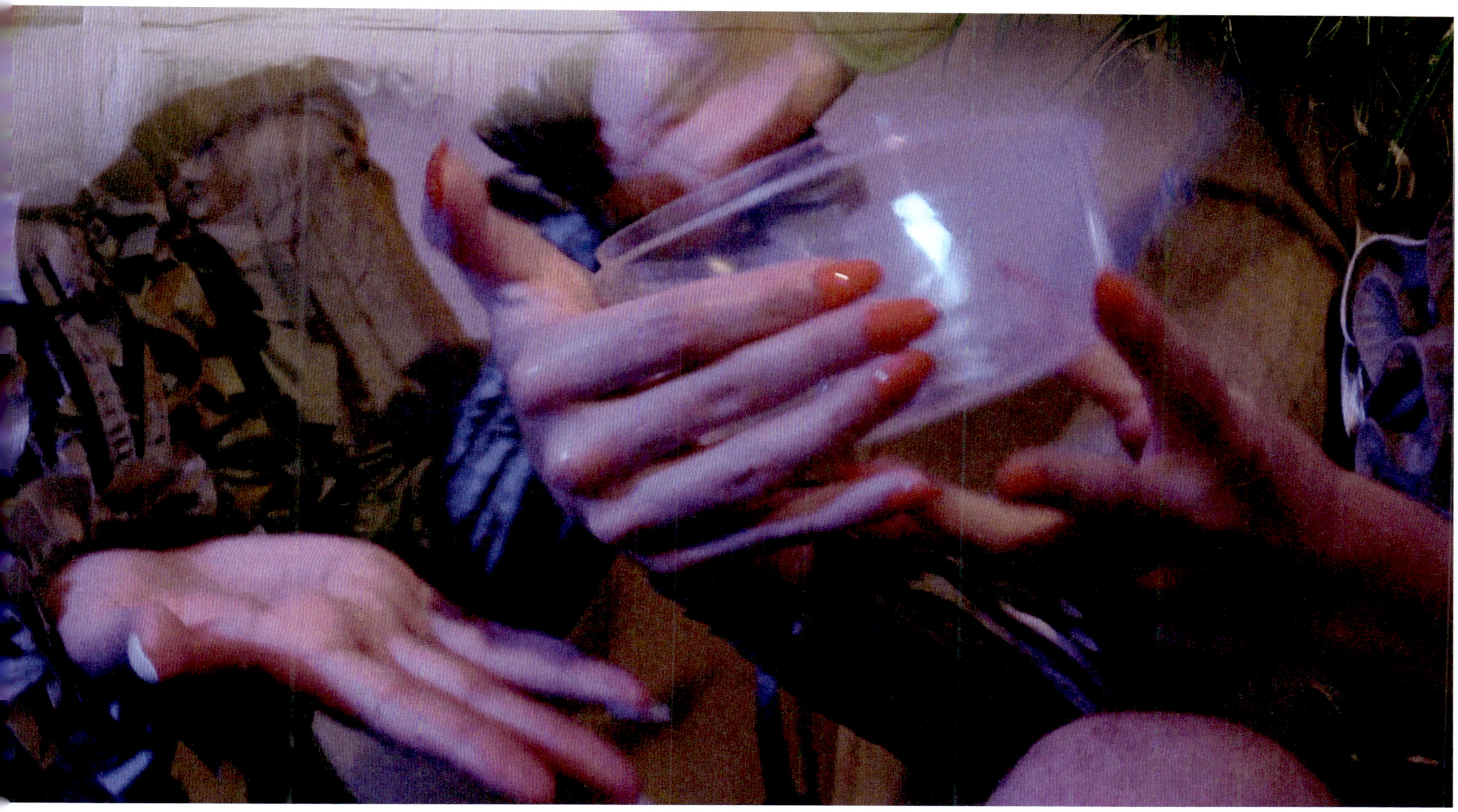

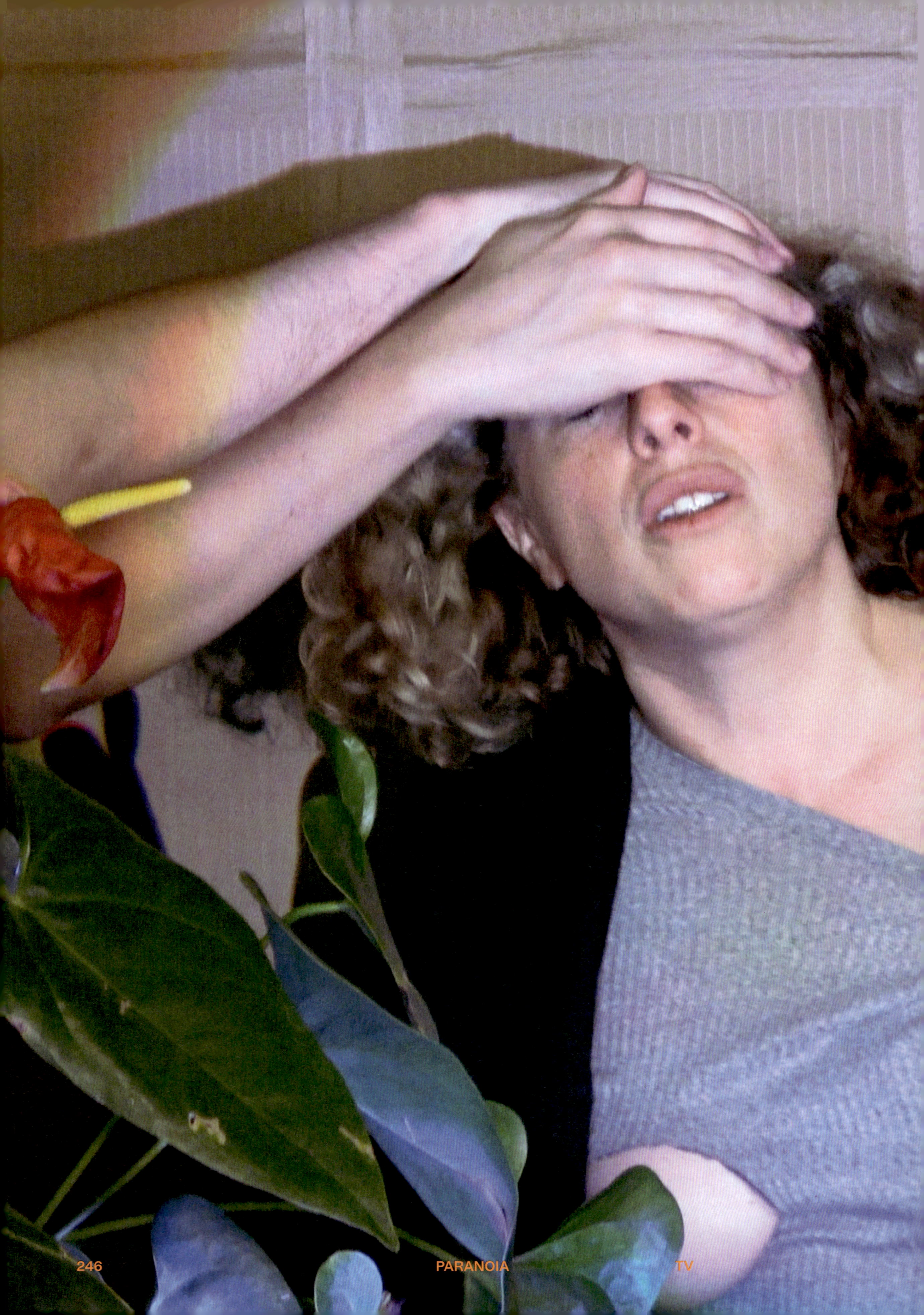

Liv Schulman was born in 1985 and grew up in Buenos Aires. She now lives and works in Paris as a visual artist and writer. Through the constant use of writing in her video works and live performances, she focuses on how language affects individual and social bodies. Using written words or dialogue to be performed as a starting point, she addresses the affects that material and immaterial economies produce in us.

Liv Schulman studied art practice and art writing at École nationale supérieure d'arts de Paris-Cergy, Goldsmiths, University of London, and École nationale supérieure d'arts de Lyon. Her works have been shown and performed at Schirn Kunsthalle, Frankfurt; Centre Pompidou, Paris; Ricard Foundation, Paris; Reina Sofía, Madrid; Friche Belle de Mai, Marseille; Galerie Noisy-le-Sec; SixtyEight Art Institute, Copenhagen; and the 2016 Biennale de Rennes. She is a recipient of the Cité internationale des arts Visual Arts Committees and of the 2018 Ricard Corporate Foundation Award. She teaches at HEAR in Strasbourg.

Brown, yellow, white and dead (2020)
Video series, 4 episodes,
ca. 22 / 17 / 13 / 19 min., French
Online

Line Producer: Visage Productions
Producers: Pauline Ghersi, Quentin Goujout
Directed by Liv Schulman
With: Pauline Ghersi, Quentin Goujout, Nicole Mercey Ortega (Episode 3–4), Guilhem Monceaux, Liv Schulman
Extras (Episode 2): Xavier Cormier, Clara Lemercier, Garance Eva Oliveras, Enzo Pernet

Shooting crew
Director of photography and camera operator: Ariela Bergman, assisted by Clara Lemercier
Sound recording: Marion Leyrahoux
Script boy: Enzo Pernet
Catering: Clara Pasteau
Technical means: Synaps collectif audiovisuel (special thanks to Florian Debu)

Postproduction
Editing and color grading: Ariela Bergman, assisted by Clara Lemercier
Sound engineer: Prisco Langlet
Theme song: Fernando Manassero
Credits: Quentin Goujout

Commissioned by steirischer herbst '20
Produced by Liv Schulman in coproduction with steirischer herbst '20

John Smith

Citadel / Twice / Magic
2020

Videos

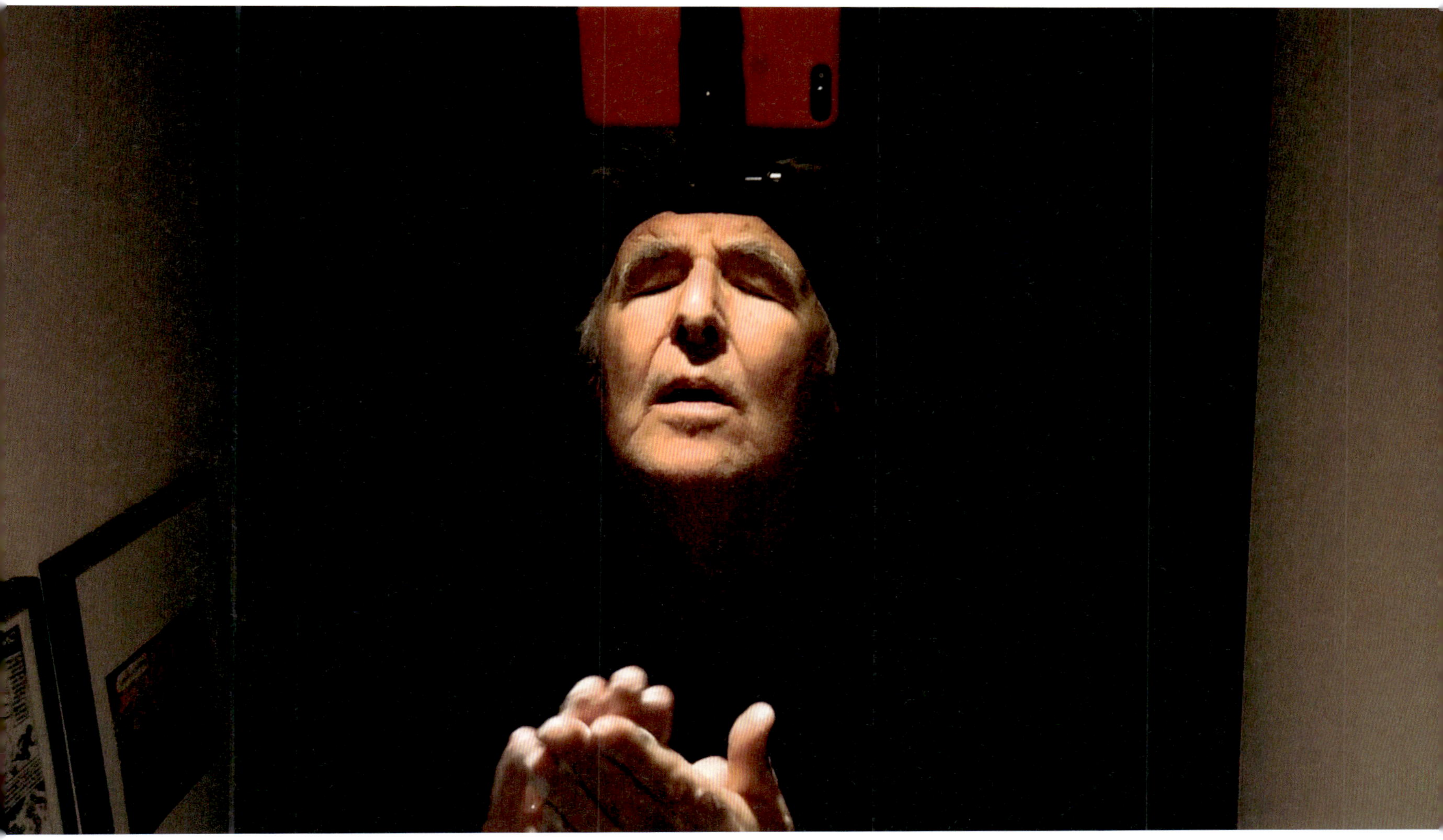

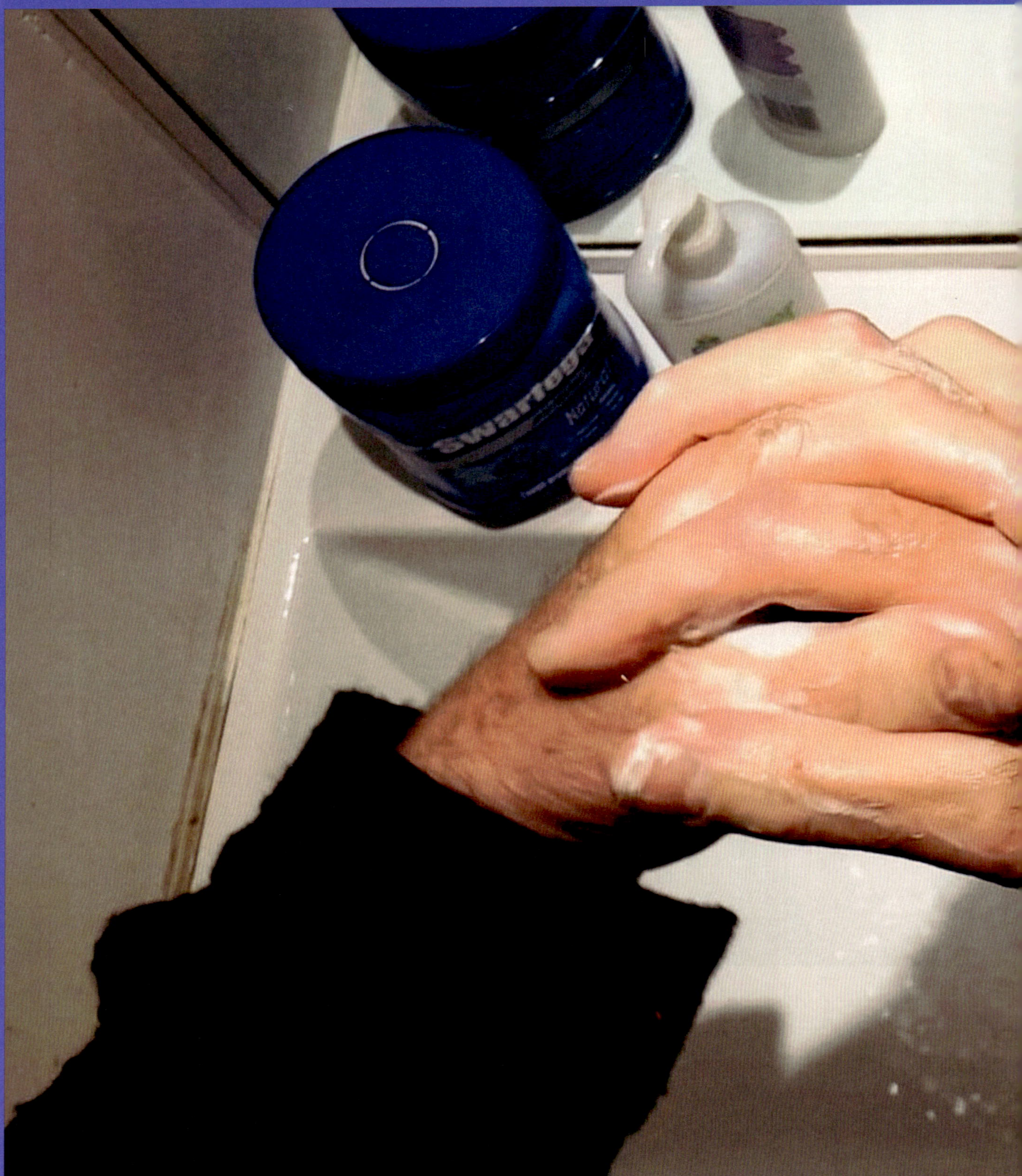

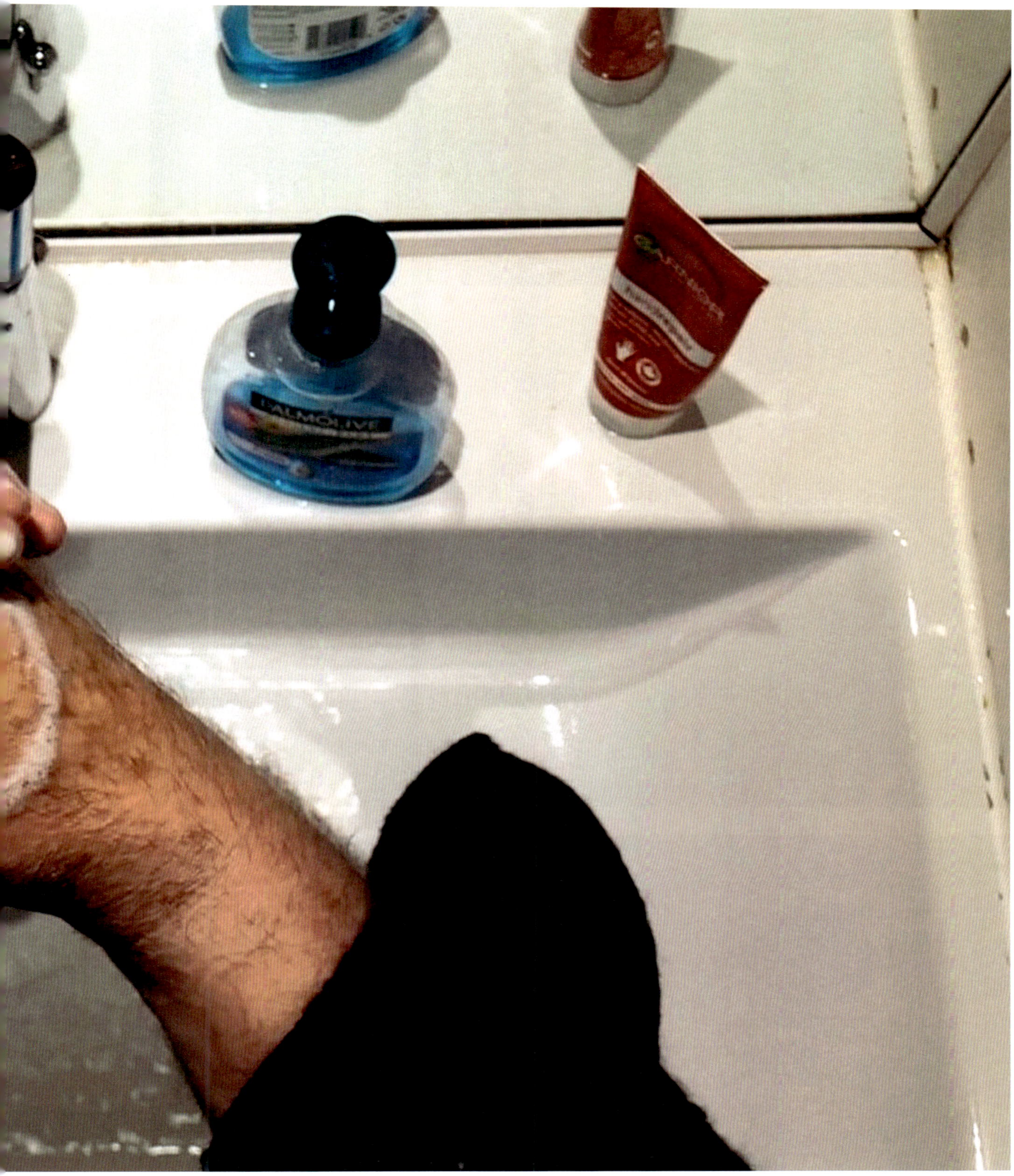

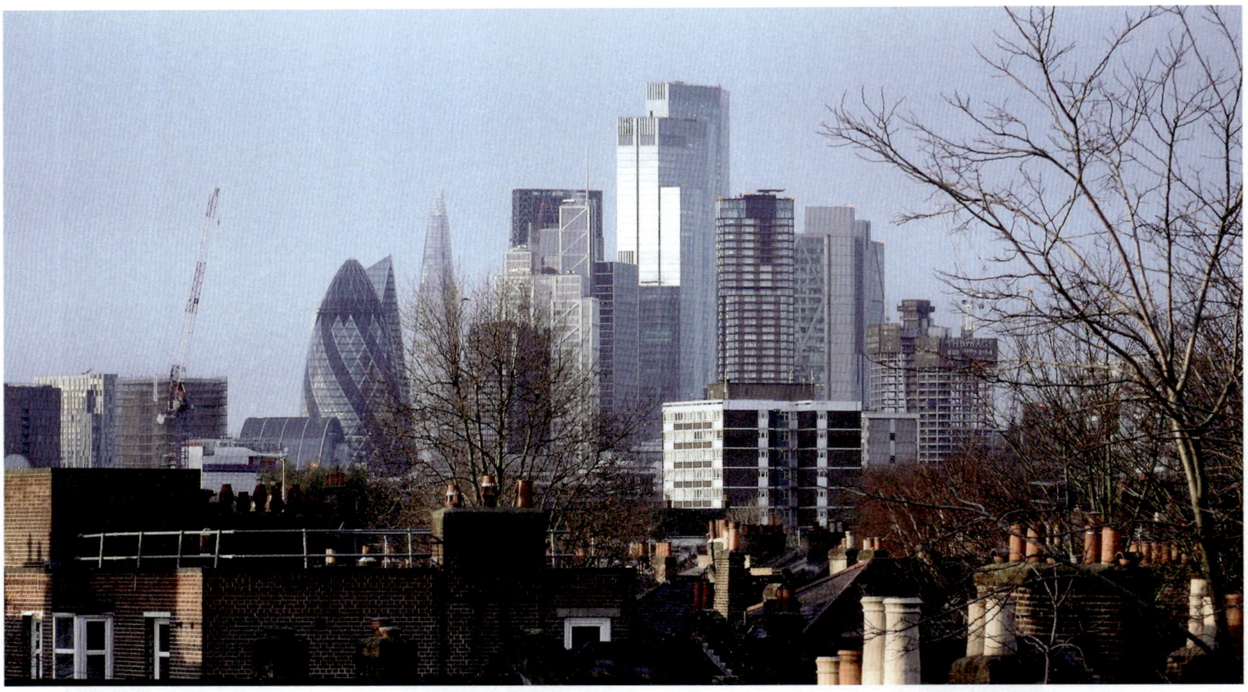

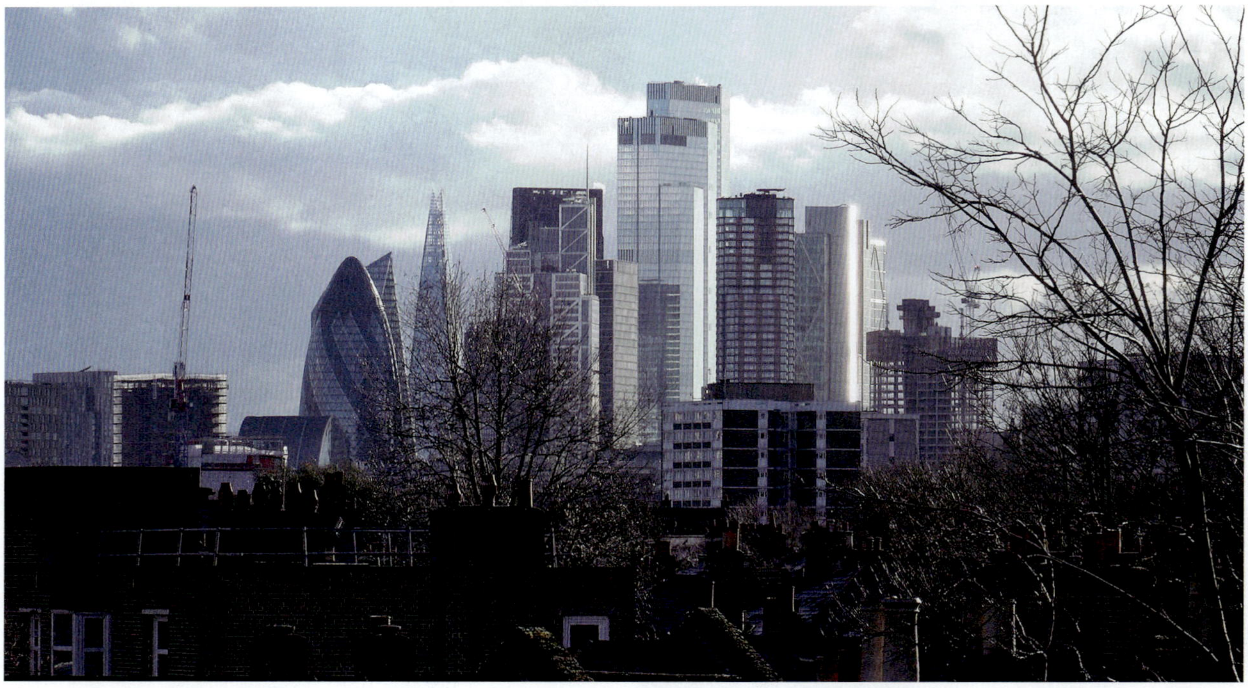

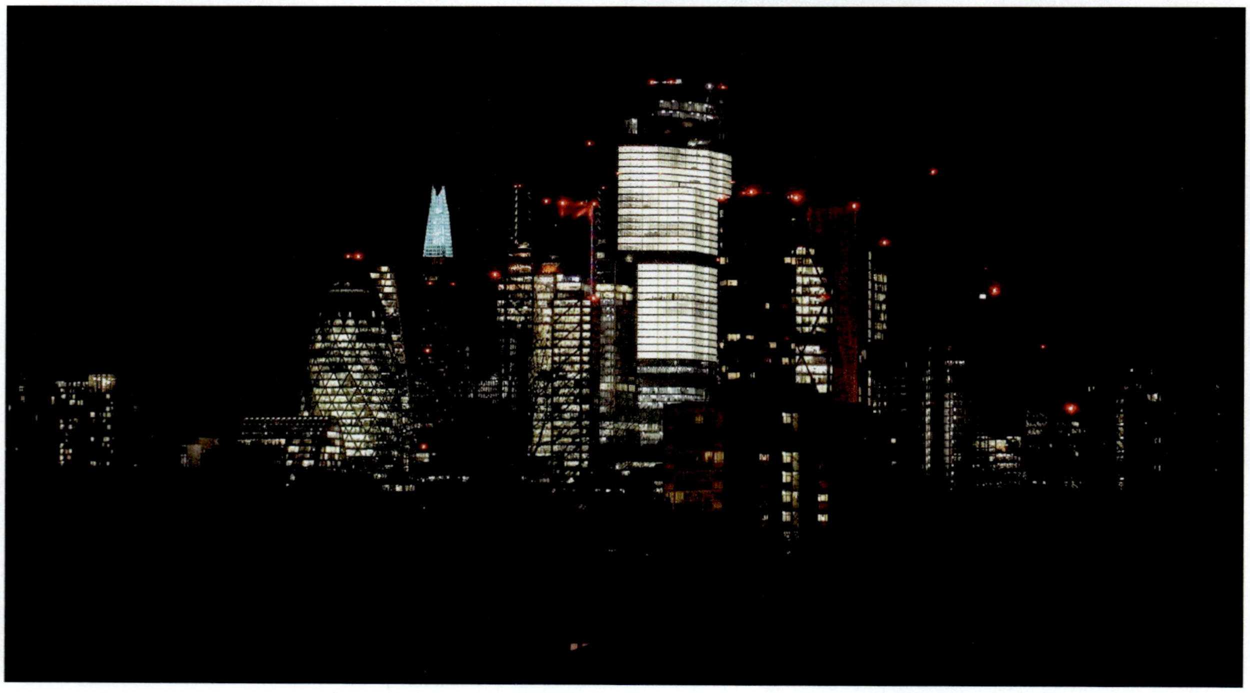

When barriers are going up, and when there is a risk that new diseases such as coronavirus will trigger a panic and a desire for market segregation that goes beyond what is medically rational, to the point of doing real and unnecessary economic damage, then, at that moment, humanity needs some government somewhere that is willing at least to make the case powerfully for freedom of exchange. Some country ready to take off its Clark Kent spectacles and leap into the phone booth and emerge with its cloak flowing as the supercharged champion of the right of populations of the earth to buy and sell freely among each other. And here in Greenwich in the first week of February 2020 I can tell you in all humility that the UK is ready for that role.

—Boris Johnson, UK Prime Minister, February 3, 2020

Filmed from my bedroom window during lockdown, *Citadel* combines short fragments from Boris Johnson's speeches relating to coronavirus with views of the London skyline. Recognizing the government's decision to place business interests before public health, it relocates the center of power from Parliament to the financial district of the City of London. Presenting the city as a site of both horror and aesthetic beauty, the film documents the dramatic effects of changing light conditions upon its architecture. As it shifts its focus from the city's gleaming skyscrapers to the inhabitants of the dense urban housing that lies in their shadow, *Citadel* contrasts faceless corporate power with individual lived experience.

I had wanted to film the view from my window for several years. My interest originated in the spectacular changes in light and shadow that transform the architecture in different weather conditions, but there was always one issue that held me back. Although I had made numerous films in the past that were concerned primarily with the aesthetics of the image, this was something that I could no longer feel comfortable with. I couldn't look at the buildings of the City of London without thinking about what they represented and feeling a need to present them critically. Then COVID-19 shook the world and I discovered the speech that Boris Johnson had made to UK business leaders on February 3. Everything fell into place and I knew that I had a starting point for my film.

In *Twice* I diligently followed the British government's COVID-19 advice while self-isolating, washing my hands for the length of time it took me to sing "Happy Birthday" twice. This official instruction seemed to reflect the absurdity and unreality of our current experience. I asked myself: "Why not choose a song that's long enough to sing only once?" and "Wouldn't something less upbeat be more appropriate?" My rendition of "Happy Birthday" to the tune of Chopin's funeral march seems much more fitting.

Magic follows on from *Twice* by treating Boris Johnson's speeches to the British people as if they were magic spells, asserting that nepotistic neoliberal impulses lurk beneath their surface. *Magic* and *Twice* now form part of an ongoing series which applies a supernatural interpretation to the prime minister's press conferences.

John Smith

John Smith was born in Walthamstow, London, in 1952, and studied at the Royal College of Art. Renowned mainly for his films and videos, Smith has shown his work in independent cinemas, galleries, and on television around the world. He received a Paul Hamlyn Foundation Award for Artists in 2011, and in 2013 he was the winner of the Jarman Award. He took part in the Paris Biennale (1982); the International Biennale of Photography, Turin (2003); the Biennale of Film & Architecture, Graz (2005); the Venice Biennale (2007); KunstFilmBiennale, Cologne (2007); the Berlin Biennale (2010); the Biennale de l'Image en Mouvement, Geneva (2010); the Marrakech Biennale (2012); and the Biennale für aktuelle Fotografie, Heidelberg (2017), among others. Smith lives and works in London and is professor emeritus of fine art at the University of East London.

Citadel / Twice / Magic (2020)
Videos, ca. 16 / 3 / 3 min., English
Online

Citadel commissioned and produced by steirischer herbst '20

studio ASYNCHROME

Vienna from Memory
2020

Map

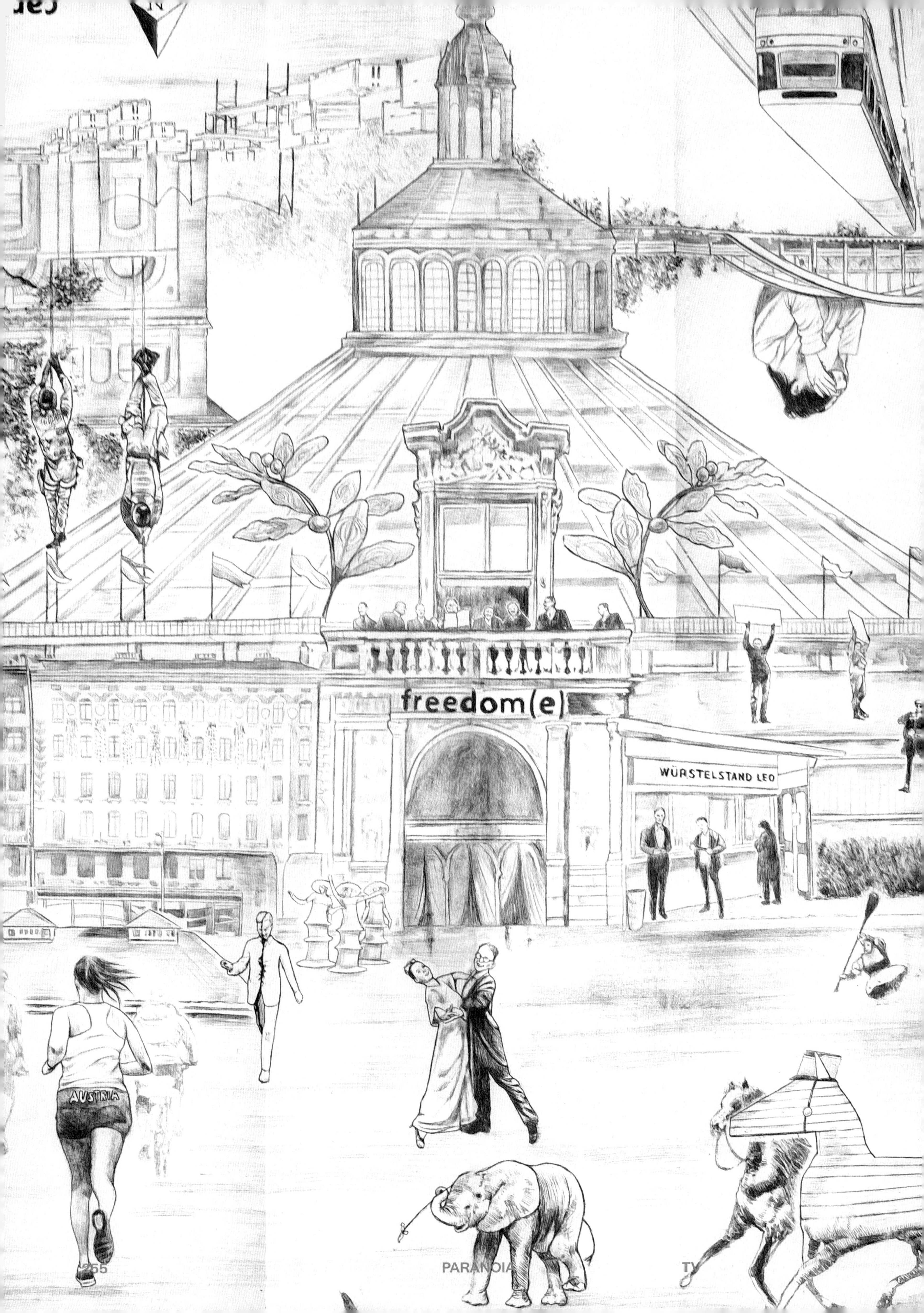
freedom(e)
WÜRSTELSTAND LEO
AUSTRIA

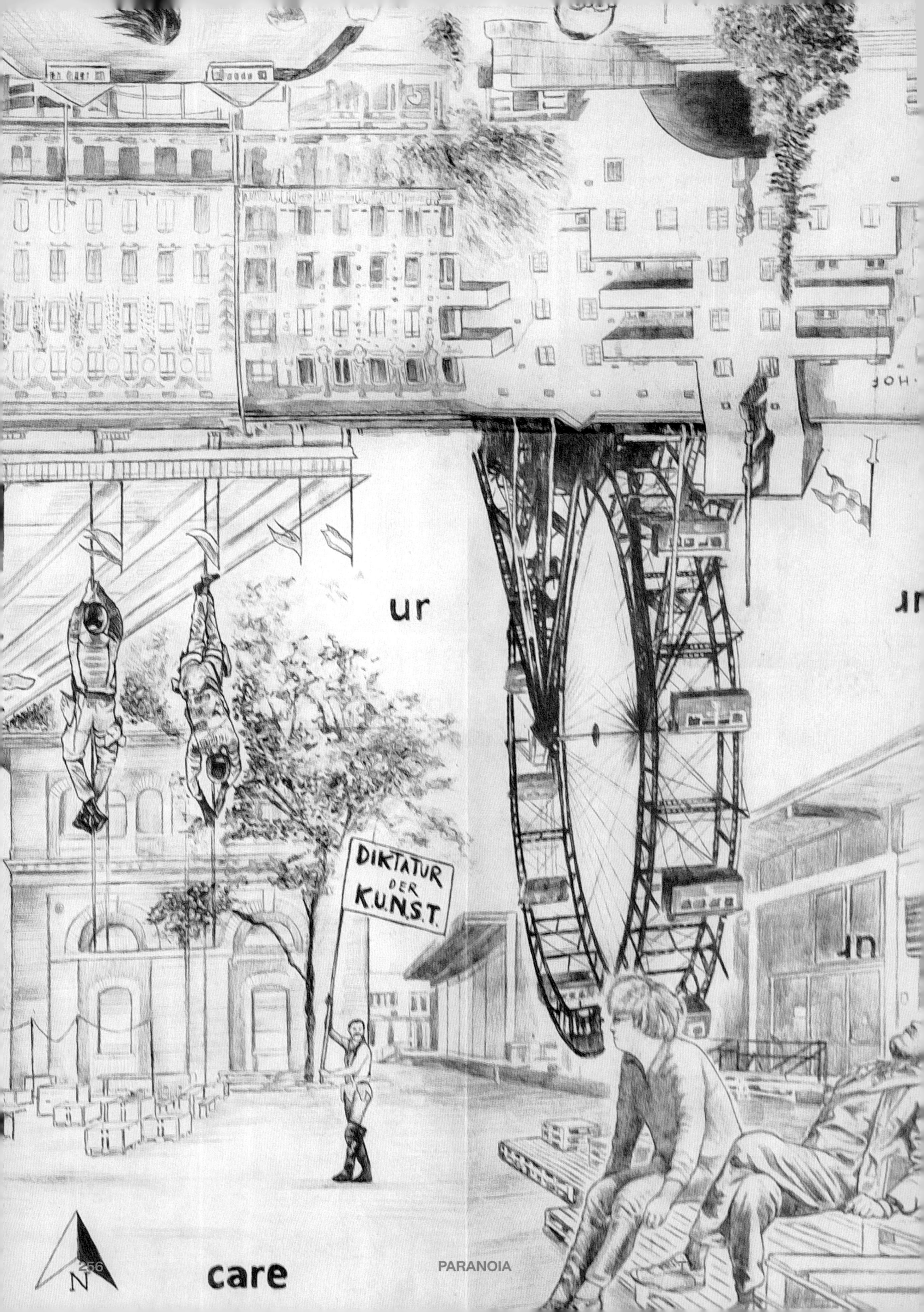
ur
DIKTATUR DER K.U.N.S.T.
care

What stories do we need to tell? Which ones should we forget in order to be free? What happens to the stories and what happens to people when systems change? As its starting point for creating the map *Vienna from Memory*, studio ASYNCHROME assumed that traveling between the cities of Vienna and Graz would no longer be possible due to the pandemic.

The duo, consisting of Marleen Leitner and Michael Schitnig, explored the vantage point from which they would like to draw the map and which perspectives the two of them would take on it. In accordance with the concept of collective memory developed by Maurice Halbwachs, they then conceived a composition that can be regarded as representing the memories of a group of people.

In this work, studio ASYNCHROME views the structure of the city as a dynamic process, a narrative work created by society in different epochs and with different cultural influences. The duo's artistic strategy was to juxtapose their individual situational perceptions of Vienna with collective narratives by people they knew and didn't know, relating these stories to one another and interweaving them in a drawing.

The same questions were asked of everyone who took part. Which memories should remain visible or invisible? What stories will be passed down to the next generations? Will this create even more borders? How does community then come about? What does it mean for the people and their stories? What is identity and what is utopia?

For Leitner and Schitnig, the medium of drawing is an ongoing, daily process. It serves them as a method for enabling complex overlaps that they can deploy as an epistemological concept. Observing people in society in their varied surroundings is always an essential part of their work. The aim is to open up possible horizons and scope for the interpretation of contemporary society.

The result in this case was a collective superimposition created from the memories of many different people. Buildings, areas, and people that no longer exist find a place on the map, as do stories of freedom, espionage, love, and the demand for distance. Walks are linked with urban changes and forge new paths in the overall composition.

Just as most stories are not linear, there is no linear direction prescribed for reading the map *Vienna from Memory*.

studio ASYNCHROME is a transdisciplinary experiment founded by Marleen Leitner and Michael Schitnig in 2013. They demand that utopia is conceived as a contemporary space of possibilities. Their work has been exhibited at the Vienna Biennale (2017), in solo exhibitions in Brussels, Rome, and Graz, and in group exhibitions in New York, Oslo, Athens, Sarajevo, and Salzburg, among other places. The duo were nominated for the Kardinal-König-Kunstpreis and received the Kunstförderpreis der Stadt Graz, the BKA START-Stipendium, as well as the Atelier-Auslandsstipendium des Landes Steiermark.

Vienna from Memory (2020)
Map

Commissioned and produced by steirischer herbst '20

Theater im Bahnhof

The Permit
2020

Video series

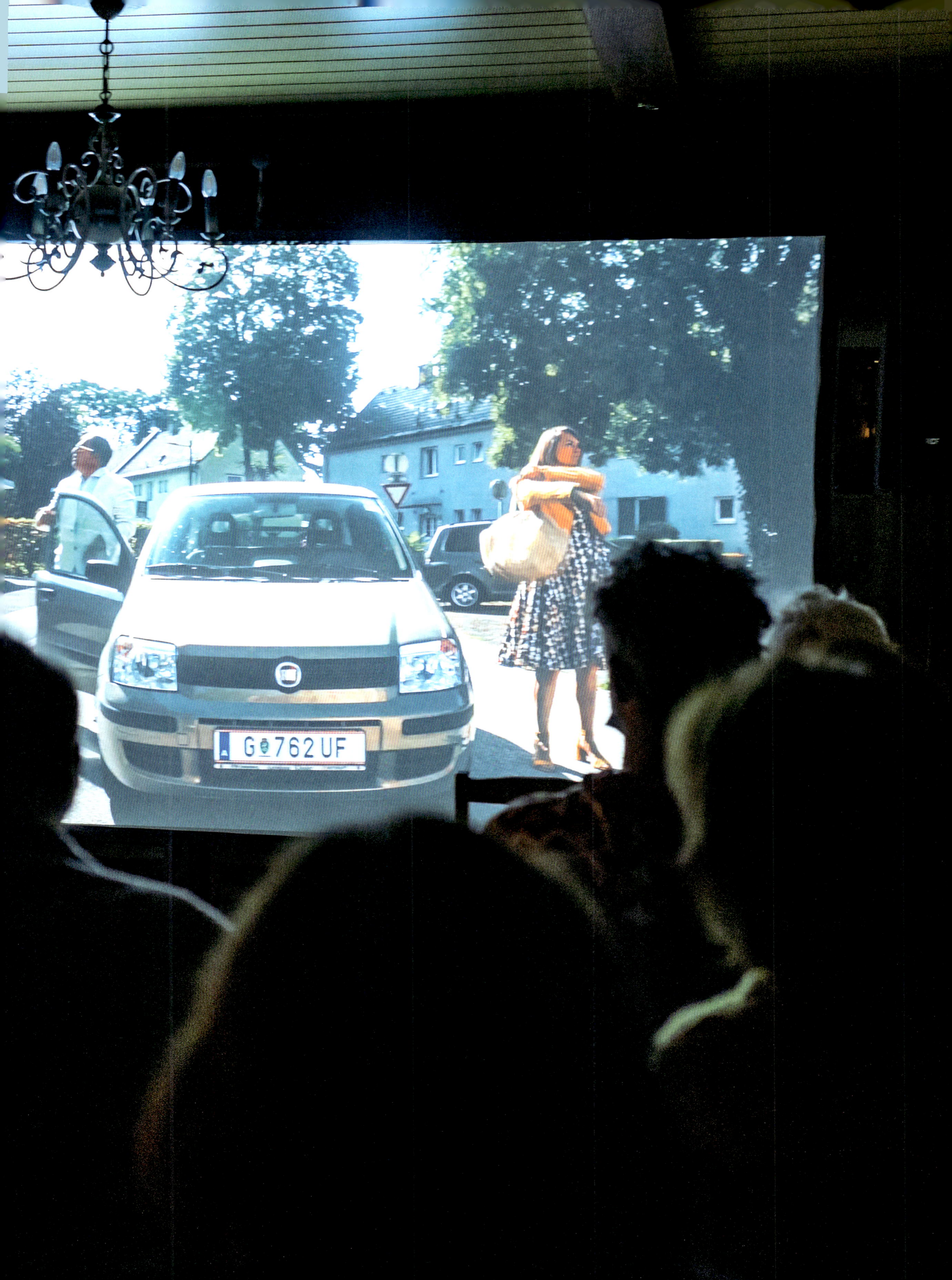
G 762 UF

High-rise buildings in the south of Graz: A couple perhaps near the end of their midlife crisis has agreed to stay together and remain a team, even if they no longer have sex. They have been commissioned to stage a theater performance in collaboration with the residents of a particular housing estate. While the husband is getting lost in the area, the wife acts as a production manager and struggles to collect signatures in the neighborhood in order to secure the necessary permits.

The Theater im Bahnhof collective uses real-life models as a template for creating performative work. We worked in spite of the difficult coronavirus situation and took the opportunity to explore various layers that are exposed when meeting people where they live.

The buildings we visited were built in the early 1960s. They were built in the middle of open fields, promising a prosperous Austrian future. There were a lot of children, a lot of progress, and a lot of hope on the horizon.

But these plans did not bear fruit in the way people thought at first. Everything changed. Now we meet some of the older people—their children did not stay, having had to change homes, even change cities, for their jobs. So there is slight disillusionment here; in some moments we feel the disappointment. Yet there are also good memories of the original plan and the original vision. We wanted to get a feeling for the motives of the artists, and also for the motives of the people we met.

Theater im Bahnhof

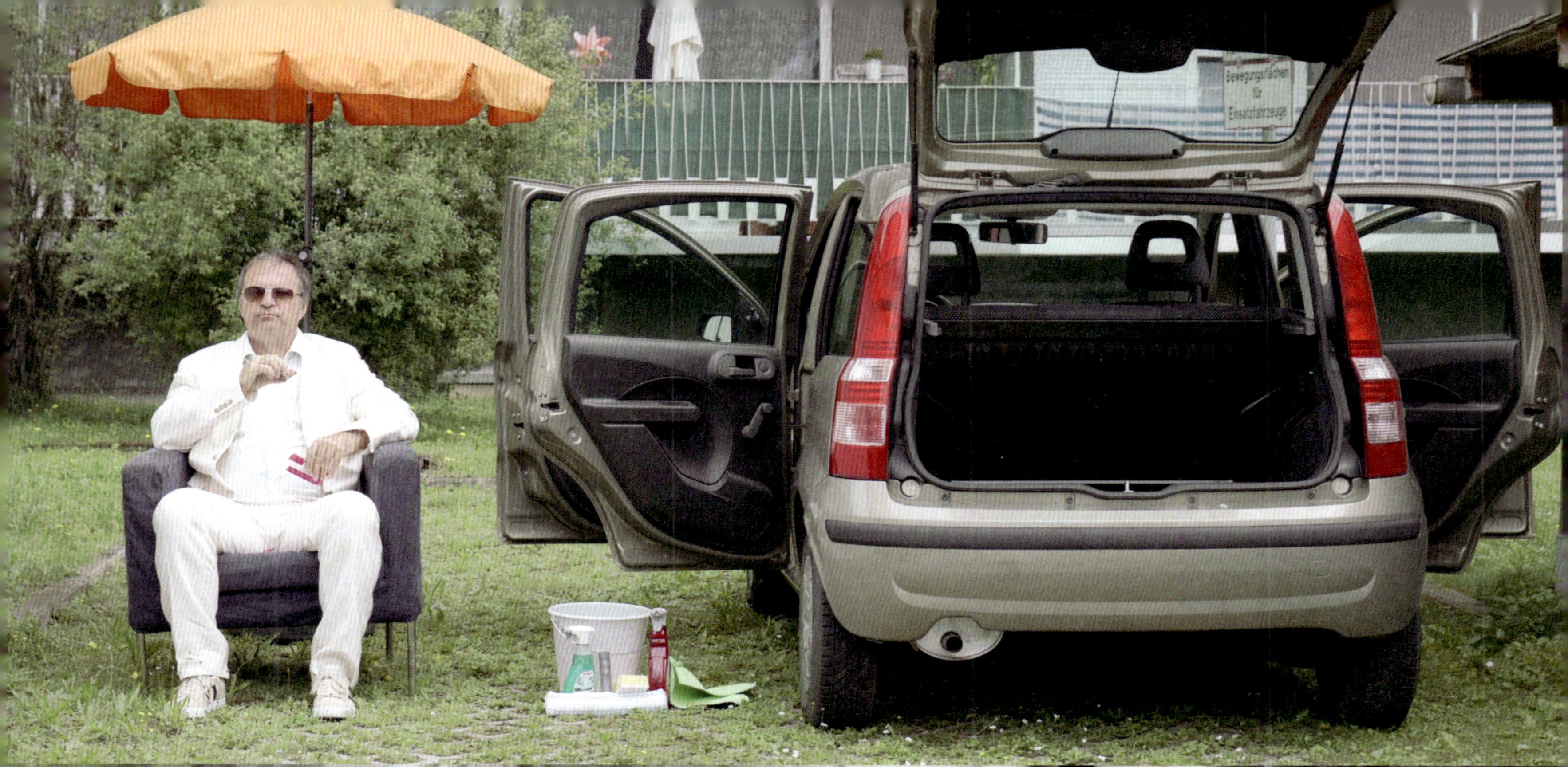

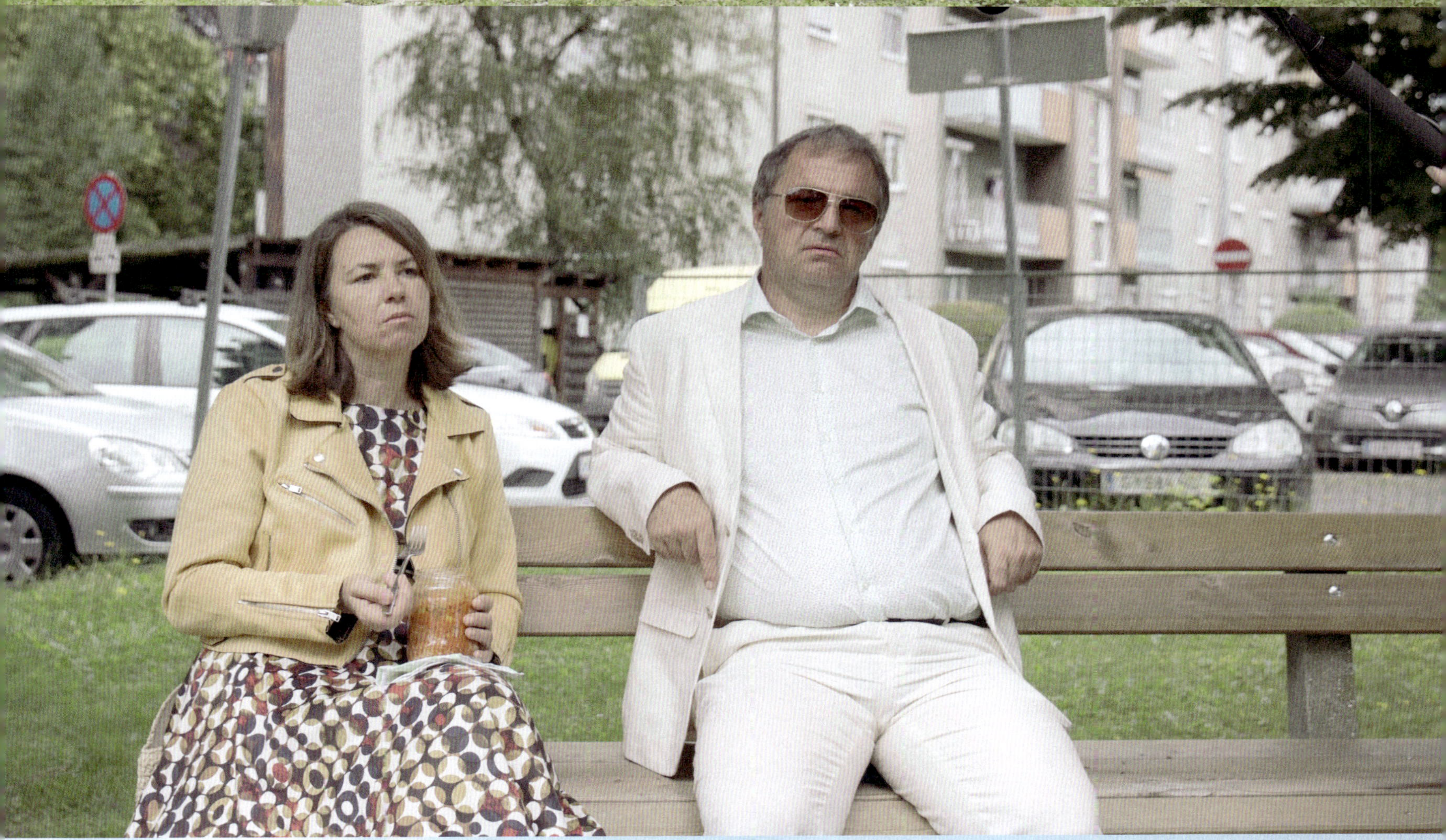

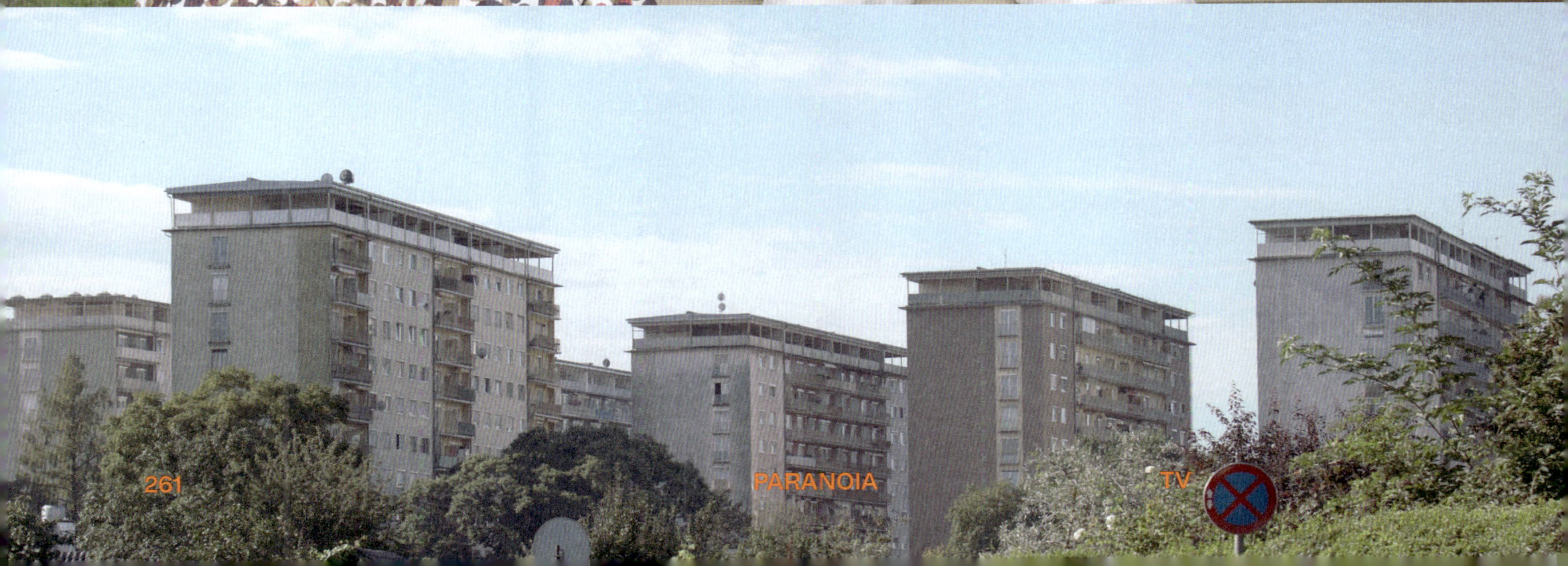

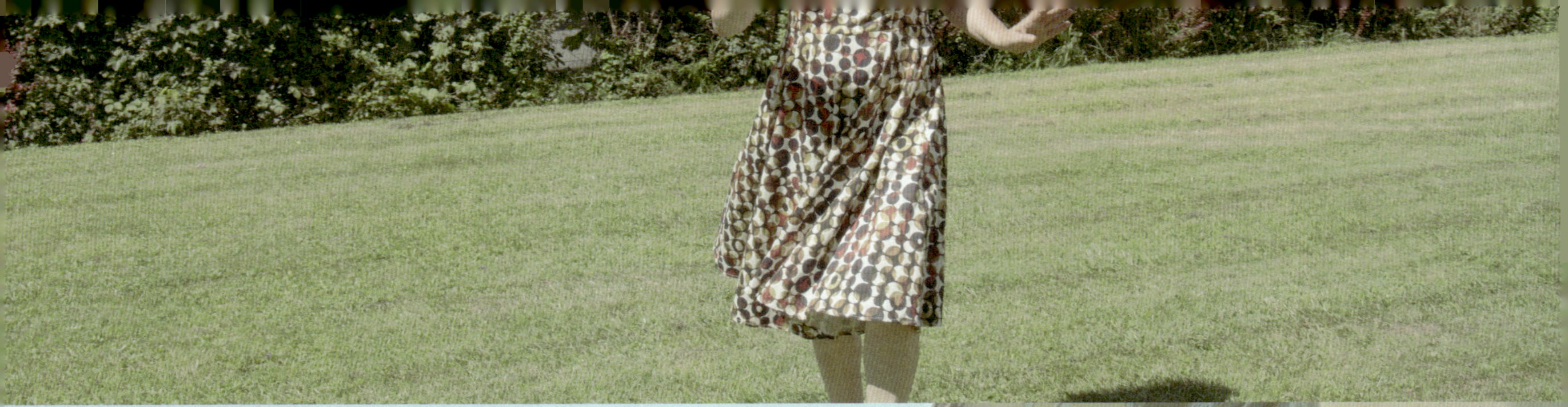

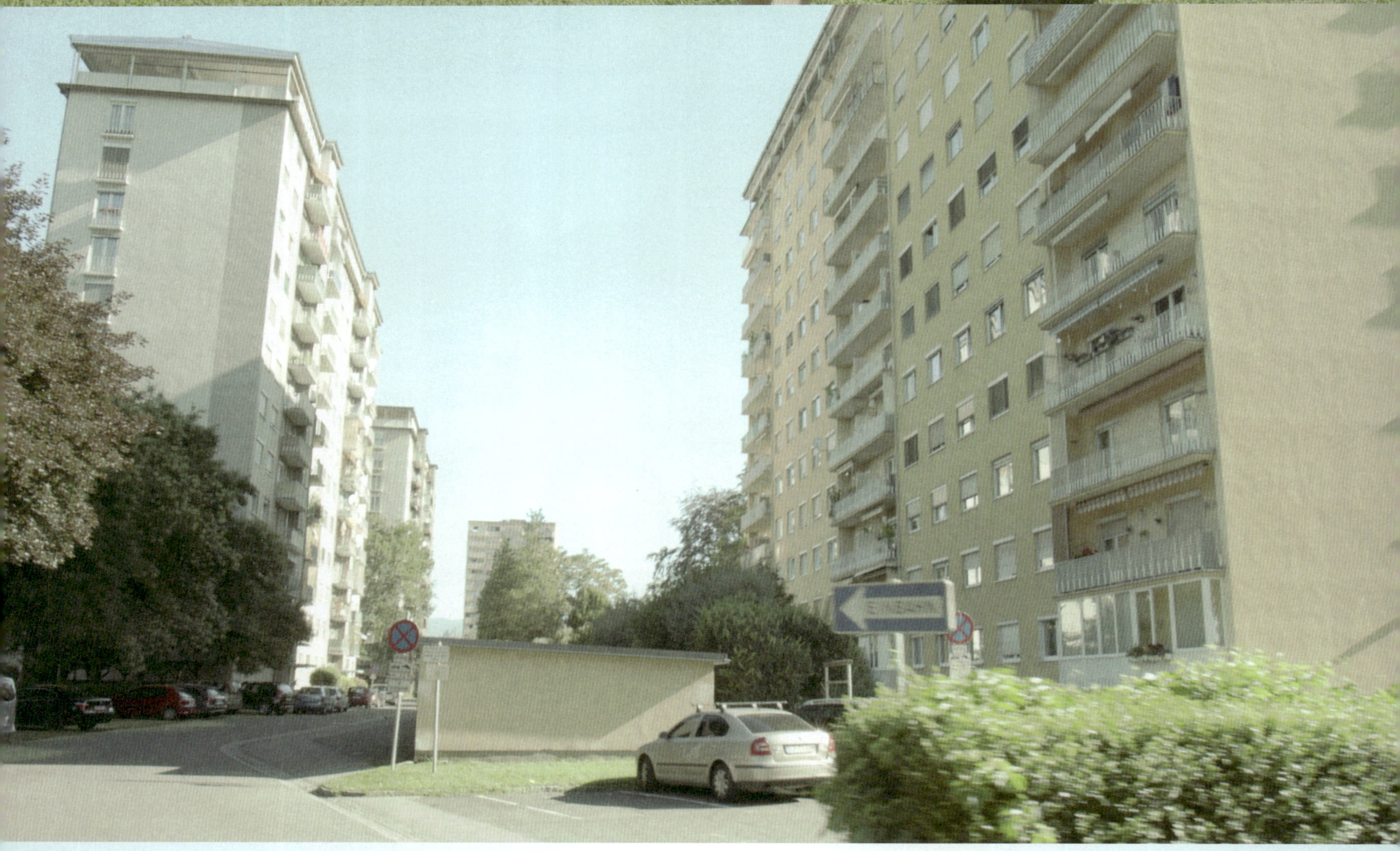

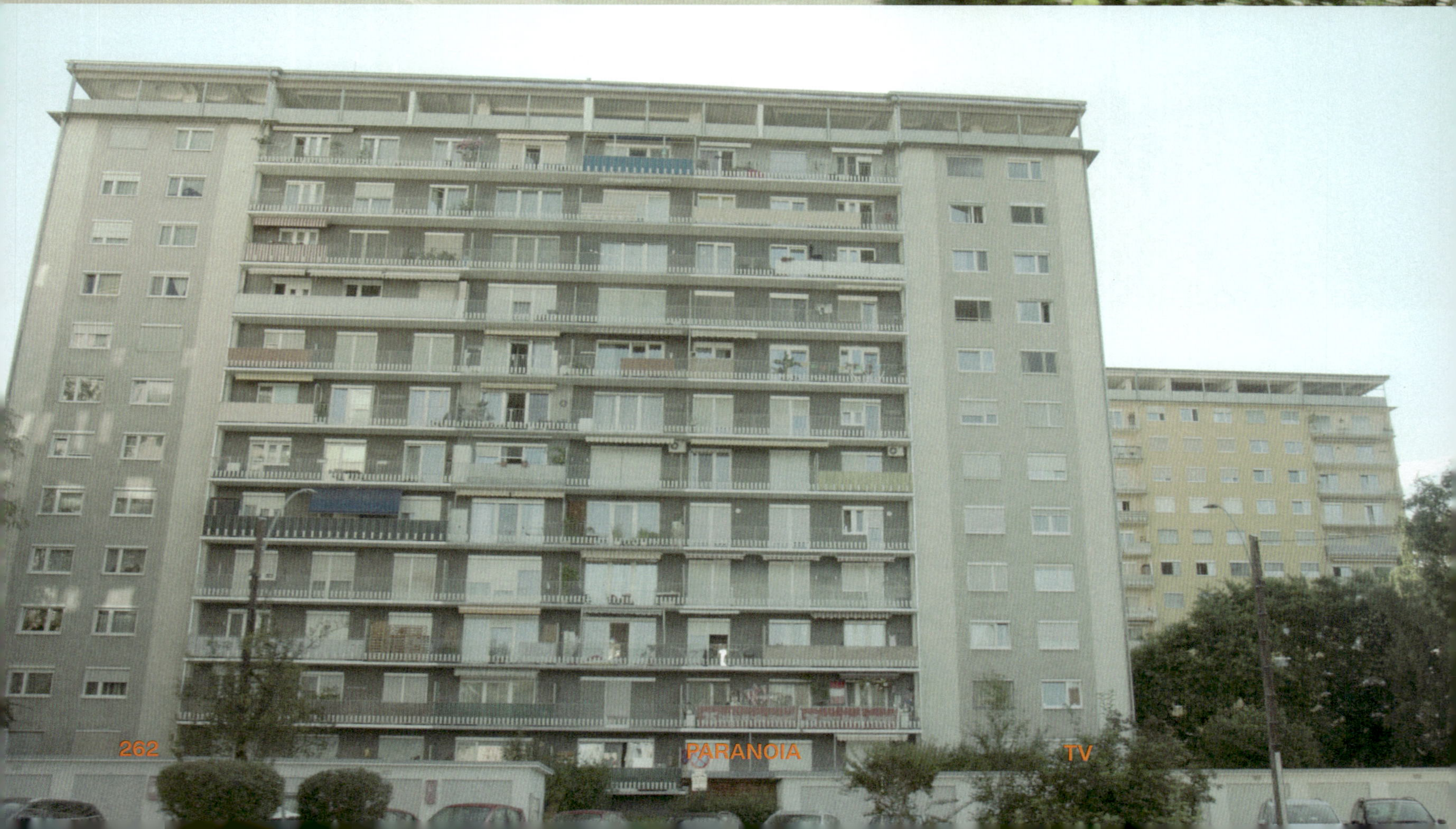

Theater im Bahnhof, founded in Graz in 1989, is a contemporary people's theater. Its focus is on researching and writing its own productions for both the stage and public space, questioning Austrian identity between popular culture and tradition.

The Permit (2020)
Video series, 3 episodes,
ca. 16 / 17 / 10 min., German
Online

By and with: Jacob Banigan, Heike Barnard, Ed. Hauswirth, Benno Hiti, Gabriela Hiti, Monika Klengel, Helmut Köpping, Rupert Lehofer, Christina Romirer, Stefan Schmid, Mario Shehata, and the residents of the co-op apartments

Commissioned by steirischer herbst '20
Produced by Theater im Bahnhof in coproduction with steirischer herbst '20

263

Sung Tieu

Untitled
2020

Newspaper intervention

am nächsten Morgen den ersten Flug oder Zug nahm, um mit meinem Partner, der er seit 15 Jahren ist, zusammen zu sein. Als junge Sängerin reist man ja viel herum. Zu Hause mit einem geliebten Menschen Zeit zu verbringen, und seien es auch nur zwei Tage, ist dann ein kostbares Gut.

Sie scheinen bei Ihren Kollegen sehr beliebt zu sein. Einer hat einmal, als Sie zur Probe erschienen, gesagt: „Jetzt geht die Sonne auf!" Darauf waren Sie sicher besonders stolz?
Ich glaube, ich bin einfach ein anständiger Mensch. Ich habe viel Respekt vor den Kollegen, bin sehr harmoniebedürftig, und Aufführungen sind immer Ensembleleistungen. Das Team ist alles. Deshalb versuche ich stets, den Kollegen meine Wertschätzung zu zeigen. Und ja, prinzipiell glaube ich, dass ich ein leichtes Gemüt habe, dass ich positiv an alles herangehe. Der Beruf ist schwer genug, da hilft es sicher, wenn man eine gewisse Leichtigkeit mitbringt, ohne von der Ernsthaftigkeit der Arbeit abzulenken.

Sind Sie süchtig nach Applaus?
Nein. Süchtig bin ich nach dem, was vor dem Applaus ist. Was mich glücklich macht, ist das gemeinsame Musizieren und die starke Energie, die dann plötzlich in einem Raum entstehen kann. Natürlich auch zwischen Publikum und Bühne.

Haben Sie noch große Wünsche, große Pläne?
Ich lebe sehr stark im Jetzt und habe große Freude mit meinem Beruf. Das hat mich, denke ich, dorthin gebracht, wo ich jetzt bin. Und ich hoffe, dass ich mir diese Freude und Faszination bewahren kann. Ich bin glücklich mit meinem Leben, habe immer öfter das Gefühl, dass ich mit mir im Reinen, irgendwie „angekommen" bin. Es gibt keine offenen, unausgesprochenen Dinge, und das bringt sehr viel Ruhe in mein Leben.

STEIRISCHE KINOS

Schließtage häufen sich

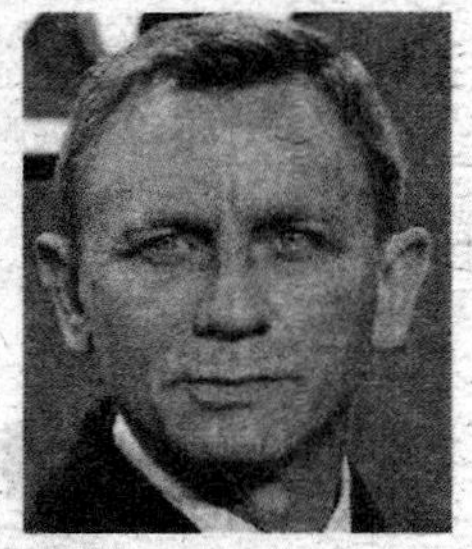

Bond Daniel Craig kehrt erst 2021 zurück AP

Kein „Bond", kein „Dune", kein „Batman" – einzig „Wonder Woman" hält 2020 die Stellung. Nebst Sitzplatzbeschränkungen machen den Kinobetreibern verschobene Blockbuster zu schaffen. Etliche Kinos haben auf die schwierige Geschäftslage im Coronajahr bereits mit mehr Schließtagen reagiert und spielen nur noch an den publikumsträchtigeren Wochenenden. Auch die Cineplexx-Kette zieht nach: In Graz hat aktuell das Annenhofkino von Montag bis Donnerstag zu, das Geidorf am Dienstag und Mittwoch. Auch das Cineplexx in Puntigam bleibt mittwochs geschlossen, das Cineplexx Leoben meldet bereits seit Wiedereröffnung der Kinos im Juli täglich „Heute spielfrei". Durchgespielt wird vorerst in den unabhängigen Grazer Kinos KIZ, Schubert und Rechbauer.

STEIRISCHE AUTOREN

Wachablöse

Wentila De La Marre, 22 Jahre lang Vorsitzende des Vereins „Steirische Autoren", hat die Geschicke der Körperschaft in jüngere Hände gelegt. Die Publizistin, für ihr Engagement unlängst mit dem Großen Ehrenzeichen des Landes Steiermark ausgezeichnet, übergab die Leitung des Vereins an Birgit Winkler. Die „Steirischen Autoren" geben unter anderem die Literaturzeitschrift „Die Feder" heraus.

AUSZEICHNUNG

Lessing-Preis

Die Autorin und Publizistin Ines Geipel (60) hat den Lessing-Preis für Kritik erhalten. Geipels Schreiben befasst sich u. a. mit ihren Erfahrungen in der DDR-Diktatur sowie den NS-Verstrickungen ihrer Familie. Ihr Werdegang ist ungewöhnlich: Sie wurde als DDR-Spitzensportlerin bekannt und war später scharfe Doping-Kritikerin. Das „Archiv unterdrückter Literatur in der DDR" geht auf ihre Arbeit zurück.

ANZEIGE

Unendlicher Widerstand
ist der Alptraum, den ich injiziere.
Unempfindlichkeit der Tagtraum.

Immunität

Die Sterblichkeit im Verborgenen praktizieren.
Die Verschonung vom Tod wird keinem gewährt.

PRÄSIDENTSCHAFTSKANZLEI WIEN

Vorhofer-Preis wird vergeben

In der Hofburg werden heute von Bundespräsident Alexander Van der Bellen der Kurt-Vorhofer-Preis und der Robert-Hochner-Preis überreicht. Der eine ist benannt nach dem Doyen des österreichischen Innenpolitik-Journalismus (1929–1995), der fast 40 Jahre für die Kleine Zeitung arbeitete. Und der andere nach dem legendären ORF-Fernsehmoderator (1945–2001). Den von unserer Zeitung vergebenen Vorhofer-Preis (7500 Euro) erhält Petra Stuiber (53), Politjournalistin und stellvertretende Chefredakteurin des „Standard". Mit dem von der Journalistengewerkschaft vergebenen Hochner-Preis (7500) geehrt wird Ulla Kramar-Schmid (54), zuvor im „profil" tätig und seit 2015 Investigativjournalistin des ORF.

Die Kleine Zeitung überträgt die Verleihungen ab 17 Uhr live: kleinezeitung.at/kultur

STEIRISCHER HERBST

Veränderte Wahrnehmung

Sung Tieus Interventionsprojekt in der Kleinen Zeitung.

Ein „Photoautomat", am Eisernen Tor in Graz, der mehr als die gewohnten Porträtbilder auswirft, flüsternde Nahrungsmittel in Supermärkten, sprechende Straßenlaternen: Etliche Interventionsprojekte kennzeichnen diesen steirischen herbst. Eines davon findet derzeit auf den Kulturseiten der Kleinen Zeitung statt (siehe unten): „Ohne Titel" nennt die vietnamesisch-deutsche Künstlerin Sung Tieu (33) eine Serie von Arbeiten, die nicht von ungefähr an das gängige Format von Todesanzeigen erinnern. „Ohne Titel" unternimmt lyrische Nachrufe auf Begriffe wie Solidarität, Nähe, Verantwortung, deren Wahrnehmung sich im Zuge der Corona-Pandemie in den letzten Monaten dramatisch verändert hat. Bis 18. Oktober hier.

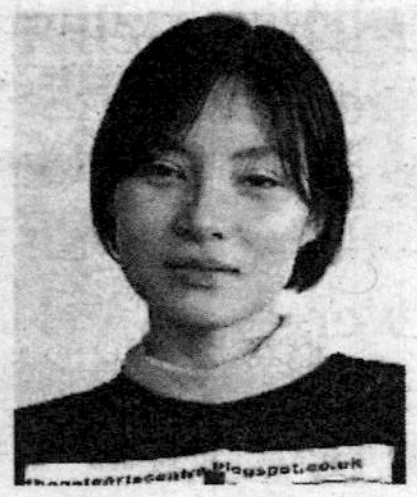

Künstlerin Sung Tieu
HAUS DER KUNST BERLIN

— ANZEIGE —

Die Vorhersage für gestern, heute, morgen ist der Tod.

Wirklichkeit

Die Asche klopft mit dem Wind.
Geister einer Kreuzung durchbrechen
den klaren Nachthimmel,
hinterlassen unsichtbare Schatten vor deiner Tür.

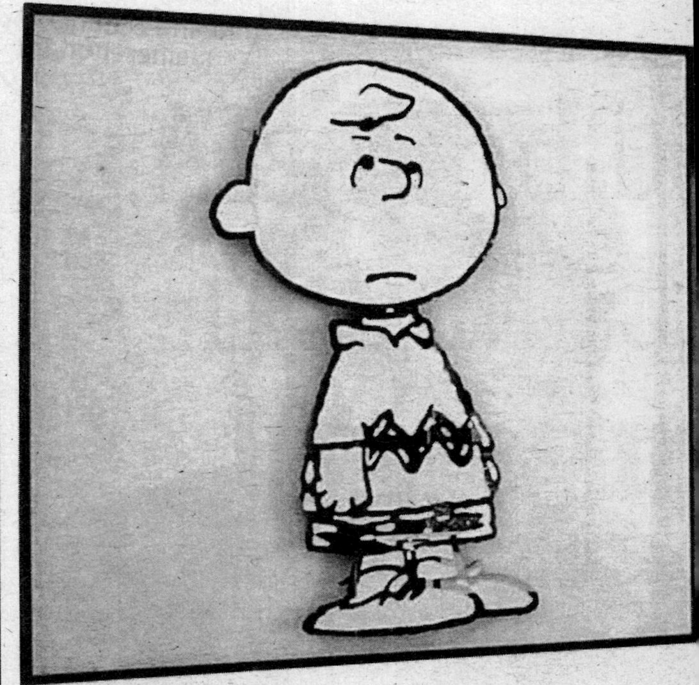

JUBILÄUM

Die Peanut kleine Leu ganz groß

Die Comicfiguren Peanuts wer Seit dem ersten Erscheinen dr 2600 Zeitungen ihre Abenteue Erfinder Charles Schulz war „vo großen Fragen des Lebens fas

Von Andreas Kanatschnig

Manche Psychiater sagen, dass Menschen, die Erdnussbutter-Sandwiches essen, einsam sind." Als Charlie Brown das sagt, sitzt er auf einer Parkbank und isst sein Jausenbrot. „Wenn du wirklich einsam bist, klebt die Erdnussbutter auf deinem Gaumen", fügt er noch hinzu und blickt verdrießlich in die Welt.

Am 2. Oktober 1950 lernten die Peanuts in sieben Tageszeitungen Amerikas als Comic-Strip das Laufen, um auf der Höhe ihres Erfolges in 2600 Zeitungen und 75 Ländern dieser Welt gedruckt zu werden. Charles Monroe Schulz war ein

Genie, das „vo gen des Leben wie Benjamin des Schulz-M USA, der Klei „Und er hatte unseren größt ist der Sinn de wenn die and lieben? Und n Glück?"

Clark sieht Faktoren, war so erfolgreich Brown ist die wie sein Kün Sohn eines Fri in gewisser W typ. Peppermi cie sind in ihn merkt es nich

In her intervention in the local newspaper *Kleine Zeitung* (Styrian edition), artist Sung Tieu conceives eight handwritten poems addressing those abstract terms that have undergone irreversible changes over the recent months of instability. These poems on notions such as “Immunity,” “Evidence,” “Intimacy,” and “Solidarity,” among others, contemplate the shifting reality of our crisis-ridden times. Her writing points to the mystery and grief that pervades our current human existence.

These half-page ads make use of conventional newspaper typography often used for obituaries. But upon closer inspection they reveal themselves as drawings, creating a contrast with the computer-generated graphics and statistics usually deployed to explain the present crisis in the media.

Released every few days throughout the length of the festival, Tieu’s intervention appears and disappears with each new newspaper edition and its large readership. With no control over the rest of the information within *Kleine Zeitung*, Tieu’s work embeds itself ambiguously, leaving the viewer to encounter the work by chance. Their subtle presentation as pencil drawings on a larger newspaper spread resonate with the fragile and tender nature of this critical moment in time.

Sung Tieu, born in Hai Duong, Vietnam, in 1987, is an artist based between London and Berlin. Recent solo exhibitions have been at Emalin, London; Haus der Kunst, Munich; and at Nottingham Contemporary. Forthcoming solo exhibitions include shows at the Kunstmuseum Bonn and Gesellschaft für Zeitgenössische Kunst Leipzig. Forthcoming group exhibitions include the 34th São Paulo Biennial (2021); Kunsthalle Basel; and Taipei Fine Arts Museum. Tieu is also the recipient of the 2020 Ars Viva Frize for Visual Art, with exhibitions at Museum Angewandte Kunst, Frankfurt, and Kunstverein Hannover forthcoming.

Untitled (2020)
Newspaper intervention

Commissioned and produced by steirischer herbst ’20

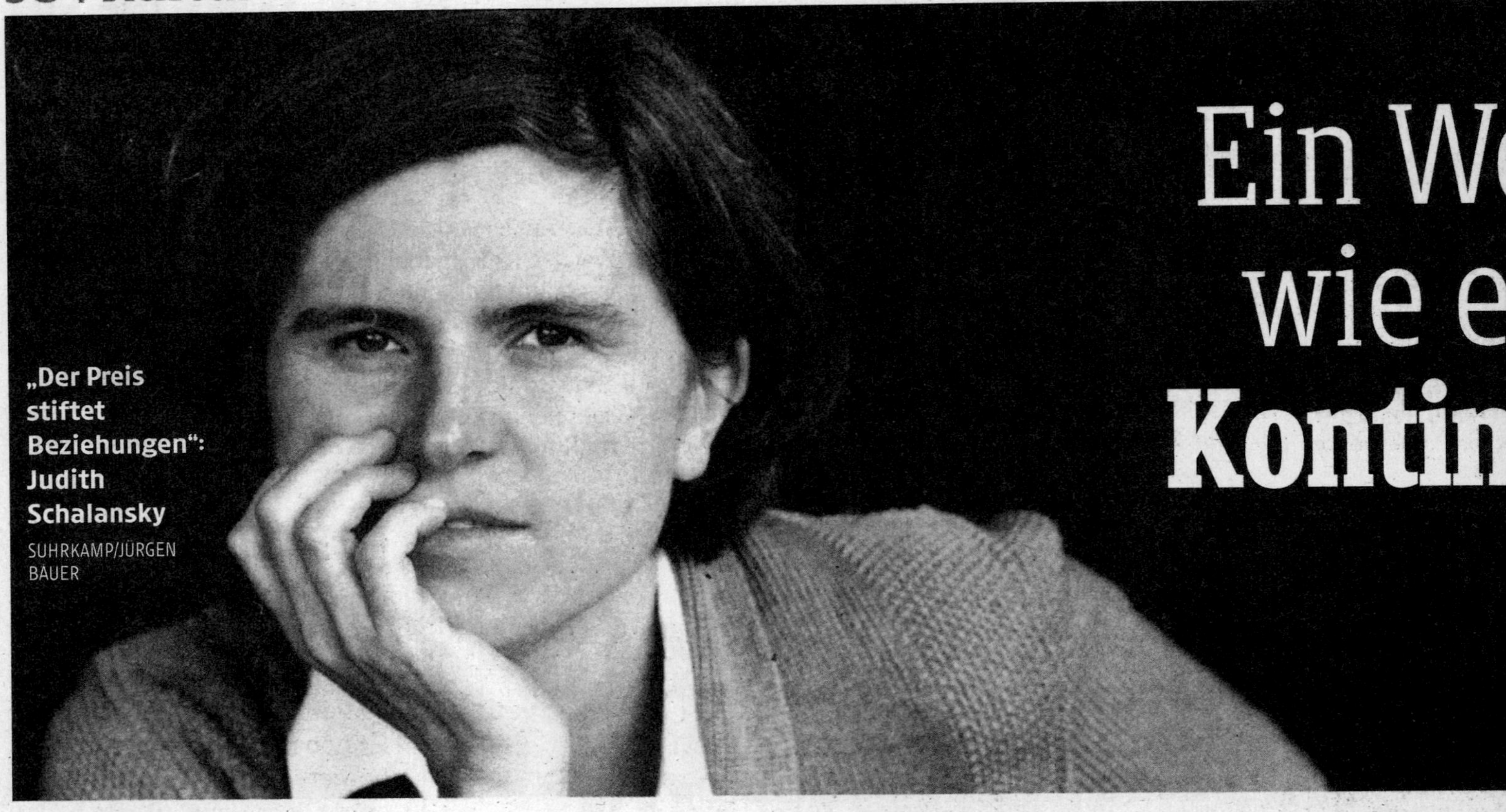

„Der Preis stiftet Beziehungen": Judith Schalansky
SUHRKAMP/JÜRGEN BAUER

Ein W
wie e
Kontin

INTERVIEW. Judith Schalansky wurde mit dem Christine-Lavant-Preis ausgezeichnet. Ein Gespräch über die Kärntner Dichterin, den Blick vom Rand auf die Gesellschaft und einen geplanten Virenatlas.

Von Marianne Fischer

Sie erhielten am Sonntag in Wien den Christine-Lavant-Preis. Welche Beziehung haben Sie zur Kärntner Autorin?
JUDITH SCHALANSKY: Das ist ja das Schöne an einem Preis. Er stiftet Beziehung, stellt Verbindungen her, spürt Verwandtschaften auf. Eine sehr lebendige Form der Denkmalspflege. Ich bin der Jury jedenfalls überaus dankbar dafür, mir mit ihrer Wahl einen der denkbar schönsten Anlässe gegeben zu haben, mich endlich rückhaltlos auf das wilde Werk der Christine Lavant einzulassen.

Sehen Sie Parallelen zu Ihrem eigenen Werk?
Durchaus. Es ist das Interesse für das vermeintlich Randständige, der Blick auf jene, die gerne an der Peripherie verortet werden: Menschen, die nicht ganz gesund, nicht vollkommen lebensfroh, nicht wohlhabend sind – arm an Möglichkeiten. Aus meiner Beschäftigung mit abgelegenen Inseln weiß ich aber, dass man gerade vom Rand einen sehr guten Blick auf die Gesellschaft hat.

Erinnern Sie sich noch daran, wann Sie erstmals mit Lavant-Werken in Berührung kamen?
Die Lavant war mir lange eine fremde Gestalt, die ich aus dem Augenwinkel wahrgenommen habe, und deren Werk und Wirken ein gewisses eingeweihtes, auch abschreckendes Raunen einhüllte. Man muss erst einmal durch diese Biografie eines geschundenen Lebens durch. Die Lavant ist eine, die auch in der Kunst mit barer Münze zahlt. Das macht sie schon allein von den Umständen her so unbestechlich. Viel entscheidender ist aber, dass ihr Werk – die Gedichte wie die Erzählungen – kühn ist, überraschend und voller Mehrdeutigkeiten. Es erscheint mir wie ein Kontinent, dessen eigentliche Erforschung mir noch bevorsteht.

Christine Lavant wird gerne als „Schmerzensfrau" bezeichnet. Sie haben selbst in Ihrem Buch „Verzeichnis einiger Verluste" geschrieben: „Am Leben zu sein be-
deutet, Verlu
deprimierend
auch eine be
Ganz klar
Ohne aufges
Leben nun
ben. Sich a
Erfahrunger
nen zu wolle
zu vermeid
ob nun für
kann dabei
Ambivalenz
Die ungar
Ágnes Helle
„Kein Gew
Kein Verlus

Derzeit erl
wegen Coro
freiheit ist ei
len Mund-N
und weniger
ben. Wie geh
Ich bin noc
davon, wie s
neue Verha
wöhnen kö
ist ein ersta
fähiges Tier
nahmezusta
sich. Imme
zu umarmen
fast schon i

Wie haben
lebt? Als Ein
Reduzierung
Das ganze
war, wie ma
Häuslichkei
viel aussor

Nicht stehen für, nicht im Gebot der
Liebe und Erkenntlichkeit
zu handeln, ist sich mit Apathie zu trennen.

Neutralität

Hier ist ein persönlicher Abschied vom Nicht-Handeln.
Ade.

Clemens von Wedemeyer

Emergency Drill Revisited
2020

Video

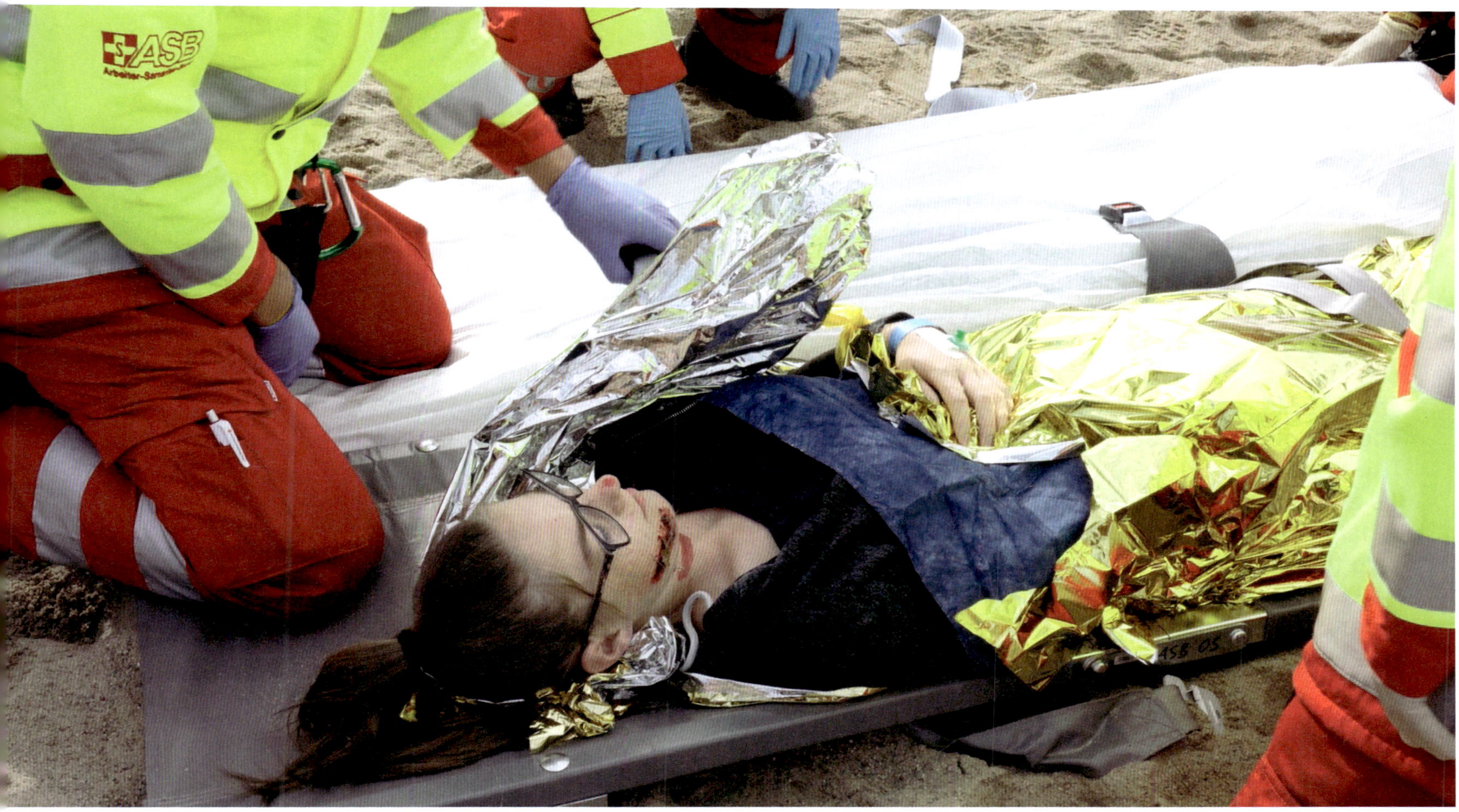
ASB

Emergency Drill documents the staging of a security procedure near Leipzig carried out by the civil protection unit in 2019. Visiting a lake surrounded by trees and beaches, I'm observing different groups of people going through the motions of helping and needing help. I find myself in the center of a fictitious play. A large group of men and women in fully equipped gear are standing by waiting for their cue. Search dogs are scanning areas systematically for "survivors." There are no random actions. On the contrary, this training is highly structured with set sequences for everyone to follow. A preparation for the unpredictable event of a catastrophe. What interests me in this scenario is the contradiction within the scripting of the emergency—as a therapeutic act, turning it into a ritual, chopping it up into bureaucratic forms to fill out and parts that can be rehearsed. With Alex Scrimgeour, I developed a dialogue on the implications of these scenarios and preparations. What do we prepare for in this fiction and what happens upon returning to normal life? What follows is the beginning of the film.

It's already begun: there's been an accident.
A ferry disaster in a lake outside Leipzig.
It's a simulation.
A scenario that has been developed for training purposes.
Not very likely, but the skills are transferable and the team-building important.
A chance to experiment in real-world conditions, test the parameters.
And the weather's good for it today.
Hey guys, I need some help here!
What are you doing there?
On the head? Back here?
Here at the belly?
Does anything hurt?
Pelvis? Does anything hurt?
This is play-acting, a break in normality.
It has a beginning, a middle, and an end.
It's a piece of theater that blocks out the structural causes, the chains of events that brought us here.
Once you have your role, you can't just switch.
Not while the simulation is running.
The role becomes more precisely defined, less open to change, during the simulation.
The people who came from the water are being helped by the people who came from the land.
The red plus hi-viz combo, the gold and silver.
The uniforms and the flashing lights make it more believable for us, too—
It's an illusion that works because everyone is taking it seriously.
What would the narrative arc look like if the same structures of power, machines, and money came to help the migrants crossing the Mediterranean?
Half a day spent practicing an emergency drill, a drop of comfort.
A semblance of activity for a catastrophe that isn't the one we think we're going through.
The exercise is an anti-catastrophe, created to provide a sense of security.

Clemens von Wedemeyer

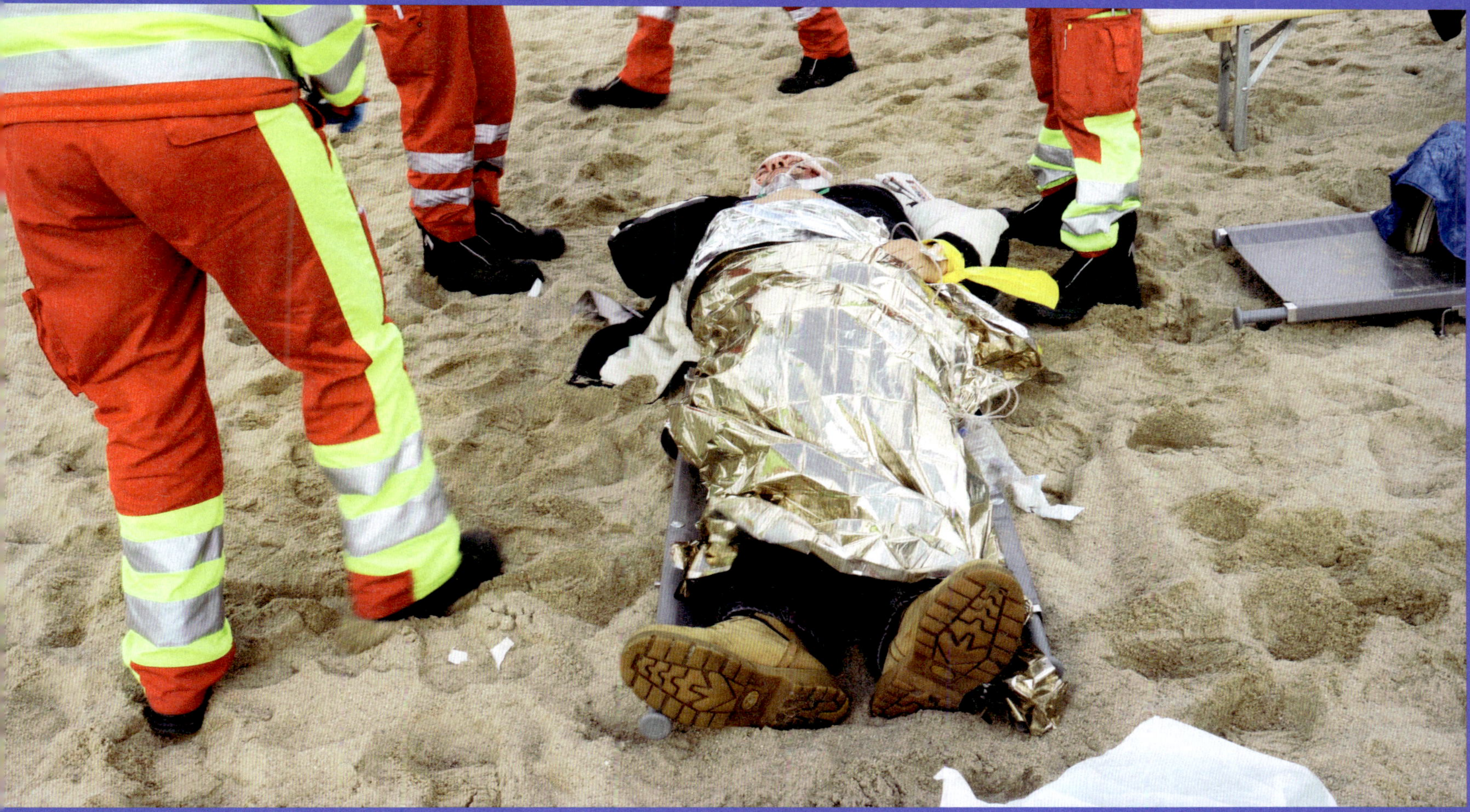

Clemens von Wedemeyer, born in Göttingen, Germany, in 1974, studied photography and media in Bielefeld and fine arts at the Academy of Visual Arts Leipzig, where he now holds a professorship for media art (expanded cinema). As a filmmaker and artist he lives in Berlin. His films and complex video installations embrace several storylines and points of view. His works explore the personal and collective history of the 20th century as well as the power and control structures of the present.

Von Wedemeyer has had solo exhibitions at Galerie für zeitgenössische Kunst Leipzig; Kunsthalle Hamburg; Museum of Contemporary Art, Chicago; and MAXXI, Rome. He took part in the Chicago Architecture Biennial (2019); the Riga Biennial (2018); the 66th Berlinale (2016); and Documenta 13, Kassel (2007), and has been awarded Villa Massimo and Villa Romana fellowships as well as the prize for the German Competition at the International Short Film Festival, Oberhausen, and a VG Bildkunst Award for Experimental Film and Video-art at Munich Film Festival.

Emergency Drill Revisited (2020)
Video, ca. 18 min., German and English
Online

Camera: Clemens von Wedemeyer, Clara Wieck
Editing: Jonas Brinker
Script consultant: Alex Scrimgeour
Voices: Megan Gay, Ian Dickinson

An exercise carried out by the Arbeiter-Samariter-Bund Deutschland e.V.

Commissioned and produced by steirischer herbst '20

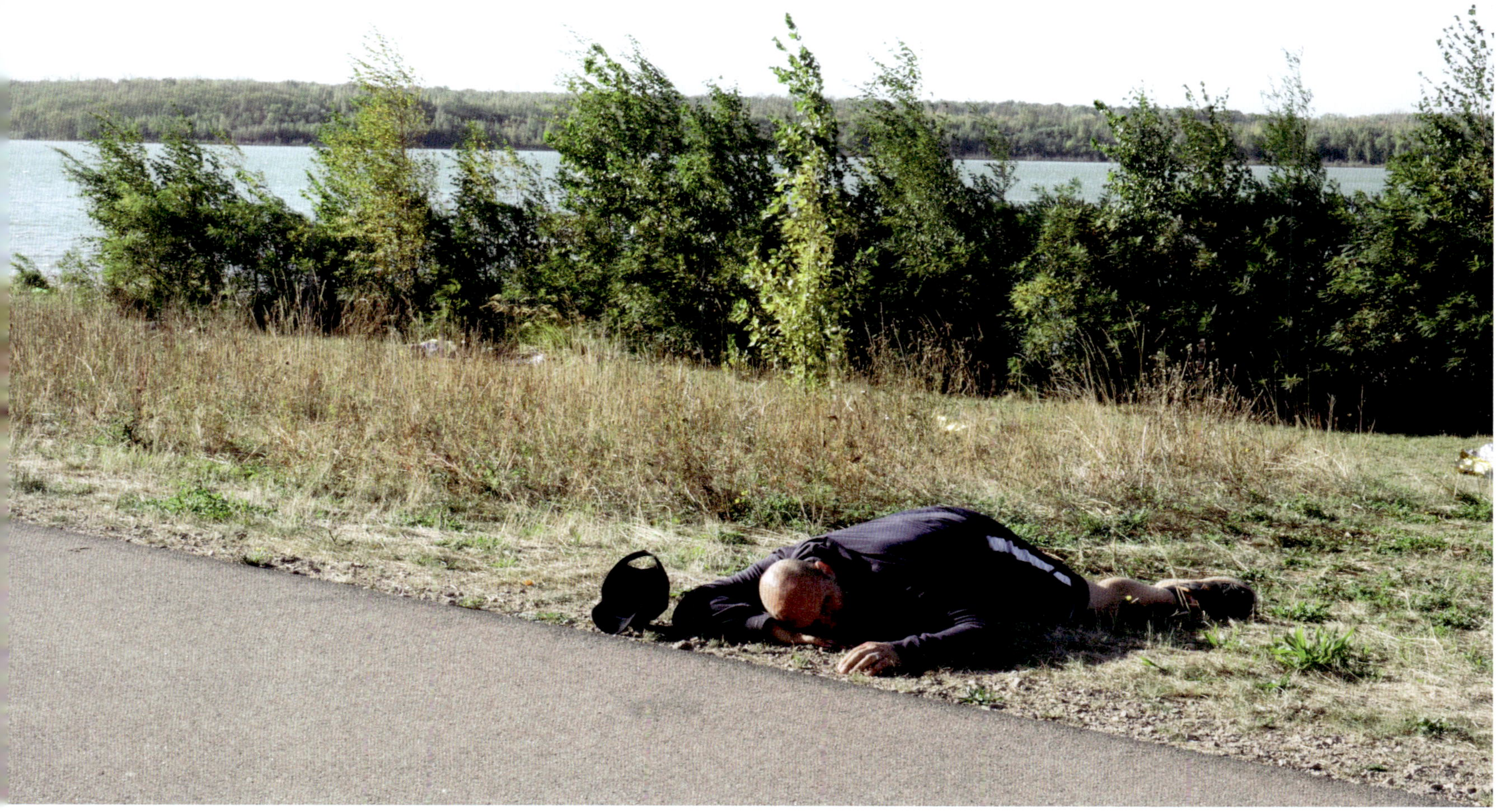

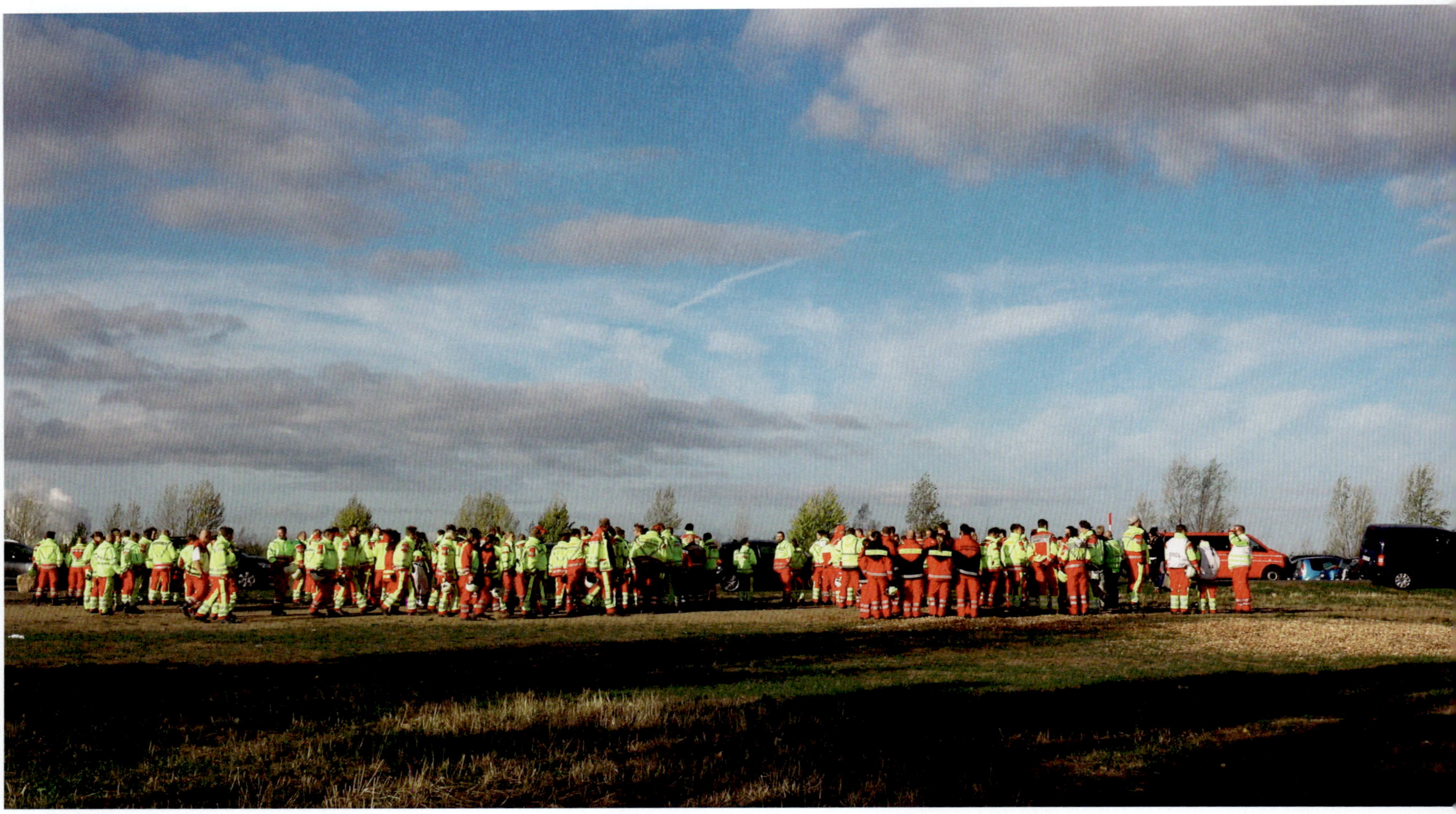

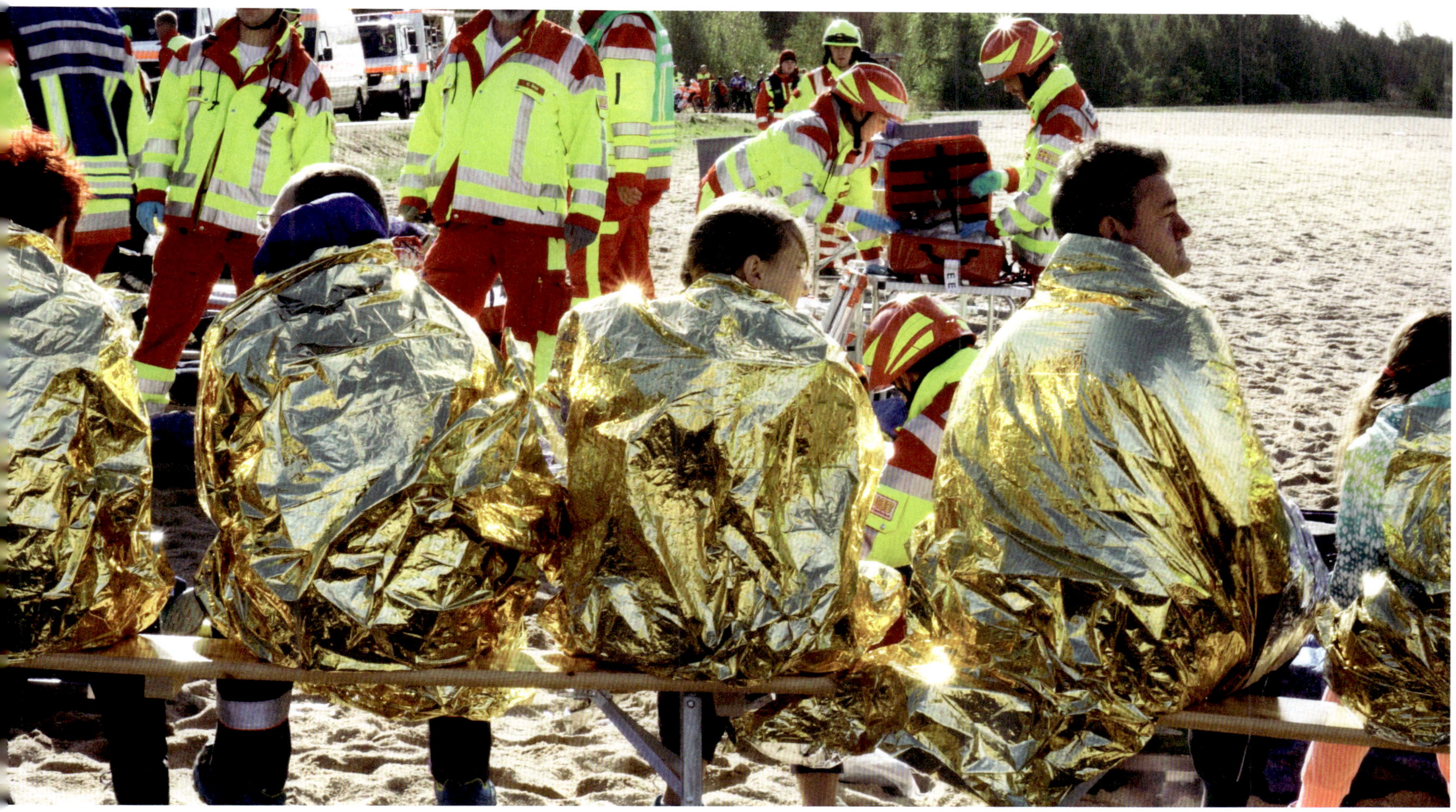

Anna Witt

Skin Front
2020

Video and public space screening

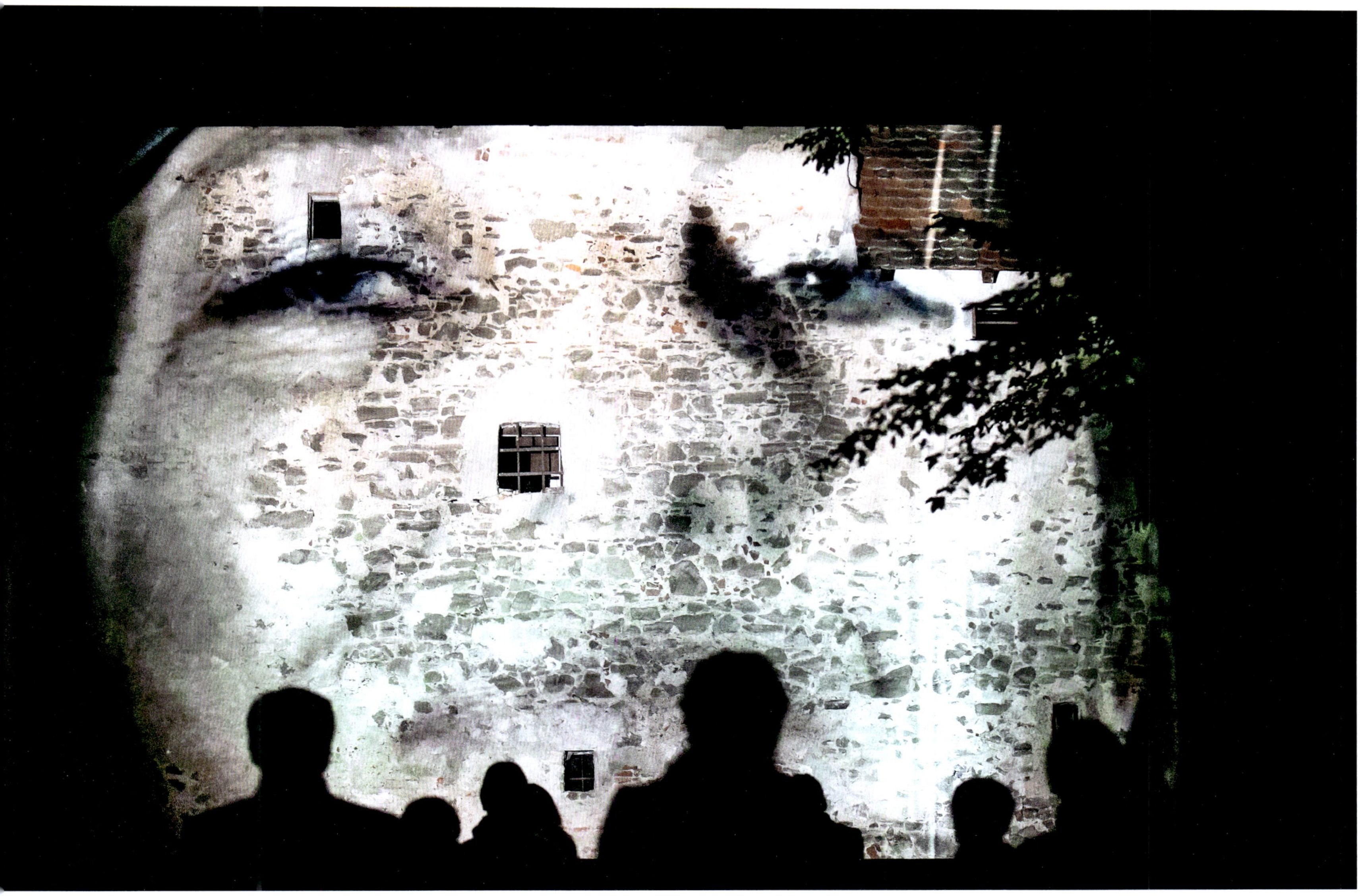

279 PARANOIA TV

Anna Witt, born in Germany in 1981, lives and works in Vienna. Her artistic practice is performative, participatory, and political. She creates situations that reflect interpersonal relationships and power structures as well as conventions of speaking and acting. Passersby in public spaces, or specifically selected people and groups, are drawn into her experimental arrangements, usually in a directly physical way. The tasks range from repeated imitation of specifically coded gestures to the development of complex choreographies and give the participants opportunities for individual articulation and authorship.

She has had solo exhibitions at Belvedere Contemporary, Vienna; Gallery Tanja Wagner, Berlin; Kunst Halle Sankt Gallen; Center for Contemporary Art, Pristina; Marabouparken Museum, Stockholm; Magazin 4, Bregenz; Salzburger Kunstverein; and Grazer Kunstverein, among others. In the last years, she took part in numerous group exhibitions, such as the Aichi Triennale 2019; 5th International Photography Festival Israel; *24/7: The Human Condition*—Vienna Biennale (2015); Off-Biennale Budapest (2017); Lux/ICA Biennial of Moving Images, London (2012); 29th Biennial of Graphic Arts, Ljubljana (2011); Triennale Linz 1.0 (2010); 6th Berlin Biennale for Contemporary Art (2010); and Manifesta 7, Trentino—Alto Adige (2008). She is the winner of the Otto Mauer Preis 2018, the Kunstpreis Europas Zukunft 2015, and the BC21 Art Award 2013.

Skin Front (2020)
Video, ca. 16 min., German
Online / public space screening
Heimat.Museum im Tabor (Feldbach) and Rösselmühle

In collaboration with Karola Sakotnik, Daniela Adler, Barbara Siegl, Sonja Skalnik, Ilse Wieser, Katharina Rungaldier, Barbara Kasper, Zuzanna Szula, Maria Raidl, Helga Kirchengast, Gabriele Grandl, Andrea Meyer, and Sadia Hammonti

Project coordinator Feldbach:
Karola Sakotnik
Camera: Caroline Bobek
Sound: Baptiste El Baz
Lights: Jürgen Mayer
Postproduction: Arthur Summereder, Alfred Lenz

Commissioned and produced by steirischer herbst '20
Screening partner Graz: Institut für Kunst im Öffentlichen Raum Steiermark / OEVERwerk

Through the pandemic, isolation became a shared experience that led to a new understanding of the body in its collective separation.

The video was created during the first lockdown in spring 2020 in a collaborative process with women of different ages from Feldbach in Styria, Austria.

For this purpose, a discussion group was created, which met online to take a joint stand in a situation of general retreat into the private sphere. Subversiveness and resistance became central concepts, which focused on the effects of the pandemic and the resulting crisis for women.

A text collage was created for the video, based on the conversations that took place during the online meetings. In addition, the women performatively interpreted experiences of physical distance and psychological closeness. Against a black background, different parts of the body enter into a dialogue and show that they are capable of physical empathy and solidarity in spite of contact bans.

For its premiere, the film was projected onto the stone wall of the Tabor, the former witches' prison in Feldbach, in a large format of approximately nine by sixteen meters. There, the largest witch trial in Styria took place at the end of the 17th century.

The coarse structure of the historical wall was visible in the projected bodies of the women, thus establishing a historical reference to the topicality of female resistance.

You didn't hear cars.
You don't hear anyone talking.
You don't hear anyone laughing.
No one was mowing the lawn—
All you heard were birds chirping.
You didn't hear any children. That was terrible.
Most of the children I heard were on TV.
And when you hear the politicians talking,
you think, what soaring language, such eloquence.
They cover things up, twist them, deny them. I hear the deformed language of hate. They are deforming my beloved language!

There's been so much in the media lately about how trendy it is to bake bread—how it's all about handling something soft and warm—but the most frequently searched recipe on the Internet was for bread you don't have to knead. What's the point of that?

My mother's doing Feldenkrais with a tablet.

In the evening at home you connected with your family digitally.
For my job, I moved everything online
and to social media to stay on the ball.
And over time I got the feeling
that my hands had been digitalized!

I scrolled through endless pictures about different issues that made me really concerned. I posted articles and expressed my own criticisms. This digital engagement combines so wonderfully with me and my life and increasingly I felt I was just entering data all the time!
But it's not effective enough for me!
I want my fingers to be a little more stubborn!
Rather than always answering emails right away and forwarding everything I'm supposed to.

And I'm always happy to provide my fingerprint.
My fingerprint opens my programs, it opens my bank account, it opens my phone. I see my fingerprint as opening doors for me!

And I must say, I've never done as well as I'm doing now.
I recognized how deeply rooted it is, this idea that human needs should be subordinate to

professional needs. That doesn't make sense for anyone!
I was always at the end of my rope—really. The whole time.

I was totally suffering, but it was a luxury quarantine.
Whenever I wanted pizza, someone brought me pizza.

Eye: What images do you see?
Hand: What are you doing?
Feet: Which way are you going?
Arm: What are you fighting for?
Mouth: What are you shouting for?

What does cooperation mean in a democracy that's actually polarized? What's the difference between subversion and resistance?
Subversion can also be private.
Resistance is always loud and public!
85% of the unemployed due to Corona are women!

Where will we save money in the future?! In the current atmosphere, we are very worried the burden will fall on women because the problem will be privatized.
We are expecting a total backlash.

Now we need to step up our efforts!
Sometimes I think if I'd lived in the old days, I'd have been burned as a witch because there are some things I just won't go along with!

Resistance is always loud and public!
85% of the unemployed due to Corona are women!
It's an existential problem.
We need more imperatives.

Are we going forward during this crisis?
Or backward? Or running in place?
I won't let them push me back!
It's a bit harder to walk now.

Anna Witt

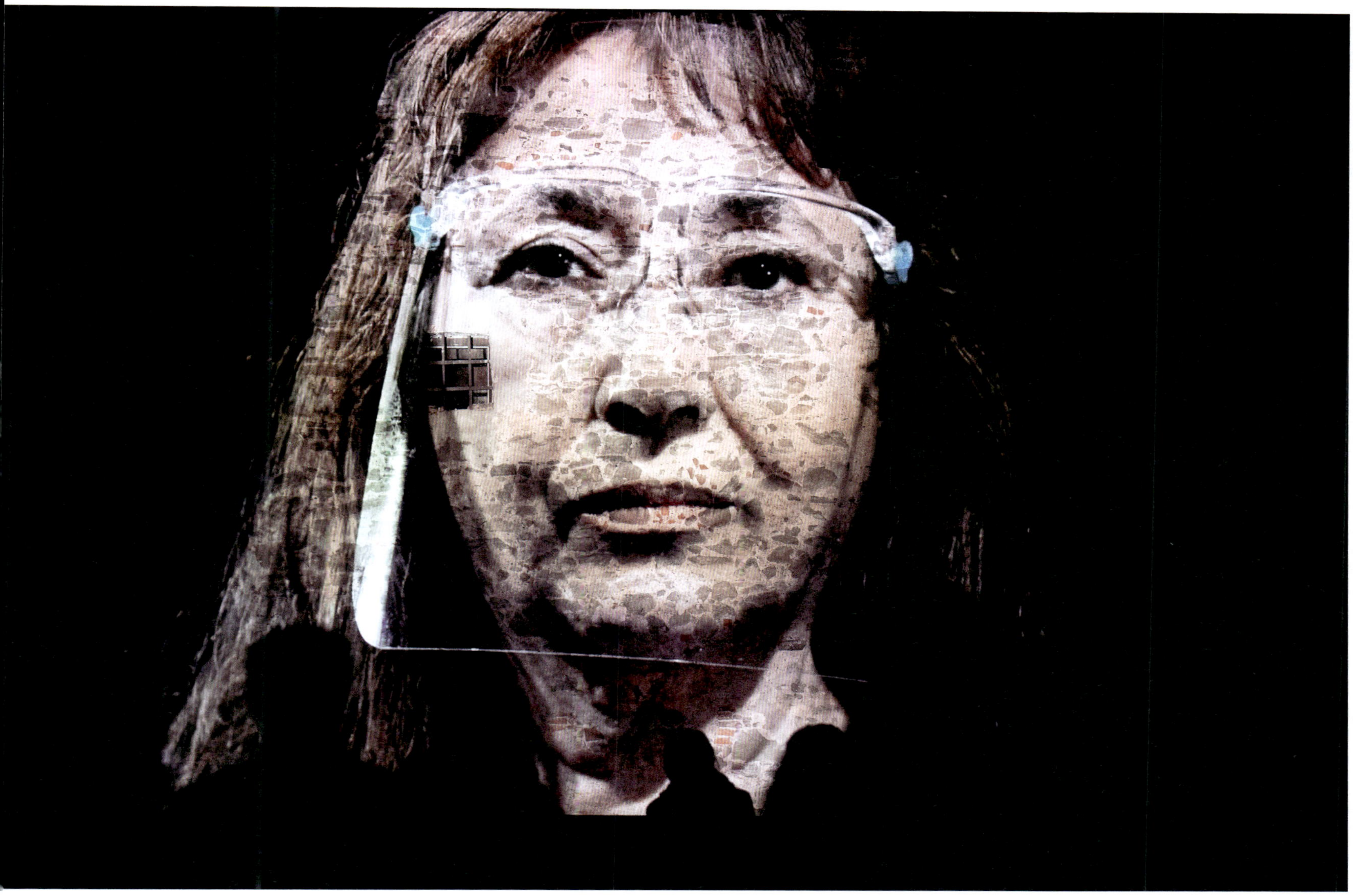

Paranoia TV News
2020

Video series

Airing from the Paranoia TV Headquarters and the streets of Graz, *Paranoia TV News* broadcast the latest information and impressions from this year's steirischer herbst festival. A series of interviews with special guests alongside coverage of real-life events and performances shed light behind the scenes and allowed the audience to tune in to the world of *Paranoia TV*.

Paranoia TV News (2020)
Video series, 13 episodes,
ca. 22 min. each, German

Concept: Ekaterina Degot
Host and writer: Rupert Lehofer
Camera: Nina Rath, Ulrich Reiterer, Daniel Baeck
Editing: Nina Rath
Sound: Fritz Hierzegger
Production: Johanna Arco, Christoph Platz
Artist interviews section: Mirela Baciak, Džana Ajanović, Barbara Seyerl
Interviewers: Mirela Baciak, Dominik Müller, Christoph Platz
Studio: AVbaby Mediastudios
Animation and CI: Grupa Ee
Animation Freud: Tobias Stärk, Simon Schmalfeld, Marc Pantenburg, Tobias Wüstefeld

Commissioned and produced by steirischer herbst '20

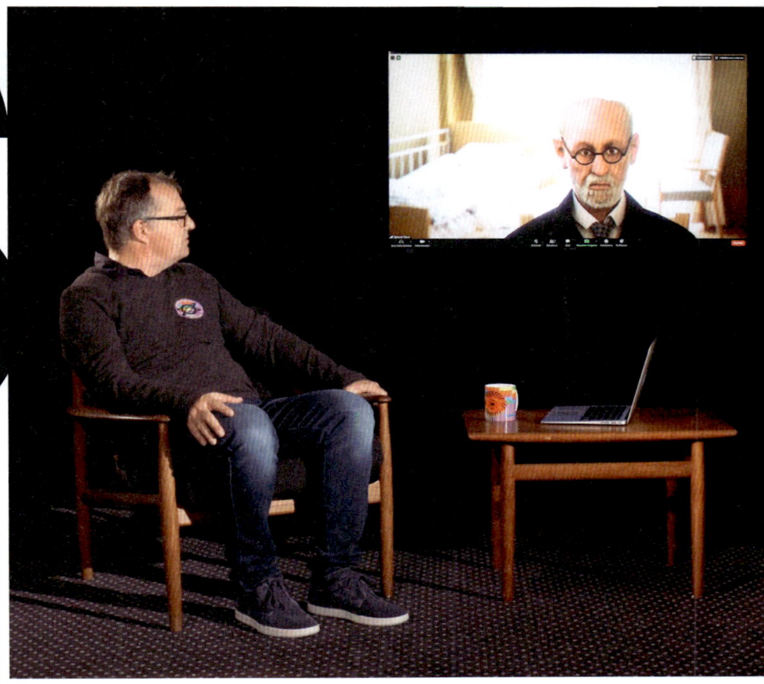

Paranoia TV Headquarters
2020

Temporary space

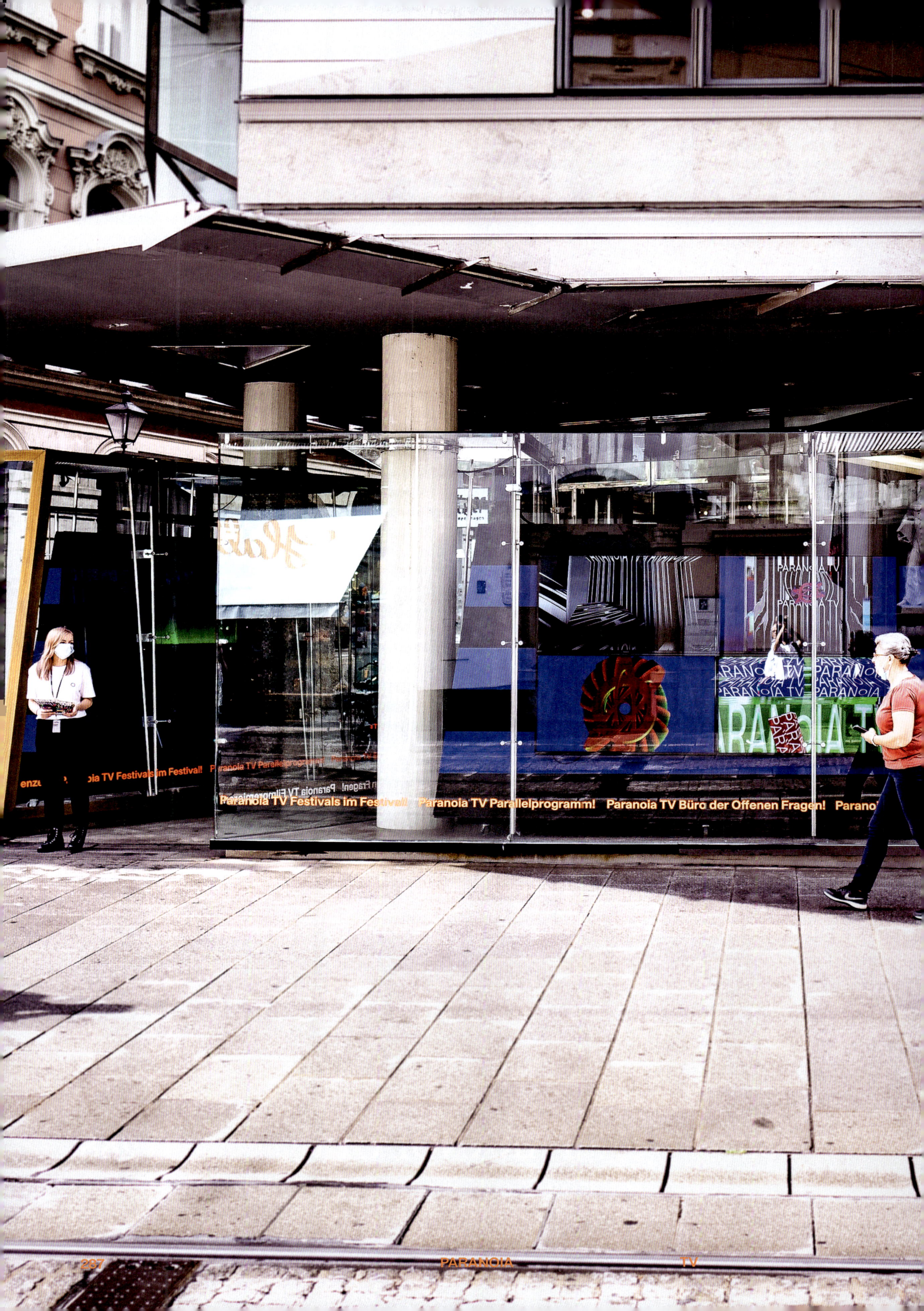
Paranoia TV Festivals im Festival!
Paranoia TV Parallelprogramm!
Paranoia TV Büro der Offenen Fragen!

Paranoia TV Zentrale, the headquarters of the temporary media conglomerate that steirischer herbst '20 created, served as a display of how the festival imagined a broadcasting center that distributed artworks internationally against the backdrop of the pandemic's new system of rules, which fostered physical borders and nationalist strategies. A whole building representing decentralized production and presentation, dense and at the same time lacking human bodies.

Located on Graz's most prominent street, Herrengasse—which is firmly in the hands of luxury brands and chain stores—it came with a touch of nostalgia for the buzzing times when video had killed the radio star.

Paranoia TV installed its broadcasting center in the old Thonethof or Generalihof from 1884. The facade still works within the 19th-century ensemble of the old town, built by architects Ferdinand Fellner and Herman Gottfried Helmer, who also designed the monumental complex that today houses Graz's Opera. Irmfried Windbichler, who worked for Eilfried Huth and contributed to an architectural and urban design discourse surrounding the renovation and preservation of business architecture, radically transformed the building in 1990 by changing its axis, splitting the ground floor walls, and adding glass and steel elements to increase transparency—a postmodern redesign.

Even today, the building is known to many Grazers as SPITZ, referring to the shoe store of the Armin Spitz family, located in Herrengasse before the Anschluss. The *Herrenrasse*, the "master race," took over the building by force at the latest after *Kristallnacht* in 1938. After the war, other shoe companies used this prime location for their flagship stores.

The Paranoia TV Headquarters was composed with elements from the building's postmodern period: at the conference table, which *Paranoia TV* acquired from the bankruptcy assets of Hypo Alpe Adria (an insurance company with a well-known scandal involving the late far-right party leader Jörg Haider), video conferences and discursive events were held, but it also projected the idea of a notorious editorial meeting room. A place where you imagined a joke starting with: Roger Ailes, Rupert Murdoch, and Steve Bannon meet in Graz . . .

A CRT television set with an AI-based avatar impersonating Sigmund Freud watched and listened to everything happening at the Paranoia TV Headquarters and progressively learned how to have consistent conversations, a Max Headroom of psychoanalysis who was able to tell stories based on real people's input.

Some elements depicted the fiction of a media conglomerate: the elevator sign claimed more stories than there were, with fictional departments that touched upon the workforce and power of media producers with echoes of "the good old times"—a projection of simplicity and crafted quality. This techno-nostalgic comment was also made by fake doors with keypads and fake studios with "on air" signs. While the real greenscreen studio on the top floor was used by the educational team, the basement was equipped with a cinematic viewing environment for the content *Paranoia TV* produced—remotely produced, virtually brought together, turned on and tuned in (also) at the Headquarters.

Christoph Platz

Concept: Christoph Platz
Architecture Christoph Platz, Sebastian Sprenger, Peter Schloss
Project Coordinators: Sebastian Sprenger, Lukas Kaiser
Art Handling: Heinz Leitner, Karl Masten
Design: Gupa Ee
Carpenter: Tischlerei Johann Gollob
A/V: Stephan Taul, Pro Video Veranstaltungstechnik
PTV HQ Café: Gatto Gasser

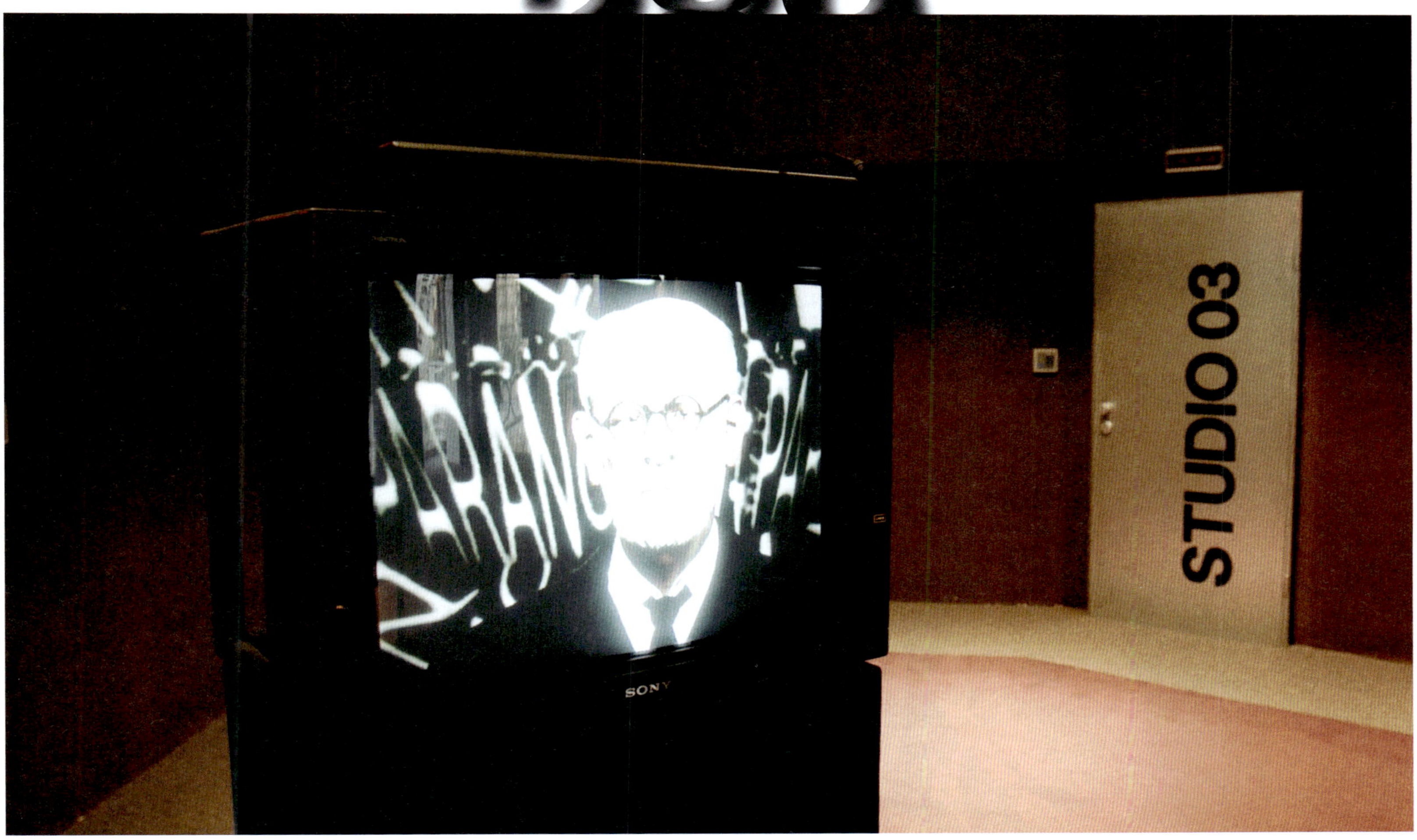

2020 PARANOIA TV

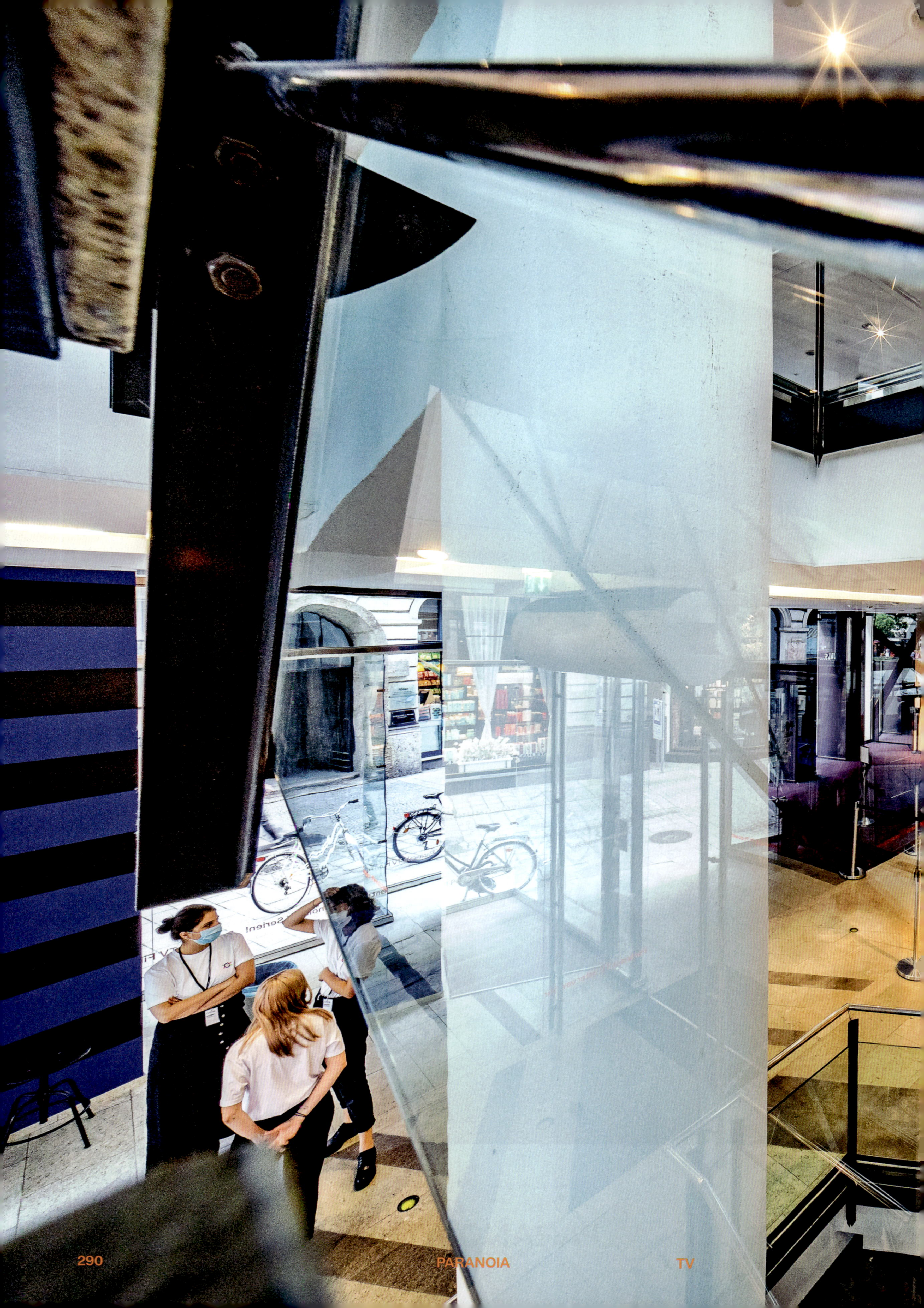

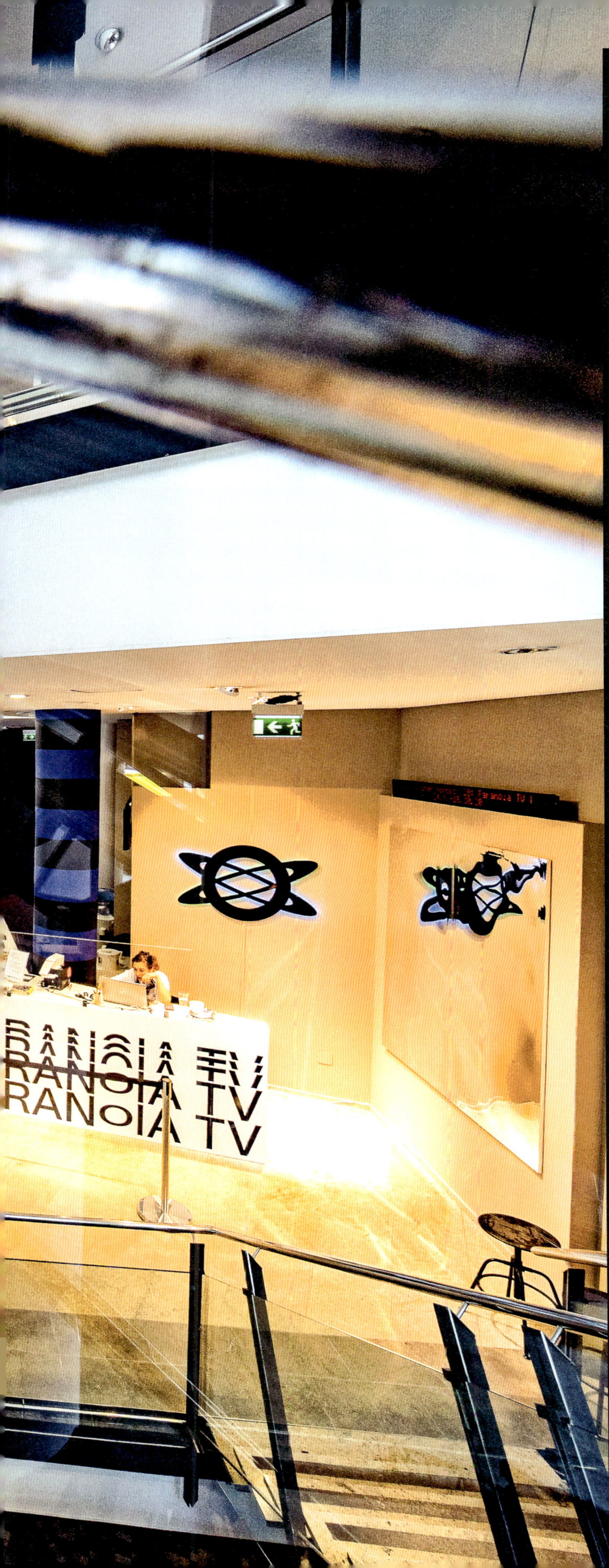

D **Büro der Offenen Fragen**
Office of Open Questions
Toiletten
Restrooms

2 **Serverraum**
Server Room

1 **Café**
Konferenzsaal
Conference Hall

EG **Foyer**
Psychoanalyse
Studio 01, 02, 03

- 1 **Vorführraum**
Screening Room

- 2 **Redaktion 01**

- 3 **Redaktion 02**

- 4 **Redaktion 03**

- 5 **Grupa Ee Entertainment**

- 6 **Schnitt**
Editing

- 7 **Tonstudio**
Sound Studio

- 8 **Statisten**
Extras

- 9 **Garderoben**
Dressing Rooms

- 10 **Maske, Friseur, Stylist**
Make-up, Hair, Stylist

- 11 **Swimming Pool**
(nur auf CEO Einladung)
(by CEO invitation only)

- 12 **Panikraum**
Panic Room

- 13 **Technikabteilung**
Tech Department

- 14 **Regie**
Direction

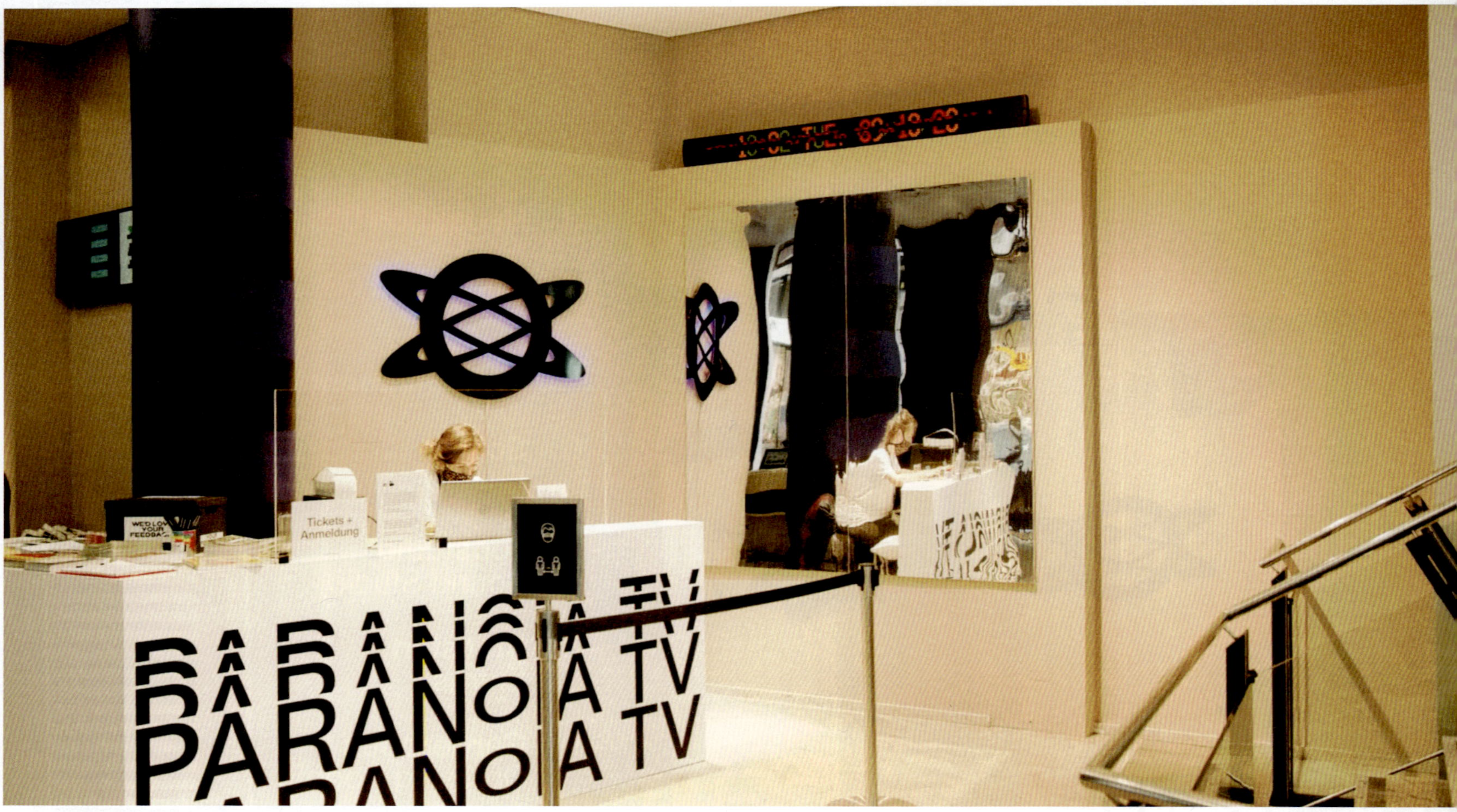
PARANOIA TV
Tickets +
Anmeldung

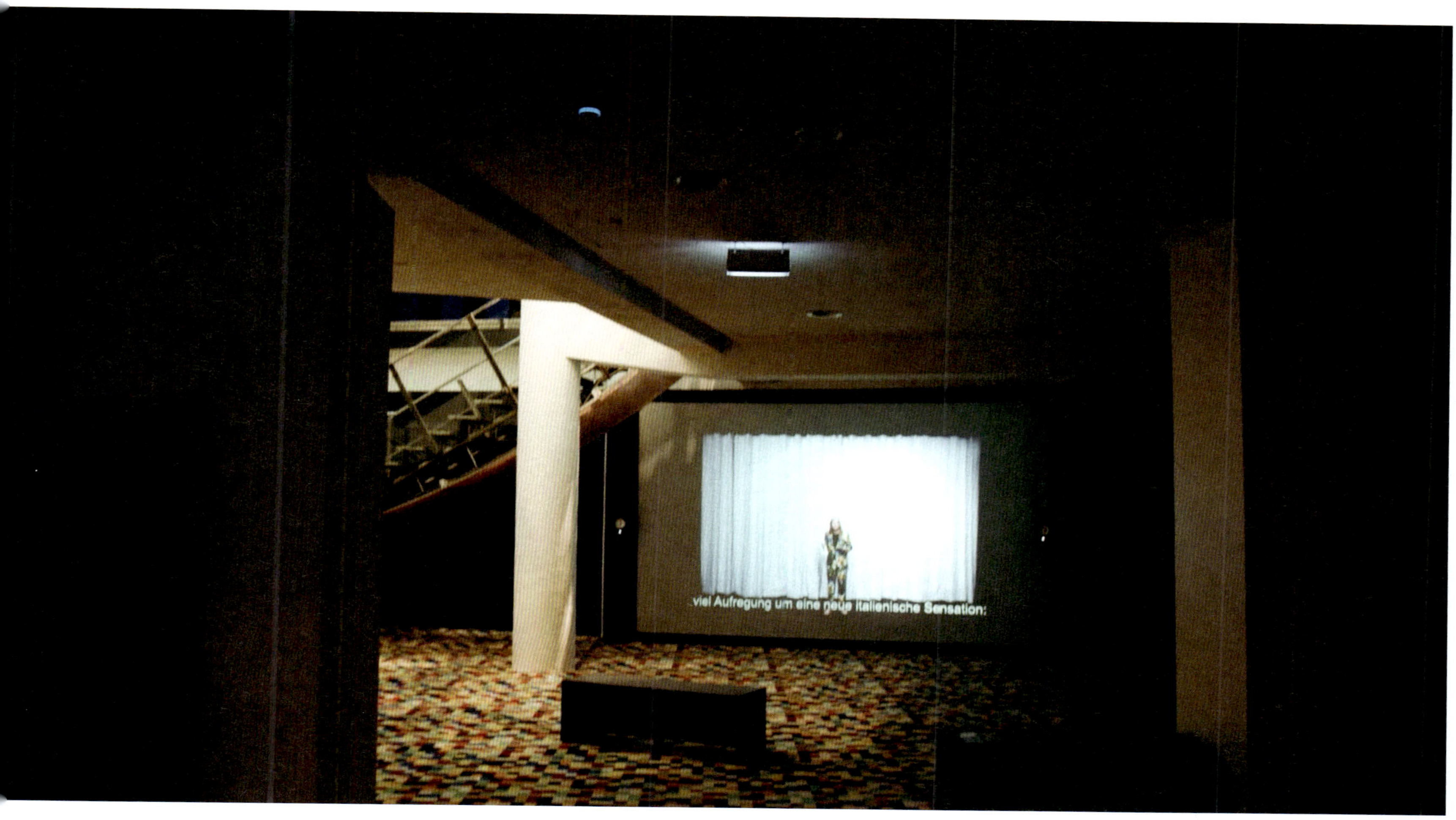
viel Aufregung um eine neue italienische Sensation:

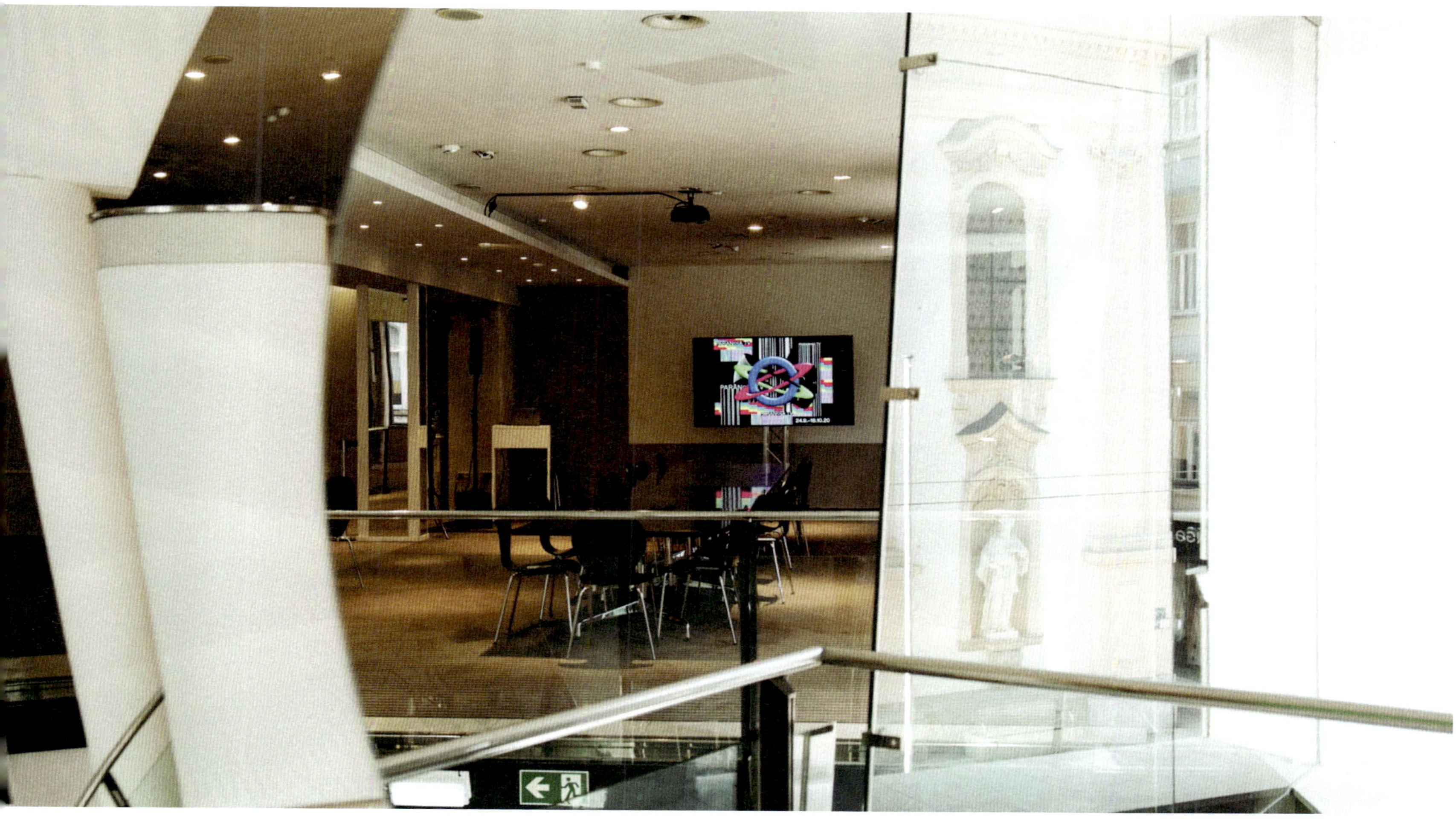

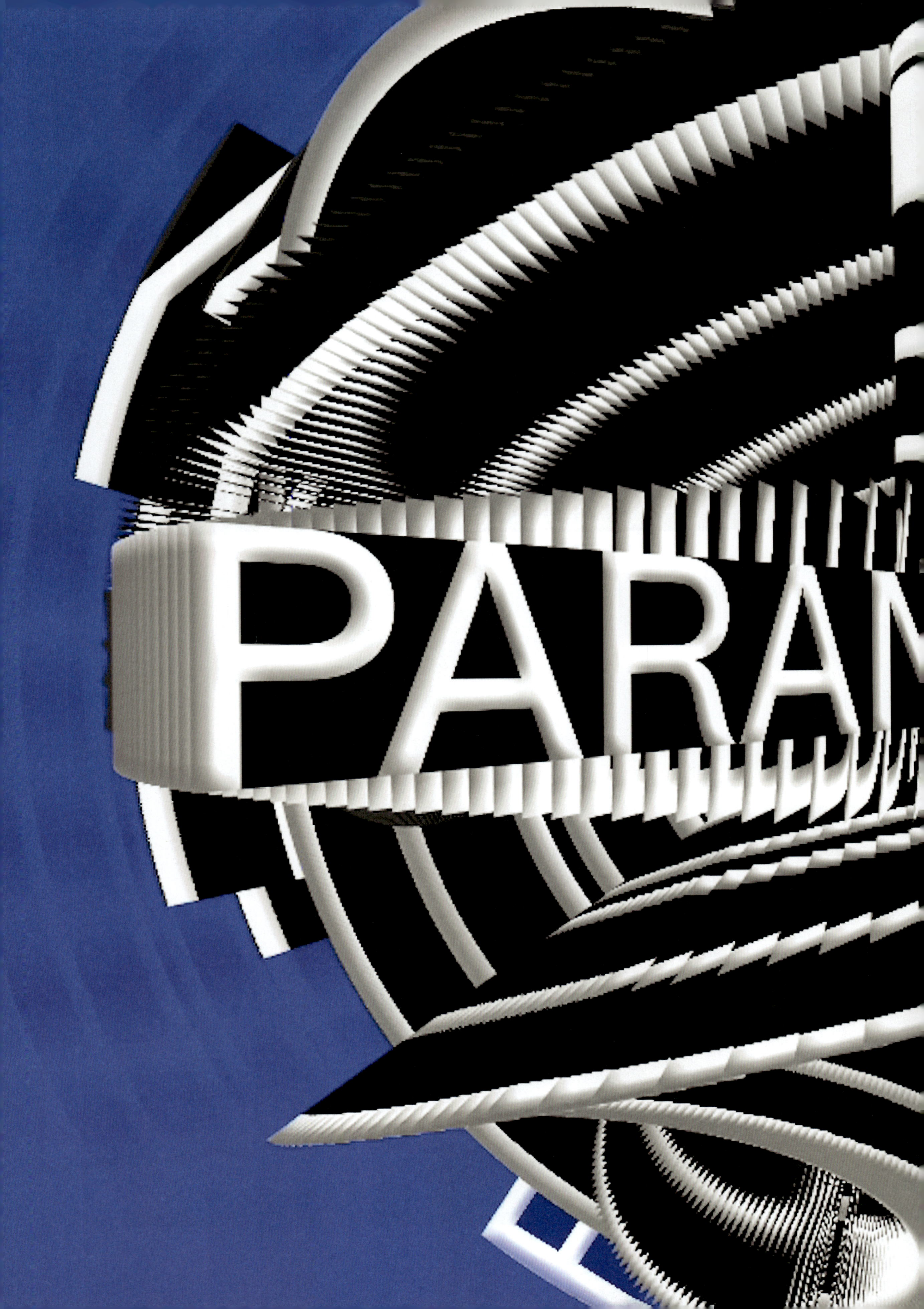
PARA

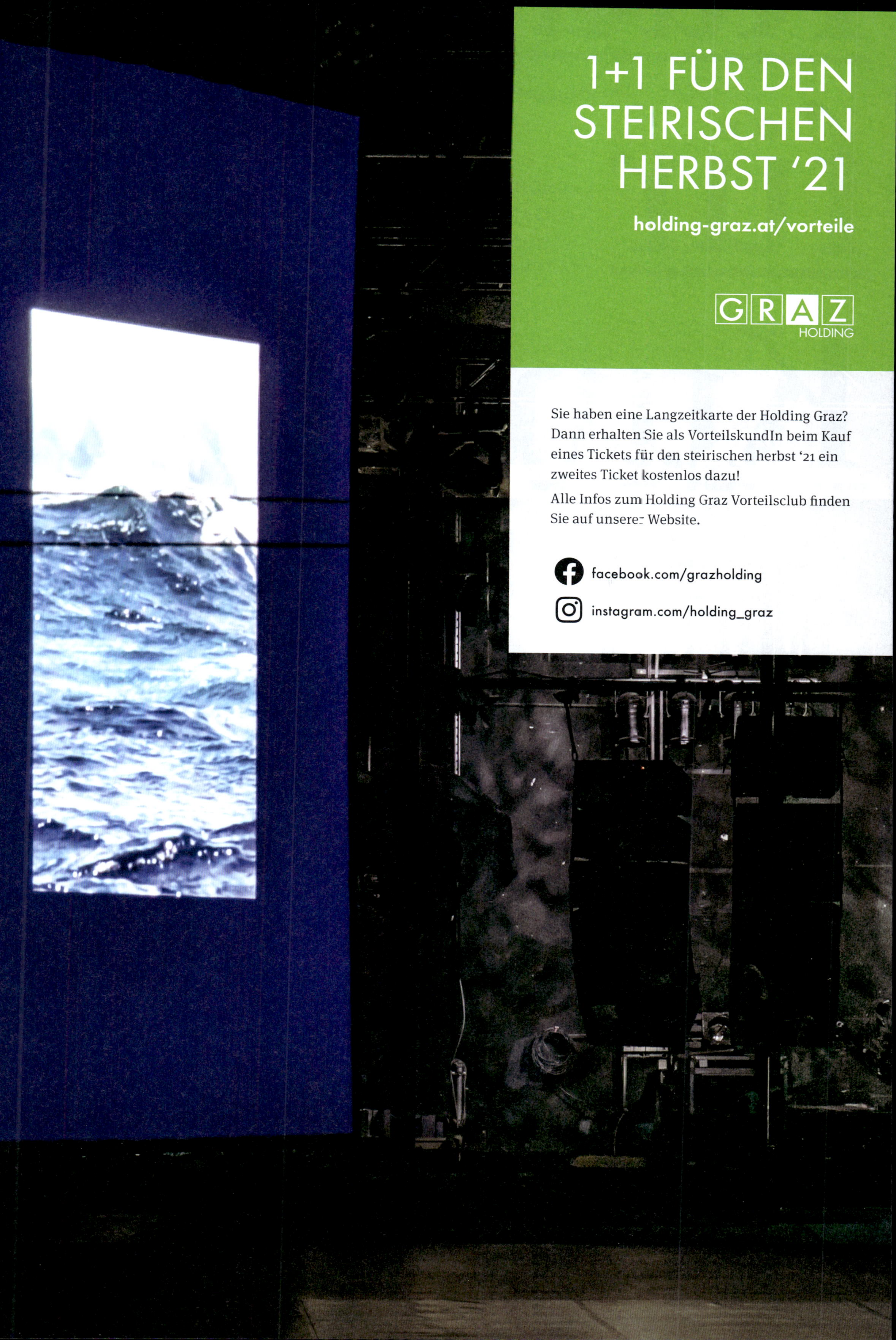
1+1 FÜR DEN STEIRISCHEN HERBST '21
holding-graz.at/vorteile
GRAZ HOLDING
Sie haben eine Langzeitkarte der Holding Graz? Dann erhalten Sie als VorteilskundIn beim Kauf eines Tickets für den steirischen herbst '21 ein zweites Ticket kostenlos dazu!
Alle Infos zum Holding Graz Vorteilsclub finden Sie auf unserer Website.
facebook.com/grazholding
instagram.com/holding_graz

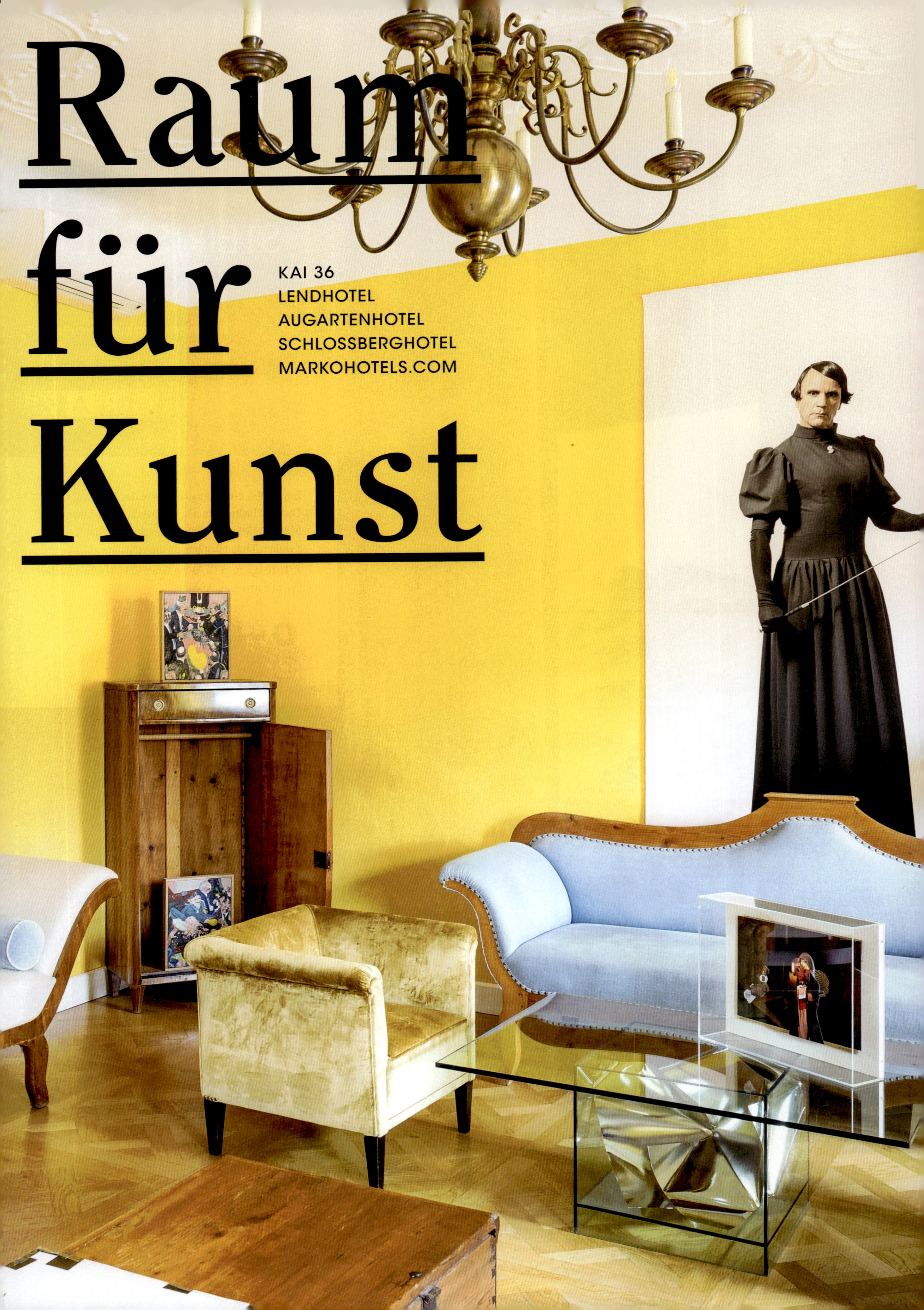
Raum
für
Kunst
KAI 36
LENDHOTEL
AUGARTENHOTEL
SCHLOSSBERGHOTEL
MARKOHOTELS.COM

steirischer herbst ’20
Curators, Artists, Speakers, Festival Team

steirischer herbst ’20—*Paranoia TV* took place from September 24 to October 18, 2020, in Graz and Styria, Austria, as well as online.

This edition of steirischer herbst was conceived by all participating artists, thinkers, and philosophers, as well as
Ekaterina Degot, Director and Chief Curator
Henriette Gallus, Deputy Director
Christoph Platz, Head of Curatorial Affairs
David Riff, Senior Curator
Dominik Müller, Curator
Mirela Baciak, Curator
and steirischer herbst team

Artists
Lawrence Abu Hamdan
Akinbode Akinbiyi
Neïl Beloufa & Bad Manner’s
Blind Date Collaboration, anulla, and monochrom
Christian von Borries and Jonathan Aner
Sergey Bratkov
Alexander Chernyshkov
Pauline Curnier Jardin
Josef Dabernig
Nika Dubrovsky and friends
Vadim Fishkin
Dani Gal
Thomas Geiger
Gelatin
Tamar Guimarães with Luisa Cavanagh and Rusi Millán Pastori
Rana Hamadeh
Janez Janša
Lina Majdalanie & Rabih Mroué
Chrystèle Nicot & Antoine Alesandrini
Ingo Niermann
Lulu Obermayer
Ahmet Öğüt
Diederik Peeters
Joanna Piotrowska
Alexandra Pirici & Jonas Lund
Hendrik Quast & Maika Knoblich
Judy Radul
Joanna Rajkowska and Robert Yerachmiel Sniderman
Roee Rosen
Susanne Sachsse / Marc Siegel / Xiu Xiu (Jamie Stewart)
Igor Samolet
Liv Schulman
John Smith
studio ASYNCHROME
Theater im Bahnhof
Sung Tieu
Clemens von Wedemeyer
Anna Witt

Speakers
manuel arturo abreu
Fahim Amir
Aaron Bastani
Franco “Bifo” Berardi
das kollektiv
Aria Dean
Lulo Demarco
Kerry Doran
Silvia Federici
Bobby Gillespie
Herwig G. Höller
Srećko Horvat
Eva Illouz
Martha Kenney
Dean Kissick
Adam Kleinman
Stephanie Krisper
Achille Mbembe
Alexander Neupert-Doppler
Robert Pfaller
Milo Rau
Drehli Robnik
Dorion Sagan
Astrid Schrader
Johann Skocek
Hito Steyerl
Natascha Strobl
Ece Temelkuran
Mark Terkessidis
Yanis Varoufakis
Jörg Vogeltanz
Martin Wabl
Mark Waschke

Festival Team

Ekaterina Degot
Director and Chief Curator

Henriette Gallus
Deputy Director

Christoph Platz
Head of Curatorial Affairs

Rita Puffer
Chief Financial Officer

Carina Hutter
Management Assistant / Coordinator National Project Funding

David Riff
Senior Curator

Mirela Baciak
Curator

Dominik Müller
Curator

Džana Ajanović
Curatorial Assistant

Barbara Seyerl
Curatorial Assistant

Jakob Schweighofer
Senior Production Manager

Amelie Brandstetter
Production Manager

Sebastian Sprenger
Production Manager

Johanna Arco
Project Coordinator

Jacqueline Emathinger
Coordinator Production Office

Kathrin Lazarus
(maternity leave)
Coordinator Production Office

Maria-Oscara Ohrenstein
Coordinator Art Projects Attendants

Project Coordinators
Elsa Chinese
Lukas Kaiser
Heinz Leitner
Martin Pelzmann
Karola Sakotnik
Eva Schmartschan
Lisa Schöttl
Stefan Tau

Video Editors
Bastian Meier
Nina Rath
Andreas Schögler
Carmen Zimmermann

Video Conference Coordinators
Ahmad Darkhabani
Marcel Masten

Karl Masten
Technical Management

Peter Schloss
Production Advisor

Christine Sbaschnigg
Coordinator Signage

Hannes Bemm
Sponsorship and Protocol Events Coordinator

Martina Heil
Editorial Coordinator / Coordinator Communications

Judith Brand
Press Officer

Arash Shahali
Coordinator International Media and Professional Visitors / International Project Funding

Vesna Pajičić
Coordinator Visitors Service

Jeff Thoss
Managing Editor

Fotini Lazaridou-Hatzigoga
Website Manager

Translations
Amy Klement
Jennifer Taylor

Editing and Proofreading
Aaron Bogart
Rainer Wieland

Press Assistants
Elisabeth Jagl
Alina Radkovic
Sarah Stoffaneller

Assistants Visitor and Press Center
Nora Blank
Anna Enge
Paulina Maitz
Paul Wolff

Elke Murlasits
Head of Office of Open Questions

Coordinators Office of Open Questions
Markus Boxler
Markus Plasencia
Lena Riecnik
Isabel Toccafondi

Team Office of Open Questions
Sedra Arab
Verena Borecky
Eva Brede
Valerentina Buljan
Kristina Gorke
Laurenz Henkel
Sonja Kinzer
Klaudia Kurta
Iryna Orlova
Martin Pobitzer
Julia Robin
Kristina Six

Trainees Office of Open Questions
Lara Hollensteiner
Stella Wolf

Marlene Obermayer
(maternity leave)
Head of Archive / Library

Tim Kirchner
(maternity leave replacement)
Head of Archive / Library

Stefanie Lazarus
Office Management

Matthias Ulbl
Accounting

Simon Resch
Office Assistant

Danica Radat
Facility Manager

Grupa Ee
(Mina Fina, Damjan Ilić, Ivian Kan Mujezinović)
Graphic Design

Documentation
Liz Eve
Johanna Lamprecht
Ulrich A. Reiterer
Mathias Völzke
Clara Wildberger

Systemantics
Website

Network Support
Datenreisebüro
digitalis

Kaya Kiocak
Database

Festival Drivers
Bernd Birnbauer
Christian Jalen

Christoph Posch
Bike Courier

Colophon

This book is published in conjunction with steirischer herbst festival steirischer herbst '20—*Paranoia TV*, September 24–October 18, 2020, Graz, Styria, Austria.

Editors:
Ekaterina Degot
David Riff

Project management:
Henriette Gallus, steirischer herbst
Nicole Rankers, Verlag der Buchhandlung Walther und Franz König

Managing editor:
Jeff Thoss

Translations:
Jennifer Taylor

Proofreading:
Aaron Bogart

Graphic design:
Grupa Ee (Mina Fina, Damjan Ilić, Ivian Kan Mujezinović)

steirischer herbst festival gmbh
Sackstraße 17
8010 Graz, Austria
www.steirischerherbst.at

Printing:
Lösch GmbH & Co. KG

Paper:
Igepa grenita 250 g/m²
Maxigloss 135 g/m²
GardaMat Eleven 90 g/m²
Opakal 50 g/m²

Published by Verlag der Buchhandlung Walther und Franz König
Ehrenstraße 4, D-50672 Cologne

ISBN 978-3-96098-998-1

Printed in Germany

Cover illustration: Grupa Ee

Bibliographic information published by the Deutsche Nationalbibliothek
The Deutsche Nationalbibliothek lists this publication in the Deutsche Nationalbibliografie; detailed bibliographic data are available at http://dnb.d-nb.de.

Distribution:

Europe
Buchhandlung Walther König
Ehrenstraße 4,
50672 Cologne, Germany
t +49 221 20 59 6 53
verlag@buchhandlung-walther-koenig.de

UK & Ireland
Cornerhouse Publications Ltd. - HOME
2 Tony Wilson Place,
Manchester M15 4FN, UK
t +44 161 212 3466
publications@cornerhouse.org

Outside Europe
D.A.P. / Distributed Art Publishers, Inc.
75 Broad Street, Suite 630,
New York, NY 10004, USA
t +1 0 212 627 1999
orders@dapinc.com

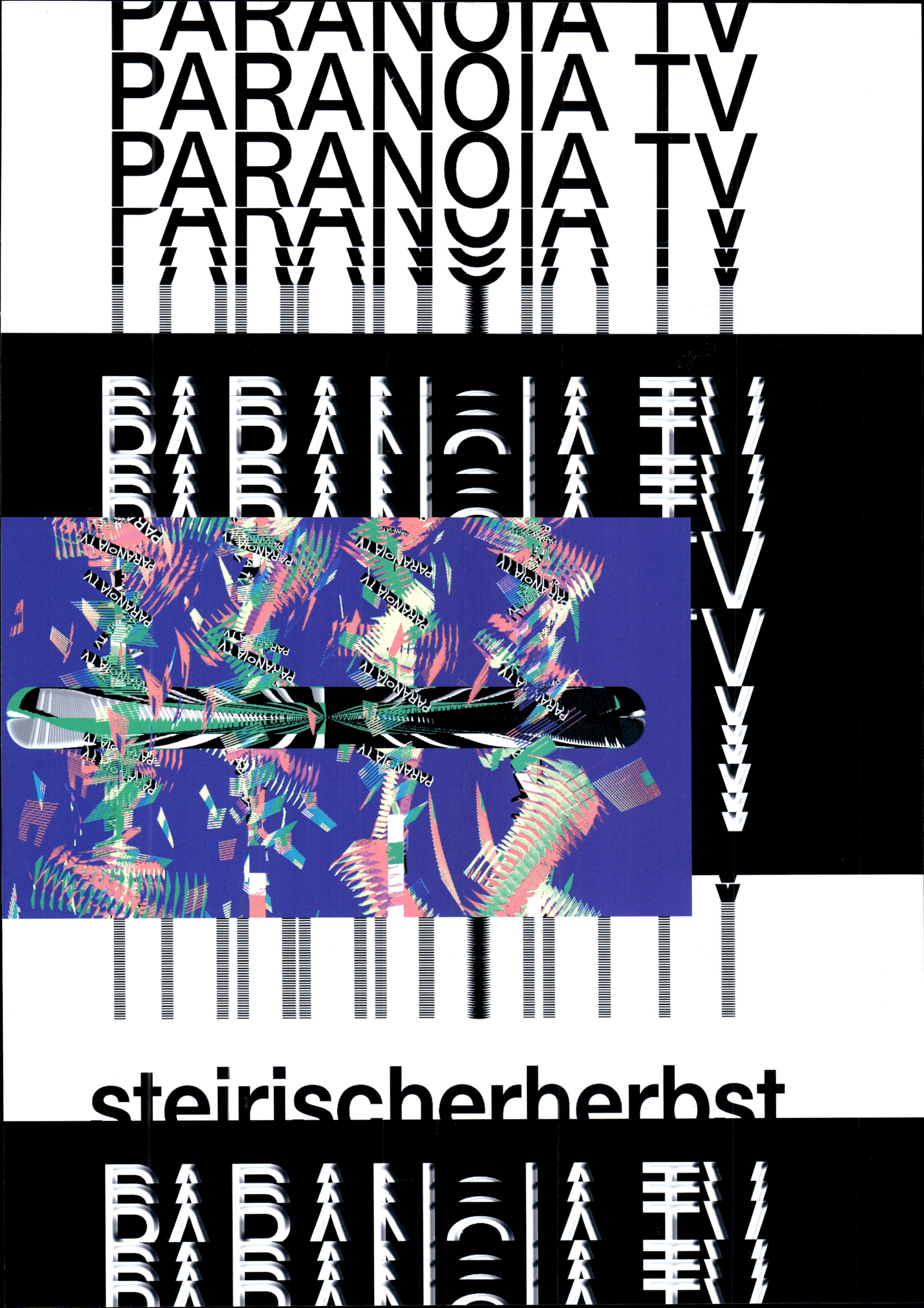
PARANOIA TV
PARANOIA TV
PARANOIA TV
steirischerherbst

Ist Lucy ein Prophet? Schon lange vor der Corona-Quarantäne hatte er nämlich die Idee gehabt, zuhause, also drinnen, eine Reihe Dokumentarfilme zu drehen, jedoch nicht biografischer, sondern eher wissenschaftlicher, natürlicher, gesellschaftlicher und politischer Art. Er hatte sich, zum Beispiel, vorgestellt, dass dort ein schlafender Mann gezeigt werden könnte, über den ein Voice-Over dann behaupten würde, dass in seinem ruhenden Körper bereits die allerersten Krebs-Metastasen entstünden.

Auf gewisse Weise hatte sich Lucy also sowohl auf seinen eigenen Krebs als auch auf eine längerfristige Praxis vorbereitet, die der Quarantäne angemessen wäre.

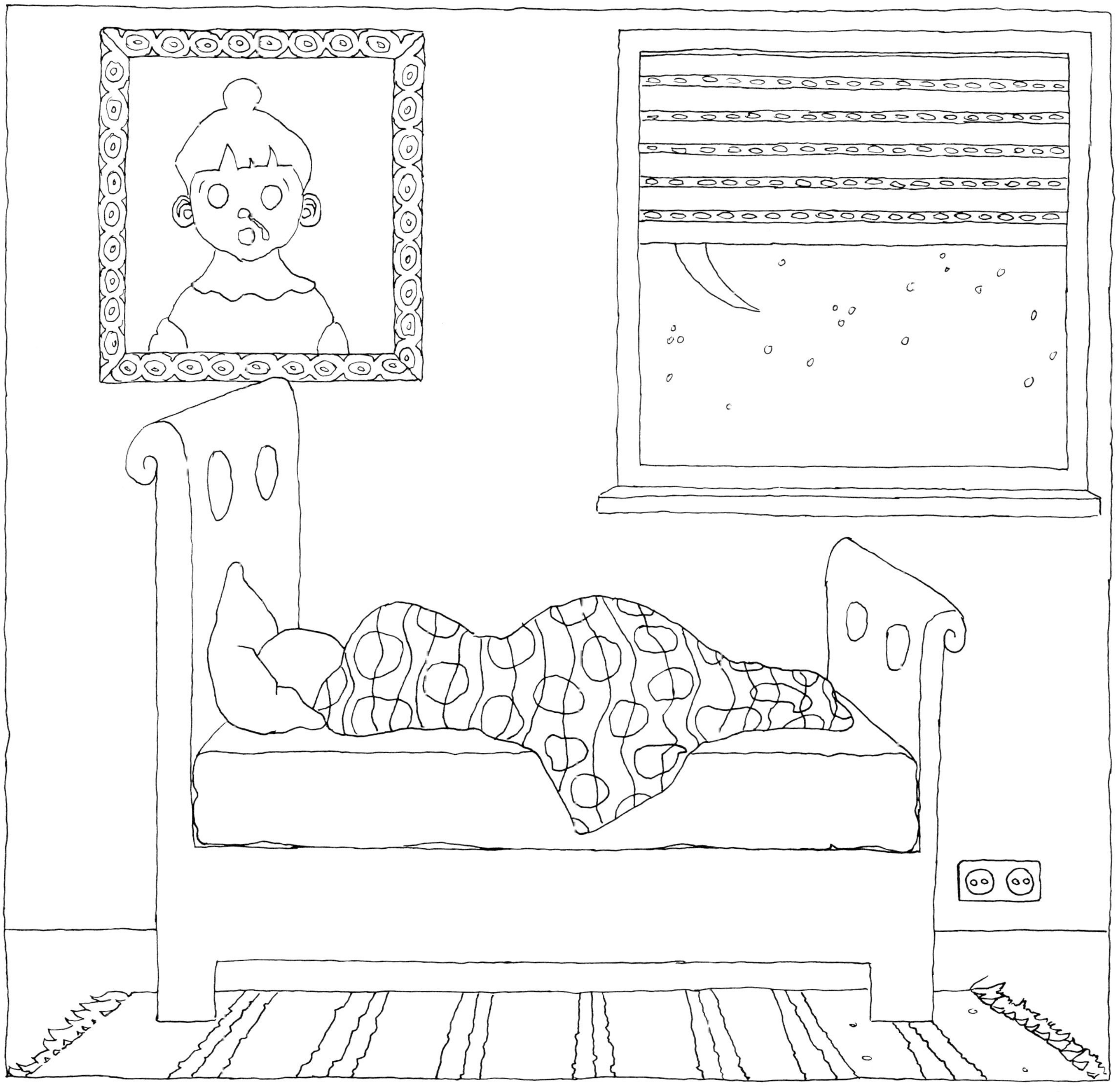

Aus *Lucy Ist Krank* (2020) ein Malbuch von Roee Rosen | steirischer herbst '20

Gesellschafter*innen/Shareholders

Das Land Steiermark
→ Culture, Europe, Sports

GRAZ

Mit großzügiger Unterstützung von/With the generous support of

Federal Ministry
Republic of Austria
Arts, Culture,
Civil Service and Sport

TOURISMUS GRAZ

Hauptsponsor/Main Sponsor

legero united
Initiator of con-tempus.eu

Veranstaltungspartner/Event Partner

HELMUT MARKO HOTELS

Exklusive Sponsorin Außenwerbung/
Exclusive Advertisment Sponsor

GRAZ HOLDING

Energiesponsor/Energy Sponsor

ENERGIE GRAZ

Ausstellungssponsor*innen/Exhibition Sponsors

hba
Held Berdnik Astner & Partner Rechtsanwälte GmbH

Gaulhofer
Fenster zum Wohnfühlen

Techniksponsor Helmut List Halle/
Technical Sponsor Helmut List Halle

Banksponsorin/Banking Sponsor

Projektförder*innen/Project Supporters

Unterstützt von/Supported by

Gastronomiepartnerin/Catering Partner

Medienpartner*innen/Media Partners

Hotelpartner*innen/Partnering Hotels

Projektpartner*innen/Project Partners

List of Illustrations

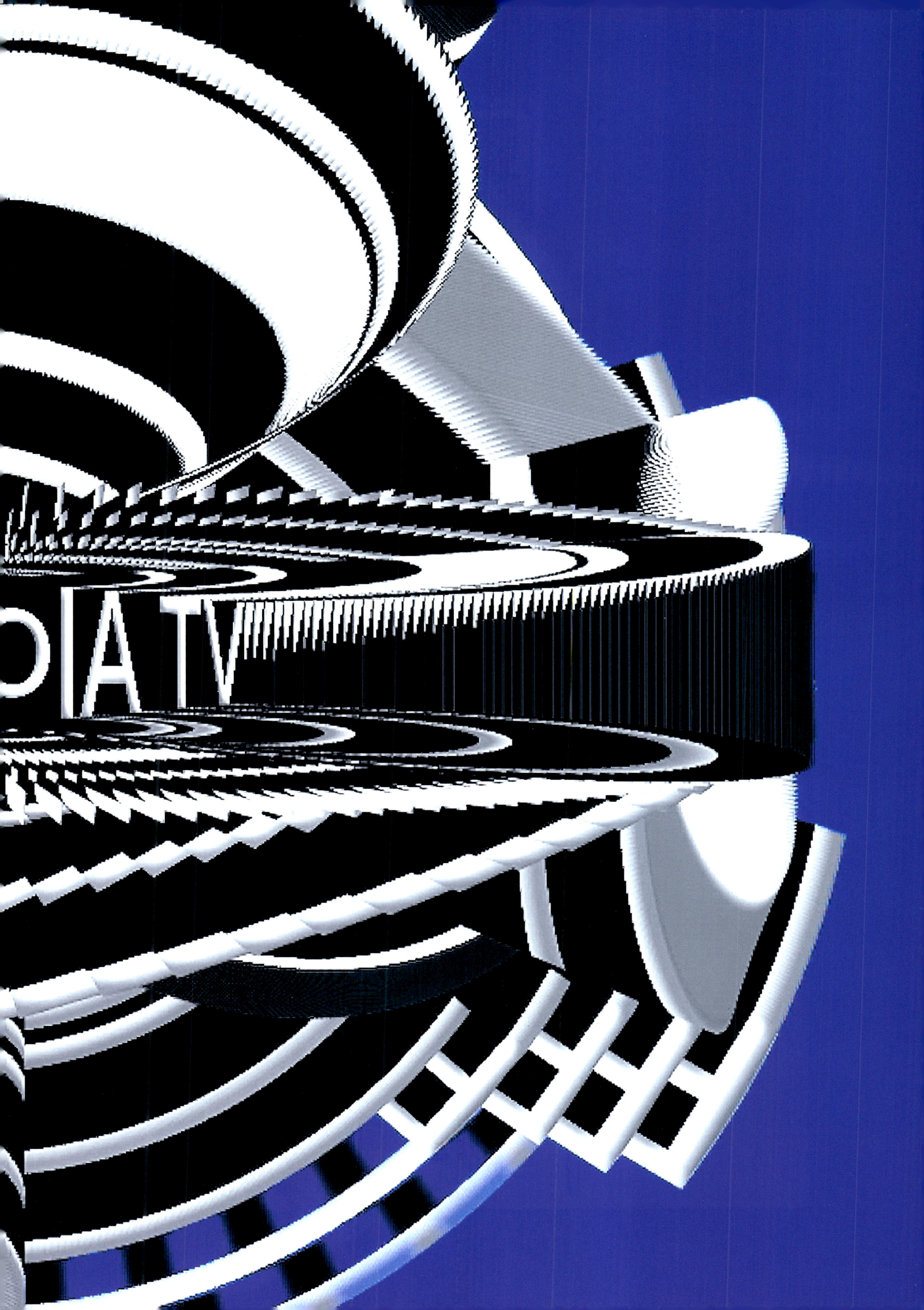
DIATV

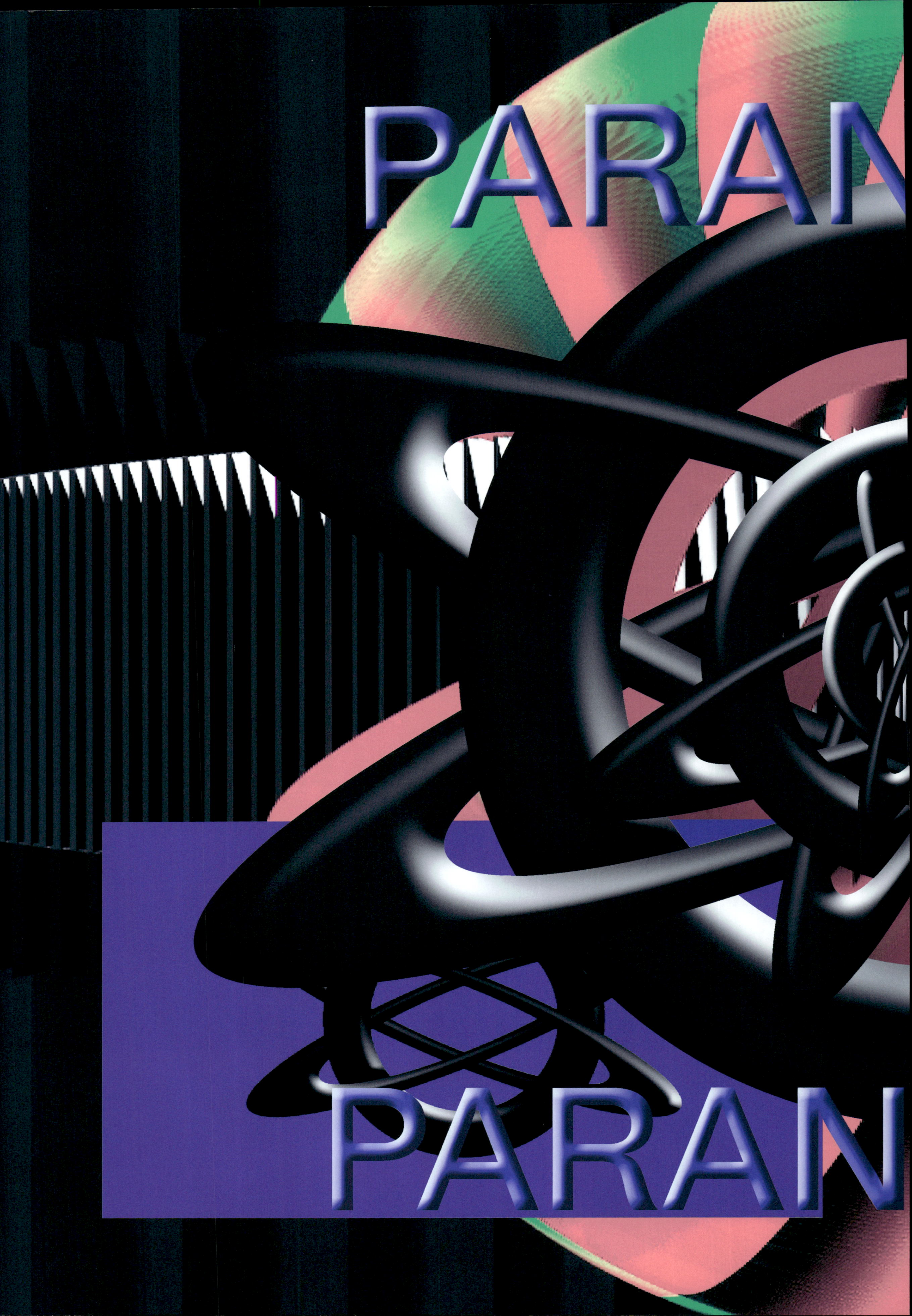
PARAN
PARAN

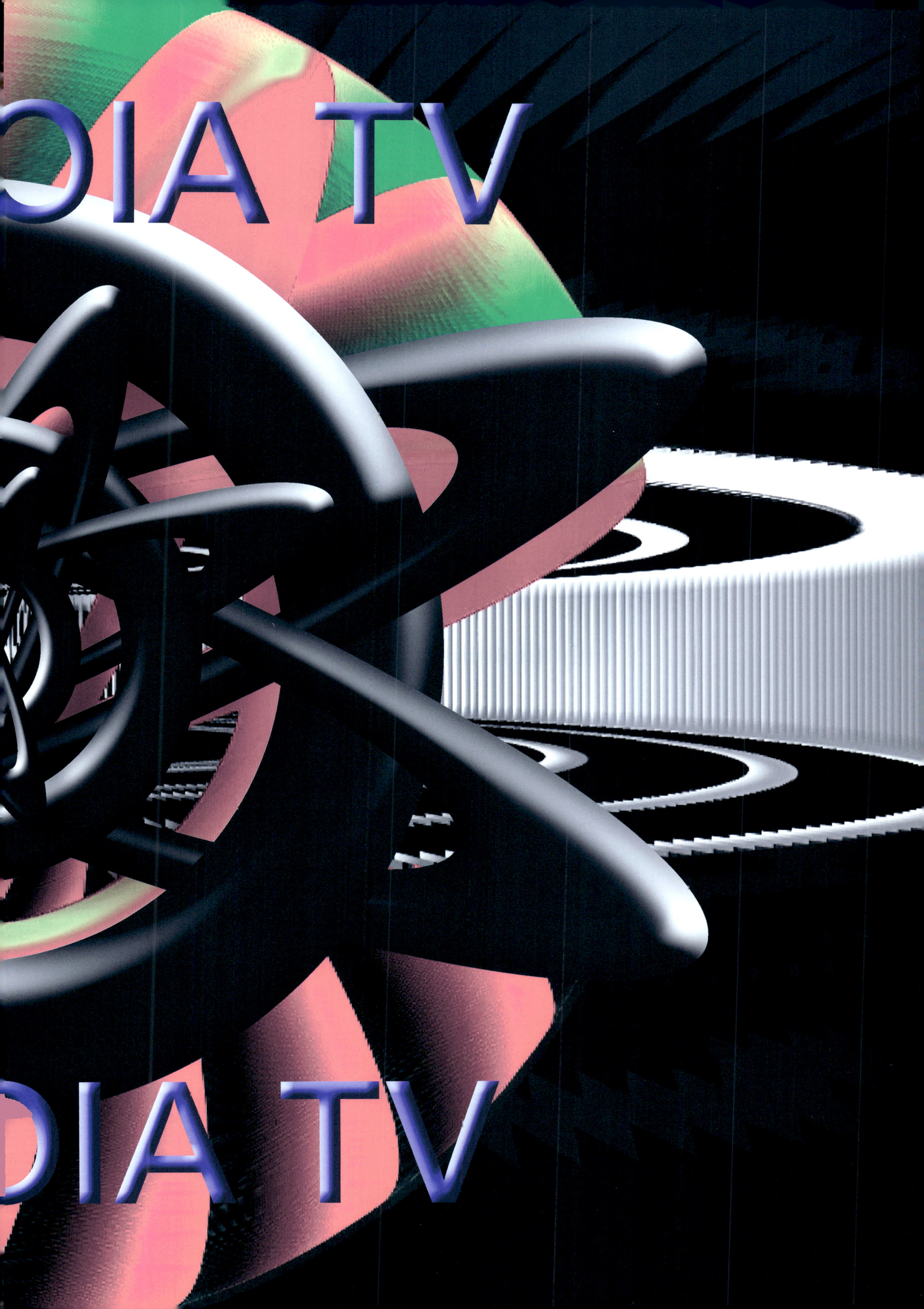
DIA TV
DIA TV

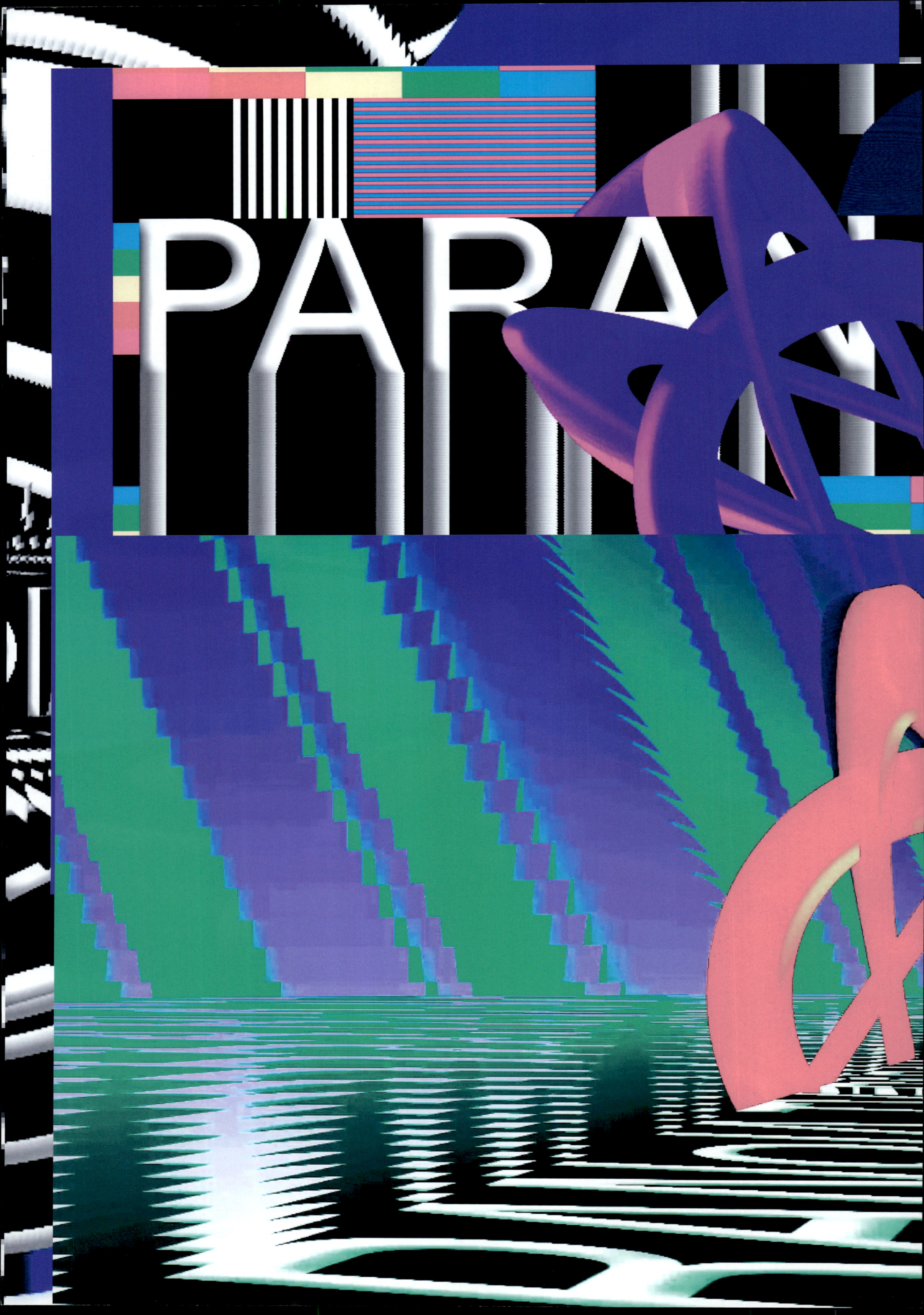
PARA

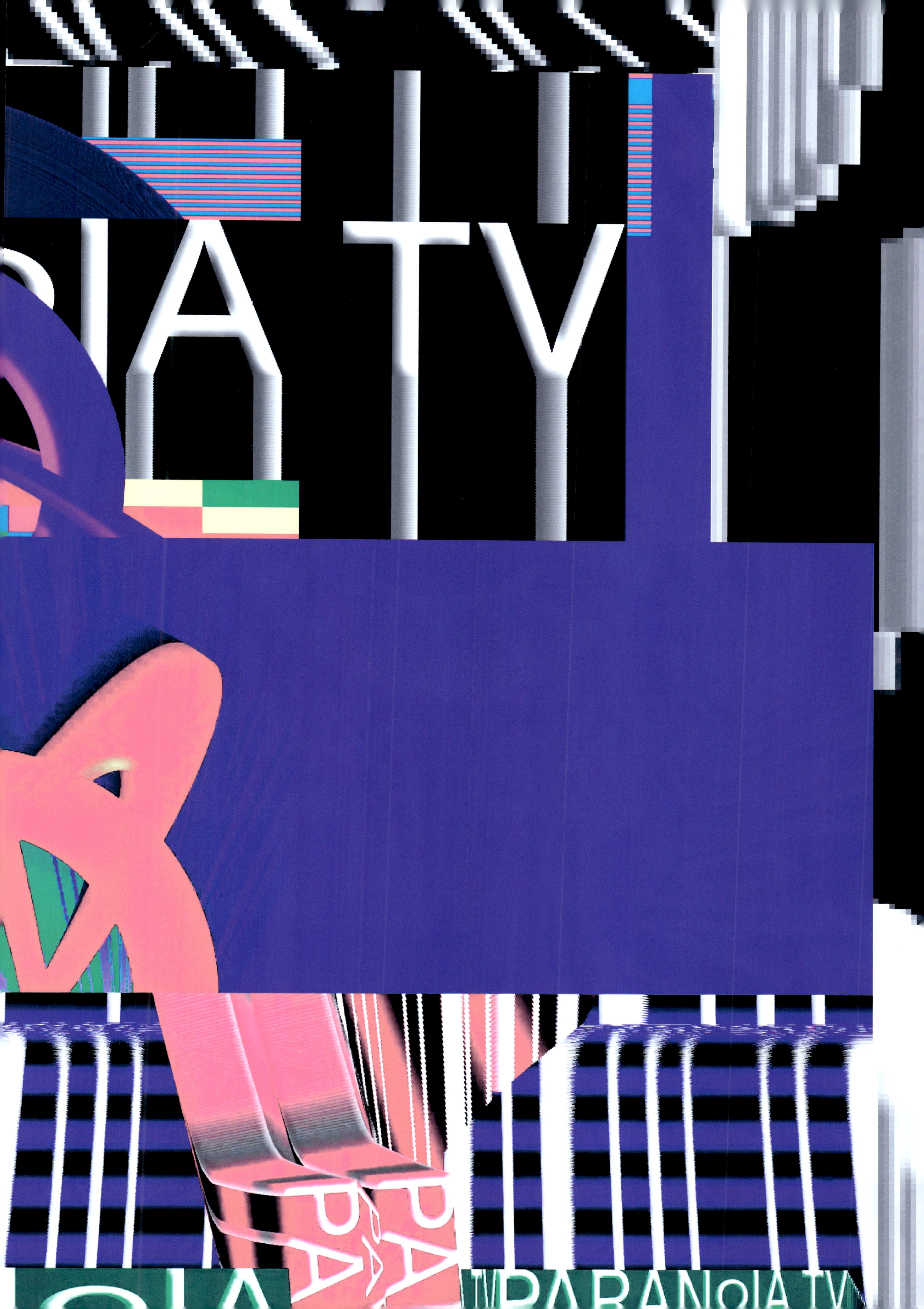
IA TV

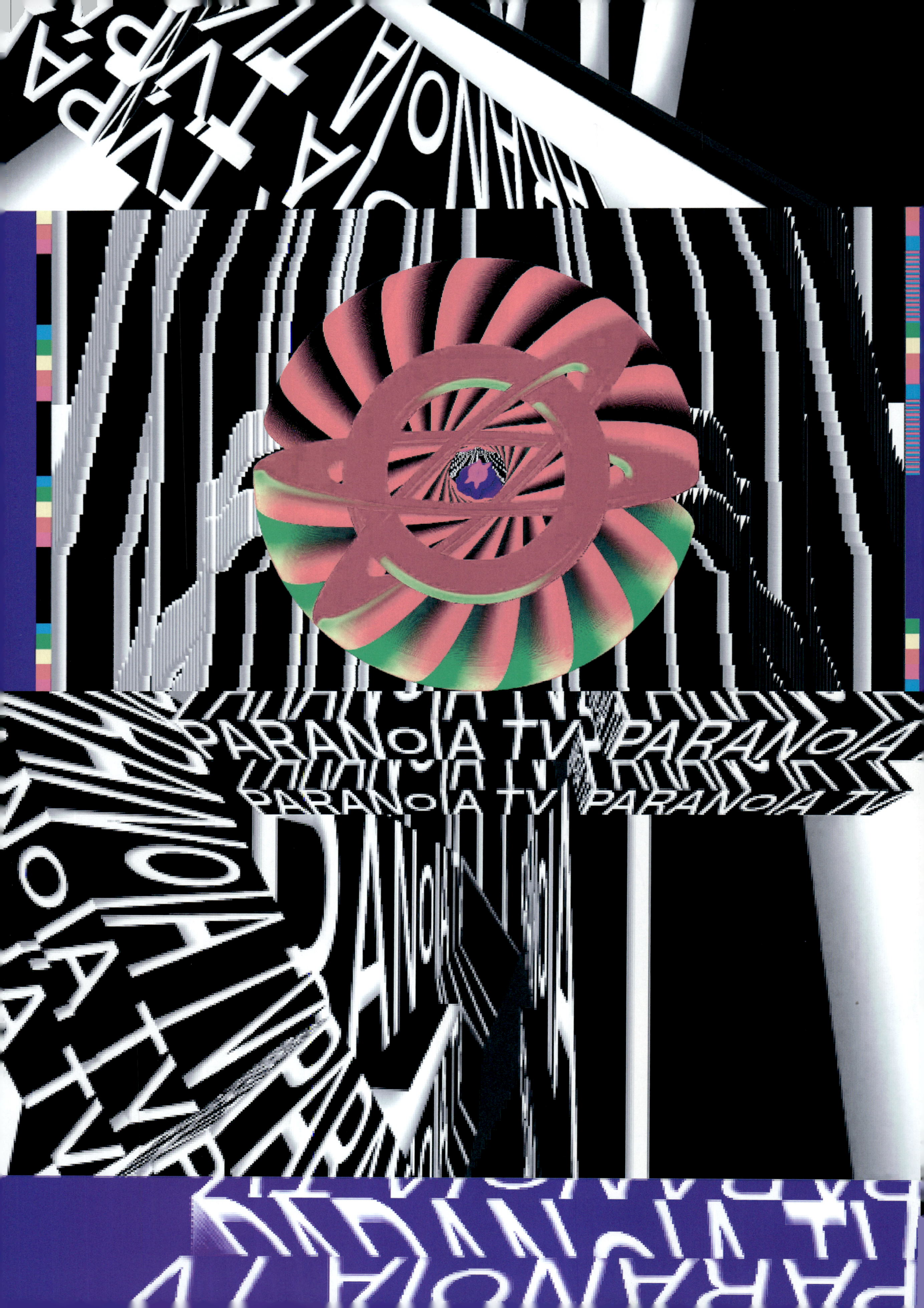
PARANOIA TV PARANOIA
PARANOIA TV PARANOIA TV

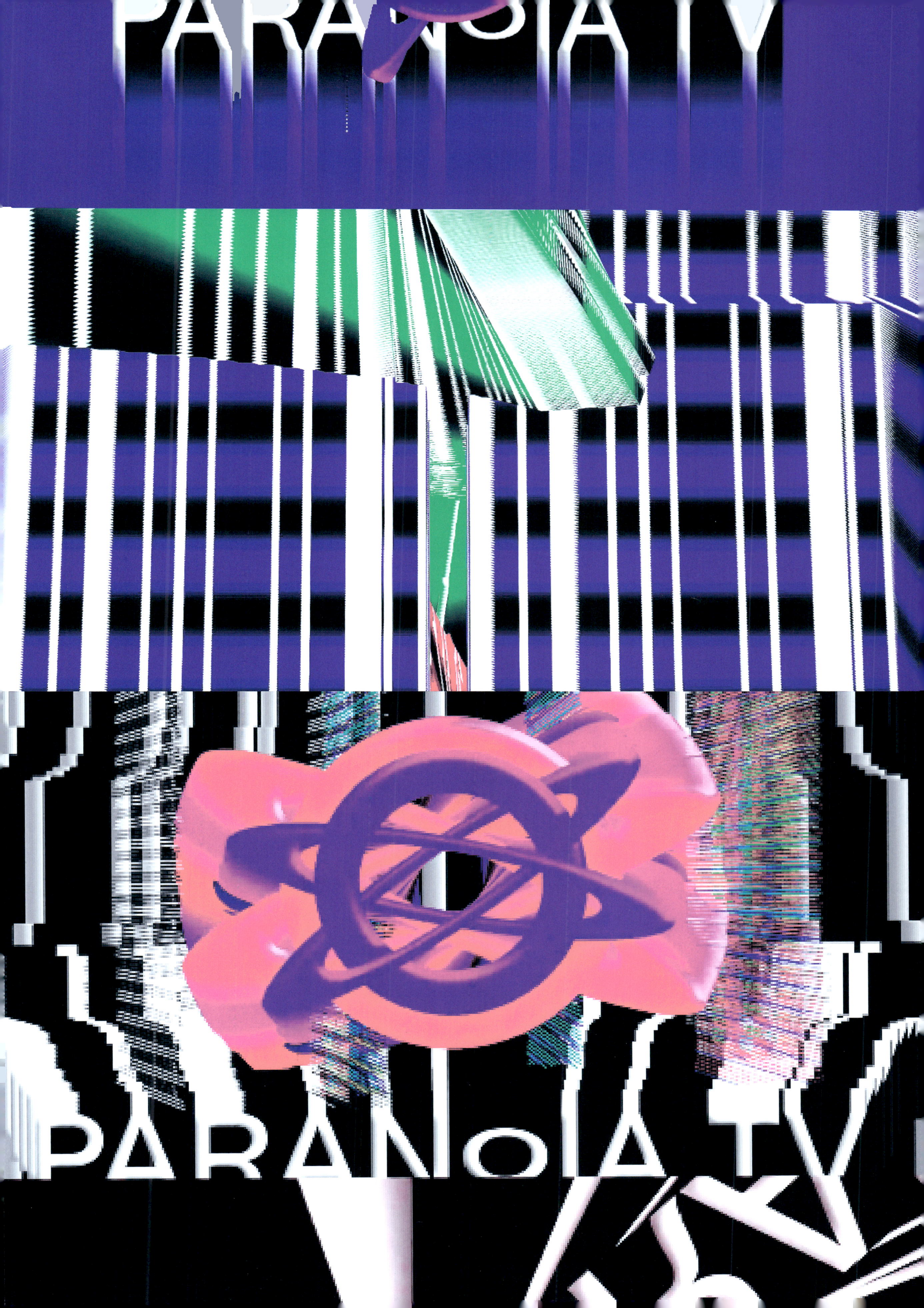
PARANOIA TV

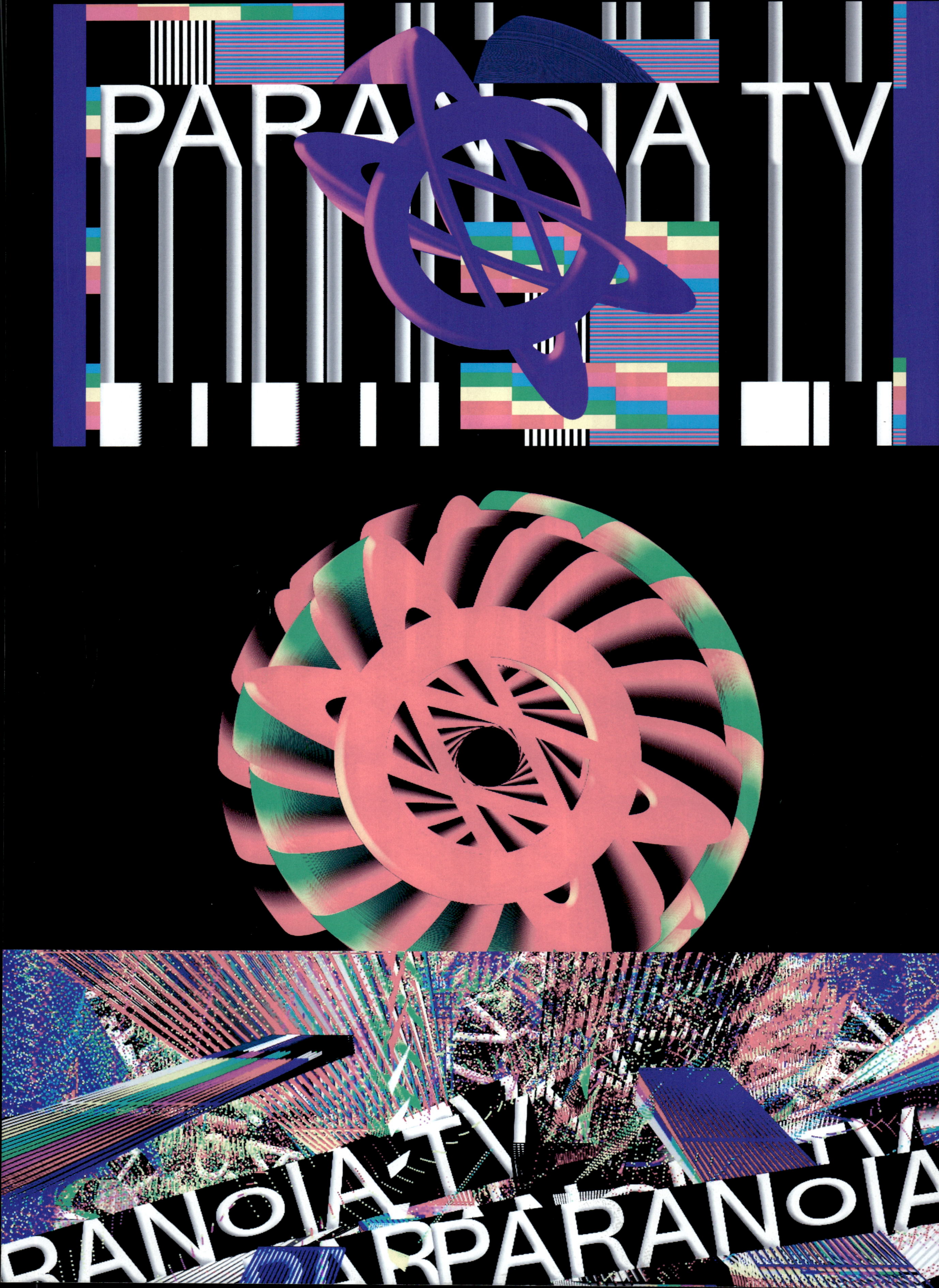
PARANOIA